MICROECONOMICS

Fourth Edition

Robert S. Pindyck

Massachusetts Institute of Technology

Daniel L. Rubinfeld

University of California, Berkeley

Prentice Hall International, Inc., Upper Saddle River, New Jersey 07458

Acquisitions Editor: Leah Bronwyn Jewell
Associate Editor: Gladys Soto
Editorial Assistant: Kristen Kaiser
Editor-in-Chief: Natalie Anderson
Marketing Manager: Patrick Lynch
Managing Editor: Dee Josephson
Production Supervisor: Arnold Vila
Production Manager: Vincent Scelta
Senior Designer: Ann France
Interior Design: Amanda Kavanaugh
Cover Design: Maureen Eide
Composition: York Production Services
Cover Illustration: Reginald Wickham

© 1998, 1995 by Prentice-Hall, Inc.
A Simon & Schuster Company
Upper Saddle River, New Jersey 07458

Previous editions copyright © 1992, 1989.

ISBN 0-13-896184-0

Prentice-Hall International (UK) Limited, London
Prentice-Hall of Australia Pty. Limited, Sydney
Prentice-Hall Canada Inc., Toronto
Prentice-Hall Hispanoamericana, S.A., Mexico
Prentice-Hall of India Private Limited, New Delhi
Prentice-Hall of Japan, Inc., Tokyo
Simon & Schuster Asia Pte. Ltd., Singapore
Editora Prentice-Hall do Brasil, Ltda., Rio de Janeiro
Prentice-Hall, Upper Saddle River, New Jersey

Printed in the United States of America
10 9 8 7 6 5 4 3 2 1

To our daughters

Maya, Talia, and Shira

Sarah and Rachel

BRIEF CONTENTS

CONTENTS

PART III Market Structure and Competitive Strategy   *331*

PART IV Information, Market Failure, and the Role of Government *577*

16 General Equilibrium and Economic Efficiency *579*

List of Examples

PREFACE

For students who care about how the world works, microeconomics is one of the most relevant and interesting subjects they study. A good grasp of microeconomics is vital for managerial decision making, for designing and understanding public policy, and more generally for appreciating how a modern economy functions.

We wrote this book, *Microeconomics*, because we believe that students need to be exposed to the new topics that have come to have a central role in microeconomics over the past decade—topics such as game theory and competitive strategy, the roles of uncertainty and information, and the analysis of pricing by firms with market power. We also felt that students need to be shown how microeconomics can be used as a practical tool for decision making. Microeconomics is an exciting and dynamic subject, but students need to be given an appreciation of its relevance and usefulness. They want and need a good understanding of how microeconomics can actually be used outside the classroom.

To respond to these needs, our book provides a fresh treatment of microeconomic theory that stresses its relevance and application to both managerial and public-policy decision making. This applied emphasis is accomplished by including more than eighty extended examples that cover such topics as the analysis of demand, cost, and market efficiency, the design of pricing strategies, investment and production decisions, and public policy analysis. Because of the importance that we attach to these examples, they are included in the flow of the text, rather than being "boxed" or screened. (A list of the examples is included in the table of contents on pages xvii–xix.)

The coverage in *Microeconomics* incorporates the dramatic changes that have occurred in the field in recent years. There is growing interest in game theory and the strategic interactions of firms (Chapters 12 and 13), in the role and implications of uncertainty and asymmetric information (Chapters 5 and 17), in the pricing strategies of firms with market power (Chapters 10 and 11), and in the design of policies to deal efficiently with externalities such as environmental pollution (Chapter 18). These topics, which have only recently received attention in most books, are covered extensively here.

That the coverage in *Microeconomics* is comprehensive and up-to-date does not mean that it is "advanced" or difficult. We have worked hard to make the exposition clear and accessible as well as lively and engaging. We believe that the study of microeconomics should be enjoyable and stimulating. We hope that our book reflects this. Except for appendices and footnotes, *Microeconomics* uses no calculus. As a result, it should be suitable for students with a broad range of backgrounds. (Those sections that are more demanding are marked with an asterisk and can be easily omitted.)

Changes in the Fourth Edition

The second and third editions of this book contained a variety of changes and additions that built on the success of the first edition. These included a number of new topics, such as the extent of a market, revealed preference, Engel curves, advertising, the theory of comparative advantage, strategic trade policy, and incentive design in vertically integrated firms. But even more importantly, with the assistance of a number of able reviewers, we heavily revised the first eight chapters of the text, and updated many of the examples. Our primary goal in revising the book has always been to make the text as clear, accessible, and interesting as possible. The fourth edition continues this tradition. We have added some new material, but we have also revised much of the existing text with the goal of improved clarity and accessibility.

Changes in this edition include a more detailed introductory discussion of supply and demand in Chapter 2, and a revised exposition of some of the core theory throughout the book, but especially in the the first ten chapters. New material on cost-of-living indexes has been added to Chapter 3, an expanded discussion of productivity growth has been added to Chapter 6, and we have expanded our discussion of costs in Chapter 7. We have also revised and expanded our discussion of the antitrust laws in Chapter 10, and we have included new material on bundling in Chapter 11. We have added a number of new examples, and most of the existing examples have been revised and updated.

Finally, we have modified many of the diagrams to improve their accuracy and clarity. This edition, like the third edition, is printed in four colors. However, this time we have tried to use those colors more effectively to make the diagrams as clear and pedagically effective as possible.

Alternative Course Designs

Microeconomics offers instructors substantial flexibility in course design. For a one-quarter or one-semester course stressing the basic core material, we would suggest using the following chapters and sections of chapters: 1, 2, 3, 4.1-4.4, 6.1-6.5, 7.1-7.4, 8, 9.1-9.4, 10.1-10.4, 11.1-11.3, 12.1-12.2, 12.5-12.6, 14, 15.1-15.4, 18.1-18.2, and 18.5. A somewhat more ambitious course might also include parts of Chapters 5 and 16, and additional sections in Chapters 6, 7, 9, 10, and 12. To emphasize uncertainty and market failure, an instructor should also include substantial parts of Chapters 5 and 17.

Depending on one's interests and the goals of the course, other sections could be added or used to replace the materials listed above. A course that emphasized modern pricing theory and business strategy would include all of Chapters 10, 11, 12, and 13, and the remaining sections of Chapter 15. A course in managerial economics might also include the appendixes to Chapters 4, 7, and 11, as well as the appendix on regression analysis at the end of the book. A course that emphasized welfare economics and public policy should include Chapter 16 and additional sections of Chapter 18.

Finally, we want to stress that those sections or subsections that are more demanding and/or are peripheral to the core material have been marked with an asterisk. These sections can easily be omitted without detracting from the flow of the book.

Supplementary Materials

Ancillaries of an exceptionally high quality are available to instructors and students using this book. The instructor's manual was written by Gilbert Davis and Valerie Suslow of the University of Michigan. It provides answers to all of the Questions for Review and all of the Exercises that appear at the end of chapters, as well as a summary of the key points in each chapter. It also contains a series of teaching suggestions. It is available from the publisher on request, as is a separate test bank, writter by Nancy Fox of Saint Joseph's University.

The study guide, written by Valerie Suslow of the University of Michigan and Jonathan Hamilton of the University of Florida, provides a wide variety of review materials and exercises for students. It can be purchased separately by students and others using the book.

For more information on the availability of the supplementary materials, contact your Prentice Hall sales representative.

Acknowledgments

Because this book has been the outgrowth of years of experience in the classroom, we owe a debt of gratitude to our students and to the colleagues with whom we often discuss microeconomics and its presentation. We have also had the help of capable research assistants, including Walter Athier, Phillip Gibbs, Jamie Jue, Kathy O'Regan, Karen Randig, Subi Rangan, and Deborah Senior. Kathy Hill helped with the art, while Assunta Kent, Mary Knott, and Dawn Elliott Linahan provided secretarial assistance with the first edition. We especially want to thank Lynn Steele and Jay Tharp, who provided considerable editorial support for the second edition. Mark Glickman and Steve Wiggins assisted with the examples in the third edition, while Andrew Guest, Jeanette Sayre, and Lynn Steele provided valuable editorial support.

Writing this book has been a painstaking and enjoyable process. At each stage we received exceptionally fine guidance from teachers of microeconomics throughout the country. After the first draft of the first edition of this book had been edited and reviewed, it was discussed at a two-day focus group meeting in New York. This provided an opportunity to get ideas from instructors with a variety of backgrounds and perspectives. We would like to thank the following focus group members for advice and criticism: Carl Davidson of Michigan State University; Richard Eastin of the University of Southern California; Judith Roberts of California State University, Long Beach; and Charles Strein of the University of Northern Iowa. We would also like to thank all those who reviewed the first edition at each stage of its evolution:

Ted Amato, University of North Carolina, Charlotte
John J. Antel, University of Houston
Kerry Back, Northwestern University
Jeremy Bulow, Stanford University
Larry A. Chenault, Miami University
Jacques Cremer, Virginia Polytechnic Institute and State University
Carl Davidson, Michigan State University
Arthur T. Denzau, Washington University
Richard V. Eastin, University of Southern California
William H. Greene, New York University
George Heitman, Pennsylvania State University
George E. Hoffer, Virginia Commonwealth University
Robert Inman, The Wharton School, University of Pennsylvania
B. Patrick Joyce, Michigan Technological University
Leonard Lardaro, University of Rhode Island
Peter Linneman, University of Pennsylvania
R. Ashley Lyman, University of Idaho
Wesley A. Magat, Duke University
Anthony M. Marino, University of Southern Florida
Michael J. Moore, Duke University
Daniel Orr, Virginia Polytechnic Institute and State University
Judith Roberts, California State University, Long Beach
Geoffrey Rothwell, Stanford University
Edward L. Sattler, Bradley University
Charles T. Strein, University of Northern Iowa
Michael Wasylenko, Syracuse University
Lawrence J. White, New York University

We had a good deal of feedback and assistance in the development of the second edition. We would like to thank the following reviewers of the second edition for the extremely valuable advice they provided:

Dale Ballou, University of Massachusetts, Amherst
Henry Chappel, University of South Carolina
John Coupe, University of Maine at Orono
Richard Eastin, University of Southern California
Otis Gilley, Louisiana Tech University
John Gross, University of Wisconsin at Milwaukee
Jonathan Hamilton, University of Florida

Claire Hammond, Wake Forest University
James Hartigan, University of Oklahoma
Robert Inman, The Wharton School, University of Pennsylvania
Joyce Jacobsen, Rhodes College
Richard Mills, University of New Hampshire
Julianne Nelson, Stern School of Business, New York University
Michael Podgursky, University of Massachusetts, Amherst
Charles Ratliff, Davidson College
Nestor Ruiz, University of California, Davis
Valerie Suslow, University of Michigan
David Vrooman, St. Lawrence University

We would like to thank a thoughtful and talented group of reviewers whose comments and ideas greatly improved the third edition:

Jack Adams, University of Arkansas, Little Rock
William Baxter, Stanford University
James A. Brander, University of British Columbia
Charles Clotfelter, Duke University
Kathryn Combs, California State University, Los Angeles
Richard Corwall, Middlebury College
Tran Dung, Wright State University
Carl E. Enomoto, New Mexico State University
Ray Farrow, Seattle University
Gary Ferrier, Southern Methodist University
David Kaserman, Auburn University
Michael Kende, INSEAD, France
Anthony Krautman, DePaul University
James MacDonald, Rensselaer Polytechnical Institute
David Mills, University of Virginia, Charlottesville
Jennifer Moll, Fairfield University
Sharon J. Pearson, University of Alberta Edmonton
Ivan P'ng, University of California, Los Angeles
Roger Sherman, University of Virginia
Abdul Turay, Radford University
Robert Whaples, Wake Forest University
Arthur Woolf, University of Vermont
Chiou-nan Yeh, Alabama State University
Joseph Ziegler, University of Arkansas, Fayetteville

We would also like to thank the reviewers who provided comments and ideas that have contributed so much to this fourth edition:

Sheri Aggarwal, Dartmouth College
Winston Chang, State University of New York, Buffalo
Gilbert Davis, University of Michigan
Philip G. King, San Francisco State University

Tetteh A. Kofi, University of San Francisco
Richard D. McGrath, College of William and Mary
George Norman, Tufts University
Nachum Sicherman, Columbia University
Houston H. Stokes, University of Illinois, Chicago
Richard W. Stratton, University of Akron

Apart from the formal review process, we are especially grateful to Jean Andrews, Paul Anglin, J. C. K. Ash, Ernst Berndt, George Bittlingmayer, Severin Borenstein, Paul Carlin, Whewon Cho, Setio Angarro Dewo, Frank Fabozzi, Joseph Farrell, Frank Fisher, Jonathan Hamilton, Robert Inman, Joyce Jacobsen, Stacey Kole, Jeannette Mortensen, John Mullahy, Krishna Pendakur, Jeffrey Perloff, Ivan P'ng, A. Mitchell Polinsky, Judith Roberts, Geoffrey Rothwell, Garth Saloner, Joel Schrag, Daniel Siegel, Thomas Stoker, David Storey, and James Walker, who were kind enough to provide comments, criticisms, and suggestions as the various editions of this book developed. We also want to thank Masaya Okoshi, Ashesh Shah, and Wilson Tai for their research assistance on the fourth edition, and Lynn Steele for her invaluable editorial assistance.

Finally, we wish to express our sincere thanks for the extraordinary effort those at Macmillan and Prentice Hall made in the development of our book. Throughout the writing of the first edition, Bonnie Lieberman provided invaluable guidance and encouragement; Ken MacLeod kept the progress of the book on an even keel; Gerald Lombardi provided masterful editorial assistance and advice; and John Molyneux ably oversaw the book's production.

In the development of the second edition, we were fortunate to have the encouragement and support of David Boelio, and the organizational and editorial help of two Macmillan editors, Caroline Carney and Jill Lectka. The second edition also benefited greatly from the superb development editing of Gerald Lombardi, and from John Travis, who managed the book's production.

Jill Lectka and Denise Abbott were our editors for the third edition, and we benefited greatly from their input. We also want to thank Valerie Ashton, John Sollami, and Sharon Lee for their superb handling of the production of the third edition.

Leah Jewell was our editor for the fourth edition; her patience, thoughtfulness, and perserverance were greatly appreciated. We also want to thank our production editor, Dee Josephson, for managing the production process so effectively, and Patricia Wosczyk, Prentice Hall's Design Manager, for her help with all aspects of the book's design.

R.S.P.
D.L.R.

PART I

Introduction:
Markets and Prices

Part I surveys the scope of microeconomics and introduces some basic concepts and tools. Chapter 1 discusses the range of problems that microeconomics addresses, and the kinds of answers it can provide. It also explains what a market is, how we determine the extent of a market, and how we measure market price.

Chapter 2 covers one of the most important tools of microeconomics: supply-demand analysis. We explain how a competitive market works and how supply and demand determine the prices and quantities of goods. We also show how supply-demand analysis can be used to determine the effects of changing market conditions, including government intervention.

CHAPTER 1

Preliminaries

Economics is divided into two main branches: microeconomics and macroeconomics. Microeconomics deals with the behavior of individual economic units. These units include consumers, workers, investors, owners of land, business firms—in fact, any individual or entity that plays a role in the functioning of our economy.[1] Microeconomics explains how and why these units make economic decisions. For example, it explains how consumers make purchasing decisions and how their choices are affected by changing prices and incomes. It also explains how firms decide how many workers to hire and how workers decide where to work and how much work to do.

Another important concern of microeconomics is how economic units interact to form larger units—markets and industries. Microeconomics helps us to understand, for example, why the American automobile industry developed the way it did and how producers and consumers interact in the market for automobiles. It explains how au-

---

[1] The prefix *micro-* is derived from the Greek word meaning "small." However, many of the individual economic units that we will study are small only in relation to the U.S. economy as a whole. For example, the annual sales of General Motors, IBM, or Exxon are larger than the gross national products of many countries.

tomobile prices are determined, how much automobile companies invest in new factories, and how many cars are produced each year. By studying the behavior and interaction of individual firms and consumers, microeconomics reveals how industries and markets operate and evolve, why they differ from one another, and how they are affected by government policies and global economic conditions.

By contrast, macroeconomics, the other major branch of economics, deals with aggregate economic quantities, such as the level and growth rate of national output, interest rates, unemployment, and inflation. But the boundary between macroeconomics and microeconomics has become less and less distinct in recent years. The reason is that macroeconomics also involves the analysis of markets—for example, the aggregate markets for goods and services, for labor, and for corporate bonds. To understand how these aggregate markets operate, we must first understand the behavior of the firms, consumers, workers, and investors who make up these markets. Thus macroeconomists have become increasingly concerned with the microeconomic foundations of aggregate economic phenomena, and much of macroeconomics is actually an extension of microeconomic analysis.

1.1 The Use and Limitations of Microeconomic Theory

Like any science, economics is concerned with the *explanation* and *prediction* of observed phenomena. Why, for example, do firms tend to hire or lay off workers when the prices of raw materials needed in the production process change? How many workers are likely to be hired or laid off by a firm or an industry if the price of raw materials increases by, say, 10 percent?

In economics, as in other sciences, explanation and prediction are based on *theories*. Theories are developed to explain observed phenomena in terms of a set of basic rules and assumptions. The theory of the firm, for example, begins with a simple assumption—firms try to maximize their profits. The theory uses this assumption to explain how firms choose the amounts of labor, capital, and raw materials that they use for production, as well as the amount of output they produce. It also explains how these choices depend on the *prices* of inputs, such as labor, capital, and raw materials, as well as the price the firm can receive for its output.

Economic theories are also the basis for making predictions. Thus the theory of the firm tells us whether a firm's output level will increase or decrease in response to an increase in wage rates or a decrease in the price of raw materials. With the application of statistical and econometric techniques, theories can be used to construct *models*, from which quantitative predictions can be made. A model is a mathematical representation, based on economic theory, of a firm, a market, or some other entity. For example, we might develop a model of a particular firm and use it to predict by *how much* the firm's output level will change as a result of, say, a 10 percent drop in the price of raw materials.[2]

No theory, whether it be in economics, physics, or any other science, is perfectly correct. The usefulness and validity of a theory depend on whether it succeeds in explaining and predicting the set of phenomena that it is intended to explain and predict. Consistent with this goal, theories are continually tested against observation. As a result of this testing, theories are often modified or refined and occasionally even discarded. The process of testing and refining theories is central to the development of economics as a science.

When evaluating a theory, it is important to keep in mind that it is invariably imperfect. This is the case in every branch of science. For example, in physics, Boyle's law relates the volume, temperature, and pressure of a gas.[3] The law is based on the assumption that individual molecules of a gas behave as though they were tiny, elastic billiard balls. Physicists today know that gas molecules do not, in fact, always behave like billiard balls, and partly because of this, Boyle's law breaks down under extremes of pressure and temperature. Nonetheless, under most conditions it does an excellent job of predicting how the temperature of a gas will change when the pressure and volume change, and it is therefore an essential tool for engineers and scientists.

The situation is much the same in economics. For example, firms do not maximize their profits all the time. Perhaps because of this, the theory of the firm has had only limited success in explaining certain aspects of firms' behavior, such as the timing of capital investment decisions. Nonetheless, the theory does explain a broad range of phenomena regarding the behavior, growth, and evolution of firms and industries, and so it has become an important tool for managers and policymakers.[4]

1.2 Positive Versus Normative Analysis

Microeconomics deals with both *positive* and *normative* questions. Positive questions have to do with explanation and prediction, normative questions with what ought to be. Suppose the U.S. government imposes a quota on the import of foreign cars. What will happen to the price of cars and to their production and sales? What impact will this have on American consumers? On workers in the automobile industry? These questions are all in the realm of positive analy-

---

[2] Statistics and econometrics also let us measure the *accuracy* of our predictions. For example, suppose we predict that a 10 percent drop in the price of raw materials will lead to a 5 percent increase in output. Are we sure that the increase in output will be exactly 5 percent, or might it be between 3 and 7 percent? Quantifying the accuracy of a prediction can be as important as the prediction itself.

[3] Robert Boyle (1627–1691) was a British chemist and physicist who discovered experimentally that pressure (P), volume (V), and temperature (T) were related in the following way: $PV = RT$, where R is a constant. Later, physicists derived this relationship as a consequence of the kinetic theory of gases, which describes the movement of gas molecules in statistical terms.

[4] A recent study shows that the managers of large American corporations make increasing use of microeconomic concepts. See Giuseppe A. Forgionne, "Economic Tools Used by Management in Large American Operated Corporations," *Business Economics* 19 (April 1984): 5–17.

sis. Positive analysis is central to microeconomics. As we explained above, theories are developed to explain phenomena, are tested against observations, and are used to construct models from which predictions are made.

The use of economic theory for prediction is important both for the managers of firms and for public policy. Suppose the federal government is considering raising the tax on gasoline. The tax would affect the price of gasoline, consumers' preferences for small or large cars, the amount of driving that people do, and so on. To plan sensibly, oil companies, automobile companies, producers of automobile parts, and firms in the tourist industry would all want to know how large the various effects of this tax will be. Government policymakers would also need quantitative estimates of the effects of the tax. They would want to determine the costs imposed on consumers (perhaps broken down by income categories); the effects on profits and employment in the oil, automobile, and tourist industries; and the amount of tax revenue likely to be collected each year.

Sometimes we want to go beyond explanation and prediction to ask questions, such as "What is best?" This involves *normative* analysis, which is also important both for managers of firms and for designers of new public policies. Again, consider a new tax on gasoline. Automobile companies would want to determine the best (profit-maximizing) mix of large and small cars to produce once the tax is in place, or how much money should be invested to make cars more fuel-efficient. For policymakers, the primary issue is likely to be whether this tax is in the public interest. The same policy objectives (say, an increase in tax revenues and a decrease in our dependence on imported oil) might be met more cheaply with a different kind of tax, such as a tariff on imported oil.

Normative analysis is not only concerned with alternative policy options; it also involves the design of particular policy choices. For example, suppose it has been decided that a gasoline tax is desirable. Balancing costs and benefits, we then ask what is the optimal size of the tax?

Normative analysis is often supplemented by value judgments. For example, a comparison between a gasoline tax and an oil import tariff might conclude that the gasoline tax is easier to administer but has a greater impact on lower-income consumers. At that point society must make a value judgment, weighing equity against economic efficiency.[5] When value judgments are involved, microeconomics cannot tell us what the best policy is. However, it can clarify the trade-offs and thereby help to illuminate and sharpen the debate.

1.3 Why Study Microeconomics?

We think that after reading this book, you will have no doubt about the importance and broad applicability of microeconomics. In fact, one of our major goals is to show you how to apply microeconomic principles to actual de-

---

[5] Most of the value judgments involving economic policy boil down to just this trade-off—equity versus economic efficiency. This conflict and its implications are discussed clearly and in depth in Arthur M. Okun, *Equality and Efficiency: The Big Tradeoff* (Washington: Brookings Institution, 1975).

cision-making problems. Nonetheless, some extra motivation early on never hurts. Here are two examples that show the use of microeconomics in practice and also provide a preview of the book.

Corporate Decision Making: Ford Introduces the Taurus

In late 1985 Ford introduced the Taurus—a newly designed, aerodynamically styled, front-wheel-drive automobile. The car was a huge success at the time and helped Ford almost to double its profits by 1987. The design and efficient production of this car involved not only some impressive engineering advances but a lot of economics as well.

First, Ford had to think carefully about how the public would react to the Taurus's design. Would consumers be swayed by the styling and performance of the car? How strong would demand be initially, how fast would it grow, and how would demand depend on the price Ford charged? Understanding consumer preferences and trade-offs and predicting demand and its responsiveness to price were essential parts of the Taurus program. (We discuss consumer preferences and demand in Chapters 3, 4, and 5.)

Next, Ford had to be concerned with the cost of the car. How high would production costs be, and how would this depend on the number of cars Ford produced each year? How would union wage negotiations or the prices of steel and other raw materials affect costs? How much and how fast would costs decline as managers and workers gained experience with the production process? And to maximize profits, how many cars should Ford plan to produce each year? (We discuss production and cost in Chapters 6 and 7 and the profit-maximizing choice of output in Chapter 8.)

Ford also had to design a pricing strategy for the car and consider how its competitors would react to this strategy. For example, should Ford charge a low price for the basic stripped-down version of the car but high prices for individual options, such as air conditioning and power steering? Or would it be more profitable to make these options "standard" items and charge a high price for the whole package? Whatever prices Ford chose, how were its competitors likely to react? Would GM and Chrysler try to undercut Ford by lowering prices? Might Ford be able to deter GM and Chrysler from lowering prices by threatening to respond with its own price cuts? (We discuss pricing in Chapters 10 and 11 and competitive strategy in Chapters 12 and 13.)

The Taurus program required a large investment in new capital equipment, and Ford had to consider the risks involved and the possible outcomes. Some of this risk was due to uncertainty over the future price of gasoline (higher gasoline prices would shift demand to smaller cars), and some was due to uncertainty over the wages that Ford would have to pay its workers. What would happen if world oil prices doubled or tripled again, or if the government imposed a new tax on gasoline? How much bargaining power would the unions have, and how might this affect wage rates? How should Ford take these uncertainties into account when making its investment decisions? (Commodity markets and the effects of taxes are discussed in Chapters 2 and 9. Labor markets and union power are discussed in Chapter 14. Investment decisions and the role of uncertainty are discussed in Chapters 5 and 15.)

Ford also had to worry about organizational problems. Ford is an integrated firm—separate divisions produce engines and parts, then assemble finished cars. How should the managers of the different divisions be rewarded? What price should the assembly division be charged for engines it receives from another division? Should all the parts be obtained from the upstream divisions, or should some of them be purchased from outside firms? (We discuss internal pricing and organizational incentives for the integrated firm in Chapters 11 and 17.)

Finally, Ford had to think about its relationship to the government and the effects of regulatory policies. For example, the Taurus had to meet federal emission standards, and production line operations had to comply with health and safety regulations. How were these regulations and standards likely to change over time? How would they affect the company's costs and profits? (We discuss the role of government in limiting pollution and promoting health and safety in Chapter 18.)

Public Policy Design: Automobile Emission Standards

In 1970, the federal Clean Air Act imposed strict tailpipe emission standards on new automobiles. These standards have become increasingly stringent, so that by 1995, the 1970 levels of nitrogen oxides, hydrocarbons, and carbon monoxide emitted by automobiles had been reduced by about 90 percent.

The design of a program like the Clean Air Act involves a careful analysis of the ecological and health effects of auto emissions. But it also involves a good deal of economics. First, the government has to evaluate the monetary impact of the program on consumers. The emission standards affect the cost both of purchasing a car (catalytic converters would be necessary, which would raise the cost of cars) and of operating it (gas mileage would be lower, and the catalytic converters would have to be repaired and maintained). Consumers ultimately bear much of this added cost, so it is important to know how it affects their standards of living. This requires an analysis of consumer preferences and demand. For example, would consumers drive less and spend more of their income on other goods? If so, would they be nearly as well off? (Consumer preferences and demand are discussed in Chapters 3 and 4.)

To answer these questions, the government needs to determine how the standards would affect the cost of producing cars. Might automobile producers use other materials to produce cars, so that cost increases would be small? (Production and cost are discussed in Chapters 6 and 7.) Then the government needs to know how the changes in production costs affect the level of production and the prices of new automobiles—are the additional costs absorbed or passed on to consumers in the form of higher prices? (Output determination is discussed in Chapter 8, and pricing in Chapters 10 through 13.)

Finally, the government needs to ask why the problems related to air pollution are not solved by our market-oriented economy. The answer is that much of the cost of air pollution is external to the firm. If firms do not find it in their self-interest to deal with auto emissions adequately, then what is the best way to alter their incentives? Should standards be set, or is it more economical to impose air pollution fees? How do we decide what people will pay to clean up the environment when there is no explicit market for clean air? Is the political process likely to solve these problems? The ultimate question is whether the auto emissions control program makes sense on a cost-benefit basis. Are the aesthetic, health, and other benefits of clean air worth the higher cost of automobiles? (These problems are discussed in Chapter 18.)

These are just two examples of how microeconomics can be applied; you will see more applications throughout this book. Many of these applications deal with markets and prices. These two words are a part of our everyday language, but it is important to be clear about their meaning.

1.4 What Is a Market?

We can divide individual economic units into two broad groups according to function—*buyers* and *sellers*. Buyers include consumers, who purchase goods and services, and firms, which buy labor, capital, and raw materials that they use to produce goods and services. Sellers include firms, which sell their goods and services; workers who sell their labor services; and resource owners, who rent land or sell mineral resources to firms. Clearly, most people and most firms act as both buyers and sellers, but we will find it helpful to think of them as simply buyers when they are buying something, and sellers when they are selling something.

Together, buyers and sellers interact to form *markets. A market is the collection of buyers and sellers that, through their actual or potential interactions, determine the price of a product or set of products.* Thus we can think of a market as the "place" where price is determined. Note that a market includes more than an *industry. An industry is a collection of firms that sell the same or closely related products.* In effect, an industry is the supply side of the market.

Economists are often concerned with *market definition*—that is, identifying which buyers and sellers should be included in a particular market. When defining a market, *potential* interactions of buyers and sellers can be just as important as *actual* ones. An example of this is the market for gold. A New Yorker who wants to buy gold is unlikely to travel to Zurich to do so. Most buyers of gold in New York will interact only with sellers of gold in New York. But buyers of gold in New York *could* purchase their gold in Zurich if the prices in that city were significantly lower than in New York because the cost of transporting gold is small relative to its value. Significant differences in the price of a commodity create a potential for *arbitrage*—buying at a low price in one location and selling at a higher price somewhere else. It is precisely this possibility of arbitrage that prevents the prices of gold in New York and Zurich from differing significantly and creates a world market for gold.

Markets are at the center of economic activity, and many of the most interesting questions and issues in economics concern how markets work. For example, why do only a few firms compete with one another in some markets, while in other markets a great many firms compete? Are consumers necessarily better off if there are many firms? If so, should the government intervene in markets with only a few firms? Why have prices in some markets risen or fallen rapidly, while in other markets prices have hardly changed at all? And which markets offer the best opportunities for an entrepreneur thinking of going into business?

Competitive Versus Noncompetitive Markets

In this book we study the behavior of both competitive and noncompetitive markets. A *perfectly competitive market* has many buyers and sellers, so that no single buyer or seller has a significant impact on price. Most agricultural markets are close to being perfectly competitive. For example, thousands of farmers produce wheat, which thousands of buyers purchase to produce flour and other products. As a result, no single farmer and no single buyer can significantly affect the price of wheat.

Many other markets are competitive enough to be treated as if they were perfectly competitive. The world market for copper, for example, contains a few dozen major producers. That is enough for the impact on price to be negligible if any one producer goes out of business. The same is true for many other natural resource markets, such as those for coal, iron, tin, or lumber.

Other markets containing only several producers may still be treated as competitive for purposes of analysis. For example, the airline industry in the United States contains several dozen firms, but most routes are served by only a few firms. Nonetheless, competition among those firms is often (but not always!) fierce enough, so that for some purposes (but not others) the market can be treated as competitive. Finally, some markets contain many producers but are *noncompetitive*; that is, individual firms can jointly affect the price. The world oil market is one example; since the early 1970s, the market has been dominated by the OPEC cartel. (A *cartel* is a group of producers that acts collectively.)

Market Price

Markets provide the possibility of transactions between buyers and sellers. Quantities of a good are sold at specific prices. In a perfectly competitive market, a single price—the *market price*—will usually prevail. The price of wheat in Kansas City and the price of gold in New York are two examples. These prices are also usually easy to measure. For example, you can find the price of corn, wheat, or gold each day in the business section of a newspaper.

In markets that are not perfectly competitive, different firms might charge different prices for the same product. This might happen because one firm is trying to win customers from its competitors, or because customers have brand loyalties that allow some firms to charge higher prices than their competitors. For example, two brands of laundry detergent might be sold in the same supermarket at different prices. Or, two supermarkets in the same town might be selling the same brand of laundry detergent at different prices. In cases like this, when we refer to the market price, we will mean the price averaged across brands or supermarkets.

The market prices of most goods will fluctuate over time, and for many goods the fluctuations can be rapid. This is particularly true for goods sold in competitive markets. The stock market, for example, is highly competitive—there are typically many buyers and sellers for any one stock. As anyone who has invested in the stock market knows, the price of any particular stock fluctuates from minute to minute and can rise or fall substantially during a single day. Similarly, the prices of commodities such as wheat, soybeans, coffee, oil, gold, silver, or lumber can also rise or fall dramatically in a day or a week.

Market Definition—The Extent of a Market

As we saw, *market definition* identifies which buyers and sellers should be included in the market. However, to determine which buyers and sellers to include, we must first determine the *extent of the market*. The *extent of a market* refers to the *boundaries*, both *geographic* and in terms of the *range of products* to be included in it.

When we refer to the market for gasoline, for example, we must be clear about its geographic boundaries. Are we referring to downtown Los Angeles, southern California, or the entire United States? And we must also be clear about the range of products we are referring to. Should regular octane and high octane premium gasoline be included in the same market? Leaded and unleaded gasoline? Gasoline and diesel fuel?

For some goods, it makes sense to talk about a market only in terms of very restrictive geographic boundaries. Housing is a good example. Most people who work in downtown Chicago will look for housing within commuting distance of that city. They will not look at homes that are 200 or 300 miles away, even though those homes might be much cheaper. And homes (together with the land they are sitting on) 200 miles away cannot easily be moved closer to Chicago. Hence the housing market in Chicago is separate and distinct from, say, the housing markets in Cleveland, Houston, Atlanta, or Philadelphia. Retail gasoline markets, on the other hand, are less limited geographically, but are still regional because of the expense of shipping gasoline long distances. Thus the market for gasoline in southern California is distinct from the market in northern Illinois. But as we mentioned earlier, gold is bought and sold in a world market; the possibility of arbitrage prevents its price from differing significantly from one location to another.

When discussing a market, we must also be clear about the range of products that we mean to include in it. For example, there is a market for 35-millimeter single lens reflex (SLR) cameras, and many brands compete in that market. But what about Polaroid instant cameras? Should they be considered part of the same market? Probably not, because they are used for different purposes, and so do not compete with SLR cameras. Gasoline is another example. Regular and premium octane gasolines might be considered part of the same market because most consumers can use either in their cars. Diesel fuel, however, is not part of this market because cars that use regular gasoline cannot use diesel fuel, and vice versa.[6]

Market definition is important for a number of reasons. A company, for example, has to understand what its actual and potential competitors are for the various products it now sells or might sell in the future. A company also has to know the product-characteristic boundaries and geographical boundaries of its market in order to be able to set price, determine advertising budgets, and make capital investment decisions. Market definition is likewise important for public-policy decisions. Should the government allow a merger or acquisition involving companies that produce similar products, or should it challenge it? The answer depends on the impact of that merger or acquisition on future competition and prices, and often this can only be evaluated by defining the market.

1.5 Real Versus Nominal Prices

We often want to compare the price of a good today with what it was in the past or is likely to be in the future. To make such a comparison meaningful, we need to measure prices relative to the overall price level. In absolute terms, the price of a dozen eggs is many times higher today than it was 50 years ago, but relative to prices overall, it is actually lower. Therefore, we must be careful to correct for inflation when comparing prices across time. This means measuring prices in *real* rather than *nominal* terms.

The *nominal price* of a good (sometimes called its "current dollar" price) is just its absolute price. For example, the nominal price of a quart of milk was about 40 cents in 1970, about 65 cents in 1980, and about 95 cents in 1996. These are the prices you would have seen in supermarkets in those years. The *real price* of a good (sometimes called its "constant dollar" price) is the price relative to an aggregate measure of prices.

The aggregate measure most often used is the Consumer Price Index (CPI). The CPI is calculated by the U.S. Bureau of Labor Statistics and is published monthly. It records how the cost of a large market basket of goods purchased by a "typical" consumer in some base year changes over time. (Currently the base is 1983.) Percentage changes in the CPI measure the rate of inflation in the economy.[7]

After correcting for inflation, was milk more expensive in 1996 than in 1970? To find out, let's calculate the 1996 price of milk in terms of 1970 dollars. The

---

[6] How can we determine the extent of a market? Since the market is where the price of a good is established, one approach focuses on market prices. We ask whether product prices in different geographic regions (or for different product types) are approximately the same, or whether they tend to move together. If either is the case, we place them in the same market. For a more detailed discussion, see George J. Stigler and Robert A. Sherwin, "The Extent of the Market," *Journal of Law and Economics* 27 (Oct. 1985): 555–585.

[7] Because the market basket is fixed, the CPI can tend to overstate inflation. The reason is that when the prices of some goods rise substantially, consumers will shift some of their purchases to goods whose prices have not risen as much, and the CPI ignores this.

CPI was 38.8 in 1970 and rose to about 157 in 1996.[8] (There was considerable inflation in the United States during the 1970s and early 1980s.) In 1970 dollars, the price of milk was therefore

$$\frac{38.8}{157} \times \$0.95 = \$0.23$$

In real terms the price of milk was lower in 1996 than it was in 1970. Put another way, the nominal price of milk went up by about 138 percent, but the CPI went up 305 percent, which means that milk prices fell relative to inflation.

In this book we will usually be concerned with real rather than nominal prices because consumer choices involve an analysis of how one price compares with another. These relative prices can most easily be evaluated if there is a common basis of comparison. Stating all prices in real terms achieves this objective. Thus, even though we will often measure prices in dollars, we will be thinking in terms of the real purchasing power of those dollars.

EXAMPLE 1.1 The Price of Eggs and the Price of a College Education

In 1970 Grade A large eggs cost about 61 cents a dozen. In the same year, the average annual cost of a college education in a private four-year college, including room and board, was about $2,530. By 1995 the price of eggs had risen to 96 cents a dozen, and the average cost of a college education was $16,685. In real terms, were eggs more expensive in 1995 than in 1970? Had a college education become more expensive?

Table 1.1 shows the nominal price of eggs, the nominal cost of a college education, and the CPI for 1970–1995. (The CPI is based on 1983 = 100.) Also

Table 1.1 The Real Prices of Eggs and of a College Education

	1970	1975	1980	1985	1990	1995
Consumer Price Index	38.8	53.8	82.4	107.6	130.7	152.4
Nominal Prices						
Grade A Large Eggs	$0.61	$0.77	$0.84	$0.80	$0.98	$0.96
College Education	$2530	$3403	$4912	$8156	$12,800	$16,685
Real Prices ($1970)						
Grade A Large Eggs	$0.61	$0.56	$0.40	$0.29	$0.30	$0.24
College Education	$2530	$2454	$2313	$2941	$3800	$4248

[8] Two good sources of data on the national economy are the *Economic Report of the President* and the *Statistical Abstract of the United States*. Both are published annually and are available from the U.S. Government Printing Office.

shown are the *real* prices of eggs and a college education in 1970 dollars, calculated as follows:

$$\text{Real price of eggs in 1975} = \frac{\text{CPI}_{1970}}{\text{CPI}_{1975}} \times \text{nominal price in 1975}$$

$$\text{Real price of eggs in 1980} = \frac{\text{CPI}_{1970}}{\text{CPI}_{1980}} \times \text{nominal price in 1980}$$

and so forth.

The table shows clearly that the real cost of a college education rose (by 68 percent) during this period, while the real cost of eggs fell (by 61 percent). It is these relative changes in the prices of eggs and college that are important for the choices that consumers must make, not the fact that both eggs and college cost more in dollars today than they did in 1970.

In the table, we calculated real prices in terms of 1970 dollars, but we could have just as easily calculated them in terms of the dollars of some other base year. For example, suppose we want to calculate the real price of eggs in *1980 dollars*. Then:

$$\text{Real price of eggs in 1975} = \frac{\text{CPI}_{1980}}{\text{CPI}_{1975}} \times \text{nominal price in 1975}$$

$$\text{Real price of eggs in 1985} = \frac{\text{CPI}_{1980}}{\text{CPI}_{1985}} \times \text{nominal price in 1985}$$

and so forth. By going through the calculations, you can check that in terms of 1980 dollars, the real price of eggs was $1.30 in 1970, $1.18 in 1975, 84 cents in 1980, 61 cents in 1985, 62 cents in 1990, and 52 cents in 1995. You can also check that the percentage declines in real price are the same no matter which base year we use.

EXAMPLE 1.2 The Minimum Wage

The federal minimum wage—first instituted in 1938 at a level of 25 cents per hour—has been increased periodically over the years. From 1981 through 1989, for example, the minimum wage was $3.35 an hour and was raised to $4.25 an hour in 1990. In 1996, after much deliberation and debate, the Congress voted to raise the minimum wage to $4.70 in 1996 and then to $5.15 in 1997.[9]

Figure 1.1 shows the minimum wage from 1938 through 1997, both in nominal terms and in 1990 constant dollars. Note that although the legislated minimum wage has steadily increased, in real terms the minimum wage today is not very different from what it was in the 1950s.

[9] Some states also have a minimum wage that is higher than the federal minimum wage.

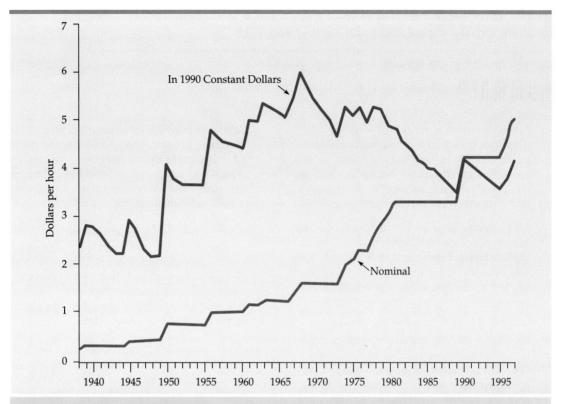

Figure 1.1 The Minimum Wage In nominal terms, the minimum wage has increased steadily over the past 60 years. However, in real terms its level in 1997 is below that of the 1970s.

Nonetheless, the decision made in 1996 to increase the minimum wage was a difficult one. Although the higher minimum wage would provide a better standard of living for those workers who had been paid below the minimum, it was feared that it would also lead to increased unemployment of young and unskilled workers. The decision to increase the minimum wage raises both normative and positive issues. The normative issue is whether any loss of teenage and low-skilled jobs is outweighed by the direct benefits to those workers who now earn more as a result, and by any indirect benefits to other workers whose wages might be increased along with the wages of those at the bottom of the pay scale.

An important positive issue associated with the minimum wage is how many fewer workers (if any) would be able to get jobs with a higher minimum wage. As we will see in Chapter 14, this issue is still hotly debated. Statistical studies have suggested that an increase in the minimum wage of about 10 percent would increase teenage unemployment 1 to 2 percent. (The actual increase from $4.25 to $5.15 represents a $0.90/$4.25 or 21 percent increase.) However, a recent review of the evidence has questioned whether there are any significant unemployment effects at all.[10]

Summary

1. Microeconomics is concerned with the decisions made by small economic units—consumers, workers, investors, owners of resources, and business firms. It is also concerned with the interaction of consumers and firms to form markets and industries.

2. Microeconomics relies heavily on the use of theory, which can (by simplification) help to explain how economic units behave and predict what that behavior will be in the future. Models are mathematical representations of theory that can help in this explanation and prediction process.

3. Microeconomics is concerned with positive questions that have to do with the explanation and prediction of phenomena. But microeconomics is also important for normative analysis, in which we ask what choices are best—for a firm or for society as a whole. Normative analyses must often be combined with individual value judgments because issues of equity and fairness as well as of economic efficiency may be involved.

4. A *market* refers to a collection of buyers and sellers who interact and to the possibility for sales and purchases that results from that interaction. Microeconomics involves the study of both perfectly competitive markets in which no single buyer or seller has an impact on price and noncompetitive markets in which individual entities can affect price.

5. The market price is established by the interaction of buyers and sellers. In a perfectly competitive market, a single price will usually prevail. In markets that are not perfectly competitive, different sellers might charge different prices. Then the market price refers to the average prevailing price.

6. When discussing a market, we must be clear about its extent in terms both of its geographic boundaries and of the range of products to be included in it. Some markets (e.g., housing) are highly localized, whereas others (e.g., gold) are worldwide.

7. To eliminate the effects of inflation, we measure real (or constant dollar) prices, rather than nominal (or current dollar) prices. Real prices use an aggregate price index, such as the CPI, to correct for inflation.

Questions for Review

1. What is the difference between a market and an industry? Are there interactions among firms in different industries that you might describe as taking place within a single market?

2. It is often said that a good theory is one that can in principle be refuted by an empirical, data-oriented study. Explain why a theory that cannot be evaluated empirically is not a good theory.

3. Which of the following two statements involves positive economic analysis and which normative? How do the two kinds of analysis differ?

---

[10] The first study is David Neumark and William Wascher, "Employment Effects of Minimum and Subminimum Wages: Panel Data on State Minimum Wage Laws," *Industrial and Labor Relations Review* 46 (Oct. 1992): 55–81. The review of the literature appears in David Card and Alan Krueger, *Myth and Measurement: The New Economics of the Minimum Wage* (Princeton: Princeton University Press, 1995).

a. Gasoline rationing (allocating to each individual a maximum amount of gasoline that can be purchased each year) is a poor social policy because it interferes with the workings of the competitive market system.

b. Gasoline rationing is a policy under which more people are made worse off than are made better off.

4. Suppose the price of unleaded regular octane gasoline were 20 cents per gallon higher in New Jersey than in Oklahoma. Do you think there would be an opportunity for arbitrage (i.e., that firms could buy gas in Oklahoma and then sell it at a profit in Jersey)? Why or why not?

5. In Example 1.1, what economic forces explain why the real price of eggs has fallen, while the real price of a college education has increased? How have these changes affected consumer choices?

6. Suppose that the Japanese yen rises against the U.S. dollar; that is, it now takes more dollars to buy any given amount of Japanese yen. Explain why this simultaneously increases the real price of Japanese cars for U.S. consumers and lowers the real price of U.S. automobiles for Japanese consumers.

Chapter Outline

List of Examples

CHAPTER 2

The Basics of Supply and Demand

One of the best ways to appreciate the relevance of economics is to begin with the basics of supply and demand. Supply-demand analysis is a fundamental and powerful tool that can be applied to a wide variety of interesting and important problems. To name a few: understanding and predicting how changing world economic conditions affect market price and production; evaluating the impact of government price controls, minimum wages, price supports, and production incentives; and determining how taxes, subsidies, tariffs, and import quotas affect consumers and producers.

We begin with a review of how supply and demand curves are used to describe the market mechanism. Without government intervention (e.g., through the imposition of price controls or some other regulatory policy), supply and demand will come into equilibrium to determine the market price of a good and the total quantity produced. What that price and quantity will be depends on the particular characteristics of supply and demand. And how price and quantity vary over time depends on how supply and demand respond to other economic variables, such as aggregate economic activity and labor costs, which are themselves changing.

We will, therefore, discuss the characteristics of supply and demand and how those characteristics may differ from one market to another. Then we can begin to use supply and demand curves to understand a variety of phenomena—why the prices of some basic commodities have fallen steadily over a long period, while the prices of others have experienced sharp gyrations; why shortages occur in certain markets; and why announcements about plans for future government policies or predictions about future economic conditions can affect markets well before those policies or conditions become reality.

Besides understanding *qualitatively* how market price and quantity are determined and how they can vary over time, it is also important to learn how they can be analyzed *quantitatively*. We will see how simple "back of the envelope" calculations can be used to analyze and predict evolving market conditions, and how markets respond both to domestic and international macroeconomic fluctuations and to the effects of government interventions. We will try to convey this understanding through simple examples and by urging you to work through some exercises at the end of the chapter.

2.1 The Market Mechanism

Let us begin with a brief review of the basic supply-demand diagram as shown in Figure 2.1. The vertical axis shows the price of a good, P, measured in dollars per unit. This is the price that sellers receive for a given quantity supplied

Figure 2.1 **Supply and Demand** The market clears at price P_0 and quantity Q_0. At the higher price P_1 a surplus develops, so price falls. At the lower price P_2 there is a shortage, so price is bid up.

and that buyers will pay for a given quantity demanded. The horizontal axis shows the total quantity demanded and supplied, Q, measured in number of units per period.

The *supply curve S* tells us how much producers are willing to sell for each price that they receive in the market. We can write this relationship between the quantity supplied and the price as an equation:

$$Q_S = Q_S(P)$$

or we can draw it graphically as in Figure 2.1. In that figure, the supply curve slopes upward because the higher the price, the more firms are usually able and willing to produce and sell. For example, a higher price may enable existing firms to expand production in the short run by hiring extra workers or by having existing workers work overtime (at greater cost to the firm), and in the long run by increasing the size of their plants. A higher price may also attract into the market new firms that face higher costs because of their inexperience and that therefore would have found entry into the market uneconomical at a lower price.

The *demand curve D* tells us how much consumers are willing to buy for each price per unit that they must pay. We can write it mathematically as

$$Q_D = Q_D(P)$$

or we can draw it graphically as in Figure 2.1. In the figure, it slopes downward because consumers are usually ready to buy more if the price is lower. For example, a lower price may encourage consumers who have already been buying the good to consume a larger quantity, and it may enable other consumers who previously might not have been able to afford the good to begin buying it.

The two curves intersect at the *equilibrium*, or *market-clearing*, price and quantity. At this price P_0, the quantity supplied and the quantity demanded are just equal (to Q_0). The *market mechanism* is the tendency in a free market for the price to change until the market clears (i.e., until the quantity supplied and the quantity demanded are equal). At this point there is neither shortage nor excess supply, so there is also no pressure for the price to change further. Supply and demand might not always be in equilibrium, and some markets might not clear quickly when conditions change suddenly, but the *tendency* is for markets to clear.

To understand why markets tend to clear, suppose the price were initially above the market-clearing level, say, P_1 in Figure 2.1. Then producers would try to produce and sell more than consumers were willing to buy. A surplus would accumulate, and to sell this surplus or at least prevent it from growing producers would begin to lower their prices. Eventually price would fall, quantity demanded would increase, and quantity supplied would decrease until the equilibrium price P_0 was reached.

The opposite would happen if the price were initially below P_0, say, at P_2. A shortage would develop because consumers would be unable to purchase all they would like at this price. This would put upward pressure on price as consumers tried to outbid one another for existing supplies and producers reacted by increasing price and expanding output. Again, the price would eventually reach P_0.

When we draw and use supply and demand curves, we are assuming that at any given price, a given quantity will be produced and sold. This makes sense only if a market is at least roughly *competitive*. By this we mean that both sellers and buyers should have little *market power* (i.e., little ability *individually* to affect the market price). Suppose instead that supply were controlled by a single producer—a monopolist. In this case there would no longer be a simple one-to-one relationship between price and quantity supplied. The reason is that a monopolist's behavior depends on the shape and position of the demand curve. If the demand curve shifted in a particular way, it might be in the monopolist's interest to keep the quantity fixed but change the price, or keep the price fixed and change the quantity. (How this could occur is explained in Chapter 10.) So when we work with supply and demand curves, we implicitly assume that we are referring to a competitive market.

2.2 Shifts in Supply and Demand

Supply and demand curves tell us how much competitive producers and consumers are willing to sell and buy as functions of the price they receive and pay. But supply and demand are also determined by other variables besides price. For example, the quantity that producers are willing to sell depends not only on the price they receive but also on their production costs, including wages, interest charges, and costs of raw materials. And in addition to price, quantity demanded depends on the total disposable income available to consumers, the prices of other products, and other variables.

Individual supply and demand curves, such as those shown in Figure 2.1, are drawn for particular values of the supply-determining variables (e.g., production costs) and demand-determining variables (e.g., income, tastes). A change in the values of one or more of the supply-determining variables translates into a shift in the supply curve; correspondingly, a change in the values of the demand-determining variables shifts the demand curve. Later we will want to determine how changes in economic conditions or tax or regulatory policy affect market prices and quantities. To do this, we must understand how supply and demand curves shift in response to changes in such variables as wage rates, capital costs, and income.

Let's begin with the supply curve S in Figure 2.2. This curve shows how much producers are willing to sell as a function of market price.[1] For example at a price P_1, the quantity produced and sold would be Q_1. Now suppose that the cost of raw materials *falls*. How does this affect the supply curve?

---

[1] We can write the supply curve mathematically as
$$Q_S = S(P, \text{COSTS})$$
where COSTS represents wages and raw materials costs. In Figure 2.2, we have drawn the relationship between the quantity supplied and the price, *holding these costs constant*.

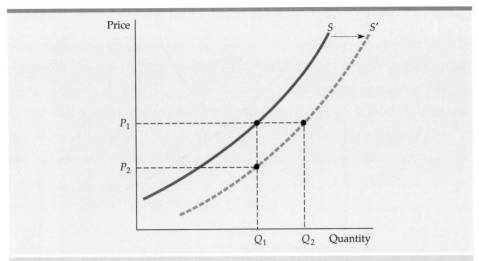

Figure 2.2 Shift in Supply If production costs fall, firms can produce the same quantity at a lower price or a larger quantity at the same price. The supply curve shifts to the right.

Lower raw material costs, indeed lower costs of any kind, make production more profitable, encouraging existing firms to expand production and enabling new firms to enter the market and produce. So if the market price stayed constant at P_1, we would expect to observe a greater supply of output than before. Figure 2.2 shows this as an increase from Q_1 to Q_2. Output increases no matter what the market price happens to be, *so the entire supply curve shifts to the right*, which is shown in the figure as a shift from S to S'.

Another way of looking at the effect of lower raw material costs is to imagine that the quantity produced stays fixed at Q_1 and to consider what price firms would require to produce this quantity. Because their costs are lower, the price they would require would also be lower—P_2 in Figure 2.2. This will be the case no matter what quantity is produced. Again, we see in the figure that the supply curve must shift to the right.

Of course, neither price nor quantity will always remain fixed when costs fall. Usually both will change as the new supply curve comes into equilibrium with the demand curve. This is illustrated in Figure 2.3, where the supply curve has shifted from S to S' as it did in Figure 2.2. As a result, the market price drops (from P_1 to P_3), and the total quantity produced increases (from Q_1 to Q_3). This is just what we would expect: Lower costs result in lower prices and increased sales. (And indeed, gradual decreases in costs resulting from technological progress and better management are an important driving force behind economic growth.)

We have seen that the response of the quantity supplied of a good to changes in the price of that good can be represented by movements *along a supply curve*. However, the response of supply to changes in other supply-determining variables is shown graphically as a *shift of the supply curve*. To distinguish these

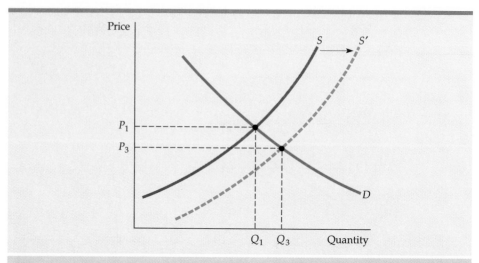

Figure 2.3 New Equilibrium Following Shift in Supply When the supply curve shifts to the right, the market clears at a lower price P_3 and a larger quantity Q_3.

two graphical depictions of supply changes, economists often use the phrase *change in supply* to refer to shifts in the supply curve, while reserving the phrase *change in the quantity supplied* to apply to movements along the supply curve.

Now let's turn to Figure 2.4 and the demand curve labeled D. How would an *increase in disposable income* affect demand?

With greater disposable income, consumers can spend more money on any good, and some consumers will do so for most goods. If the market price were held constant at P_1, we would, therefore, expect to see an increase in quantity demanded, say, from Q_1 to Q_2. This would happen no matter what the market price was, so that the result would be a *shift to the right of the entire demand curve*. In the figure, this is shown as a shift from D to D'. Alternatively, we can ask what price consumers would pay to purchase a given quantity Q_1. With greater disposable income, they should be willing to pay a higher price, say, P_2 instead of P_1 in Figure 2.4. Again, *the demand curve will shift to the right*. As we did with supply, we will use the phrase *change in demand* to refer to shifts in the demand curve, while reserving the phrase *change in the quantity demanded* to apply to movements along the demand curve.[2]

In general, neither price nor quantity remains constant when demand changes as disposable income increases. A new price and quantity result after demand comes into equilibrium with supply. As shown in Figure 2.5, we would expect to see consumers pay a higher price P_3 and firms produce a greater quantity Q_3 as a result of an increase in disposable income.

---

[2] Mathematically, we can write the demand curve as
$$Q_D = D(P, I)$$
where I is disposable income. When we draw a demand curve, we are keeping I fixed.

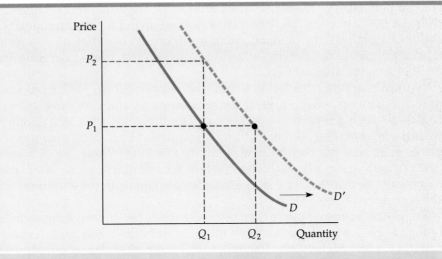

Figure 2.4   Shift in Demand   The demand for a product depends on its price but may also depend on other variables, such as income, the weather, and the prices of other goods. For most products, demand increases when income rises. A higher income level shifts the demand curve to the right.

Changes in the prices of related goods also affect demand. For example, copper and aluminum are substitute goods. Because one can often be substituted for the other in industrial use, the demand for copper will increase if the price of aluminum increases. Automobiles and gasoline, on the other hand,

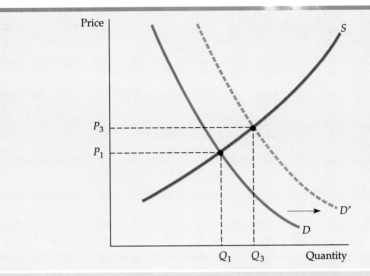

Figure 2.5   New Equilibrium Following Shift in Demand   When the demand curve shifts to the right, the market clears at a higher price P_3 and a larger quantity Q_3.

are complementary goods (i.e., they tend to be used together). Therefore, a decrease in the price of gasoline increases the demand for automobiles. So the shift to the right of the demand curve in Figure 2.5 could also have resulted from an increase in the price of a substitute good or from a decrease in the price of a complementary good.

In most markets both the demand and supply curves shift from time to time. Consumers' disposable incomes change as the economy grows (or contracts, during economic recessions). The demands for some goods shift with the seasons (e.g., fuels, bathing suits, umbrellas), with changes in the prices of related goods (an increase in oil prices increases the demand for natural gas), or simply with changing tastes. Similarly wage rates, capital costs, and the prices of raw materials also change from time to time, which shifts supply.

Supply and demand curves can be used to trace the effects of these changes. In Figure 2.6, for example, shifts to the right of both supply and demand result in a slightly higher price (from P_1 to P_2) and a much larger quantity (from Q_1 to Q_2). In general, price and quantity will change depending both on how much the supply and demand curves shift and on the shapes of those curves. To predict the sizes and directions of such changes, we must be able to quantitatively characterize the dependence of supply and demand on price and other variables. We will turn to this in the next section.

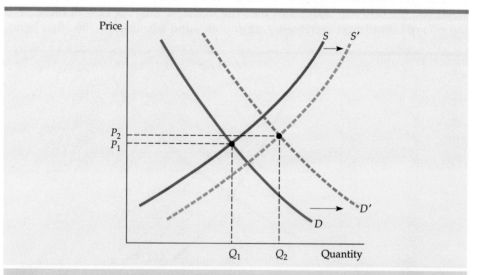

Figure 2.6 New Equilibrium Following Shifts in Supply and Demand
Supply and demand curves shift over time as market conditions change. In this example, rightward shifts of the supply and demand curves lead to slightly higher price and a much larger quantity. In general, changes in price and quantity depend on the amount by which each curve shifts and the shape of each curve.

EXAMPLE 2.1	The Price of Eggs and the Price of a College Education

In Example 1.1, we saw that from 1970 to 1995, the real (constant dollar) price of eggs fell by 61 percent, whereas the real price of a college education rose by 68 percent. What caused this large decline in egg prices and large increase in the price of college?

We can understand these price changes by examining the behavior of supply and demand for each good, as shown in Figure 2.7. For eggs, the mechanization of poultry farms sharply reduced the cost of producing eggs, shifting the supply curve downward over this period. At the same time, the demand curve for eggs shifted to the left as a more health (and cholesterol) conscious population changed its eating habits, tending to avoid eggs. As a result, not only did the real price of eggs decline sharply, but total annual consumption fell somewhat (from 5300 million dozen to 5100 million dozen).

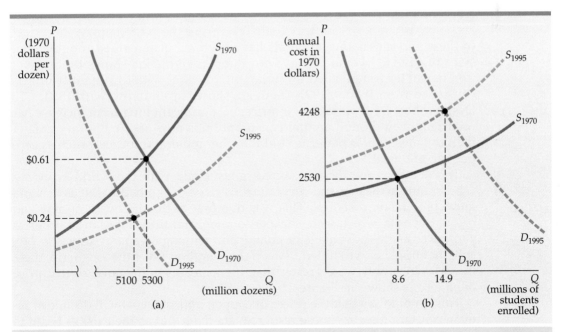

(a)

(b)

Figure 2.7(a)   Market for Eggs   The supply curve for eggs shifted down as production costs fell, and the demand curve shifted to the left as consumer preferences changed. As a result, the real price of eggs fell sharply, and egg consumption fell slightly.

Figure 2.7(b)   Market for College Education   The supply curve for a college education shifted up as the costs of equipment, maintenance, and staffing rose. The demand curve shifted to the right as a growing number of high school graduates desired a college education. As a result, both price and enrollments rose sharply.

For college, supply and demand shifted in the opposite directions. Increases in the costs of equipping and maintaining modern classrooms, laboratories, and libraries, along with increases in faculty salaries, pushed the supply curve up. At the same time, the demand curve shifted to the right as a larger and larger percentage of a growing number of high school graduates decided that a college education was essential. Thus, despite the increase in price, 1995 found nearly 15 million students enrolled in college degree programs, compared with 8.6 million in 1970.

EXAMPLE 2.2 The Long-Run Behavior of Mineral Prices

The early 1970s was a period of public concern about the earth's natural resources. Groups like the Club of Rome predicted that our energy and mineral resources would soon be depleted, so that prices would skyrocket and bring an end to economic growth.[3] But these predictions ignored basic microeconomics. The earth does indeed have only a finite amount of minerals, such as copper, iron, and coal. Yet during the past century, the prices of these and most other minerals have declined or remained roughly constant relative to overall prices. For example, Figure 2.8 shows the price of iron in real terms (adjusted for inflation), together with the quantity of iron consumed from 1880 to 1995. (Both are shown as an index, with 1880 = 1.) Despite short-term variations in price, no significant long-term increase has occurred, even though annual consumption is now about 20 times greater than in 1880. Similar patterns hold for other mineral resources, such as copper, oil, and coal.[4]

The demands for these resources grew along with the world economy. (These shifts in the demand curve are illustrated in Figure 2.9.) But as demand grew, production costs fell. This was due first to the discovery of new and bigger deposits, which were cheaper to mine, and then to technical progress and the economic advantage of mining and refining on a large scale. As a result, the supply curve shifted to the right over time. Over the long term, these increases in supply were greater than the increases in demand, so that price often fell, as shown in Figure 2.9.

This is not to say that the prices of copper, iron, and coal will decline or remain constant forever—these resources are *finite*. But as their prices begin to

---

[3] See, for example, Dennis Meadows et al., *The Limits to Growth* (New York: Potomac Associates, 1972). This book and others like it struck a resonant chord in the public consciousness. Unfortunately these studies ignored such basic economic phenomena as cost reduction resulting from technical progress, experience, and economies of scale, and substitution of alternative resources (including nondepletable ones) in response to higher prices. For a discussion of these issues, see Julian L. Simon, *The Ultimate Resource* (Princeton, N.J.: Princeton University Press, 1981).

[4] The data in Figure 2.8 are from Robert S. Manthy, *Natural Resource Commodities—A Century of Statistics* (Baltimore: Johns Hopkins University Press, 1978), supplemented after 1973 with data from the U.S. Bureau of Mines, and from the World Bank.

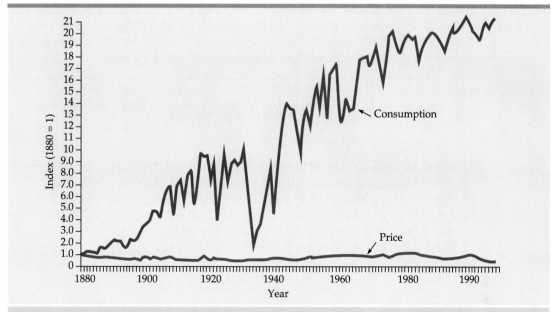

Figure 2.8 Consumption and Price of Iron, 1880–1995 Annual consumption has increased about twentyfold, but the real (inflation-adjusted) price has not changed much.

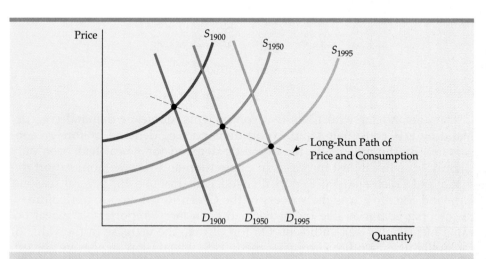

Figure 2.9 Long-Run Movements of Supply and Demand for Mineral Resources Demand for most resources has increased dramatically over the past century, but prices have fallen or risen only slightly in real (inflation-adjusted) terms because cost reductions have shifted the supply curve to the right just as dramatically.

rise, consumption will likely shift at least in part to substitute materials. For example, copper has already been replaced in many applications by aluminum, and more recently in electronic applications by fiber optics. (See Example 2.6 for a more detailed discussion of copper prices.)

E X A M P L E   2.3   **The Market for Wheat**

Wheat is an important agricultural commodity, and the market for it has been studied extensively by agricultural economists. During the 1980s and 1990s, changes in the wheat market had major implications for American farmers and for U.S. agricultural policy. To understand what happened, let us examine the behavior of supply and demand over this period.

From statistical studies, we know that for 1981 the supply curve for wheat was approximately as follows[5]

$$\text{Supply:} \qquad Q_S = 1800 + 240P$$

where price is measured in dollars per bushel and quantities are in millions of bushels per year. These studies also indicate that in 1981 the demand curve for wheat was

$$\text{Demand:} \qquad Q_D = 3550 - 266P$$

By setting the quantity supplied equal to the quantity demanded, we can determine the market-clearing price of wheat for 1981:

$$Q_S = Q_D$$

$$1800 + 240P = 3550 - 266P$$

$$506P = 1750$$

$$P = \$3.46 \text{ per bushel}$$

The demand for wheat has two components: domestic demand (i.e., demand by U.S. consumers) and export demand (i.e., demand by foreign consumers). By the mid-1980s, the domestic demand for wheat had risen only slightly (due to modest increases in population and income), but export demand had fallen sharply. Export demand had dropped for several reasons. First and foremost was the success of the Green Revolution in agriculture—developing countries like India that had been large importers of wheat became increasingly self-sufficient. On top of this, the increase in the value of the dollar against other currencies made U.S. wheat more expensive abroad. Finally, European countries adopted protectionist policies that subsidized their

---

[5] For a survey of statistical studies of the demand and supply of wheat and an analysis of evolving market conditions, see Larry Salathe and Sudchada Langley, "An Empirical Analysis of Alternative Export Subsidy Programs for U.S. Wheat," *Agricultural Economics Research* 38, No. 1 (Winter 1986). The supply and demand curves in this example are based on the studies they survey.

own production and imposed tariff barriers against imported wheat. In 1985, for example, the demand curve for wheat was

Demand: $Q_D = 2580 - 194P$

(The supply curve remained more or less the same as in 1981.)

Now we can again equate the quantity supplied and the quantity demanded and determine the market-clearing price for 1985:

$$1800 + 240P = 2580 - 194P$$

$$P = \$1.80 \text{ per bushel}$$

We see, then, that the major shift in export demand led to a sharp drop in the market-clearing price of wheat—from $3.46 in 1981 to $1.80 in 1985.

By 1993, the demand for U.S. wheat was much stronger. Although domestic demand had not changed much from 1985, annual exports had increased by nearly 350 million bushels. The supply curve for wheat had shifted only slightly. In 1993, demand and supply were

Demand: $Q_D = 3385 - 279P$

Supply: $Q_S = 1728 + 228P$

Once again, equating the quantity supplied and the quantity demanded yields the market-clearing price for 1993:

$$1728 + 228P = 3385 - 279P$$

$$P = \$3.27 \text{ per bushel}$$

Thus by 1993, the market-clearing price had rebounded to $3.27 per bushel.

Was the price of wheat actually $3.46 in 1981? Did it actually fall to $1.80 in 1985, and then rise to $3.27 in 1993? No—consumers paid about $3.70 in 1981, about $3.20 in 1985, and about $3.30 in 1993. Furthermore, throughout this period American farmers received more than $4 for each bushel they produced. Why? Because the U.S. government has propped up the price of wheat and has paid subsidies to farmers. We discuss exactly how this is done and evaluate the costs and benefits for consumers, farmers, and the federal budget in Chapter 9.

2.3 Elasticities of Supply and Demand

We have seen that the demand for a good depends on its price, as well as on consumer income and on the prices of other goods. Similarly, supply depends on price, as well as on variables that affect production cost. For example, if the price of coffee increases, the quantity demanded will fall, and the quantity supplied will rise. Often, however, we want to know *how much* the quantity supplied or demanded will rise or fall. How sensitive is the demand for coffee to its price? If price increases by 10 percent, how much will the quantity demanded change? How much will it change if income rises by 5 percent? We use *elasticities* to answer questions like these.

An elasticity is a measure of the sensitivity of one variable to another. Specifically, it is a number that tells us *the percentage change that will occur in one variable in response to a 1 percent change in another variable.* For example, the *price elasticity of demand* measures the sensitivity of quantity demanded to price changes. It tells us what the percentage change in the quantity demanded for a good will be following a 1 percent increase in the price of that good.

Let's look at this in more detail. Denoting quantity and price by Q and P, we write the price elasticity of demand as

$$E_p = (\%\Delta Q)/(\%\Delta P)$$

where $\%\Delta Q$ simply means "percentage change in Q" and $\%\Delta P$ means "percentage change in P."[6] But the percentage change in a variable is just the absolute change in the variable divided by the original level of the variable. (If the Consumer Price Index were 200 at the beginning of the year and increased to 204 by the end of the year, the percentage change—or annual rate of inflation—would be $4/200 = .02$, or 2 percent.) So we can also write the price elasticity of demand as[7]

$$E_P = \frac{\Delta Q/Q}{\Delta P/P} = \frac{P}{Q}\frac{\Delta Q}{\Delta P} \tag{2.1}$$

The price elasticity of demand is usually a negative number. When the price of a good increases, the quantity demanded usually falls, so $\Delta Q/\Delta P$ (the change in quantity for a change in price) is negative, and therefore E_p is negative.

When the price elasticity is greater than 1 in magnitude, we say that demand is *price elastic* because the percentage decline in quantity demanded is greater than the percentage increase in price. If the price elasticity is less than 1 in magnitude, demand is said to be *price inelastic*. In general, the elasticity of demand for a good depends on the availability of other goods that can be substituted for it. When there are close substitutes, a price increase will cause the consumer to buy less of the good and more of the substitute. Demand will then be highly price elastic. When there are no close substitutes, demand will tend to be price inelastic.

Equation (2.1) says that the price elasticity of demand is the change in quantity associated with a change in price $(\Delta Q/\Delta P)$ times the ratio of price to quantity (P/Q). But as we move down the demand curve, $\Delta Q/\Delta P$ may change, and the price and quantity will always change. Therefore, the price elasticity of demand must be measured *at a particular point on the demand curve* and will generally change as we move along the curve.

This is easiest to see for a *linear* demand curve, that is, a demand curve of the form

$$Q = a - bP$$

---

[6] The symbol Δ is the Greek capital letter delta; it means "the change in." So ΔX means "the change in the variable X," say, from one year to the next.

[7] In terms of infinitesimal changes (letting the ΔP become very small), $E_p = (P/Q)(dQ/dP)$.

As an example, consider the demand curve

$$Q = 8 - 2P$$

For this curve, $\Delta Q/\Delta P$ is constant and equal to -2 (a ΔP of 1 results in a ΔQ of -2). However, the curve does *not* have a constant elasticity. Observe from Figure 2.10 that as we move down the curve, the ratio P/Q falls, and therefore the elasticity decreases in magnitude. Near the intersection of the curve with the price axis, Q is very small, so $E_p = -2(P/Q)$ is large in magnitude. When $P = 2$ and $Q = 4$, $E_p = -1$. And at the intersection with the quantity axis, $P = 0$ so $E_p = 0$.

Because we draw demand (and supply) curves with price on the vertical axis and quantity on the horizontal axis, $\Delta Q/\Delta P = (1/\text{slope of curve})$. As a result, for any price and quantity combination, the steeper the slope of the curve, the less elastic demand is. Figures 2.11(a) and (b) show two special cases. Figure 2.11(a) shows a demand curve that is *infinitely elastic*. There is only a single price P^* at which consumers will buy the good; for even the smallest increase in price above this level, quantity demanded drops to zero, and for any decrease in price, quantity demanded increases without limit. The demand curve in Figure 2.11(b), on the other hand, is *completely inelastic*. Consumers will buy a fixed quantity Q^*, no matter what the price.

We will also be interested in elasticities of demand with respect to other variables besides price. For example, demand for most goods usually rises when aggregate income rises. The *income elasticity of demand* is the percent-

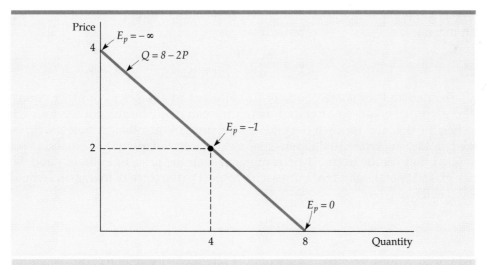

Figure 2.10 Linear Demand Curve The price elasticity of demand depends not only on the slope of the demand curve but also on the price and quantity. The elasticity, therefore, varies along the curve as price and quantity change. Slope is constant for this linear demand curve. Near the top, price is high and quantity is small, so the elasticity is large in magnitude. The elasticity becomes smaller as we move down the curve.

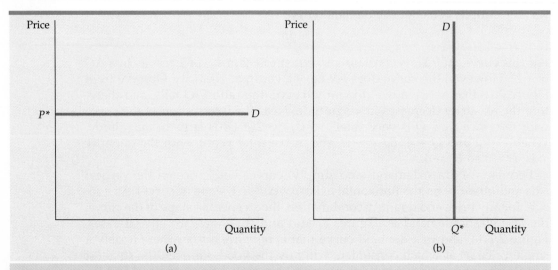

Figure 2.11(a) Infinitely Elastic Demand For a horizontal demand curve, $\Delta Q/\Delta P$ is infinite. (A tiny change in price leads to an enormous change in demand.) The elasticity of demand is, therefore, infinite.

Figure 2.11(b) Completely Inelastic Demand For a vertical demand curve, $\Delta Q/\Delta P$ is zero. The quantity demanded is the same no matter what the price, so the elasticity of demand is zero.

age change in the quantity demanded Q resulting from a 1 percent increase in income I:

$$E_I = \frac{\Delta Q/Q}{\Delta I/I} = \frac{I}{Q}\frac{\Delta Q}{\Delta I} \tag{2.2}$$

The demand for some goods is also affected by the prices of other goods. For example, because butter and margarine can easily be substituted for each other, the demand for each depends on the price of the other. A *cross-price elasticity of demand* refers to the percentage change in the quantity demanded for a good that results from a 1 percent increase in the price of another good. So the elasticity of demand for butter with respect to the price of margarine would be written as

$$E_{Q_b P_m} = \frac{\Delta Q_b/Q_b}{\Delta P_m/P_m} = \frac{P_m}{Q_b}\frac{\Delta Q_b}{\Delta P_m} \tag{2.3}$$

where Q_b is the quantity of butter and P_m is the price of margarine.

In this example of butter and margarine, the cross-price elasticities will be positive because the goods are *substitutes*—they compete in the market, so a rise in the price of margarine, which makes butter cheaper relative to margarine than it was before, leads to an increase in the demand for butter. (The demand curve for butter will shift to the right, so its price will rise.) But this is not always the case. Some goods are *complements*; they tend to be used together, so that an increase in the price of one tends to push down the consumption of the other. Gasoline and motor oil are an example. If the price of gasoline goes up, the quantity of gasoline demanded falls—motorists will drive less. But the demand for motor oil also falls. (The entire demand curve for motor oil shifts to the left.) Thus, the cross-price elasticity of motor oil with respect to gasoline is negative.

Elasticities of supply are defined in a similar manner. The *price elasticity of supply* is the percentage change in the quantity supplied resulting from a 1 percent increase in price. This elasticity is usually positive because a higher price gives producers an incentive to increase output.

We can also refer to elasticities of supply with respect to such variables as interest rates, wage rates, and the prices of raw materials and other intermediate goods used to manufacture the product in question. For example, for most manufactured goods, the elasticities of supply with respect to the prices of raw materials are negative. An increase in the price of a raw material input means higher costs for the firm, so other things being equal, the quantity supplied will fall.

2.4 Short-Run Versus Long-Run Elasticities

When analyzing demand and supply, it is important to distinguish between the short run and the long run. In other words, if we ask how much demand or supply changes in response to a change in price, we must be clear about *how much time is allowed to pass before measuring the changes in the quantity demanded or supplied.* If we allow only a short time to pass, say, one year or less, then we are dealing with the short run. In general, short-run demand and supply curves look very different from their long-run counterparts.

Demand

For many goods, demand is much more price elastic in the long run than in the short run. One reason is that people take time to change their consumption habits. For example, even if the price of coffee rises sharply, the quantity demanded will fall only gradually as consumers slowly begin to drink less of it. Another reason is that the demand for a good might be linked to the stock of another good, which changes only slowly. For example, the demand for gasoline is much more elastic in the long run than in the short run. A sharply higher price of gasoline reduces the quantity demanded in the short run by causing motorists to drive less, but it has its greatest impact on demand by inducing consumers to buy smaller and more fuel-efficient cars. But the stock of cars changes only slowly, so that the quantity of gasoline demanded falls only slowly. Figure 2.12(a) shows short-run and long-run demand curves for goods such as these.

On the other hand, for some goods just the opposite is true—demand is more elastic in the short run than in the long run. These goods (automobiles, refrigerators, televisions, or the capital equipment purchased by industry) are *durable*,

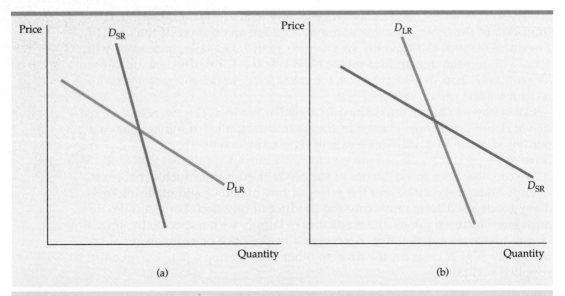

Figure 2.12(a)   Gasoline: Short-Run and Long-Run Demand Curves   In the short run, an increase in price has only a small effect on the quantity of gasoline demanded. Motorists may drive less, but they will not change the kind of car they are driving overnight. In the longer run, however, they will shift to smaller and more fuel-efficient cars, so the effect of the price increase will be larger. Demand is, therefore, more elastic in the long run than in the short run.

Figure 2.12(b)   Automobiles: Short-Run and Long-Run Demand Curves   The opposite is true for automobile demand. If price increases, consumers initially defer buying a new car, so that annual quantity demanded falls sharply. In the longer run, however, old cars wear out and must be replaced, so that annual quantity demanded picks up. Demand is, therefore, less elastic in the long run than in the short run.

so that the total stock of each good owned by consumers is large relative to the annual production. As a result, a small change in the total stock that consumers want to hold can result in a large percentage change in the level of purchases. Suppose, for example, that price goes up 10 percent, causing the total stock of the good consumers want to hold to drop 5 percent. Initially, this will cause purchases to drop much more than 5 percent. But eventually, as the stock depreciates (and units must be replaced), the quantity demanded will increase again, so that in the long run the total stock of the good owned by consumers will be about 5 percent less than before the price increase.

Automobiles are an example. (Annual U.S. demand—new car purchases—is about 8 to 11 million, but the stock of cars is around 120 million.) If automobile prices rise, many people will delay buying new cars, and the quantity demanded will fall sharply (even though the total stock of cars that consumers want to hold falls only a small amount). But eventually, old cars wear out and have to be replaced, so demand picks up again. As a result, the long-run change in the quantity demanded is much smaller than the short-run change. Figure 2.12(b) shows demand curves for a durable good like automobiles.

Income elasticities also differ from the short run to the long run. For most goods and services—foods, beverages, fuel, entertainment, etc.—the income elasticity of demand is larger in the long run than in the short run. For example, consider the behavior of gasoline consumption during a period of strong economic growth when aggregate income rises by 10 percent. Eventually people will increase their gasoline consumption—they can afford to take more trips and perhaps own a larger car. But this change in consumption takes time, and initially demand increases only a small amount. Thus, the long-run elasticity will be larger than the short-run elasticity.

For a durable good, the opposite is true. Again, consider automobiles. If aggregate income rises by 10 percent, the stock of cars that consumers will want to hold will also rise, say, by 5 percent. But this means a much larger increase in *current purchases* of cars. (If the stock is 120 million, a 5 percent in-

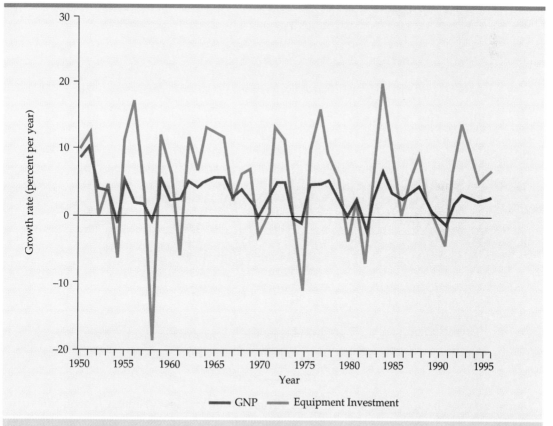

Figure 2.13   GNP and Investment in Durable Equipment   Annual growth rates are compared for GNP and investment in durable equipment. The short-run GNP elasticity of demand is larger than the long-run elasticity for long-lived capital equipment, so changes in investment in equipment magnify changes in GNP. Hence, capital goods industries are considered "cyclical."

crease is 6 million, which might be about 60 percent of normal demand in a single year.) Eventually consumers succeed in building up the stock of cars, after which new purchases are largely to replace old cars. (These new purchases will still be greater than before because with a larger stock of cars outstanding, more cars need to be replaced each year.) Clearly, the short-run income elasticity of demand will be much larger than the long-run elasticity.

Because the demands for durable goods fluctuate so sharply in response to short-run changes in income, the industries that produce these goods are very vulnerable to changing macroeconomic conditions, and in particular to the business cycle—recessions and booms. Hence, these industries are often called *cyclical* industries—their sales tend to magnify cyclical changes in gross national product (GNP) and national income.

Figures 2.13 and 2.14 illustrate this. Figure 2.13 plots two variables over time, the annual real (inflation-adjusted) rate of growth of GNP, and the annual real rate of growth of investment in producers' durable equipment (i.e., machinery and other equipment purchased by firms). Note that the durable

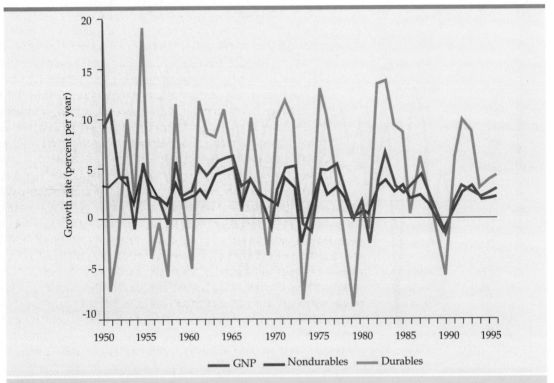

Figure 2.14   Consumption of Durables Versus Nondurables   Annual growth rates are compared for GNP, consumer expenditures on durable goods (automobiles, appliances, furniture, etc.), and consumer expenditures on nondurable goods (food, clothing, services, etc.). The stock of durables is large compared with annual demand, so short-run demand elasticities are larger than long-run elasticities. Like capital equipment, industries that produce consumer durables are "cyclical" (i.e., changes in GNP are magnified). This is not true for nondurables.

equipment series follows the same pattern as the GNP series, but the changes in GNP are magnified. For example, in 1961–1966 GNP grew by at least 4 percent each year. Purchases of durable equipment also grew but by much more (over 10 percent in 1963–1966). On the other hand, during the recessions of 1974–1975, 1982, and 1991, equipment purchases fell by much more than GNP.

Figure 2.14 also shows the real rate of growth of GNP, and in addition, the annual real rates of growth of spending by consumers on durable goods (automobiles, appliances, etc.), and on nondurable goods (food, fuel, clothing, etc.). Note that both consumption series follow GNP, but only the durable goods series tends to magnify the changes in GNP. Changes in consumption of nondurables are roughly the same as changes in GNP, but changes in consumption of durables are usually several times larger. It should be clear from this why companies such as General Motors and General Electric are considered "cyclical"—sales of cars and of electrical appliances are strongly affected by changing macroeconomic conditions.

EXAMPLE 2.4   The Demands for Gasoline and Automobiles

Gasoline and automobiles exemplify some of the different characteristics of demand discussed above. They are complementary goods—an increase in the price of one tends to reduce the demand for the other. And their respective dynamic behaviors (long-run versus short-run elasticities) are just the opposite from each other—for gasoline the long-run price and income elasticities are larger than the short-run elasticities; for automobiles the reverse is true.

There have been a number of statistical studies of the demands for gasoline and automobiles. Here we report estimates of price and income elasticities from two studies that emphasize the dynamic response of demand.[8] Table 2.1 shows price and income elasticities of demand for gasoline in the United States for the short run, the long run, and just about everything in between.

Table 2.1   Demand For Gasoline

Elasticity	Years Following Price or Income Change					
	1	2	3	5	10	20
Price	−0.11	−0.22	−0.32	−0.49	−0.82	−1.17
Income	0.07	0.13	0.20	0.32	0.54	0.78

[8] The study of gasoline demand is in Robert S. Pindyck, *The Structure of World Energy Demand* (Cambridge, Mass.: MIT Press, 1979). The estimates of automobile demand elasticities are based on the article by Saul H. Hymans, "Consumer Durable Spending: Explanation and Prediction," *Brookings Papers on Economic Activity* 1 (1971): 173–199.

Table 2.2	Demand For Automobiles					
	Years Following Price or Income Change					
Elasticity	**1**	**2**	**3**	**5**	**10**	**20**
Price	−1.20	−0.93	−0.75	−0.55	−0.42	−0.40
Income	3.00	2.33	1.88	1.38	1.02	1.00

Note the large differences between the long-run and the short-run elasticities. Following the sharp increases that occurred in the price of gasoline with the rise of the OPEC cartel in 1974, many people (including executives in the automobile and oil industries) claimed that the demand for gasoline would not change much—that demand was not very elastic. Indeed, for the first year after the price rise, they were right—the quantity demanded did not change much. But demand did eventually change. It just took time for people to alter their driving habits and to replace large cars with smaller and more fuel-efficient ones. This response continued after the second sharp increase in oil prices that occurred in 1979–1980. It is partly because of this that OPEC could not maintain oil prices above $30 per barrel, and prices fell.

Table 2.2 shows price and income elasticities of demand for automobiles. Note that the short-run elasticities are much larger than the long-run elasticities. It should be clear from the income elasticities why the automobile industry is so highly cyclical. For example, GNP fell by nearly 3 percent in real (inflation-adjusted) terms during the 1982 recession, but automobile sales fell by about 8 percent in real terms.[9] Auto sales recovered, however, during 1983–1985. Auto sales also fell by about 8 percent during the 1991 recession (when GNP fell 2 percent), but began to recover in 1993.

Supply

Elasticities of supply also differ from the long run to the short run. For most products, long-run supply is much more price elastic than short-run supply because firms face *capacity constraints* in the short run and need time to expand their capacity by building new production facilities and hiring workers to staff them. This is not to say that the quantity supplied will not increase in the short run if price goes up sharply. Even in the short run, firms can increase output by using their existing facilities more hours per week, paying workers to work overtime, and hiring some new workers immediately. But firms will be able to expand output much more given the time to expand their facilities and hire a larger permanent work force.

---

[9] This includes imports, which were capturing a growing share of the U.S. market. Domestic auto sales fell by even more.

For some goods and services, short-run supply is completely inelastic. Rental housing in most cities is an example. In the very short run, because there is only a fixed number of rental units, an increase in demand only pushes rents up. In the longer run, and without rent controls, higher rents provide an incentive to renovate existing buildings and construct new ones, so that the quantity supplied increases.

For most goods, however, firms can find ways to increase output even in the short run, if the price incentive is strong enough. The problem is that because of the constraints that firms face, it is costly to increase output rapidly, so that it may require a large price increase to elicit a small short-run increase in the quantity supplied. We discuss these characteristics of supply in more detail in Chapter 8, but for now it should be clear why for many goods, short-run and long-run supply curves resemble those in Figure 2.15(a). (The figure refers to the supply of primary [newly mined] copper, but it could also apply to many other goods.)

For some goods, supply is more elastic in the short run than in the long run. Such goods are durable and can be recycled as part of supply if price goes up. An example is the *secondary supply* of metals (i.e., the supply from *scrap metal*, which is often melted down and refabricated). When the price of

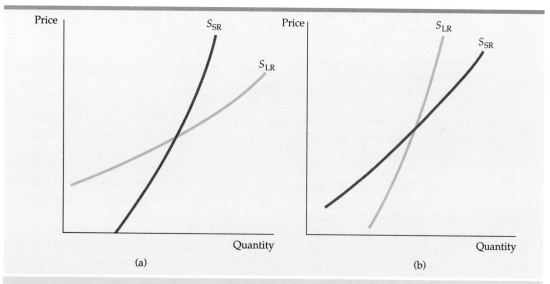

Figure 2.15(a)   Primary Copper: Short-Run and Long-Run Supply Curves   Like most goods, supply is more elastic in the long run. If price increases, firms would like to produce more but are limited by capacity constraints in the short run. In the longer run, they can add to capacity and produce more.

Figure 2.15(b)   Secondary Copper: Short-Run and Long-Run Supply Curves   If price increases, there is a greater incentive to convert scrap copper into new supply, so initially secondary supply (i.e., supply from scrap) increases sharply. But later, as the stock of scrap falls, secondary supply contracts. Secondary supply is therefore less elastic in the long run than in the short run.

Table 2.3 Supply of Copper		
Price Elasticity of:	**Short-run**	**Long-run**
Primary supply	0.20	1.60
Secondary supply	0.43	0.31
Total supply	0.25	1.50

copper goes up, it increases the incentive to convert scrap copper into new supply, so that initially secondary supply increases sharply. But eventually the stock of good-quality scrap will fall, making the melting, purifying, and refabricating more costly, so that secondary supply will contract. Thus the long-run price elasticity of secondary supply is smaller than the short-run elasticity.

Figures 2.15(a) and 2.15(b) show short-run and long-run supply curves for primary (production from the mining and smelting of ore) and secondary copper production. Table 2.3 shows estimates of the elasticities for each component of supply, and then for total supply, based on a weighted average of the component elasticities.[10] Because secondary supply is only about 20 percent of total supply, the price elasticity of total supply is larger in the long run than in the short run.

EXAMPLE 2.5 **The Weather in Brazil and the Price of Coffee in New York**

Droughts or subfreezing weather occasionally destroy or damage many of Brazil's coffee trees. Because Brazil produces much of the world's coffee, the result is a decrease in the supply of coffee and a sharp run-up in its price.

For example, in July 1975, a frost destroyed most of Brazil's 1976–1977 coffee crop. (Remember that it is winter in Brazil when it is summer in the northern hemisphere.) As Figure 2.16 shows, the price of a pound of coffee in New York went from 68 cents in 1975 to $1.23 in 1976, and then to $2.70 in 1977. Prices fell, but then jumped again in 1986, after a seven-month drought in 1985 ruined much of Brazil's coffee crop. Finally, starting in June 1994, freezing weather followed by a drought destroyed nearly half of Brazil's 1995–1996 coffee crop. As a result, the price of coffee in 1994–1995 was about double the 1993 level.

The run-up in price following a freeze or drought is usually short-lived, however. Within a year, price begins to fall; within three or four years, it returns to its earlier levels. For example, in 1978 the price of coffee in New York

---

10 These estimates were obtained by aggregating the regional estimates reported in Franklin M. Fisher, Paul H. Cootner, and Martin N. Baily, "An Econometric Model of the World Copper Industry," *Bell Journal of Economics* 3 (Autumn 1972): 568–609.

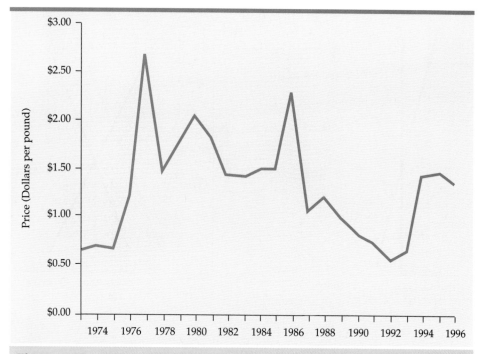

Figure 2.16 Price of Brazilian Coffee When droughts or freezes damage Brazil's coffee trees, the price of coffee can soar. But the price usually falls again after a few years, as demand and supply adjust.

fell to $1.48 per pound, and by 1983 it had fallen in real (inflation-adjusted) terms to within a few cents of its prefreeze 1975 price.[11] Likewise, in 1987 the price of coffee fell to below its predrought 1984 level, and then continued declining until the 1994 freeze.

Coffee prices behave this way because both demand and supply (especially supply) are much more elastic in the long run than in the short run. Figure 2.17 shows this. Note that in the very short run (within one or two months after a freeze), supply is completely inelastic; there are simply a fixed number of coffee beans, some of which have been damaged by the frost. Demand is also relatively inelastic. As a result of the frost, the supply curve shifts to the left, and price increases sharply, from P_0 to P_1.

In the intermediate run, say, one year after the freeze, both supply and demand are more elastic, supply because existing trees can be harvested more intensively (with some decrease in quality), and demand because consumers have had time to change their buying habits. The intermediate-run supply

---

[11] During 1980, however, prices temporarily went just above $2 per pound as a result of export quotas imposed under the International Coffee Agreement (ICA). The ICA is essentially a cartel agreement implemented by the coffee-producing countries in 1968. It has been largely ineffective and has seldom had an affect on the price. We discuss cartel pricing in detail in Chapter 12.

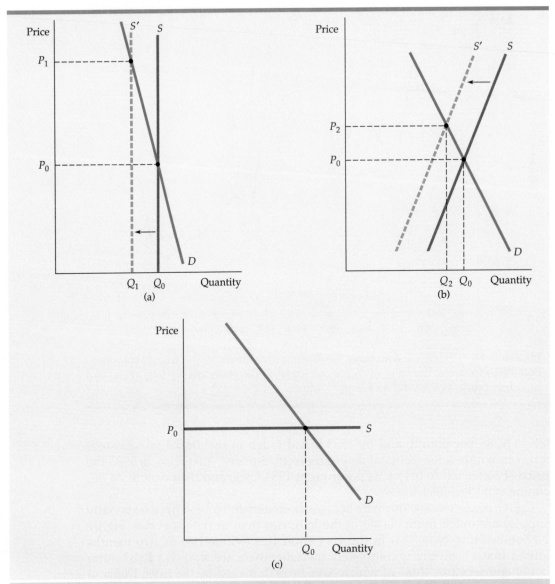

Figure 2.17 Supply and Demand for Coffee (a) A freeze or drought in Brazil causes the supply curve to shift to the left. In the short run, supply is completely inelastic; only a fixed number of coffee beans can be harvested. Demand is also relatively inelastic; consumers change their habits only slowly. As a result, the initial effect of the freeze is a sharp increase in price, from P_0 to P_1. (b) In the intermediate run, supply and demand are both more elastic, so price falls part way back, to P_2. (c) In the long run, supply is extremely elastic; new coffee trees will have had time to mature, so the effect of the freeze will have disappeared. Price returns to P_0.

curve also shifts to the left, but price has come down from P_1 to P_2. The quantity supplied has also increased somewhat from the short run, from Q_1 to Q_2. In the long run, price returns to its normal level; coffee growers have had time to replace the trees damaged by the freeze. The long-run supply curve, then, simply reflects the cost of producing coffee, including the costs of land, of planting and caring for the trees, and of a competitive rate of profit.

*2.5 Understanding and Predicting the Effects of Changing Market Conditions

We have discussed the meaning and characteristics of supply and demand, but our treatment has been largely qualitative. To use supply and demand curves to analyze and predict the effects of changing market conditions, we must begin to attach numbers to them. For example, to see how a 50 percent reduction in the supply of Brazilian coffee may affect the world price of coffee, we need to write down actual supply and demand curves and then calculate how those curves will shift, and how price will then change.

In this section we will see how to do simple "back of the envelope" calculations with linear supply and demand curves. Although they are often an approximation to more complex curves, we use linear curves because they are the easiest to work with. It may come as a surprise, but one can do some informative economic analyses on the back of a small envelope with a pencil and a pocket calculator.

First, we must learn how to "fit" linear demand and supply curves to market data. (By this we do not mean statistical fitting in the sense of linear regression or other statistical techniques, which we discuss later in the book.) Suppose we have two sets of numbers for a particular market. First are the price and quantity that generally prevail in the market (i.e., the price and quantity that prevail "on average," or when the market is in equilibrium, or when market conditions are "normal"). We call these numbers the equilibrium price and quantity, and we denote them by P^* and Q^*. Second are the price elasticities of supply and demand for the market (at or near the equilibrium), which we denote by E_S and E_D, as before.

These numbers might come from a statistical study done by someone else; they might be numbers that we simply think are reasonable; or they might be numbers that we want to try out on a "what if" basis. What we want to do is *write down the supply and demand curves that fit (i.e., are consistent with) these numbers.* Then we can determine numerically how a change in a variable such as GNP, the price of another good, or some cost of production will cause supply or demand to shift and thereby affect the market price and quantity.

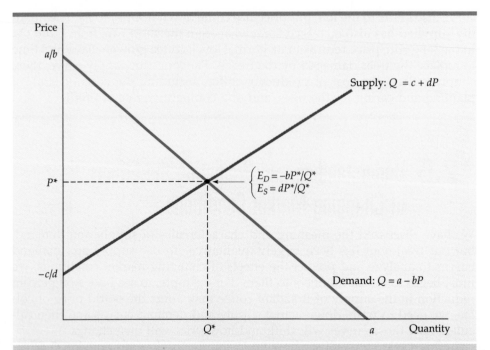

Price

a/b

Supply: $Q = c + dP$

P^*

$\begin{cases} E_D = -bP^*/Q^* \\ E_S = dP^*/Q^* \end{cases}$

$-c/d$

Demand: $Q = a - bP$

Q^* a Quantity

Figure 2.18   Fitting Linear Supply and Demand Curves to Data   Linear supply and demand curves provide a convenient tool for analysis. Given data for the equilibrium price and quantity P^* and Q^*, and estimates of the elasticities of demand and supply E_D and E_S, we can calculate the parameters c and d for the supply curve, and a and b for the demand curve. (In the case drawn here, $c < 0$.) The curves can then be used to analyze the behavior of the market quantitatively.

Let's begin with the linear curves shown in Figure 2.18. We can write these curves algebraically as

Demand:	$Q = a - bP$	(2.4a)
Supply:	$Q = c + dP$	(2.4b)

The problem is to choose numbers for the constants a, b, c, and d. This is done, for supply and for demand, in a two-step procedure:

- *Step 1:* Recall that each price elasticity, whether of supply or demand, can be written as

$$E = (P/Q)(\Delta Q/\Delta P)$$

where $\Delta Q/\Delta P$ is the change in quantity demanded or supplied resulting from a small change in price. For linear curves, $\Delta Q/\Delta P$ is constant. From equations (2.4a) and (2.4b), we see that $\Delta Q/\Delta P = d$ for supply, and $\Delta Q/\Delta P = -b$ for demand. Now, let's substitute these values for $\Delta Q/\Delta P$ into the elasticity formula:

Demand:	$E_D = -b(P^*/Q^*)$	(2.5a)
Supply:	$E_S = d(P^*/Q^*)$	(2.5b)

where P^* and Q^* are the equilibrium price and quantity for which we have data and to which the curves will be fit. Because we have numbers for E_S, E_D, P^*, and Q^*, we can substitute these numbers in equations (2.5a) and (2.5b) and solve for b and d.

■ *Step 2*: Since we now know b and d, we can substitute these numbers, as well as P^* and Q^*, into equations (2.4a) and (2.4b) and solve for the remaining constants a and c. For example, we can rewrite equation (2.4a) as

$$a = Q^* + bP^*$$

and then use our data for Q^* and P^*, together with the number we calculated in Step 1 for b, to obtain a.

Let's do this for a specific example—long-run supply and demand for the world copper market. The relevant numbers for this market are as follows:[12] quantity $Q^* = 7.5$ million metric tons per year (mmt/yr); price $P^* = 75$ cents per pound; elasticity of supply $E_S = 1.6$; elasticity of demand $E_D = -0.8$. (The price of copper has fluctuated during the past decade between 50 cents and more than \$1.30, but 75 cents is a reasonable average price for 1980–1990.)

We begin with the supply curve equation (2.4b) and use our two-step procedure to calculate numbers for c and d. The long-run price elasticity of supply is 1.6, $P^* = .75$, and $Q^* = 7.5$.

■ *Step 1*: Substitute these numbers in equation (2.5b) to determine d:

$$1.6 = d(0.75/7.5) = 0.1d$$

so that $d = 1.6/0.1 = 16$.

■ *Step 2*: Substitute this number for d, together with the numbers for P^* and Q^*, into equation (2.4b) to determine c:

$$7.5 = c + (16)(0.75) = c + 12$$

so that $c = 7.5 - 12 = -4.5$. We now know c and d, so we can write our supply curve:

$$\textit{Supply:} \quad Q = -4.5 + 16P$$

We can now follow the same steps for the demand curve equation (2.4a). An estimate for the long-run elasticity of demand is -0.8. First, substitute this number, and the values for P^* and Q^*, in equation (2.5a) to determine b:

$$-0.8 = -b(0.75/7.5) = -0.1b$$

so that $b = 0.8/0.1 = 8$. Second, substitute this value for b and the values for P^* and Q^* in equation (2.4a) to determine a:

$$7.5 = a - (8)(0.75) = a - 6$$

---

[12] The supply elasticity is for total supply, as shown in Table 2.3. The demand elasticity is a regionally aggregated number based on Fisher, Cootner, and Baily, "An Econometric Model." Quantities refer to what was then the non-Communist world market.

so that $a = 7.5 + 6 = 13.5$. Thus, our demand curve is

$$Demand: \quad Q = 13.5 - 8P$$

To check that we have not made a mistake, set the quantity supplied equal to the quantity demanded and calculate the equilibrium price that results:

$$Supply = -4.5 + 16P = 13.5 - 8P = Demand$$

$$16P + 8P = 13.5 + 4.5$$

or $P = 18/24 = 0.75$, which is indeed the equilibrium price we began with.

We have written supply and demand so that they depend only on price, but they could easily depend on other variables as well. For example, demand might depend on income as well as price. We would then write demand as

$$Q = a - bP + fI \tag{2.6}$$

where I is an index of aggregate income or GNP. (For example, I might equal 1.0 in a base year and then rise or fall to reflect percentage increases or decreases in aggregate income.)

For our copper market example, a reasonable estimate for the long-run income elasticity of demand is 1.3. For the linear demand curve (2.6), we can then calculate f by using the formula for the income elasticity of demand: $E = (I/Q)(\Delta Q/\Delta I)$. Taking the base value of I as 1.0, we have

$$1.3 = (1.0/7.5)(f)$$

so $f = (1.3)(7.5)/(1.0) = 9.75$. Finally, substituting the values $b = 8$, $f = 9.75$, $P^* = 0.75$, and $Q^* = 7.5$ into (2.6), we can calculate that a must equal 3.75.

We have seen how to fit linear supply and demand curves to data. Now, to see how these curves can be used to analyze markets, look at Example 2.6 on the behavior of copper prices and Example 2.7 on the world oil market.

EXAMPLE 2.6   **Declining Demand and the Behavior of Copper Prices**

After reaching a level of about $1.00 per pound in 1980, the price of copper fell sharply to about 60 cents per pound in 1986. In real (inflation-adjusted) terms, this price was even lower than during the Great Depression 50 years earlier. Only in 1988–1989 did prices recover somewhat, as a result of strikes by miners in Peru and Canada that disrupted supplies. Figure 2.19 shows the behavior of copper prices in 1965–1996 in both real and nominal terms.

The world-wide recessions of 1980 and 1982 contributed to the decline of copper prices; as mentioned above, the income elasticity of copper demand is about 1.3. But copper demand did not pick up as the industrial economies recovered during the mid-1980s. Instead, the 1980s saw a steep decline in the demand for copper.

This decline occurred for two reasons. First, a large part of copper consumption is for the construction of equipment for electric power generation

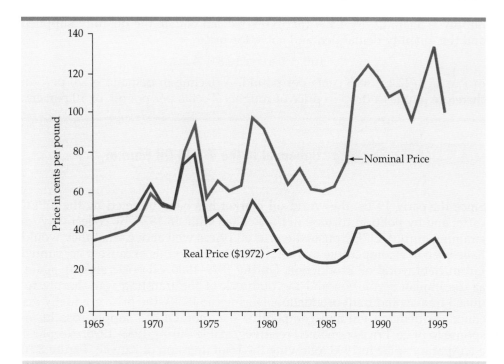

Figure 2.19 Copper Prices 1965–1996 Copper prices are shown in both nominal (no adjustment for inflation) and real (inflation-adjusted) terms. In real terms copper prices declined steeply from the early 1970s through the mid-1980s as demand fell. In 1988–1990 copper prices rose in response to supply disruptions caused by strikes in Peru and Canada, but prices later fell after the strikes ended.

and transmission. But by the late 1970s, the growth rate of electric power generation had fallen dramatically in most industrialized countries. (For example, in the United States the growth rate fell from over 6 percent per annum in the 1960s and early 1970s to less than 2 percent in the late 1970s and 1980s.) This meant a big drop in what had been a major source of copper demand. Second, in the 1980s other materials, such as aluminum and fiber optics, were increasingly substituted for copper.

Copper producers are concerned about the possible effects of further declines in demand, particularly as strikes end and supplies increase. Declining demand will depress prices; to find out how much, we can use the linear supply and demand curves that we just derived. Let us calculate the effect on price of a 20 percent decline in demand. Because we are not concerned here with the effects of GNP growth, we can leave the income term fI out of demand.

We want to shift the demand curve to the left by 20 percent. In other words, we want the quantity demanded to be 80 percent of what it would be otherwise for every value of price. For our linear demand curve, we simply multiply the right-hand side by 0.8:

$$Q = (0.8)(13.5 - 8P) = 10.8 - 6.4P$$

Supply is again $Q = -4.5 + 16P$. Now we can equate the quantity supplied and the quantity demanded and solve for price:

$$16P + 6.4P = 10.8 + 4.5$$

or $P = 15.3/22.4 = 68.3$ cents per pound. A decline in demand of 20 percent therefore implies a drop in price of roughly 7 cents per pound, or 10 percent.

EXAMPLE 2.7   Upheaval in the World Oil Market

Since the early 1970s, the world oil market has been buffeted by the OPEC cartel and by political turmoil in the Persian Gulf. In 1974, by collectively restraining output, OPEC pushed world oil prices well above what they would have been in a competitive market. OPEC could do this because it accounted for much of world oil production. During 1979–1980, oil prices shot up again, as the Iranian revolution and the outbreak of the Iran-Iraq war sharply reduced Iranian and Iraqi production. During the 1980s, the price gradually declined, as demand fell and competitive (i.e., non-OPEC) supply rose in response to price. Prices remained relatively stable during 1988–1996, except for a temporary spike in 1990 following the Iraqi invasion of Kuwait. Figure 2.20 shows the world price of oil from 1970 to 1996, in both nominal and real terms.

The Persian Gulf is one of the less stable regions of the world, and this has led to concern over the possibility of new oil supply disruptions and sharp increases in oil prices. What would happen to oil prices—in the short run and the longer run—if a war or revolution in the Persian Gulf caused a sharp cutback in oil production? Let's see how simple supply and demand curves can be used to predict the outcome of such an event.

This example is set in 1995, so all prices are measured in 1995 dollars. Here are some rough figures: 1995 world price = $18 per barrel, world demand and total supply = 23 billion barrels per year (bb/yr), 1995 OPEC supply = 10 bb/yr, and competitive (non-OPEC) supply = 13 bb/yr.[13] And here are price elasticity estimates for oil supply and demand:[14]

	Short-Run	Long-Run
World Demand:	−0.05	−0.40
Competitive Supply:	0.10	0.40

---

[13] Non-OPEC supply includes the production of China and the former Soviet republics.

[14] For the sources of these numbers and a more detailed discussion of OPEC oil pricing, see Robert S. Pindyck, "Gains to Producers from the Cartelization of Exhaustible Resources," *Review of Economics and Statistics* 60 (May 1978): 238–251; James M. Griffin and David J. Teece, *OPEC Behavior and World Oil Prices* (London: Allen and Unwin, 1982); and Hillard G. Huntington, "Inferred Demand and Supply Elasticities from a Comparison of World Oil Models," in T. Sterner, ed., *International Energy Economics* (London: Chapman and Hall, 1992).

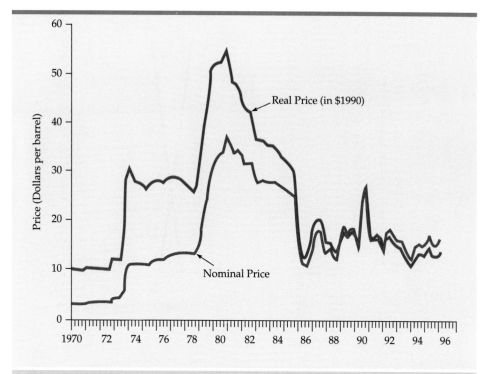

Figure 2.20   The Price of Crude Oil   The OPEC cartel and political events caused the price of oil to rise sharply at times, but it later fell as supply and demand adjusted.

You should verify that these numbers imply the following for demand and competitive supply in the *short run*:

Short-Run Demand: $D = 24.08 - 0.06P$

Short-Run Competitive Supply: $S_C = 11.74 + 0.07P$

Of course, *total* supply is competitive supply *plus* OPEC supply, which we take as constant at 10 bb/yr. Adding this 10 bb/yr to the competitive supply curve above, we obtain the following for the total short-run supply:

Short-Run Total Supply: $S_T = 21.74 + 0.07P$

You should verify that the quantity demanded and the total quantity supplied are equal at an equilibrium price of $18 per barrel.

You should also verify that the corresponding demand and supply curves for the *long run* are

Long-Run Demand: $D = 32.18 - 0.51P$

Long-Run Competitive Supply: $S_C = 7.78 + 0.29P$

Long-Run Total Supply: $S_T = 17.78 + 0.29P$

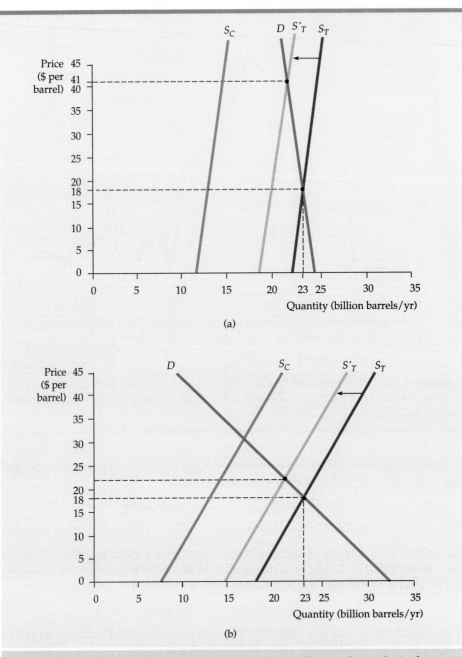

Figure 2.21 **Impact of Saudi Production Cut** The total supply is the sum of competitive (non-OPEC) supply and the 10 bb/yr of OPEC supply. Part (a) shows the short-run supply and demand curves. If Saudi Arabia stops producing, the supply curve will shift to the left by 3 bb/yr. In the short-run, price will increase sharply. Part (b) shows long-run curves. In the long run, demand and competitive supply are much more elastic, so the impact on price will be much smaller.

Again, you can check that the quantities supplied and demanded equate at a price of $18.

Saudi Arabia is one of the world's largest oil producers, accounting for roughly 3 bb/yr, which is nearly one third of OPEC production and about 13 percent of total world production. What would happen to the price of oil if, because of war or political upheaval, Saudi Arabia stopped producing oil? We can use our supply and demand curves to find out.

For the *short run*, simply subtract 3 from total supply:

$$\text{Short-Run Demand:} \qquad D = 24.08 - 0.15P$$

$$\text{Short-Run Total Supply:} \qquad S_T = 18.74 + 0.07P$$

By equating this total quantity supplied with the quantity demanded, we can see that in the short run, the price will more than double to $30.79 per barrel. Figure 2.21 shows this supply shift and the resulting short-run increase in price. The initial equilibrium is at the intersection of S_T and D. After the drop in Saudi production, the equilibrium occurs where S_T' and D cross.

In the *long run*, however, things will be different. Because both demand and competitive supply are more elastic in the long run, the 3 bb/yr cut in oil production will no longer support such a high price. Subtracting 3 from long-run total supply and equating with long-run demand, we can see that the price will fall to $21.75, only $3.75 above the initial $18 price.

Hence, if Saudi Arabia suddenly stops producing oil, we should expect to see more than a doubling in price. However, we should also expect to see the price gradually decline afterward, as demand falls and competitive supply rises. As Figure 2.20 shows, this is indeed what happened following the sharp decline in Iranian and Iraqi production during 1979–1980. History may or may not repeat itself, but if it does, we can at least predict the impact on oil prices.

2.6 Effects of Government Intervention— Price Controls

In the United States and most other industrial countries, markets are rarely free of government intervention. Besides imposing taxes and granting subsidies, governments often regulate markets (even competitive markets) in a variety of ways. Here we will see how to use supply and demand curves to analyze the effects of one common form of government intervention: price controls. Later, in Chapter 9, we examine the effects of price controls and other forms of government intervention and regulation in more detail.

Figure 2.22 illustrates the effects of price controls. Here P_0 and Q_0 are the equilibrium price and quantity that would prevail without government regulation. The government, however, has decided that P_0 is too high and has mandated that the price can be no higher than a maximum allowable *ceiling price*, denoted by P_{max}. What is the result? At this lower price, producers (particularly those with higher costs) will produce less, and supply will be Q_1. Consumers, on the other hand, will demand more at this low price; they would like to purchase the quantity Q_2. So demand exceeds supply, and a shortage develops, known as *excess demand*. The amount of excess demand is $Q_2 - Q_1$.

This excess demand sometimes takes the form of queues, as when drivers lined up to buy gasoline during the winter of 1974 and the summer of 1979. (In both instances, the gasoline lines were the result of price controls; the government prevented domestic oil and gasoline prices from rising along with world oil prices.) Sometimes it takes the form of curtailments and supply rationing, as with natural gas price controls and the resulting gas shortages of the mid-1970s, when industrial consumers of gas had their supplies cut off, forcing factories to close. And sometimes it spills over to other markets, where it artificially increases demand. For example, natural gas price controls caused potential buyers of gas to use oil instead.

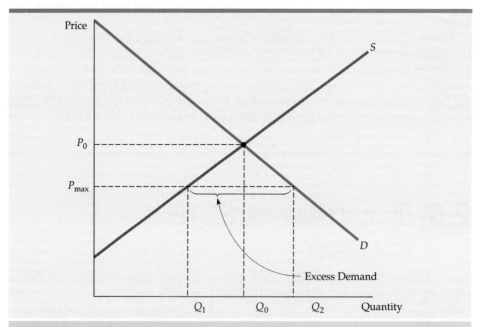

Figure 2.22   Effects of Price Controls   Without price controls the market clears at the equilibrium price and quantity P_0 and Q_0. If price is regulated to be no higher than P_{max}, supply falls to Q_1, demand increases to Q_2, and a shortage develops.

Some people gain and some lose from price controls. As Figure 2.22 suggests, producers lose—they receive lower prices, and some leave the industry. Some but not all consumers gain. Consumers who can purchase the good at a lower price are clearly better off, but those who have been "rationed out" and cannot buy the good at all are worse off. How large are the gains to the winners, how large are the losses to the losers, and do the total gains exceed the total losses? To answer these questions we need a method to measure the gains and losses from price controls and other forms of government intervention. We discuss such a method in Chapter 9.

EXAMPLE 2.8 **Price Controls and Natural Gas Shortages**

In 1954, the federal government began regulating the wellhead price of natural gas. Initially the controls were not binding; the ceiling prices were above those that cleared the market. But in about 1962, these ceiling prices did become binding, and excess demand for natural gas developed and slowly began to grow. In the 1970s, this excess demand, spurred by higher oil prices, became severe and led to widespread curtailments. Ceiling prices were far below those that would have prevailed in a free market.[15]

Today, producers and industrial consumers of natural gas, oil, and other commodities are concerned that the government might respond, once again, with price controls if prices rise sharply. Hence, it is important to understand the likely impact of such price controls. To see how this can be done, we will go back to the year 1975 and calculate the impact of natural gas price control at that time.

Based on econometric studies of natural gas markets and the behavior of those markets as controls were gradually lifted during the 1980s, the following data describe the market in 1975. The free market price of natural gas would have been about $2.00 per mcf (thousand cubic feet), and production and consumption would have been about 20 Tcf (trillion cubic feet). The average price of oil (including both imports and domestic production), which affects both supply and demand for natural gas, was about $8/barrel.

A reasonable estimate for the price elasticity of supply is 0.2. Higher oil prices also lead to more natural gas production because oil and gas are often discovered and produced together; an estimate of the cross-price elasticity of supply is 0.1. As for demand, the price elasticity is about −0.5, and the cross-

---

[15] This regulation began with the Supreme Court's 1954 decision requiring the then Federal Power Commission to regulate wellhead prices on natural gas sold to interstate pipeline companies. These price controls were largely removed during the 1980s, under the mandate of the Natural Gas Policy Act of 1978. For a detailed discussion of natural gas regulation and its effects, see Paul W. MacAvoy and Robert S. Pindyck, *The Economics of the Natural Gas Shortage* (Amsterdam: North-Holland, 1975); R. S. Pindyck, "Higher Energy Prices and the Supply of Natural Gas," *Energy Systems and Policy* 2 (1978): 177–209; and Arlon R. Tussing and Connie C. Barlow, *The Natural Gas Industry* (Cambridge, Mass.: Ballinger, 1984).

price elasticity with respect to oil price is about 1.5. You can verify that the following linear supply and demand curves fit these numbers:

$$\text{\textit{Supply:}} \qquad Q = 14 + 2P_G + .25P_O$$

$$\text{\textit{Demand:}} \qquad Q = -5P_G + 3.75P_O$$

where Q is the quantity of natural gas (in Tcf), P_G is the price of natural gas (in dollars per mcf), and P_O is the price of oil (in dollars per barrel). You can also verify, by equating the quantities supplied and demanded and substituting $8.00 for P_O, that these supply and demand curves imply an equilibrium free market price of $2.00 for natural gas.

The regulated price of gas in 1975 was about $1.00 per mcf. Substituting this price for P_G in the supply function gives a quantity supplied (Q_1 in Figure 2.22) of 18 Tcf. Substituting for P_G in the demand function gives a demand (Q_2 in Figure 2.22) of 25 Tcf. Price controls thus created an excess demand of $25 - 18 = 7$ Tcf, which manifested itself in the form of widespread curtailments.

Price regulation was a major component of U.S. energy policy during the 1960s and 1970s, and it continued to influence the evolution of natural gas markets in the 1980s. In Example 9.1 of Chapter 9, we show how to measure the gains and losses that result from price controls.

Summary

1. Supply-demand analysis is a basic tool of microeconomics. In competitive markets, supply and demand curves tell us how much will be produced by firms and how much will be demanded by consumers as a function of price.

2. The market mechanism is the tendency for supply and demand to equilibrate (i.e., for price to move to the market-clearing level), so that there is neither excess demand nor excess supply.

3. Elasticities describe the responsiveness of supply and demand to changes in price, income, or other variables. For example, the price elasticity of demand measures the percentage change in the quantity demanded resulting from a 1 percent increase in price.

4. Elasticities pertain to a time frame, and for most goods it is important to distinguish between short-run and long-run elasticities.

5. If we can estimate, at least roughly, the supply and demand curves for a particular market, we can calculate the market-clearing price by equating the quantity supplied with the quantity demanded. Also, if we know how supply and demand depend on other economic variables, such as income or the prices of other goods, we can calculate how the market-clearing price and quantity will change as these other variables change. This is a means of explaining or predicting market behavior.

6. Simple numerical analyses can often be done by fitting linear supply and demand curves to data on price and quantity and to estimates of elasticities. For many markets such data and estimates are available, and simple "back of the envelope" calculations can help us understand the characteristics and behavior of the market.

Questions for Review

1. Suppose that unusually hot weather causes the demand curve for ice cream to shift to the right. Why will the price of ice cream rise to a new market-clearing level?

2. Use supply and demand curves to illustrate how each of the following events would affect the price of butter and the quantity of butter bought and sold: (a) an increase in the price of margarine; (b) an increase in the price of milk; (c) a decrease in average income levels.

3. Suppose a 3 percent increase in the price of corn flakes causes a 6 percent decline in the quantity demanded. What is the elasticity of demand for corn flakes?

4. Why do long-run elasticities of demand differ from short-run elasticities? Consider two goods: paper towels and televisions. Which is a durable good? Would you expect the price elasticity of demand for paper towels to be larger in the short run or in the long run? Why? What about the price elasticity of demand for televisions?

5. Explain why for many goods, the long-run price elasticity of supply is larger than the short-run elasticity.

6. Suppose the government regulates the prices of beef and chicken and sets them below their market-clearing levels. Explain why shortages of these goods will develop and what factors will determine the sizes of the shortages. What will happen to the price of pork? Explain briefly.

7. In a discussion of tuition rates, a university official argues that the demand for admission is completely price inelastic. As evidence she notes that while the university has doubled its tuition (in real terms) over the past 15 years, neither the number nor quality of students applying has decreased. Would you accept this argument? Explain briefly. (*Hint:* The official makes an assertion about the demand for admission, but does she actually observe a demand curve? What else could be going on?)

8. Use supply and demand curve shifts to illustrate the effect of the following events on the market for apples. Make clear the direction of the change in both price and quantity sold.
   a. Scientists find that an apple a day does indeed keep the doctor away.
   b. The price of oranges triples.
   c. A drought shrinks the apple crop to one-third its normal size.
   d. Thousands of college students abandon the academic life to become apple pickers.
   e. Thousands of college students abandon the academic life to become apple growers.

Exercises

1. Consider a competitive market for which the quantities demanded and supplied (per year) at various prices are given as follows:

Price ($)	Demand (millions)	Supply (millions)
60	22	14
80	20	16
100	18	18
120	16	20

   a. Calculate the price elasticity of demand when the price is $80, and when the price is $100.

   b. Calculate the price elasticity of supply when the price is $80, and when the price is $100.

   c. What are the equilibrium price and quantity?

   d. Suppose the government sets a price ceiling of $80. Will there be a shortage, and if so, how large will it be?

2. Refer to Example 2.3 on the market for wheat. Suppose that in 1985 the Soviet Union had bought an additional 200 million bushels of U.S. wheat. What would the free market price of wheat have been and what quantity would have been produced and sold by U.S. farmers?

3. The rent control agency of New York City has found that aggregate demand is $Q_D = 100 - 5P$, with quantity measured in tens of thousands of apartments, and price, the average monthly rental rate, measured in hundreds of dollars. The agency also noted that the increase in Q at lower P results from more three-person families coming into the city from Long Island and demanding apartments. The city's board of realtors acknowledges that this is a good demand estimate and has shown that supply is $Q_S = 50 + 5P$.

   a. If both the agency and the board are right about demand and supply, what is the free market price? What is the change in city population if the agency sets a maximum average monthly rental of $100, and all those who cannot find an apartment leave the city?

   b. Suppose the agency bows to the wishes of the board and sets a rental of $900 per month on all apartments to allow landlords a "fair" rate of return. If 50 percent of any long-run increases in apartment offerings comes from new construction, how many apartments are constructed?

4. Much of the demand for U.S. agricultural output has come from other countries. From Example 2.3, total demand is $Q = 3,550 - 266P$. In addition, we are told that domestic demand is $Q_D = 1,000 - 46P$. Domestic supply is $Q = 1,800 + 240P$. Suppose the export demand for wheat falls by 40 percent.

   a. U.S. farmers are concerned about this drop in export demand. What happens to the free market price of wheat in the United States? Do the farmers have much reason to worry?

   b. Now suppose the U.S. government wants to buy enough wheat each year to raise the price to $3.00 per bushel. Without export demand, how much wheat would the government have to buy each year? How much would this cost the government?

5. In Example 2.6 we examined the effect of a 20 percent decline in copper demand on the price of copper, using the linear supply and demand curves developed in Section 2.5.

Suppose the long-run price elasticity of copper demand were -0.4 instead of -0.8.

   a. Assuming, as before, that the equilibrium price and quantity are $P^* = 75$ cents per pound and $Q^* = 7.5$ million metric tons per year, derive the linear demand curve consistent with the smaller elasticity.

   b. Using this demand curve, recalculate the effect of a 20 percent decline in copper demand on the price of copper.

6. Example 2.7 analyzes the world oil market. Using the data given in that example,

   a. Show that the short-run demand and competitive supply curves are indeed given by

$$D = 24.08 - 0.06P$$

$$S_C = 11.74 + 0.07P$$

   b. Show that the long-run demand and competitive supply curves are indeed given by

$$D = 32.18 - 0.51P$$

$$S_C = 7.78 + 0.29P$$

   c. Use this model to calculate what would happen to the price of oil in the short run *and* the long run if OPEC were to cut its production by 6 billion barrels per year.

7. Refer to Example 2.8, which analyzes the effects of price controls on natural gas.

   a. Using the data in the example, show that the following supply and demand curves did indeed describe the market in 1975:

   Supply: $Q = 14 + 2P_G + 0.25P_O$

   Demand: $Q = -5P_G + 3.75P_O$

   where P_G and P_O are the prices of natural gas and oil, respectively. Also, verify that if the price of oil is $8.00, these curves imply a free market price of $2.00 for natural gas.

   b. Suppose the regulated price of gas in 1975 had been $1.50 per million cubic feet, instead of $1.00. How much excess demand would there have been?

   c. Suppose that the market for natural gas had *not* been regulated. If the price of oil had increased from $8 to $16, what would have happened to the free market price of natural gas?

PART II
Producers, Consumers, and Competitive Markets

Part II presents the theoretical core of microeconomics.

Chapters 3 and 4 explain the principles underlying consumer demand. We see how consumers make consumption decisions, how their preferences and budget constraints determine their demands for various goods, and why different goods have different demand characteristics. Chapter 5 contains somewhat more advanced material that shows how to analyze consumer choice under uncertainty. We explain why people usually dislike risky situations, and show how they can reduce risk, and choose among risky alternatives.

Chapters 6 and 7 develop the theory of the firm. We see how firms combine inputs, such as capital, labor, and raw materials, to produce goods and services, in a way that minimizes the costs of production. We also see how a firm's costs depend on its rate of production and on its production experience. Chapter 8 then shows how firms choose their profit-maximizing rate of production. We also see how the production decisions of individual firms combine to determine the competitive market supply curve and its characteristics.

Chapter 9 applies supply and demand curves to the analysis of competitive markets. Government policies, such as price controls, quotas, taxes, and subsidies, can have wide-ranging effects on consumers and producers. We explain how supply-demand analysis can be used to evaluate these effects.

CHAPTER 3

Consumer Behavior

In 1962, Pillsbury Co. acquired a company in Woodbridge, New Jersey, that produced a new premium ice cream. The ice cream was marketed under the name Haagen-Dazs. The inclusion of more cream and eggs made the ice cream richer and more flavorful than most other brands, and the Scandinavian-sounding name suggested that it was a quality product worth a higher price. But before Haagen-Dazs could be extensively marketed, the company had to resolve an important problem—*how high a price should it charge*? No matter how good the ice cream was, its profitability would be affected considerably by the company's pricing decision. Knowing that consumers would pay more for a premium ice cream was not enough; at issue was *how much more*. Pillsbury, therefore, had to conduct a careful analysis of consumer preferences to determine the demand for ice cream and its dependence on both price and quality.

In the early 1960s, reports showing the extent to which the poor were underfed and malnourished aroused public concern. In response, Congress passed the Food Stamp Act of 1964, which directed the federal government to fund a program in which households with sufficiently low incomes would receive coupons that could be exchanged for food. But a problem arose in the design and evaluation of this program. To what extent would food stamps provide people with more food, as opposed to simply subsidizing food that they would have bought anyway? In other words, would the program turn out to be little more than an income supplement that would be spent largely on nonfood items, instead of a solution to the nutritional problems of the poor? Once again, an analysis of consumer behavior was needed. In this case, the federal government had to determine how spending on food, as opposed to other goods, is affected by changing income levels and prices.

These two problems—one involving corporate policy and the other public policy—exemplify the importance of the economic theory of consumer behavior and the kinds of issues it can help resolve. In this chapter and the next, we will see how consumers allocate their incomes and how this determines the demands for various goods and services. This, in turn, will help us understand how changes in income and prices affect demands for goods and services and why the demands for some products are more sensitive than others to price and income changes.

Consumer behavior is best understood in three steps. The first step is to examine *consumer preferences*. Specifically, we need a practical way to describe how people might prefer one good to another. But preferences ignore prices. Therefore as a second step, we must account for the fact that consumers face *budget constraints*—they have limited incomes that restrict the quantities of goods that they can buy. The third step is to put consumer preferences and budget constraints together to determine *consumer choices*. In other words, given their preferences and limited incomes, what combinations of goods will consumers buy to maximize their satisfaction? We will go through each of these steps in turn.

3.1 Consumer Preferences

Given the vast number of goods and services that our industrial economy provides for purchase and given the wide diversity of personal tastes, how can we describe consumer preferences in a coherent way? A good way to begin is to think of preferences in terms of comparisons of market baskets. A *market basket* is just a collection of one or more commodities. For example, it might contain the various food items in a bag of groceries or the combination of food, clothing, and fuel that a consumer buys each month.

Because people purchase combinations of goods, we can ask whether one market basket is preferred to another. Table 3.1 shows several market baskets consisting of various amounts of food and clothing purchased monthly. For example, market basket *A* consists of 20 units of food and 30 units of clothing, basket *B* consists of 10 units of food and 50 units of clothing, and so on. By asking consumers to compare these different baskets, we can describe their preferences for food and clothing.

Some Basic Assumptions

The theory of consumer behavior begins with three basic assumptions regarding people's preferences for one market basket versus another. We believe that these assumptions hold for most people in most situations:

1. Preferences are *complete*, which means that consumers can compare and rank all market baskets. In other words, for any two market baskets *A* and *B*, a consumer will prefer *A* to *B*, will prefer *B* to *A*, or will be indifferent between the two. (By "indifferent" we mean that a person would be equally happy with either basket.) Note that these preferences ignore costs. A consumer might prefer steak to hamburger but would buy hamburger because it is cheaper.

2. Preferences are *transitive*. Transitivity means that if a consumer prefers market basket *A* to market basket *B*, and prefers *B* to *C*, then the consumer also prefers *A* to *C*. For example, if a Rolls Royce is preferred to a Cadillac and a Cadillac is preferred to a Chevrolet, then a Rolls Royce is also preferred to a Chevrolet. Transitivity is normally regarded as necessary for consumer rationality.

3. All goods are "good" (i.e., desirable), so that leaving costs aside, *consumers always prefer more of any good to less*. This assumption is made for pedagogic reasons; it simplifies the graphical analysis. Of course, some goods, such as air pollution, may be undesirable, and consumers will always prefer less. We ignore these "bads" in the context of our current discussion of consumer choice because most consumers would not choose to purchase them. We will, however, discuss them later in the book.

These three assumptions form the basis of consumer theory. They do not explain consumers' preferences, but they do impose a degree of rationality and reasonableness on them. Building on these assumptions, we will now explore consumer behavior.

Table 3.1 Alternative Market Baskets		
Market Basket	**Units of Food**	**Units of Clothing**
A	20	30
B	10	50
D	40	20
E	30	40
G	10	20
H	10	40

NOTE: We will avoid the use of the letters *C* and *F* to represent market baskets, whenever market baskets might be confused with the number of units of food and clothing.

Indifference Curves

We can show a consumer's preferences graphically with the use of *indifference curves. An indifference curve represents all combinations of market baskets that provide the same level of satisfaction to a person.* That person is therefore indifferent among the market baskets represented by the points on the curve.

Given our three assumptions about preferences, we know that a consumer can always indicate a preference for one market basket over another or indifference between the two. This information can then be used to rank all possible consumption choices. To see this in graphic form, we assume there are only two goods, food F and clothing C, available for consumption. In this case, market baskets describe combinations of food and clothing that a person might wish to consume. Table 3.1 provides some examples of market baskets containing various amounts of food and clothing.

Figure 3.1 shows the same market baskets that are in Table 3.1. The horizontal axis measures the number of units of food purchased each week, and the vertical axis measures the number of units of clothing. Market basket A, with 20

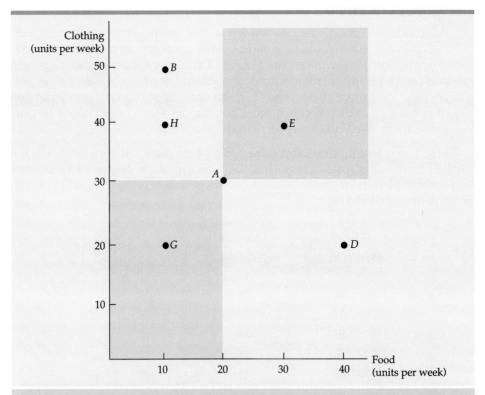

Figure 3.1   Describing Individual Preferences   Because more of each good is preferred to less, we can compare market baskets in the shaded areas. Market basket A is clearly preferred to market basket G, while E is clearly preferred to A. However, A cannot be compared with B, D, or H without additional information.

units of food and 30 units of clothing, is preferred to market basket G because A contains more food *and* more clothing (recall our third assumption that more is better than less). Similarly, market basket E, which contains still more food and more clothing, is preferred to A. In fact, we can easily compare all market baskets in the two shaded areas (such as E and G) to A because they contain either more or less of both food and clothing. However, comparisons of market basket A with market baskets B, D, and H are not possible without more information about the consumer's ranking because B contains more clothing but less food, and D contains more food but less clothing than A.

This additional information is provided in Figure 3.2, which shows an indifference curve, labeled U_1, that passes through points A, B, and D. This curve indicates that the consumer is indifferent among these three market baskets. It tells us that the consumer feels neither better nor worse off in giving up 10 units of food to obtain 20 additional units of clothing in moving from market basket A to B. Likewise, the consumer is indifferent between points A and D (i.e., will give up 10 units of clothing to obtain 20 units of food). On the other hand, the consumer prefers A to H, which lies below U_1.

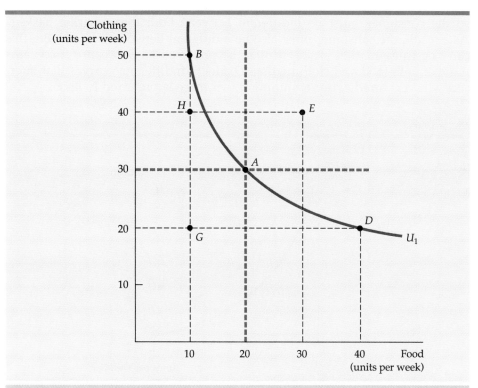

Figure 3.2 **An Indifference Curve** A person's indifference curve U_1 shows all market baskets that generate the same level of satisfaction as does market basket A; these include market baskets B and D. The person prefers market basket E, which lies above U_1 to A, but prefers A to H or G, which lie below U_1.

The indifference curve in Figure 3.2 slopes downward from left to right. To understand why this must be the case, suppose instead that the indifference curve sloped upward from A to E. This would violate the assumption that more of any commodity is preferred to less. Because market basket E has more of both food and clothing than market basket A, it must be preferred to A and therefore cannot be on the same indifference curve as A. In fact, any market basket lying above and to the right of indifference curve U_1 in Figure 3.2 is preferred to any market basket on U_1.

To describe a person's preferences for all combinations of food and clothing, we can graph a set of indifference curves. This is called an *indifference map*. Each indifference curve in the map shows the market baskets among which the person is indifferent. Figure 3.3 shows three indifference curves that form part of an indifference map. Indifference curve U_3 generates the highest level of satisfaction, followed by indifference curves U_2 and U_1.

Indifference curves cannot intersect. To see why, we will assume the contrary and see how it violates the assumptions about consumer behavior. Figure 3.4 shows two indifference curves, U_1 and U_2, that intersect at A. Because A and B are both on indifference curve U_1, the consumer must be indifferent between the two market baskets. Both A and D lie on indifference curve U_2, so the consumer must be indifferent between both these market baskets. As a result, the consumer must also be indifferent between B and D. But this can't be true—market basket B must be preferred to D because it contains more of both food and clothing than D. Hence indifference curves that intersect would contradict our assumption that more is preferred to less.

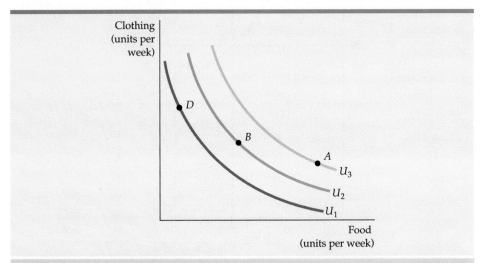

Figure 3.3   An Indifference Map   An indifference map is a set of indifference curves that describes a person's preferences. Any market basket on indifference curve U_3, such as market basket A, is preferred to any market basket on curve U_2 (e.g., basket B), which in turn is preferred to any market basket on U_1, such as D.

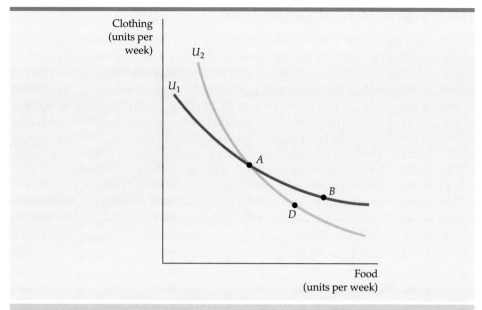

Figure 3.4 **Indifference Curves Cannot Cross** If indifference curves U_1 and U_2 intersected, one of the assumptions of consumer theory would be violated. According to this diagram, the consumer should be indifferent among market baskets A, B, and D. Yet B is preferred to D because B has more of both goods.

Of course, there are an infinite number of nonintersecting indifference curves, one for every possible level of satisfaction. In fact, every possible market basket (corresponding to a point on the graph) has an indifference curve passing through it.

Ordinal Versus Cardinal Rankings

For simplicity, we have shown only three indifference curves in Figure 3.3. The three curves provide an ordinal ranking of market baskets. An *ordinal ranking places market baskets in the order of most preferred to least preferred,* but it does not indicate by *how much* one market basket is preferred to another. For example, we know that consumption of any basket on U_3, such as A, is preferred to consumption of any basket on U_2, such as B. However, the amount by which A is preferred to B (and B to D) is not revealed by the indifference map.

By contrast, when economists first studied utility, they hoped that individual preferences could be easily quantified or measured in terms of basic units and could therefore provide a *cardinal ranking* of alternatives. Today, however, we know that the particular unit of measurement of utility is unimportant. For example, although we cannot say that consumers on U_2 are twice as happy as they might be on U_1, an ordinal ranking is sufficient to help us explain how most individual decisions are made. In the few instances where it is not, we will discuss an alternative approach to describing preferences.

The Marginal Rate of Substitution

People face trade-offs when choosing among two or more goods, and indifference curves can help to clarify those trade-offs. The indifference curve in Figure 3.5 illustrates this. Starting at market basket *A* and moving to market basket *B*, we see that the consumer is willing to give up six units of clothing to obtain one extra unit of food. However, moving from *B* to *D*, he is willing to give up only four units of clothing to obtain an additional unit of food, and in moving from *D* to *E*, he will give up two units of clothing for one unit of food. The more clothing and the less food a person consumes, the more clothing he will give up to obtain more food. Similarly, the more food that a person possesses, the less clothing he will give up for more food.

To quantify the amount of one good a consumer will give up to obtain more of another good, we use a measure called the *marginal rate of substitution* (MRS). The MRS of food *F* for clothing *C* is the maximum amount of clothing that a person is willing to give up to obtain one additional unit of food. If the MRS

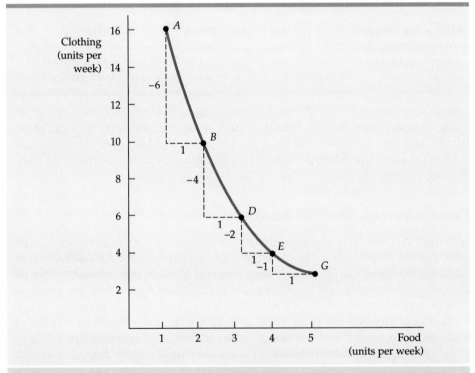

Figure 3.5   The Marginal Rate of Substitution   The slope of an indifference curve measures the consumer's marginal rate of substitution (MRS) between two goods. In the figure, the MRS between clothing (*C*) and food (*F*), $-\Delta C/\Delta F$, falls from 6 (between *A* and *B*) to 4 (between *B* and *D*) to 2 (between *D* and *E*) to 1 (between *E* and *G*). When the MRS diminishes along an indifference curve, the indifference curve is convex.

is 3, the consumer will give up 3 units of clothing to obtain an additional unit of food, while if the MRS is 1/2, only 1/2 a unit of clothing will be given up.

To be consistent throughout the book, we will describe the MRS in terms of the amount of the good drawn on the vertical axis that must be given up to obtain one extra unit of the good drawn on the horizontal axis. Thus in Figure 3.5 we refer to the amount of clothing given up to obtain an additional unit of food. If we denote the change in clothing by ΔC and the change in food by ΔF, the MRS can be written as $-\Delta C/\Delta F$. The negative sign is included to make the marginal rate of substitution a positive number (ΔC is always negative). As a result, the marginal rate of substitution at any point is equal in magnitude to the slope of the indifference curve at that point.

At this point it is useful to add an additional assumption regarding consumer preferences to the three we discussed earlier in the chapter:

4. Along an indifference curve there is a *diminishing marginal rate of substitution*. In mathematical terms, this implies that indifference curves are *convex* or bowed inward. The term convex means that the slope of the indifference curve increases (i.e., becomes less negative) as we move down along the curve. In other words, an indifference curve is convex if the MRS diminishes along the curve. The indifference curve in Figure 3.5 is convex. Starting with market basket A in Figure 3.5 and moving to market basket B, we note that the MRS of food F for clothing C is $-\Delta C/\Delta F = -(-6)/1 = 6$. However, when starting at market basket B and moving from B to D, the MRS falls to 4. Starting at market basket D and moving to E, the MRS is 2, and starting at E and moving to G, the MRS is 1. As food consumption increases, the slope of the indifference curve falls in magnitude, so the MRS also falls.[1]

Is it reasonable to assume that indifference curves are convex? Yes. As more and more of one good is consumed, we would expect that a consumer would prefer to give up fewer and fewer units of a second good to get additional units of the first one. As we move down along the indifference curve in Figure 3.5 and consumption of food increases, the consumer's desire for still more food should diminish. Thus, he should be willing to give up less and less clothing to obtain additional food.

Another way of describing this is to say that consumers generally prefer a balanced market basket to market baskets that contain all of one good and none of the other. Note from Figure 3.5 that a relatively balanced market basket containing 3 units of food and 6 units of clothing (basket D) generates as much satisfaction as another market basket that contains only 1 unit of food, but 16 units of clothing (basket A). It follows that a balanced market basket containing (for example) 6 units of food and 8 units of clothing would generate a higher level of satisfaction.

---

[1] With nonconvex preferences, the MRS increases as the amount of the good measured on the horizontal axis increases along any indifference curve. This unlikely possibility might arise if one or both goods are addictive. For example, the willingness to substitute an addictive drug for other goods might increase as the use of the addictive drug increased.

Perfect Substitutes and Perfect Complements

The shapes of indifference curves can imply different degrees of willingness to substitute one good for another. To see this, look at the two polar cases illustrated in Figure 3.6. Figure 3.6(a) shows Philip's preferences for apple juice and orange juice. These two goods are perfect substitutes for Philip, since he is entirely indifferent between having a glass of one or the other. In this case, the marginal rate of substitution of apple juice for orange juice is 1; Philip is always willing to trade a glass of one for a glass of the other. In general, we say that two goods are *perfect substitutes* when the marginal rate of substitution of one good for the other is a constant; that is, the indifference curves that describe the trade-off between the consumption of the goods are straight lines.

Figure 3.6(b) illustrates Jane's preferences for left shoes and right shoes. For Jane, the two goods are perfect complements, since a left shoe will not increase her satisfaction unless she can obtain the matching right shoe. In this case, the marginal rate of substitution of left shoes for right shoes is zero whenever there are more right shoes than left shoes, since Jane would not give up any left shoes to get additional right shoes. Correspondingly, the marginal rate of substitution is infinite whenever there are more left shoes than right, since Jane will give up all but one of the excess left shoes she has in order to obtain an additional right shoe. Two goods are *perfect complements* when the indifference curves for the goods are shaped as right angles.

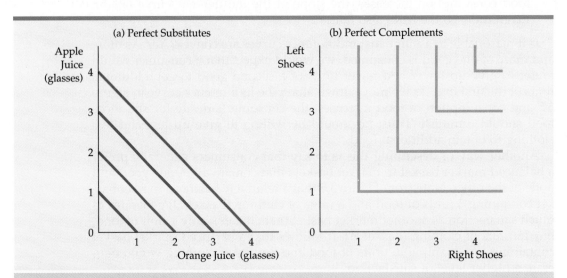

Figure 3.6   Perfect Substitutes and Perfect Complements   In (a), Philip views orange juice and apple juice as perfect substitutes; he is always indifferent between a glass of one and a glass of the other. In (b), Jane views left shoes and right shoes as perfect complements. An additional left shoe gives her no extra satisfaction unless she also obtains the matching right shoe.

| EXAMPLE 3.1 | **Designing New Automobiles** |

If you were an automobile company executive, how would you decide when to introduce new models and how much money to invest in restyling? You would probably know that two of the most important attributes of a car are its styling (e.g., design and interior features) and its performance (e.g., gas mileage and handling). Both styling and performance are desirable attributes; the better the styling and the better the performance, the greater will be the demand for a car. However, it costs money to restyle a car and to improve its performance. How much of each attribute should you include in the car?

The answer depends in part on the costs of production, but it also depends on consumer preferences for automobile attributes. Two characterizations of consumer preferences are shown in Figure 3.7. People with preferences shown in Figure 3.7(a) prefer performance to styling—they are willing to give up quite a bit of styling to get better performance. Compare these preferences to those of a different segment of the population shown in Figure 3.7(b). These people prefer styling to performance, and will put up with poor gas mileage or handling to get a more stylish car.

Knowing which preference group is most prevalent in the population can help automobile company executives make strategic production decisions. One way to determine this is by conducting surveys in which individuals

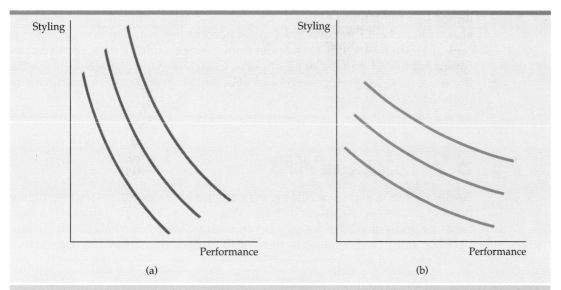

(a)   (b)

Figure 3.7 Preferences for Automobile Attributes Preferences for automobile attributes can be described by indifference curves. Each curve shows the combinations of performance and styling that give the same satisfaction. Consumers in (a) are willing to give up a considerable amount of styling for additional performance. The opposite is true for consumers in (b).

are asked about their preferences for a number of automobiles with differing combinations of styling and performance. Another way is to statistically analyze past consumer purchases of cars that varied in styling and performance. By relating the prices paid for different cars to the levels of the cars' attributes, one can determine the relative value attached to each attribute by various groups of consumers.[2] Either approach can help determine whether the largest group of consumers values performance more highly (as in Figure 3.7a) or styling more highly (as in Figure 3.7b), and to what extent people in each group are willing to trade off one attribute for the other.

A recent study of automobile demand in the United States shows that over the past two decades most consumers have preferred styling over performance.[3] The study divided all cars sold in the United States from 1977 through 1991 into nine market classes, ranging from subcompact to luxury sport. Within each class, the degree of styling change was indexed from 1 (no visible exterior change, as in the 1991 Honda Accord) to 5 (a complete sheet metal change, as in the 1989 Buick Century) to 9 (a complete new body, a change in size, and a conversion of rear-wheel to front-wheel drive, as in the 1980 Chevrolet Citation). The study found that automobile companies that emphasized style changes grew more rapidly than companies that emphasized performance. In particular, those cars undergoing major style changes enjoyed a significantly higher growth in sales than cars not undergoing such changes. (The major effect occurred immediately after the style change, but smaller effects were felt in subsequent years.)

The importance of styling helps explain the growing share of Japanese imports in the United States—U.S. domestic sales grew at 1.3 percent per year, while sales of imports grew at 6.4 percent per year. On average, 15 percent of all domestic U.S. cars underwent a major style change each year, as compared to 23.4 percent of all imports. Clearly, styling changes (along with improvements in performance and reliability) spurred the growth of imported cars.

3.2 Budget Constraints

An indifference map describes a person's preferences for various combinations of goods and services. But preferences do not explain all of consumer behavior. Individual choices are also affected by *budget constraints*, which limit people's ability to consume in light of the prices they must pay for various goods and services.

---

[2] For an example, see Vladimir Bajic, "Automobiles and Implicit Markets: An Estimate of a Structural Demand Model for Automobile Characteristics," *Applied Economics* 25 (1993): 541–551.

[3] See Edward L. Millner and George E. Hoffer, "A Reexamination of the Impact of Automotive Styling on Demand," *Applied Economics* 25 (1993): 101–110.

The Budget Line

To see how a budget constraint limits a consumer's choices, let's consider a situation in which a woman has a fixed amount of income, I, that can be spent on food and clothing. Let F be the amount of food purchased, and C the amount of clothing. We will denote the prices of the two goods P_F and P_C. Then $P_F F$ (i.e., price of food times the quantity) is the amount of money spent on food, and $P_C C$ is the amount of money spent on clothing.

The *budget line* indicates all combinations of F and C for which total money spent is equal to income. Since there are only two goods, the woman will spend her entire income on food and clothing. As a result, the combinations of food and clothing that she can buy will all lie on this line:

$$P_F F + P_C C = I \tag{3.1}$$

For example, suppose the consumer has a weekly income of $80, the price of food is $1 per unit, and the price of clothing is $2 per unit. Table 3.2 shows various combinations of food and clothing that she can purchase each week with her $80. If all her budget were allocated to clothing, the most that she could buy would be 40 units (at a price of $2 per unit), as represented by market basket A. If she spent all her budget on food, she could buy 80 units (at $1 per unit), as given by market basket G. Market baskets B, D, and E show three additional ways in which $80 could be spent on food and clothing.

Figure 3.8 shows the budget line associated with the market baskets given in Table 3.2. Because giving up a unit of clothing saves $2 and buying a unit of food costs $1, the amount of clothing given up for food along the budget line must be the same everywhere. As a result, the budget line is a straight line from point A to point G. In this particular case, the budget line is given by the equation $F + 2C = \$80$.

The intercept of the budget line is represented by market basket A. As she moves along the line from market basket A to market basket G, the consumer spends less on clothing and more on food. It is easy to see that the extra clothing that must be given up to consume an additional unit of food is given by the ratio of the price of food to the price of clothing ($1/$2 = 1/2). Since clothing costs $2 per unit, while food is only $1 per unit, 1/2 a unit of clothing must

Table 3.2 Market Baskets and the Budget Line			
Market Basket	**Food (F)**	**Clothing (C)**	**Total Spending**
A	0	40	$80
B	20	30	$80
D	40	20	$80
E	60	10	$80
G	80	0	$80

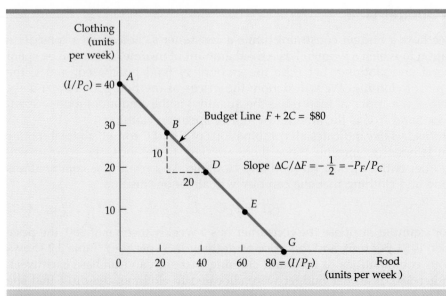

Figure 3.8 **A Budget Line** The consumer's budget line describes the combinations of goods that can be purchased given the consumer's income and the prices of the goods. Line AG (which passes through points B, D, and E) shows the budget associated with an income of $80, a price of food of $P_F = \$1$ per unit, and a price of clothing of $P_C = \$2$ per unit. The slope of the budget line (measured between points B and D) is $-P_F/P_C = -10/20 = -1/2$.

be given up to get 1 unit of food. In Figure 3.8 the slope of the line, $\Delta C/\Delta F = -1/2$, measures the relative cost of food and clothing.

Using equation (3.1), we can see how much of C must be given up to consume more of F by dividing both sides of the equation by P_C and then solving for C:

$$C = (I/P_C) - (P_F/P_C)F \qquad (3.2)$$

Equation (3.2) is the equation for a straight line; it has a vertical intercept of I/P_C and a slope of $-(P_F/P_C)$.

The slope of the budget line, $-(P_F/P_C)$, is the negative of the ratio of the prices of the two goods. The magnitude of the slope tells us the rate at which the two goods can be substituted for each other without changing the total amount of money spent. The vertical intercept (I/P_C) represents the maximum amount of C that can be purchased with income I. Finally, the horizontal intercept (I/P_F) tells us how many units of F could be purchased if all income were spent on F.

The Effects of Changes in Income and Prices

We have seen that the budget line depends on income and on the prices of the goods P_F and P_C. Prices and income often change, however. Let's see how such changes affect the budget line.

Income Changes

What happens to the budget line when income changes? From the equation for the straight line, we can see that a change in income alters the vertical intercept of the budget line but does not change the slope (because the price of neither good changed). Figure 3.9 shows that if income is doubled (from $80 to $160), the budget line shifts outward (from budget line L_1 to budget line L_2). Note, however, that L_2 remains parallel to L_1. If she desires, the consumer could now double her purchases of both food and clothing. Likewise, if her income is cut in half (from $80 to $40), the budget line shifts inward, from L_1 to L_3.

Price Changes

What happens to the budget line if the price of one good changes, but the price of the other good does not? We can use the equation $C = (I/P_C) - (P_F/P_C)F$ to describe the effects of a change in the price of food on the budget line. Suppose the price of food falls by half, from $1 to $0.50. Then the vertical intercept of the budget line remains unchanged, but the slope changes from $-P_F/P_C = -1/\$2 = -1/2$ to $-\$0.50/\$2 = -1/4$. In Figure 3.10 we obtain the new budget line L_2 by rotating the original budget line L_1 outward, pivoting from the C-intercept. This rotation makes sense because a person who consumes only clothing and no food is unaffected by the price change.

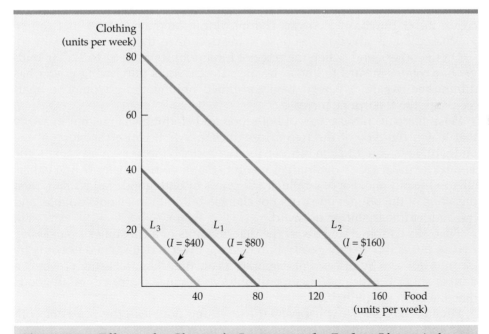

Figure 3.9 Effects of a Change in Income on the Budget Line A change in income (with prices unchanged) causes the budget line to shift parallel to the original line (L_1). When the income of $80 (on L_1) is increased to $160, the budget line shifts outward to L_2. If the income falls to $40, the line shifts inward to L_3.

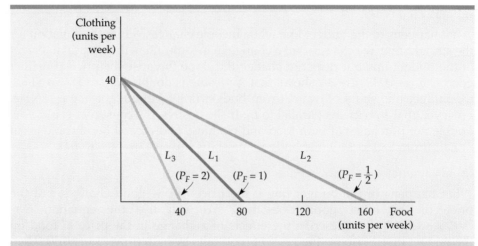

Figure 3.10 Effects of a Change in Price on the Budget Line A change in the price of one good (with income unchanged) causes the budget line to rotate about one intercept. When the price of food falls from $1.00 to $0.50, the budget line rotates outward from L_1 to L_2. However, when the price increases from $1.00 to $2.00, the line rotates inward from L_1 to L_3.

However, someone who consumes a large amount of food will have an increase in his purchasing power. The maximum amount of food that can be purchased has doubled in response to the decline in the price of food.

On the other hand, when the price of food doubles from $1 to $2, the budget line rotates inward to line L_3 because the person's purchasing power has diminished. Again, a person who consumed only clothing would be unaffected by the food price increase.

What happens if the prices of both food and clothing change, but in a way that leaves the *ratio* of the two prices unchanged? Because the slope of the budget line is equal to the ratio of the two prices, the slope will remain the same. The intercept of the budget line must shift so that the new line is parallel to the old one. For example, if the prices of both goods fall by half, then the slope of the budget line does not change, but both intercepts double, and the budget line is shifted outward.

This tells us something about the determinants of a consumer's *purchasing power*—her ability to buy goods. Purchasing power is determined not only by income, but also by prices. For example, a consumer's purchasing power can double either because her income doubles *or* because the prices of all goods that she buys fall by half.

Finally, consider what happens if everything doubles—the prices of both food and clothing *and* the consumer's income. (This can happen in an inflationary economy.) Because both prices have doubled, the ratio of the prices has not changed and, therefore, neither has the slope of the budget line. Because the price of clothing has doubled as has income, the maximum amount of clothing that can be purchased (represented by the vertical intercept of the budget line) is unchanged. The same is true for food. Therefore, an inflation in which all prices and income levels rise proportionately will not affect the consumer's budget line or purchasing power.

3.3 Consumer Choice

Given preferences and budget constraints, we can now determine how individual consumers choose how much of each good to buy. We assume that consumers make this choice in a rational way—that they choose goods to *maximize the satisfaction they can achieve, given the limited budget available to them.*

The maximizing market basket must satisfy two conditions. First, *it must be located on the budget line.* To see why, note that any market basket to the left of and below the budget line leaves some income unallocated, which if spent could increase the consumer's satisfaction. Of course, consumers can—and sometimes do—save some of their incomes for future consumption. But this means that the choice is not just between food and clothing, but between consuming food or clothing now and consuming food or clothing in the future. At this point we will keep things simple by assuming that all income is spent now. Note also that any market basket to the right of and above the budget line cannot be purchased with available income. Thus the only rational and feasible choice is a market basket on the budget line.

The second condition is that *the maximizing market basket must give the consumer the most preferred combination of goods and services.* These two conditions reduce the problem of maximizing consumer satisfaction to one of picking an appropriate point on the budget line.

In our food and clothing example, as with any two goods, we can graphically illustrate the solution to the consumer's choice problem. Figure 3.11 shows how the problem is solved. Here, three indifference curves describe a consumer's preferences for food and clothing. Remember that of the three curves, the outermost curve U_3 yields the greatest amount of satisfaction, the curve U_2 yields the next greatest amount, and the curve U_1 yields the least.

First, note that point B on indifference curve U_1 is not the most preferred choice, because a reallocation of income in which more is spent on food and less on clothing can increase the consumer's satisfaction. In particular, by moving to point A, the consumer spends the same amount of money and achieves the increased level of satisfaction associated with indifference curve U_2. Second, note that market baskets to the right and above indifference curve U_2, like the market basket associated with D on indifference curve U_3, achieve a higher level of satisfaction but cannot be purchased with the available income. Therefore, A maximizes the consumer's satisfaction.

We see from this that the market basket that maximizes satisfaction must lie on the highest indifference curve that touches the budget line. Point A is the point of tangency between indifference curve U_2 and the budget line. At A the slope of the budget line is exactly equal to the slope of the indifference curve. Because the MRS ($-\Delta C/\Delta F$) is the negative of the slope of the indif-

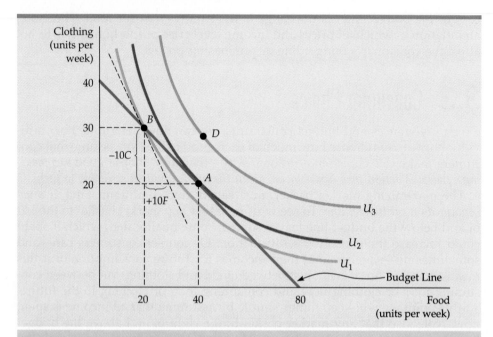

Figure 3.11 **Maximizing Consumer Satisfaction** Consumers maximize their satisfaction by choosing market basket *A*. At this point the budget line and indifference curve U_2 are tangent, and no higher level of satisfaction (e.g., with market basket *D*) can be attained. At *A*, the point of maximization, the MRS between the two goods equals the price ratio. At *B*, however, the MRS ($-(-10/10) = 1$) is greater than the price ratio (1/2), so satisfaction is not maximized.

ference curve; we can say that satisfaction is maximized (given the budget constraint) at the point where

$$\text{MRS} = P_F/P_C \qquad (3.3)$$

This is an important result: Satisfaction is maximized when *the marginal rate of substitution* (of *F* for *C*) *is equal to the ratio of the prices* (of *F* to *C*). Thus the consumer can obtain maximum satisfaction by adjusting his consumption of goods *F* and *C*, so that the MRS equals the price ratio.

The condition given in equation (3.3) is an example of the kinds of optimization conditions that arise in economics. In this instance, maximization is achieved when the *marginal benefit*—that is, the benefit associated with the consumption of one additional unit of food—is equal to the *marginal cost*. The marginal benefit is measured by the MRS. At point *A* it equals 1/2 (the magnitude of the slope of the indifference curve), which implies that the consumer is willing to give up 1/2 unit of clothing to obtain 1 unit of food. At the same point, the marginal cost is measured by the value of the slope of the budget line; it also equals 1/2 because the cost of getting one unit of food is to give up 1/2 unit of clothing ($P_F = 1$ and $P_C = 2$ on the budget line).

If the MRS is less or greater than the price ratio, the consumer's satisfaction has not been maximized. For example, compare point B in Figure 3.11 to point A. At point B, the consumer is purchasing 20 units of food and 30 units of clothing. The price ratio (or marginal cost) is equal to 1/2 because food costs $1 and clothing costs $2. However, the MRS (or marginal benefit) is greater than 1/2. (It is approximately 1.) As a result, the consumer is willing to substitute one unit of food for one unit of clothing without loss of satisfaction. Because food is cheaper than clothing, it is in his interest to buy more food and less clothing. If the consumer purchases one less unit of clothing, for example, that $2 can be allocated to two units of food, when only one unit is needed to maintain his level of satisfaction.[4]

The reallocation of the budget continues in this manner (moving along the budget line), until we reach point A, because at A the price ratio of 1/2 just equals the MRS of 1/2, which implies that the consumer is willing to trade one unit of clothing for two units of food. Only when the condition MRS $= 1/2 = P_F/P_C$ holds is he maximizing his satisfaction.

EXAMPLE 3.2 **Designing New Automobiles**

Our analysis of consumer choice allows us to see how the differing preferences of consumer groups for automobiles can affect their purchasing decisions. Following up on Example 3.1, we consider two groups of consumers; each group wishes to spend $10,000 on the styling and performance of cars (additional money could be allocated to other attributes of automobiles not discussed here), but each group has different preferences for styling and performance.

Figure 3.12 shows the car-buying budget constraint that individuals in each group face. The first group, with preferences similar to those in Figure 3.7(a), prefers performance to styling. By finding the point of tangency between a typical individual's indifference curve and the budget constraint, we see that consumers in this group would prefer to buy a car whose performance was worth $7,000 and whose styling was worth $3,000. Individuals in the second group, however, would prefer cars with $2,500 worth of performance and $7,500 worth of styling. (Recall from Example 3.1 that statistical studies have shown that the majority of consumers belong to the second group.)

With knowledge of group preferences, an automobile company can design a production and marketing plan. One potentially profitable option is to manufacture a model that emphasizes styling to a somewhat lesser degree than

---

[4] The result that the MRS equals the price ratio is deceptively powerful. Imagine two consumers who have just purchased various quantities of food and clothing. Without looking at their purchases, you can tell both persons (if they are maximizing) the value of their MRS (by looking at the prices of the two goods). What you cannot tell, however, is the quantity of each good purchased, because that is determined by their individual preferences. If the two consumers have different tastes, they will consume different quantities of food and clothing, even though each MRS is the same.

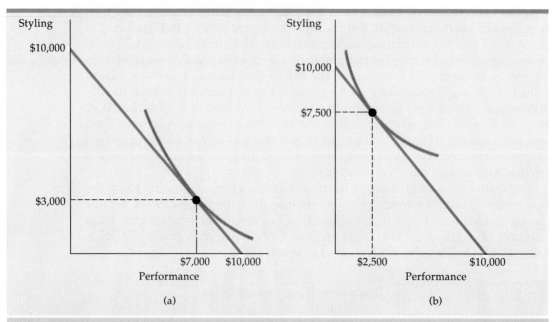

Figure 3.12   Consumer Choice of Automobile Attributes   The consumers in (a) are willing to trade off a considerable amount of styling for some additional performance. Given a budget constraint, they will choose a car that emphasizes performance. The opposite is true for consumers in (b).

individuals in Figure 3.12(b) would prefer, but to a much greater degree than individuals in Figure 3.12(a) would like (so as to appeal to both groups). A second option is to produce a relatively large number of cars that emphasize styling, and a smaller number that emphasize performance. Either choice would follow from knowledge of the car-buying preferences discussed above.

E X A M P L E   3 . 3   The Decision Making of a Local Public Official

Grant programs from the federal government to state and local governments serve many purposes. One program might seek to increase school spending, another to redistribute income from relatively wealthy states and localities to those that are relatively poor, and a third to ensure that individual governments provide minimum service levels to their constituents.

Which kinds of grant programs are best suited to achieve these different objectives? The answer depends on the incentive effects that each program generates; by changing the constraints that local public officials face, a grant program can alter the official's decision about how much the local government should spend. We can use consumer theory to see how two types of grant programs evoke different responses from public officials.

Suppose that a public official is in charge of the police budget, which is paid for by local taxes. Her preferences reflect what she believes should be allocated for police spending and what she feels citizens would prefer to have available for private consumption. Before the introduction of the grant program, the city's budget line is PQ in Figure 3.13(a). This budget line represents the *total* amount of resources available for public police spending (shown on the horizontal axis) and private spending (shown on the vertical axis).[5] The preference-maximizing market basket A on indifference curve U_1 shows that OR is spent on private expenditures and OS on police expenditures. Since

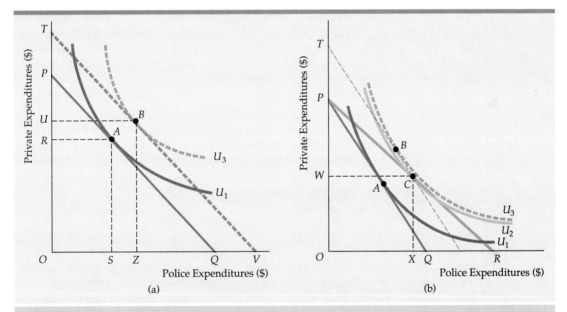

(a)

(b)

Figure 3.13(a)   A Nonmatching Grant   A nonmatching grant from the federal government to a local government acts just like an increase in income in the traditional consumer analysis. The local government official moves from A to B, allocating a portion of the grant to public expenditures and a portion to lower taxes and therefore to an increase in private expenditures.

Figure 3.13(b)   A Matching Grant   A matching grant acts just like a price decrease in the traditional consumer analysis. The local government official moves from A to C, allocating some of the grant to public expenditures and some to private expenditures. Relatively more money, however, is spent on public expenditures than would be with a nonmatching grant of the same total amount.

---

[5] This sum would approximately equal the per capita income of the jurisdiction (say $10,000) times the number of taxpayers (say, 50,000).

public expenditures are paid for by local taxes, these private expenditures represent spending after local taxes have been paid.

The first type of grant program, a *nonmatching grant*, is simply a check from the federal government that the local government can spend without restriction. An unconditional grant of this sort expands the community budget line outward from *PQ* to *TV* in Figure 3.13(a), where *PT* = *QV* is the dollar amount of the grant. The response to this influx of dollars is to move to a higher indifference curve by selecting market basket *B*, with more of both goods (*OU* of private expenditures and *OZ* of police expenditures). But more private expenditures means that some of the money for police that came previously from taxes now comes from government grants.

The second type of program is the *matching grant*. Matching funds are offered as a form of subsidy to local spending. For example, the federal government might offer to pay $1 for every $2 that the local government raises to pay for police. As a result, a matching grant lowers the relative cost of the publicly provided good. In terms of Figure 3.13(b), the matching grant rotates the budget line outward from *PQ* to *PR*. If no local money is spent on police, the budget line is unchanged. However, if the local public official decides to spend money on the public sector, the budget increases.

In response to the matching grant, the official chooses market basket *C* rather than *A*. As with a nonmatching grant, there is an increase in both police and private expenditures. At *C*, *OX* dollars are allocated to police and *OW* to private expenditures. However, the spending effects of the two types of grant are different. The diagram shows that the matching grant leads to greater police spending than does the nonmatching grant, even when the two programs involve identical government expenditures.[6]

A Corner Solution

Sometimes consumers buy in extremes, at least within categories of goods. For example, some people spend no money on travel and entertainment. The indifference curve analysis can be used to show conditions under which consumers choose not to consume a particular good.

In Figure 3.14, faced with budget line *AB*, a man chooses to purchase only food and no clothing. This is called a *corner solution* because when one of the goods is not consumed, the consumption bundle appears at the corner of the graph. At *B*, which is the point of maximum satisfaction, the marginal rate of substitution of food for clothing is greater than the slope of the budget line. This suggests that if the consumer had more clothing to give up, he would gladly trade it for additional food. However, at this point the consumer is already consuming all food and no clothing, and it is impossible to consume *negative* amounts of clothing!

---

6 Note also that point *B*, attained with a nonmatching grant, is on a higher indifference curve than point *C*, which is attained with a matching grant. The nonmatching grant leads to greater satisfaction for the same level of expenditure. In other words, there is a trade-off between encouraging a particular change in expenditure and achieving the highest level of satisfaction for a given expenditure.

When a corner solution arises, the consumer's MRS does not necessarily equal the price ratio. Unlike equation (3.3) the necessary condition for satisfaction to be maximized is given by the inequality[7]

$$\text{MRS} \geq P_F/P_C \tag{3.4}$$

The marginal benefit–marginal cost equality that we described in the previous section holds only when positive quantities of all goods are consumed.

An important lesson here is that predictions about how much of a product consumers will purchase when faced with changing economic conditions depend on the nature of consumer preferences for that product and related products and on the slope of the consumer's budget line. If the MRS of food for clothing is substantially greater than the price ratio, as in Figure 3.14, then a small decrease in the price of clothing will not alter the consumer's choice—he will still choose to consume only food. But if the price of clothing falls far enough, the consumer could quickly choose to consume a lot of clothing.

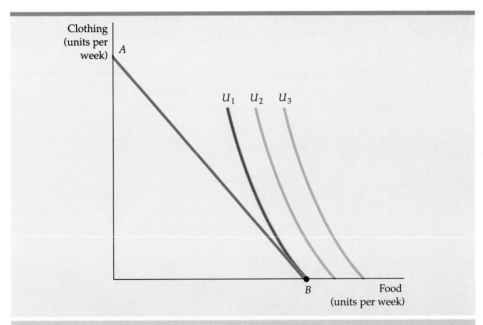

Figure 3.14   A Corner Solution   When the consumer's marginal rate of substitution is not equal to the price ratio for all levels of consumption, then a corner solution arises. The consumer maximizes satisfaction by consuming only one of the two goods. Given budget line AB, the highest level of satisfaction is achieved at B on indifference curve U_1, where MRS (of food for clothing) $> P_F/P_C$.

---

[7] Strict equality could hold if the slope of the budget constraint happened to equal the slope of the indifference curve, which is unlikely. Note that the inequality would be reversed if the corner solution were at point A rather than B.

EXAMPLE 3.4 **A College Trust Fund**

Jane Doe's parents have provided a trust fund for her college education. Jane, who is 18, can receive the entire trust fund on the condition that she spend it only on education. The trust fund is a welcome gift to Jane but perhaps not as welcome as an unrestricted trust would be. To see this, consider Figure 3.15, in which dollars per year spent on education are shown on the horizontal axis, and dollars spent on other forms of consumption are on the vertical axis.

The budget line that Jane faces before being awarded the trust is given by line *PQ*. The trust fund expands the budget line outward so long as the full amount of the fund, shown by distance *PB*, is spent on education. By accepting the trust fund and going to college, Jane increases her satisfaction, moving from A on indifference curve U_1 to B on indifference curve U_2.

Note that B represents a corner solution because Jane's marginal rate of substitution of other consumption for education is lower than the relative price of other consumption. Jane would prefer to spend a portion of the trust fund on other goods as well as education. Without the restriction on the trust fund, she would move to C on indifference curve U_3, decreasing her spending on

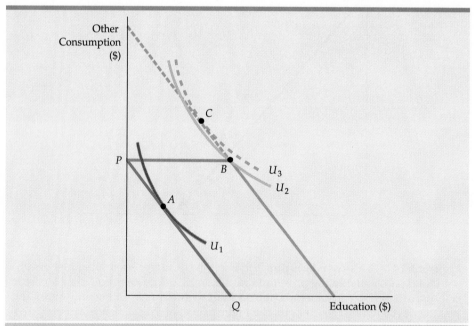

Figure 3.15 A College Trust Fund A student is given a college trust fund that must be spent on education. The student moves from A to B, a corner solution. If, however, the trust fund could be spent on other consumption as well as education, the student would be better off at C.

education (perhaps going to a junior college rather than a four-year college) but increasing her spending on items that she enjoys more than education.

Recipients usually prefer an unrestricted trust to a restricted one. Restricted trusts are popular, however, because they allow parents to control their children's expenditures in ways that they believe are in the children's long-run best interests.

3.4 Revealed Preference

In Section 3.1 we saw how an individual's preferences could be represented by a series of indifference curves. Then in Section 3.3, we saw how preferences determine choices, given a budget constraint. Can this process be reversed? If we know the choices a consumer has made, can we determine her preferences?

We can, if we have information about a sufficient number of choices that are made when prices and income levels vary. The basic idea is simple. If a consumer chooses one market basket over another, and the chosen market basket is more expensive than the alternative one, then the consumer must prefer the chosen market basket.

Suppose that an individual, facing the budget constraint given by line l_1 in Figure 3.16, chooses market basket A. Let's compare this to baskets B and D. Since the individual could have purchased market basket B (and all market baskets below line l_1) and did not, we say that A is *preferred* to B.

It might seem at first glance that we cannot make a direct comparison between market baskets A and D because D is not on l_1. But suppose the relative prices of food and clothing change, so that the new budget line is l_2, and the individual then chooses market basket B. Because D lies on budget line l_2 and was not chosen, B is preferred to D (and B is preferred to all market baskets below line l_2). Because A is preferred to B and B is preferred to D, we conclude that A is preferred to D. Furthermore, note in Figure 3.16 that market basket A is preferred to all of the market baskets that appear in the green-shaded areas. However, since food and clothing are "goods" rather than "bads," all market baskets that lie in the pink-shaded area in the rectangle above and to the right of A are preferred to A. Hence, the indifference curve passing through A must lie in the unshaded area.

Given more information about choices when prices and income levels vary, we can get a better fix on the shape of the indifference curve. Consider Figure 3.17. Suppose that facing line l_3 (which was chosen to pass through A), the individual chooses market basket E. Because E was chosen, even though A was equally expensive (it lies on the same budget line), E is preferred to A, as are all points in the rectangle above and to the right of E. Now suppose that facing line l_4 (which passes through A) the individual chooses market basket G. Because G was chosen and A was not, G is preferred to A, as are all market baskets above and to the right of G.

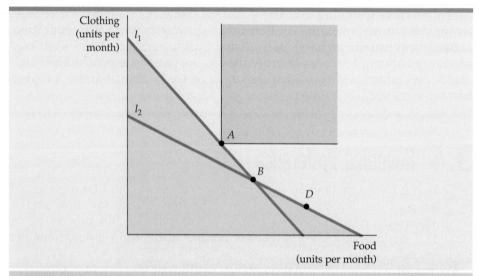

Figure 3.16 **Revealed Preference—Two Budget Lines** If an individual facing budget line l_1 has chosen market basket A rather than market basket B, A is revealed preferred to B. Likewise, facing budget line l_2, the individual chooses market basket B, which is then revealed preferred to market basket D. A is preferred to all market baskets in the green-shaded area, whereas all market baskets in the pink-shaded area are preferred to A.

We can go further by making use of the assumption that preferences are convex. Then, because E is preferred to A, all market baskets above and to the right of line AE in Figure 3.17 must be preferred to A. (Otherwise the indifference curve passing through A would have to pass through a point above and to the right of AE and then fall below the line at E, and the indifference curve would not be convex.) By a similar argument, all points on AG or above are also preferred to A. Therefore, the indifference curve must lie within the unshaded area.

The revealed preference approach is valuable as a means of checking whether individual choices are consistent with the assumptions of consumer theory. It has even been applied to the study of animal behavior. By changing an animal's environment, we can test whether the animal's consumption choices are consistent with consumer theory. One study of rats varied the "price" of different foods according to the number of times the rats had to push a lever to obtain the foods. The rats' behavior was consistent with consumer theory—they were shown to have relatively low "price" elasticities for essential foods and higher elasticities for nonessentials.[8]

Finally, revealed preference analysis can help us understand the implications of choices that consumers must make in particular circumstances, as Example 3.5 shows.

---

[8] See John H. Kagel, Raymond C. Battalio, Howard Rachlin, and Leonard Green, "Demand Curves for Animal Consumers," *Quarterly Journal of Economics* 96 (Feb. 1981): 1–15.

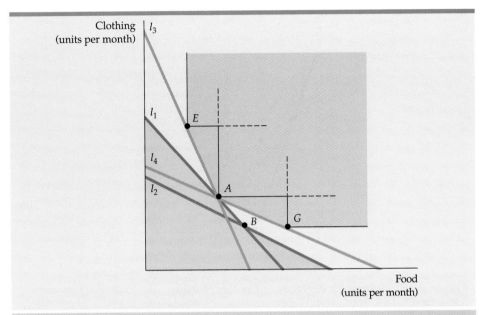

Figure 3.17 Revealed Preference—Four Budget Lines Facing budget line l_3 the individual chooses E, which is revealed preferred to A (since A could have been chosen). Likewise, facing line l_4, G is chosen, which is also revealed preferred to A. A is preferred to all market baskets in the green-shaded area, whereas all market baskets in the pink-shaded area are preferred to A.

EXAMPLE 3.5 Revealed Preference for Recreation

A health club has been offering the use of its facilities to anyone who is willing to pay an hourly fee. Now the club decides to alter its pricing policy by charging an annual membership fee along with a lower hourly fee. Does this new financial arrangement make individuals better off or worse off than the old arrangement? The answer depends on people's preferences.

Suppose that Roberta has $100 of income available each week for recreational activities, including exercise, movies, restaurant meals, and so on. When the health club charged a fee of $4 per hour, Roberta used the facility 10 hours per week. Under the new arrangement, she is required to pay $30 per week for access to the facilities, but can use the club for only $1 per hour.

Is this change beneficial for Roberta? Revealed preference analysis provides the answer. In Figure 3.18 line l_1 represents the budget constraint that Roberta faced under the original pricing arrangement. In this case she maximized her satisfaction by choosing market basket A, with 10 hours of exercise and $60 of other recreational activities. Under the new arrangement, which shifts the budget line to l_2, she could still choose market basket A. But since U_1 is clearly not tangent to l_2, Roberta will be better off choosing another market basket,

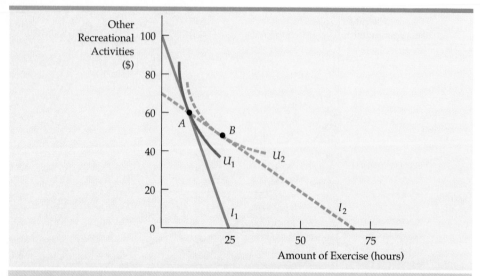

Figure 3.18 **Revealed Preference for Recreation** An individual chooses to use a health club for 10 hours per week at point *A*, when facing budget line l_1. When the fees are altered, the individual faces budget line l_2. She is then made better off, because market basket *A* can still be purchased, as can market basket *B*, which lies on a higher indifference curve.

such as *B*, with 25 hours of exercise and $45 of other recreational activities. Because she would choose *B* when she could still choose *A*, she prefers *B* to *A*. The new pricing arrangement therefore makes Roberta better off.

We could also ask whether this new pricing system—called a *two-part tariff*—will increase the profits of the health club. If all members are like Roberta and more use generates more profit, then the answer is yes. In general, however, the answer depends on the preferences of all members, and on the costs of operating the facility. We discuss the two-part tariff in detail in Chapter 11 when we study how firms with market power set prices.

3.5 The Concept of Utility

Indifference curves allow us to describe consumer preferences graphically, and build on the assumption that consumers can rank alternatives. But consumer preferences can also be described using the concepts of utility and marginal utility. We will explain what each of these concepts means and then relate them to indifference curve analysis.

Utility and Satisfaction

Utility is the level of satisfaction that a person gets from consuming a good or undertaking an activity. Utility has an important psychological compo-

nent because people obtain utility by getting things that give them pleasure and by avoiding things that give them pain. In economic analysis, however, utility is most often used to summarize the preference ranking of market baskets. If buying three books makes a person happier than the purchase
of one shirt, then we say that the books give that person more utility than
the shirt.

A *utility function* is obtained by attaching a number to each market basket,
so that if market basket A is preferred to market basket B, the number will be
higher for A than for B. For example, market basket A on the highest of three
indifference curves U_3 might have a utility level of 3, while market basket B
on the second-highest indifference curve U_2 might have a utility level of 2,
and market basket C, on the lowest indifference curve U_1, a utility level of 1.
Thus the utility function provides the same information about preferences that
an indifference map does. Both utility functions and indifference maps order
consumer choices in terms of levels of satisfaction.

The utility function is more easily applied to the analysis of choices involving three or more goods simply because it is difficult to graph indifference curves in this case. But it is important to distinguish between the cardinal and ordinal properties of utility functions. For example, the levels of
utility associated with the three market baskets A, B, and C might be 4, 2,
and 1, or they might be 6, 4, and 3. Because most choices can be explained
simply by the ordinal ranking of utility levels, the indicators 4, 2, and 1 provide the same information as the indicators 6, 4, and 3. What is important
is the *relative* rankings that are given when a particular set of numbers is
chosen.

Bearing in mind that we are using the ordinal properties of utility functions, let's examine one in particular. The function $u(F,C) = FC$ tells us that
the level of satisfaction obtained from consuming F units of food and C units
of clothing is the product of F and C. Figure 3.19 shows indifference curves
associated with this function. The graph was drawn by initially choosing one
particular market basket, say, $F = 5$ and $C = 5$, which generates a utility level
of 25. Then the indifference curve (also called an *isoutility curve*) was drawn
by finding all market baskets for which $FC = 25$ (e.g., $F = 10, C = 2.5; F = 2.5,$
$C = 10$). The second indifference curve contains all market baskets for which
$FC = 50$, and the third all baskets such that $FC = 100$.

The important point is that the numbers attached to the indifference curves
are for convenience only. Suppose the utility function were changed to
$u(F,C) = 4FC$. Consider any market basket that previously generated a utility
level of 25, say, $F = 5$ and $C = 5$. Now the level of utility has increased, by a
factor of 4, to 100. Thus the indifference curve labeled 25 looks the same, but
it should now be labeled 100 rather than 25. In fact, the only difference between the indifference curves associated with the utility function $4FC$ and the
utility function FC is that the curves are numbered 100, 200, and 400, rather
than 25, 50, and 100. Most often when we use utility functions, we care about
their ordinal rather than cardinal properties. On the few occasions in this book
when we do plan to use the stronger assumption that utility has cardinal
meaning, we will let you know.

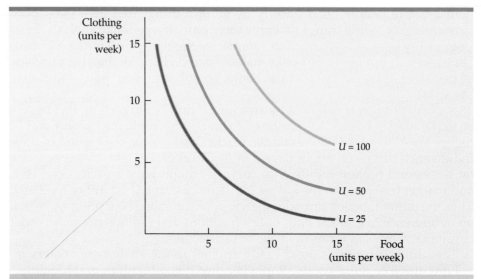

Figure 3.19 Utility Functions and Indifference Curves A utility function can be represented by a set of indifference curves, each with a numerical indicator. The figure shows three indifference curves, with utility levels of 25, 50, and 100.

Marginal Utility

By introducing the concept of marginal utility, our previous analysis of consumer choice can be recast in a way that provides additional insight. To begin, let's distinguish between the total utility obtained by consumption and the satisfaction obtained from the last item consumed. *Marginal utility* (MU) measures the additional satisfaction obtained from consuming an additional amount of a good. For example, the marginal utility associated with a consumption increase from 0 to 10 units of food might be 9; from 10 to 20, it might be 7; and from 20 to 30, it might be 5.

These numbers are consistent with the principle of *diminishing marginal utility*: As more and more of a good is consumed, consuming additional amounts will yield smaller and smaller additions to utility. Imagine, for example, the consumption of television—marginal utility might fall after the second or third hour (and could become negative after the fourth or fifth).

We can relate the concept of marginal utility to the consumer's utility maximization problem in the following way. Consider a small movement down an indifference curve in Figure 3.19. The additional consumption of F, ΔF, will generate marginal utility MU_F. This results in a total increase in utility of $MU_F\Delta F$. At the same time, the loss of consumption of C, ΔC, will lower utility per unit by MU_C, resulting in a total loss of $MU_C\Delta C$.

Because all points on an indifference curve generate the same level of utility, the total gain in utility associated with the increase in F must balance the loss due to the lower consumption of C. Formally,

$$0 = MU_F(\Delta F) + MU_C(\Delta C)$$

Now we can rearrange this equation so that

$$-(\Delta C/\Delta F) = MU_F/MU_C$$

But since $-(\Delta C/\Delta F)$ is the marginal rate of substitution of F for C, it follows that

$$MRS = MU_F/MU_C \qquad (3.5)$$

Equation (3.5) tells us that the marginal rate of substitution is the ratio of the marginal utility of F to the marginal utility of C. As the consumer gives up more and more of C to obtain more of F, the marginal utility of F falls and the marginal utility of C increases.

We saw earlier in this chapter that when consumers maximize their satisfaction, the marginal rate of substitution of F for C is equal to the ratio of the prices of the two goods:

$$MRS = P_F/P_C \qquad (3.6)$$

Since the MRS is also equal to the ratio of the marginal utilities of consuming F and C (from equation 3.4), it follows that

$$MU_F/MU_C = P_F/P_C$$

or

$$MU_F/P_F = MU_C/P_C \qquad (3.7)$$

According to equation (3.7), utility maximization is achieved when the budget is allocated so that *the marginal utility per dollar of expenditure is the same for each good.* To see why this must hold, note that if a person gets more utility from spending an additional dollar on food than on clothing, her utility will be increased by spending more on food. So long as the marginal utility of spending an extra dollar on food exceeds the marginal utility of spending an extra dollar on clothing, she should shift her budget toward food and away from clothing. Eventually, the marginal utility of food will decrease (because there is diminishing marginal utility in consumption) and the marginal utility of clothing will increase (for the same reason). Only when the consumer has equalized the marginal utility per dollar of expenditure across all goods will she have maximized utility. This *equal marginal principle* is an important concept in microeconomics. It will reappear in different forms throughout our analysis of consumer and producer behavior.

EXAMPLE 3.6   Gasoline Rationing

In 1974 and again in 1979, the government imposed price controls on gasoline, and many gas stations had to reduce their prices (world oil prices rose but controls kept domestic prices low). As a result, motorists wanted to buy more gasoline than was available at the controlled prices, and gasoline was rationed. Nonprice rationing is an alternative to the market that some people consider fair. Under one form of rationing everyone has an equal chance to purchase a rationed good, whereas under a market system those with higher incomes can outbid those with lower incomes to obtain goods that are in scarce supply.

In this case gasoline was allocated by long lines at the gas pumps: Those who were willing to give up their time waiting got the gas they wanted, while others did not. By guaranteeing every person a minimum amount of gasoline, rationing can provide some people with access to a product that they could not otherwise afford. But rationing hurts others by limiting the amount of gasoline that they can buy.[9]

We can see this clearly in Figure 3.20, which applies to a woman with an annual income of $20,000. The horizontal axis shows her annual consumption of gasoline, and the vertical axis shows her remaining income after purchas-

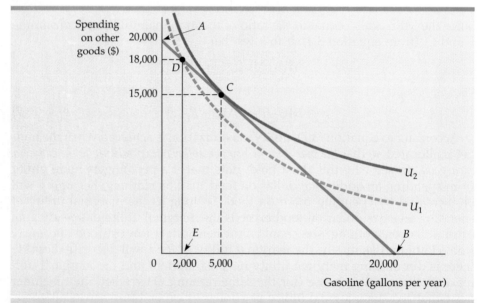

Figure 3.20 **Inefficiency of Gasoline Rationing** When a good is rationed, less is available than consumers would like to buy, and consumers may be worse off. Without gasoline rationing, up to 20,000 gallons of gasoline are available for consumption (at point B). The consumer chooses point C on indifference curve U_2, consuming 5,000 gallons of gasoline. However, with a limit of 2,000 gallons of gasoline under rationing (at point E), the consumer moves to D on the lower indifference curve U_1.

[9] For a more extensive discussion of gasoline rationing, see H. E. Frech III and William C. Lee, "The Welfare Cost of Rationing-By-Queuing Across Markets: Theory and Estimates from the U.S. Gasoline Crises," *Quarterly Journal of Economics* (1987): 97–108. Other, more general examples of rationing appear in Martin L. Weitzman, "Is the Price System or Rationing More Effective in Getting a Commodity to Those Who Need it Most?" *Bell Journal of Economics* 8 (Autumn 1977): 517–525.

ing gasoline. Suppose the controlled gasoline price is $1 per gallon. Because her income is $20,000, she is limited to the points on budget line *AB*, which has a slope of −1. At $1 per gallon, the woman might wish to buy 5,000 gallons of gasoline per year and spend $15,000 on other goods, represented by *C*. At this point, she has maximized her utility (by being on the highest possible indifference curve U_2), given her budget constraint of $20,000.

Because of rationing, the woman can purchase only 2,000 gallons of gasoline. As a result, she now faces budget line *ADE*. The budget line is no longer a straight line because purchases above 2,000 gallons are not possible. The figure shows that her choice to consume at *D* involves a lower level of utility, U_1, than would be achieved without rationing, U_2, because she is consuming less gasoline and more of other goods than she would otherwise prefer.

3.6 Cost-of-Living Indexes

The Social Security system has been the subject of heated debate lately. Under this system, a retired person receives an annual benefit that is initially determined at the time of retirement and is based on the person's work history. The benefit then increases from year to year at a rate equal to the rate of increase of the Consumer Price Index (CPI). *The CPI is calculated each year by the U.S. Bureau of Labor Statistics as the ratio of the cost of a typical bundle of consumer goods and services today in comparison to the cost during a base period.* Does the CPI accurately reflect the cost of living for retirees? Is it appropriate to use the CPI as we now do—as a cost-of-living index for other government programs, for private union pensions, and for other private wage agreements? The answers to these questions lie in the economic theory of consumer behavior. In this section we describe the theoretical underpinnings of cost indexes such as the CPI, using an example that describes the hypothetical price changes that students and their parents might face.

Let's look at two sisters, Rachel and Sarah, whose preferences are identical. When Sarah began her college education in 1987, her parents gave her a "discretionary" budget of $500 per quarter, to be spent on food, which was available at a price of $2.00 per pound, and on books, which were available at a price of $20 each. Sarah bought 100 pounds of food (at a cost of $200) and 15 books (at a cost of $300). Ten years later, in 1997 when Rachel (who had worked during the interim) is about to start college, her parents promise her a budget that is equilvalent in buying power to that of her older sister. Unfortunately, prices in the college town have increased, with food now $2.20 per pound, and books $100 each. By how much should the discretionary budget be increased to leave Rachel as well off in 1997 as her sister Sarah was in 1987? Table 3.3 summarizes the relevant data and Figure 3.21 provides the answer.

The initial budget constraint facing Sarah in 1987 is given by line l_1 in Figure 3.21, and her utility-maximizing combination of food and books is at point *A* on indifference curve U_1. We can check that the cost of achieving this level of utility is $500 as stated in the table:

Table 3.3 Cost-of-Living Index		
	1987 (Sarah)	**1997 (Rachel)**
Price of books	$20/book	$100/book
Number of books	15	6
Price of food	$2.00/lb.	$2.20/lb.
Pounds of food	100	300
Expenditure	$500	$1,260

$500 = 100 lbs. of food × $2.00/pound + 15 books × $20/book

As Figure 3.21 shows, for Rachel to achieve the same level of utility as Sarah, while facing the new higher prices, she requires a budget sufficient for her to purchase the food-book consumption bundle given by point B on line l_2 (and tangent to indifference curve U_1), where she chooses 300 lbs. of food and 6 books. Note that in doing so, Rachel has taken into account that the price of books has increased relative to food, and therefore has sustituted toward food and away from books.

The cost to Rachel of attaining the same level of utility as Sarah is given by:

$1,260 = 300 lbs. of food × $2.20/pound + 6 books × $100/book

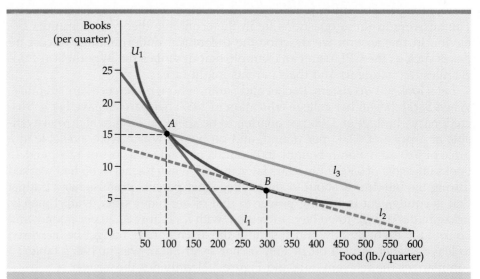

Figure 3.21 Cost-of-Living Indexes The Laspeyres price index, which represents the cost of buying bundle A at current prices relative to the cost of bundle A at base year prices, overstates the ideal cost-of-living index.

The ideal *cost-of-living adjustment* for Rachel is therefore $760 (which is $1,260 less than the $500 that was given to Sarah), and the ideal cost-of-living index is $1,260/$500 = 2.52. Much like the CPI, we set the index in the base year of 1987 to 100, so that the value of the index in 1997 is 252. A value of 252 implies a 152% increase in the cost of living, whereas a value of 100 would imply that the cost of living has not changed. *This ideal cost-of-living index represents the cost of attaining a given level of utility at current (1997) prices relative to the cost of attaining the same utility at base (1987) prices.*

Unfortunately, the informational needs for such an ideal cost-of-living index to be calculated on an economy-wide basis are huge—we would need to know individual preferences (which vary across the population) as well as prices and expenditures. Actual price indexes are, therefore, based on consumer *purchases,* not preferences. A price index, such as the CPI, which uses a *fixed consumption bundle in the base period,* is called a *Laspeyres price index.* The Laspeyres index answers the question: *What is the amount of money at current year prices that an individual requires to purchase the bundle of goods and servics that was chosen in the base year divided by the cost of purchasing the same bundle at base year prices?*

To calculate a Laspeyres cost of living index for Rachel is straightforward in this case. To buy 100 pounds of food and 15 books in 1997 would require an expenditure of $1,720 (100 × $2.20 + 15 × $100). This expenditure allows Rachel to choose bundle A on budget line l_3 (or any other bundle on that line). Note that l_3 is the budget line that allows Rachel to purchase the same consumption bundle as her sister at the current 1997 prices. (Line l_3 was constructed by shifting line l_2 outward until it intersected point A.) It would thus require a $1,220 increase in Rachel's discretionary budget for her to be compensated for the increased cost of living. The Laspeyres index is therefore $1,720/$500 = 344 (using 100 as the base in 1987).

In our example, the Laspeyres price index is clearly much higher than the ideal price index. But, does a Laspeyres index always overstate the true cost-of-living index? The answer is yes, as can be seen from the figure. Suppose that Rachel was given the budget associated with line l_3 during the base year of 1987. She could choose bundle A, but clearly she could achieve a higher level of utility if she purchased more food and fewer books (by moving to the right on line l_3). Because A and B generate equal utility, it follows that Rachel is better off receiving a Laspeyres cost-of-living adjustment rather than an ideal adjustment. The Laspeyres index overcompensates Rachel for the higher cost of living, and the Laspeyres cost-of-living index is, therefore, greater than the ideal cost-of-living-index. This result holds generally, and applies to the CPI in particular. The reason is that the Laspeyres price index assumes that consumers do not alter their consumption patterns as prices change. By changing consumption, increasing their purchases of those items that have become relatively cheaper, and decreasing their purchases of the relatively more expensive items, however, consumers can achieve the same level of utility without having to consume the same bundle of goods that they did before the price change.

Economic theory shows us that the Laspeyres cost-of-living index overstates the amount needed to compensate individuals for price increases. With respect to Social Security and other government programs, this means that *us-*

ing the CPI to adjust retirement benefits will tend to overcompensate most recipients and will require greater government expenditure than would otherwise be needed. This is why the U.S. government has considered changing the construction of the CPI, switching from a Laspeyres price index to a more complex price index that reflects changing consumption patterns.

Another commonly used cost-of-living index is the *Paasche index*. Unlike the Laspeyres index, which focuses on the cost of buying a base-year bundle, the Paasche index focuses on the cost of buying the *current year's bundle*. In particular, the Paasche index answers another question: *What is the amount of money at current year prices that an individual requires to purchase the current bundle of goods and services divided by the cost of purchasing the same bundle in the base year?*

It is helpful to compare the Laspeyres and the Paasche cost-of-living indexes.

■ *Laspeyres index:* The amount of money at current year prices that an individual requires to purchase the bundle of goods and services that was *chosen in the base year* divided by the cost of purchasing the same bundle at base year prices.

■ *Paasche index:* The amount of money at current year prices that an individual requires to purchase the bundle of goods and services *chosen in the current year* divided by the cost of purchasing the same bundle in the base year.

We can compare the Laspeyres and Paasche indexes algebraically for any two goods—for example, food (F) and clothing (C). Both involve ratios that utilize today's current year prices P_{Ft} and P_{Ct}. However, the Laspeyres index LI relies on base year consumption, F_b and C_b, whereas the Paasche index PI relies on today's current consumption, F_t and C_t. Formally:

$$LI = \frac{P_{Ft}F_b + P_{Ct}C_b}{P_{Fb}F_b + P_{Cb}C_b}$$

$$PI = \frac{P_{Ft}F_t + P_{Ct}C_t}{P_{Fc}F_t + P_{Cb}C_t}$$

Just as the Laspeyres index will overstate the ideal cost of living, the Paasche index will understate it because it assumes that the individual will buy the current year bundle in the base period. In actuality, facing base year prices, the consumer would have been able to achieve the same level of utility at a lower cost by changing her consumption bundle. Since the Paasche index is a ratio of the cost of buying the current bundle divided by the cost of buying a base year bundle, overstating the cost of the base year bundle (the denominator in the ratio) will cause the index itself to be overstated.

Neither the Laspeyres nor the Paasche index provides a perfect cost-of-living index, and the informational needs for the ideal index are too great. What is the best solution in practice? The U.S. government's most recent answer to this difficult question came in 1995, when it adopted the use of a *chain-weighted* price index to deflate its measure of gross domestic product (GDP) and thereby to obtain an estimate of real GDP. Chain weighting was introduced to overcome problems that arose when long-term comparisons of real

GDP were made using fixed-weight price indexes (such as Paasche and Laspeyres) and prices were rapidly changing.

Economists have known for years that Laspeyres cost-of-living indexes overstate inflation. However, it was not until the energy price shocks of the 1970s, the more recent fluctuations in food prices, and the concern surrounding the federal deficit that the move away from the Laspeyres index grew. It has been estimated, for example, that a failure to take into account the changes in consumers' computer purchases in responses to the sharp decreases in computer prices has in recent years caused the CPI to overstate the cost of living by about 0.3 percent per year. Hopefully, the U.S. government will eventually improve the way it calculates the CPI.

Summary

1. The theory of consumer choice is built on the assumption that people behave rationally in an attempt to maximize the satisfaction that they can obtain by purchasing a particular combination of goods and services.

2. Consumer choice has two related parts: the study of the consumer's preferences and the analysis of the budget line, which constrains the choices a person can make.

3. Consumers make choices by comparing market baskets or bundles of commodities. Their preferences are assumed to be complete (they can compare all possible market baskets) and transitive (if they prefer market basket A to B, and B to C, then they prefer A to C). In addition, we have assumed that more of each good is always preferred to less.

4. Indifference curves, which represent all combinations of goods and services that give the same level of satisfaction, are downward-sloping and cannot intersect one another.

5. Consumer preferences can be completely described by a set of indifference curves, or an indifference map. This indifference map provides an ordinal ranking of all choices that the consumer might make.

6. The marginal rate of substitution of F for C is the maximum amount of C that a person is willing to give up to obtain one additional unit of F. The marginal rate of substitution diminishes as we move down along an indifference

curve. When there is a diminishing marginal rate of substitution, preferences are convex.

7. Budget lines represent all combinations of goods for which consumers expend all their income. Budget lines shift outward in response to an increase in consumer income, but they pivot and rotate about a fixed point (on the vertical axis) when the price of one good (on the horizontal axis) changes but income and the price of the other good do not.

8. Consumers maximize satisfaction subject to budget constraints. When a consumer maximizes satisfaction by consuming some of each of two goods, the marginal rate of substitution is equal to the ratio of the prices of the two goods being purchased.

9. This maximization is sometimes achieved at a corner solution in which one good is not consumed. In that case the marginal rate of substitution need not equal the ratio of the prices.

10. The theory of revealed preference shows how the choices that individuals make when prices and income vary can be used to determine their preferences. When an individual chooses basket A when she could afford B, we know that A is preferred to B.

11. The theory of the consumer can be presented using either an indifference curve approach, which uses the ordinal properties of utility (that is, which allows for the ranking of alternatives), or a utility function approach. A

utility function is obtained by attaching a number to each market basket; if market basket *A* is preferred to market basket *B*, *A* generates more utility than *B*.

12. When risky choices are analyzed or when comparisons must be made among individuals, the cardinal properties of the utility function can be important. Usually the utility function will show diminishing marginal utility: As more and more of a good is consumed, the consumer obtains smaller and smaller increments to utility.

13. When the utility function approach is used and both goods are consumed, utility maximization occurs when the ratio of the marginal utilities of the two goods (which is the marginal rate of substitution) is equal to the ratio of the prices.

14. An ideal cost-of-living index measures the cost of buying a bundle of goods at current prices that generates the same level of *utility* as was enjoyed by the bundle of goods that was consumed at base year prices. The Laspeyres price index, however, represents the cost of buying the bundle of goods chosen in the base year at current prices relative to the cost of buying *the same bundle* at base year prices. The CPI, like all Laspeyres price indexes, overstates the ideal cost-of-living index. By contrast, the Paasche index measures the cost at current year prices of buying a bundle of goods chosen in the current year divided by the cost of buying the same bundle at base year prices. It thus understates the ideal cost-of-living index.

Questions for Review

1. What does *transitivity of preferences* mean?

2. Suppose that a set of indifference curves was not negatively sloped. What could you say about the desirability of the two goods?

3. Explain why two indifference curves cannot intersect.

4. Draw a set of indifference curves for which the marginal rate of substitution is constant. Draw two budget lines with different slopes; show what the satisfaction-maximizing choice will be in each case. What conclusions can you draw?

5. Explain why a person's marginal rate of substitution between two goods must equal the ratio of the price of the goods for the person to achieve maximum satisfaction.

6. Explain why consumers are likely to be worse off when a product that they consume is rationed.

7. Upon merging with West Germany's economy, East German consumers indicated a

preference for Mercedes-Benz automobiles over Volkswagen automobiles. However, when they converted their savings into deutsche marks, they flocked to Volkswagen dealerships. How can you explain this apparent paradox?

8. Describe the equal marginal principle. Explain why this principle may not hold if increasing marginal utility is associated with the consumption of one or both goods.

9. What is the difference between ordinal utility and cardinal utility? Explain why the assumption of cardinal utility is not needed in order to rank consumer choices.

10. The price of computers has fallen substantially over the past two decades. Use this drop in price to explain why the Consumer Price Index is likely to substantially understate the cost-of-living index for individuals who use computers intensively.

Exercises

1. In this chapter, consumer preferences for various commodities did not change during the analysis. Yet in some situations, preferences do change as consumption occurs. Discuss why and how preferences might change over time with consumption of these two commodities:
   a. cigarettes
   b. dinner for the first time at a restaurant with a special cuisine.

2. Draw the indifference curves for the following individuals' preferences for two goods: hamburgers and beer.
   a. Al likes beer but hates hamburgers. He always prefers more beer no matter how many hamburgers he has.
   b. Betty is indifferent between bundles of either three beers or two hamburgers. Her preferences do not change as she consumes any more of either food.
   c. Chris eats one hamburger and washes it down with one beer. He will not consume an additional unit of one item without an additional unit of the other.
   d. Doreen loves beer but is allergic to beef. Every time she eats a hamburger she breaks out in hives.

3. The price of records is $8, and the price of tapes is $10. Philip has a budget of $80 and has already purchased 4 records. He thus has $48 more to spend on additional records and tapes. Draw his budget line. If his remaining expenditure is made on 1 record and 4 tapes, show Philip's consumption choice on the budget line.

4. Suppose Bill views butter and margarine as perfectly substitutable for each other.
   a. Draw a set of indifference curves that describes Bill's preferences for butter and margarine.
   b. Are these indifference curves convex? Why?
   c. If butter costs $2 per package, while margarine costs only $1, and Bill has a $20 budget to spend for the month, which butter-margarine market basket will he choose? Can you show this graphically?

5. Suppose Jones and Smith have decided to allocate $1,000 per year on liquid refreshment in the form of alcoholic or nonalcoholic drinks. Jones and Smith differ substantially in their preferences for these two forms of refreshment. Jones prefers alcoholic to nonalcoholic drinks, while Smith prefers the nonalcoholic option.
   a. Draw a set of indifference curves for Jones and a second set for Smith.
   b. Discuss why the two sets of curves are different from each other using the concept of marginal rate of substitution.
   c. If both Smith and Jones pay the same prices for their refreshments, will their marginal rates of substitution of alcoholic for nonalcoholic drinks be the same or different? Explain.

6. Anne is a frequent flyer whose fares are reduced (through coupon giveaways) by 25 percent after she flies 25,000 miles a year, and then by 50 percent after she flies 50,000 miles. Can you graph the budget line that Anne faces in making her flight plans for the year?

7. Antonio buys 8 new college textbooks during his first year at school at a cost of $50 each. Used books cost only $30 each. When the bookstore announces that there will be a 20 percent price increase in new texts and a 10 percent increase in used texts for the next year, Antonio's father offers him $80 extra. Is Antonio better off or worse off after the price change?

8. Suppose that Samantha and Jason both spend $24 per week on video and movie entertainment. When the prices of videos and movies are both $4, they each rent 3 videos and buy 3 movie tickets. Following a video price war and an increased cost of movie tickets, the video price falls to $2 and the movie ticket increases to $6. Samantha now rents 6 videos and buys 2 movie tickets; Jason, however, buys 1 movie ticket and rents 9 videos.
   a. Is Samantha better off or worse off after the price change?
   b. Is Jason better off or worse off?

9. Connie Consumer has a monthly income of $200, which she allocates between two goods: meat and potatoes.
   a. Suppose meat costs $4 per pound and potatoes cost $2 per pound. Draw her budget constraint.
   b. Suppose also that her utility function is given by the equation $u(M,P) = 2M + P$. What combination of meat and potatoes should she buy to maximize her utility? (*Hint:* Meat and potatoes are perfect substitutes.)
   c. Connie's supermarket has a special promotion. If she buys 20 pounds of potatoes (at $2 per pound), she gets the next 10 pounds for free. This offer applies only to the first 20 pounds she buys. All potatoes in excess of the first 20 pounds (excluding bonus potatoes) are still $2 per pound. Draw her budget constraint.
   d. An outbreak of potato rot raises the price of potatoes to $4 per pound. The supermarket ends its promotion. What does her budget constraint look like now? What combination of meat and potatoes maximizes her utility?

10. The utility that Jane receives by consuming food F and clothing C is given by $u(F,C) = FC$.
   a. Draw the indifference curve associated with a utility level of 12, and the indifference curve associated with a utility level of 24. Are the indifference curves convex?
   b. Suppose that food costs $1 a unit, clothing costs $3 a unit, and Jane has $12 to spend on food and clothing. Graph the budget line that she faces.
   c. What is the utility-maximizing choice of food and clothing? (*Hint:* Solve the problem graphically.)
   d. What is the marginal rate of substitution of food for clothing when utility is maximized?
   e. Suppose that Jane buys 3 units of food and 3 units of clothing with her $12 budget. Would her marginal rate of substitution of food for clothing be greater or less than 1/3? Explain.

11. The utility that Meredith receives by consuming food F and clothing C is given by $u(F,C) = FC$. Suppose that her income in 1990 is $1,200 and the prices of food and clothing are $1 per unit of each. However, by 1995 the price of food has increased to $2 and the price of clothing to $3. Let 100 represent the cost-of-living index for 1990. Calculate the ideal and the Laspeyres cost-of-living index for Meredith for 1995. (*Hint:* Meredith will spend equal amounts on food and clothing.)

Chapter Outline

List of Examples

CHAPTER 4

Individual and Market Demand

Chapter 3 laid the foundation for the theory of consumer demand. We discussed the nature of consumers' preferences and saw how, given a budget constraint, consumers choose a consumption basket that maximizes their satisfaction. From here it's a short step to analyzing demand itself and how the demand for a good depends on its price, the prices of other goods, and income.

We begin by examining the demands of individual consumers. Since we know how changes in price and income affect a person's budget line, we can determine how they affect consumption choice. In this way we can also determine a person's demand curve for a good. Next, we will see how individual demand curves can be aggregated to determine the market demand curve. We will also study the characteristics of demand and see why the demands for some kinds of goods differ considerably from the demands for others. In addition, we will show how demand curves can be used to measure the benefits that people receive when they consume a product, above and beyond the expenditure they make. Finally, we will briefly describe some of the methods that can be used to obtain useful empirical information about demand.

4.1 Individual Demand

This section shows how the demand curve of an individual consumer follows from the consumption choices that a person makes when faced with a budget constraint. To illustrate the concepts graphically, we will limit the available goods to food and clothing, as in Chapter 3.

Price Changes

We begin by examining how consumption of food and clothing changes when the price of food changes. Figure 4.1 shows the consumption choices that a person would make when allocating a fixed amount of income between the two goods as the price of food changes.

Initially, the price of food is $1, the price of clothing is $2, and the consumer's income is $20. The utility-maximizing consumption choice is at point B in Figure 4.1(a). Here, the consumer buys 12 units of food and 4 units of clothing, which achieves the level of utility associated with indifference curve U_2.

Now look at Figure 4.1(b), which shows the relationship between the price of food and the quantity demanded. The horizontal axis measures the quantity of food consumed, just as in Figure 4.1(a), but the vertical axis now measures the price of food. Point G in Figure 4.1(b) corresponds to point B in Figure 4.1(a). At G the price of food is $1, and the consumer purchases 12 units of food.

Suppose the price of food increases to $2. As we saw in Chapter 3, the budget line in Figure 4.1(a) rotates inward about the vertical intercept, becoming twice as steep as before. The higher relative price of food has increased the magnitude of the slope of the budget line. The consumer now achieves maximum utility at A, which is on a lower indifference curve U_1. (Because the price of food has risen, the consumer's purchasing power, and hence attainable utility, has fallen.) At A, the consumer chooses 4 units of food and 6 units of clothing. In Figure 4.1(b), this modified consumption choice is at E, which shows that at a price of $2, 4 units of food are demanded. Finally, what will happen if the price of food *decreases* to 50 cents? Now the budget line rotates outward, so the consumer can achieve the higher level of utility associated with indifference curve U_3 in Figure 4.1(a) by selecting D, with 20 units of food and 5 units of clothing. Point H in Figure 4.1(b) shows the price of 50 cents and the quantity demanded of 20 units of food.

The Demand Curve

We can go on to include all possible changes in the price of food. In Figure 4.1(a), the *price-consumption curve* traces the utility-maximizing combinations of food and clothing associated with each and every price of food. Note that as the price of food falls, attainable utility increases, and the consumer buys more food. This pattern of increasing consumption of a good in response to a decrease in price almost always holds. But what happens to the consump-

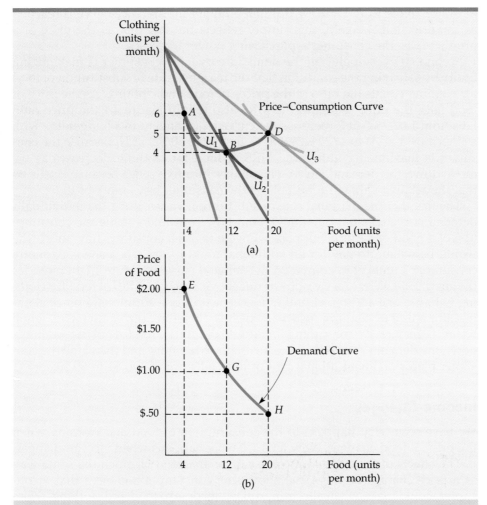

Figure 4.1   Effect of Price Changes   A reduction in the price of food, with income and the price of clothing fixed, causes this consumer to choose a different market basket. In (a) the market baskets that maximize utility for various prices of food (point A, $2; B, $1; D, $0.50) trace out the price-consumption curve. Part (b) gives the demand curve, which relates the price of food to the quantity demanded. (Points E, G, and H correspond to points A, B, and D, respectively.)

tion of clothing as the price of food falls? As Figure 4.1(a) shows, the consumption of clothing may either increase or decrease. Both food *and* clothing consumption can increase because the decrease in the price of food has increased the consumer's ability to purchase both goods.

   The *demand curve* shown in Figure 4.1(b) relates the quantity of food that the consumer will buy to the price of food. The demand curve has two important properties. First, the level of utility that can be attained changes as we move along the curve. The lower the price of the product, the higher the level of utility. (Note from Figure 4.1(a) that a higher indifference curve is reached as the price falls.) Again, this simply reflects the fact that as the price of a product falls, the consumer's purchasing power increases.

Second, at every point on the demand curve, the consumer is maximizing utility by satisfying the condition that the marginal rate of substitution of food for clothing equals the ratio of the prices of food and clothing. As the price of food falls, the price ratio and the MRS also fall. In Figure 4.1 the price ratio falls from 1 ($2/$2) at E (because the curve U_1 is tangent to a budget line with a slope of -1 at A) to 1/2 ($1/$2) at G, to 1/4 ($0.50/$2) at H. Because the consumer is maximizing utility, the MRS of food for clothing decreases as we move down the demand curve. This makes intuitive sense because it tells us that the relative value of food falls as the consumer buys more of it.

The fact that the marginal rate of substitution varies along the individual's demand curve tells us something about how consumers value the consumption of a good or service. Suppose we were to ask a consumer how much she would be willing to pay for an additional unit of food when she is currently consuming 4 units of it. Point E on the demand curve in Figure 4.1(b) provides the answer: $2. Why? As we pointed out above, since the MRS of food for clothing is 1 at E, one additional unit of food is worth one additional unit of clothing. But a unit of clothing costs $2, which is, therefore, the value (or marginal benefit) obtained by consuming an additional unit of food. Thus, as we move down the demand curve in Figure 4.1(b), the MRS falls, and the value the consumer places on an additional unit of food falls from $2 to $1 to $0.50.

Income Changes

We have seen what happens to the consumption of food and clothing when the price of food changes. Now let's see what happens when income changes.

The effects of a change in income can be analyzed in much the same way as a price change. Figure 4.2(a) shows the consumption choices that a consumer would make when allocating a fixed income to food and clothing, when the price of food is $1 and the price of clothing is $2. Initially the consumer's income is $10. The utility-maximizing consumption choice is then at A, at which she buys 4 units of food and 3 units of clothing.

This choice of 4 units of food is also shown in Figure 4.2(b) as E on demand curve D_1. Demand curve D_1 is the curve that would be traced out if we held income fixed at $10 *but varied the price of food*. Because we are holding the price of food constant, we will observe only a single point E on this demand curve.

What happens if the consumer's income is increased to $20? Her budget line then shifts outward parallel to the original budget line, allowing her to attain the utility level associated with indifference curve U_2. Her optimal consumption choice is now at B, where she buys 10 units of food and 5 units of clothing. In Figure 4.2(b) her consumption of food is shown as G on demand curve D_2. (D_2 is the demand curve that would be traced out if we held income fixed at $20 but varied the price of food.) Finally, note that if her income increases to $30, she chooses D, with a market basket containing 16 units of food (and 7 units of clothing), represented by H in Figure 4.2(b).

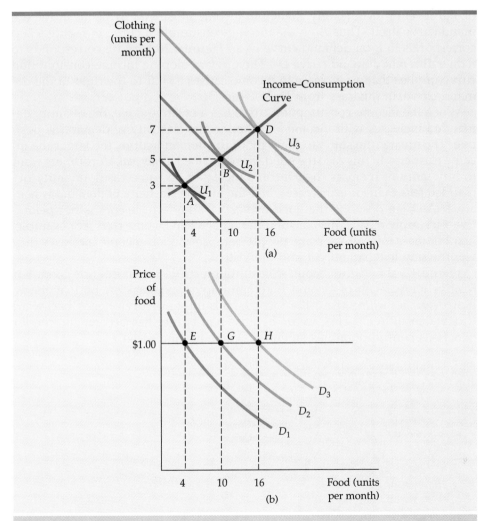

Figure 4.2   Effect of Income Changes   An increase in income, with the prices of all goods fixed, causes consumers to alter their choice of market basket. In part (a) the market baskets that maximize consumer satisfaction for various incomes (point *A*, $10; *B*, $20; *D*, $30) trace out the income-consumption curve. The shift to the right of the demand curve in response to the increases in income is shown in part (b). (Points *E*, *G*, and *H* correspond to points *A*, *B*, and *D*, respectively.)

We could go on to include all possible changes in income. In Figure 4.2(a) the *income-consumption curve* traces out the utility-maximizing combinations of food and clothing associated with every income level. This income-consumption curve is upward sloping because the consumption of both food and clothing increases as income increases. Previously, we saw that a change in the price of a good corresponded to a movement along a demand curve. Here, the story is different. Because each demand curve is measured for a particular level of income, any change in income must lead to a shift in the demand curve itself. Thus A on the income-consumption curve in Figure 4.2(a) corresponds to E on demand curve D_1 in Figure 4.2(b), and B corresponds to F on a different demand curve D_2. The upward-sloping income-consumption curve implies that an increase in income causes a shift to the right in the demand curve, in this case from D_1 to D_2 to D_3.

When the income-consumption curve has a positive slope, the quantity demanded increases with income and the income elasticity of demand is positive. The greater the shifts to the right of the demand curve, the larger the income elasticity. In this case the goods are described as *normal*: Consumers want to buy more of them as their income increases. In some cases, quantity demanded *falls* as income increases, and the income elasticity of demand is negative. We then describe the good as *inferior*. The term *inferior* is not pejorative—it simply means that consumption falls when income rises. For example, hamburger is inferior for some people because as their income increases they want to buy less hamburger and more steak.

Figure 4.3 shows the income-consumption curve for an inferior good. For relatively low levels of income, both hamburger and steak are normal goods. However, as income rises, the income-consumption curve bends backward (from point B to C). This occurs because hamburger has become an inferior good—its consumption has fallen as income has increased.

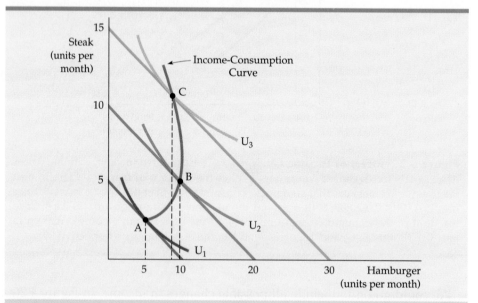

Figure 4.3   An Inferior Good   An increase in a person's income can lead to less consumption of one of the two goods being purchased. Here, hamburger is a normal good between A and B, but becomes an inferior good when the income-consumption curve bends backward between B and C.

Engel Curves

Income-consumption curves can be used to construct *Engel curves,* which relate the quantity of a good consumed to income. Figure 4.4 shows how such curves are constructed for two different goods. Figure 4.4(a), which shows an upward-sloping Engel curve, is derived directly from Figure 4.2(a). In both figures, as income increases from $10 to $20 to $30, the consumption of food increases from 4 to 10 to 16 units. The upward-sloping Engel curve—like the upward-sloping income-consumption curve in Figure 4.2(a)—applies to all normal goods. Note that an Engel curve for clothing would have a similar shape (clothing consumption increases from 3 to 5 to 7 units as income increases).

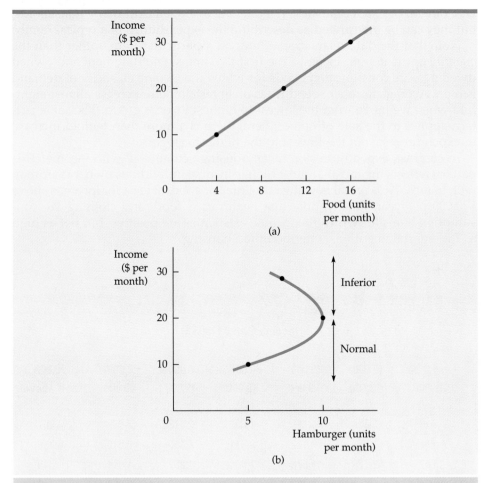

Figure 4.4 **Engel Curves** Engel curves relate the quantity of a good consumed to income. In (a) food is a normal good, and the Engel curve is upward sloping. In (b), however, hamburger is a normal good for income less than $20 per month and an inferior good for income greater than $20 per month.

Figure 4.4(b) shows the Engel curve for hamburger, derived from Figure 4.3. We see that hamburger consumption increases from 5 to 10 units as income increases from $10 to $20. As income increases further, from $20 to $30, consumption falls to 8 units. The portion of the Engel curve that is downward sloping is the income range in which hamburger is an inferior good.

EXAMPLE 4.1   Consumer Expenditures in the United States

Engel curves explain how consumer spending varies among income groups. Table 4.1 illustrates this for several items taken from a recent survey by the U.S. Bureau of Labor Statistics. The data are averaged over many households, but they can be interpreted as describing the expenditures of a typical family.

Note that the data relate *expenditures* on a particular item, rather than the *quantity* of the item to income. The first two items, entertainment and owned dwellings, are consumption goods for which the income elasticity of demand is high. Average family expenditures on entertainment increase almost eightfold when we move from the lowest to highest income group. The same pattern applies to the sale of homes; here, there is a more than tenfold increase in expenditures from the lowest to the highest category.

In contrast, expenditures on *rental* housing actually *fall* with income. This pattern reflects the fact that most higher-income individuals own, rather than rent, homes. Thus rental housing is an inferior good, at least for incomes above $20,000 per year. Finally, note that health care, food, and clothing are consumption items for which the income elasticities are positive, but not as high as for entertainment or owner-occupied housing.

Table 4.1   Annual U.S. Household Consumer Expenditures

Expenditures ($) on:	Income Group (1993 $)						
	Less than $10,000	10,000– 19,000	20,000– 29,000	30,000– 39,000	40,000– 49,000	50,000– 69,000	70,000 and above
Entertainment	520	894	1,185	1,602	2,018	2,565	4,007
Owned dwellings	854	1,370	2,122	3,314	4,450	5,616	9,736
Rented dwellings	1,642	2,128	1,978	1,884	1,802	1,514	748
Health care	1,034	1,647	1,732	1,881	2,012	2,054	2,703
Food	2,461	3,198	3,971	4,706	5,556	6,273	8,137
Clothing	867	1,068	1,394	1,778	2,215	2,316	3,668

Source: U.S. Department of Labor, Bureau of Labor Statistics, "Consumer Expenditure Survey: 1992–1993."

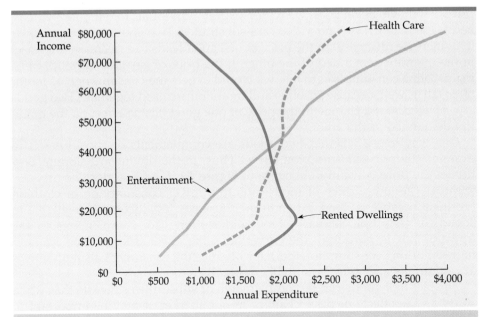

Figure 4.5 Engel Curves for U.S. Consumers Average per capita expenditures on rented dwellings, health care, and entertainment are plotted as functions of annual income. Health care and entertainment are superior goods—expenditures increase with income. Rental housing, however, is an inferior good.

The data in Table 4.1 can be plotted to characterize the expenditure Engel curves graphically. We have done this in Figure 4.5, for rented dwellings, health care, and entertainment. Observe that as income rises, expenditures on entertainment increase rapidly, while expenditures on rental housing decrease.

Substitutes and Complements

The demand curves that we graphed in Chapter 2 showed the relationship between the price of a good and the quantity demanded, with preferences, income, and the prices of all other goods held constant. For many goods, demand is related to the consumption and to the prices of other goods. Baseball bats and baseballs, hot dogs and mustard, and computer hardware and software are all examples of goods whose consumption is complementary—when the consumption of one increases, the consumption of the other is likely to increase as well. Other goods, such as cola and diet cola, owner-occupied houses and rental apartments, and movie tickets and videocassette rentals, are substitutable—when the consumption of one increases, the consumption of the other is likely to decrease.

We call two goods *substitutes* if an increase (decrease) in the price of one leads to an increase (decrease) in the quantity demanded of the other. If the price of a movie ticket rises, we would expect individuals to rent more videos, because movie tickets and videos are substitutes. Two goods are *complements* if an increase (decrease) in the price of one good leads to a decrease (increase) in the quantity demanded of the other. If the price of gasoline goes up, causing gasoline consumption to fall, we would expect the consumption of motor oil to fall as well, because gasoline and motor oil are used together. (Two goods are *independent* if a change in the price of one good has no effect on the quantity demanded of the other.)

One way to see whether two goods are complements or substitutes is to examine the price-consumption curve. Thus, in the downward-sloping portion of the price-consumption curve of Figure 4.1, food and clothing are substitutes—the lower price of food leads to a lower consumption of clothing (perhaps because as food expenditures increase, less income is available to spend on clothing). Similarly, food and clothing are complements in the upward-sloping portion of the curve; here, the lower price of food leads to higher clothing consumption (perhaps because the consumer eats more meals at restaurants and must be suitably dressed).

The fact that goods can be complements or substitutes suggests that when studying the effects of price changes in one market, it may be important to look at the consequences in related markets. The interrelationships among markets are discussed in more detail in Chapter 16.

4.2 Income and Substitution Effects

A fall in the price of a good has two effects. First, consumers enjoy an increase in real purchasing power; they are better off because they can buy the same amount of the good for less money and thus have money left over for additional purchases. Second, they will tend to consume more of the good that has become cheaper, and less of those goods that are now relatively more expensive. These two effects normally occur simultaneously, but it will be useful to distinguish between them in our analysis. The specifics are illustrated in Figure 4.6, where the initial budget line is RS and there are two goods, food and clothing. Here, the consumer maximizes utility by choosing the market basket at A, thereby obtaining the level of utility associated with the indifference curve U_1.

Now, let's see what happens if the price of food falls, causing the budget line to rotate outward to line RT. The consumer now chooses the market basket at B on indifference curve U_2. Since market basket B was chosen even though market basket A was feasible, we know by revealed preference that B is preferred to A. Thus the reduction in the price of food allows the consumer to increase her level of satisfaction—her purchasing power has increased. The total change in the consumption of food caused by the lower price is given by F_1F_2. Initially, the consumer purchased OF_1 units of food, but after the price change, food consumption has increased to OF_2. Line segment F_1F_2, therefore, represents the increase in desired food purchases.

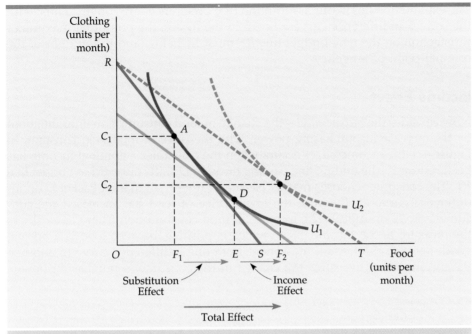

Figure 4.6 Income and Substitution Effects—Normal Good A decrease in the price of food has an income effect and a substitution effect. The consumer is initially at A on budget line RS. When the price of food falls, consumption increases by F_1F_2 as the consumer moves to B. The substitution effect, F_1E (associated with a move from A to D) changes the relative prices of food and clothing but keeps real income (satisfaction) constant. The income effect EF_2 (associated with a move from D to B) keeps relative prices constant but increases purchasing power. Food is a normal good because the income effect EF_2 is positive.

Substitution Effect

The drop in price has a substitution effect and an income effect. The *substitution effect* is the change in food consumption associated with a change in the price of food, *with the level of utility held constant*. The substitution effect captures the change in food consumption that occurs as a result of the price change that makes food relatively cheaper than clothing. This substitution is marked by a movement along an indifference curve. In Figure 4.6, the substitution effect can be obtained by drawing a budget line parallel to the new budget line RT (reflecting the lower relative price of food), but that is just tangent to the original indifference curve U_1 (holding the level of satisfaction constant). The new lower budget line reflects the fact that nominal income was subtracted in order to isolate the substitution effect. Given that budget line, the consumer chooses market basket D and consumes OE units of food. The line segment F_1E thus represents the substitution effect.

Figure 4.6 makes it clear that when the price of food declines, the substitution effect always leads to an increase in the quantity of food demanded.

The explanation lies in our assumption that preferences are convex. Thus, with the convex indifference curves shown in the figure, the point that maximizes satisfaction on the new budget line RT must lie below and to the right of the original point of tangency.

Income Effect

Now consider the *income effect*—the change in food consumption brought about by the increase in purchasing power, with the price of food held constant. In Figure 4.6, the income effect occurs when the consumer's nominal income has been restored—the budget line passing through D shifts outward to budget line RT. The consumer chooses market basket B rather than market basket D on indifference curve U_2 (because the lower price of food has increased the consumer's level of utility). The increase in food consumption from OE to OF_2 is the measure of the income effect, which is positive, because food is a normal good. Because it reflects a movement from one indifference curve to another, the income effect measures the change in the consumer's purchasing power.

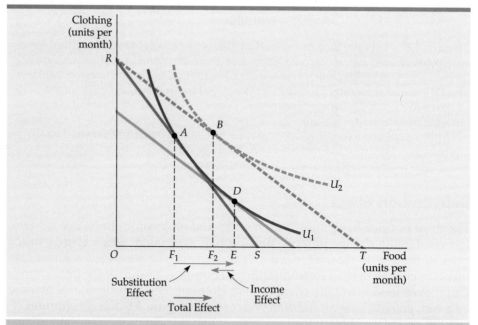

Figure 4.7   Income and Substitution Effects—Inferior Good   The consumer is initially at A on budget line RS. With a decrease in the price of food, the consumer moves to B. The resulting change in food purchased can be broken down into a substitution effect F_1E (associated with a move from A to D) and an income effect EF_2 (associated with a move from D to B). In this case, food is an inferior good because the income effect is negative. However, the substitution effect exceeds the income effect, so the decrease in the price of food leads to an increase in the quantity of food demanded.

When a good is inferior, the income effect is negative—as income rises, consumption falls. Figure 4.7 shows income and substitution effects for an inferior good. The negative income effect is measured by line segment EF_2. Even with inferior goods, the income effect is rarely large enough to outweigh the substitution effect. As a result, when the price of an inferior good falls, its consumption almost always increases.

A Special Case—The Giffen Good

The income effect may theoretically be large enough to cause the demand curve for a good to slope upward. We call such a good a *Giffen good*, and Figure 4.8 shows the income and substitution effects. Initially, the consumer is at A, consuming relatively little clothing and much food. Now the price of food declines. The decline in the price of food frees enough income so that the consumer desires to buy more clothing and fewer units of food, as illustrated by B. By revealed preference, the consumer is better off at B rather than A even though less food is consumed.

Although intriguing, the Giffen good is rarely of practical interest. It requires a large negative income effect. But the income effect is usually small—

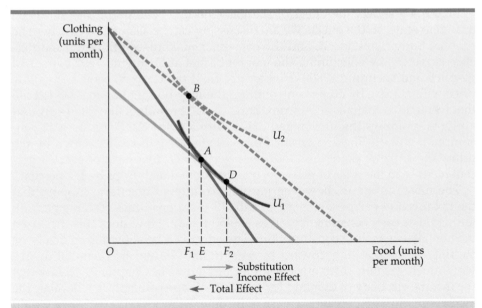

Figure 4.8 **Upward-Sloping Demand Curve: The Giffen Good** When food is an inferior good, and the income effect is large enough to dominate the substitution effect, the demand curve will be upward-sloping. The consumer is initially at point A. But after the price of food falls, the consumer moves to B and consumes less food. The income effect F_2F_1 is larger than the substitution effect EF_2, so that the decrease in the price of food leads to a lower quantity of food demanded.

most goods individually account for only a small part of the consumer's budget. And large income effects are often associated with normal rather than inferior goods (e.g., for housing, food, or transportation).

EXAMPLE 4.2 **The Effects of a Gasoline Tax**

For years after the oil crisis of 1973–1974, the U.S. government considered increasing the federal tax on gasoline. In 1993, a modest 7 1/2 cent tax increase was enacted as part of a larger budget reform package. This increase was much less than the $1 to $2 tax increase that would have been necessary to put U.S. gasoline prices on a par with those in Europe. Because an important goal of higher gasoline taxes has been to discourage the consumption of gasoline (and not to raise revenue), the government has also considered ways of passing the resulting income back to consumers. One popular suggestion is a rebate program in which the tax revenues would be returned to households on an equal per capita basis. What would be the effect of such a program?

To begin, let's focus on the effect of the program over a period of five years. The relevant price elasticity of demand is about −0.5.[1] Suppose that a low-income consumer uses about 1200 gallons of gasoline a year, that gasoline costs $1 per gallon, and that the consumer's annual income is $9000.

Figure 4.9 shows the effect of the gasoline tax. (The graph has not been drawn to scale, so the effects we are discussing can be seen more clearly.) The original budget line is *AB*, and the consumer maximizes utility (on indifference curve U_2) by consuming the market basket at *C*, buying 1200 gallons of gasoline and spending $7800 on other goods. If the tax is 50 cents per gallon, price will increase by 50 percent, shifting the new budget line to *AD*.[2] (Recall that when price changes and income stays fixed, the budget line rotates around a pivotal point on the unchanged axis.) With a price elasticity of −0.5, consumption will decline 25 percent from 1200 to 900 gallons, as shown by the utility-maximizing point *E* on indifference curve U_1 (because for every 1 percent increase in the price of gasoline, quantity demanded drops by 1/2 percent).

The rebate program, however, partially counters this effect. Suppose that the tax revenue per person is about $450 (900 gallons times 50 cents per gallon), so that each consumer receives a $450 rebate. How does this increased income affect gasoline consumption? The effect can be shown graphically by shifting the budget line upward by $450 to line *FJ*, which is parallel to *AD*. How much gasoline does our consumer buy now? In Chapter 2 we saw that the income elasticity of demand for gasoline is approximately 0.3. Because the $450 represents a 5 percent increase in income ($450/$9000 = 0.05), we would expect the rebate to increase consumption by 1.5 percent (0.3 times 5 percent)

---

[1] We saw in Chapter 2 that the price elasticity of demand for gasoline varied substantially from the short run to the long run, ranging from −0.11 in the short run to −1.17 in the long run.

[2] To simplify the example, we have assumed that all of the gasoline tax is paid by consumers in the form of a higher price. A more general analysis of tax shifting is presented in Chapter 9.

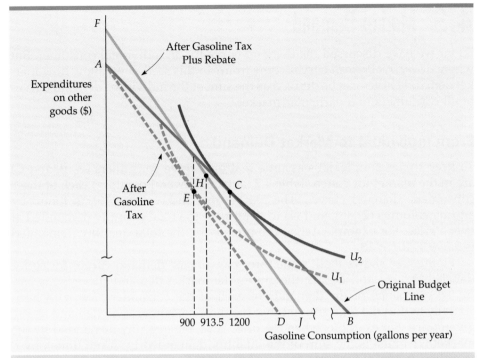

Figure 4.9 Effect of a Gasoline Tax with a Rebate A gasoline tax is imposed when the consumer is initially buying 1200 gallons of gasoline at point C. After the tax the budget line shifts from AB to AD and the consumer maximizes his preferences by choosing E, with a gasoline consumption of 900 gallons. However, when the proceeds of the tax are rebated to the consumer, his consumption increases somewhat to 913.5 gallons at H. Despite the rebate program, the consumer's gasoline consumption has fallen, as has his level of satisfaction.

of 900 gallons, or 13.5 gallons. The new utility-maximizing consumption choice at H illustrates this. (We omitted the indifference curve that is tangent at H to simplify the diagram.) Despite the rebate program, the tax would reduce gasoline consumption by 286.5 gallons, from 1200 to 913.5. Because the income elasticity of demand for gasoline is relatively low, the income effect of the rebate program is dominated by the substitution effect, and the program with a rebate does reduce consumption.

Figure 4.9 reveals that a gasoline tax program with a rebate makes the average low-income consumer slightly worse off, because H lies just below indifference curve U_2.[3] Why introduce such a program? Those who support gasoline taxes argue that they promote national security (by reducing dependence on foreign oil) and encourage conservation, thus helping to weaken OPEC. We will examine the impact of a gasoline tax further in Chapter 9.

---

[3] Of course, some consumers (those who spend little on gasoline) will be better off after receiving the rebate, while others (those who spend a lot on gasoline) will be worse off.

4.3 Market Demand

So far we have discussed the demand curve for an individual consumer. But where do *market demand* curves come from? In this section we show how market demand curves can be derived as the sum of the individual demand curves of all consumers in a particular market.

From Individual to Market Demand

To keep things simple, let's assume that only three consumers (A, B, and C) are in the market for coffee. Table 4.2 tabulates several points on each of these consumers' demand curves. The market demand, column (5), is found by adding columns (2), (3), and (4) to determine the total quantity demanded at every price. For example, when the price is $3, the total quantity demanded is 2 + 6 + 10, or 18.

Figure 4.10 shows these same three consumers' demand curves for coffee (labeled D_A, D_B, and D_C). In the graph, the market demand curve is the *horizontal summation* of the demands of each of the consumers. We sum horizontally to find the total amount that the three consumers will demand at any given price. For example, when the price is $4, the quantity demanded by the market (11 units) is the sum of the quantity demanded by A (no units), by B (4 units), and by C (7 units). Because all the individual demand curves slope downward, the market demand curve will also slope downward. However, the market demand curve need not be a straight line, even though each of the individual demand curves is. In Figure 4.10, for example, the market demand curve is *kinked* because one consumer makes no purchases at prices the other consumers find inviting (those above $4).

Two points should be noted. First, the market demand curve will shift to the right as more consumers enter the market. Second, factors that influence the demands of many consumers will also affect the market demand. Suppose, for example, that most consumers in a particular market

Table 4.2	Determining the Market Demand Curve			
(1) Price ($)	(2) Individual A (units)	(3) Individual B (units)	(4) Individual C (units)	(5) Market (units)
1	6	10	16	32
2	4	8	13	25
3	2	6	10	18
4	0	4	7	11
5	0	2	4	6

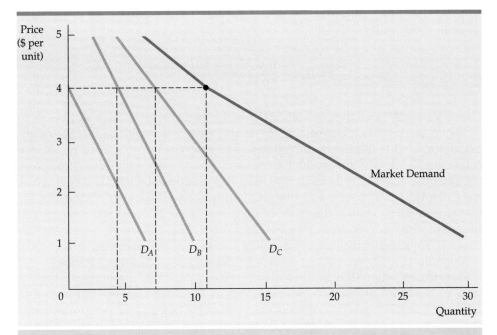

Figure 4.10   Summing to Obtain a Market Demand Curve   The market demand curve is obtained by summing the consumers' demand curves D_A, D_B, and D_C. At each price, the quantity of food demanded by the market is the sum of the quantity demanded by each consumer. For example, at a price of $4, the quantity demanded by the market (11 units) is the sum of the quantity demanded by A (no units), by B (4 units), and by C (7 units).

earn more income, and as a result, increase their demands for coffee. Because each consumer's demand curve shifts to the right, so will the market demand curve.

The aggregation of individual demands into market demands is not just a theoretical exercise. It becomes important in practice when market demands are built up from the demands of different demographic groups or from consumers located in different areas. For example, we might obtain information about the demand for home computers by adding independently obtained information about the demands of (i) households with children, (ii) households without children, and (iii) single individuals. Or we might determine the U.S. demand for natural gas by aggregating the demands for natural gas of the major regions (East, South, Midwest, Mountain, and West, for example).

Point and Arc Elasticities of Demand

Recall from Chapter 2 that the price elasticity of demand measures the percentage change in the quantity demanded resulting from a percentage change in price. Denoting the quantity of a good by Q and its price by P, the *price elasticity of demand* is

$$E_P = \frac{\Delta Q/Q}{\Delta P/P} = \frac{\Delta Q/\Delta P}{Q/P} \qquad (4.1)$$

(Here Δ means "a change in" so $\Delta Q/Q$ is the percentage change in Q.)

When demand is inelastic (i.e., E_P is less than 1 in magnitude), the quantity demanded is relatively unresponsive to changes in price. As a result, the total expenditure on the product increases when the price increases. Suppose, for example, that a family currently uses 1000 gallons of gasoline a year when the price is $1 per gallon, and that the family's price elasticity of demand for gasoline is -0.5. Then if the price of gasoline increases to $1.10 (a 10 percent increase), the consumption of gasoline falls to 950 gallons (a 5 percent decrease). Total expenditures on gasoline, however, will increase from $1000 (1000 gallons $\times$ $1 per gallon) to $1045 (950 gallons $\times$ $1.10 per gallon).

In contrast, when demand is elastic (E_P is greater than 1 in magnitude), the total expenditure on the product decreases as the price goes up. Suppose that a family buys 100 pounds of chicken a year, at a price of $2 per pound, and that the price elasticity of demand for chicken is -1.5. Then if the price of chicken increases to $2.20 (a 10 percent increase), the family's consumption of chicken falls to 85 pounds a year (a 15 percent decrease). Total expenditures on chicken will fall as well, from $200 (100 pounds $\times$ $2 per pound) to $187 (85 pounds $\times$ $2.20 per pound).

If the elasticity of demand is -1 (the *unit elastic* case), total expenditure remains the same after a price change. Then a price increase leads to a decrease in quantity demanded that is just sufficient to leave the total expenditure on the good unchanged.

Table 4.3 summarizes the relationship between elasticity and expenditure. It is useful to review the table from the point of view of the seller of the good rather than the buyer. When demand is inelastic, a price increase leads only to a small decrease in quantity demanded, so that the total revenue received

Table 4.3   Price Elasticity and Consumer Expenditures

Demand	If Price Increases, Expenditures	If Price Decreases, Expenditures
Inelastic	Increase	Decrease
Unit elastic	Are unchanged	Are unchanged
Elastic	Decrease	Increase

by the seller increases. But when demand is elastic, a price increase leads to a large decline in quantity demanded, and total revenue falls.

When calculating demand elasticities, we must be careful about the price change or quantity change that is in question. For a large price change (say, 20 percent), the value of the elasticity will depend on just where along the demand curve we measure the price and quantity. For this reason, it is useful to distinguish between a *point elasticity of demand* and an *arc elasticity of demand.*

The point elasticity of demand is defined as the price elasticity at a particular point on the demand curve. It is calculated by substituting for $\Delta P/\Delta Q$ in the elasticity formula the magnitude of the slope of the demand curve at that point. ($\Delta P/\Delta Q$ is the slope for small ΔP because price is measured on the vertical axis and quantity demanded on the horizontal axis.)

As a result, Equation (4.1) becomes

$$\text{Point Elasticity:} \qquad E_P = (P/Q)(1/\text{slope}) \qquad\qquad (4.2)$$

Because the slope of the demand curve may change from point to point, the point elasticity is defined only for very small changes in price, ΔP. Because both (P/Q) and the slope of the demand curve can change as we move along the demand curve, so will the point elasticity of demand.

There are times when we want to calculate a price elasticity over some portion of the demand curve rather than at a single point. For example, suppose that we are contemplating an increase in the price of a product from \$8 to \$10 and expect the quantity demanded to fall from 6 units to 4. How should we calculate the price elasticity of demand? Is the price increase 25 percent (a \$2 increase divided by the original price of \$8), or is it 20 percent (a \$2 increase divided by the new price of \$10)? Likewise, is the percentage decrease in quantity demanded 33 1/3 percent (2/6) or 50 percent (2/4)?

There is no correct answer to this question. We could calculate the price elasticity using the original price and quantity, in which case we would find that $E_P = (-33\ 1/3\ \text{percent}/20\ \text{percent}) = -1.67$. Alternatively, we could use the new price and quantity, in which case we would find that $E_P = (-50\ \text{percent}/25\ \text{percent}) = -2.0$. The difference between these two calculated elasticities is large, and neither seems preferable to the other.

We can resolve this problem by using the *arc elasticity of demand.* Rather than choose either the initial or the final price, we use an average of the two, $\overline{P}$; similarly for the quantity demanded, we use $\overline{Q}$. Thus the arc elasticity of demand is given by

$$\text{Arc Elasticity:} \qquad E_P = (\Delta Q/\Delta P)(\overline{P}/\overline{Q}) \qquad\qquad (4.3)$$

In our example, the average price is \$9 and the average quantity is 5 units, so the arc elasticity is $E_P = (-2/\$2)(\$9/5) = -1.8$. The arc elasticity will always lie somewhere (but not necessarily halfway) between the point elasticities calculated at the lower and the higher prices.

EXAMPLE 4.3 **The Aggregate Demand for Wheat**

In Chapter 2 (Example 2.2), we discussed the two components of the demand for U.S. wheat: domestic demand (by U.S. consumers) and export demand (by foreign consumers). Let us see how the total demand for wheat in 1993 can be obtained by aggregating the domestic and foreign demands.

The domestic demand for wheat is given by the equation $Q_{DD} = 1354 - 70P$, where Q_{DD} is the number of bushels (in millions) demanded domestically, and P is the price in dollars per bushel. Export demand is given by $Q_{DE} = 2031 - 209P$, where Q_{DE} is the number of bushels (in millions) demanded from abroad. As shown in Figure 4.11, the domestic demand for wheat, given by AB, is relatively price inelastic. In fact, statistical studies have shown that the price elasticity of domestic demand is about -0.2. However, export demand, given by CD, is more price elastic, with an elasticity of -0.4 to -0.5. Export demand is more elastic than domestic demand because poorer countries that import U.S. wheat turn to other grains and foodstuffs if wheat prices rise.[4]

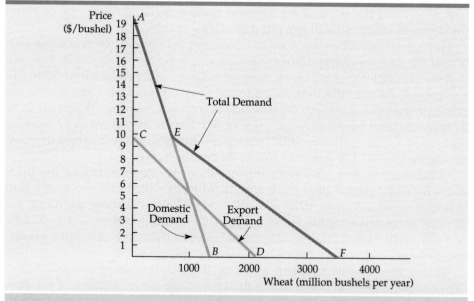

Figure 4.11 **The Aggregate Demand for Wheat** The total world demand for wheat is the horizontal sum of the domestic demand AB and the export demand CD. Even though each individual demand curve is linear, the market demand curve is kinked, reflecting that there is no export demand when the price of wheat is greater than $12 per bushel.

---

[4] For a survey of statistical studies of demand and supply elasticities and an analysis of the U.S. wheat market, see Larry Salathe and Sudchada Langley, "An Empirical Analysis of Alternative Export Subsidy Programs for U.S. Wheat," *Agricultural Economics Research* 38, no. 1 (Winter 1986).

To obtain the world demand for wheat, we set the left side of each demand equation equal to the quantity of wheat (the variable on the horizontal axis). We then add the right side of the equations, to obtain $Q_{DD} + Q_{DE} = (1354 - 70P) + (2031 - 209P) = 3385 - 279P$. (Note that this is the same total demand equation for 1993 given in Example 2.3.) This generates the line segment EF in Figure 4.11.

However, at all prices above point C, there is no export demand, so world demand and domestic demand are identical. As a result, for all prices above C, world demand is given by line segment AE. (If we were to add Q_{DE} for prices above C, we would be incorrectly adding a negative export demand to a positive domestic demand.) As the figure shows, the resulting world demand for wheat, given by AEF, is kinked. The kink occurs at point E, the price level above which there is no export demand.

EXAMPLE 4.4 The Demand for Housing

A family's demand for housing depends on the age and status of the household making the purchasing decision. One approach to housing demand is to relate the number of rooms per house for each household (the quantity demanded) to an estimate of the price of an additional room in a house and to the household's family income.[5] (Prices of rooms vary across the United States because of differences in construction costs.) Table 4.4 lists some of the price and income elasticities obtained for different demographic groups.

In general, the elasticities show that the size of houses that consumers demand (as measured by the number of rooms) is relatively insensitive to dif-

Table 4.4 Price and Income Elasticities of the Demand for Rooms

Group	Price Elasticity	Income Elasticity
Single individuals	−0.14	0.19
Married, head of household age less than 30, 1 child	−0.22	0.07
Married, head age 30–39, 2 or more children	0	0.11
Married, head age 50 or older, 1 child	−0.08	0.18

---

[5] See Mahlon Strazheim, *An Econometric Analysis of the Urban Housing Market* (New York: National Bureau of Economic Research, 1975), chap. 4.

ferences in either income or price. However, differences among subgroups of the population are important. For example, families with young heads of households have a price elasticity of −0.22, substantially greater than those with older household heads. Presumably, families buying houses are more price sensitive when the parents and their children are younger and the parents may plan on having more children. Among married households, the income elasticity of demand for rooms also increases with age, which tells us that older households buy larger houses than younger households.

Price and income elasticities of demand for housing also depend on where people live.[6] Demand in the central cities is substantially more price elastic than the suburban elasticities. Income elasticities, however, increase as one moves farther from the central city. Thus poorer (on average) central city residents (who live where the price of land is relatively high) are more price sensitive in their housing choices than their wealthier suburban counterparts.

4.4 Consumer Surplus

Consumers buy goods because the purchase makes them better off. *Consumer surplus* measures how much better off individuals in the aggregate are by being able to buy a good in the market. Because different consumers value consumption of particular goods differently, the maximum amount they are willing to pay for those goods also differs. *Consumer surplus is the difference between what a consumer is willing to pay for a good and what the consumer actually pays when buying it.* Suppose, for example, that a student would have been willing to pay $13 for a rock concert ticket, even though she had to pay only $12. The $1 that she saved is her consumer surplus.[7] When we add the consumer surpluses of all consumers who buy a good, we obtain a measure of the aggregate consumer surplus.

Consumer surplus can be calculated easily if we know the demand curve. To see the relationship between demand and consumer surplus, examine the individual demand curve for concert tickets shown in Figure 4.12.[8] Drawing the demand curve to look more like a stepladder than a straight

---

[6] See Allen C. Goodman and Masahiro Kawai, "Functional Form, Sample Selection, and Housing Demand," *Journal of Urban Economics* 20 (Sept. 1986): 155–167.

[7] Measuring consumer surplus in dollars involves an implicit assumption about the shape of the consumers' indifference curves—that a consumer's marginal utility associated with increases in income remains constant within the range of income in question. In many cases, this is a reasonable assumption, although it might be suspect when large changes in income are involved. See Robert D. Willig, "Consumer Surplus Without Apology," *American Economic Review* 65 (1976): 589–597.

[8] The following discussion applies to an individual demand curve, but a similar argument would also apply to a market demand curve.

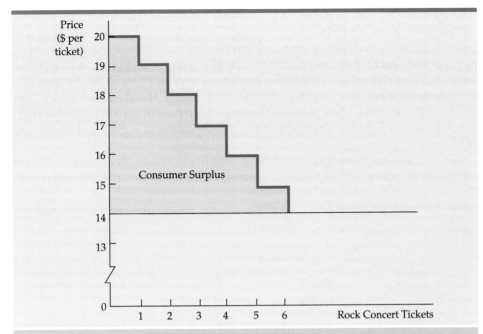

Figure 4.12 Consumer Surplus Consumer surplus is the total benefit from the consumption of a product, net of the total cost of purchasing it. In this figure the consumer surplus associated with six concert tickets (purchased at $14 per ticket) is given by the yellow-shaded area.

line allows us to measure the value that this consumer obtains from buying tickets.

When deciding how many tickets to buy, the student might calculate as follows: The first ticket costs $14 but is worth $20. This $20 valuation is obtained by using the demand curve to find the maximum amount that the student will pay for each additional ticket ($20 is the maximum this student will pay for the first ticket). The ticket is worth purchasing because it generates $6 of surplus value above and beyond the cost of the purchase. The second ticket is also worth buying because it generates a surplus of $5 ($19 − $14). The third ticket generates a surplus of $4. However, the fourth generates a surplus of only $3, the fifth a surplus of $2, and the sixth a surplus of just $1. The student is indifferent about purchasing the seventh ticket (since it generates zero surplus) and prefers not to buy any more than that, as the value of each additional ticket is less than its cost.

In Figure 4.12, consumer surplus is obtained by adding the excess values or surpluses for all units purchased. In this case, consumer surplus = $6 + $5 + $4 + $3 + $2 + $1 = $21.

In a more general case, the stepladder demand curve can be easily transformed into a straight-line demand curve by making the units of the good smaller and smaller. In Figure 4.13, the stepladder is drawn when half-tickets are sold (two students share a ticket), and the stepladder begins to approximate the straight-line demand curve. We use such demand curves as approximations and correspondingly use the triangle in Figure 4.13 to measure consumer surplus. When the demand curve is not a straight line, the consumer surplus is measured by the area below the demand curve and above the price line.[9] To calculate the aggregate consumer surplus in a market, we simply find the area below the *market* demand curve and above the price line.

Consumer surplus has important applications in economics. When added over many individuals, consumer surplus measures the aggregate

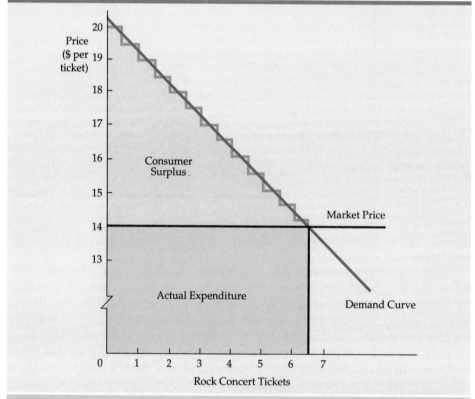

Figure 4.13   Consumer Surplus Generalized   When the units of consumption of a good (here, tickets) are small, the consumer surplus can be measured by the area under the demand curve and above the line representing the purchase price of the good. In the figure the consumer surplus is given by the shaded triangle.

---

[9] In the demand curve drawn in Figure 4.13, the consumer surplus is $21 1/8, a close approximation to the $21 previously determined. This demand curve involves a maximum price of $20.50 and a quantity sold of 6 1/2. In this case, the triangle has a base of 6 1/2, a height of $6.50, and an area of $21 1/8.

benefit that consumers obtain from buying goods in a market. When we combine consumer surplus with the aggregate profits that producers obtain, we can evaluate the costs and benefits of alternative market structures and of public policies that alter the behavior of consumers and firms in those markets.

EXAMPLE 4.5   The Value of Clean Air

Air is free in the sense that we need not pay to breathe it. Yet the absence of a market for air may help explain why the air quality in some cities has been deteriorating for decades. In 1970 Congress amended the Clean Air Act to tighten automobile emissions controls. Were these controls worth it? Were the benefits of cleaning up the air sufficient to outweigh the costs that would be imposed directly on car producers and indirectly on car buyers?

To answer this question, Congress asked the National Academy of Sciences to evaluate these emissions controls in a cost-benefit study. The benefits portion of that study examined how much people value clean air, using empirically determined estimates of the demand for clean air.

Although there is no explicit market for clean air, people do pay more to buy houses where the air is clean than they pay to buy comparable houses in areas with dirtier air. This information was used to estimate the demand for clean air.[10] Detailed data for house prices among neighborhoods of Boston and Los Angeles were compared with the levels of various air pollutants, while the effects of other variables that might affect house value were taken into account statistically. The study determined a demand curve for clean air that looked approximately like that shown in Figure 4.14.

The horizontal axis measures the amount of air *pollution reduction,* and the vertical axis measures the increased value of a home associated with those pollution reductions. For example, consider the demand for cleaner air of a homeowner in a city in which the air is rather dirty, as exemplified by a level of nitrogen oxides (NOX) of 10 parts per 100 million (pphm). If the family were required to pay $1000 for each 1 pphm reduction in air pollution, it would choose A on the demand curve to obtain a pollution reduction of 5 pphm.

How much is a 50 percent, or 5 pphm, reduction in pollution worth to the typical family just described? We can measure this value by calculating the consumer surplus associated with reducing air pollution. Since the price for this reduction is $1000 per unit, the family would pay $5000. However, the family values all but the last unit of reduction by more than $1000. As a result, the shaded triangle in Figure 4.14 gives the value of the cleanup (above and beyond the payment). Because the demand curve is a straight line, the surplus can be calculated from the area of the triangle whose height is $1000

---

[10] The results are summarized in Daniel L. Rubinfeld, "Market Approaches to the Measurement of the Benefits of Air Pollution Abatement," in Ann Friedlaender, ed., *The Benefits and Costs of Cleaning the Air* (Cambridge: MIT Press, 1976), 240–273.

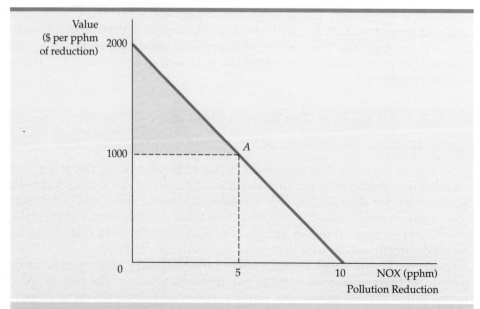

Figure 4.14 Valuing Cleaner Air The shaded triangle gives the consumer surplus generated when air pollution is reduced by 5 parts per 100 million of nitrogen oxide at a cost of $1000 per part reduced. The surplus is created because most consumers are willing to pay more than $1000 for each unit reduction of nitrogen oxide.

($2000 − $1000) and whose base is 5 pphm. Therefore, the value to the household of the pollution reduction is $2500.

A complete cost-benefit analysis would use a measure of the total benefit of the cleanup (the benefit per household times the number of households). This could be compared with the total cost of the cleanup to determine whether such a project were worthwhile. We will discuss clean air further in Chapter 18 when we describe the tradeable emissions permits that were introduced by the Clean Air Act of 1990.

4.5 Network Externalities

So far we have assumed that people's demands for a good are independent of one another. In other words, Tom's demand for coffee depends on Tom's tastes, his income, the price of coffee, and perhaps the price of tea, but it does not depend on Dick's or Harry's demands for coffee. This assumption enabled us to obtain the market demand curve by simply summing individuals' demands.

For some goods, however, a person's demand also depends on the demands of *other* people. In particular, a person's demand may be affected by the number of other people who have purchased the good. If this is the case, there is a *network externality*. Network externalities can be positive or negative. A *positive* network externality exists if the quantity of a good demanded by a typical consumer increases in response to the growth in purchases of other consumers. If the opposite is true, there is a *negative* network externality.

The Bandwagon Effect

One example of a positive network externality is the *bandwagon effect*.[11] This refers to the desire to be in style, to have a good because almost everyone else has it, or to indulge in a fad. The bandwagon effect often arises with children's toys (Barbie dolls or Nintendo video games, for example). Creating this effect is a major objective in marketing and advertising these toys. Building a bandwagon effect is also often the key to success in selling clothing.

The bandwagon effect is illustrated in Figure 4.15, where the horizontal axis measures the sales of some fashionable good in thousands per month. Suppose

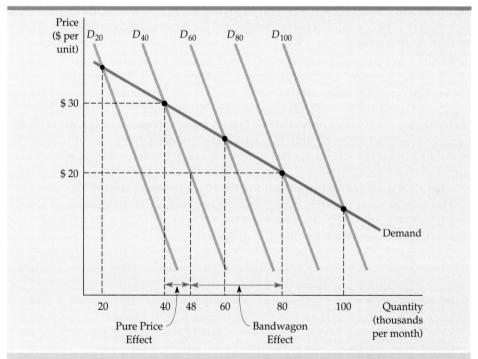

Figure 4.15   Positive Network Externality: Bandwagon Effect   A bandwagon effect is an example of a positive network externality, in which the quantity of a good that an individual demands grows in response to the growth of purchases by other individuals. Here the demand for a good shifts to the right from D_{40} to D_{80} due to the bandwagon effect as the price of the product falls from $30 to $20.

---

[11] The bandwagon effect and the snob effect (discussed below) were introduced by Harvey Liebenstein, "Bandwagon, Snob, and Veblen Effects in the Theory of Consumers' Demand," *Quarterly Journal of Economics* 62 (Feb. 1948): 165–201.

consumers think that only 20,000 people have bought the good. This is a small number relative to the U.S. population, so consumers would have little motivation to buy the good to be in style. Some consumers may still buy it (depending on its price), but only for its intrinsic value. In this case, demand is given by the curve D_{20}.

Suppose instead that consumers think that 40,000 people have bought the good. Now they find the good more attractive and want to buy more. The demand curve is D_{40}, which is to the right of D_{20}. Similarly, if consumers thought that 60,000 people had bought the good, the demand curve would be D_{60}, and so on. The more people consumers believe have bought the good, the farther to the right is the demand curve.

Ultimately, consumers would get a good sense of how many people *have* purchased the good. This number would, of course, depend on its price. In Figure 4.15, for example, if the price were $30, 40,000 people would buy the good, so the relevant demand curve would be D_{40}. Or if the price were $20, 80,000 people would buy the good, and the relevant demand curve would be D_{80}. *The market demand curve is therefore found by joining the points on the curves* $D_{20}, D_{40}, D_{60}, D_{80}$, *and* D_{100} *that correspond to the quantities 20,000; 40,000; 60,000; 80,000; and 100,000.*

The market demand curve is relatively elastic compared with the curves D_{20}, etc. To see why the bandwagon effect leads to a more elastic demand curve, consider the effect of a drop in price from $30 to $20, with a demand curve of D_{40}. If there were no bandwagon effect, quantity demanded would increase from 40,000 to only 48,000. But as more people buy the good, it becomes stylish to own it, and the bandwagon effect increases quantity demanded further, to 80,000. So the bandwagon effect increases the response of demand to price changes (i.e., makes demand more elastic). As we'll see later, this result has important implications for firms' pricing strategies.

The bandwagon effect is associated with fads and stylishness, but a positive network externality can arise for other reasons. The intrinsic value of some goods to their owners is greater the greater the number of other people who own the goods. For example, if I am the only person to own a compact disc (CD) player, it will not be economical for companies to manufacture compact discs, and without the discs, the CD player will be of little value to me. The more people who own players, the more discs will be manufactured, and the greater will be the value of the player to me. The same is true for personal computers; the more people who own them, the more software will be written, and thus the more useful the computer will be to me.

The Snob Effect

Network externalities are sometimes negative. Consider the *snob effect*, which refers to the desire to own exclusive or unique goods. The quantity demanded of a snob good is higher the *fewer* the people who own it. Rare works of art, specially designed sports cars, and made-to-order clothing are snob goods. Here, the value I get from a painting or sports car is in part the prestige, status, and exclusivity resulting from the fact that few other people own one like it.

Figure 4.16 illustrates the snob effect. D_2 is the demand curve that would apply if consumers believed only 2000 people owned the good. If people believe that 4000 people own the good, it is less exclusive, and its snob value is reduced. Quantity demanded will therefore be lower; the curve D_4 applies. Similarly, if people believe that 6000 people own the good, demand is even smaller, and D_6 applies. Eventually consumers learn how widely owned the good actually is, so the market demand curve is found by joining the points on the curves D_2, D_4, D_6, etc., that actually correspond to the quantities 2000, 4000, 6000, etc.

The snob effect makes market demand less elastic. To see why, suppose the price were initially $30,000, with 2000 people purchasing the good, and was then lowered to $15,000. If there were no snob effect, the quantity purchased would increase to 14,000 (along curve D_2). But as a snob good, its value is greatly reduced if more people own it. The snob effect dampens the increase

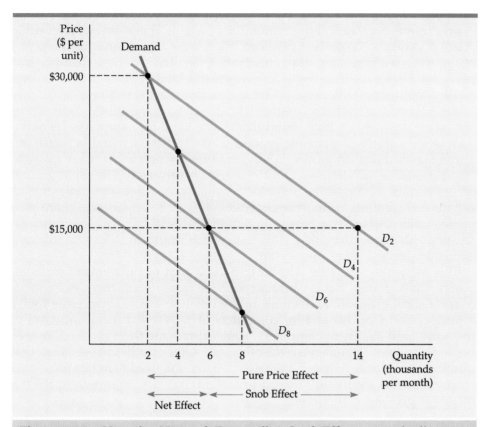

Figure 4.16 **Negative Network Externality: Snob Effect** A snob effect is an example of a negative network externality, in which the quantity of a good that an individual demands falls in response to the growth of purchases by other individuals. Here the demand for a good shifts to the left from D_2 to D_6 as the price falls from $30,000 to $15,000 and more people buy the good.

in quantity demanded, cutting it by 8000 units, so the net increase in sales is only to 6000 units. For many goods, marketing and advertising are geared to creating a snob effect. This means that demand will be less elastic—a result that has important implications for pricing.

Negative network externalities can arise for other reasons. The effect of congestion is a common one. The value I obtain from a lift ticket at a ski resort is lower the more people there are who have bought tickets because I prefer short lines and fewer skiers on the slopes. And likewise for entry to an amusement park, skating rink, or beach.[12]

EXAMPLE 4.6 **Network Externalities and the Demands for Computers and Fax Machines**

The 1950s and 1960s saw phenomenal growth in the demand for mainframe computers. From 1954 to 1965, for example, annual revenues from the leasing of mainframes increased at the extraordinary rate of 78 percent per year, while prices declined by 20 percent per year. Prices were falling, and the quality of computers was increasing dramatically, but the elasticity of demand would have to have been quite large to account for this kind of growth. IBM, among other computer manufacturers, wanted to know what was going on.

An econometric study by Gregory Chow, then working at IBM, helped provide some answers.[13] Chow found that the demand for computers follows a "saturation curve"—a dynamic process where at first demand is small and grows slowly, but then grows rapidly, until finally nearly everyone likely to buy a computer has done so, and the market is saturated. The rapid growth occurs because of a positive network externality. As more and more organizations own computers, more and better software is written, and more people are trained to use computers, so that the value of having a computer increases. This causes demand to increase, which results in still more software and better trained users, and so on.

This network externality was an important part of the demand for computers. Chow found that it could account for close to half the rapid growth of rentals in 1954–1965. Reductions in the inflation-adjusted price (he found a price elasticity of demand for computers of -1.44) and major increases in the power and quality of computers, which also made them much more useful and effective, accounted for the other half. Other studies have shown that this process continued through the decades that followed.[14] In fact, this same kind of network externality helped to fuel a rapid rate of growth in the demand for personal computers.

---

[12] Tastes differ. Some people associate a *positive* network externality with skiing or a day on the beach; they enjoy crowds and might find the mountain or beach lonely without them.

[13] See Gregory Chow, "Technological Change and the Demand for Computers," *American Economic Review* 57, no. 5 (Dec. 1967): 1117–1130.

[14] See Robert J. Gordon, "The Postwar Evolution of Computer Prices," in *Technology and Capital Formation*, Dale W. Jorgenson and Ralph Landau, eds. (Cambridge: MIT Press, 1989).

Another product that has experienced explosive growth in recent years is the fax machine. Clearly a strong positive network externality is at work here. Since a fax machine can only transmit to or receive a document from another fax machine, the value of owning one depends crucially on how many other people own them. By the early 1990s, nearly all business offices in the United States had fax machines, and the fax had become a standard means of communicating. This made it essential equipment for almost every business firm.

*4.6 Empirical Estimation of Demand

Later in this book, we discuss how demand information is used as an input to firms' economic decision making. For example, General Motors needs to understand automobile demand to decide whether to offer rebates or below-market-interest-rate loans for new cars. Knowledge about demand is also important for public policy decisions—understanding the demand for oil can help Congress decide whether to pass an oil import tax. Here, we briefly examine some methods for evaluating and forecasting demand. The more basic statistical tools needed to estimate demand curves and demand elasticities are described in the appendix to this book.

Interview and Experimental Approaches to Demand Determination

The most direct way to obtain information about demand is through *interviews* in which consumers are asked how much of a product they might be willing to buy at a given price. Direct approaches such as these, however, are unlikely to succeed because people may lack information or interest, or may want to mislead the interviewer. Therefore, market researchers have designed more successful indirect interview approaches. Consumers might be asked, for example, what their current consumption behavior is and how they would respond if a certain product were available at a 10 percent discount. Or interviewees might be asked how they would expect others to behave. Although indirect survey approaches to demand estimation can be fruitful, the difficulties of the interview approach have forced economists and marketing specialists to look to alternative methods.

In *direct marketing experiments,* actual sales offers are posed to potential customers. An airline, for example, might offer a reduced price on certain flights for six months, partly to learn how this price change affects demand for its flights and how other firms will respond.

Direct experiments are real, not hypothetical, but substantial problems remain. The wrong experiment can be costly, and even if profits and sales rise, the firm cannot be sure that the increase was the result of the experimental change because other factors probably changed at the same time. Also the response to experiments—which consumers often recognize as short-lived—may differ from the response to a permanent change. Finally, a firm can afford to try only a limited number of experiments.

The Statistical Approach to Demand Estimation

Firms often rely on market data based on actual studies of demand. Properly applied, the statistical approach to demand estimation can enable one to sort out the effects of variables, such as income and the prices of other products, on the quantity of a product demanded. Here we outline some of the conceptual issues involved in the statistical approach.

The data in Table 4.5 describe the quantity of raspberries sold in a market each year. Information about the market demand for raspberries might be valuable to an organization representing growers; it would allow them to predict sales on the basis of their own estimates of price and other demand-determining variables. To focus our attention on demand, let's suppose that the quantity of raspberries produced is sensitive to weather conditions but not to the current price in the market (because farmers make their planting decisions based on last year's price).

The price and quantity data from Table 4.5 are graphed in Figure 4.17. If we believed that price alone determined demand, it would be plausible to describe the demand for the product by drawing a straight line (or other appropriate curve), $Q = a - bP$, which "fit" the points as shown by demand curve D. The "least-squares" method of curve-fitting is described in the appendix to this book.

Does curve D (given by the equation $Q = 28.7 - 0.98P$) really represent the

Table 4.5 Demand Data			
Year	**Quantity (Q)**	**Price (P)**	**Income (I)**
1988	4	24	10
1989	7	20	10
1990	8	17	10
1991	13	17	17
1992	16	10	17
1993	15	15	17
1994	19	12	20
1995	20	9	20
1996	22	5	20

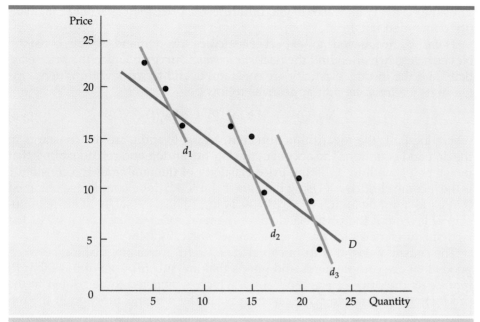

Figure 4.17   Estimating Demand   Price and quantity data can be used to determine the form of a demand relationship. But the same data could describe a single demand curve D, or three demand curves d_1, d_2, and d_3 that shift over time.

demand for the product? The answer is yes, but only if no important factors other than product price affect demand. But in Table 4.5, we have included data for one omitted variable—the average income of purchasers of the product. Note that income (I) has increased twice during the study, suggesting that the demand for agricultural products has shifted twice. Thus demand curves d_1, d_2, and d_3 in Figure 4.17 give a more likely description of demand. This demand relationship would be described algebraically as

$$Q = a - bP + cI \tag{4.4}$$

The income term in the demand equation allows the demand curve to shift in a parallel fashion as income changes. (The demand relationship, calculated using the least-squares method, is given by $Q = 5.07 - 0.40P + 0.94I$.)

The Form of the Demand Relationship

The demand relationships discussed above are straight lines, so that the effect of a change in price on quantity demanded is constant. However, the price elasticity of demand varies with the price level. For the demand equation $Q = a - bP$, for example, the price elasticity E_P is

$$E_P = (\Delta Q / \Delta P)(P/Q) = -b(P/Q) \tag{4.5}$$

Thus the elasticity increases in magnitude as the price increases (and the quantity demanded falls).

There is no reason to expect elasticities of demand to be constant. Nevertheless, we often find the *isoelastic demand* curve, in which the price elasticity and the income elasticity are constant, useful to work with. When written in its *log-linear form*, it appears as follows:

$$\log(Q) = a - b \log(P) + c \log(I) \qquad (4.6)$$

where log ( ) is the logarithmic function, and a, b, and c are the constants in the demand equation. The appeal of the log-linear demand relationship is that the slope of the line $-b$ is the price elasticity of demand, and the constant c is the income elasticity.[15] Using the data in Table 4.5, for example, we obtained the regression line $\log(Q) = -0.81 - 0.24 \log(P) + 1.46 \log(I)$.[16] This relationship tells us that the price elasticity of demand for raspberries is -0.24 (that is, demand is inelastic), and the income elasticity is 1.46.

The constant elasticity form can also be useful for distinguishing between goods that are complements and goods that are substitutes. Suppose that P_2 represents the price of a second good, which is believed to be related to the product we are studying. We can then write the demand function in the following form:

$$\log(Q) = a - b \log(P) + b_2 \log(P_2) + c \log(I)$$

When b_2, the cross-price elasticity, is positive, the two goods are substitutes, and when b_2 is negative the two goods are complements.

Summary

1. Individual consumers' demand curves for a commodity can be derived from information about their tastes for all goods and services and from their budget constraints.

2. Engel curves, which describe the relationship between the quantity of a good consumed and income, can be useful for discussions of how consumer expenditures vary with income.

3. Two goods are substitutes if an increase in the price of one good leads to an increase in the quantity demanded of the other. In contrast, two goods are complements if an increase in the price of one leads to a decrease in the quantity demanded of the other.

4. The effect of a price change on the quantity demanded of a good can be broken into two

---

[15] The natural logarithmic function with base e has the property that $\Delta(\log(Q)) = \Delta Q/Q$ for any change in $\log(Q)$. Similarly, $\Delta(\log(P)) = \Delta P/P$ for any change in $\log(P)$. It follows that $\Delta(\log(Q)) = \Delta Q/Q = -b[\Delta(\log(P))] = -b(\Delta P/P)$. Therefore, $(\Delta Q/Q)/(\Delta P/P) = -b$, which is the price elasticity of demand. By a similar argument, the income elasticity of demand c is given by $(\Delta Q/Q)/(\Delta I/I)$.

[16] When reporting price and income elasticities of demand, we usually follow one of two procedures. Either we obtain their elasticities from constant elasticity demand equations, or we use other demand relationships and evaluate the price and elasticities when each of the variables is evaluated at its mean. In the equation $Q = a - bP$, for example, we would calculate the price elasticity using the mean price $\overline{P}$ and the mean quantity sold $\overline{Q}$, so that $E_p = b\,(\overline{P}/\overline{Q})$.

parts—a substitution effect, in which satisfaction remains constant but the price changes, and an income effect, in which the price remains constant but satisfaction changes. Because the income effect can be positive or negative, a price change can have a small or a large effect on quantity demanded. In one unusual but interesting case (that of a Giffen good), the quantity demanded may move in the same direction as the price change (leading to an upward-sloping individual demand curve).

5. The market demand curve is the horizontal summation of the individual demand curves of all consumers in the market for the good. The market demand curve can be used to calculate how much people value the consumption of particular goods and services.

6. Demand is price inelastic when a 1 percent increase in price leads to a less than 1 percent decrease in quantity demanded, so that the consumer's expenditure increases. Demand is price elastic when a 1 percent increase in price leads to a more than 1 percent decrease in quantity demanded, so that the consumer's expenditure decreases. Demand is unit elastic when a 1 percent increase in price leads to a 1 percent decrease in quantity demanded.

7. The concept of *consumer surplus* can be useful in determining the benefits that people receive from the consumption of a product. Consumer surplus is the difference between what a consumer is willing to pay for a good and what he actually pays when buying it.

8. There is a network externality when one person's demand is affected directly by the purchasing decisions of other consumers. One example of a positive network externality, the bandwagon effect, occurs when a typical consumer's quantity demanded increases because she considers it stylish to buy a product that others have purchased. An example of a negative network externality, the snob effect, occurs when the quantity demanded by a consumer increases when fewer people own the good.

9. A number of methods can be used to obtain information about consumer demand. These include interview and experimental approaches, direct marketing experiments, and the more indirect statistical approach. The statistical approach can be very powerful in its application, but it is necessary to determine the appropriate variables that affect demand before the statistical work is done.

Questions for Review

1. How is an individual demand curve different from a market demand curve? Which curve is likely to be more price elastic? (*Hint*: Assume that there are no network externalities.)

2. Is the demand for a particular brand of product, such as Head skis, likely to be more price elastic or price inelastic than the demand for the aggregate of all brands, such as downhill skis? Explain.

3. Tickets to a rock concert sell for $10. But at that price, the demand is substantially greater than the available number of tickets. Is the value or marginal benefit of an additional ticket greater than, less than, or equal to $10? How might you determine that value?

4. Suppose a person allocates a given budget between two goods, food and clothing. If food is an inferior good, can you tell whether clothing is inferior or normal? Explain.

5. Which of the following combinations of goods are complements and which are substitutes? Could they be either in different circumstances? Discuss.
   a. a mathematics class and an economics class
   b. tennis balls and a tennis racket
   c. steak and lobster
   d. a plane trip and a train trip to the same destination
   e. bacon and eggs

6. Which of the following events would cause a movement along the demand curve for U.S.-produced clothing, and which would cause a shift in the demand curve?
   a. the removal of quotas on the importation of foreign clothes
   b. an increase in the income of U.S. citizens
   c. a cut in the industry's costs of producing domestic clothes that is passed on to the market in the form of lower clothing prices

7. For which of the following goods is a price increase likely to lead to a substantial income (as well as substitution) effect?
   a. salt
   b. housing
   c. theater tickets
   d. food

8. Suppose that the average household in a state consumes 500 gallons of gasoline per year. A 10-cent gasoline tax is introduced, coupled with a $50 annual tax rebate per household. Will the household be better or worse off after the new program is introduced?

9. Which of the following three groups is likely to have the most and which the least price-elastic demand for membership in the Association of Business Economists?
   a. students
   b. junior executives
   c. senior executives

Exercises

1. The ACME corporation determines that at current prices the demand for its computer chips has a price elasticity of −2 in the short run, while the price elasticity for its disc drives is −1.
   a. If the corporation decides to raise the price of both products by 10 percent, what will happen to its sales? To its sales revenue?
   b. Can you tell from the available information which product will generate the most revenue for the firm? If yes, why? If not, what additional information would you need?

2. Refer to Example 4.3 on the aggregate demand for wheat. From 1981 to 1990, domestic demand grew in response to growth in U.S. income levels. As a rough approximation, the domestic demand curve in 1990 was $Q_{DD} = 1200 − 55P$. Export demand, however, remained about the same, due to protectionist policies that limited wheat imports. Calculate and draw the aggregate demand curve for wheat in 1990.

3. Vera is shopping for a new videocassette recorder. She hears that the Betamax format is technologically superior to the VHS system. However, she asks her friends and it turns out they all have VHS machines. They agree that the Betamax format provides a better picture, but they add that at the local video store, the Beta format section seems to be getting smaller and smaller. Based on what she observes, Vera buys a VHS machine. Can you explain her decision? Speculate on what would occur if a new 8 mm video format is introduced.

4. Suppose you are in charge of a toll bridge that is essentially cost free. The demand for bridge crossings Q is given by $P = 12 − 2Q$.
   a. Draw the demand curve for bridge crossings.
   b. How many people would cross the bridge if there were no toll?
   c. What is the loss of consumer surplus associated with the charge of a bridge toll of $6?

5. a. Orange juice and apple juice are known to be perfect substitutes. Draw the appropriate price-consumption (for a variable price of orange juice) and income-consumption curves.

   b. Left shoes and rights shoes are perfect complements. Draw the appropriate price-consumption and income-consumption curves.

6. Heather's marginal rate of substitution of movie tickets for rental videos is known to be the same no matter how many rental videos she wants. Draw Heather's income consumption curve and her Engel curve for videos.

7. You are managing a $300,000 city budget in which monies are spent on schools and public safety only. You are about to receive aid from the federal government to support a special antidrug law enforcement program. Two programs that are available are (1) a $100,000 grant that must be spent on law enforcement; and (2) a 100 percent matching grant, in which each dollar of local spending on law enforcement is matched by a dollar of federal money. The federal matching program limits its payment to each city to a maximum of $100,000.

   a. Complete the table below with the amounts available for safety.

SCHOOLS	SAFETY (no govt. assistance)	SAFETY (program 1)	SAFETY (program 2)
$0			
50,000			
100,000			
150,000			
200,000			
250,000			
300,000			

   b. Which program would you (the manager) choose if you wish to maximize the satisfaction of the citizens if you allocate

$50,000 of the $300,000 to schools? What about $250,000?

   c. Draw the budget constraints for the three options: no aid, program 1, or program 2.

8. By observing an individual's behavior in the situations outlined below, determine the relevant income elasticities of demand for each good (i.e., whether the good is normal or inferior). If you cannot determine the income elasticity, what additional information might you need?

   a. Bill spends all his income on books and coffee. He finds $20 while rummaging through a used paperback bin at the bookstore. He immediately buys a new hardcover book of poetry.

   b. Bill loses $10 he was going to use to buy a double espresso. He decides to sell his new book at a discount to his friend and use the money to buy coffee.

   c. Being bohemian becomes the latest teen fad. As a result, coffee and book prices rise by 25 percent. Bill lowers his consumption of both goods by the same percentage.

   d. Bill drops out of art school and gets an M.B.A. instead. He stops reading books and drinking coffee. Now he reads the *Wall Street Journal* and drinks bottled mineral water.

9. Suppose the income elasticity of demand for food is 0.5, and the price elasticity of demand is -1.0. Suppose also that Felicia spends $10,000 a year on food, and that the price of food is $2, and that her income is $25,000.

   a. If a $2 sales tax on food were to cause the price of food to double, what would happen to her consumption of food? (*Hint*: Since a large price change is involved, you should assume that the price elasticity measures an arc elasticity, rather than a point elasticity.)

   b. Suppose that she is given a tax rebate of $5000 to ease the effect of the tax. What would her consumption of food be now?

   c. Is she better or worse off when given a rebate equal to the sales tax payments? Discuss.

APPENDIX TO CHAPTER 4

Demand Theory— A Mathematical Treatment

This appendix presents a mathematical treatment of the basics of demand theory. Our goal is to provide a short overview of the theory of demand for students who have some familiarity with the use of calculus. To do this, we will explain and then apply the concept of constrained optimization.

Utility Maximization

Demand theory is based on the premise that consumers maximize utility subject to a budget constraint. Utility is assumed to be an increasing function of the quantities of goods consumed, but marginal utility is assumed to decrease with consumption. The consumer's optimization problem when there are two goods, X and Y, may then be written as

$$\text{Maximize } U(X,Y) \tag{A4.1}$$

subject to the constraint that all income is spent on the two goods:

$$P_X X + P_Y Y = I \tag{A4.2}$$

Here, $U(\ )$ is the utility function, X and Y are the quantities of the two goods that the consumer purchases, P_X and P_Y are the prices of the goods, and I is income.[1]

To determine the individual consumer's demand for the two goods, we choose those values of X and Y that maximize (A4.1) subject to (A4.2). When we know the particular form of the utility function, we can solve to find the consumer's demand for X and Y directly. However, even if we write the utility function in its general form $U(X,Y)$, the technique of constrained optimization can be used to describe the conditions that must hold if the consumer is maximizing utility.

The Consumer's Optimum

To solve the constrained optimization problem given by equations (A4.1) and (A4.2), we use the method of Lagrange multipliers, which works as follows. We first write the "Lagrangian" for the problem. To do this, rewrite the constraint (A4.2) as $P_X X + P_Y Y - I = 0$. The Lagrangian is then

$$\Phi = U(X,Y) - \lambda(P_X X + P_Y Y - I) \tag{A4.3}$$

---

[1] To simplify the mathematics, we assume that the utility function is continuous (with continuous derivatives) and that goods are infinitely divisible.

The parameter λ is called the *Lagrange multiplier;* we will discuss its interpretation shortly.

If we choose values of X and Y that satisfy the budget constraint, then the second term in equation (A4.3) will be zero, and maximizing Φ will be equivalent to maximizing $U(X,Y)$. By differentiating Φ with respect to X, Y, and λ and then equating the derivatives to zero, we obtain the necessary conditions for a maximum:[2]

$$MU_X(X,Y) - \lambda\, P_X = 0$$

$$MU_Y(X,Y) - \lambda\, P_Y = 0 \qquad\qquad\qquad \text{(A4.4)}$$

$$P_X X + P_Y Y - I = 0$$

Here, MU is short for marginal utility (i.e., $MU_X(X,Y) = \partial U(X,Y)/\partial X$, the change in utility from a small increase in the consumption of good X).

The third condition is the original budget constraint. The first two conditions of (A4.4) tell us that each good will be consumed up to the point at which the marginal utility from consumption is a multiple (λ) of the price of the good. To see the implication of this, we combine the first two conditions to obtain the *equal marginal principle:*

$$\lambda = [MU_X(X,Y)/P_X] = MU_Y(X,Y)/P_Y \qquad\qquad \text{(A4.5)}$$

In other words, the marginal utility of each good divided by its price is the same. To be optimizing, *the consumer must be getting the same utility from the last dollar spent by consuming either X or Y*. Were this not the case, consuming more of one good and less of the other would increase utility.

To characterize the individual's optimum in more detail, we can rewrite the information in (A4.5) to obtain

$$MU_X(X,Y)/MU_Y(X,Y) = P_X/P_Y \qquad\qquad\qquad \text{(A4.6)}$$

Marginal Rate of Substitution

We can use equation (A4.6) to see the link between utility functions and indifference curves. An indifference curve represents all market baskets that give the consumer the same level of utility. If U^* is a fixed utility level, then the indifference curve that corresponds to that utility level is given by

$$U(X,Y) = U^*$$

As the market baskets are changed by adding X and subtracting Y, the total change in utility must equal zero. Therefore

$$MU_X(X,Y)\, dX + MU_Y(X,Y)\, dY = dU^* = 0 \qquad\qquad \text{(A4.7)}$$

---

[2] These conditions are necessary for an "interior" solution in which the consumer consumes positive amounts of both goods. However, the solution could be a "corner" solution in which all of one good and none of the other are consumed.

Rearranging,

$$-dY/dX = MU_X(X,Y)/MU_Y(X,Y) = MRS_{XY} \qquad (A4.8)$$

where MRS_{XY} represents the individual's marginal rate of substitution of X for Y. Because the left-hand side of (A4.8) represents the negative of the slope of the indifference curve, it follows that at the point of tangency the individual's marginal rate of substitution (which trades off goods while keeping utility constant) is equal to the individual's ratio of marginal utilities, which in turn is equal to the ratio of the prices of the two goods, from (A4.6).[3]

When the individual indifference curves are convex, the tangency of the indifference curve to the budget line solves the consumer's optimization problem. This was illustrated by Figure 3.11 in Chapter 3.

An Example

In general, the three equations in (A4.4) can be solved to determine the three unknowns X, Y, and λ as a function of the two prices and income. Substitution for λ then allows us to solve for the demands for each of the two goods in terms of income and the prices of the two commodities. This can be most easily seen in terms of an example.

A frequently used utility function is the Cobb-Douglas utility function, which can be represented in two forms:

$$U(X,Y) = a \log(X) + (1-a) \log(Y)$$

and

$$U(X,Y) = X^a Y^{1-a}$$

The two forms are equivalent for the purposes of demand theory because they both yield the identical demand functions for goods X and Y. We will derive the demand functions for the first form and leave the second as an exercise for the reader.

To find the demand functions for X and Y, given the usual budget constraint, we first write the Lagrangian:

$$\Phi = a \log(X) + (1-a)\log(Y) - \lambda(P_X X + P_Y Y - I)$$

Now differentiating with respect to X, Y, and λ, and setting the derivatives equal to zero, we obtain

$$\partial\Phi/\partial X = a/X - \lambda P_X = 0$$
$$\partial\Phi/\partial Y = (1-a)/Y - \lambda P_Y = 0$$
$$\partial\Phi/\partial\lambda = P_X X + P_Y Y - I = 0$$

---

[3] We are implicitly assuming that the "second-order conditions" for a utility maximum hold, so that the consumer is maximizing rather than minimizing utility. The convexity condition is sufficient for the second-order conditions to be satisfied. In mathematical terms, the condition is that $d(MRS)/dX < 0$, or that $dY^2/dX^2 > 0$, where $-dY/dX$ is the slope of the indifference curve. It is important to note that diminishing marginal utility is not sufficient to ensure that indifference curves are convex.

The first two conditions imply that

$$P_X X = a/\lambda \qquad\qquad (A4.9)$$

$$P_Y Y = (1 - a)/\lambda \qquad\qquad (A4.10)$$

Combining these with the last condition (the budget constraint) gives: $a/\lambda + (1 - a)/\lambda - I = 0$, or $\lambda = 1/I$. Now we can substitute this expression for λ back into (A4.9) and (A4.10) to obtain the demand functions:

$$X = (a/P_X)I$$

$$Y = [(1 - a)/P_Y]I$$

In this example the demand for each good depends only on the price of that good and on income, and not on the price of the other good. Thus, the cross-price elasticities of demand are 0.

Marginal Utility of Income

Whatever the form of the utility function, the Lagrange multiplier λ represents the extra utility generated when the budget constraint is relaxed—in this case by adding one dollar to the budget. To see this, we differentiate the utility function $U(X,Y)$ totally with respect to I:

$$dU/dI = MU_X(X,Y)(dX/dI) + MU_Y(X,Y)(dY/dI) \qquad (A4.11)$$

Because any increment in income must be divided between the two goods, it follows that

$$dI = P_X dX + P_Y dY \qquad\qquad (A4.12)$$

Substituting from (A4.5) into (A4.11), we get

$$dU/dI = \lambda P_X(dX/dI) + \lambda P_Y(dY/dI) = \lambda(P_X \, dX + P_Y \, dY)/dI \qquad (A4.13)$$

and substituting (A4.12) into (A4.13), we get

$$dU/dI = (\lambda P_X \, dX + \lambda P_Y \, dY)/(P_X \, dX + P_Y \, dY) = \lambda \qquad (A4.14)$$

Thus the Lagrange multiplier is the extra utility that results from an extra dollar of income.

Going back to our original analysis of the conditions for utility maximization, we see from equation (A4.5) that maximization requires that the utility obtained from the consumption of every good, per dollar spent on that good, be equal to the marginal utility of an additional dollar of income. If this were not the case, utility could be increased by spending more on the good with the higher ratio of marginal utility to price, and less on the other good.

To help clarify these results, let's go back to our Cobb-Douglas utility function example. In that example, we saw that when $U = a \log(X) + (1 - a)\log Y$, the demand functions were $X = (a/P_X)I$, and $Y = [(1 - a)/P_Y]I$, and the Lagrange multiplier was $\lambda = 1/I$. Now we can see how the Lagrange multiplier can be interpreted when specific values have been chosen for each of the parameters in the problem. Let $a = 1/2$, $P_X = \$1$, $P_Y = \$2$, and $I = \$100$. Then the choices that maximize utility are $X = 50$ and $Y = 25$. Also note that $\lambda = 1/100$. The Lagrange multiplier tells us that if an additional dollar of income were available to the consumer, the level of utility achieved would increase by 1/100. This is relatively easy to check. With an income of \$101, the maximizing choices of the two goods are $X = 50.5$ and $Y = 25.25$. A bit of arithmetic tells us that the original level of utility is 3.565, and the new level of utility is 3.575. As we can see, the additional dollar of income has indeed increased utility by .01, or 1/100.

Duality in Consumer Theory

One important feature of consumer theory is the *dual* nature of the consumer's decision. The optimum choice of X and Y can be analyzed not only as the problem of choosing the highest indifference curve (the maximum value of $U(\ )$) that touches the budget line, but also as the problem of choosing the lowest budget line (the minimum budget expenditure) that touches a given indifference curve. To see this, consider the following dual consumer optimization problem, the problem of minimizing the cost of achieving a particular level of utility:

$$\text{Minimize } P_X X + P_Y Y$$

subject to the constraint that

$$U(X,Y) = U^*$$

The corresponding Lagrangian is given by

$$\Phi = P_X X + P_Y Y - \mu(U(X,Y) - U^*) \tag{A4.15}$$

where μ is the Lagrange multiplier. Differentiating Φ with respect to X, Y, and μ, and setting the derivatives equal to zero, we find the following necessary conditions for expenditure minimization:

$$P_X - \mu MU_X(X,Y) = 0$$
$$P_Y - \mu MU_Y(X,Y) = 0$$

and

$$U(X,Y) = U^*$$

By solving the first two equations, we see that

$$\mu = [P_X/MU_X(X,Y)] = [P_Y/MU_Y(X,Y)] = 1/\lambda$$

Because it is also true that $MU_X(X,Y)/MU_Y(X,Y) = MRS_{XY} = P_X/P_Y$, the cost-minimizing choice of X and Y must occur at the point of tangency of the budget line and the indifference curve that generates utility U^*. Because this is the same point that maximized utility in our original problem, the dual expenditure minimization problem yields the same demand functions that are obtained from the direct utility maximization problem.

To see how the dual approach works, let's reconsider the Cobb-Douglas example again. The algebra is somewhat easier to follow if we use the exponential form of the Cobb-Douglas utility function, $U(X,Y) = X^a Y^{1-a}$. In this case, the Lagrangian is given by

$$\Phi = P_X X + P_Y Y - \mu[X^a Y^{1-a} - U^*] \tag{A4.16}$$

Differentiating with respect to X, Y, and μ and equating to zero, we obtain

$$P_X = \mu a U^*/X$$

$$P_Y = \mu(1-a)U^*/Y$$

Multiplying the first equation by X and the second by Y and adding, we get

$$P_X X + P_Y Y = \mu U^*$$

If we let I be the cost-minimizing expenditure (the individual must spend all of his income to get utility level U^* or U^* would not have maximized utility in the original problem), then it follows that $\mu = I/U^*$. Substituting in the equations above, we obtain

$$X = aI/P_X \quad \text{and} \quad Y = (1-a)I/P_Y$$

These are the same demand functions that we obtained before.

Income and Substitution Effects

The demand function tells us how any individual's utility-maximizing choices respond to changes in income and in the prices of goods. It is important, however, to distinguish that portion of any price change that involves the movement along an indifference curve and that portion that involves a movement to a different indifference curve (and therefore a change in purchasing power). To do this, we consider what happens to the demand for good X when the price of X changes. The change in demand can be divided into a substitution effect (the change in quantity demanded when the level of utility is fixed) and an income effect (the change in the quantity demanded with the level of utility changing but the relative price of good X unchanged). We denote the *Slutsky demand*—the change in X that results from a unit change in the price of X holding utility constant—by $\partial X/\partial P_X|_{u=u}*$. Thus the total change in X resulting from a unit change in P_X is

$$dX/dP_X = \partial X/\partial P_X|_{u=u}* + (\partial X/\partial I)(\partial I/\partial P_X) \tag{A4.17}$$

The first term on the right side of equation (A4.17) is the substitution effect (because utility is fixed), and the second term is the income effect (because income increases).

From the consumer's budget constraint, $I = P_X X + P_Y Y$, we know by differentiation that

$$\partial I/\partial P_X = X \tag{A4.18}$$

Suppose for the moment that the consumer owned goods X and Y. Then equation (A4.18) would tell us that when the price of good X increases by \$1, the amount of income the consumer can obtain by selling the good increases by $X. In our theory of the consumer, however, the consumer does not own the good. As a result, equation (A4.18) tells us how much additional income the consumer would need to leave him as well off after the price change as before. For this reason, it is customary to write the income effect as negative (reflecting a loss of purchasing power) rather than positive. Equation (A4.17) then appears as follows:

$$dX/dP_X = \partial X/\partial P_X \big|_{u=u^*} - X(\partial X/\partial I) \qquad (A4.19)$$

In this new form, called the *Slutsky equation*, the first term represents the substitution effect, the change in demand for good X obtained by keeping utility fixed. The second term is the income effect, the change in purchasing power resulting from the price change times the change in demand resulting from that change in purchasing power.

An alternative way to decompose a price change into substitution and income effects does not involve indifference curves; the approach is usually attributed to Hicks. In Figure A4.1, the consumer initially chooses market basket A on budget line RS. Suppose that after the price of food falls (and the

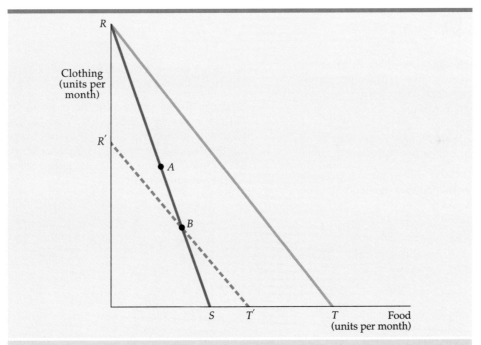

Figure A4.1 Hicksian Substitution Effect The individual initially consumes market basket A. A decrease in the price of food shifts the budget line from RS to RT. If a sufficient amount of income is taken away from the individual to make him no better off than he was at A, the new market basket chosen must lie on line segment BT' of budget line $R'T'$ (which intersects RS to the right of A), and the quantity of food consumed must be greater than at A.

budget line moves to RT), we take away enough income from the individual, so that he is no better off (and no worse off) than he was before. To do so, we draw a budget line parallel to RT. If the budget line passed through A, then the consumer would be at least as satisfied as before the price change because he has the option to purchase market basket A if he wishes. Therefore, the budget line that leaves him equally as well off must be a line such as $R'T'$, which is parallel to RT and which intersects RS at a point B below and to the right of point A.

Revealed preference tells us that the new market basket that is chosen must lie on line segment BT', since all market baskets on line segment $R'B$ could have been chosen but were not when the original budget line was RS. (Recall that the consumer preferred market basket A to any other feasible market basket.) Now note that all points on line segment $R'B$ involve more food consumption than does market basket A. It follows that the quantity of food demanded increases whenever there is a decrease in the price of food, holding utility constant. This negative substitution effect holds for all price changes and does not rely on the assumption of convexity of preferences.

Exercises

1. Which of the following utility functions are consistent with convex indifference curves, and which are not?
   a. $U(X,Y) = 2X + 5Y$
   b. $U(X,Y) = (XY)^{.5}$
   c. $U(X,Y) = \text{Min } (X,Y)$, where Min is the minimum of the two values of X and Y

2. Show that the two utility functions given below generate the identical demand functions for goods X and Y:

   a. $U(X,Y) = \log(X) + \log(Y)$
   b. $U(X,Y) = (XY)^{.5}$

3. Assume that a utility function is given by $\text{Min}(X,Y)$, as in Exercise 1(c). What is the Slutsky equation that decomposes the change in the demand for X in response to a change in its price? What is the income effect? What is the substitution effect?

CHAPTER 5

Choice Under Uncertainty

So far we have assumed that prices, incomes, and other variables are known with certainty. However, many of the choices that people make involve considerable uncertainty. For example, most people borrow to finance large purchases, such as a house or a college education, and plan to pay for the purchase out of future income. But for most of us, future incomes are uncertain. Our earnings can go up or down; we can be promoted, demoted, or even lose our jobs. Or if we delay buying a house or investing in a college education, we risk having its price rise in real terms, making it less affordable. How should we take these uncertainties into account when making major consumption or investment decisions?

Sometimes we must choose how much risk to bear. What, for example, should you do with your savings? Should you invest your money in something safe, such as a savings account, or something riskier but potentially more lucrative, such as the stock market? Another example is the choice of a job or even a career. Is it better to work for a large, stable company where job security is good but the chances for advancement are limited, or to join (or form) a new venture, which offers less job security but more opportunity for advancement?

147

To answer questions such as these, we must be able to quantify risk so we can compare the riskiness of alternative choices. We therefore begin this chapter by discussing measures of risk. Afterward, we will examine people's preferences toward risk. (Most people find risk undesirable, but some people find it more undesirable than others.) Next, we will see how people can deal with risk. Sometimes risk can be reduced—by diversification, by buying insurance, or by investing in additional information. In other situations (e.g., when investing in stocks or bonds), people must choose the amount of risk they wish to bear.

5.1 Describing Risk

To describe risk quantitatively, we need to know all the possible outcomes of a particular action and the likelihood that each outcome will occur.[1] Suppose, for example, that you are considering investing in a company that is exploring for offshore oil. If the exploration effort is successful, the company's stock will increase from $30 to $40 per share; if it is not, it will fall to $20 per share. Thus there are two possible future outcomes: a $40 per share price and a $20 per share price.

Probability

Probability refers to the likelihood that an outcome will occur. In our example, the probability that the oil exploration project is successful might be 1/4, and the probability that it is unsuccessful 3/4. Probability is a difficult concept to formalize because its interpretation can depend on the nature of the uncertain events and on the beliefs of the people involved. One *objective* interpretation of probability relies on the frequency with which certain events tend to occur. Suppose we know that of the last 100 offshore oil explorations 25 have succeeded and 75 have failed. Then the probability of success of 1/4 is objective because it is based directly on the frequency of similar experiences.

But what if there are no similar past experiences to help measure probability? In these cases objective measures of probability cannot be deduced, and a more *subjective* measure is needed. Subjective probability is the perception that an outcome will occur. This perception may be based on a person's judgment or experience, but not necessarily on the frequency with which a particular outcome has actually occurred in the past. When probabilities are subjectively determined, different people may attach different probabilities to different outcomes and thereby make different choices. For example, if the search for oil were to take place in an area where no previous searches had

---

[1] Some people distinguish between uncertainty and risk along the lines suggested by the economist Frank Knight some 60 years ago. *Uncertainty* can refer to situations in which many outcomes are possible but their likelihoods are unknown. *Risk* then refers to situations in which we can list all possible outcomes, and we know the likelihood that each outcome will occur. We will always refer to risky situations but will simplify the discussion by using uncertainty and risk interchangeably.

ever occurred, I might attach a higher subjective probability than you to the chance that the project will succeed because I know more about the project, or because I have a better understanding of the oil business and can therefore make better use of our common information. Either different information or different abilities to process the same information can explain why subjective probabilities vary among individuals.

Whatever the interpretation of probability, it is used in calculating two important measures that help us describe and compare risky choices. One measure tells us the *expected value* and the other the *variability* of the possible outcomes.

Expected Value

The *expected value* associated with an uncertain situation is a weighted average of the *payoffs* or values associated with all possible outcomes, with the probabilities of each outcome used as weights. The expected value measures the *central tendency*—that is, the average payoff. Our offshore oil exploration example has two possible outcomes: success yields a payoff of $40 per share, while failure yields a payoff of $20 per share. Denoting "probability of" by Pr, the expected value in this case is given by

$$\text{Expected value} = \text{Pr(success)}(\$40/\text{share}) + \text{Pr(failure)}(\$20/\text{share})$$
$$= (1/4)(\$40/\text{share}) + (3/4)(\$20/\text{share}) = \$25/\text{share}$$

More generally, if there are two possible outcomes having payoffs X_1 and X_2 and the probabilities of each outcome are given by Pr_1 and Pr_2, then the expected value is $E(X) = Pr_1 X_1 + Pr_2 X_2$.[2]

Variability

Suppose you are choosing between two part-time sales jobs that have the same expected income ($1500). The first job is based entirely on commission—the income earned depends on how much you sell. The second job is salaried. There are two equally likely incomes under the first job—$2000 for a good sales effort and $1000 for one that is only modestly successful. The second job pays $1510 most of the time, but you would earn $510 in severance pay if the company goes out of business. Table 5.1 summarizes these possible outcomes, their payoffs, and their probabilities.

Note that the two jobs have the same expected income because .5($2000) + .5($1000) = .99 ($1510) + .01 ($510) = $1500. But the *variability* of the possible payoffs is different for the two jobs. This variability can be measured by recognizing that large differences (whether positive or negative) between actual payoffs and the expected payoff, called *deviations*, signal greater risk. Table 5.2 gives the deviations of actual incomes from the expected income for each of the two sales jobs.

---

[2] When there are n possible outcomes, the expected value becomes $E(X) = Pr_1 X_1 + Pr_2 X_2 + \cdots + Pr_n X_n$.

Table 5.1 Income from Sales Jobs

	Outcome 1		Outcome 2	
	Probability	Income ($)	Probability	Income ($)
Job 1: Commission	.5	2000	.5	1000
Job 2: Fixed salary	.99	1510	.01	510

In the first commission job, the average deviation is $500, which is obtained by weighting each deviation by the probability that each outcome occurs. Thus

$$\text{Average deviation} = .5(\$500) + .5(\$500) = \$500$$

For the second fixed-salary job, the average deviation is

$$\text{Average deviation} = .99(\$10) - .01(\$990) = \$19.80$$

The first job is thus substantially more risky than the second because its average deviation of $500 is much greater than the average deviation of $19.80 for the second job.

Despite its simplicity, the average deviation can be difficult to use for some purposes because all negative differences have to be translated into positive deviations. One easy way to avoid confusion is to square each difference; then, the square root of the resulting number will always be positive. We will, therefore, replace the average deviation with the standard deviation. The *standard deviation* measures the square root of the average of the *squares* of the deviations of the payoffs associated with each outcome from their expected value.[3]

Table 5.3 illustrates the calculation of the standard deviation for our example. Note that the average of the squared deviations under Job 1 is given by

$$.5(\$250,000) + .5(\$250,000) = \$250,000$$

The standard deviation is therefore equal to the square root of $250,000, or $500. Similarly, the average of the squared deviations under Job 2 is given by

$$.99(\$100) + .01(\$980,100) = \$9900$$

Table 5.2 Deviations from Expected Income ($)

	Outcome 1	Deviation	Outcome 2	Deviation
Job 1	$2000	$500	$1000	$500
Job 2	1510	10	510	990

---

[3] Another measure of variability, *variance*, is the square of the standard deviation.

		Deviation		Deviation	Average Deviation
Table 5.3	**Calculating Variance ($)**				
	Outcome 1	Squared	Outcome 2	Squared	Squared
Job 1	$2000	$250,000	$1000	$250,000	$250,000
Job 2	1510	100	510	980,100	9,900

The standard deviation is the square root of $9,900, or $99.50. Once again, we see that the second job is much less risky than the first; the standard deviation of the incomes earned is lower.[4]

The concept of standard deviation applies equally well when there are many outcomes rather than just two. Suppose, for example, that the first job yields incomes ranging from $1000 to $2000 in increments of $100 that are all equally likely. The second job yields incomes from $1300 to $1700 (again in increments of $100) that are also all equally likely. Figure 5.1 shows the alternatives graphically. (If there had been only two outcomes that were equally probable, then the figure would be drawn as two vertical lines, each with a height of 0.5.)

You can see from Figure 5.1 that the first job is riskier than the second. The "spread" of possible payoffs for the first job is much greater than the spread of payoffs for the second. And the standard deviation of the payoffs associated with the first job is greater than the standard deviation associated with the second.

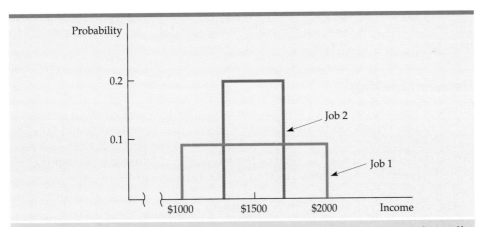

Figure 5.1   Outcome Probabilities for Two Jobs   The distribution of payoffs associated with Job 1 has a greater spread and a greater standard deviation than the distribution of payoffs associated with Job 2. Both distributions are flat because all outcomes are equally likely.

---

[4] In general, when there are two outcomes with payoffs X_1 and X_2, each occurring with probability Pr_1 and Pr_2, and $E(X)$ is the expected value of the outcomes, the standard deviation is given by σ, where $\sigma^2 = Pr_1[(X_1 - E(X))^2] + Pr_2[(X_2 - E(X))^2]$.

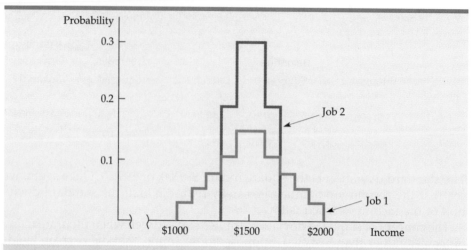

Figure 5.2   Unequal Probability Outcomes   The distribution of payoffs associated with Job 1 has a greater spread and a greater standard deviation than the distribution of payoffs associated with Job 2. Both distributions are peaked because the extreme payoffs are less likely than those near the middle of the distribution.

In this particular example, all payoffs are equally likely, so the curves describing the payoffs under each job are flat. But in many cases, some payoffs are more likely than others. Figure 5.2 shows a situation in which the more extreme payoffs are the least likely. Again, the salary from Job 1 has a greater variance. From this point on we will use the standard deviation of payoffs to measure the degree of risk.

Decision Making

Suppose you are choosing between the two sales jobs described in our original example. Which job would you take? If you dislike risk, you will take the second job. It offers the same expected income as the first but with less risk. But suppose we add $100 to each of the payoffs in the first job, so that the expected payoff increases from $1500 to $1600. Table 5.4 gives the new earnings and the squared deviations.

The jobs can then be described as follows:

Job 1:   Expected income = $1600   Standard deviation = $5,000
Job 2:   Expected income = $1500   Standard deviation = $99.50

Job 1 offers a higher expected income but is much riskier than Job 2. Which job is preferred depends on the individual. An aggressive entrepreneur may opt for the higher expected income and higher standard deviation, but a more conservative person might opt for the second job. To see how people might decide between incomes that differ in both expected value and in riskiness, we need to develop our theory of consumer choice further.

Table 5.4 Incomes from Sales Jobs—Modified ($)				
	Outcome 1	**Deviation Squared**	**Outcome 2**	**Deviation Squared**
Job 1	$2100	$250,000	$1100	$250,000
Job 2	1510	100	510	980,100

5.2 Preferences Toward Risk

We used a job example to describe how people might evaluate risky outcomes, but the principles apply equally well to other choices. In this section we concentrate on consumer choices generally, and on the utility that consumers obtain from choosing among risky alternatives. To simplify things, we'll consider the consumption of a single commodity—the consumer's income, or more appropriately, the market basket that the income can buy. We assume that consumers know all probabilities, and (for much of this section) that payoffs are now measured in terms of utility rather than dollars.

Figure 5.3(a) shows how we can describe a woman's preferences toward risk. The curve 0E, which gives her utility function, tells us the level of utility (on the vertical axis) that she can attain for each level of income (measured in thousands of dollars on the horizontal axis). The level of utility increases from 10 to 16 to 18 as income increases from $10,000 to $20,000 to $30,000. But note that marginal utility is diminishing, falling from 10 when income increases from 0 to $10,000, to 6 when income increases from $10,000 to $20,000, and to 2 when income increases from $20,000 to $30,000.

Now suppose she has an income of $15,000 and is considering a new but risky sales job that will either double her income to $30,000 or cause it to fall to $10,000. Each possibility has a probability of .5. As Figure 5.3(a) shows, the utility level associated with an income of $10,000 is 10 (at point A), and the utility associated with a level of income of $30,000 is 18 (at E). The risky job must be compared with the current job, for which the utility is 13 (at B).

To evaluate the new job, she can calculate the expected value of the resulting income. Because we are measuring value in terms of the woman's utility, we must calculate the *expected utility* $E(u)$ she can obtain. The expected utility is the sum of the utilities associated with all possible outcomes, weighted by the probability that each outcome will occur. In this case, expected utility is

$$E(u) = (1/2)u(\$10,000) + (1/2)u(\$30,000) = 0.5(10) + 0.5(18) = 14$$

The new risky job is thus preferred to the original job because the expected utility of 14 is greater than the original utility of 13.

The old job involved no risk—it guaranteed an income of $15,000 and a utility level of 13. The new job is risky, but it offers both a higher expected income ($20,000) and, more important, a higher expected utility. If the woman wished to increase her expected utility, she would take the risky job.

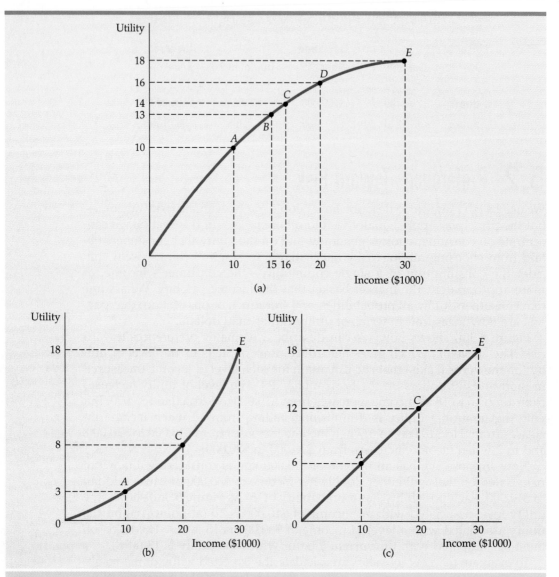

Figure 5.3 **Risk Aversion** People differ in their preferences toward risk. In (a) a consumer's marginal utility diminishes as income increases. The consumer is risk averse because she would prefer a certain income of $20,000 (with a utility of 16) to a gamble with a .5 probability of $10,000 and a .5 probability of $30,000 (and expected utility of 14). In (b) the consumer is risk loving, because she would prefer the same gamble (with expected utility of 10.5) to the certain income (with a utility of 8). Finally, in (c) the consumer is risk neutral and is indifferent between certain events and uncertain events with the same expected income.

Different Preferences Toward Risk

People differ in their willingness to bear risk. Some are risk averse, some risk loving, and some risk neutral. A person who prefers a certain given income to a risky job with the same expected income is described as being *risk averse*. (Such a person has a diminishing marginal utility of income.) Risk aversion is the most common attitude toward risk. To see that most people are risk averse most of the time, note the vast number of risks that people insure against. Most people not only buy life insurance, health insurance, and car insurance, but also seek occupations with relatively stable wages.

Figure 5.3(a) applies to a woman who is risk averse. Suppose she can have a certain income of $20,000, or a job yielding an income of $30,000 with probability .5 and an income of $10,000 with probability .5 (so that the expected income is $20,000). As we saw, the expected utility of the uncertain income is 14, an average of the utility at point *A* (10) and the utility at *E* (18), and is shown by *C*. Now we can compare the expected utility associated with the risky job to the utility generated if $20,000 were earned without risk. This utility level, 16, is given by *D* in Figure 5.3(a). It is clearly greater than the expected utility associated with the risky job.

A person who is *risk neutral* is indifferent between a certain income and an uncertain income with the same expected value. In Figure 5.3(c) the utility associated with a job generating an income of either $10,000 or $30,000 with equal probability is 12, as is the utility of receiving a certain income of $20,000.[5]

Figure 5.3(b) shows the third possibility—*risk loving*. In this case the expected utility of an uncertain income that will be either $10,000 with probability .5 or $30,000 with probability .5 is *higher* than the utility associated with a certain income of $20,000. Numerically,

$$E(u) = .5u(\$10,000) + .5u(\$30,000) = .5(3) + .5(18) = 10.5 > u(\$20,000) = 8$$

The primary evidence for risk loving is that many people enjoy gambling. Some criminologists might describe criminals as risk lovers, especially when a robbery is committed that has a high prospect of apprehension and punishment. These special cases aside, few people are risk loving, at least with respect to major purchases or large amounts of income or wealth.[6]

The *risk premium* is the amount of money that a risk-averse person would pay to avoid taking a risk. The magnitude of the risk premium depends in general on the risky alternatives that the person faces. To determine the risk

---

[5] When people are risk neutral, the marginal utility of income is constant, so the income they earn can be used as an indicator of well-being. A government policy that doubled people's incomes would then also double their utility. At the same time, government policies that alter the risks that people face, without changing their expected incomes, would not affect their well-being. Risk neutrality allows a person to avoid the complications that might be associated with the effects of governmental actions on the riskiness of outcomes.

[6] People may be averse to some risks and act like risk lovers with respect to others. This issue was treated by Milton Friedman and Leonard J. Savage in "The Utility Analysis of Choices Involving Risk," *Journal of Political Economy* (1948): 279–304.

premium, we have reproduced the utility function of Figure 5.3(a) in Figure 5.4. Recall that an expected utility of 14 is achieved by a woman who is going to take a risky job with an expected income of $20,000. This is shown graphically by drawing a horizontal line to the vertical axis from point *F*, which bisects straight line *AE* (thus representing an average of $10,000 and $30,000). But the utility level of 14 can also be achieved if the woman has a *certain* income of $16,000, as shown by dropping a vertical line from point *C*. Thus the risk premium of $4000, given by line segment *CF*, is the amount of income ($20,000 minus $16,000) she would give up to leave her indifferent between the risky job and the safe one.

How risk averse a person is depends on the nature of the risk and on the person's income. Generally, risk-averse people prefer a smaller variability of outcomes. We saw that when there are two outcomes, an income of $10,000 and an income of $30,000, the risk premium is $4000. Now consider a second risky job, involving a .5 probability of receiving an income of $40,000 and a utility level of 20 and a .5 probability of getting an income of $0. The expected income is again $20,000, but the expected utility is only 10:

$$\text{Expected utility} = .5u(\$0) + .5u(\$40,000) = 0 + .5(20) = 10$$

Because the utility of having a certain income of $20,000 is 16, the woman loses 6 units of utility if she is required to accept the job. The risk premium in this case

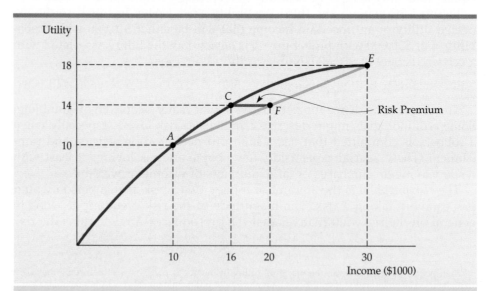

Figure 5.4 Risk Premium The risk premium, *CF*, measures the amount of income an individual would give up to leave her indifferent between a risky choice and a certain one. Here, the risk premium is $4000 because a certain income of $16,000 (at point *C*) gives her the same expected utility (14) as the uncertain income (a .5 probability of being at point *A* and a .5 probability of being at point *E*) that has an expected value of $20,000.

is equal to $10,000 because the utility of a certain income of $10,000 is 10. She can afford to give up $10,000 of her $20,000 expected income to have the certain income of $10,000 and will have the same level of expected utility. Thus the greater the variability, the more a person is willing to pay to avoid the risky situation.

| EXAMPLE 5.1 | **Business Executives and the Choice of Risk** |

Are business executives more risk loving than most people? When they are presented with alternative strategies, some risky, some safe, which do they choose? In one study, 464 business executives were asked to respond to a questionnaire that described risky situations that the executive might face as the vice president of a hypothetical company.[7] The executives were presented with four risky items, each of which had a given probability of a favorable and an unfavorable outcome. The payoffs and probabilities were chosen so that each item had the same expected value. In increasing order of the risk involved (as measured by the difference between the favorable and unfavorable outcomes), the four items were (1) a lawsuit involving a patent violation, (2) a customer threat concerning the supplying of a competitor, (3) a union dispute, and (4) a joint venture with a competitor. The executives were asked a series of questions to learn their willingness to take or avoid risks. Thus in some situations the executives could opt to delay a choice, to collect information, to bargain, or to delegate a decision, so as to avoid taking risks or to modify the risks that they would take later.

The study found that executives vary substantially in their preferences toward risk. Roughly 20 percent of those answering indicated that they were relatively neutral toward risk, while 40 percent opted for the more risky alternatives, and 20 percent were clearly risk averse (20 percent did not respond). More important, executives (including those who chose risky alternatives) made substantial efforts to reduce or eliminate risk, usually by delaying decisions and by collecting more information.

In general, risk can arise where the expected gain is either positive (e.g., a chance for a large reward versus a small one) or negative (e.g., a chance for a large loss or for no loss). The study found that executives differ in their preferences toward risk, depending on whether the risk involved gains or losses. In general, those executives who liked risky situations did so when losses were involved. (Perhaps they were willing to gamble against a large loss in the hope of breaking even.) However, when the risks involved gains, the same executives were more conservative, opting for the less risky alternatives.[8]

---

[7] This example is based on Kenneth R. MacCrimmon and Donald A. Wehrung, "The Risk In-Basket," *Journal of Business* 57 (1984): 367–387.

[8] It is interesting that some people treat the risk of a small gain in income very differently from the risk of a small loss. Prospect theory, developed by psychologists Daniel Kahneman and Amos Tversky, helps to explain this phenomenon. See "Rational Choice and the Framing of Decisions," *Journal of Business* 59 (1986): S251–S278, and "Prospect Theory: An Analysis of Decision Under Risk," *Econometrica* 47 (1979): 263–292.

EXAMPLE 5.2 Deterring Crime

Fines may deter certain types of crimes, such as speeding, double-parking, tax evasion, and air polluting, better than incarceration.[9] The party choosing to violate the law in these ways has good information and can reasonably be assumed to be behaving rationally.

Other things being equal, the greater the fine, the more a potential criminal will be discouraged from engaging in the crime. For example, if it were costless to catch criminals and if the crime imposed a calculable cost of $1000 on society, we might choose to catch all violators and impose a fine of $1000 on each. That would discourage people whose benefit from engaging in the activity was less than the fine.

In practice, however, it is very costly to catch lawbreakers. Therefore, we save on administrative costs by imposing relatively high fines (which are no more costly to collect than low fines), but allocating resources so that the probability of a violator's being apprehended is much less than one. Thus the size of the fine that needs to be imposed to discourage criminal behavior depends on the risk preferences of the potential violators. The more risk averse a person is, the smaller the fine that must be imposed to discourage him or her, as the following example demonstrates.

Suppose that a city wants to deter people from double-parking. By double-parking, a typical resident saves $5 in terms of his own time available to engage in activities that are more pleasant than searching for a parking space. If the driver is risk neutral and if it were costless to catch violators, a fine of just over $5, say, $5.01, would need to be assessed every time he double-parked. This would ensure that the net benefit of double-parking to the driver (the $5 benefit less the $5.01 fine) would be less than zero, so that he would choose to obey the law. In fact, all potential violators whose benefit was less than or equal to $5 would be discouraged, while a few whose benefit was greater than $5 would violate the law (they might have to double-park in an emergency).

Extensive monitoring is expensive but fortunately may not be necessary. The same deterrence effect can be obtained by assessing a fine of $50 and catching only one in ten violators (or perhaps a fine of $500 with a one-in-100 chance of being caught). In each case the expected penalty is $5 ([$50][.1] or [$500][.01]). A policy of a high fine and a low probability of catching a violator is likely to reduce enforcement costs.

The fines to be assessed need not be large. If drivers were very risk averse, a much lower fine could be used because they would be willing to forgo the

[9] This discussion builds indirectly on Gary S. Becker, "Crime and Punishment: An Economic Approach," *Journal of Political Economy* (Mar./Apr. 1968): 169–217. See also Mitchell Polinsky and Steven Shavell, "The Optimal Tradeoff Between the Probability and the Magnitude of Fines," *American Economic Review* 69 (Dec. 1979): 880–891.

activity in part because of the risk associated with the enforcement process. In the previous example, a $25 fine with a .1 probability of catching the violator might discourage most people from violating the law.

5.3 Reducing Risk

Sometimes consumers choose risky alternatives that suggest risk-loving rather than risk-averse behavior, as the recent growth in state lotteries shows. Nonetheless, in the face of a broad variety of risky situations, consumers are generally risk averse. In this section we describe three ways by which consumers commonly reduce risks: diversification, insurance, and obtaining more information about choices and payoffs.

Diversification

Suppose that you plan to take a part-time job selling appliances on a commission basis. You can decide to sell only air conditioners or only heaters, or you can spend half your time selling each. Of course, you can't be sure how hot or cold the weather will be next year. How should you apportion your time to minimize the risk involved in the sales job?

The answer is that risk can be minimized by *diversification*—by allocating your time toward selling two or more products (whose sales are not closely related), rather than a single product. Suppose that there is a fifty-fifty chance that it will be a relatively hot year, and a fifty-fifty chance that it will be cold. Table 5.5 gives the earnings that you can make selling air conditioners and heaters.

If you sell only air conditioners or only heaters, your actual income will be either $12,000 or $30,000 but your expected income will be $21,000 (.5[$30,000] + .5[$12,000]). But suppose you diversify by dividing your time evenly between the two products. Then your income will certainly be $21,000, whatever the weather. If the weather is hot, you will earn $15,000 from air conditioner sales and $6000 from heater sales; if it is cold, you will earn $6000 from air conditioner sales and $15,000 from heater sales. Hence, by diversifying you eliminate all risk.

Diversification is not always this easy. In our example heater and air conditioner sales were inversely related—whenever the sales of one were strong, the sales of the other were weak. But the principle of diversification is a gen-

Table 5.5 Income from Sales of Appliances		
	Hot Weather	**Cold Weather**
Air conditioner sales	$30,000	$12,000
Heater sales	12,000	30,000

eral one. As long as you can allocate your effort or your investment funds toward a variety of activities whose outcomes are not closely related, you can eliminate some risk.

Insurance

We have seen that risk-averse people will be willing to give up income to avoid risk. In fact, if the cost of insurance is equal to the expected loss (e.g., a policy with an expected loss of $1000 will cost $1000), risk-averse people will want to buy enough insurance to allow them to fully recover from any financial losses they might suffer.

The reasoning is implicit in our discussion of risk aversion. Buying insurance assures a person of having the same income whether or not there is a loss. Because the insurance cost is equal to the expected loss, this certain income is equal to the expected income from the risky situation. For a risk-averse consumer, the guarantee of the same income whatever the outcome generates more utility than would be the case if that person had a high income when there was no loss and a low income when a loss occurred.

To clarify this argument, suppose a homeowner faces a 10 percent probability that his house will be burglarized and he will suffer a $10,000 loss. Let's assume he has $50,000 worth of property. Table 5.6 shows his wealth with two possibilities—to insure or not to insure.

The decision to purchase insurance does not alter his expected wealth. It does, however, smooth it out over both possible outcomes. This is what generates a higher level of expected utility for the homeowner. Why? We know that the marginal utility in both the no-loss and loss situations is the same for the man who buys insurance (because his wealth is the same). But when there is no insurance, the marginal utility in the event of a loss is higher than if no loss occurs (recall that with risk aversion there is diminishing marginal utility). Therefore, a transfer of wealth from the no-loss to the loss situation must increase total utility. And this transfer of wealth is exactly what the purchase of insurance accomplishes.

Consumers usually buy insurance from companies that specialize in selling it. In general, insurance companies are profit-maximizing firms that offer insurance because they know that when they pool policies, they face relatively little risk. The ability to avoid risk by operating on a large scale is based on the *law of large numbers*, which tells us that although single events may be random and largely unpredictable, the average outcome of many similar events

Table 5.6 The Decision to Insure			
Insurance	**Burglary (Pr = .1)**	**No Burglary (Pr = .9)**	**Expected Wealth**
No	$40,000	$50,000	$49,000
Yes	49,000	49,000	49,000

can be predicted. For example, I may not be able to predict whether a coin toss will come out heads or tails, but I know that when many coins are flipped, approximately half will turn up heads and half tails. Similarly, if I am selling automobile insurance, I cannot predict whether a particular driver will have an accident, but I can be reasonably sure, judging from past experience, about how many accidents a large group of drivers will have.

By operating on a large scale, insurance companies can assure themselves that over a large enough number of events, the total premiums paid in will be equal to the total amount of money paid out. To return to our burglary example, a man knows that there is a 10 percent probability that his house will be burgled; if it is, he will suffer a $10,000 loss. Prior to facing this risk, he calculates the expected loss to be $1000 (.10 × $10,000), but there is sub-stantial risk involved, since there is a 10 percent probability of a large loss. Now suppose 100 people are similarly situated and all of them buy burglary insurance from an insurance company. Because they are all similarly situ-ated, the insurance company charges each of them a premium of $1000 for the insurance. This $1000 premium generates an insurance fund of $100,000 from which losses can be paid. The insurance company can rely on the law of large numbers, which tells it that the expected loss over the 100 individ-uals is likely to be very close to $1000 each. Therefore, the total payout will be close to $100,000, and the company need not worry about losing more than that.

Insurance companies typically charge premiums above the expected loss because they need to cover their administrative costs. As a result, people some-times choose to self-insure rather than buy from an insurance company. One way to avoid risk is to self-insure by diversifying. For example, self-insurance against the risks associated with investing usually takes the form of diversi-fying one's portfolio, say, by buying a mutual fund. Self-insurance against other risks can be achieved by spending money. For example, a person can self-insure against the risk of loss by putting money into a fund to cover fu-ture loss. Another person may self-insure against the loss of future earnings by putting funds into an individual retirement account.

EXAMPLE 5.3   The Value of Title Insurance When Buying a House

Suppose a family is buying its first house. The family knows that to close the sale of the house they will need a deed that gives them the clear "title" to the house. Without such a clear title, there is always a chance that the seller of the house is not its true owner. Of course, the seller could be engaging in fraud but is more likely to be unaware of the exact nature of his or her ownership rights. For example, the owner may have borrowed heavily, using the house as "collateral" for the loan. Or the property might carry with it a legal re-quirement that limits the use to which it may be put.

Suppose the family is willing to pay $150,000 for the house but believes there is a one in ten chance that careful research will show that the current seller does not own the property. The property would then be worth only $50,000. If there were no insurance available, a risk-neutral family would bid at most $140,000 for the property (.9[$150,000] + .1[$50,000]). However, a family that expects to tie up most of their assets in their house would most likely be risk averse and would, therefore, bid substantially less to buy the house, say, $120,000.

In situations such as this, it is clearly in the interest of the seller to assure the buyer that there is no risk of a lack of full ownership. The seller does this by purchasing "title insurance." The title insurance company researches the history of the property, checks to see whether any legal liabilities are attached to it, and generally assures itself that there is no ownership problem. The insurance company then agrees to bear any remaining risk that might exist.[10]

Because the title insurance company is a specialist in such insurance and can collect the relevant information relatively easily, the cost of title insurance is often less than the expected value of the loss involved. A fee of $1,000 for title insurance is not unusual, and the expected loss can be substantially higher. Clearly, it is in the interest of the sellers of homes to provide such insurance, because all but the most risk-loving buyers will pay much more for the house when it is insured than when it is not. In fact, most states require sellers to provide title insurance before the sale of a house can be complete.

The Value of Information

The decision a consumer makes when outcomes are uncertain is based on limited information. If more information were available, the consumer could make better predictions and reduce risk. Because information is a valuable commodity, people will pay for it. The *value of complete information* is the difference between the expected value of a choice when there is complete information and the expected value when information is incomplete.

To see how valuable information can be, suppose you are a store manager and must decide how many suits to order for the fall season. If you order 100 suits, your cost is $180 per suit, but if you order only 50 suits, your cost increases to $200. You know you will be selling the suits for $300 each, but you are not sure what total sales will be. All suits not sold can be returned, but for only half of what you paid for them. Without additional information, you will act on your belief that there is a .5 probability that 100 suits will be sold and a .5 probability that sales will be 50. Table 5.7 gives the profit that you would earn in each of the two cases.

Without additional information, you would choose to buy 100 suits if you were risk neutral, taking the chance that your profit might be either $12,000 or $1500. But if you were risk averse, you might buy 50 suits because then you would know for sure that your profit would be $5000.

---

[10] Because mortgage lenders are also concerned about such risks, they usually require new buyers to have title insurance before they will issue a mortgage.

Table 5.7	Profits from Sales of Suits		
	Sales of 50	**Sales of 100**	**Expected Profit**
1. Buy 50 suits	$5000	$5000	$5000
2. Buy 100 suits	1500	12,000	6750

With complete information, you can make the correct suit order whatever the sales might be. If sales were going to be 50 and you ordered 50 suits, your profit would be $5000. If, on the other hand, sales were going to be 100 and you ordered 100 suits, your profit would be $12,000. Since both outcomes are equally likely, your expected profit with complete information would be $8500. The value of information is computed as

	Expected value with complete information:	$8500
Less:	Expected value with uncertainty (buy 100 suits):	−$6750
	Value of complete information	$1750

Thus it is worth paying up to $1750 to obtain an accurate prediction of sales. Even though forecasting is inevitably imperfect, it may be worth investing in a marketing study that provides a better forecast of next year's sales.

E X A M P L E 5.4 **The Value of Information in the Dairy Industry**

Historically, the U.S. dairy industry has allocated its advertising expenditures more or less uniformly throughout the year.[11] But per capita consumption of milk declined by 24 percent between 1955 and 1980, which stirred milk producers to look for a new sales strategy to encourage milk consumption. One strategy would be to increase advertising expenditures and to continue to advertise at a uniform rate throughout the year. A second strategy is to invest in market research to obtain more information about the seasonal demand for milk, and then reallocate expenditures, so that advertising is most intense when the demand for milk is greatest.

Research into milk demand shows that sales follow a seasonal pattern, with demand the greatest during the spring and lowest during summer and early fall. The price elasticity of milk demand is negative but small and the income elasticity positive and large. Most important is that milk advertising has the most effect on sales when consumers have the strongest preference for milk (March, April, and May), and the least when preferences are weakest (August, September, and October).

---

[11] This example is based on Henry Kinnucan and Olan D. Forker, "Seasonality in the Consumer Response to Milk Advertising with Implications for Milk Promotion Policy," *American Journal of Agricultural Economics* 68 (1986): 562–571.

In this case, the cost of obtaining the seasonal information about milk demand is relatively low, and the value of the information is substantial. To estimate this value, we can compare the actual sales of milk during 1972–1980 with what the sales would have been had the advertising expenditures been made in proportion to the strength of the seasonal demand. In the latter case, 30 percent of the advertising budget would be allocated in the first quarter of the year, and only 20 percent in the third quarter.

Making these calculations for the New York metropolitan area shows that the value of information—the value of the additional milk sales—was $4,046,557. This means a 9 percent increase in the profit to producers.

*5.4 The Demand for Risky Assets

Most people are risk averse. Given a choice, they prefer a fixed monthly income to one that is as large on average but that fluctuates randomly from month to month. Yet many of these same people will invest all or part of their savings in stocks, bonds, and other assets that carry some risk. Why do risk-averse people invest in the stock market, and thereby risk losing part or all of their investment?[12] How do people decide how much risk to bear when making investments and planning for the future? To answer these questions, we need to examine the demand for risky assets.

Assets

An *asset* is something that provides a monetary flow to its owner. For example, apartments in an apartment building can be rented out, providing a flow of rental income to the owner of the building. Another example is a savings account in a bank that pays interest (usually every day or every month). Typically, these interest payments are reinvested in the account.

The monetary flow that one receives from owning an asset can take the form of an explicit payment, such as the rental income from an apartment building: Every month the landlord receives rent checks from the tenants. Another explicit payment is the dividend on shares of common stock: Every three months the owner of a share of General Motors stock receives a quarterly dividend payment.

But sometimes the monetary flow from ownership of an asset is implicit; it takes the form of an increase or decrease in the price or value of the asset. (An increase in the value of an asset is a *capital gain*, a decrease a *capital loss*.) For example, as the population of a city grows, the value of an apartment building may increase. The owner of the building will then earn a capital gain

---

[12] Most Americans have at least some money invested in stocks or other risky assets, but often the investment is made indirectly. For example, many people who hold full-time jobs have shares in a pension fund, funded in part by their own salary contributions, and in part by contributions made by their employers. Usually these pension funds are invested partly in the stock market.

beyond the rental income he or she receives. Although the capital gain is *un-realized* until the building is sold because no money is actually received until then, there is an implicit monetary flow because the building *could* be sold at any time. The monetary flow from owning General Motors stock is also partly implicit. The price of the stock changes from day to day, and each time it changes, the owner of the stock gains or loses.

A *risky asset* provides a monetary flow that is at least in part random. In other words, the monetary flow is not known with certainty in advance. A share of General Motors stock is an obvious example of a risky asset—one cannot know whether the price of the stock will rise or fall over time, and one cannot even be sure that the company will continue to pay the same (or any) dividend per share. But although people often associate risk with the stock market, most other assets are also risky.

The apartment building is one example of this. One cannot know how much land values will rise or fall, whether the building will be fully rented all the time, or even whether the tenants will pay their rent promptly. Corporate bonds are another example—the corporation that issued the bonds could go bankrupt and fail to pay bond owners their interest and principal. Even long-term U.S. government bonds that mature in 10 or 20 years are risky. Although it is highly unlikely that the federal government will go bankrupt, the rate of inflation could unexpectedly increase and make future interest payments and the eventual repayment of principal worth less in real terms, and thereby reduce the value of the bonds.

In contrast to a risky asset, we call an asset *riskless* (or risk free) if it pays a monetary flow that is known with certainty. Short-term U.S. government bonds—called Treasury bills—are a riskless, or almost riskless, asset. Because these bonds mature in a few months, there is very little risk from an unexpected increase in the rate of inflation. And one can be reasonably confident that the U.S. government will not default on the bond (i.e., refuse to pay back the holder when the bond comes due). Other examples of riskless or almost riskless assets include passbook savings accounts in a bank and short-term certificates of deposit.

Asset Returns

People buy and hold assets because of the monetary flows they provide. To compare assets with each other, it helps to think of this monetary flow relative to the asset's price or value. The *return* on an asset is the total monetary flow it yields as a fraction of its price. For example, a bond worth $1000 today that pays out $100 this year (and every year) has a return of 10 percent.[13] If an apartment building was worth $10 million last year, increased in value to $11 million this year,

---

[13] The price of a bond often changes during a year. If the bond appreciated (depreciated) in value during the year, its return would be greater than (less than) 10 percent. Also, the definition of return given above should not be confused with the "internal rate of return" sometimes used to compare monetary flows occurring over some time. We discuss other return measures in Chapter 15, when we deal with present discounted values.

and also provided a net (of expenses) rental income of $0.5 million, it would have yielded a return of 15 percent over the past year. Or if a share of General Motors stock had been worth $80 at the beginning of the year, fell to $72 by the end of the year, and paid a dividend of $4, it would have yielded a return of −5 percent (the dividend yield of 5 percent less the capital loss of 10 percent).

When people invest their savings in stocks, bonds, land, or other assets, they usually hope to earn a return that exceeds the rate of inflation, so that by delaying consumption, they can buy more in the future than they could by spending all their income now. As a result, we often express the return on an asset in real (inflation-adjusted) terms. The *real return* on an asset is its simple (or nominal) return *less* the rate of inflation. For example, if the annual rate of inflation had been 5 percent, the bond, the apartment building, and the share of GM stock described above would have yielded real returns of 5 percent, 10 percent, and −10 percent, respectively.

Because most assets are risky, an investor cannot know in advance what returns they will yield over the coming year. For example, the apartment building might have depreciated in value instead of appreciating, and the price of GM stock might have risen instead of falling. However, we can still compare assets by looking at their *expected returns*. The expected return on an asset is just the expected value of its return (i.e., the return that it should earn on average). In some years the *actual* return that an asset earns may be much higher than its expected return, and in some years much lower, but over a long period the average return should be close to the expected return.

Different assets have different expected returns. For example, Table 5.8 shows that the expected real return on a U.S. Treasury bill has been less than 1 percent, while the real return for a representative stock on the New York Stock Exchange has been almost 9 percent.[14] Why would anyone buy a Treasury bill when the expected return on stocks is so much higher? The answer is that the demand for an asset depends not just on its expected return, but also on its *risk*. Although stocks have a higher expected return than Treasury bills, they also carry much more risk. One measure of risk, the stan-

Table 5.8 Investments—Risk and Return (1926–1994)		
	Real Rate of Return (%)	Risk (standard deviation, %)
Common stocks (S&P 500)	8.9	20.2
Long-term corporate bonds	2.7	8.3
U.S. Treasury bills	0.6	3.3

---

[14] For some stocks the expected return is higher, and for some it is lower. Stocks of smaller companies (e.g., some of those traded on the NASDAQ) have higher expected rates of return—and higher return standard deviations.

dard deviation of the real return, is equal to 20.2 percent for common stocks, but only 8.3 percent for corporate bonds, and 3.3 percent for U.S. Treasury bills. Clearly, the higher the expected return on the investment, the greater the risk involved. As a result, a risk-averse investor must balance expected return against risk. We examine this trade-off in more detail below.

The Trade-off Between Risk and Return

Suppose a woman wants to invest her savings in two assets—Treasury bills, which are almost risk free, and a representative group of stocks.[15] She has to decide how much of her savings to invest in each of these two assets—she might invest only in Treasury bills, only in stocks, or in some combination of the two. As we will see, this is analogous to the consumer's problem of allocating a budget between purchases of food and clothing.

Denote the risk-free return on the Treasury bill by R_f. Because the return is risk free, the expected and actual returns are the same. Also, let the expected return from investing in the stock market be R_m, and the *actual* return be r_m. The actual return is risky. At the time of the investment decision, we know the set of possible outcomes and the likelihood of each, but we do not know what particular outcome will occur. The risky asset will have a higher expected return than the risk-free asset $(R_m > R_f)$. Otherwise, risk-averse investors would buy only Treasury bills and no stocks would be sold.

To determine how much money the investor should put in each asset, let's set b equal to the fraction of her savings placed in the stock market, and $(1 - b)$ the fraction used to purchase Treasury bills. The expected return on her total portfolio, R_p, is a weighted average of the expected return on the two assets:[16]

$$R_p = bR_m + (1 - b)R_f \tag{5.1}$$

Suppose, for example, that Treasury bills pay 4 percent $(R_f = .04)$, the stock market's expected return is 12 percent $(R_m = .12)$, and $b = 1/2$. Then $R_p = 8$ percent. How risky is this portfolio? One measure of its riskiness is the standard deviation of the portfolio's return. Let's describe the standard deviation of the risky stock market investment by σ_m. With some algebra, we can show that the standard deviation of the portfolio (with one risky and one risk-free asset) is the fraction of the portfolio invested in the risky asset times the standard deviation of that asset:[17]

$$\sigma_p = b\sigma_m \tag{5.2}$$

---

[15] The easiest way to invest in a representative group of stocks is to buy shares in a *mutual fund*. A mutual fund invests in many stocks, so that by buying the fund, one effectively buys a portfolio of many stocks.

[16] The expected value of the sum of two variables is the sum of the expected values, so $R_p = E[br_m] + E[(1 - b)R_f] = bE[r_m] + (1 - b)R_f = bR_m - (1 - b)R_f$.

[17] To see why, note from footnote 4 that we can write the variance of the portfolio return as $\sigma_p^2 = E[br_m + (1 - b)R_f - R_p]^2$. Substituting equation (5.1) for the expected return on the portfolio, R_p, we have
$$\sigma_p^2 = E[br_m + (1 - b)R_f - bR_m - (1 - b)R_f]^2 = E[b(r_m - R_m)]^2 = b\sigma_m^2.$$
The standard deviation of a random variable is the square root of its variance, so $\sigma_p = b\sigma_m$.

The Investor's Choice Problem

We have still not determined how this investor should choose this fraction b. To do this, we must first show that she faces a risk-return trade-off analogous to the budget line of a consumer. To see what this trade-off is, note that equation (5.1) for the expected return on the portfolio can be rewritten as

$$R_p = R_f + b(R_m - R_f)$$

Now, from equation (5.2) we see that $b = \sigma_p/\sigma_m$, so that

$$R_p = R_f + \frac{(R_m - R_f)}{\sigma_m}\, \sigma_p \tag{5.3}$$

This equation is a *budget line* because it describes the trade-off between risk (σ_p) and expected return (R_p). Note that it is the equation for a straight line; R_m, R_f, and σ_m are constants, so the slope $(R_m - R_f)/\sigma_m$ is a constant, as is the intercept R_f. The equation says that *the expected return on the portfolio R_p increases as the standard deviation of that return σ_p increases*. We call the slope of this budget line, $(R_m - R_f)/\sigma_m$, the *price of risk* because it tells us how much extra risk an investor must incur to enjoy a higher expected return.

The budget line is drawn in Figure 5.5. As the figure shows, if the investor wants no risk, she can invest all her funds in Treasury bills ($b = 0$), and earn an expected return R_f. To receive a higher expected return, she must incur some risk. For example, she could invest all her funds in stocks ($b = 1$), and earn an expected return R_m, but incur a standard deviation σ_m. Or she might invest some fraction of her funds in each type of asset, earn an expected return somewhere between R_f and R_m, and face a standard deviation less than σ_m but greater than zero.

Figure 5.5 also shows the solution to the investor's problem. Three indifference curves are drawn in the figure. Each curve describes combinations of risk and return that leave the investor equally satisfied. (The curves are upward-sloping because risk is undesirable, so with a greater amount of risk, it takes a greater expected return to make the investor equally well-off.) The curve U_3 yields the greatest amount of satisfaction, and U_1 the least amount. (For a given amount of risk, the investor earns a higher expected return on U_3 than on U_2, and a higher expected return on U_2 than on U_1.) Of the three indifference curves, the investor would prefer to be on U_3, but this is not feasible because it does not touch the budget line. Curve U_1 is feasible, but the investor can do better. Like the consumer choosing quantities of food and clothing, our investor does best by choosing a combination of risk and return at the point where an indifference curve (in this case U_2) is tangent to the budget line. At that point, the investor's return has an expected value R^* and a standard deviation σ^*.

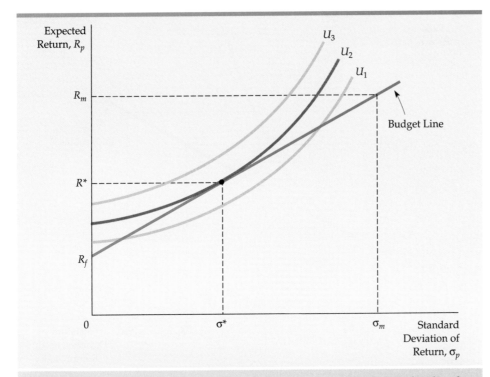

Figure 5.5 **Choosing Between Risk and Return** An investor is dividing her funds between two assets, Treasury bills, which are risk free, and stocks. The budget line describes the trade-off between the expected return and the riskiness of that return, as measured by its standard deviation. The slope of the budget line is $(R_m - R_f)/\sigma_m$, which is the price of risk. Three indifference curves are shown; each curve shows combinations of risk and return that leave an investor equally satisfied. The curves are upward-sloping because a risk-averse investor will require a higher expected return if she is to bear a greater amount of risk. The utility-maximizing investment portfolio is at the point where indifference curve U_2 is tangent to the budget line.

People differ in their attitudes toward risk. This is illustrated in Figure 5.6, which shows how two different investors choose their portfolios. Investor A is very risk averse. His indifference curve U_A is tangent to the budget line at a point of low risk, so he will invest almost all his funds in Treasury bills and earn an expected return R_A just slightly larger than the risk-free return R_f. Investor B is less risk averse. She will invest most of her funds in stocks, and the return on her portfolio will have a higher expected value R_B but also a higher standard deviation σ_B.

In Chapters 3 and 4, we simplified the problem of consumer choice by assuming the consumer had only two goods to choose from, food and clothing. In the same spirit, we have simplified the investor's choice between only

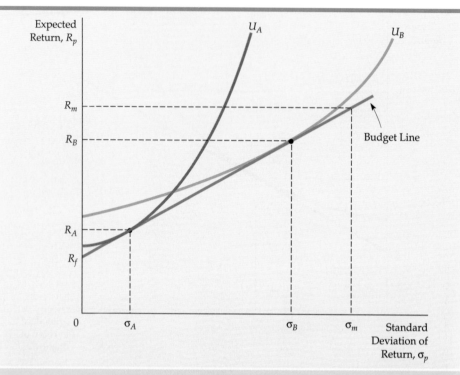

Figure 5.6   The Choices of Two Different Investors   Investor *A* is very risk averse. His portfolio will consist mostly of the risk-free asset, so his expected return R_A will be only slightly greater than the risk-free return, but the risk σ_A will be small. Investor *B* is less risk averse. She will invest a large fraction of her funds in stocks. The expected return on her portfolio R_B will be larger, but the return will also be riskier.

Treasury bills and stocks. However, the basic principles would be the same if we had more assets (e.g., corporate bonds, land, and different types of stocks). Every investor faces a trade-off between risk and return.[18] How much extra risk an investor is willing to bear to earn a higher expected return depends on how risk averse that investor is. Less risk-averse investors tend to include a larger fraction of risky assets in their portfolios.

---

[18] Although we have not discussed this point, what matters is "systematic" or nondiversifiable risk, since investors can eliminate "nonsystematic" risk by holding a well-diversified portfolio (e.g., via a mutual fund). We discuss systematic versus nonsystematic risk in Chapter 15. For a more detailed treatment, see a standard text on finance. A good one is Richard Brealey and Stewart Myers, *Principles of Corporate Finance*, 5th ed. (New York: McGraw-Hill, 1996).

Summary

1. Consumers and managers frequently make decisions in which there is uncertainty about the future. This uncertainty is characterized by the term risk, when each of the possible outcomes and its probability of occurrence is known.

2. Consumers and investors are concerned about the expected value and the variability of uncertain outcomes. The expected value is a measure of the central tendency of the value of the risky outcomes. The variability is frequently measured by the standard deviation of outcomes, which is the square root of the average of the squares of the deviations of each possible outcome from its expected value.

3. Facing uncertain choices, consumers maximize their expected utility, an average of the utility associated with each outcome, with the associated probabilities serving as weights.

4. A person who would prefer a certain return of a given amount to a risky investment whose expected return is the same amount is risk averse. The maximum amount of money that a risk-averse person would pay to avoid taking a risk is the risk premium.

5. A person who is indifferent between a risky investment and the certain receipt of the expected return on that investment is risk neutral.

6. A risk-loving consumer would prefer a risky investment with a given expected return to the certain receipt of that expected sum.

7. Risk can be reduced by (a) diversification, (b) purchasing insurance, and (c) obtaining additional information.

8. The *law of large numbers* enables insurance companies to provide actuarially fair insurance for which the premium paid equals the expected value of the loss being insured against.

9. Consumer theory can be applied to decisions to invest in risky assets. The budget line reflects the price of risk, and consumers' indifference curves reflect their attitudes toward risk.

Questions for Review

1. What does it mean to say that a person is risk averse? Why are some people likely to be risk averse, while others are risk lovers?

2. Why is the variance a better measure of variability than the range?

3. What does it mean for consumers to maximize expected utility? Can you think of a case where a person might not maximize expected utility?

4. Why do people want to fully insure against uncertain situations when insurance is actuarially fair?

5. Why is an insurance company likely to behave *as if* it is risk neutral even if its managers are risk-averse individuals? (*Hint*: How many projects are insured by an entire insurance company? How many does each individual manager deal with?)

6. When is it worth paying to obtain more information to reduce uncertainty?

7. How does the diversification of an investor's portfolio avoid risk?

8. Why do some investors put a large portion of their portfolios into risky assets, while others invest largely in risk-free alternatives? (*Hint*: Do the two investors receive exactly the same return on average? Why?)

Exercises

1. Consider a lottery with three possible outcomes: $100 will be received with probability .1, $50 with probability .2, and $10 with probability .7.
   a. What is the expected value of the lottery?
   b. What is the variance of the outcomes of the lottery?
   c. What would a risk-neutral person pay to play the lottery?

2. Suppose you have invested in a new computer company whose profitability depends on (1) whether the U.S. Congress passes a tariff that raises the cost of Japanese computers, and (2) whether the U.S. economy grows slowly or quickly. What are the four mutually exclusive states of the world that you should be concerned about?

3. Richard is deciding whether to buy a state lottery ticket. Each ticket costs $1, and the probability of winning payoffs is given as follows:

Probability	Return
.5	$0.00
.25	$1.00
.2	$2.00
.05	$7.50

   a. What is the expected value of Richard's payoff if he buys a lottery ticket? What is the variance?
   b. Richard's nickname is "No-risk Rick." He is an extremely risk-averse individual. Would he buy the ticket?
   c. Suppose Richard was offered insurance against losing any money. If he buys 1,000 lottery tickets, how much would he be willing to pay to insure his gamble?
   d. In the long run, given the price of the lottery ticket and the probability/return table, what do you think the state would do about the lottery?

4. Suppose an investor is concerned about a business choice in which there are three prospects, whose probability and returns are given below:

Probability	Return
0.2	$100
0.4	50
0.4	−25

   What is the expected value of the uncertain investment? What is the variance?

5. You are an insurance agent who has to write a policy for a new client named Sam. His company, Society for Creative Alternatives to Mayonnaise (SCAM), is working on a low-fat, low-cholesterol mayonnaise substitute for the sandwich condiment industry. The sandwich industry will pay top dollar to whoever invents such a mayonnaise substitute first. Sam's SCAM seems like a very risky proposition to you. You have calculated his possible returns table as follows:

Probability	Return	
.999	−$1,000,000	(he fails)
.001	$1,000,000,000	(he succeeds and sells the formula)

   a. What is the expected return of his project? What is the variance?
   b. What is the most Sam is willing to pay for insurance? Assume Sam is risk neutral.
   c. Suppose you found out that the Japanese are on the verge of introducing their own mayonnaise substitute next month. Sam does not know this and has just turned down your final offer of $1000 for the insurance. If Sam tells you his SCAM is only six months away from perfecting his mayonnaise substitute *and* knowing what you know about the Japanese, would you raise

or lower your policy premium on any subsequent proposal to Sam? Based on his information, would Sam accept?

6. Suppose that Natasha's utility function is given by $u(I) = y^5$, where I represents annual income in thousands of dollars.
   a. Is Natasha risk loving, risk neutral, or risk averse? Explain.
   b. Suppose that Natasha is currently earning an income of $10,000 ($I = 10$) and can earn that income next year with certainty. She is offered a chance to take a new job that offers a .5 probability of earning $16,000, and a .5 probability of earning $5000. Should she take the new job?
   c. In (b), would Natasha be willing to buy insurance to protect against the variable income associated with the new job? If so, how much would she be willing to pay for that insurance? (*Hint*: What is the risk premium?)

7. Draw a utility function over income $u(I)$ that has the property that a man is a risk lover when his income is low but a risk averter when his income is high. Can you explain why such a utility function might reasonably describe a person's tastes?

8. A city is considering how much to spend monitoring parking meters. The following information is available to the city manager:
   i. Hiring each meter-monitor costs $10,000 per year.
   ii. With one monitoring person hired, the probability of a driver getting a ticket each time he or she parks illegally is equal to .25.
   iii. With two monitors hired, the probability of getting a ticket is .5, with three monitors the probability is .75, and with four the probability is equal to 1.
   iv. The current fine for overtime parking with two metering persons hired is $20.
   a. Assume first that all drivers are risk neutral. What parking fine would you levy and how many meter monitors would you hire (1, 2, 3, or 4) to achieve the current level of deterrence against illegal parking at the minimum cost?
   b. Now assume that drivers are very risk averse. How would your answer to (a) change?
   c. (For discussion) What if drivers could insure themselves against the risk of parking fines? Would it make good public policy to allow such insurance to be available?

CHAPTER 6

Production

In the last three chapters, we focused on the demand side of the market—the preferences and behavior of consumers. Now we turn to the supply side and examine the behavior of producers. We will see how firms can organize their production efficiently and how their costs of production change as input prices and the level of output change. We will also see that there are strong similarities between the optimizing decisions of firms and those of consumers—understanding consumer behavior will help us understand producer behavior.

The theory of production and cost is central to the economic management of the firm. Just consider some of the problems that a company like General Motors faces regularly. How much assembly-line machinery and how much labor should it use in its new automobile plants? If it wants to increase production, should it hire more workers, or should it also construct new plants? Does it make more sense for one automobile plant to produce different models, or should each model be manufactured in a separate plant? What should GM expect its costs to be during the coming year, and how are these costs likely to change over time and be affected by the level of production? These questions apply not only to business firms, but also to other producers of goods and services, such as governments and nonprofit agencies.

In this chapter we study the firm's production technology—the physical relationship that describes how inputs (such as labor and capital) are transformed into outputs (such as cars and televisions). We do this in several steps. First, we show how the production technology can be represented in the form of a production function—a compact description that facilitates the analysis. Then, we use the production function to show how the firm's output changes when first one and then all the inputs are varied. We will be particularly concerned with the scale of the firm's operation. Are there technological advantages that make the firm more productive as its scale increases?

6.1 The Technology of Production

In the production process, firms turn *inputs*, which are also called *factors of production*, into *outputs* (or products). For example, a bakery uses inputs that include the labor of its workers; raw materials, such as flour and sugar; and the capital invested in its ovens, mixers, and other equipment to produce such outputs as bread, cakes, and pastries.

We can divide inputs into the broad categories of labor, materials, and capital, each of which might include more narrow subdivisions. Labor inputs include skilled workers (carpenters, engineers) and unskilled workers (agricultural workers), as well as the entrepreneurial efforts of the firm's managers. Materials include steel, plastics, electricity, water, and any other goods that the firm buys and transforms into a final product. Capital includes buildings, equipment, and inventories.

The relationship between the inputs to the production process and the resulting output is described by a production function. A *production function* indicates the output Q that a firm produces for every specified combination of inputs. For simplicity, we will assume that there are two inputs, labor L and capital K. We can then write the production function as

$$Q = F(K, L) \tag{6.1}$$

This equation relates the quantity of output to the quantities of the two inputs, capital and labor. For example, the production function might describe the number of personal computers that can be produced each year with a 10,000-square-foot plant and a specific amount of assembly-line labor employed during the year. Or it might describe the crop that a farmer can obtain with a specific amount of machinery and workers.

The production function allows for inputs to be combined in varying proportions to produce an output in many ways. For example, wine can be produced in a labor-intensive way by people stomping the grapes, or in a capital-intensive way by machines squashing the grapes. Note that equation (6.1) applies to a *given technology* (i.e., a given state of knowledge about the various methods that might be used to transform inputs into outputs). As the technology becomes more advanced and the production function changes, a firm can obtain more output for a given set of inputs. For example, a new, faster computer chip may allow a hardware manufacturer to produce more high-speed computers in a given period of time.

Production functions describe what is *technically feasible* when the firm operates *efficiently*; that is, when the firm uses each combination of inputs as effectively as possible. Because production functions describe the maximum output feasible for a given set of inputs in a *technically efficient* manner, it follows that inputs will not be used if they decrease output. The presumption that production is always technically efficient need not always hold, but it is reasonable to expect that profit-seeking firms will not waste resources.

6.2 Isoquants

Let's begin by examining the firm's production technology when it uses two inputs and can vary both of them. Suppose, for example, that the inputs are labor and capital, and that they are used to produce food. Table 6.1 tabulates the output achievable for various combinations of inputs.

Labor inputs are listed across the top row, capital inputs down the column on the left. Each entry in the table is the maximum (technically efficient) output that can be produced per time period (say, a year) with each combination of labor and capital used over that time period. (For example, 4 units of labor per year and 2 units of capital per year yield 85 units of food per year.) Reading along each row, we see that output increases as labor inputs are increased, with capital inputs fixed. Reading down each column, we see that output also increases as capital inputs are increased, with labor inputs fixed.

The information contained in Table 6.1 can also be represented graphically using isoquants. *An isoquant is a curve that shows all the possible combinations of inputs that yield the same output.* Figure 6.1 shows three isoquants. (Each axis in the figure measures the quantity of inputs.) These isoquants are based on the data in Table 6.1, but have been drawn as smooth curves to allow for the use of fractional amounts of inputs.

Table 6.1 Production with Two Variable Inputs					
	Labor Input				
Capital Input	**1**	**2**	**3**	**4**	**5**
1	20	40	55	65	(75)
2	40	60	(75)	85	90
3	55	(75)	90	100	105
4	65	85	100	110	115
5	(75)	90	105	115	120

Figure 6.1 Production with Two Variable Inputs Production isoquants show the various combinations of inputs necessary for the firm to produce a given output. A set of isoquants, or isoquant map, describes the firm's production function. Output increases as we move from isoquant Q_1, (at which 55 units per year are produced at points such as A and D) to isoquant Q_2 (75 units per year at points such as B) and to isoquant Q_3 (90 units per year at points such as C and E).

For example, isoquant Q_1 shows all combinations of labor per year and capital per year that together yield 55 units of output per year. Two of these points, A and D, correspond to Table 6.1. At A, 1 unit of labor and 3 units of capital yield 55 units of output; whereas at D, the same output is produced from 3 units of labor and 1 unit of capital. Isoquant Q_2 shows all combinations of inputs that yield 75 units of output and corresponds to the four combinations of labor and capital circled in the table (e.g., at B, where 2 units of capital and 3 units of labor are combined). Isoquant Q_2 lies above and to the right of Q_1 because it takes more labor and/or capital to obtain a higher level of output. Finally, isoquant Q_3 shows labor-capital combinations that yield 90 units of output. Point C involves 3 units of labor and 3 units of capital, whereas Point E involves 2 units of labor and 5 units of capital. Note that inputs and output are *flows*. The firm uses certain amounts of labor and capital *each year* to produce an amount of output over that year. To simplify, we will frequently ignore the reference to time, and just refer to amounts of labor, capital, and output.

Isoquants are similar to the indifference curves that we used to study consumer theory. Where indifference curves order levels of satisfaction from low to high, isoquants order levels of output. However, unlike indifference curves, each isoquant is associated with a *specific level of output*. By contrast, the numerical labels attached to indifference curves are meaningful only in an ordinal way—higher levels of utility are associated with higher indifference curves, but we cannot measure a specific level of utility the way we can measure a specific level of output with an isoquant.

An *isoquant map* is a set of isoquants, each of which shows the maximum output that can be achieved for any set of inputs. An isoquant map is another way of describing a production function, just as an indifference map is a way of describing a utility function. Each isoquant corresponds to a different level of output, and the level of output increases as we move up and to the right in the figure.

Isoquants show the flexibility that firms have when making production decisions—firms can usually obtain a particular output using various combinations of inputs. It is important for the managers of a firm to understand the nature of this flexibility. For example, fast-food restaurants have recently faced shortages of young, low-wage employees. The companies have responded by automating—adding self-service salad bars and introducing more sophisticated cooking equipment. They have also recruited older people to fill these positions. As we discuss in Chapters 7 and 8, by taking this flexibility in the production process into account, managers can choose input combinations that minimize cost and maximize profit.

The Short Run Versus the Long Run

It is important to distinguish between the short and long run when analyzing production. The *short run* refers to a period of time in which one or more factors of production cannot be changed. Factors that cannot be varied over this period are called *fixed inputs*. A firm's capital, for example, usually requires time to change—a new factory must be planned and built, machinery and other equipment must be ordered and delivered, all of which can take a year or more. The *long run* is the amount of time needed to make all inputs variable. In the short run, firms vary the intensity with which they utilize a given plant and machinery; in the long run, they vary the size of the plant. All fixed inputs in the short run represent the outcomes of previous long-run decisions based on firms' estimates of what they could profitably produce and sell.

There is no specific time period, such as one year, that separates the short run from the long run. Rather, one must distinguish them on a case-by-case basis. For example, the long run can be as brief as a day or two for a child's lemonade stand, or as long as five or ten years for a petrochemical producer or an automobile manufacturer.

6.3 Production with One Variable Input (Labor)

Let's consider the case in which capital is fixed, but labor is variable, so that the firm can produce more output by increasing its labor input. Imagine, for example, that you are managing a clothing plant. You have a fixed amount of

Table 6.2   Production with One Variable Input

Amount of Labor (L)	Amount of Capital (K)	Total Output (Q)	Average Product (Q/L)	Marginal Product (ΔQ/ΔL)
0	10	0	—	—
1	10	10	10	10
2	10	30	15	20
3	10	60	20	30
4	10	80	20	20
5	10	95	19	15
6	10	108	18	13
7	10	112	16	4
8	10	112	14	0
9	10	108	12	−4
10	10	100	10	−8

equipment, but you can hire more labor or less to sew and to run the machines. You have to decide how much labor to hire and how much clothing to produce. To make the decision, you will need to know how the amount of output Q increases (if at all), as the input of labor L increases.

Table 6.2 gives this information. The first three columns show the amount of output that can be produced in one month with different amounts of labor, and with capital fixed at 10 units. (The first column shows the amount of labor, the second the fixed amount of capital, and the third total output.) When labor input is zero, output is also zero. Then output increases as labor is increased up to an input of 8 units. Beyond that point, total output declines: While initially each unit of labor can take greater and greater advantage of the existing machinery and plant, after a certain point, additional labor is no longer useful and indeed can be counterproductive. (Five people can run an assembly line better than two, but ten people may get in each other's way.)

Average and Marginal Products

The contribution that labor makes to the production process can be described in terms of the average and marginal products of labor. The fourth column in Table 6.2 shows the *average product of labor* AP_L, which is the output per unit of labor input. The average product is calculated by dividing the total output Q by the total input of labor, L. In our example the average product increases initially but falls when the labor input becomes greater than 4. The fifth column shows the *marginal product of labor* MP_L. This is the *additional* output produced as the labor input is increased by 1 unit. For example, with capital fixed at 10 units, when the labor input increases from 2 to 3, total output increases from 30 to 60, creating an additional output of 30 (60 − 30) units. The marginal product of labor can be written as $\Delta Q/\Delta L$ (i.e., the change in output ΔQ resulting from a 1-unit increase in labor input ΔL).

Remember that the marginal product of labor depends on the amount of capital used. If the capital input increased from 10 to 20, for example, the marginal product of labor would most likely increase. The reason is that additional workers are likely to be more productive if they have more capital to use. Like the average product, the marginal product first increases then falls, in this case after the third unit of labor.

To summarize:

> Average product of labor = Output/labor input = Q/L
>
> Marginal product of labor = Change in output/change in labor input = $\Delta Q/\Delta L$

Figure 6.2 plots the information contained in Table 6.2. (We have connected all the points in the figure with solid lines.) Figure 6.2(a) shows that output increases until it reaches the maximum output of 112; thereafter it diminishes. That portion of the total output is dashed to denote that production past an output of 8 is not technically efficient and therefore is not part of the production function; technical efficiency rules out negative marginal products. Figure 6.2(b) shows the average and marginal product curves. (The units of the vertical axis have changed from output to output per unit of labor.) Note that the marginal product is always positive when output is increasing, and it is negative when output is decreasing.

It is no coincidence that the marginal product curve crosses the horizontal axis of the graph at the point of maximum total product. This happens because adding a worker to a production line in a manner that slows up the line and decreases total output implies a negative marginal product for that worker.

The average product and marginal product curves are closely related. *When the marginal product is greater than the average product, the average product is increasing,* as shown between outputs 1 and 4 in Figure 6.2(b). For example, suppose that the only employee of an advertising firm can write 10 advertisements per day, so that initially 10 is the average product of labor. Now, a more productive employee is hired who can produce 20 ads per day. The marginal product of labor, 20 ads, is greater than the average, 10. And because both workers combine to produce 30 ads in two days of labor, the new average product has increased to 15 ads.

Similarly, *when the marginal product is less than the average product, the average product is decreasing,* as shown between outputs 4 and 10 in Figure 6.2(b). In our previous example, had the first worker been the more productive of the two, the marginal product of the first worker would have been 20 ads and the marginal product of the second worker 10 ads. Since the marginal prod-

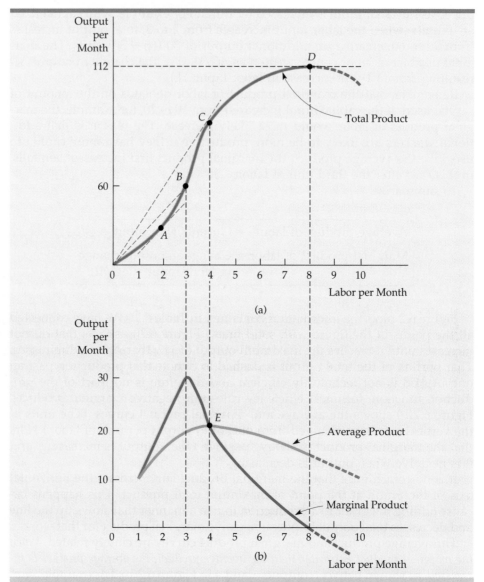

Figure 6.2 **Production with One Variable Input** When all inputs other than labor are fixed, the total product curve in (a) shows the output produced for different amounts of labor input. The average and marginal products in (b) are obtained directly from the total product curve. At point A, the marginal product is 20 because the tangent to the total product curve has a slope of 20. At point B in (a) the average product of labor is 20, which is the slope of the line from the origin to B. The average product of labor at point C in (a) is given by the slope of the line $0C$. To the left of point E in (b) the marginal product is above the average product and the average is increasing, while to the right of E the marginal product is below the average and the average is decreasing. As a result, E represents the point at which the average and marginal products are equal and the average product reaches its maximum.

uct (10 ads) would then be less than the average product (20 ads), the new average product would have fallen to 15 ads.

Because the marginal product is above the average product when the average product is increasing, and below the average product when the average product is decreasing, it follows that the marginal product must equal the average product when the average product reaches its maximum. This happens at point *E* in Figure 6.2(b).

The geometric relationship between the total product and the average and marginal product curves is shown in Figure 6.2(a). The average product of labor is the total product divided by the quantity of labor input. For example, at *B* the average product is equal to the output of 60 divided by the input of 3, or 20 units of output per unit of labor input. But this is just the slope of the line running from the origin to *B* in Figure 6.2(a). In general, *the average product of labor is given by the slope of the line drawn from the origin to the corresponding point on the total product curve.*

The marginal product of labor is the change in the total product resulting from an increase of one unit of labor. For example, at *A* the marginal product is 20 because the tangent to the total product curve has a slope of 20. In general, *the marginal product of labor at a point is given by the slope of the total product at that point.* We can see in Figure 6.2(a) that the marginal product of labor increases initially, peaks at an input of 3, and then declines as we move up the total product curve to *C* and *D*. At *D*, when total output is maximized, the slope of the tangent to the total product curve is 0, as is the marginal product. Beyond that point, the marginal product becomes negative.

Note the graphical relationship between average and marginal products. At *B*, the marginal product of labor (the slope of the tangent to the total product curve at *B*—not shown explicitly) is greater than the average product (dashed line 0*B*). As a result, the average product of labor increases as we move from *B* to *C*. At *C*, the average and marginal products of labor are equal—the average product is the slope of the line from the origin 0*C*, while the marginal product is the tangent to the total product curve at *C* (note the equality of the average and marginal products at point *E* in Figure 6.2b). Finally, as we move beyond *C* toward *D*, the average marginal product falls below the average product; you can check that the slope of the tangent to the total product curve at any point between *C* and *D* is lower than the slope of the line from the origin.

The Law of Diminishing Returns

A diminishing marginal product of labor (and a diminishing marginal product of other inputs) holds for most production processes; the phrase "the law of diminishing returns" is often used to describe this phenomenon. The *law of diminishing returns* states that as the use of an input increases (with other inputs fixed), a point will eventually be reached at which the resulting additions to output decrease. When the labor input is small (and capital is fixed), small increments in labor input add substantially to output as workers are allowed to develop specialized tasks. Eventually, however, the law of diminishing returns applies. When there are too many workers, some workers become ineffective, and the marginal product of labor falls.

The law of diminishing returns usually applies to the short run where at least one input is fixed. However, it can also apply to the long run. Even though inputs are generally variable in the long run, a manager may still want to analyze production choices for which one or more inputs are unchanged. Suppose, for example, that only two plant sizes are feasible, and a manager must decide which to build. Then, the manager would want to know when diminishing returns will set in for each of the two options.

Do not confuse the law of diminishing returns with possible changes in the *quality* of labor as labor inputs are increased (as, for example, if the most highly qualified laborers are hired first, and the least qualified last). In our analysis of production, we have assumed that all labor inputs are of equal quality; diminishing returns result from limitations on the use of other fixed inputs (e.g., machinery), not from declines in worker quality. Also, do not confuse diminishing returns with negative returns. The law of diminishing returns describes a *declining* marginal product but not necessarily a negative one.

The law of diminishing returns applies to a given production technology. Over time, however, inventions and other improvements in technology may allow the entire total product curve in Figure 6.2(a) to shift upward, so that

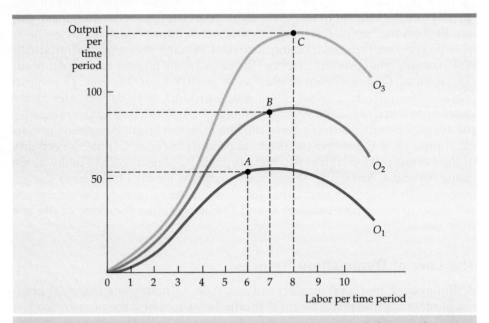

Figure 6.3 **The Effect of Technological Improvement** Labor productivity (output per unit of labor) can increase if there are improvements in the technology, even though any given production process exhibits diminishing returns to labor. As we move from point *A* on curve O_1 to *B* on curve O_2 to *C* on curve O_3 over time, labor productivity increases.

more output can be produced with the same inputs. Figure 6.3 illustrates this. Initially the output curve is given by O_1, but improvements in technology may allow the curve to shift upward, first to O_2, and later to O_3.

Suppose that over time as labor is increased in production, technological improvements are also being made. Then, output changes from A (with an input of 6 on curve O_1) to B (with an input of 7 on curve O_2) to C (with an input of 8 on curve O_3). The move from A to B to C relates an increase in labor input to an increase in output and makes it appear that there are no diminishing returns when there are. For inputs greater than 6, each of the individual product curves exhibits diminishing returns to labor.

The shifting of the total product curve hides the presence of diminishing returns and suggests that they need not have any negative long-run implications for economic growth. In fact, as we discuss in Example 6.1, the failure to account for improvements in technology in the long run led British economist Thomas Malthus wrongly to predict dire consequences from continued population growth.

EXAMPLE 6.1 **Malthus and the Food Crisis**

The law of diminishing returns was central to the thinking of economist Thomas Malthus (1766–1834).[1] Malthus believed that the limited amount of land on our globe would not be able to supply enough food as population grew and more laborers began to farm the land. Eventually as both the marginal and average productivity of labor fell and there were more mouths to feed, mass hunger and starvation would result. Fortunately, Malthus was wrong (although he was right about the diminishing returns to labor).

Table 6.3 Index of World Food Consumption Per Capita[2]	
Year	**Index**
1948–1952	100
1960	115
1970	123
1980	128
1990	137
1995	135

---

[1] Thomas Malthus, *Essay on the Principle of Population*, 1798.

[2] All but the data for 1990 and 1995 appear as Table 4.1 in Julian Simon, *The Ultimate Resource* (Princeton: Princeton University Press, 1981). The original source for all the data is the UN Food and Agriculture Organization, *Production Yearbook*, and *World Agricultural Situation*.

Over the past century, technological improvements have dramatically altered the production of food in most countries (including developing countries, such as India), so that the average product of labor has increased. These improvements include new high-yielding and disease-resistant strains of seeds, better fertilizers, and better harvesting equipment. As Table 6.3 shows, overall food consumption throughout the world has outpaced population growth more or less continually since the end of World War II. This increase in world agricultural productivity is also illustrated in Figure 6.4, which shows average cereal yields from 1970 through 1995, along with a world price index for food.[3] Note that cereal yields have increased steadily over the 25-year period. Growth in agricultural productivity led to increases in food supplies that outstripped the growth in demand, so that apart from a temporary increase in the early 1970s, prices have been declining.

Some of the increase in food production has been due to small increases in the amount of land devoted to farming. For example, from 1961 to 1975, the percentage of land devoted to agriculture increased from 32.9 percent to 33.3 percent in Africa, from 19.6 percent to 22.4 percent in Latin America, and from 21.9 percent to 22.6 percent in the Far East.[4] However, during the same period the percentage of land devoted to agriculture fell from 26.1 percent to

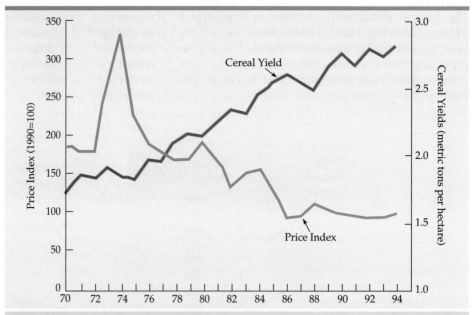

Figure 6.4   Cereal Yields and World Price of Food   Cereal yields have increased steadily. The average world price of food increased temporarily in the early 1970s, but has declined since.

---

[3] Data are from the UN Food and Agriculture Organization and the World Bank.

[4] See Julian Simon, *The Ultimate Resource* (Princeton: Princeton University Press, 1981) 83.

25.5 percent in North America, and from 46.3 percent to 43.7 percent in Western Europe. Clearly most of the improvement in food output is due to improved technology, not to increases in land used for agriculture.

Hunger remains a severe problem in some areas, such as the Sahel region of Africa, in part because of the low productivity of labor there. Although other countries produce an agricultural surplus, mass hunger still occurs because of the difficulty of redistributing foods from more to less productive regions of the world, and because of the low incomes of those less productive regions.

Labor Productivity

We sometimes measure the average product of labor for an industry or for the economy as a whole; then we refer to the results as *labor productivity*. Because the average product measures output per unit of labor input, it is relatively easy to measure (because total labor input and total output are the only pieces of information you need), and can provide useful comparisons across industries and for one industry over a long period. But productivity is especially important because it determines the real standard of living that a country can achieve for its citizens.

There is a simple link between productivity and the standard of living. In any particular year, the aggregate value of goods and services produced by an economy is equal to the payments made to all factors of production, including wages, rental payments to capital, and profit to firms. But consumers ultimately receive these factor payments, whatever their form. As a result, consumers in the aggregate can increase their rate of consumption in the long run only by increasing the total amount they produce.

As Table 6.4 shows, the level of output per person in the United States in 1995 was higher than in other leading developed nations. But two patterns over the post-World War II period have been disturbing for Americans. First, productivity in the United States has grown less rapidly than productivity in most other developed nations. Second, productivity growth in the past two decades has been much lower in all developed coutries than it had been in the past. Both of these patterns can be seen in the table and in Figure 6.5. The figure shows productivity, measured in 1991 U.S. dollars per worker, for the United States and for other countries. Observe that in 1960 productivity in the United States was more than three times as large as productivity in Japan and about twice as large as productivity in Germany, France, and the United Kingdom. However, by 1995 the differences had narrowed considerably.

Throughout most of the 1960–1995 period, Japan has enjoyed the highest rate of productivity growth, followed by Germany and France. United States productivity growth has been the lowest, even lower than that of the United Kingdom. How can this slowdown in growth be explained? And why has productivity growth in the United States been lower than elsewhere? The most important source of growth in labor productivity is the growth in the *stock of capital*. An increase in capital means more and better machinery, so

Table 6.4	Labor Productivity in Developed Countries[5]				
	France	West Germany	Japan	United Kingdom	United States
	Output per Person (1995)				
	$21,529	$22,373	$21,269	$19,925	$26,183
Years	**Annual Rate of Growth of Labor Productivity (%)**				
1960–1973	4.72	4.06	8.20	2.87	1.93
1974–1986	2.09	1.86	2.73	1.80	0.35
1987–1995	1.85	1.60	1.77	1.41	1.01

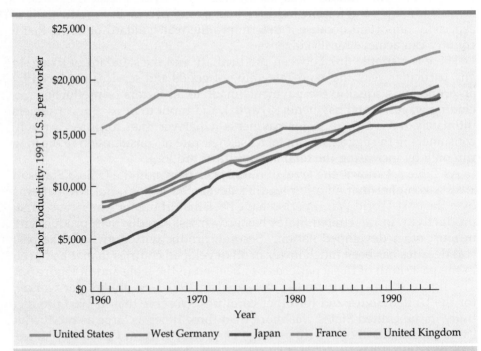

Figure 6.5   Labor Productivity in Five Countries   During the 1960s and 1970s, productivity growth in the United States was lower than in Germany, France, the United Kingdom, and Japan, although the *level* of productivity was higher. In the 1980s and 1990s, productivity growth slowed in all of these countries.

---

[5] See Angus Maddison, "Growth and Slowdown in Advanced Capitalist Countries," *Journal of Economic Literature* 25 (1987): 649–698. The more recent growth numbers are based on data from *Industrial Policy in OECD Countries, Annual Review*.

that each worker can produce more output for each hour worked. Differences in the rate of growth of capital help to explain much of the data in Table 6.4. The greatest capital growth during the postwar period was in Japan and France, which were rebuilt substantially after World War II. To some extent, therefore, the lower rate of growth of productivity in the United States as compared with Japan, France, and West Germany is the result of these countries catching up after the war.

Productivity growth is also tied to the natural resource sector of the economy. As oil and other resources began to be depleted, output per worker fell somewhat. Environmental regulations (e.g., the need to restore land to its original condition after strip mining for coal) magnified this effect as the public became more concerned with the importance of cleaner air and water.

These factors explain part, but not all, of productivity growth over time and across different countries. A full understanding of these differences remains an important research problem in economics.

| EXAMPLE 6.2 | Will the Standard of Living in the United States Improve? |

Will the standard of living in the United States continue to improve, or will the economy barely keep future generations from being worse off than we are today? The answer depends on the labor productivity of U.S. workers, because the real incomes of U.S. consumers increase only as fast as productivity does.

As we saw in Table 6.4, from 1974 to 1986, productivity growth in the United States was 0.35 percent, the lowest of all major developed countries. U.S. productivity growth increased only slightly, to about 1 percent per year, during 1987–1995 but remained well below its pre-1974 rates. What does this mean for the average U.S. worker? In a competitive international economy, this slow growth will eventually lead to lower increases in workers' wages; otherwise, higher wages would have to be matched by higher prices. But these higher prices would not be competitive in today's world economy. Workers will thus have to absorb most of the impact of low productivity growth.

We have seen how slow growth of capital investment can lead to low labor productivity growth. But the decline in productivity growth in the United States has other causes particular to this country. For example, during 1945–1965, many workers left farms for manufacturing. Agriculture has lower productivity than manufacturing, so the shift created productivity growth. (The ratio of agricultural to industrial productivity was about 0.40 in 1948 and has not changed much since.) By 1965 few people were left on the farms who could move to manufacturing, so this source of growth was exhausted.[6]

---

[6] See the discussion in Lester Thurow, "The Productivity Problem," *Technology Review* (1980): 40–51; and Martin N. Baily, "What Has Happened to Productivity Growth?" *Science* (Oct. 1986): 443–451.

Table 6.5 U.S. Productivity Growth in Key Sectors

	Mining	Construction	Durable Goods Manufacturing	Nondurables Manufacturing	Services
Average Rate of Productivity Growth (percent per year)					
1967–1970	3.14	−1.17	0.62	2.85	0.21
1971–1974	−2.93	−0.45	3.21	4.12	0.02
1975–1978	−2.93	−0.45	3.21	4.12	−0.26
1979–1982	−6.16	−4.81	2.21	1.23	0.07
1983–1986	6.99	4.21	5.80	3.47	0.31
1987–1990	2.47	−2.84	3.47	1.67	0.12
1991–1994	3.54	1.49	5.30	3.32	0.05

Much of the decline in productivity growth can be traced to several key industries. Table 6.5 shows U.S. productivity growth in five key sectors: mining, construction, durable goods manufacturing, nondurables manufacturing, and services. Observe that productivity growth in mining fell sharply after 1970; this was the result of stringent environmental and safety regulations that went into effect at that time. The productivity of the U.S. construction sector also declined substantially. There is no consensus about the source of this decline—it may be due in part to problems with nuclear reactor construction and in part to problems with the interstate highway system. Whatever the cause, it contributed to the overall slowdown in U.S. productivity growth. And although productivity growth in durables manufacturing was strong, this sector represented a small and shrinking share of the overall economy.

The movement of workers into the service sector of the economy has also dampened productivity growth in the United States, since productivity in the service sector is approximately 60 percent of the national average. By the early 1990s, for example, over 35 percent of all hours of work were spent on service industry jobs, with a substantial portion of these hours devoted to nursing and health care and to lawyers and accountants. As Table 6.5 shows, the rate of productivity growth in services has always been low.

Overall, this suggests that at least part of the slowdown in productivity growth was inevitable. Because the sources of low productivity growth are varied and complex, the standard of living cannot be increased simply by reversing what has happened in the past. But the future need not be bleak. Capital investment can be increased by tax policies that stimulate investment, and greater and more creative efforts can be made to encourage productivity-enhancing research and development.

6.4 Production with Two Variable Inputs

Now that we have seen the relationship between production and productivity, let's consider the firm's production technology in the long run, where both capital and labor inputs (instead of just labor) are variable. We can examine alternative ways of producing by looking at the shape of a series of isoquants.

Recall that an isoquant describes all combinations of inputs that yield the same level of output. The isoquants shown in Figure 6.6 are reproduced from Figure 6.1; they all slope downward because both labor and capital have positive marginal products. More of either input increases output; so if output is to be kept constant as more of one input is used, less of the other input must be used.

Diminishing Returns

In Figure 6.6, there are diminishing returns to both labor and capital. We can see why there are diminishing returns to labor by drawing a horizontal line at a particular level of capital, say 3. Reading the levels of output from each isoquant as labor is increased, we note that each additional unit of labor generates less and less additional output. For example, when labor is increased

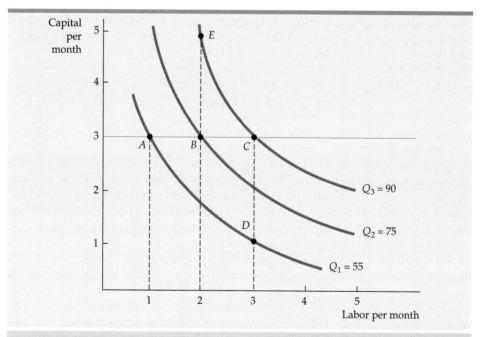

Figure 6.6 The Shape of Isoquants In the long run when both labor and capital are variable, both factors of production can exhibit diminishing returns. As we move from *A* to *C*, there are diminishing returns to labor, and as we move from *D* to *C*, there are diminishing returns to capital.

from 1 unit to 2 (from A to B), output increases by 20 (from 55 to 75). However, when labor is increased by an additional unit (from B to C), output increases by only 15 (from 75 to 90). Thus there are diminishing returns to labor both in the long and short run. Because adding one factor while holding the other factor constant eventually leads to lower and lower increments to output, the isoquant must become steeper, as more capital is added in place of labor, and flatter when labor is added in place of capital.

There are also diminishing returns to capital. With labor fixed, the marginal product of capital decreases as capital is increased. For example, when capital is increased from 1 to 2 and labor is held constant at 3, the marginal product of capital is initially 20 (75 − 55), but the marginal product falls to 15 (90 − 75) when capital is increased from 2 to 3.

Substitution Among Inputs

With two inputs that can be varied, a manager will want to consider substituting one input for another. The slope of each isoquant indicates how the quantity of one input can be traded off against the quantity of the other, while keeping output constant. When the negative sign is removed, we call the slope the marginal rate of technical substitution (MRTS). The *marginal rate of technical substitution of labor for capital* is the amount by which the input of capital can be reduced when one extra unit of labor is used, so that output remains constant. This is analogous to the marginal rate of substitution (MRS) in consumer theory. Like the MRS, the MRTS is always measured as a positive quantity. In formal terms,

$$\text{MRTS} = -\text{Change in capital input/change in labor input}$$

$$= -\Delta K/\Delta L \text{ (for a fixed level of } Q)$$

where ΔK and ΔL are small changes in capital and labor along an isoquant.

Note that in Figure 6.7 the MRTS is equal to 2 when labor increases from 1 unit to 2, and output is fixed at 75. However, the MRTS falls to 1 when labor is increased from 2 units to 3, and then declines to 2/3 and to 1/3. Clearly, as more and more labor replaces capital, labor becomes less productive and capital becomes relatively more productive. So less capital needs to be given up to keep constant the output from production, and the isoquant becomes flatter.

We assume that there is a *diminishing MRTS*. In other words, the MRTS falls as we move down along an isoquant. The mathematical implication is that isoquants are convex, or bowed inward. The diminishing MRTS tells us that the productivity that any one input can have is limited. As more and more labor is added to the production process in place of capital, the productivity of labor falls. Similarly, when more capital is added in place of labor, the productivity of capital falls. Production needs a balanced mix of both inputs.

As our discussion has just suggested, the MRTS is closely related to the marginal products of labor MP_L and capital MP_K. To see how, imagine adding some labor and reducing the amount of capital to keep output constant. The addition to output resulting from the increased labor input is equal to the ad-

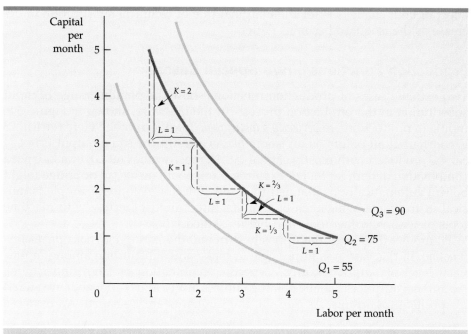

Figure 6.7 Marginal Rate of Technical Substitution Isoquants are downward sloping and convex like indifference curves. The slope of the isoquant at any point measures the marginal rate of technical substitution, the ability of the firm to replace capital with labor while maintaining the same level of output. On isoquant Q_2, the MRTS falls from 2 to 1 to 2/3 to 1/3.

ditional output per unit of additional labor (the marginal product of labor) times the number of units of additional labor:

$$\text{Additional output from increased use of labor} = (\text{MP}_L)(\Delta L)$$

Similarly, the decrease in output resulting from the reduction in capital is the loss of output per unit reduction in capital (the marginal product of capital) times the number of units of capital reduction:

$$\text{Reduction in output from decreased use of capital} = (\text{MP}_K)(\Delta K)$$

Because we are keeping output constant by moving along an isoquant, the total change in output must be zero. Thus,

$$(\text{MP}_L)(\Delta L) + (\text{MP}_K)(\Delta K) = 0$$

Now, by rearranging terms we see that

$$(\text{MP}_L)/(\text{MP}_K) = -(\Delta K/\Delta L) = \text{MRTS} \qquad (6.2)$$

Equation (6.2) tells us that as we move along an isoquant, continually replacing capital with labor in the production process, the marginal product of capital increases and the marginal product of labor decreases. The combined effect of both changes is for the marginal rate of technical substitution to decrease as the isoquant becomes flatter.

Production Functions—Two Special Cases

Two extreme cases of production functions show the possible range of input substitution in the production process. In the first case, shown in Figure 6.8, inputs to production are *perfectly substitutable* for one another. Here the MRTS is constant at all points on an isoquant. As a result the same output (say Q_3) can be produced with mostly capital (at A), mostly labor (at C), or a balanced combination of both (at B). For example, a toll booth on a road or bridge might be run automatically or manned by a toll collector. Another example is musical instruments, which can be manufactured almost entirely with machine tools or with very few tools and highly skilled labor.

Figure 6.9 illustrates the opposite extreme, the *fixed-proportions production function*. In this case it is impossible to make any substitution among inputs. Each level of output requires a specific combination of labor and capital. Additional output cannot be obtained unless more capital and labor are added in specific proportions. As a result, the isoquants are L-shaped. An example

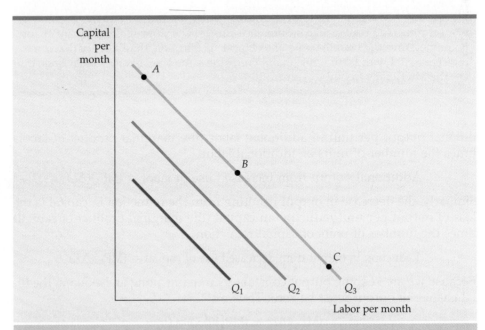

Figure 6.8   Isoquants When Inputs Are Perfectly Substitutable   When the isoquants are straight lines, the MRTS is constant. Hence the rate at which capital and labor can be substituted for each other is the same no matter what level of inputs is being used. Points A, B, and C represent three different capital-labor combinations that generate the same output Q_3.

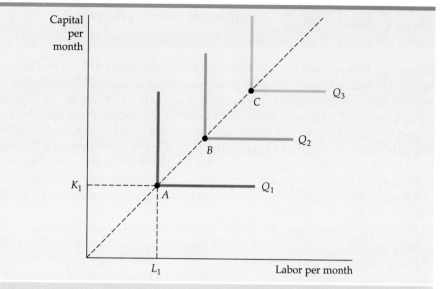

Figure 6.9 **Fixed-Proportions Production Function** When the isoquants are L-shaped, only one combination of labor and capital can be used to produce a given output (as at point A on isoquant Q_1, point B on isoquant Q_2, and point C on isoquant Q_3). Adding more labor alone does not increase output, nor does adding more capital alone.

is the reconstruction of concrete sidewalks using jackhammers. It takes one person to use a jackhammer—neither two people and one jackhammer nor one person and two jackhammers is likely to increase production.

In Figure 6.9 points A, B, and C represent technically efficient combinations of inputs. For example, to produce output Q_1, a quantity of labor L_1 and capital K_1 can be used, as at A. If capital stays fixed at K_1, adding more labor does not change output. Nor does adding capital with labor fixed at L_1. Thus on the vertical and the horizontal segments of the L-shaped isoquants, either the marginal product of capital or the marginal product of labor is zero. Higher output results only when both labor and capital are added, as in the move from input combination A to input combination B.

The fixed-proportions production function describes situations in which the methods of production available to firms are limited. For example, the production of a television show might involve a certain mix of capital (camera and sound equipment, etc.) and labor (producer, director, actors, etc.). To make more television shows, all inputs to production must be increased proportionally. In particular, it would be difficult to increase capital inputs at the expense of labor, since actors are necessary inputs to production (except perhaps for animated films). Likewise, it would be difficult to substitute labor for capital, since filmmaking today requires sophisticated film equipment.

E X A M P L E   6 . 3   **A Production Function for Wheat**

Crops can be produced using different methods. Food grown on large farms in the United States is usually produced with a *capital-intensive technology*, which involves substantial investments in capital, such as buildings and equipment, and relatively little input of labor. However, food can also be produced using very little capital (a hoe) and a lot of labor (several people with the patience and stamina to work the soil). One way to describe the agricultural production process is to show one isoquant (or more) that describes the combination of inputs that generates a given level of output (or several output levels). The description that follows comes from a production function for wheat that was estimated statistically.[7]

Figure 6.10 shows one isoquant, associated with the production function, corresponding to an output of 13,800 bushels of wheat per year. The manager of the farm can use this isoquant to decide whether it is profitable to hire more labor or use more machinery. Assume the farm is currently operating at A, with a labor input L of 500 hours and a capital input K of 100 machine hours. The manager decides to experiment by using fewer hours of machine time. To produce the same crop per year, he finds that he needs to replace this machine time by adding 260 hours of labor.

The results of this experiment tell the manager about the shape of the wheat production isoquant. When comparing points A (where $L = 500$ and $K = 100$) and B (where $L = 760$ and $K = 90$) in Figure 6.10, both of which are on the same isoquant, the manager finds that the marginal rate of technical substitution is equal to 0.04 $(-\Delta K/\Delta L = -(-10)/260 = .04)$.

The MRTS tells the manager the nature of the trade-off between adding labor and reducing the use of farm machinery. Because the MRTS is substantially less than 1 in value, the manager knows that when the wage of a laborer is equal to the cost of running a machine, he ought to use more capital. (At his current level of production, he needs 260 units of labor to substitute for 10 units of capital.) In fact, he knows that unless labor is much less expensive than the use of a machine, his production process ought to become more capital-intensive.

The decision about how many laborers to hire and machines to use cannot be fully resolved until we discuss the costs of production in the next chapter. However, this example illustrates how knowledge about production isoquants and the marginal rate of technical substitution can help a manager. It also suggests why most farms in the United States and Canada, where labor is relatively expensive, operate in the range of production in which the MRTS is relatively high (with a high capital-to-labor ratio), whereas farms in developing countries in which labor is cheap operate with a lower MRTS (and a lower

---

[7] The food production function on which this example is based is given by the equation $Q = 100(K^{.8}L^{.2})$, where Q is the rate of output in bushels of food per year, K is the quantity of machines in use per year, and L is the number of hours of labor per year.

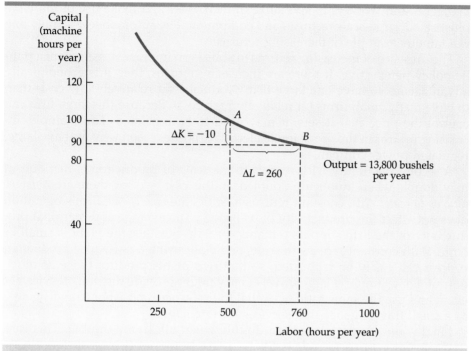

Figure 6.10 Isoquant Describing the Production of Wheat A wheat output of 13,800 bushels per year can be produced with different combinations of labor and capital. The more capital-intensive production process is shown as point A, and the more labor-intensive process as B. The marginal rate of technical substitution between A and B is 10/260 = 0.04.

capital-to-labor ratio).[8] The exact labor/capital combination to use depends on the input prices, a subject we discuss in Chapter 7.

6.5 Returns to Scale

The measure of increased output associated with increases in *all* inputs is fundamental to the long-run nature of the firm's production process. How does the output of the firm change as its inputs are proportionately increased? If output more than doubles when inputs are doubled, there are *increasing returns to scale*. This might arise because the larger scale of operation allows

---

[8] With the production function given in footnote 7, it is not difficult (using calculus) to show that the marginal rate of technical substitution is given by MRTS = $(MP_L/MP_K) = (1/4)(K/L)$. Thus the MRTS decreases as the capital-to-labor ratio falls. For an interesting study of agricultural production in Israel, see Richard E. Just, David Zilberman, and Eithan Hochman, "Estimation of Multicrop Production Functions," *American Journal of Agricultural Economics* 65 (1983): 770–780.

managers and workers to specialize in their tasks and make use of more sophisticated, large-scale factories and equipment. The automobile assembly line
is a famous example of increasing returns.

The presence of increasing returns to scale is an important issue from a public policy perspective. If there are increasing returns, then it is economically
advantageous to have one large firm producing (at relatively low cost) than
to have many small firms (at relatively high cost). Because this large firm can
control the price that it sets, it may need to be regulated. For example, increasing returns in the provision of electricity is one reason why we have large,
regulated power companies.

A second possibility with respect to the scale of production is that output
may double when inputs are doubled. In this case, we say there are *constant
returns to scale*. With constant returns to scale, the size of the firm's operation
does not affect the productivity of its factors. The average and marginal productivity of the firm's inputs remains constant whether the plant is small or
large. With constant returns to scale, one plant using a particular production
process can easily be replicated, so that two plants produce twice as much
output. For example, a large travel agency might provide the same service per
client and use the same ratio of capital (office space) and labor (travel agents)
as a small travel agency that services fewer clients.

Finally, output may less than double when all inputs double. This case
of *decreasing returns to scale* is likely to apply to any firm with large-scale
operations. Eventually, difficulties of management associated with the com-
plexities of organizing and running a large-scale operation may lead to decreased productivity of both labor and capital. Communication between
workers and managers can become difficult to monitor and the workplace
more impersonal. Thus the decreasing-returns case is likely to be associated with the problems of coordinating tasks and maintaining a useful line
of communication between management and workers. Or it may result because individuals cannot exhibit their entrepreneurial abilities in a large-
scale operation.

The presence or absence of returns to scale is seen graphically in the two
parts of Figure 6.11. The ray $0A$ from the origin in each panel describes a production process in which labor and capital are used as inputs to produce various levels of output in the ratio of 5 hours of labor to 2 hours of machine
time. In (a) the firm's production function exhibits constant returns to scale.
When 5 hours of labor and 2 hours of machine time are used, an output of 10
units is produced. When both inputs double, output doubles from 10 to 20
units, and when both inputs triple, output triples, from 10 to 30 units. Put differently, twice as much of both inputs is needed to produce 20 units, and three
times as much is needed to produce 30 units.

In Figure 6.11(b) the firm's production function exhibits increasing returns
to scale. Now the isoquants become closer together as we move away from
the origin along $0A$. As a result, less than twice the amount of both inputs is
needed to increase production from 10 units to 20, and substantially less than
three times the inputs are needed to produce 30 units. The reverse would be
true if the production function exhibited decreasing returns to scale (not

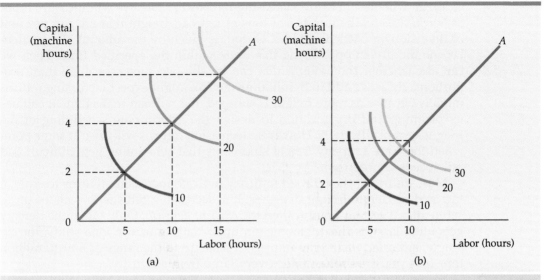

Figure 6.11 Returns to Scale When a firm's production process exhibits constant returns to scale as shown by a movement along ray $0A$ in part (a), the isoquants are equally spaced as output increases proportionally. However, when there are increasing returns to scale as shown in (b), the isoquants move closer together as inputs are increased along the ray.

shown here). With decreasing returns, the isoquants become increasingly distant from one another as output levels proportionally increase.

Returns to scale vary considerably across firms and industries. Other things being equal, the greater the returns to scale, the larger firms in an industry are likely to be. Manufacturing industries are more likely to have increasing returns to scale than service-oriented industries because manufacturing involves large investments in capital equipment. Services are more labor-intensive and can usually be provided as efficiently in small quantities as they can on a large scale.

EXAMPLE 6.4 Returns to Scale in the Rail Industry

During most of this century, railroads have grown larger and larger, yet their financial problems have continued to mount.[9] Does this increase in size make good economic sense? If so, why do railroads continue to have difficulty competing with other forms of transportation? We can get some insight into these questions by looking at the economics of rail freight transportation.

---

[9] This example draws on the analysis of railroad freight regulation by Theodore Keeler, *Railroads, Freight, and Public Policy* (Washington: Brookings Institution, 1983), chap. 3.

To see whether there are increasing returns to scale, we will measure input as *freight density*, the number of tons of railroad freight that are run per unit of time along a particular route. Output is given by the amount of a particular commodity shipped along this route within the specified time. Then we can ask whether the amount that can be shipped increases more than proportionately as we add to freight tonnage. We might expect increasing returns initially because as more freight is shipped, the railroad management can use its planning and organization to design the appropriate scheduling of the freight system efficiently. However, decreasing returns will arise at some point when there are so many freight shipments that scheduling gets difficult and rail speeds are reduced.

Most studies of the railroad industry indicate increasing returns to scale at low and moderate freight densities, but decreasing returns to scale begin to set in after a certain point (called the *efficient density*). Only when the density gets quite large is this phenomenon important, however. One study, for example, indicated increasing returns to scale up to the range of 8 to 10 million tons (per year) per route-mile, a very large freight density.

To see the practical importance of these numbers, we have tabulated the freight densities of major U.S. railroads in Table 6.6. Some railroads such as Colorado & Southern and Union Pacific have reached or surpassed the point of minimum efficient size (the point at which increasing returns to scale disappear). But many railroads operate at freight densities below this.

Because most railroads have not surpassed their optimum size, it appears that the growth in the size of most of them has been economically advantageous. Indeed, economies of scale relating to density have been an important efficiency reason supporting the recent merger of Burlington Northern

Table 6.6 Freight Densities of Major Railroads (million tons per route-mile)	
Railroad	**Density**
Atchison, Topeka & Santa Fe	6.03
Baltimore & Ohio	4.46
Burlington Northern	6.11
Chicago & Northwestern	3.10
Colorado & Southern	10.66
Fort Worth & Denver	6.55
Kansas City Southern	5.96
Missouri Pacific	5.01
Southern Pacific	5.35
Union Pacific	7.87
Western Pacific	3.20

Railroad and the Atchison, Topeka and Sante Fe Railroad, and the acquisition of Chicago & Northwestern by the Union Pacific Railroad. Whether these acquisitions have also led to an increase in the market power of the railroads, and whether any increased market power can be justified in light of the financial problems that have plagued the railroad industry, are public policy issues that are likely to be discussed for years to come.

Summary

1. A *production function* describes the maximum output a firm can produce for each specified combination of inputs.

2. An *isoquant* is a curve that shows all combinations of inputs that yield a given level of output. A firm's production function can be represented by a series of isoquants associated with different levels of output.

3. In the short run, one or more inputs to the production process are fixed, whereas in the long run all inputs are potentially variable.

4. Production with one variable input, labor, can be usefully described in terms of the *average product of labor* (which measures the productivity of the average worker), and the *marginal product of labor* (which measures the productivity of the last worker added to the production process).

5. According to the *law of diminishing returns,* when one or more inputs are fixed, a variable input (usually labor) is likely to have a marginal product that eventually diminishes as the level of input increases.

6. Isoquants always slope downward because the marginal product of all inputs is positive. The shape of each isoquant can be described by the marginal rate of technical substitution at each point on the isoquant. The *marginal rate of technical substitution of labor for capital* (MRTS) is the amount by which the input of capital can be reduced when one extra unit of labor is used, so that output remains constant.

7. The standard of living that a country can attain for its citizens is closely related to its level of labor productivity. Recent decreases in the rate of productivity growth in developed countries are due in part to the lack of growth of capital investment.

8. The possibilities for substitution among inputs in the production process range from a production function in which inputs are perfectly substitutable to one in which the proportions of inputs to be used are fixed (a fixed-proportions production function).

9. In long-run analysis, we tend to focus on the firm's choice of its scale or size of operation. Constant returns to scale means that doubling all inputs leads to doubling output. Increasing returns to scale occurs when output more than doubles when inputs are doubled, whereas decreasing returns to scale applies when output less than doubles.

Questions for Review

1. What is a production function? How does a long-run production function differ from a short-run production function?

2. Why is the marginal product of labor likely to increase and then decline in the short run?

3. Diminishing returns to a single factor of production and constant returns to scale are not inconsistent. Discuss.

4. You are an employer seeking to fill a vacant position on an assembly line. Are you more

concerned with the average product of labor or the marginal product of labor for the last person hired? If you observe that your average product is just beginning to decline, should you hire any more workers? What does this situation imply about the marginal product of your last worker hired?

5. Faced with constantly changing conditions, why would a firm ever keep *any* factors fixed? What determines whether a factor is fixed or variable?

6. How does the curvature of an isoquant relate to the marginal rate of technical substitution?

7. Can a firm have a production function that exhibits increasing returns to scale, constant returns to scale, and decreasing returns to scale as output increases? Discuss.

8. Give an example of a production process in which the short run involves a day or a week, and the long run any period longer than a week.

Exercises

1. Suppose a chair manufacturer is producing in the short run when equipment is fixed. The manufacturer knows that as the number of laborers used in the production process increases from 1 to 7, the number of chairs produced changes as follows: 10, 17, 22, 25, 26, 25, 23.
   a. Calculate the marginal and average product of labor for this production function.
   b. Does this production function exhibit diminishing returns to labor? Explain.
   c. Explain intuitively what might cause the marginal product of labor to become negative.

2. Fill in the gaps in the table below.

Quantity of Variable Input	Total Output	Marginal Product of Variable Input	Average Product of Variable Input
0	0	—	—
1	150		
2			200
3		200	
4	760		
5		150	
6			150

3. A political campaign manager has to decide whether to emphasize television advertisements or letters to potential voters in a re-

election campaign. Describe the production function for campaign votes. How might information about this function (such as the shape of the isoquants) help the campaign manager to plan strategy?

4. A firm has a production process in which the inputs to production are perfectly substitutable in the long run. Can you tell whether the marginal rate of technical substitution is high or low, or is further information necessary? Discuss.

5. The marginal product of labor is known to be greater than the average product of labor at a given level of employment. Is the average product increasing or decreasing? Explain.

6. The marginal product of labor in the production of computer chips is 50 chips per hour. The marginal rate of technical substitution of hours of labor for hours of machine-capital is 1/4. What is the marginal product of capital?

7. Do the following production functions exhibit decreasing, constant, or increasing returns to scale?
   a. $Q = .5KL$
   b. $Q = 2K + 3L$

8. The production function for the personal computers of DISK, Inc., is given by $Q = 10K^{.5}L^{.5}$, where Q is the number of computers produced per day, K is hours of machine time, and L is hours of labor input.

DISK's competitor, FLOPPY, Inc., is using the production function $Q = 10K^{.6}L^{.4}$.

a. If both companies use the same amounts of capital and labor, which will generate more output?

b. Assume that capital is limited to 9 machine hours, but labor is unlimited in supply. In which company is the marginal product of labor greater? Explain.

9. In Example 6.3, wheat is produced according to the production function $Q = 100(K^{.8}L^{.2})$.

a. Beginning with a capital input of 4 and a labor input of 49, show that the marginal product of labor and the marginal product of capital are both decreasing.

b. Does this production function exhibit increasing, decreasing, or constant returns to scale?

Chapter Outline

List of Examples

CHAPTER 7

The Cost of Production

In the last chapter, we examined the firm's production technology—the relationship that shows how factor inputs can be transformed into outputs. Now we will see how the production technology, together with the prices of factor inputs, determine the firm's cost of production.

Given a firm's production technology, managers must decide *how* to produce. As we saw, inputs can be combined in different ways to yield the same amount of output. For example, one can produce a certain output with a lot of labor and very little capital, with very little labor and a lot of capital, or with some other combination of the two. In this chapter we see how the *optimal* (cost-minimizing) combination of inputs is chosen. We will also see how a firm's costs depend on its rate of output, and how these costs are likely to change over time.

We begin by explaining how cost is defined and measured, distinguishing between the concept of cost used by economists, who are concerned about the firm's performance, and by accountants, who focus on the firm's financial statements. We then examine how the characteristics of the firm's production technology affect costs, both in the short run when the firm can do little to change its capital stock, and in the long run when the firm can change all its factor inputs.

We then show how the concept of returns to scale can be modified to apply to the process of producing many different outputs. We also show how cost sometimes falls over time as managers and workers learn from experience, so that the production process becomes more efficient. Finally, we show how empirical information can be used to estimate cost functions and predict future cost.

7.1 Measuring Cost: Which Costs Matter?

Before we can analyze how cost is determined, we need to be clear about what we mean by cost and how we measure it. What items should be included as part of a firm's cost? Cost obviously includes the wages a firm pays its workers and the rent it pays for office space. But what if the firm already owns an office building and doesn't have to pay rent? And how should we treat money that the firm spent two or three years ago (and can't recover) for equipment or for research and development? We'll answer these questions in the context of the economic decisions that managers make.

Economic Cost Versus Accounting Cost

An economist thinks of cost differently from an accountant, who is concerned with the firm's financial statements. Accountants tend to take a retrospective look at a firm's finances because they have to keep track of assets and liabilities and evaluate past performance. Accounting cost includes depreciation expenses for capital equipment, which are determined on the basis of the allowable tax treatment by the Internal Revenue Service.

Economists—and we hope managers—take a forward-looking view of the firm. They are concerned with what cost is expected to be in the future, and with how the firm might be able to rearrange its resources to lower its cost and improve its profitability. They must therefore be concerned with *opportunity cost*, the cost associated with opportunities that are foregone by not putting the firm's resources to their highest value use.

For example, consider a firm that owns a building, and therefore pays no rent for office space. Does this mean that the cost of office space is zero? Although an accountant would treat this cost as zero, an economist would note that the firm could have earned rent on the office space by leasing it to another company. This foregone rent is an opportunity cost of utilizing the office space and should be included as part of the cost of doing business.

Accountants and economists both include actual outlays, called *explicit costs*, in their calculations. Explicit costs include wages, salaries, and the cost of materials and property rentals. For accountants, explicit costs are important because they involve direct payments by a company to other firms and individuals that it does business with. These costs are relevant for the economist because the cost of wages and materials represents money that could have usefully been spent elsewhere.

Let's take a look at how economic cost can differ from accounting cost in the treatment of wages and economic depreciation. For example, consider an owner who manages her own retail store but chooses not to pay herself a salary. Although no monetary transaction has occurred (and thus would not appear as an accounting cost), the business nonetheless incurs an opportunity cost because the owner could have earned a competitive salary by working elsewhere.

Accountants and economists also treat depreciation differently. When estimating the future profitability of a business, an economist or manager is concerned with the capital cost of plant and machinery. This involves not only the explicit cost of buying and then running the machinery, but also the cost associated with wear and tear. When evaluating past performance, accountants use tax rules that apply to broadly defined types of assets to determine allowable depreciation in their cost and profit calculations. But these depreciation allowances need not reflect the actual wear and tear on the equipment, which is likely to vary asset by asset.

Sunk Costs

Although opportunity cost is often hidden, it should be taken into account when making economic decisions. Just the opposite is true of sunk cost—it is usually visible, but after it has been incurred, it should always be ignored when making future economic decisions.

A *sunk cost* is an expenditure that has been made and cannot be recovered. Because it cannot be recovered, it should not influence the firm's decisions. For example, consider the purchase of specialized equipment designed specially for a plant. We assume the equipment can be used to do only what it was originally designed for and cannot be converted for alternative use. The expenditure on this equipment is a sunk cost. Because it has no alternative use, its opportunity cost is zero. Thus it should not be included as part of the firm's costs.[1] The decision to buy this equipment may have been good or bad. It doesn't matter. It's water under the bridge and shouldn't affect the firm's current decisions.

What about a *prospective* sunk cost? For example, suppose the firm has not yet bought the specialized equipment and is considering whether to do so. A prospective sunk cost is an *investment*. Here the firm must decide whether that investment in specialized equipment is economical. In Chapter 15 we explain in detail how to make investment decisions of this kind.

As an example, suppose a firm is considering moving its headquarters to a new city. Last year it paid $500,000 for an option to buy a building in the city; the option gives it the right to buy the building at a cost of $5,000,000, so that its total expenditure will be $5,500,000 if it indeed buys the building. Now it finds that a comparable building has become available in the same

---

[1] If, on the other hand, the equipment could be put to other use, or be sold or rented to another firm, its current economic cost would be measured by the value from its next most profitable use.

city at a price of $5,250,000. Which building should it buy? The answer is the original building. The $500,000 option is a cost that has been sunk and that should not affect the firm's current decision. The economic cost of the original property is $5,000,000 to the firm (because the sunk cost of the option is not part of the economic cost), while the newer property has an economic cost of $5,250,000. Of course, if the new building cost $4,750,000, the firm should buy it, and forgo its option.

EXAMPLE 7.1 Choosing the Location for a New Law School Building

The Northwestern University Law School has long been located in Chicago, along the shores of Lake Michigan. However, the main campus of the university is located in the suburb of Evanston. In the mid-1970s, the law school began planning the construction of a new building and needed to decide on an appropriate location. Should it be built on the current site in the city, where it would remain near the downtown law firms? Or should it be moved to Evanston, where it would become physically integrated with the rest of the university?

The downtown location had many prominent supporters. They argued in part that it was cost-effective to locate the new building in the city because the university already owned the land, whereas a large parcel of land would have to be purchased in Evanston if the building were to be built there. Does this argument make economic sense?

No. It makes the common mistake of failing to distinguish accounting costs from economic costs. From an economic point of view, it is very expensive to locate downtown because the opportunity cost of the valuable lakeshore location is high—that property could have been sold for enough money to buy the Evanston land with substantial funds left over.

In the end, Northwestern decided to keep the law school in Chicago. This was a costly decision. It may have been appropriate if the Chicago location was particularly valuable to the law school, but the decision was inappropriate if it was made on the presumption that the downtown land was without cost.

7.2 Cost in the Short Run

In the short run, some of a firm's inputs to production are fixed, while others can be varied as the firm changes its output. Various measures of the cost of production can be distinguished on this basis.

Total Cost (TC)

The total cost of production has two components: the *fixed cost* (FC), which is borne by the firm whatever level of output it produces, and the *variable cost* (VC), which varies with the level of output. Depending on circumstances, fixed cost may include expenditures for plant maintenance, insurance, and perhaps a minimal number of employees—this cost remains the same no matter how much the firm produces. Variable cost includes expenditures for wages, salaries, and raw materials—this cost increases as output increases.

Fixed cost does not vary with the level of output—it must be paid even if there is no output. It can be eliminated only by shutting down altogether. (In Chapter 8 we will see that a firm may decide to go out of business and thereby forgo its (future) outlays on fixed costs.)

Which costs are variable and which costs are fixed depends on the time horizon that we are dealing with. For a short time horizon—say, one or two months—most costs are fixed. The reason is that over such a short time horizon, a firm is typically obligated to receive and pay for contracted shipments of materials, and the firm cannot easily lay off workers. On the other hand, over a long time horizon—say two or three years—most costs are variable. Over a long time horizon, if the firm wanted to reduce its output, it could probably reduce its workforce, purchase less raw material, and perhaps even sell off some of its capital.

To decide how much to produce, managers of firms need to know how variable cost increases with the level of output. To address this issue, we need to develop some additional cost measures. We will use a specific example that typifies the cost situation of many firms. After we explain each of the cost concepts, we will describe how they relate to our previous analysis of the firm's production process.

The data in Table 7.1 describe a firm with a fixed cost of $50. Variable cost increases with output, as does total cost. The total cost is the sum of the fixed cost in column 1 and the variable cost in column 2. From the figures given in columns 1 and 2, a number of additional cost variables can be defined.

Marginal Cost (MC)

Marginal cost—sometimes called incremental cost—is the increase in cost that results from producing one extra unit of output. Because fixed cost does not change as the firm's level of output changes, marginal cost is equal to the increase in variable cost or the increase in total cost that results from an extra unit of output. We can therefore write marginal cost as

$$MC = \Delta VC/\Delta Q = \Delta TC/\Delta Q$$

Marginal cost tells us how much it will cost to expand the firm's output by one unit. In Table 7.1, marginal cost is calculated from either the variable cost (column 2) or the total cost (column 3). For example, the marginal cost of increasing output from 2 to 3 units is $20 because the variable cost of the firm increases from $78 to $98. (Total cost of production also increases by $20, from $128 to $148. Total cost differs from variable cost only by the fixed cost, which by definition does not change as output changes.)

Average Cost (AC)

Average cost is the cost per unit of output. Average total cost (ATC) is the firm's total cost divided by its level of output TC/Q. Thus the average total cost of

Table 7.1	A Firm's Short-Run Costs ($)						
Rate of Output	Fixed Cost	Variable Cost	Total Cost	Marginal Cost	Average Fixed Cost	Average Variable Cost	Average Total Cost
	(FC) (1)	(VC) (2)	(TC) (3)	(MC) (4)	(AFC) (5)	(AVC) (6)	(ATC) (7)
0	50	0	50	—	—	—	—
1	50	50	100	50	50	50	100
2	50	78	128	28	25	39	64
3	50	98	148	20	16.7	32.7	49.3
4	50	112	162	14	12.5	28	40.5
5	50	130	180	18	10	26	36
6	50	150	200	20	8.3	25	33.3
7	50	175	225	25	7.1	25	32.1
8	50	204	254	29	6.3	25.5	31.8
9	50	242	292	38	5.6	26.9	32.4
10	50	300	350	58	5	30	35
11	50	385	435	85	4.5	35	39.5

producing at a rate of five units is $36, $180/5. Basically, average total cost tells us the per-unit cost of production. By comparing the average total cost to the price of the product, we can determine whether production is profitable.

ATC has two components. *Average fixed cost* (AFC) is the fixed cost (column 1) divided by the level of output, FC/Q. For example, the average fixed cost of producing 4 units of output is $12.50 ($50/4). Because fixed cost is constant, average fixed cost declines as the rate of output increases. *Average variable cost* (AVC) is variable cost divided by the level of output VC/Q. The average variable cost of producing 5 units of output is $26, $130 divided by 5.

The Determinants of Short-Run Cost

Table 7.1 shows that variable and total costs increase with output. The rate at which these costs increase depends on the nature of the production process, and in particular on the extent to which production involves diminishing returns to variable factors. Recall from Chapter 6 that diminishing returns to labor occurs when the marginal product of labor is decreasing. If labor is the only variable factor, what happens as we increase the firm's rate of output? To produce more output, the firm has to hire more labor. Then, if the marginal product of labor decreases rapidly as the amount of labor hired is increased (owing to diminishing returns), greater and greater expenditures must be made to produce output at the faster rate. As a result, variable and total costs increase rapidly as the rate of output is increased. On the other hand, if the marginal product of labor decreases only slightly as the amount of labor is increased, costs will not rise so fast when the rate of output is increased.[2]

Let's look at the relationship between production and cost in more detail by concentrating on the costs of a firm that can hire as much labor as it wishes at a fixed wage w. Recall that marginal cost MC is the change in variable cost for a 1-unit change in output (i.e., $\Delta VC/\Delta Q$). But the variable cost is the per-unit cost of the extra labor w times the amount of extra labor ΔL. It follows, then, that

$$MC = \Delta VC/\Delta Q = w\Delta L/\Delta Q$$

The marginal product of labor MPL is the change in output resulting from a 1-unit change in labor input, or $\Delta Q/\Delta L$. Therefore, the extra labor needed to obtain an extra unit of output is $\Delta L/\Delta Q = 1/MP_L$. As a result,

$$MC = w/MP_L \tag{7.1}$$

Equation (7.1) states that in the short run, marginal cost is equal to the price of the input that is being varied divided by its marginal product. Suppose, for example, that the marginal product of labor is 3 and the wage rate is $30 per hour. Then, 1 hour of labor will increase output by 3 units, so that 1 unit of output will require 1/3 hour of labor, and will cost $10. The marginal cost of producing that unit of output is $10, which is equal to the wage, $30, divided by the marginal product of labor, 3. A low marginal product of labor means that a large amount of additional labor is needed to produce more output, which leads to a high marginal cost. A high marginal product means that the labor requirement is low, as is the marginal cost. More generally, whenever the marginal product of labor decreases, the marginal cost of production increases, and vice versa.[3]

The effect of the presence of diminishing returns in the production process can also be seen by looking at the data on marginal costs in Table 7.1. The marginal cost of additional output is high at first because the first few inputs to production are not likely to raise output much in a large plant with a lot of equipment. However, as the inputs become more productive, the marginal cost decreases substantially. Finally, marginal cost increases again for relatively high levels of output, owing to the effect of diminishing returns.

The law of diminishing returns also creates a direct link between the average variable cost of production and the average productivity of labor. Average variable cost AVC is the variable cost per unit of output, or VC/Q. When L units of labor are used in the production process, the variable cost is wL. Thus,

$$AVC = wL/Q$$

---

[2] We are implicitly assuming that labor is hired in competitive markets, so that the payment per unit of factor used is the same no matter what the firm's output.

[3] With two or more variable inputs, the relationship is more complex, but still the greater the productivity of factors, the less the variable cost that the firm must incur to produce any given level of output.

Recall from Chapter 6 that the average product of labor AP_L is given by the output per unit of input Q/L. As a result

$$AVC = w/AP_L \qquad (7.2)$$

Since the wage rate is fixed from the firm's perspective, there is an inverse relationship between average variable cost and the average product of labor. Suppose, for example, that the average product of labor is 5 and the wage rate is $30 per hour. Then, each hour of labor will increase output on average by 5 units, so that each unit of output will require 1/5 hour of labor, and will cost $6. The average variable cost of producing each unit of output is $6, which is equal to the wage, $30, divided by the average product of labor, 5. A lower marginal product of labor means that a lot of labor is needed to produce the firm's output, which leads to a high average variable cost. A high average product of labor means that the labor required for production is low, as is the average variable cost.

We have seen that with both marginal cost and average variable cost, there is a direct link between the productivity of factors of production and the costs of production. Marginal and average product tell us about the relationship between inputs and output. The comparable cost variables tell us about the budgetary implications of that production information.

The Shapes of the Cost Curves

Figure 7.1 shows two sets of continuous cost curves; they show how costs vary with small changes in output, and therefore provide different information from Table 7.1. The fixed cost, variable cost, and total cost curves are shown in Figure 7.1(a). Fixed cost FC does not vary with output and is shown as a horizontal line at $50. Variable cost VC is zero when output is zero, and then increases continuously as output increases. The total cost curve TC is determined by vertically adding the fixed cost curve to the variable cost curve. Because fixed cost is constant, the vertical distance between the two curves is always $50.

Figure 7.1(b) shows the corresponding set of marginal and average variable cost curves.[4] Because total fixed cost is $50, the average fixed cost curve AFC falls continuously from $50 when output is 1 toward zero for large output. The shapes of the remaining curves are determined by the relationship between the marginal and average cost curves. Whenever marginal cost lies below average cost, the average cost curve falls. Whenever marginal cost lies above average cost, the average cost curve rises. And when average cost is at a minimum, marginal cost equals average cost. Marginal and average costs are another example of the average-marginal relationship described in Chapter 6 (with respect to marginal and average product). For example, at $20 marginal

---

[4] The curves do not exactly match the numbers in Table 7.1. Because marginal cost represents the change in cost associated with a change in output, we have plotted the MC curve for the first unit of output by setting output equal to ½, for the second unit by setting output equal to 1½, and so on.

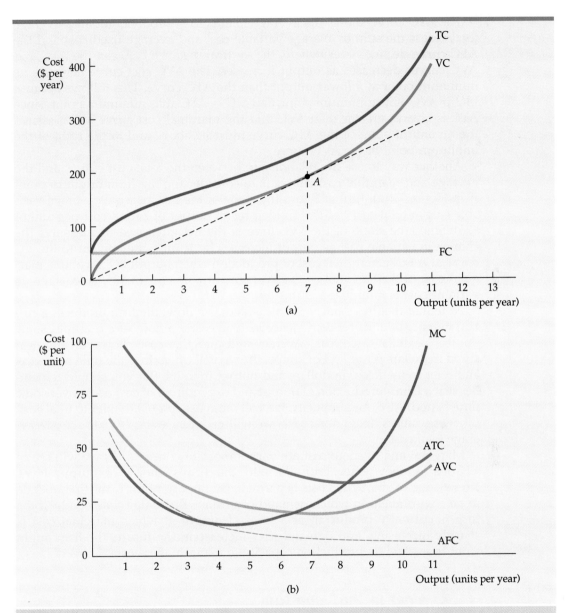

Figure 7.1   Cost Curves for a Firm   In (a) total cost TC is the vertical sum of fixed cost FC and variable cost VC. In (b) average total cost ATC is the sum of average variable cost AVC and average fixed cost AFC. Marginal cost MC crosses the average variable cost and average total cost curves at their minimum points.

cost is below the average variable cost of $25, and the average is lowered. But when marginal cost is $30, which is greater than average variable cost ($25), the average increases. Finally, when marginal cost ($25) and average cost ($25) are the same, the average variable cost remains unchanged (at about $25).

The ATC curve shows the average total cost of production. Since average total cost is the sum of average variable cost and average fixed cost and the AFC curve declines everywhere, the vertical distance between the ATC and AVC curves decreases as output increases. The AVC cost curve achieves its minimum point at a lower output than the ATC curve. This follows because MC = AVC at its minimum point, and MC = ATC at its minimum point. Since ATC is always greater than AVC and the marginal cost curve MC is rising, the minimum point of the ATC curve must lie above and to the right of the minimum point of the AVC curve.

Another way to see the relationship between the total cost curves and the average and marginal cost curves is to consider the ray from origin to point *A* in Figure 7.1(a). In that figure the slope of the ray measures average variable cost (a total cost of $175 divided by an output of 7, or a cost per unit of $25). Since the slope of the VC curve is the marginal cost (it measures the change in variable cost as output increases by 1 unit), the tangent to the VC curve at *A* is the marginal cost of production when output is 7. At *A* this marginal cost of $25 is equal to the average variable cost of $25, since average variable cost is minimized at this output.[5]

Note that the firm's output is measured as a flow; the firm produces a certain number of units *per year*. Hence its total cost is a flow—for example, some number of dollars per year. (Average and marginal costs, however, are measured in dollars *per unit*.) For simplicity, we will often drop the time reference, and refer to total cost in dollars and output in units. But you should remember that a firm's production of output and expenditure of cost occur over some time period. Also, for simplicity, we will often use *cost* (C) to refer to total cost. Likewise, unless noted otherwise, we will use *average cost* (AC) to refer to average total cost.

Marginal and average cost are very important concepts. As we will see in Chapter 8, they enter critically into the firm's choice of output level. Knowledge of short-run costs is particularly important for firms that operate in an environment in which demand conditions fluctuate considerably. If the firm is currently producing at a level of output at which marginal cost is sharply increasing, and demand may increase in the future, the firm might want to expand its production capacity to avoid higher costs.

7.3 Cost in the Long Run

In the long run, the firm can change all its inputs. In this section we show how to choose the combination of inputs that minimizes the cost of producing a given output. We will also examine the relationship between long-run cost and the level of output.

---

[5] The relationships just described hold only approximately when we are describing discrete rather than infinitesimal changes in output. Thus, at an output of 8, average total cost is approximately, but not identically, equal to marginal cost.

The Cost-Minimizing Input Choice

Let's begin by considering a fundamental problem that all firms face: *how to select inputs to produce a given output at minimum cost.* For simplicity, we will work with two variable inputs: labor (measured in hours of work per year) and capital (measured in hours of use of machinery per year). We assume that both labor and capital can be hired (or rented) in competitive markets. The price of labor is the wage rate w, and the price of capital is the rental rate for machinery r. We assume that capital is rented rather than purchased, so that we can put all business decisions on a comparable basis. For example, labor services might be hired at a wage of $12,000 per year, or capital might be "rented" for $75,000 per machine per year.

Because capital and labor inputs are hired in competitive factor markets, we can take the price of these inputs as fixed. We can then focus on the firm's optimal combination of factors, without worrying about whether large purchases will cause the price of an input to increase.[6]

The Isocost Line

We begin by looking at the cost of hiring factor inputs, which can be represented by a firm's isocost lines. An *isocost line* includes all possible combinations of labor and capital that can be purchased for a given total cost. To see what an isocost line looks like, recall that the total cost C of producing any particular output is given by the sum of the firm's labor cost wL and its capital cost rK:

$$C = wL + rK \qquad (7.3)$$

For each different level of total cost, equation (7.3) describes a different isocost line. For example, in Figure 7.2, the isocost line C_0 describes all possible combinations of inputs that cost C_0 to purchase.

If we rewrite the total cost equation (7.3) as an equation for a straight line, we get:

$$K = C/r - (w/r)L$$

It follows that the isocost line has a slope of $\Delta K/\Delta L = -(w/r)$, which is the ratio of the wage rate to the rental cost of capital. This slope is similar to the slope of the budget line that the consumer faces (because it is determined solely by the prices of the goods in question, whether inputs or outputs). It tells us that if the firm gave up a unit of labor (and recovered w dollars in cost) to buy w/r units of capital at a cost of r dollars per unit, its total cost of production would remain the same. For example, if the wage rate were $10 and the rental cost of capital $5, the firm could replace one unit of labor with two units of capital, with no change in total cost.

---

[6] This might happen because of overtime or a relative shortage of capital equipment. We discuss the possibility of a relationship between the prices of factor inputs and the quantities demanded by a firm in Chapter 14.

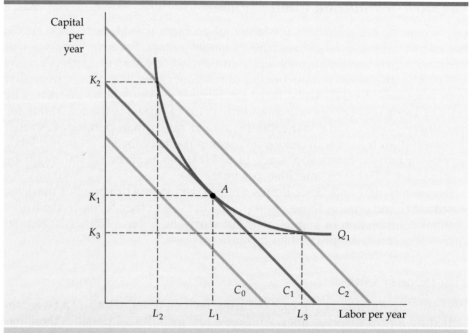

Figure 7.2 **Producing a Given Output at Minimum Cost** Isocost curves describe the combination of inputs to production that cost the same amount to the firm. Isocost curve C_1 is tangent to isoquant Q_1 at A and shows that output Q_1 can be produced at minimum cost with labor input L_1 and capital input K_1. Other input combinations—L_2, K_2 and L_3, K_3—yield the same output at higher cost.

Choosing Inputs

Suppose we wish to produce output level Q_1. How can we do this at minimum cost? Look at the firm's production isoquant, labeled Q_1, in Figure 7.2. The problem is to choose the point on this isoquant that minimizes total costs.

Figure 7.2 illustrates the solution to this problem. Suppose the firm were to spend C_0 on inputs. Unfortunately, no combination of inputs can be purchased for expenditure C_0 that will allow the firm to achieve output Q_1. Output Q_1 can be achieved with the expenditure of C_2, however, either by using K_2 units of capital and L_2 units of labor, or by using K_3 units of capital and L_3 units of labor. But C_2 is not the minimum cost. The same output Q_1 can be produced more cheaply than this, at a cost of C_1, by using K_1 units of capital and L_1 units of labor. In fact, isocost line C_1 is the lowest isocost line that allows output Q_1 to be produced. The point of tangency of the isoquant Q_1 and the isocost line C_1 at point A tells us the cost-minimizing choice of inputs, L_1 and K_1, which can be read directly from the diagram. At this point, the slopes of the isoquant and the isocost line are just equal.

When the expenditure on all inputs increases, the slope of the isocost line does not change (because the prices of the inputs have not changed), but the intercept increases. Suppose, however, that the price of one of the inputs, such as labor, were to increase. Then, the slope of the isocost line $-(w/r)$ would increase in magnitude, and the isocost line would become steeper. Figure 7.3 shows this. Initially, the isocost line is C_1, and the firm minimizes its costs of producing output Q_1 at A by using L_1 units of labor and K_1 units of capital. When the price of labor increases, the isocost line becomes steeper. The isocost line C_2 reflects the higher price of labor. Facing this higher price of labor, the firm minimizes its cost of producing output Q_1 by producing at B, using L_2 units of labor and K_2 units of capital. The firm has responded to the higher price of labor by substituting capital for labor in the production process.

How does this relate to the firm's production process? Recall that in our analysis of production technology, we showed that the marginal rate of technical substitution MRTS of labor for capital is the negative of the slope of the isoquant, and is equal to the ratio of the marginal products of labor and capital.

$$\text{MRTS} = -\Delta K/\Delta L = \text{MP}_L/\text{MP}_K \qquad (7.4)$$

Figure 7.3   Input Substitution When an Input Price Changes   Facing an isocost curve C_1, the firm produces output Q_1 at point A using L_1 units of labor and K_1 units of capital. When the price of labor increases, the isocost curves become steeper. Output Q_1 is now produced at point B on isocost curve C_2 by using L_2 units of labor and K_2 units of capital.

Above, we noted that the isocost line has a slope of $\Delta K/\Delta L = -w/r$. It follows that when a firm minimizes the cost of producing a particular output, the following condition holds:

$$MP_L/MP_K = w/r$$

Rewriting this condition slightly,

$$MP_L/w = MP_K/r \tag{7.5}$$

Equation (7.5) tells us that when cost is minimized, each dollar of input added to the production process will add an equivalent amount to output. Assume, for example, that the wage rate is $10 and the rental rate on capital is $2. If the firm chooses inputs so that the marginal product of labor and the marginal product of capital are equal to ten, it will want to hire less labor and rent more capital because capital is five times less expensive than labor. The firm can minimize its cost only when the production of an additional unit of output costs the same regardless of which additional input is used.

EXAMPLE 7.2 **The Effect of Effluent Fees on Firms' Input Choices**

Steel plants are often built on or near a river. A river offers readily available, inexpensive transportation for both the iron ore that goes into the production process and the finished steel itself. A river also provides a cheap method of disposing of by-products of the production process, called effluent. For example, a steel plant processes its iron ore for use in blast furnaces by grinding taconite deposits into a fine consistency. During this process, the ore is extracted by a magnetic field as a flow of water and fine ore passes through the plant. One by-product of this process—fine taconite particles—can be dumped in the river at relatively little cost to the firm, whereas alternative removal methods or private treatment plants are relatively expensive.

Because the taconite particles are a nondegradable waste that can harm vegetation and fish, the Environmental Protection Agency (EPA) has imposed an effluent fee—a per-unit fee that the steel firm must pay for the effluent that goes into the river. How should the manager of the firm respond to the imposition of this effluent fee to minimize the costs of production?

Suppose that without regulation the steel firm is producing 2000 tons of steel per month, while using 2000 machine-hours of capital and 10,000 gallons of water (which contains taconite particles when returned to the river). The manager of the firm estimates that a machine-hour costs $40, and dumping each gallon of wastewater in the river costs the firm $10. (The total cost of production is, therefore, $180,000: $80,000 for capital and $100,000 for wastewater.) How should the manager respond to an EPA-imposed effluent fee of $10 per gallon of wastewater dumped?

Figure 7.4 shows the cost-minimizing response. The vertical axis measures the firm's input of capital in machine-hours per month, and the horizontal axis measures the quantity of wastewater in gallons per month. First, consider

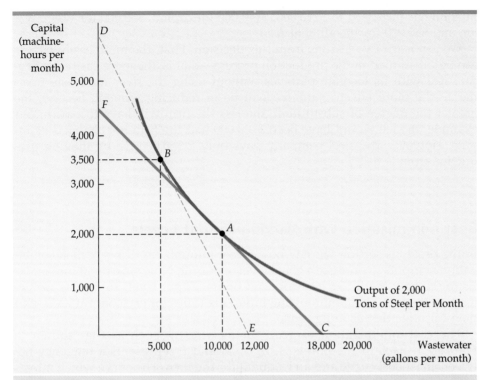

Figure 7.4   The Cost-Minimizing Response to an Effluent Fee   When the firm is not charged for dumping its wastewater in a river, it chooses to produce a given output using 10,000 gallons of wastewater and 2000 machine-hours of capital at *A*. However, an effluent fee raises the cost of wastewater, shifts the isocost curve from *FC* to *DE*, and causes the firm to produce at *B*, with much less effluent.

how the firm produces when there is no effluent fee. Point *A* represents the input of capital and the level of wastewater that allows the firm to produce its quota of steel at minimum cost. Because the firm is minimizing cost, *A* lies on the isocost line *FC*, which is tangent to the isoquant. The slope of the isocost line is equal to −$10/$40 = −0.25 because a unit of capital costs four times more than a unit of wastewater.

When the effluent fee is imposed, the cost of wastewater increases from $10 per gallon to $20, because for every gallon of wastewater (which costs $10), the firm has to pay the government an additional $10. The effluent fee increases the cost of wastewater relative to capital. To produce the same output at the lowest possible cost, the manager must choose the isocost line with a slope of −$20/$40 = −0.5 that is tangent to the isoquant. In Figure 7.4, *DE* is the appropriate isocost line, and *B* gives the appropriate choice of capital and wastewater. The move from *A* to *B* shows that with an effluent fee the use of an alternative production technology, which emphasizes the use of capital (3500 machine-hours) and uses less wastewater (5000 gallons), is cheaper than the original process, which did not emphasize recycling. (The total cost of production has increased to $240,000: $140,000 for capital, $50,000 for waste-water, and $50,000 for the effluent fee.)

We can learn two lessons from this decision. First, the more easily factors can be substituted in the production process—that is, the more easily the firm can deal with its taconite particles without using the river for waste treatment—the more effective the fee will be in reducing effluent. Second, the greater the degree of substitution, the less the firm will have to pay. In our example, the fee would have been $100,000 had the firm not changed its inputs. However, the steel company pays only a $50,000 fee by moving production from *A* to *B*.

Cost Minimization with Varying Output Levels

In the previous section we saw how a cost-minimizing firm selects a combination of inputs to produce a given level of output. Now we extend this analysis to see how the firm's costs depend on its output level. To do this we determine the firm's cost-minimizing input quantities for each output level, and then calculate the resulting cost.

The cost-minimization exercise yields a result such as that shown in Figure 7.5. Each of the points *A*, *B*, *C*, *D*, and *E* represents a tangency between an isocost curve and an isoquant for the firm. The curve which moves upward and to the right from the origin, tracing out the points of tangency, is the firm's *expansion path*. The expansion path describes the combinations of labor and capital that the firm will choose to minimize costs for every output level. As long as the use of both inputs increases as output increases, the curve will look approximately as shown in Figure 7.5. The firm's expansion path shows the lowest long-run total cost of producing each level of output.

7.4 Long-Run Versus Short-Run Cost Curves

We saw earlier (see Figure 7.1) that short-run average cost curves are U-shaped. We will see that long-run average cost curves can also be U-shaped, but different economic factors explain the shapes of these curves. In this section, we discuss long-run average and marginal cost curves and highlight the differences between these curves and their short-run counterparts.

The Inflexibility of Short-Run Production

Recall that in the long run all inputs to the firm are variable, because its planning horizon is long enough to allow for a change in plant size. This added flexibility allows the firm to produce at a lower average cost than in the short run. To see why, we might compare the situation in which capi-

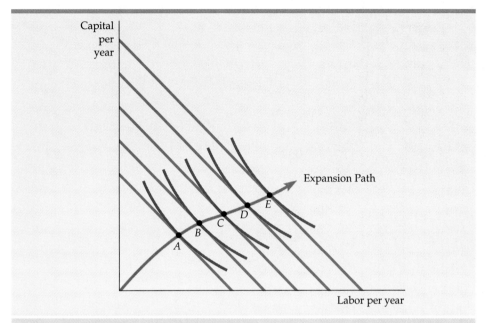

Figure 7.5 A Firm's Expansion Path The expansion path (from the origin through points *A*, *B*, *C*, *D*, and *E*) illustrates the least-cost combinations of labor and capital that can be used to produce each level of output in the long run when both inputs to production can be varied.

tal and labor are both flexible to the case in which capital is fixed in the short run.

Figure 7.6 shows the firm's production isoquants. Suppose capital is fixed at a level K_1 in the short run. To produce output Q_1, the firm would minimize costs by choosing labor equal to L_1, corresponding to the point of tangency with the isocost line *AB*. The inflexibility appears when the firm decides to increase its output to Q_2. If capital were not fixed, it would produce this output with capital K_2 and labor L_2. Its cost of production would be reflected by isocost line *CD*. However, the fixed capital forces the firm to increase its output by using capital K_1 and labor L_3 at *P*. Point *P* lies on the isocost line *EF*, which represents a higher cost than isocost line *CD*. The cost of production is higher when capital is fixed because the firm is unable to substitute relatively inexpensive capital for more costly labor when it expands its production.

Long-Run Average Cost

In the long run, the ability to change the amount of capital allows the firm to reduce costs. To see how costs vary as the firm moves along its expansion path in the long run, we can look at the long-run average and marginal cost

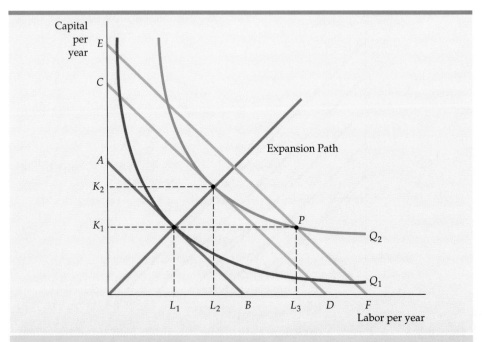

Figure 7.6 **The Inflexibility of Short-Run Production** When a firm operates in the short run, its cost of production may not be minimized because of inflexibility in the use of capital inputs. Output is initially at level Q_1. In the short run, output Q_2 can be produced only by increasing labor from L_1 to L_3 because capital is fixed at K_1. In the long run, the same output can be produced more cheaply by increasing labor from L_1 to L_2 and capital from K_1 to K_2.

curves.[7] The most important determinant of the shape of the long-run average and marginal cost curves is whether there are increasing, constant, or decreasing returns to scale. Suppose, for example, that the firm's production process exhibits constant returns to scale at all levels of output. Then a doubling of inputs leads to a doubling of output. Because input prices remain unchanged as output increases, the average cost of production must be the same for all levels of output.

Suppose instead that the firm's production process is subject to increasing returns to scale. A doubling of inputs leads to more than a doubling of output. Then the average cost of production falls with output because a doubling of costs is associated with a more than twofold increase in output. By the same logic, when there are decreasing returns to scale, the average cost of production must be increasing with output.

In the last chapter, we saw that in the long run most firms' production technologies first exhibit increasing returns to scale, then constant returns to scale,

---

[7] We saw that in the short run the shapes of the average and marginal cost curves were determined primarily by diminishing returns. As we showed in Chapter 6, diminishing returns to each factor are consistent with constant (or even increasing) returns to scale.

and eventually decreasing returns to scale. Figure 7.7 shows a typical long-run average cost curve LAC consistent with this description of the production process. The long-run average cost curve is U-shaped, just like the short-run average cost curve, but the source of the U-shape is increasing and decreasing returns to scale, rather than diminishing returns to a factor of production.

The long-run marginal cost curve LMC is determined from the long-run average cost curve; it measures the change in long-run total costs as output is increased incrementally. LMC lies below the long-run average cost curve when LAC is falling, and above the long-run average cost curve when LAC is rising.[8] The two curves intersect at A, where the long-run average cost curve achieves its minimum. And in the special case in which LAC is constant, LAC and LMC are equal.

Economies and Diseconomies of Scale

In the long run, it may be in the firm's interest to change the input proportions as the level of output changes. When input proportions do change, the concept of returns to scale no longer applies. Rather, we say that a firm enjoys *economies of scale* when it can double its output for less than twice the cost. Correspondingly, there are *diseconomies of scale* when a doubling of output requires more than twice the cost. The term *economies of scale* includes increasing returns to scale as a special case, but it is more general because it allows input combinations to be altered as the firm changes its level of

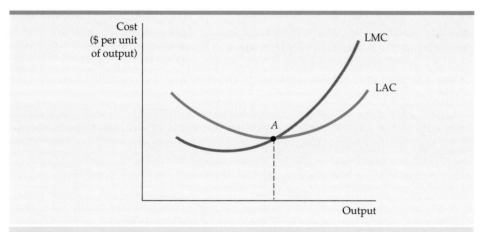

Figure 7.7   Long-Run Average and Marginal Cost   When a firm is producing at an output at which the long-run average cost LAC is falling, the long-run marginal cost LMC is less than LAC. When LAC is increasing, LMC is greater than LAC. The two curves intersect at A, where the LAC curve achieves its minimum.

---

[8] Recall that $AC = TC/Q$, which means that, $\Delta AC/\Delta Q = [Q(\Delta TC/\Delta Q) - TC]/Q^2 = (MC - AC)/Q$. Clearly, when AC is increasing, $\Delta AC/\Delta Q$ is positive and $MC > AC$. Correspondingly, when AC is decreasing, $\Delta AC/\Delta Q$ is negative and $MC < AC$.

production. In this more general setting, a U-shaped long-run average cost curve is consistent with the firm facing economies of scale for relatively low output levels and diseconomies of scale for higher levels.

Economies of scale are often measured in terms of a cost-output elasticity, E_c. E_c is the percentage change in the cost of production resulting from a 1 percent increase in output:

$$E_c = (\Delta C/C)/(\Delta Q/Q) \tag{7.6}$$

To see how E_c relates to our traditional measures of cost, rewrite equation (7.6) as follows:

$$E_c = (\Delta C/\Delta Q)/(C/Q) = MC/AC \tag{7.7}$$

Clearly, E_c is equal to one when marginal and average costs are equal; then costs increase proportionately with output, and there are neither economies nor diseconomies of scale (constant returns to scale would apply if input proportions were fixed). When there are economies of scale (costs increase less than proportionately with output), marginal cost is less than average cost (both are declining), and E_c is less than one. Finally, when there are diseconomies of scale, marginal cost is greater than average cost, and E_c is greater than one.

The Relationship Between Short-Run and Long-Run Cost

Figures 7.8 and 7.9 show the relationship between short-run and long-run cost. Assume a firm is uncertain about the future demand for its product and is considering three alternative plant sizes. The short-run average cost curves for the three plants are given by SAC_1, SAC_2, and SAC_3 in Figure 7.8. The decision is important because, once built, the firm may not be able to change the plant size for some time.

Figure 7.8 shows the case in which there are constant returns to scale in the long run. If the firm expects to produce Q_1 units of output, then it should build the smallest plant. Its average cost of production would be $10; this is the minimum cost because the short-run marginal cost SMC crosses short-run average cost SAC when both equal $10. If the firm expects to produce Q_2, the middle-sized plant is best, and its average cost of production is again $10. If it is to produce Q_3, the third plant is best. With only these plant sizes, any production choice between Q_1 and Q_2 will entail an increase in the average cost of production, as will any level of production between Q_2 and Q_3.

What is the firm's long-run cost curve? In the long run, the firm can change the size of its plant, so if it was initially producing Q_1 and wanted to increase output to Q_2 or Q_3, it could do so with no increase in average cost. With three possible plant sizes, the long-run average cost curve is therefore given by the cross-hatched portions of the short-run average cost curves because these show the minimum cost of production for any output level. The long-run average cost curve is the *envelope* of the short-run average cost curves—it envelops or surrounds the short-run curves.

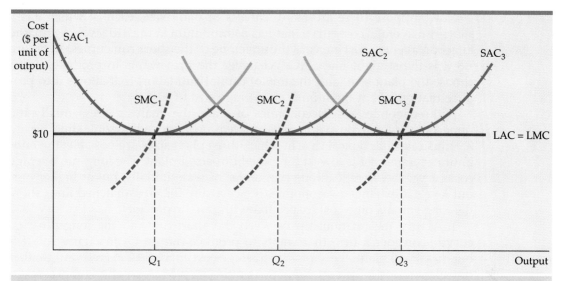

Figure 7.8   Long-Run Cost with Constant Returns to Scale   The long-run average cost curve LAC, which is identical to the long-run marginal cost curve LMC, is the envelope of the short-run average cost curves (SAC$_1$, SAC$_2$, and SAC$_3$ are shown). With constant returns to scale, the long-run average cost curve consists of the minimum points of the short-run average cost curves.

Figure 7.9   Long-Run Cost with Economies and Diseconomies of Scale   The long-run average cost curve LAC is the envelope of the short-run average cost curves (SAC$_1$, SAC$_2$, and SAC$_3$). With economies and diseconomies of scale, the minimum points of the short-run average cost curves do not lie on the long-run average cost curve.

Now suppose there are many choices of plant size, each of which has a short-run average cost curve that has its minimum at the $10 level. Again, the long-run average cost curve is the envelope of the short-run curves. In Figure 7.8 it is the straight line LAC. Whatever the firm wants to produce, it can choose the plant size (and the mix of capital and labor) that allows it to produce that output at the minimum average cost of $10.

With economies or diseconomies of scale, the analysis is essentially the same, but the long-run average cost curve is no longer a horizontal line. Figure 7.9 illustrates the typical case in which three plant sizes are possible; the minimum average cost is lowest for a medium-sized plant. The long-run average cost curve, therefore, exhibits economies of scale initially, but at higher output levels it exhibits diseconomies. Once again, the cross-hatched lines show the long-run average cost associated with the three plants.

To clarify the relationship between the short-run and the long-run cost curves, consider a firm that wants to produce output Q_1 in Figure 7.9. If it builds a small plant, the short-run average cost curve SAC_1 is relevant, so that the average cost of production (at B on SAC_1) is $8. A small plant is a better choice than a medium-sized plant with an average cost of production of $10 ($A$ on curve SAC_2). Point B would therefore become one point on the long-run cost function when only three plant sizes are possible. If plants of other sizes could be built, and at least one size allowed the firm to produce Q_1 at less than $8 per unit, then B would no longer be on the long-run cost curve.

In Figure 7.9, the envelope that would arise if plants of any size could be built is given by the LAC curve, which is U-shaped. Note, once again, that the LAC curve never lies above any of the short-run average cost curves. Also note that the points of minimum average cost of the smallest and largest plants do *not* lie on the long-run average cost curve because there are economies and diseconomies of scale in the long run. For example, a small plant operating at minimum average cost is not efficient because a larger plant can take advantage of increasing returns to scale to produce at a lower average cost.

Finally, note that the long-run marginal cost curve LMC is not the envelope of the short-run marginal cost curves. Short-run marginal costs apply to a particular plant; long-run marginal costs apply to all possible plant sizes. Each point on the long-run marginal cost curve is the short-run marginal cost associated with the most cost-efficient plant. Consistent with this relationship, SMC_1 intersects LMC in Figure 7.9 at the output level at which SAC_1 is tangent to LAC.

7.5 Production with Two Outputs— Economies of Scope

Many firms produce more than one product. Sometimes a firm's products are closely linked to one another—a chicken farm produces poultry and eggs, an automobile company produces automobiles and trucks, and a university produces teaching and research. Other times, firms produce products that are physically unrelated. In both cases, however, a firm is likely to enjoy production or cost advantages when it produces two or more products. These advantages could result from the joint use of inputs or production facilities, joint marketing programs, or possibly the cost savings of a common administration. In some cases, the production of one product gives an automatic and unavoidable by-product that is valuable to the firm. For example, sheet metal manufacturers produce scrap metal and shavings they can sell.

To study the economic advantages of joint production, let's consider an automobile company that produces two products, cars and tractors. Both products use capital (factories and machinery) and labor as inputs. Cars and tractors are not typically produced at the same plant, but they do share management resources, and both rely on similar machinery and skilled labor. The managers of the company must choose how much of each product to produce. Figure 7.10 shows two *product transformation curves*. Each curve shows the various combinations of cars and tractors that can be produced with a given input of labor and machinery. Curve O_1 describes all combinations of the two outputs that can be produced with a relatively low level of inputs, and curve O_2 describes the output combinations associated with twice the inputs.

The product transformation curve has a negative slope because to get more of one output, the firm must give up some of the other output. For example, a firm that emphasizes car production will devote less of its resources to producing tractors. In this case, curve O_2 lies twice as far from the origin as curve O_1, signifying that this firm's production process exhibits constant returns to scale in the production of both commodities.[9]

If curve O_1 were a straight line, joint production would entail no gains (or losses). One smaller company specializing in cars and another in tractors would generate the same output as the single company that produces both. However, the product transformation curve is bowed outward (or *concave*) because joint production usually has advantages that enable a single company to produce more cars and tractors with the same resources than would two companies producing each product separately. These production advantages involve the joint sharing of inputs. A single management is often able to schedule and organize production and to handle accounting and financial aspects more effectively than separate managements could.

In general, *economies of scope* are present when the *joint output of a single firm is greater than the output that could be achieved by two different firms each producing a single product* (with equivalent production inputs allocated between the two firms). If a firm's joint output is *less* than that which could be achieved by separate firms, then its production process involves *diseconomies of scope*. This could occur if the production of one product somehow conflicted with the production of the second product.

---

[9] For a more general analysis of economies of scope, see Elizabeth E. Bailey and Ann F. Friedlaender, "Market Structure and Multiproduct Industries: A Review Article," *Journal of Economic Literature* 20 (Sept. 1982): 1024–1048, or John C. Panzar and Robert D. Willig, "Economies of Scope," *American Economic Review* 71 (May 1981): 268–272.

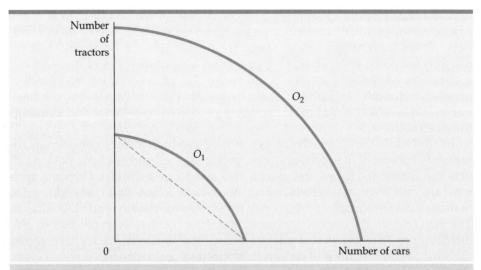

Figure 7.10 Product Transformation Curve The product transformation curve describes the different combinations of two outputs that can be produced with a fixed amount of production inputs. The product transformation curves O_1 and O_2 are bowed out (or concave) because there are economies of scope in production.

There is no direct relationship between economies of scale and economies of scope. A two-output firm can enjoy economies of scope even if its production process involves diseconomies of scale. Suppose, for example, that manufacturing flutes and piccolos jointly is cheaper than producing both separately. Yet the production process involves highly skilled labor and is most effective if undertaken on a small scale. Likewise, a joint-product firm can have economies of scale for each individual product, yet not enjoy economies of scope. Imagine, for example, a large conglomerate that owns several firms that produce efficiently on a large scale but that do not take advantage of economies of scope because they are administered separately.

The extent to which there are economies of scope can also be determined by studying a firm's costs. If a combination of inputs used by one firm generates more output than two independent firms would produce, then it costs less for a single firm to produce both products than it would cost the independent firms. To measure the degree to which there are economies of scope, we should ask what percentage of the cost of production is saved when two (or more) products are produced jointly rather than individually. Equation (7.8) gives the *degree of economies of scope* (SC) that measures this savings in cost:

$$SC = \frac{C(Q_1) + C(Q_2) - C(Q_1, Q_2)}{C(Q_1, Q_2)} \tag{7.8}$$

$C(Q_1)$ represents the cost of producing output Q_1, $C(Q_2)$ the cost of producing output Q_2, and $C(Q_1, Q_2)$ the joint cost of producing both outputs. (When the physical units of output can be added, as in the car-tractor example, the expression becomes $C(Q_1 + Q_2)$.) With economies of scope, the joint cost is less than the sum of the individual costs, so that SC is greater than 0. With diseconomies of scope, SC is negative. In general, the larger the value of SC, the greater the economies of scope.

| E X A M P L E   7.3 | **Economies of Scope in the Trucking Industry** |

Suppose that you are managing a trucking firm that hauls loads of different sizes between cities.[10] In the trucking business, several related but distinct products can be offered, depending on the size of the load and the length of the haul. First, any load, small or large, can be taken directly from one location to another without intermediate stops. Second, a load can be combined with other loads, which may go between different locations, and eventually be shipped indirectly from its origin to the appropriate destination. And each type of load, partial or full, may involve different lengths of haul.

This raises questions about both economies of scale and economies of scope. The scale question is whether large-scale, direct hauls are cheaper and more profitable than individual hauls by small truckers. The scope question is whether a large trucking firm enjoys cost advantages from operating both direct quick hauls and indirect, slower (but less expensive) hauls. Central planning and organization of routes could provide for economies of scope. The key to the presence of economies of scale is the fact that the organization of routes and the types of hauls we have described can be accomplished more efficiently when many hauls are involved. Then it will be more likely that hauls can be scheduled that allow most truckloads to be full, rather than half-full.

Studies of the trucking industry show that economies of scope are present. For example, one analysis of 105 trucking firms looked at four distinct outputs: (1) short hauls with partial loads, (2) intermediate hauls with partial loads, (3) long hauls with partial loads, and (4) hauls with total loads. The results indicate that the degree of economies of scope SC was 1.576 for a reasonably large firm. However, the degree of economies of scope falls to 0.104 when the firm becomes very large. Large firms carry sufficiently large truckloads, so there is usually no advantage to stopping at an intermediate terminal to fill a partial load. A direct trip from the origin to the destination is sufficient. Apparently, however, other disadvantages are associated with the management of very large firms, so the economies of scope get smaller as the firm gets bigger. In any event, the ability to combine partial loads at an intermediate location lowers the firm's costs and increases its profitability.

The study suggests, therefore, that to compete in the trucking industry a firm must be large enough to be able to combine loads at intermediate stopping points.

---

[10] This example is based on Judy S. Wang Chiang and Ann F. Friedlaender, "Truck Technology and Efficient Market Structure," *Review of Economics and Statistics* 67 (1985): 250–258.

*7.6 Dynamic Changes in Costs— The Learning Curve

Our discussion has suggested one reason a large firm may have a lower long-run average cost than a small firm—increasing returns to scale in production. It is tempting to conclude that firms that enjoy lower average cost over time are growing firms with increasing returns to scale. But this need not be true. In some firms, long-run average cost may decline over time because workers and managers absorb new technological information as they become more experienced at their jobs.

As management and labor gain experience with production, the firm's marginal and average costs of producing a given level of output fall for four reasons. First, workers often take longer to accomplish a given task the first few times they do it. As they become more adept, their speed increases. Second, managers learn to schedule the production process more effectively, from the flow of materials to the organization of the manufacturing itself. Third, engineers, who are initially very cautious in their product designs, may gain enough experience to be able to allow for tolerances in design that save cost without increasing defects. Better and more specialized tools and plant organization may also lower cost. Fourth, suppliers of materials may learn how to process materials required by the firm more effectively and may pass on some of this advantage to the firm in the form of lower materials cost.

As a consequence, a firm "learns" over time as cumulative output increases. Managers can use this learning process to help plan production and to forecast future costs. Figure 7.11 illustrates this process, in the form of a learning curve. A *learning curve* describes the relationship between a firm's cumulative output and the amount of inputs needed to produce a unit of output.

Figure 7.11 shows a learning curve for the production of machine tools by a manufacturer.[11] The horizontal axis measures the *cumulative* number of lots of machine tools that the firm has produced (a lot is a group of approximately 40 machines), and the vertical axis the number of hours of labor needed to produce each lot. Labor input per unit of output directly affects the firm's cost of production because the fewer the hours of labor needed, the lower the marginal and average cost of production.

The learning curve in the figure is based on the relationship

$$L = A + BN^{-\beta} \tag{7.9}$$

where N is the cumulative units of output produced, L is the labor input per units of output, and A, B, and β are constants, with A and B positive, and β between 0 and 1. When N is equal to 1, L is equal to $A + B$, so that $A + B$ measures the labor input required to produce the first unit of output. When β equals 0, labor input per unit of output remains the same as the cumulative

---

[11] See Werner Z. Hirsch, "Manufacturing Progress Functions," *Review of Economics and Statistics* 34 (May 1952): 143–155.

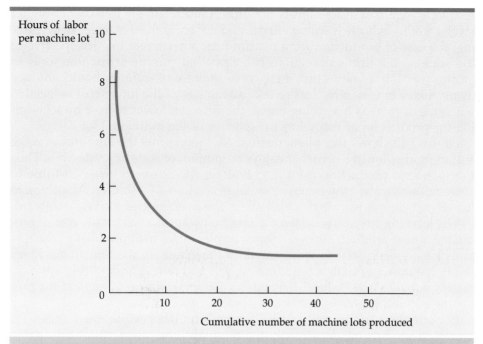

Figure 7.11   The Learning Curve   A firm's cost of production may fall over time as the managers and workers become more experienced and more effective at using the available plant and equipment. The learning curve shows the extent to which the hours of labor needed per unit of output fall as the cumulative output produced increases.

level of output increases, so there is no learning. When β is positive and N gets larger and larger, L becomes arbitrarily close to A, so that A represents the minimum labor input per unit of output after all learning has taken place.

The larger is β, the more important is the learning effect. With β equal to 0.5, for example, the labor input per unit of output falls proportionally to the square root of the cumulative output. This degree of learning can substantially reduce the firm's production costs as the firm becomes more experienced.

In this machine tool example, the value of β is 0.31. For this particular learning curve, every doubling in cumulative output causes the difference between the input requirement and the minimum attainable input requirement to fall by about 20 percent.[12] As Figure 7.11 shows, the learning curve drops sharply as the cumulative number of lots produced increases to about 20. Beyond an output of 20 lots, the cost savings are relatively small.

Once the firm has produced 20 or more machine lots, the entire effect of the learning curve would be complete, and the usual analysis of cost could be employed. If, however, the production process were relatively new, then

---

[12] Because $(L - A) = BN^{-.31}$, we can check that $0.8(L - A)$ is approximately equal to $B(2N)^{-.31}$.

relatively high cost at low levels of output (and relatively low cost at higher levels) would indicate learning effects, and not economies of scale. With learning, the cost of production for a mature firm is relatively low irrespective of the scale of the firm's operation. If a firm that produces machine tools in groups (or "lots") knows that it enjoys economies of scale, it should produce its machines in very large lots to take advantage of the lower cost associated with size. If there is a learning curve, the firm can lower its cost by scheduling the production of many lots irrespective of the individual lot size.

Figure 7.12 shows this phenomenon. AC_1 represents the long-run average cost of production of a firm that enjoys economies of scale in production. Thus the change in production from A to B along AC_1 leads to lower cost due to economies of scale. However, the move from A on AC_1 to C on AC_2 leads to lower cost due to learning, which shifts the average cost curve downward.

The learning curve is crucial for a firm that wants to predict the cost of producing a new product. Suppose, for example, that a firm producing machine tools knows that its labor requirement per machine for the first 10 machines is 1.0, the minimum labor requirement A is equal to zero, and β is approximately equal to 0.32. Table 7.2 calculates the total labor requirement for producing 80 machines.

Because there is a learning curve, the per-unit labor requirement falls with increased production. As a result, the total labor requirement for producing more and more output increases in smaller and smaller increments. Therefore, a firm looking at the high initial labor requirement will obtain an overly pes-

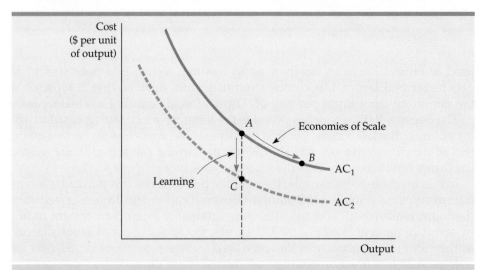

Figure 7.12 **Economies of Scale Versus Learning** A firm's average cost of production can decline over time because of growth of sales when increasing returns are present (a move from A to B on curve AC_1), or it can decline because there is a learning curve (a move from A on curve AC_1 to C on curve AC_2).

Table 7.2 Predicting the Labor Requirements of Producing a Given Output		
Cumulative Output (N)	**Per-Unit Labor Requirement for each 10 units of Output (L)[13]**	**Total Labor Requirement**
10	1.00	10.0
20	.80	18.0 (10.0 + 8.0)
30	.70	25.0 (18.0 + 7.0)
40	.64	31.4 (25.0 + 6.4)
50	.60	37.4 (31.4 + 6.0)
60	.56	43.0 (37.4 + 5.6)
70	.53	48.3 (43.0 + 5.3)
80	.51	53.4 (48.3 + 5.1)

simistic view of the business. Suppose the firm plans to be in business for a long time, producing 10 units per year, and the total labor requirement for the first year's production is 10. In the first year of production, the firm's cost will be high as it learns the business. But once the learning effect has taken place, production costs will be lower. After 8 years, the labor required to produce 10 units will be only 5.1, and per-unit cost will be roughly half what it was in the first year of production. Thus the learning curve can be important for a firm deciding whether it is profitable to enter an industry.

EXAMPLE 7.4 The Learning Curve in Practice

Suppose that as the manager of a firm that has just entered the chemical processing industry you face the following problem: Should you produce a relatively low level of output (and sell at a high price), or should you price your product lower and increase your rate of sales? The second alternative is appealing if there is a learning curve in this industry. Then the increased volume will lower your average production costs over time and increase the firm's profitability.

To decide what to do, you can examine the available statistical evidence that distinguishes the components of the learning curve (learning new processes by labor, engineering improvements, etc.) from increasing returns to scale. For example, a study of 37 chemical products reveals that cost reductions in the

---

[13] The numbers in this column were calculated from the equation $\log(L) = -0.322 \log(N/10)$, where L is the unit labor input and N is cumulative output.

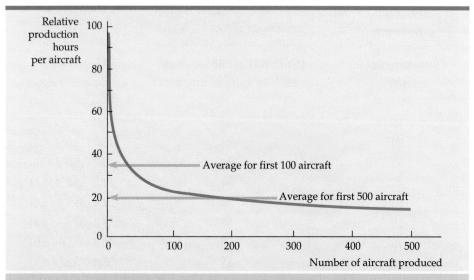

Figure 7.13 Learning Curve for Airbus Industrie The learning curve relates the labor requirement per aircraft to the cumulative number of aircraft produced. As the production process becomes better organized and workers gain familiarity with their jobs, labor requirements fall dramatically.

chemical processing industry were directly tied to the growth of cumulative industry output, to investment in improved capital equipment, and to a lesser extent to economies of scale.[14] In fact, for the entire sample of chemical products, average costs of production fell at 5.5 percent per year.[15] The study reveals that for each doubling of plant scale, the average cost of production falls by 11 percent. For each doubling of cumulative output, however, the average cost of production falls by 27 percent. The evidence shows clearly that learning effects are more important than economies of scale in the chemical processing industry.[16]

The learning curve has also been shown to be important in the semiconductor industry. A study of seven generations of dynamic random-access memory (DRAM) semiconductors from 1974 to 1992 found that the learning

[14] The study was by Marvin Lieberman, "The Learning Curve and Pricing in the Chemical Processing Industries," *RAND Journal of Economics* 15 (1984): 213–228.

[15] The author used the average cost AC of the chemical products, the cumulative industry output X, and the average scale of a production plant Z and estimated the relationship log (AC) = -0.387 log (X) $- 0.173$ log (Z). The -0.387 coefficient on cumulative output tells us that for every 1 percent increase in cumulative output, average cost decreases 0.387 percent. The -0.173 coefficient on plant size tells us that for every 1 percent increase in plant size, cost decreases 0.173 percent.

[16] By interpreting the two coefficients in the previous footnote in light of the levels of the output and plant size variables, we can allocate about 15 percent of the cost reduction to increases in the average scale of plants, and 85 percent to increases in cumulative industry output. (Suppose plant scale doubled, while cumulative output increased by a factor of 5 during the study. Then costs would fall by 11 percent from the increased scale and by 62 percent from the increase in cumulative output.)

rates averaged about 20 percent (so that a 10 percent increase in cumulative production would lead to a 2 percent decrease in cost).[17] The study also compared learning by firms in Japan to firms in the United States, and found that there was no distinguishable difference in the speed of learning.

Another example is the aircraft industry, where studies have found learning rates that are as high as 40 percent.[18] This is illustrated in Figure 7.13, which shows the labor requirements for production of aircraft by Airbus Industrie. Observe that the first 10 or 20 airplanes require far more labor to produce than the hundredth or two hundredth airplane. Also note how the learning curve flattens out after a certain point; in this case, nearly all learning is complete after 200 airplanes have been built.

Learning curve effects can be important in determining the shape of long-run cost curves and can thus help guide the firm's management. Managers can use learning curve information to decide whether a production operation is profitable, and if it is, to plan how large the plant operation and the volume of cumulative output need be to generate a positive cash flow.

*7.7 Estimating and Predicting Cost

A business that is expanding or contracting its operation needs to predict how costs will change as output changes. Estimates of future costs can be obtained from a *cost function*, which relates the cost of production to the level of output and other variables that the firm can control.

Suppose we wanted to characterize the short-run cost of production in the automobile industry. We could obtain data on the number of automobiles Q produced by each car company and relate this information to the variable cost of production VC. The use of variable cost, rather than total cost, avoids the problem of trying to allocate the fixed cost of a multiproduct firm's production process to the particular product being studied.[19]

Figure 7.14 shows a typical pattern of cost and output data. Each point on the graph relates the output of an auto company to that company's variable cost of production. To predict cost accurately, we need to determine the underlying relationship between variable cost and output. Then, if a company expands its production, we can calculate what the associated cost is likely to be. The curve in the figure is drawn with this in mind—it provides a reasonably close fit to the cost data. (Typically, least-squares regression analysis would be used to fit the curve to the data.) But what shape of curve is the most appropriate, and how do we represent that shape algebraically?

---

[17] The study was by D. A. Irwin and P. J. Klenow, "Learning-by-Doing Spillovers in the Semiconductor Industry," Graduate School of Business, University of Chicago, 1993.

[18] See, for example, N. K. Womer and J. W. Patterson, "Estimation and Testing of Learning Curves," *Journal of Business and Economic Statistics* (Oct. 1983).

[19] If an additional piece of equipment is needed as output increases, then annual rental cost of the equipment should be counted as a variable cost. If, however, the same machine can be used at all output levels, then its cost is fixed and should not be included.

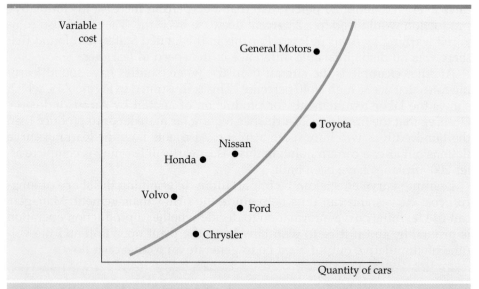

Figure 7.14 Total Cost Curve for the Automobile Industry An empirical estimate of the total cost curve can be obtained by using data for individual firms in an industry. The total cost curve for automobile production is obtained by determining statistically the curve that best fits the points that relate the output of each firm to the total cost of production.

One cost function that might be chosen is

$$VC = \beta Q \tag{7.10}$$

This *linear* relationship between cost and output is easy to use but is applicable only if marginal cost is constant.[20] For every unit increase in output, variable cost increases by β, so marginal cost is constant and equal to β.

If we wish to allow for a U-shaped average cost curve and a marginal cost that is not constant, we must use a more complex cost function. One possibility is the *quadratic* cost function, which relates variable cost to output and output squared:

$$VC = \beta Q + \gamma Q^2 \tag{7.11}$$

This implies a straight-line marginal cost curve of the form $MC = \beta + 2\gamma Q$.[21] Marginal cost increases with output if γ is positive, and decreases with output if γ is negative.

If the marginal cost curve is not linear, we might use a *cubic* cost function:

$$VC = \beta Q + \gamma Q^2 + \delta Q^3 \tag{7.12}$$

---

[20] In statistical cost analyses, other variables might be added to the cost function to account for differences in input costs, production processes, product mix, etc., among firms.

[21] Short-run marginal cost is given by $\Delta VC/\Delta Q = \beta + \gamma \Delta(Q^2)/\Delta Q$. But $\Delta(Q^2)/\Delta Q = 2Q$. (Check this using calculus or by numerical example.) Therefore, $MC = \beta + 2\gamma Q$.

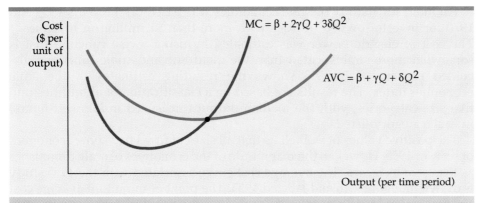

Figure 7.15 Cubic Cost Function A cubic cost function implies that the average and the marginal cost curves are U-shaped.

Figure 7.15 shows this cubic cost function. It implies U-shaped marginal as well as average cost curves.

Cost functions can be difficult to measure. First, output data often represent an aggregate of different types of products. Total automobiles produced by General Motors, for example, involves different models of cars. Second, cost data are often obtained directly from accounting information that fails to reflect opportunity costs. Third, allocating maintenance and other plant costs to a particular product is difficult when the firm is a conglomerate that produces more than one product line.

Cost Functions and the Measurement of Scale Economies

Recall that the cost-output elasticity E_c is less than one when there are economies of scale and greater than one when there are diseconomies of scale. An alternative index, the *scale economies index* (SCI), is defined as follows:

$$SCI = 1 - E_c \qquad (7.13)$$

When $E_c = 1$, SCI $= 0$, and there are no economies or diseconomies of scale. When E_c is greater than one, SCI is negative, and there are diseconomies of scale. Finally, when E_c is less than 1, SCI is positive, and there are economies of scale.

E X A M P L E 7.5   Cost Functions for Electric Power

In 1955, consumers bought 369 billion kilowatt-hours (kwh) of electricity; in 1970 they bought 1083 billion. Because there were fewer electric utilities in 1970, the output per firm had increased substantially. Was this increase due to economies of scale or other reasons? If it was the result of economies of scale, it would be economically inefficient for regulators to "break up" electric utility monopolies.

An interesting study of scale economies was based on the years 1955 and 1970 for investor-owned utilities with more than $1 million in revenues.[22] The cost of electric power was estimated by using a cost function that is somewhat more sophisticated than the quadratic and cubic functions discussed earlier.[23] Table 7.3 shows the resulting estimates of the scale economies index. The results are based on a classification of all utilities into five size categories, with the median output (measured in kilowatt-hours) in each category listed.

The positive values of SCI tell us that all sizes of firms had some economies of scale in 1955. However, the magnitude of the economies of scale diminishes as firm size increases. The average cost curve associated with the 1955 study is drawn in Figure 7.16 and labeled 1955. The point of minimum average cost occurs at point A at an output of approximately 20 billion kilowatts. Because there were no firms of this size in 1955, no firm had exhausted the opportunity for returns to scale in production. Note, however, that the average cost curve is relatively flat from an output of 9 billion kilowatts and higher, a range in which 7 of 124 firms produced.

When the same cost functions were estimated with 1970 data, the cost curve labeled 1970 in Figure 7.16 was the result. The graph shows clearly that the average costs of production fell from 1955 to 1970. (The data are in real 1970 dollars.) But the flat part of the curve now begins at about 15 billion kwh. By 1970, 24 of 80 firms were producing in this range. Thus many more firms were operating in the flat portion of the average cost curve in which economies of scale are not an important phenomenon. More important, most of the firms were producing in a portion of the 1970 cost curve that was flatter than their point of operation on the 1955 curve. (Five firms were at a point of diseconomies of scale: Consolidated Edison [SCI = −0.003], Detroit Edison [SCI = −0.004], Duke Power [SCI = −0.012], Commonwealth Edison [SCI = −0.014], and Southern [SCI = −0.028].) Thus unexploited scale economies were much smaller in 1970 than in 1955.

This cost function analysis makes it clear that the decline in the cost of producing electric power cannot be explained by the ability of larger firms to take advantage of economies of scale. Rather, improvements in technology unrelated to the scale of the firms' operation and the decline in the real cost of energy inputs, such as coal and oil, are important reasons for the lower costs. The tendency toward lower average cost caused by a movement to the right

Table 7.3 Scale Economies in the Electric Power Industry					
Output (million kwh)	43	338	1109	2226	5819
Value of SCI, 1955	.41	.26	.16	.10	.04

---

[22] This example is based on Laurits Christensen and William H. Greene, "Economies of Scale in U.S. Electric Power Generation," *Journal of Political Economy* 84 (1976): 655–676.

[23] The translog cost function that was used provides a more general functional relationship than any of those we have discussed.

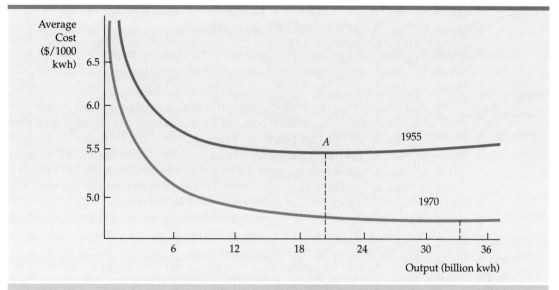

Figure 7.16 Average Cost of Production in the Electric Power Industry The average cost of electric power in 1955 achieved a minimum at approximately 20 billion kilowatt-hours. By 1970 the average cost of production had fallen sharply and achieved a minimum at an output of more than 33 billion kilowatt-hours.

along an average cost curve is minimal compared with the effect of technological improvement.

E X A M P L E   7 . 6 **A Cost Function for the Savings and Loan Industry**

Understanding returns to scale in the savings and loan industry is important for regulators who must decide how savings and loans should be restructured in light of the failure of numerous institutions. In this regard, the empirical estimation of a long-run cost function can be useful.[24]

Data were collected for 86 savings and loan associations for 1975 and 1976 in a region that includes Idaho, Montana, Oregon, Utah, Washington, and Wyoming. Output is difficult to measure in this case because a savings and loan association provides a service to its customers, rather than a physical product. The output Q measure reported here (and used in other studies) is the total assets of each savings and loan association. In general, the larger the asset base of an association, the higher its profitability. Long-run average cost LAC is measured by average operating expense. Output and total operating

---

[24] This example builds on J. Holton Wilson, "A Note on Scale Economies in the Savings and Loan Industry," *Business Economics* (Jan. 1981): 45–49.

costs are measured in hundreds of millions of dollars. Average operating costs are measured as a percentage of total assets.

A quadratic long-run average cost function was estimated for the year 1975, yielding the following relationship:

$$LAC = 2.38 - 0.6153Q + 0.0536Q^2$$

The estimated long-run average cost function is U-shaped and reaches its point of minimum average cost when the total assets of the savings and loan reach \$574 million.[25] (At this point the average operating expenses of the savings and loan are 0.61 percent of its total assets.) Because almost all savings and loans in the region being studied had substantially less than \$574 million in assets, the cost function analysis suggests that an expansion of savings and loans through either growth or mergers would be valuable.

How appropriate such a policy is cannot be fully evaluated here, however. To do so, we would need to take into account the possible social costs associated with the lessening of competition from growth or mergers, and we would need to assure ourselves that this particular cost function analysis accurately estimated the point of minimum average cost.

Summary

1. Managers, investors, and economists must take into account the opportunity cost associated with the use of the firm's resources—the cost associated with the opportunities foregone when the firm uses its resources in its next best alternative.

2. In the short run, one or more of the inputs of the firm are fixed. Total cost can be divided into fixed cost and variable cost. A firm's *marginal cost* is the additional variable cost associated with each additional unit of output. The *average variable cost* is the total variable cost divided by the number of units of output.

3. When there is a single variable input, as in the short run, the presence of diminishing returns determines the shape of the cost curves. In particular, there is an inverse relationship between the marginal product of the variable input and the marginal cost of production. The average variable cost and average total cost curves are U-shaped. The short-run mar-

ginal cost curve increases beyond a certain point, and cuts both average cost curves from below at their minimum points.

4. In the long run, all inputs to the production process are variable. As a result, the choice of inputs depends both on the relative costs of the factors of production and on the extent to which the firm can substitute among inputs in its production process. The cost-minimizing input choice is made by finding the point of tangency between the isoquant representing the level of desired output and an isocost line.

5. The firm's expansion path describes how its cost-minimizing input choices vary as the scale or output of its operation increases. As a result, the expansion path provides useful information relevant for long-run planning decisions.

6. The long-run average cost curve is the envelope of the firm's short-run average cost

---

[25] This can be seen by graphing the curve, or by differentiating the average cost function with respect to Q, setting it equal to 0, and solving for Q.

curves, and it reflects the presence or absence of returns to scale. When there are constant returns to scale and many plant sizes are possible, the long-run cost curve is horizontal, and the envelope consists of the points of minimum short-run average cost. However, when there are increasing returns to scale initially and then decreasing returns to scale, the long-run average cost curve is U-shaped, and the envelope does not include all points of minimum short-run average cost.

7. A firm enjoys economies of scale when it can double its output at less than twice the cost. Correspondingly, there are diseconomies of scale when a doubling of output requires more than twice the cost. Scale economies and diseconomies apply even when input proportions are variable; returns to scale applies only when input proportions are fixed.

8. When a firm produces two (or more) outputs, it is important to note whether there are economies of scope in production. Economies

of scope arise when the firm can produce any combination of the two outputs more cheaply than could two independent firms that each produced a single product. The degree of economies of scope is measured by the percentage in reduction in cost when one firm produces two products relative to the cost of producing them individually.

9. A firm's average cost of production can fall over time if the firm "learns" how to produce more effectively. The *learning curve* describes how much the input needed to produce a given output falls as the cumulative output of the firm increases.

10. Cost functions relate the cost of production to the level of output of the firm. The functions can be measured in both the short run and the long run by using either data for firms in an industry at a given time or data for an industry over time. A number of functional relationships including linear, quadratic, and cubic can be used to represent cost functions.

Questions for Review

1. A firm pays its accountant an annual retainer of $10,000. Is this an explicit or an implicit cost?

2. The owner of a small retail store does her own accounting work. How would you measure the opportunity cost of her work?

3. Suppose a chair manufacturer finds that the marginal rate of technical substitution of capital for labor in his production process is substantially greater than the ratio of the rental rate on machinery to the wage rate for assembly-line labor. How should he alter his use of capital and labor to minimize the cost of production?

4. Why are isocost lines straight lines?

5. If the marginal cost of production is increasing, does this tell you whether the average variable cost is increasing or decreasing? Explain.

6. If the marginal cost of production is greater than the average variable cost, does this tell you whether the average variable cost is increasing or decreasing? Explain.

7. If the firm's average cost curves are U-shaped, why does its average variable cost curve achieve its minimum at a lower level of output than the average total cost curve?

8. If a firm enjoys increasing returns to scale up to a certain output level, and then constant returns to scale, what can you say about the shape of the firm's long-run average cost curve?

9. How does a change in the price of one input change the firm's long-run expansion path?

10. Distinguish between economies of scale and economies of scope. Why can one be present without the other?

Exercises

1. Assume a computer firm's marginal costs of production are constant at $1000 per computer. However, the fixed costs of production are equal to $10,000.
   a. Calculate the firm's average variable cost and average total cost curves.
   b. If the firm wanted to minimize the average total cost of production, would it choose to be very large or very small? Explain.

2. If a firm hires a currently unemployed worker, the opportunity cost of utilizing the worker's service is zero. Is this true? Discuss.

3. a. Suppose a firm must pay an annual franchise fee or tax, which is a fixed sum, independent of whether it produces any output. How does this tax affect the firm's fixed, marginal, and average costs?
   b. Now suppose the firm is charged a tax that is proportional to the number of items it produces. Again, how does this tax affect the firm's fixed, marginal, and average costs?

4. A recent issue of *Business Week* reported the following:

   During the recent auto sales slump, GM, Ford, and Chrysler decided it was cheaper to sell cars to rental companies at a loss than to lay off workers. That's because closing and reopening plants is expensive, partly because the automakers' current union contracts obligate them to pay many workers even if they're not working.

   When the article discusses selling cars "at a loss," is it referring to accounting profit or economic profit? How will the two differ in this case? Explain briefly.

5. A chair manufacturer hires its assembly-line labor for $22 an hour and calculates that the rental cost of its machinery is $110 per hour. Suppose that a chair can be produced using 4 hours of labor or machinery in any combination. If the firm is currently using 3 hours of labor for each hour of machine time, is it minimizing its costs of production? If so, why? If not, how can it improve the situation?

6. Suppose the economy takes a downturn, and labor costs fall by 50 percent and are expected to stay at that level for a long time. Show graphically how this change in the relative price of labor and capital affects the firm's expansion path.

7. You are in charge of cost control in a large metropolitan transit district. A consultant you have hired comes to you with the following report:

   Our research has shown that the cost of running a bus for each trip down its line is $30 regardless of the number of passengers it carries. Each bus can carry 50 people. At rush hour, when the buses are full, the average cost per passenger is 60 cents. However, during off-peak hours, average ridership falls to 18 people, and average cost soars to $1.67 per passenger. As a result, we should encourage more rush-hour business when costs are cheaper and discourage off-peak business when costs are higher.

   Do you follow the consultant's advice? Discuss.

8. An oil refinery consists of different pieces of processing equipment, each of which differs in its ability to break down heavy sulfurized crude oil into final products. The refinery process is such that the marginal cost of producing gasoline is constant up to a point as crude oil is put through a basic distilling unit. However, as the unit fills up, the firm finds that in the short run the amount of crude oil that can be processed is limited. The marginal cost of producing gasoline is also constant up to a capacity limit when crude oil is put through a more sophisticated hydrocracking unit. Graph the marginal cost of gasoline production when a basic distilling unit and a hydrocracker are used.

9. You manage a plant that mass produces engines by teams of workers using assembly

machines. The technology is summarized by the production function

$$Q = 4 \, KL$$

where Q is the number of engines per week, K is the number of assembly machines, and L is the number of labor teams. Each assembly machine rents for $r = \$12{,}000$ per week and each team costs $w = \$3000$ per week. Engine costs are given by the cost of labor teams and machines, plus $\$2000$ per engine for raw materials. Your plant has a fixed installation of 10 assembly machines as part of its design.

a. What is the cost function for your plant— namely, how much will it cost to produce Q engines? What are average and marginal costs for producing Q engines? How do average costs vary with output?

b. How many teams are required for producing 80 engines? What is the average cost per engine?

c. You are asked to make recommendations for the design of a new production facility. What would you suggest? In particular, what capital/labor (K/L) ratio should the new plant accommodate? If lower average cost were your only criterion, should you suggest that the new plant have more production capacity or less production capacity than the plant you currently manage?

*10. A computer company's cost function, which relates its average cost of production AC to its cumulative output in thousands of computers CQ and its plant size in terms of thousands of computers produced per year Q, within the production range of 10,000 to 50,000 computers, is given by

$$AC = 10 - 0.1CQ + 0.3Q$$

a. Is there a learning curve effect?

b. Are there increasing or decreasing returns to scale?

c. During its existence, the firm has produced a total of 40,000 computers and is producing 10,000 computers this year. Next year it plans to increase its production to 12,000 computers. Will its average cost of production increase or decrease? Explain.

11. The total short-run cost function of a company is given by the equation $C = 190 + 53Q$, where C is the total cost and Q is the total quantity of output, both measured in tens of thousands.

a. What is the company's fixed cost?

b. If the company produces 100,000 units, what is its average variable cost?

c. What is its marginal cost *per unit* produced?

d. What is its average fixed cost?

e. Suppose the company borrows money and expands its factory. Its fixed cost rises by $\$50{,}000$, but its variable cost falls to $\$45{,}000$ per 10,000 units. The cost of interest (I) also enters into the equation. Each one-point increase in the interest rate raises costs by $\$30{,}000$. Write the new cost equation.

*12. Suppose the long-run total cost function for an industry is given by the cubic equation $TC = a + bQ + cQ^2 + dQ^3$. Show (using calculus) that this total cost function is consistent with a U-shaped average cost curve for at least some values of the parameters a, b, c, d.

*13. A computer company produces hardware and software using the same plant and labor. The total cost of producing computer processing units H and software programs S is given by

$$TC = aH + bS - cHS$$

where $a, b,$ and c are positive. Is this total cost function consistent with the presence of economies or diseconomies of scale? With economies or diseconomies of scope?

This appendix presents a mathematical treatment of the basics of production and cost theory. As in the appendix to Chapter 4, we use the method of Lagrange multipliers to solve the firm's cost-minimizing problem.

Cost Minimization

The theory of the firm relies on the assumption that firms choose inputs to the production process that minimize the cost of producing output. If there are two inputs, capital K and labor L, the production function $F(K, L)$ describes the maximum output that can be produced for every possible combination of inputs. We assume that each of the factors in the production process has positive but decreasing marginal products. Writing the marginal product of capital as $MP_K(K, L) = \partial F(K, L)/\partial K$, we assume that $MP_K(K, L) > 0$ and $\partial MP_K(K, L)/\partial K < 0$. Similarly, if the marginal product of labor is given by $MP_L(K, L) = \partial F(K, L)/\partial L$, we assume that $MP_L(K, L) > 0$ and $\partial MP_L(K, L)/\partial L < 0$.

A competitive firm takes the prices of both labor w and capital r as given. Then the cost-minimization problem can be written as

$$\text{Minimize } C = wL + rK \tag{A7.1}$$

subject to the constraint that a fixed output Q_0 be produced:

$$F(K, L) = Q_0 \tag{A7.2}$$

C represents the cost of producing the fixed level of output Q_0, and w and r are the wage rate and price of capital, respectively.

To determine the firm's demand for the inputs capital and labor, we choose the values of K and L that minimize (A7.1) subject to (A7.2). We can solve this constrained optimization problem using the method discussed in Appendix 4. The Lagrangian is

$$\Phi = wL + rK - \lambda[F(K, L) - Q_0] \tag{A7.3}$$

where λ is the Lagrange multiplier. By differentiating with respect to K, L, and then λ, and equating the derivatives to zero, we obtain the necessary conditions for a maximum:[1]

$$\partial\Phi/\partial K = r - \lambda MP_K(K, L) = 0$$
$$\partial\Phi/\partial L = w - \lambda MP_L(K, L) = 0 \tag{A7.4}$$
$$\partial\Phi/\partial\lambda = F(K, L) = Q_0$$

---

[1] These conditions are necessary for a solution involving positive amounts of both inputs.

245

By combining the first two conditions we obtain

$$MP_K(K, L)/r = MP_L(K, L)/w \tag{A7.5}$$

Equation (A7.5) tells us that if the firm is minimizing costs it will choose its factor inputs to equate the ratio of the marginal product of each factor divided by its price. To see that this makes sense, suppose MP_K/r were greater than MP_L/w. Then the firm could reduce its cost while still producing the same output by using more capital and less labor.

Finally, we can combine the first two conditions of (A7.4) in a different way to evaluate the Lagrange multiplier:

$$\lambda = r/MP_K(K, L) = w/MP_L(K, L) \tag{A7.6}$$

Suppose output increases by one unit. Because the marginal product of capital measures the extra output associated with an additional input of capital, $1/MP_K(K, L)$ measures the extra capital needed to produce one unit of output. Therefore, $r/MP_K(K, L)$ measures the additional input cost of producing an additional unit of output by increasing capital. Likewise, $w/MP_L(K, L)$ measures the additional cost of producing a unit of output using additional labor as an input. In both cases, the Lagrange multiplier is equal to the marginal cost of production, because it tells us how much the cost increases if the amount is increased by one unit.

Marginal Rate of Technical Substitution

Recall that an isoquant is a curve that represents the set of all input combinations that give the firm the same level of output, say, Q^*. Thus the condition that $F(K, L) = Q^*$ represents a production isoquant. As input combinations are changed along an isoquant, the change in output, given by the total derivative of $F(K, L)$, equals zero (i.e., $dQ = 0$). Thus

$$MP_K(K, L)dK + MP_L(K, L)dL = dQ = 0 \tag{A7.7}$$

It follows by rearrangement that

$$-dK/dL = MRTS_{LK} = MP_L(K, L)/MP_K(K, L) \tag{A7.8}$$

where $MRTS_{LK}$ is the firm's marginal rate of technical substitution between labor and capital.

Now, rewrite the condition given by (A7.5) to get

$$MP_L(K, L)/MP_K(K, L) = w/r \tag{A7.9}$$

Because the left side of (A7.8) represents the negative of the slope of the isoquant, it follows that at the point of tangency of the isoquant and the isocost line, the firm's marginal rate of technical substitution (which trades off inputs while keeping output constant) is equal to the ratio of the input prices (which represents the slope of the firm's isocost line).

We can look at this result another way by rewriting (A7.9) again:

$$MP_L/w = MP_K/r \qquad \text{(A7.10)}$$

Equation (A7.10) tells us that the marginal products of all production inputs must be equal when these marginal products are adjusted by the unit cost of each input. If the cost-adjusted marginal products were not equal, the firm could change its inputs to produce the same output at a lower cost.

Duality in Production and Cost Theory

As in consumer theory, the firm's input decision has a dual nature. The optimum choice of K and L can be analyzed not only as the problem of choosing the lowest isocost line tangent to the production isoquant, but also as the problem of choosing the highest production isoquant tangent to a given isocost line. To see this, consider the following dual producer problem:

$$\text{Maximize } F(K, L)$$

subject to the cost constraint that

$$wL + rK = C_0 \qquad \text{(A7.11)}$$

The corresponding Lagrangian is given by

$$\Phi = F(K, L) - \mu(wL + rK - C_0) \qquad \text{(A7.12)}$$

where μ is the Lagrange multiplier. The necessary conditions for output maximization are

$$MP_K(K, L) - \mu r = 0$$
$$MP_L(K, L) - \mu w = 0 \qquad \text{(A7.13)}$$
$$wL + rK - C_0 = 0$$

By solving the first two equations, we see that

$$MP_K(K, L)/r = MP_L(K, L)/w \qquad \text{(A7.14)}$$

which is identical to the condition that was necessary for cost minimization.

The Cobb-Douglas Cost and Production Functions

Given a specific production function $F(K, L)$, conditions (A7.13) and (A7.14) can be used to derive the *cost function* $C(Q)$. To see this, let's work through the example of a Cobb-Douglas production function. This production function is

$$F(K, L) = AK^\alpha L^\beta$$

or, by taking the logs of both sides of the production function equation:

$$\log [F(K, L)] = \log A + \alpha \log K + \beta \log L$$

We assume that $\alpha < 1$ and $\beta < 1$, so that the firm has decreasing marginal products of labor and capital.[2] If $\alpha + \beta = 1$, the firm has *constant returns to scale*, because doubling K and L doubles F. If $\alpha + \beta > 1$, the firm has *increasing returns to scale*, and if $\alpha + \beta < 1$, it has *decreasing returns to scale*.

To find the amounts of capital and labor that the firm should utilize to minimize the cost of producing an output Q_0, we first write the Lagrangian

$$\Phi = wL + rK - \lambda(AK^{\alpha}L^{\beta} - Q_0) \tag{A7.15}$$

Differentiating with respect to L, K, and λ, and setting those derivatives equal to 0, we obtain

$$\partial\Phi/\partial L = w - \lambda(\beta AK^{\alpha}L^{\beta-1}) = 0 \tag{A7.16}$$

$$\partial\Phi/\partial K = r - \lambda(\alpha AK^{\alpha-1}L^{\beta}) = 0 \tag{A7.17}$$

$$\partial\Phi/\partial\lambda = AK^{\alpha}L^{\beta} - Q_0 = 0 \tag{A7.18}$$

From equation (A7.16) we have

$$\lambda = w/A\beta K^{\alpha}L^{\beta-1} \tag{A7.19}$$

Substituting this into equation (A7.17) gives us

$$r\beta AK^{\alpha}L^{\beta-1} = w\alpha AK^{\alpha-1}L^{\beta} \tag{A7.20}$$

or

$$L = \beta rK/\alpha w \tag{A7.21}$$

Now, use equation (A7.21) to eliminate L from equation (A7.18):

$$AK^{\alpha}\beta^{\beta}r^{\beta}K^{\beta}/\alpha^{\beta}w^{\beta} = Q_0 \tag{A7.22}$$

Rewrite this as

$$K^{\alpha+\beta} = (\alpha w/\beta r)^{\beta}Q_0/A \tag{A7.23}$$

or

$$K = [(\alpha w/\beta r)^{\beta/(\alpha+\beta)}](Q_0/A)^{1/(\alpha+\beta)} \tag{A7.24}$$

We have now determined the cost-minimizing quantity of capital. To determine the cost-minimizing quantity of labor, we simply substitute equation (A7.24) into equation (A7.21):

$$L = [(\beta r/\alpha w)^{\alpha/(\alpha+\beta)}](Q_0/A)^{1/(\alpha+\beta)} \tag{A7.25}$$

Note that if the wage rate w rises relative to the price of capital r, the firm will use more capital and less labor. If, say because of technological change, A increases (so the firm can produce more output with the same inputs), both K and L will fall.

---

[2] For example, the marginal product of labor is given by $MP_L = \partial[F(K,L)]/\partial L = \beta AK^{\alpha}L^{\beta-1}$, so that MP_L falls as L increases.

We have shown how cost-minimization subject to an output constraint can be used to determine the firm's optimal mix of capital and labor. Now we will determine the firm's cost function. The total cost of producing *any output Q* can be obtained by substituting equations (A7.24) for *K* and (A7.25) for *L* into the equation $C = wL + rK$. After some algebraic manipulation we find that

$$C = w^{\beta/(\alpha+\beta)} \, r^{\alpha/(\alpha+\beta)} \left[\left(\frac{\alpha}{\beta} \right)^{\beta/(\alpha+\beta)} + \left(\frac{\alpha}{\beta} \right)^{-\alpha/(\alpha+\beta)} \right] \left(\frac{Q}{A} \right)^{1/(\alpha+\beta)} \qquad \text{(A7.26)}$$

This *cost function* tells both how the total cost of production increases as the level of output *Q* increases, and also how cost changes as input prices change. When $\alpha + \beta$ equals 1, cost will increase proportionately with output, which means that the production process exhibits constant returns to scale. Likewise if $\alpha + \beta$ is greater than 1, there are decreasing returns to scale, and if $\alpha + \beta$ is less than 1, there are increasing returns to scale.

Now consider the dual problem of maximizing the output that can be produced with the expenditure of C_0 dollars. We leave it to you to work through this problem for the Cobb-Douglas production function, and show that equations (A7.24) and (A7.25) describe the cost-minimizing input choices. To get you started, note that the Lagrangian for this dual problem is $\Phi = AK^\alpha L^\beta - \mu(wL + rK - C_0)$.

Exercises

1. Of the following production functions, which exhibit increasing, constant, or decreasing returns to scale?
   a. $F(K, L) = K^2 L$
   b. $F(K, L) = 10K + 5L$
   c. $F(K, L) = (KL)^{.5}$

2. The production function for a product is given by $Q = 100KL$. If the price of capital is $120 per day and the price of labor is $30 per day, what is the minimum cost of producing 1000 units of output?

3. Suppose a production function is given by $F(K, L) = KL^2$, and that the price of capital is $10 and the price of labor $15. What combination of labor and capital minimizes the cost of producing any given output?

4. Suppose the process of producing lightweight parkas by Polly's Parkas is described by the function

$$Q = 10K^{.8} \, (L - 40)^{.2}$$

where *Q* is the number of parkas produced, *K* is the number of computerized stitching-machine hours, and *L* is the number of per-son-hours of labor. In addition to capital and labor, $10 worth of raw materials are used in the production of each parka.

   a. By minimizing cost subject to the production function, derive the cost-minimizing demands for *K* and *L* as a function of output (*Q*), wage rates (*w*), and rental rates on machines (*r*). Use these to derive the total cost function (costs as a function of *Q*, *r*, *w*, and the constant $10 per unit materials cost).

   b. This process requires skilled workers, who earn $32 per hour. The rental rate on the machines used in the process is $64 per hour. At these factor prices, what are total costs as a function of *Q*? Does this technology exhibit decreasing, constant, or increasing returns to scale?

   c. Polly's Parkas plans to produce 2000 parkas per week. At the factor prices given above, how many workers should they hire (at 40 hours per week) and how many machines should they rent (at 40 machine-hours per week)? What are the marginal and average costs at this level of production?

Chapter Outline

List of Examples

CHAPTER 8

Profit Maximization and Competitive Supply

A cost curve describes the minimum cost at which a firm can produce various amounts of output. With this knowledge, we can now turn to a fundamental problem faced by every firm: How much should be produced? In this chapter, we will see how a perfectly competitive firm chooses the level of output that maximizes its profit. We will also see how the output choice of individual firms leads to a supply curve for the entire industry.

Our discussion of production and cost in Chapters 6 and 7 applies to firms in all kinds of markets, but in this chapter we discuss only firms in perfectly competitive markets. In a perfectly competitive market all firms produce the identical product, and each firm is so small in relation to the industry that its production decisions have no effect on market price. New firms can easily enter the industry if they perceive a potential for profit, and existing firms can exit the industry if they start losing money.

We begin by explaining why it makes sense to assume that firms maximize profit. We provide a rule for choosing the profit-maximizing output for firms in all markets—

competitive or otherwise. Then we show how a competitive firm chooses its output in the short and long run. We see how this output choice changes as the cost of production or the prices of inputs change. In this way, we show how to derive the firm's *supply curve*. We then aggregate the supply curves of individual firms to obtain the *industry* supply curve. In the short run, firms in an industry choose which level of output to produce to maximize profit. In the long run, firms not only make output choices, but also decide whether to be in a market at all. We will see that the prospect of high profits encourages firms to enter an industry, while losses encourage them to leave.

8.1 Profit Maximization

In this section we analyze profit maximization by firms. First, we ask whether firms do indeed seek to maximize profit. Then, we describe a rule that any firm—whether in a competitive market or not—can use to find its profit-maximizing output level. Next, we consider the special case of a firm in a competitive market. We distinguish the demand curve facing a competitive firm from the market demand curve, and then use this information to describe the competitive firm's profit-maximization rule.

Do Firms Maximize Profit?

The assumption of profit maximization is frequently used in microeconomics because it predicts business behavior reasonably accurately and avoids unnecessary analytical complications. But whether firms do maximize profit has been controversial.

For smaller firms managed by their owners, profit is likely to dominate almost all the firm's decisions. In larger firms, however, managers who make day-to-day decisions usually have little contact with the owners (i.e., the stockholders). As a result, the owners of the firm cannot monitor the managers' behavior on a regular basis. Managers then have some leeway in how they run the firm and can deviate from profit-maximizing behavior to some extent.

Managers may be more concerned with goals such as revenue maximization to achieve growth or the payment of dividends to satisfy shareholders than with profit maximization. Managers might also be overly concerned with the firm's short-run profit (perhaps to earn a promotion or a large bonus) at the expense of its longer-run profit, even though long-run profit maximization better serves the interests of the stockholders.[1] (We discuss the implications of differences between the incentives of managers and owners of firms in greater detail in Chapter 17.)

Even so, managers' freedom to pursue goals other than long-run profit maximization is limited. If they do pursue such goals, shareholders or the boards

---

[1] To be more exact, maximizing the market value of the firm is a more appropriate goal than profit maximization because market value includes the stream of profits that the firm earns over time. It is the stream of profits that is of direct interest to the stockholders.

of directors can replace them, or the firm can be taken over by new management. In any case, firms that do not come close to maximizing profit are not likely to survive. Firms that do survive in competitive industries make long-run profit maximization one of their highest priorities.

Thus our working assumption of profit maximization is reasonable. Firms that have been in business for a long time are likely to care a lot about profit, whatever else their managers may appear to be doing. For example, a firm that subsidizes public television may seem public-spirited and altruistic. Yet this beneficence is likely to be in the long-run financial interest of the firm because it generates goodwill for the firm and its products.

8.2 Marginal Revenue, Marginal Cost, and Profit Maximization

Let's begin by looking at the profit-maximizing output decision for *any* firm, whether the firm operates in a perfectly competitive market or is one that can influence price. Since profit is the difference between (total) revenue and (total) cost, to find the firm's profit-maximizing output level, we must analyze its revenue. Suppose that the firm's output is q, and that it obtains revenue R. This revenue is equal to the price of the product P times the number of units sold: $R = Pq$. The cost of production C also depends on the level of output. The firm's profit is the difference between revenue and cost:

$$\pi(q) = R(q) - C(q)$$

(Here we show explicitly that π, R, and C depend on output. Usually we will omit this reminder.)

To maximize profit, the firm selects the output for which the difference between revenue and cost is the greatest. This is shown in Figure 8.1. Revenue $R(q)$ is a curved line, which accounts for the possibility that an increased output may be accomplished only with a lower price. The slope of the line, which shows how much revenue increases when output increases by one unit, is *marginal revenue*. Because there are fixed and variable costs, $C(q)$ is not a straight line; its slope, which measures the additional cost associated with an additional unit of output, is *marginal cost*. $C(q)$ is positive when output is zero because there is a fixed cost in the short run.

For low levels of output, profit is negative—revenue is insufficient to cover fixed and variable costs. (Profit is negative when $q = 0$ because of fixed cost.) Here marginal revenue is greater than marginal cost, which tells us that increases in output will increase profit. As output increases, profit eventually becomes positive (for q greater than q_0) and increases until output reaches q^* units. Here the marginal revenue and marginal cost are equal, and q^* is the profit-maximizing output. Note that the vertical distance between revenue and cost, AB, is greatest at this point; equivalently $\pi(q)$ reaches its peak. Beyond q^* units of production, marginal revenue is less than marginal cost, and profit falls, reflecting the rapid increase in the total cost of production.

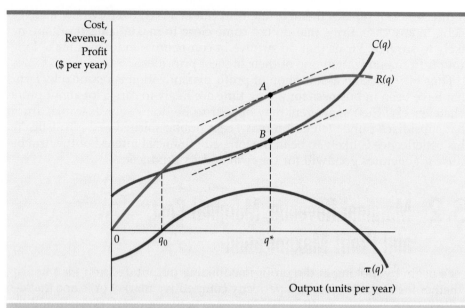

Figure 8.1 Profit Maximization in the Short Run A firm chooses output q^*, so that profit, the difference AB between revenue R and cost C, is maximized. At that output, marginal revenue (the slope of the revenue curve) is equal to marginal cost (the slope of the cost curve).

To see why q^* maximizes profit another way, suppose output is less than q^*. Then, if the firm increases output slightly, it will add more to revenues than it adds to costs. In other words, the marginal revenue (the additional revenue from producing one more unit of output) is greater than marginal cost. Similarly, when output is greater than q^*, marginal revenue is less than the marginal cost. Only when marginal revenue and marginal cost are equal has profit been maximized.

The rule that profit is maximized when marginal revenue is equal to marginal cost holds for all firms, whether competitive or not. This important rule can also be derived algebraically. Profit, $\pi = R - C$, is maximized at the point at which an additional increment to output just leaves profit unchanged (i.e., $\Delta\pi/\Delta q = 0$):

$$\Delta\pi/\Delta q = \Delta R/\Delta q - \Delta C/\Delta q = 0$$

$\Delta R/\Delta q$ is marginal revenue MR and $\Delta C/\Delta q$ is marginal cost MC. Thus we conclude that profit is maximized when MR − MC = 0, so that

$$\boxed{MR(q) = MC(q)}$$

Demand and Marginal Revenue for a Competitive Firm

Because each firm in a competitive industry sells only a small fraction of the entire industry sales, *how much output the firm decides to sell will have no effect on the market price of the product*. The market price is determined by the industry demand and supply curves. Therefore, the competitive firm is a *price taker*: It knows that its production decision will have no effect on the price of the product. For example, when a farmer is deciding how many acres of wheat to plant in a given year, he can take the market price of wheat as given. That price will not be affected by his acreage decision.

Often we will want to distinguish between market demand curves and the demand curves that individual firms face. In this chapter we will denote market output and demand by capital letters (Q and D), and the firm's output and demand by lowercase letters (q and d).

Because the firm is a price taker, the revenue curve $R(q)$ is a straight line, since for a given P, revenue increases proportionately with output. In addition, *the demand curve d facing an individual competitive firm is given by a horizontal line*. In Figure 8.2(a) the farmer's demand curve corresponds to a price of $4 per bushel of wheat. The horizontal axis measures the amount of wheat that the farmer can sell, and the vertical axis measures the price. Compare the demand curve facing the firm (in this case the farmer) in Figure 8.2(a) with the market demand curve D in Figure 8.2(b).

The market demand curve shows how much wheat *all consumers* will buy at each possible price. The market demand curve is downward sloping because consumers buy more wheat at a lower price. The demand curve facing the firm, however, is horizontal because the firm's sales will have no effect on

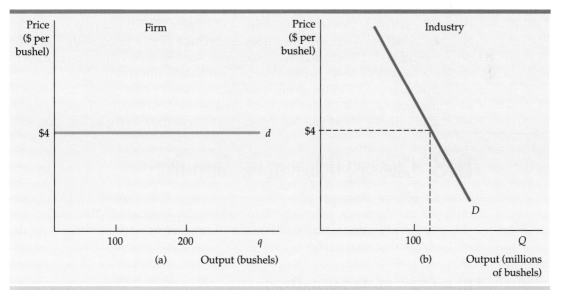

Figure 8.2 Demand Curve Faced by a Competitive Firm A competitive firm supplies only a small portion of the total output of all the firms in an industry. Therefore the firm takes the market price of the product as given, choosing its output on the assumption that the price will be unaffected by the output choice. In (a) the demand curve facing the firm is perfectly elastic, even though the market demand curve in (b) is downward sloping.

the price. Suppose the firm increased its sales from 100 to 200 bushels of wheat. This would have almost no effect on the market because the industry output of wheat is 100 million bushels at $4 per bushel. Price is determined by the interaction of all firms and consumers in the market, not by the output decision of a single firm.

When an individual firm faces a horizontal demand curve, it can sell an additional unit of output without lowering price. As a result, the total revenue increases by an amount equal to the price (one bushel of wheat sold for $4 yields additional revenue of $4). At the same time, the average revenue received by the firm is also $4 because each bushel of wheat produced will be sold at $4. Therefore, *the demand curve d facing an individual firm in a competitive market is both its average revenue curve and its marginal revenue curve. Along this demand curve, marginal revenue and price are equal.*

Profit Maximization by a Competitive Firm

Because MR = P, and the demand curve facing a competitive firm is horizontal, the general profit-maximizing rule that applies to any firm can be simplified. A perfectly competitive firm should choose its output so that *marginal cost equals price*:

$$MC(q) = MR = P$$

Note that this is a rule for setting output, not price, since competitive firms take price as fixed. However, we show in Chapter 10 that the rule is a useful benchmark when we compare a noncompetitive firm's price with what the price would be if the market were competitive. The rule can help regulators decide what prices to set when they are regulating noncompetitive firms.

Because the choice of the profit-maximizing output by a competitive firm is so important, we will devote most of the rest of this chapter to analyzing it. We begin with the short-run output decision, and then move to the long run.

8.3 Choosing Output in the Short Run

How should the manager of a profit-maximizing firm choose a level of output over the short run when the firm's plant size is fixed? In this section we show how a firm can use information about revenue and cost to make a profit-maximizing output decision.

Short-Run Profit Maximization by a Competitive Firm

In the short run, a firm operates with a fixed amount of capital and must choose the levels of its variable inputs (labor and materials) to maximize profit. Figure 8.3 shows the firm's short-run decision. The average and marginal revenue curves are drawn as horizontal lines at a price equal to $40. In this fig-

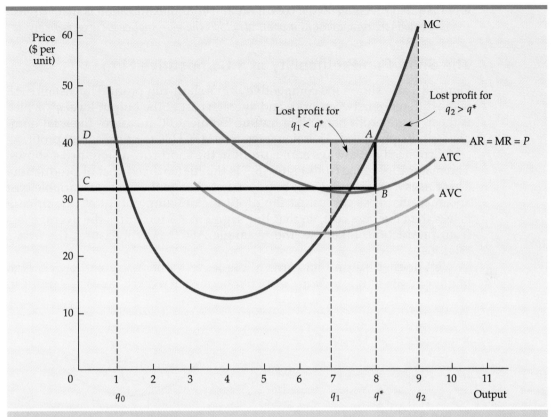

Figure 8.3 A Competitive Firm Making a Positive Profit In the short run, the competitive firm maximizes its profit by choosing an output q^* at which its marginal cost MC is equal to the price P (or marginal revenue MR) of its product. The profit of the firm is measured by the rectangle $ABCD$. Any lower output q_1, or higher output q_2, will lead to lower profit.

ure, we have drawn the average total cost curve ATC, the average variable cost curve AVC, and the marginal cost curve MC, so that we can see the firm's profit more easily.

Profit is maximized at point A, associated with an output $q^* = 8$ and a price of $40, because marginal revenue is equal to marginal cost at this point. At a lower output, say $q_1 = 7$, marginal revenue is greater than marginal cost, so profit could be increased by increasing output. The shaded area between $q_1 = 7$ and q^* shows the lost profit associated with producing at q_1. At a higher output, say q_2, marginal cost is greater than marginal revenue; thus, reducing output saves a cost that exceeds the reduction in revenue. The shaded area between q^* and $q_2 = 9$ shows the lost profit associated with producing at q_2.

The MR and MC curves cross at an output of q_0 as well as q^*. At q_0, however, profit is clearly not maximized. (This can be easily seen in Figure 8.1.) An increase in output beyond q_0 increases profit because marginal cost is well below marginal revenue. So the condition for profit maximization is that *marginal revenue equals marginal cost at a point at which the marginal cost curve is rising.*

The Short-Run Profitability of a Competitive Firm

Figure 8.3 also shows the competitive firm's short-run profit. The distance *AB* is the difference between price and average cost at the output level *q**, which is the average profit per unit of output. Segment *BC* measures the total number of units produced. Therefore rectangle *ABCD* is the firm's total profit.

A firm need not always earn a profit in the short run, as Figure 8.4 shows. The major difference from Figure 8.3 is the higher fixed cost of production. This raises average total cost but does not change the average variable cost and marginal cost curves. At the profit-maximizing output *q**, the price *P* is less than average cost, so that line segment *AB* measures the average *loss* from production. Likewise, the rectangle *ABCD* now measures the firm's total loss.

Why doesn't a firm that earns a loss leave the industry entirely? A firm might operate at a loss *in the short run* because it expects to earn a profit in

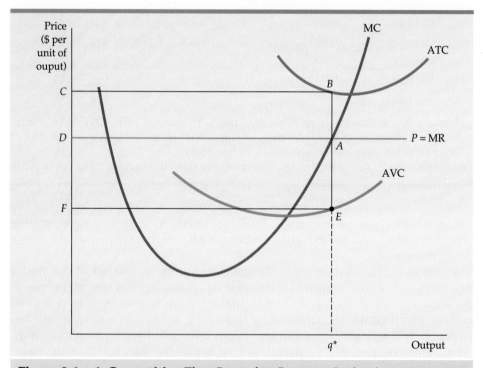

Figure 8.4 A Competitive Firm Incurring Losses In the short run, a competitive firm may produce at a loss (because its fixed cost is high), if it can still generate revenues that more than cover its variable cost. The firm minimizes its losses by producing at *q**, with losses *ABCD*. If the firm were to produce nothing, it would incur even greater losses equal to the fixed cost of production *CBEF*.

the future as the price of its product increases or the cost of production falls. In fact, a firm has two choices in the short run: It can produce some output, or it can shut down its production temporarily. It will choose the more profitable (or the less unprofitable) of the two alternatives. In particular, *a firm will find it profitable to shut down (produce no output) when the price of its product is less than the minimum average variable cost.* In this situation, revenues from production will not cover variable costs, and losses will increase.

Figure 8.4 illustrates the case in which some production is appropriate. The output q^* is at the point where short-run losses are minimized. The firm's losses are smaller at q^* in comparison to the no-output alternative because price exceeds average variable cost at q^*. Each unit produced yields more revenue than cost, thereby increasing profits. (Total profit is still negative, however, because the *fixed cost* is high.) Line segment *AE* measures the difference between price and average variable cost, and rectangle *AEFD* measures the reduction in losses that can be achieved by producing at q^* rather than at 0.

To see this another way, recall that the difference between average total cost ATC and average variable cost AVC is average fixed cost AFC. Therefore, in Figure 8.4, line segment *BE* represents the average fixed cost, and rectangle *CBEF* represents the total fixed cost of production. When the firm produces no output, its loss is equal to its total fixed cost *CBEF*. But when it produces at q^*, its loss is reduced to the rectangle *ABCD*. Fixed cost, which is irrelevant to the firm's production decision in the short run, is crucial when determining whether the firm ought to leave the industry in the long run.

To summarize: The competitive firm produces no output if price is less than minimum average variable cost. When it does produce, it maximizes profit by choosing the output level at which price is equal to marginal cost. At this output level, profit is positive if price is greater than average total cost. The firm may operate at a loss in the short run. However, if it expects to continue to lose money over the long run, it will go out of business.

EXAMPLE 8.1 **Some Cost Considerations for Managers**

The application of the rule that marginal revenue should equal marginal cost depends on the manager's ability to estimate marginal cost.[2] To obtain useful measures of cost, managers should keep three guidelines in mind.

First, when possible, *average variable cost should not be used as a substitute for marginal cost.* When marginal and average cost are nearly constant, there is little difference between them. However, when marginal and average cost are increasing sharply, the use of average variable cost can be misleading when

[2] This example draws on the discussion of costs and managerial decision making in Thomas Nagle, *The Strategy and Tactics of Pricing* (Englewood Cliffs, N.J.: Prentice-Hall, 1987), chap. 2.

deciding how much to produce. Suppose, for example, that a company has the following cost information:

Current output: 100 units per day, of which 25 units are produced during overtime
Materials cost: $500 per day
Labor cost: $2000 per day (regular) plus $1000 per day (overtime)

Average variable cost is easily calculated—it is the labor and materials cost ($3500) divided by 100 units per day, or $35 per unit. But the appropriate cost is marginal cost, which could be calculated as follows: Materials cost per unit is likely to be constant whatever the output level, so that marginal materials cost is $500/100 = $5 per unit. Since the marginal cost of labor is likely to involve overtime work only, it is obtained by noting that 25 of the 100 units were produced during the overtime period. The average overtime pay per unit of production, $1000/25 = $40 per unit, provides a good estimate of the marginal cost of labor. Therefore, the marginal cost of producing an additional unit of output is $45 per unit (the marginal materials cost plus the marginal labor cost); this is much larger than the average variable cost of $35. If the manager relied on average variable cost, too much output would be produced.

Second, *a single item on a firm's accounting ledger may have two components, only one of which involves marginal cost.* Suppose, for example, that a manager is trying to cut back production. She reduces the number of hours that some employees work and lays off others. But the salary of an employee who is laid off may not be an accurate measure of the marginal cost of production when cuts are made because union contracts often require the firm to pay laid-off employees part of their salary. In this case, the marginal cost of increasing production is not the same as the savings in marginal cost when production is decreased. The savings is the labor cost after the required layoff salary has been subtracted.

Third, *all opportunity costs should be included in determining marginal cost.* Suppose a department store wants to sell children's furniture. Instead of building a new selling area, the manager decides to use part of the third floor, which had been used for appliances, for the furniture. The marginal cost of this space is the profit that would have been earned had the store continued to sell appliances there, per unit of furniture sold. This opportunity cost measure may be much greater than what the store actually paid for that part of the building.

These three guidelines can help a manager to measure marginal cost correctly. Failure to do so can cause production to be too high or too low, and thereby reduce profit.

8.4 The Competitive Firm's Short-Run Supply Curve

A *supply curve* for a firm tells us how much output it will produce at every possible price. We have seen that competitive firms will increase output to the point at which price is equal to marginal cost, but they will shut down if price is below average variable cost. Therefore, for positive output the firm's supply curve is the portion of the marginal cost curve that lies above the average variable cost curve. Since the marginal cost curve cuts the average variable cost curve at its minimum point (recall our discussion in Chapter 7 of marginal and average cost), *the firm's supply curve is its marginal cost curve above the point of minimum average variable cost.* For any P greater than minimum AVC, the profit-maximizing output can be read directly from the graph. At a price P_1 in Figure 8.5, for example, the quantity supplied will be q_1, and at P_2 it will be q_2. For P less than (or equal to) minimum AVC, the profit-maximizing output is equal to zero. In Figure 8.5 the entire supply curve is the cross-hatched portion of the vertical axis and the marginal cost curve.

Short-run supply curves for competitive firms slope upward for the same reason that marginal cost increases—the presence of diminishing returns to one or more factors of production. As a result, an increase in the market price will induce those firms already in the market to increase the quantities they produce. The higher price makes the additional production profitable and also increases the firm's *total* profit because it applies to all units that the firm produces.

Figure 8.5 **The Short-Run Supply Curve of a Competitive Firm** In the short run, the firm chooses its output so that marginal cost MC is equal to price, so long as it covers its variable cost of production. The short-run supply curve is given by the cross-hatched portion of the marginal cost curve.

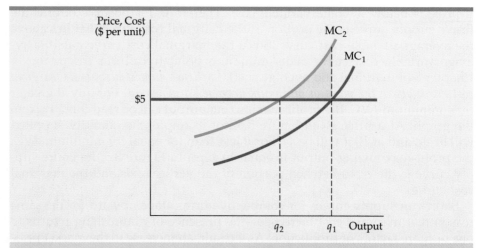

Figure 8.6 The Response of a Firm to a Change in Input Price When the marginal cost of production for a firm increases (from MC_1 to MC_2), the level of output that maximizes profit falls (from q_1 to q_2).

The Firm's Response to an Input Price Change

When the price of its product changes, the firm changes its output level, so that the marginal cost of production remains equal to the price. Often, however, the product price changes at the same time that the prices of *inputs* change. In this section we show how the firm's output decision changes in response to a change in the price of one of the firm's inputs.

Figure 8.6 shows a firm's marginal cost curve that is initially given by MC_1 when the firm faces a price of $5 for its product. The firm maximizes its profit by producing an output of q_1. Now suppose the price of one of the firm's inputs increases. This causes the marginal cost curve to shift upward from MC_1 to MC_2 because it now costs more to produce each unit of output. The new profit-maximizing output is q_2, at which $P = MC_2$. Thus, the higher input price causes the firm to reduce its output.

If the firm had continued to produce q_1, it would have incurred a loss on the last unit of production. In fact, all production beyond q_2 reduces profit. The shaded area in the figure gives the total savings to the firm (or equivalently, the reduction in lost profit) associated with the reduction in output from q_1 to q_2.

EXAMPLE 8.2	**The Short-Run Production of Petroleum Products**

Suppose you are managing an oil refinery and you decide to produce a particular combination of refinery products, including gasoline, jet fuel, and residual fuel oil for home heating. A lot of crude oil is available, but the amount that you refine depends on the capacity of the refinery and the cost of production. How much should you produce each day?[3]

Information about the refinery's marginal cost of production is essential for this decision. Figure 8.7 shows the short-run marginal cost curve (SMC). Marginal cost increases with output, but in a series of uneven segments rather than as a smooth curve. The increase is in segments because the refinery uses different processing units to turn crude oil into finished products. When a particular processing unit reaches capacity, output can be increased only by substituting a more expensive process. For example, gasoline can be produced from light crude oils rather inexpensively in a processing unit called a "thermal cracker." When this unit becomes full, additional gasoline can still be produced (from heavy as well as light crude oil) but at a higher cost. In Figure 8.7 the first capacity constraint comes into effect when production reaches about 9700 barrels a day. A second capacity constraint becomes important when production increases beyond 10,700 barrels a day.

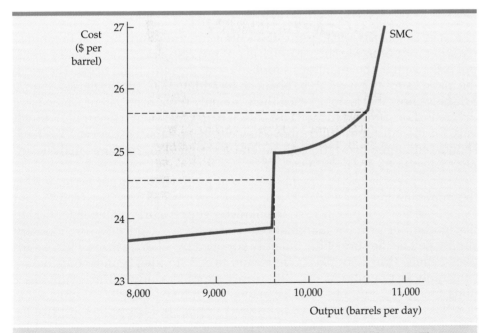

Figure 8.7   The Short-Run Production of Petroleum Products   The marginal cost of producing petroleum products from crude oil increases sharply at several levels of output as the refinery shifts from one processing unit to another. As a result, the output level can be insensitive to some changes in price and very sensitive to others.

3 This example is based on James M. Griffin, "The Process Analysis Alternative to Statistical Cost Functions: An Application to Petroleum Refining," *American Economic Review* 62 (1972): 46–56. The numbers have been updated and applied to a particular refinery.

Deciding how much output to produce now becomes relatively easy. Suppose that refined products can be sold for $23 per barrel. Since the marginal cost of production is close to $24 for the first unit of output, at a price of $23 no crude oil should be run through the refinery. If, however, the price of the product is between $24 and $25, the refinery should produce 9700 barrels a day (filling the thermal cracker). Finally, if the price is above $25, the more expensive refining unit should be used and production expanded toward 10,700 barrels a day.

Because the cost function rises in steps, you know that your production decisions need not change much in response to small changes in the price of the product. You will typically utilize sufficient crude oil to fill the appropriate processing unit until price increases (or decreases) substantially. Then you need simply calculate whether the increased price warrants using an additional, more expensive processing unit.

8.5 The Short-Run Market Supply Curve

The *short-run market supply curve* shows the amount of output that the industry will produce in the short run for every possible price. The industry's output is the sum of the quantities supplied by all the individual firms. Therefore the market supply curve can be obtained by adding their supply curves. Figure 8.8 shows how this is done when there are only three firms, all of which have different short-run production costs. Each firm's marginal cost curve is drawn only for the portion that lies above its average variable cost curve. (We have shown only three firms to keep the graph simple, but the same analysis applies when there are many firms.)

At any price below P_1, the industry will produce no output because P_1 is the minimum average variable cost of the lowest-cost firm. Between P_1 and P_2, only firm 3 will produce, so the industry supply curve will be identical to that portion of firm 3's marginal cost curve MC_3. At price P_2, the industry supply will be the sum of the quantity supplied by all three firms. Firm 1 supplies 2 units, firm 2 supplies 5 units, and firm 3 supplies 8 units; thus industry supply is 15 units. At price P_3, firm 1 supplies 4 units, firm 2 supplies 7 units, and firm 3 supplies 10 units; in total the industry supplies 21 units. Note that the industry supply curve is upward sloping but has a kink at price P_2. With many firms in the market, however, the kink becomes unimportant, so we usually draw industry supply as a smooth, upward-sloping curve.

Finding the industry supply curve is not always as simple as adding up a set of firm supply curves. As price rises, all firms in the industry expand their output. This additional output increases the demand for inputs to production and may lead to higher input prices. As we saw in Figure 8.6, increasing input prices shifts the firms' marginal cost curves upward. For example, an increased demand for beef could also increase demand for corn and soybeans (which are used to feed cattle), and thereby cause the prices of these crops to rise. In turn, the higher input prices would cause beef firms' marginal cost

Figure 8.8 Industry Supply in the Short Run The short-run industry supply curve is the horizontal summation of the supply curves of the individual firms. Because the third firm has a lower average variable cost curve than the first two firms, the market supply curve S begins at price P_1 and follows the marginal cost curve of the third firm MC_3 until price equals P_2, where there is a kink. For all prices above P_2, the industry quantity supplied is the sum of the quantities supplied by each of the three firms.

curves to shift upward. This lowers each firm's output choice (for any given market price) and causes the industry supply curve to be less responsive to changes in output price than it would otherwise be.

Elasticity of Market Supply

The price elasticity of market supply measures the sensitivity of industry output to market price. Recall from Chapter 2 that the elasticity of supply E_S is the percentage change in quantity supplied Q in response to a 1 percent change in price P:

$$E_S = (\Delta Q/Q)/(\Delta P/P)$$

Because marginal cost curves are upward sloping, the short-run elasticity of supply is always positive. When marginal costs increase rapidly in response to increases in output, the elasticity of supply is low. Firms are then capacity-constrained and find it costly to increase output. But, when marginal costs increase slowly in response to increases in output, supply is relatively elastic, and a small price increase induces firms to produce much more.

At one extreme is the case of *perfectly inelastic supply*, which arises when the industry's plant and equipment are so fully utilized that new plants must be built (as they will be in the long run) to achieve greater output. At the other extreme is the case of *perfectly elastic supply*, which arises when marginal costs are constant.

EXAMPLE 8.3   The Short-Run World Supply of Copper

In the short run, the shape of the market supply curve for a mineral such as copper depends on how the cost of mining varies within and among the world's major producers. Costs of mining, smelting, and refining copper differ because of differences in labor and transportation costs and differences in the copper content of the ore. Table 8.1 summarizes some of the relevant cost and production data for the largest copper-producing nations.

These data can be used to plot the world supply curve for copper. The supply curve is a short-run curve because it takes the existing mines as fixed. Figure 8.9 shows how this curve is constructed for the six countries listed in the table. The complete world supply curve would, of course, incorporate data for all copper-producing countries. Also, note that the curve in Figure 8.9 is an approximation. The marginal cost number for each country is an average for all copper producers in that country. In the United States, for example, some producers had a marginal cost greater than 90 cents, and some less than 90 cents.

The lowest-cost copper is mined in Zaire, where the marginal cost of refined copper was about 65 cents per pound.[4] Curve MC_Z describes this marginal cost curve. The curve is horizontal until Zaire's capacity to mine copper is reached. Curve MC_{Zm} describes Zambia's supply curve (marginal cost is 70 cents per pound). Likewise, curves MC_C, MC_{US}, MC_P, and MC_{Ca} represent the marginal cost curves for Chile, the United States, Peru, and Canada, respectively.

Table 8.1 The World Copper Industry (1996)		
Country	**Annual Production (thousand metric tons)**	**Marginal Cost (dollars per pound)**
Canada	729	1.15
Chile	2425	.80
Peru	405	1.00
United States	1860	.90
Zaire	380	.65
Zambia	342	.70

---

[4] We are presuming that marginal and average costs of production are approximately the same.

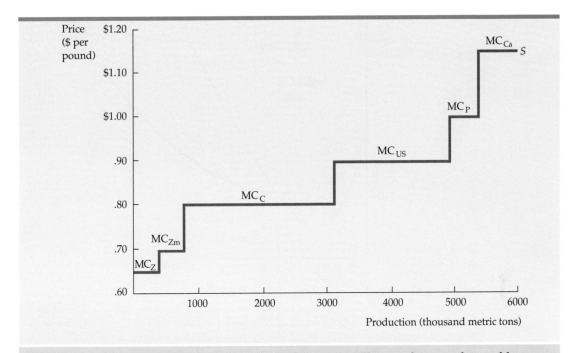

Figure 8.9 The Short-Run World Supply of Copper The supply curve for world copper is obtained by summing the marginal cost curves for each of the major copper-producing countries. The supply curve slopes upward because the marginal cost of production ranges from a low of 65 cents per pound in Zaire to a high of $1.15 per pound in Canada.

The world supply curve, denoted S, is obtained by summing each nation's supply curve horizontally. The slope and the elasticity of the supply curve depend on the price of copper. At relatively low prices, such as 70 to 90 cents per pound, the supply curve is quite elastic because small price increases lead to substantial increases in refined copper. But for higher prices, say above $1.15 per pound, the supply curve becomes quite inelastic because at such prices all producers would be operating at capacity.

Producer Surplus in the Short Run

In Chapter 4 we measured consumer surplus as the difference between the maximum that a person would pay for an item and its market price. An analogous concept applies to firms. If marginal cost is rising, the price of the product is greater than marginal cost for every unit produced except the last one. As a result, firms earn a surplus on all but the last unit of output. The *producer surplus* of a firm is the sum over all units produced of the difference between the market price of the good and the marginal cost of production. Just as consumer surplus measures the area below an individual's demand curve

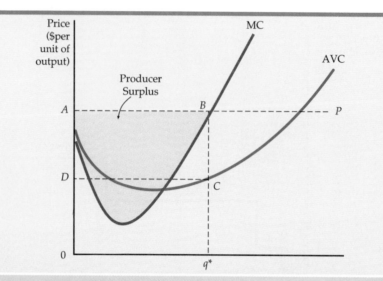

Figure 8.10 Producer Surplus for a Firm The producer surplus for a firm is measured by the shaded area below the market price and above the marginal cost curve, between outputs 0 and q^*, the profit-maximizing output. Alternatively, it is equal to rectangle $ABCD$ because the sum of all marginal costs up to q^* is equal to the variable costs of producing q^*.

and above the market price of the product, producer surplus measures the area above a producer's supply curve and below the market price.

Figure 8.10 illustrates short-run producer surplus for a firm. The profit-maximizing output is q^*, where $P = MC$. Producer surplus is given by the shaded area under the firm's horizontal demand curve and above its marginal cost curve, from zero output to the profit-maximizing output q^*.

When we add the marginal costs of producing each level of output from 0 to q^*, we find that the sum is the total variable cost of producing q^*. Marginal cost reflects increments to cost associated with increases in output; since fixed cost does not vary with output, the sum of all marginal costs must equal the sum of the firm's variable costs.[5] Thus producer surplus can alternatively be defined as the difference between the firm's revenue and its total variable cost. In Figure 8.10 producer surplus is also therefore given by the rectangle $ABCD$, which equals revenue ($0ABq^*$) minus variable cost ($0DCq^*$).

Producer surplus is closely related to profit but is not equal to it. Producer surplus is equal to revenue net of variable cost, while profit is equal to revenue net of *all* costs, both variable and fixed:

$$\text{Producer Surplus} = PS = R - VC$$
$$\text{Profit} = \pi = R - VC - FC$$

It follows that in the short run when the fixed cost is positive, producer surplus is greater than profit.

---

[5] The area under the marginal cost curve from 0 to q^* is $TC(q^*) - TC(0) = TC - FC = VC$.

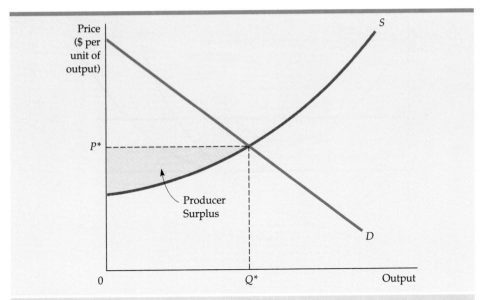

Figure 8.11 Producer Surplus for a Market The producer surplus for a market is the area below the market price and above the market supply curve, between 0 and output Q^*.

The extent to which firms enjoy producer surplus depends on their costs of production. Higher-cost firms have less producer surplus, and lower-cost firms have more. By adding up all the individual firms' producer surpluses, we can determine the producer surplus for a market. This can be seen in Figure 8.11. In the figure the market supply curve begins at the vertical axis at a point that represents the average variable cost of the lowest-cost firm in the market. Producer surplus is the area that lies below the market price of the product and above the supply curve between the output levels 0 and Q^*.

8.6 Choosing Output in the Long Run

In the long run, a firm can alter all its inputs, including the size of the plant. It can decide to shut down (i.e., to *exit* the industry) or to begin to produce a product for the first time (i.e., to *enter* an industry). Because we are concerned here with competitive markets, we allow for *free entry* and *free exit*. In other words, we are assuming that firms may enter or exit without any legal restriction or any special costs associated with entry.[6]

Figure 8.12 shows how a competitive firm makes its long-run, profit-maximizing output decision. As in the short run, it faces a horizontal demand curve. (In Figure 8.12 the firm takes the market price of $40 as given.) Its short-run average (total) cost curve SAC and short-run marginal cost curve SMC

---

[6] In Chapter 10 we discuss examples of barriers to entry in an industry.

Figure 8.12 **Output Choice in the Long Run** The firm maximizes its profit by choosing the output at which price is equal to long-run marginal cost LMC. In the diagram, the firm increases its profit from *ABCD* to *EFGD* by increasing its output in the long run.

are low enough for the firm to make a positive profit, given by rectangle *ABCD*, by producing an output of q_1, where SMC $= P =$ MR. The long-run average cost curve LAC reflects the presence of economies of scale up to output level q_2 and diseconomies of scale at higher output levels. The long-run marginal cost curve LMC cuts the long-run average cost from below at q_2, the point of minimum long-run average cost.

If the firm believes the market price will remain at $40, it will want to increase the size of its plant to produce an output q_3 at which its *long-run* marginal cost is equal to the $40 price. When this expansion is complete, the firm's profit margin will increase from *AB* to *EF*, and its total profit will increase from *ABCD* to *EFGD*. Output q_3 is profit-maximizing for the firm because at any lower output, say q_2, the marginal revenue from additional production is greater than the marginal cost, so expansion is desirable. But at any output greater than q_3, marginal cost is greater than marginal revenue, so additional production would reduce profit. In summary, *the long-run output of a profit-maximizing competitive firm is where long-run marginal cost is equal to price.*

Note that the higher the market price, the higher the profit that the firm can earn. Correspondingly, as the price of the product falls from $40 to $30, so does the profit of the firm. At a price of $30, the firm's profit-maximizing output is q_2, the point of long-run minimum average cost. In this case, since $P =$ ATC, the firm earns zero economic profit. As we show in the following sections, this means that investors in the firm earn a competitive return on their investment.

Zero Profit

As we saw in Chapter 7, it is important to distinguish between accounting profit and economic profit. Accounting profit is measured by the difference between the firm's revenues and costs, including actual outlays and depreciation expenses. Economic profit takes account of opportunity costs. One such opportunity cost is the return that the owners of the firm could make if their capital were used elsewhere. Suppose, for example, that the firm uses labor and capital inputs; its capital equipment has been purchased (and has been depreciated). The firm's accounting profit will equal its revenues R minus its labor costs wL, which is positive. However, its economic profit π equals its revenues R minus its labor costs wL and minus its opportunity cost of capital rK, measured by what it could rent the capital for in the market. Thus,

$$\pi = R - wL - rK = 0$$

A firm earning a negative economic profit should consider going out of business if it does not expect to improve its financial picture. However, a firm that earns zero economic profit need not go out of business because zero profit means the firm is earning a reasonable return on its investment. Of course, investors would like to earn a positive economic profit—that is what encourages entrepreneurs to develop and commercialize new ideas. But in competitive markets, as we will see, economic profits become zero in the long run. Zero economic profits signify not that the firms in the industry are performing poorly, but rather, that the industry is competitive.

Long-Run Competitive Equilibrium

Figure 8.12 shows how a \$40 price induces a firm to increase its output and gives the firm a positive profit. Because profit is calculated net of the opportunity cost of investment, a positive profit means an unusually high return on investment. This high return causes investors to direct resources away from other industries and into this one—there will be *entry* into the market. Eventually the increased production associated with new entry causes the market supply curve to shift to the right, so that market output increases and the market price of the product falls.[7] Figure 8.13 illustrates this. In part (b) of the figure, the supply curve has shifted from S_1 to S_2, causing the price to fall from P_1 (\$40) to P_2 (\$30). In part (a), which applies to a single firm, the long-run average cost curve is tangent to the horizontal price line at output q_2.

When a firm earns zero economic profit, it has no incentive to exit the industry, and other firms have no special incentive to enter. A *long-run competitive equilibrium* occurs when three conditions hold. First, all firms in the industry are maximizing profit. Second, no firm has an incentive either to enter

---

[7] We discuss why the long-run supply curve might be upward sloping in the next section.

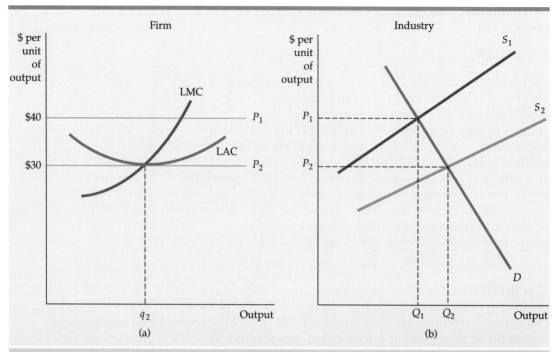

Figure 8.13 Long-Run Competitive Equilibrium Initially the long-run equilibrium price of a product is $40 per unit, as shown in (b) as the intersection of demand curve D and supply curve S_1. In (a) it is shown that firms earn a positive profit because their long-run average cost reaches a minimum of $30 (at q_2). This positive profit encourages entry of new firms and causes a shift to the right in the supply curve to S_2. The long-run equilibrium occurs at a price of $30 because each firm earns zero profit, and there is no incentive to enter or exit the industry.

or exit the industry because all firms in the industry are earning zero economic profit. Third, the price of the product is such that the quantity supplied by the industry is equal to the quantity demanded by consumers.

The dynamic process that leads to long-run equilibrium creates a puzzle. Firms enter the market because of the opportunity to earn positive profit, and they exit because of losses. Yet, in long-run equilibrium, firms earn zero economic profit. Why do firms exit or enter if they know that eventually they will be no better or worse off than if they do nothing? The answer is that it can take a long time to reach a long-run equilibrium, and a substantial profit (or loss) can be made in the short run. The first firm to enter a profitable industry can earn much more short-run profit for its investors than can firms that enter later. Similarly, the first firm to exit an unprofitable industry can save its investors lots of money. Thus the concept of long-run equilibrium tells us the *direction* that firms' behavior is likely to take. The idea of an eventual zero-profit, long-run equilibrium should not discourage a manager whose reward depends on the short-run profit that the firm earns.

To see why all the conditions for long-run equilibrium must hold, assume that all firms have identical costs, and consider what happens if too many firms enter the industry in response to an opportunity for profit. Then the supply curve in Figure 8.13(b) will shift further to the right, and price will fall below $30, say to $25. At that price, however, firms will lose money. As a result, some firms will exit the industry. Firms will continue to exit until the market supply curve shifts back to S_2. Only when there is no incentive to exit or enter the industry can a market be in long-run equilibrium.

Now suppose that all firms in the industry do not have identical cost curves. One firm has a patent or new idea that lets it produce at a lower average cost than all other firms. Then, it is consistent with long-run equilibrium for that firm to be earning a positive *accounting* profit (and to enjoy a higher producer surplus than other firms). As long as other investors and firms cannot acquire the patent or idea that lowers costs, they have no incentive to enter the industry. And as long as the process is particular to this product and this industry, the fortunate firm has no incentive to exit the industry. The distinction between accounting profit and economic profit is important here. If the new idea or invention is profitable, other firms in the industry will pay to use it. (Or they might attempt to buy the entire firm to acquire the patent.) The increased value of the patent thus represents an opportunity cost to the firm—it could sell the rights to the patent rather than use it. If all firms are equally efficient otherwise, once this opportunity cost is accounted for, the *economic* profit of the firm falls to zero.[8]

There are other instances in which firms earning positive accounting profit may be earning zero economic profit. Suppose, for example, that a clothing store happens to be located near a large shopping center. The additional flow of customers may substantially increase the store's accounting profit because the cost of the land is based on its historical cost. However, as far as economic profit is concerned, the cost of the land should reflect its opportunity cost, which in this case is its current market value. When the opportunity cost of land is included, the profitability of the clothing store is no higher than that of its competitors.

Thus the condition that economic profit be zero is essential for the market to be in a long-run equilibrium. Positive economic profit, by definition, represents an opportunity for investors and an incentive to enter the industry. Positive accounting profit, however, may signal that firms already in the industry possess valuable assets, skills, or ideas, and this will not necessarily encourage entry by other firms.

Economic Rent

We have seen that some firms earn higher accounting profit than others because they have access to factors of production that are in limited supply; these might include land and natural resources, entrepreneurial skill, or other

---

[8] If the firm with the patent is more efficient than other firms, then it will be earning a positive profit. But if the patent holder is less efficient, it should sell off the patent and go out of business.

creative talent. What makes economic profit zero in the long run in these situations is the willingness of other firms to use the factors of production that are in limited supply. The positive accounting profits are therefore translated into *economic rent* that is earned by the scarce factors. *Economic rent* is defined as the difference between what firms are willing to pay for an input to production less the minimum amount necessary to buy that input. In competitive markets, in both the short and the long run, economic rent is often positive, even though profit is zero.

For example, suppose that two firms in an industry own their land outright; the minimum cost of obtaining the land is zero. One firm is located on a river and can ship its products for $10,000 a year less than the other firm, which is inland. Then, the $10,000 higher profit of the first firm is due to the $10,000 per year economic rent associated with its river location. The rent is created because the land along the river is valuable, and other firms would be willing to pay for it. Eventually, the competition for this specialized factor of production will increase its value to $10,000. Land rent—the difference between $10,000 and the zero cost of obtaining the land—is also $10,000. Note that while the economic rent has increased, the economic profit of the firm on the river has become zero.

The zero economic profit tells the firm on the river that it should remain in the industry only if it is at least as efficient in production as other firms. It also tells possible entrants to the industry that entry will be profitable only if they can produce more efficiently than firms already producing.

Producer Surplus in the Long Run

When a firm is earning a positive accounting profit, but there is no incentive for other firms to enter or exit the industry, this profit must reflect economic rent. How then does rent relate to producer surplus? To begin, note that economic rent applies to factor inputs while producer surplus applies to outputs. Note also that producer surplus measures the difference between the market price a producer receives and the marginal cost of production. Thus, in the long run, in a competitive market, *the producer surplus that a firm earns on the output that it sells consists of the economic rent that it enjoys from all its scarce inputs.*[9]

Suppose, for example, that a baseball team has a franchise that allows it to operate in a particular city. Suppose also that the only alternative location for the team is a city in which the team will generate substantially lower revenues. The team will therefore earn an economic rent associated with its current location; this rent will reflect the difference between what the firm would be willing to pay for its current location and the amount needed to locate in the alternative city. The firm will also be earning a producer surplus associated with the sale of baseball tickets and other franchise items. This surplus will reflect not only the location rent just discussed but also any economic

---

[9] In a noncompetitive market producer surplus will reflect economic profit as well as economic rent.

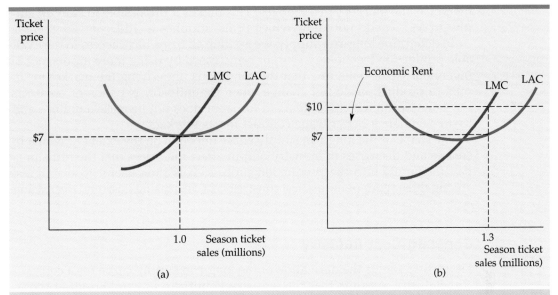

Figure 8.14 **Firms Earn Zero Profit in Long-Run Equilibrium** In long-run equilibrium, all firms earn zero economic profit. In (a) a baseball team in a moderate-size city sells enough tickets so that price ($7) is equal to marginal and average cost. In (b) the demand is greater, so a $10 price can be charged. The team increases its sales to the point at which the average cost of production plus the average economic rent is equal to the ticket price. When the opportunity cost associated with owning the franchise is taken into account, the team earns zero economic profit.

rents associated with the firm's other factor inputs, including the stadium and the players.

Figure 8.14 shows that firms that earn economic rent earn the same economic profit as firms that do not earn rent. Part (a) shows the economic profit of a baseball team located in a moderate-size city. The average price of a ticket is $7, and costs are such that the team earns zero economic profit. Part (b) shows the profit of a team with the same costs, but in a larger city. Because more people want to see baseball games, the team can sell tickets for $10 apiece, and thereby earn an accounting profit of close to $3 on each ticket. However, the rent associated with the more desirable location represents a cost to the firm—an opportunity cost—because it could sell its franchise to another team. As a result, the economic profit in the larger city is also zero.

8.7 The Industry's Long-Run Supply Curve

In our analysis of short-run supply, we first derived the firm's supply curve and then showed how the horizontal summation of individual firms' supply curves generated a market supply curve. We cannot analyze long-run supply in the same way, however, because in the long run firms enter and exit the

market as the market price changes. This makes it impossible to sum up supply curves—we do not know which firms' supplies to add.

To determine long-run supply, we assume all firms have access to the available production technology. Output is increased by using more inputs, not by
invention. We also assume that the conditions underlying the market for inputs to production do not change when the industry expands or contracts.
For example, an increased demand for labor does not increase a union's ability to negotiate a better wage contract for its workers.

The shape of the long-run supply curve depends on the extent to which increases and decreases in industry output affect the prices that the firms must
pay for inputs into the production process. It is thus useful to distinguish
among three types of industries: constant-cost, increasing-cost, and decreasing-
cost.

Constant-Cost Industry

Figure 8.15 shows the derivation of the long-run supply curve for a constant-
cost industry. Assume that the industry is initially in equilibrium at the intersection of market demand curve D_1 and the short-run market supply curve

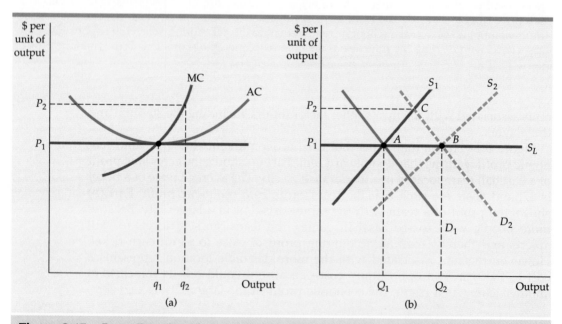

Figure 8.15   Long-Run Supply in a Constant-Cost Industry   In (b) the long-run supply
curve in a constant-cost industry is a horizontal line S_L. When demand increases, initially causing a price rise (represented by a move from point A to point C), the firm initially increases its
output from q_1 to q_2, as shown in (a). But the entry of new firms causes a shift to the right in industry supply. Because input prices are unaffected by the increased output of the industry, entry
occurs until the original price is obtained (at point B).

S_1, in part (b) of the figure. Point A at the intersection of demand and supply is on the long-run supply curve S_L because it tells us that the industry will produce Q_1 units of output when the long-run equilibrium price is P_1.

To obtain other points on the long-run supply curve, suppose the market demand for the product unexpectedly increases, say because of a reduction in personal income taxes. A typical firm is initially producing at an output of q_1, where P_1 is equal to long-run marginal cost and long-run average cost. But the firm is also in short-run equilibrium, so that price also equals short-run marginal cost. Suppose that the tax cut shifts the market demand curve from D_1 to D_2. Demand curve D_2 intersects supply curve S_1 at C. As a result, the price increases from P_1 to P_2.

Part (a) shows how this price increase affects a typical firm in the industry. When the price increases to P_2, the firm follows its short-run marginal cost curve and increases its output to q_2. This output choice maximizes profit because it satisfies the condition that price equal short-run marginal cost. If every firm responds this way, each firm will be earning a positive profit in short-run equilibrium. This profit will be attractive to investors and will cause existing firms to expand their operations and new firms to enter the market.

As a result, in Figure 8.15(b) the short-run supply curve shifts to the right, from S_1 to S_2. This shift causes the market to move to a new long-run equilibrium at the intersection of D_2 and S_2. For this intersection to be a long-run equilibrium, output must expand just enough so that firms are earning zero profit and the incentive to enter or exit the industry disappears.

In a constant-cost industry, the additional inputs necessary to produce the higher output can be purchased without an increase in the per-unit price. This might happen, for example, if unskilled labor is a major input in production, and the market wage of unskilled labor is unaffected by the increase in the demand for labor. Since the prices of inputs have not changed, the firms' cost curves are also unchanged; the new equilibrium must be at a point such as B in Figure 8.15(b), at which price is equal to P_1, the original price before the unexpected increase in demand occurred.

The long-run supply curve for a constant-cost industry is, therefore, a horizontal line at a price that is equal to the long-run minimum average cost of production. At any higher price, there would be positive profit, increased entry, increased short-run supply, and thus downward pressure on price. Remember that in a constant-cost industry, input prices do not change when conditions change in the output market. Constant-cost industries can have horizontal long-run average cost curves.

Increasing-Cost Industry

In an increasing-cost industry, the prices of some or all inputs to production increase as the industry expands and the demand for the inputs grows. This might arise, for example, if the industry uses skilled labor, which becomes in short supply as the demand for it increases. Or the firm might require mineral resources that are available only on certain types of land, so that the cost of land as an input increases with output. Figure 8.16 shows the derivation of

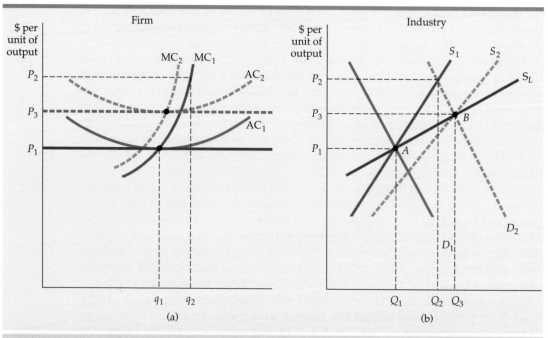

Figure 8.16 **Long-Run Supply in an Increasing-Cost Industry** In (b), the long-run supply curve in an increasing-cost industry is an upward-sloping curve S_L. When demand increases, initially causing a price rise, the firms increase their output from q_1 to q_2 in (a). Then, the entry of new firms causes a shift to the right in supply. Because input prices increase as a result, the new long-run equilibrium occurs at a higher price than the initial equilibrium.

long-run supply, which is similar to the previous constant-cost derivation. The industry is initially in equilibrium at A in part (b). When the demand curve unexpectedly shifts from D_1 to D_2, the price of the product increases in the short run to P_2, and industry output increases from Q_1 to Q_2. A typical firm shown in part (a) increases its output from q_1 to q_2 in response to the higher price by moving along its short-run marginal cost curve. The higher profit that this and other firms earn induces new firms to enter the industry.

As new firms enter and output expands, the increased demand for inputs causes some or all input prices to increase. The short-run market supply curve shifts to the right as before, but not as much, and the new equilibrium at B results in a price P_3 that is higher than the initial price P_1. The higher market price is needed to ensure that firms earn zero profit in long-run equilibrium because the higher input prices raise the firms' short-run and long-run cost curves. Figure 8.16(a) illustrates this. The average cost curve shifts up from AC_1 to AC_2, while the marginal cost curve shifts to the left from MC_1 to MC_2. The new long-run equilibrium price P_3 is equal to the new minimum average cost. As in the constant-cost case, the higher short-run profit caused by the initial increase in demand disappears in the long run as firms increase their output and input costs rise.

The new equilibrium at B in Figure 8.16(b) is, therefore, on the long-run supply curve for the industry. *In an increasing-cost industry, the long-run industry supply curve is upward sloping.* The industry produces more output, but only at the higher price needed to compensate for the increase in input costs. The term "increasing cost" refers to the upward shift in the firms' long-run average cost curves, not to the positive slope of the cost curve itself.

Decreasing-Cost Industry

The industry supply curve can also be downward sloping. In this case, the unexpected increase in demand causes industry output to expand as before. But as the industry grows larger, it can take advantage of its size to obtain some of its inputs more cheaply. For example, a larger industry may allow for an improved transportation system or for a better, less expensive financial network. In this case firms' average cost curves shift downward (even though firms do not enjoy economies of scale), and the market price of the product falls. The lower market price and the lower average cost of production induce a new long-run equilibrium with more firms, more output, and a lower price. Therefore, *in a decreasing-cost industry, the long-run supply curve for the industry is downward sloping.*

The Short-Run and Long-Run Effects of a Tax

In Chapter 6 we saw that a tax on a firm's input (in the form of an effluent fee) creates an incentive for the firm to change the way it uses inputs in its production process. Now we consider how a firm responds to a tax on its output. To simplify the analysis, assume that the firm uses a fixed-proportions production technology. If the firm is a polluter, the output tax can encourage the firm to reduce its output, and therefore its effluent, or the tax might be imposed just to raise revenue.

First, suppose the output tax is imposed only on this firm, and thus does not affect the market price of the product. We will see that the tax on output encourages the firm to reduce its output. Figure 8.17 shows the relevant short-run cost curves for a firm enjoying positive economic profit by producing an output of q_1 and selling its product at the market price P_1. Because the tax is assessed for every unit of output, it raises the firm's marginal cost curve from MC_1 to $MC_2 = MC_1 + t$, where t is the tax per unit of the firm's output. The tax also raises the average variable cost curve by the amount t.

A close look at Figure 8.17 shows us that the output tax can have two possible effects. First, if the tax is less than the firm's profit margin, the firm will maximize its profit by choosing an output at which its marginal cost plus the tax is equal to the price of the product. The firm's output falls from q_1 to q_2, and the implicit effect of the tax is to shift the firm's short-run supply curve upward (by the amount of the tax). Second, if the tax is greater than the firm's profit margin, then the average variable cost curve will rise, and the minimum average variable cost will be greater than the market price of the product. The firm will then choose not to produce.

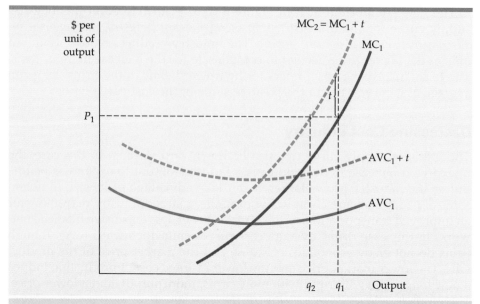

Figure 8.17   Effect of an Output Tax on a Competitive Firm's Output   An output tax raises the firm's marginal cost curve by the amount of the tax. The firm will reduce its output to the point at which the marginal cost plus the tax is equal to the price of the product.

Now suppose all firms in the industry are taxed and have increasing marginal costs. Because each firm reduces its output at the current market price, the total output supplied by the industry will also fall, causing the price of the product to increase. Figure 8.18 illustrates this, where an upward shift in the supply curve, from S_1 to $S_2 = S_1 + t$, causes the market price of the product to increase (by less than the amount of the tax) from P_1 to P_2. This increase in the price of the product diminishes some of the effects that we described previously. Firms will reduce their output less than they would without a price increase.

Output taxes may also encourage some firms (those whose costs are somewhat higher than others) to exit the industry. Figure 8.19 shows the long-run effects of the tax. The fee raises the long-run average cost curve for each firm in the industry. Part (a) shows the effect of the tax on a firm that was earning a profit in the short run (its average cost was less than P_1). The output tax makes production unprofitable for some firms, which choose to exit the industry in search of greater profit elsewhere. This in turn shifts the market supply curve to the left. In part (b) the market price of the product increases from P_1 to P_3, and the quantity sold in the market falls from Q_1 to Q_3.

When the dust settles, the long-run equilibrium will have fewer firms, a lower price (P_3 less than P_2), less output (Q_3 less than Q_2), and less effluent

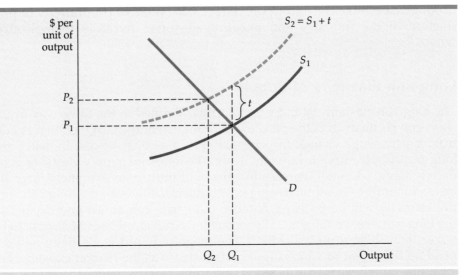

Figure 8.18 Effect of an Output Tax on Industry Output An output tax placed on all firms in a competitive market shifts the short-run supply curve for the industry upward by the amount of the tax. This raises the market price of the product and lowers the total output of the industry.

Figure 8.19 The Long-Run Effects of an Output Tax In the long run, the output tax will raise the average cost curve in (a) from LAC_1 to LAC_2. As some firms exit the industry because of lower profits, the aggregate supply curve in (b) shifts upward and to the left. In the long-run equilibrium, quantity demanded and quantity supplied are equated at a higher price and a lower output.

produced, because the output tax reduced the relative profitability of production in the industry and encouraged some investors to look elsewhere.[10]

Long-Run Elasticity of Supply

The long-run elasticity of industry supply is defined in the same way as the short-run elasticity. It is the percentage change in output ($\Delta Q/Q$) that results from a percentage change in price ($\Delta P/P$). In a constant-cost industry, the long-run supply curve is horizontal, and the long-run supply elasticity is infinitely large. (A small increase in price will induce an extremely large increase in output.) In an increasing-cost industry, however, the long-run supply elasticity will be positive. Because industries can adjust and expand in the long run, we would generally expect long-run elasticities of supply to be larger than short-run elasticities.[11] The magnitude of the elasticity will depend on the extent to which input costs increase as the market expands. For example, an industry that depends on inputs that are widely available will have a more elastic long-run supply than will an industry that uses inputs in short supply.

EXAMPLE 8.4   The Long-Run Supply of Housing

Owner-occupied and rental housing provide interesting examples of the range of possible supply elasticities. People buy or rent housing to obtain the services that a house provides—a place to eat and sleep, comfort, and so on. If the price of housing services were to rise in one area of the country, the quantity of services provided could increase substantially.

To begin, consider the supply of owner-occupied housing in suburban or rural areas where land is not scarce. Here, the price of land does not increase substantially as the quantity of housing supplied increases. Likewise, the costs associated with construction are not likely to increase because there is a national market for lumber and other materials. Therefore, the long-run elasticity of the supply of housing is likely to be very large, approximating a constant-cost industry. In fact, one study found the long-run supply curve to be nearly horizontal.[12]

---

[10] Although total market output will decline, each firm that remains in the market could produce more output and generate more effluent if the increase in the price is greater than the upward shift in the long-run average cost curve. But if policy is directed toward total industrial pollution, the response of the market, not of individual firms, is important.

[11] In some cases the opposite is true. Consider the elasticity of supply of scrap metal from a durable good like copper. Recall from Chapter 2 that because there is an existing stock of scrap, the long-run elasticity of supply will be *smaller* than the short-run elasticity.

[12] See James R. Follain, Jr., "The Price Elasticity of the Long-Run Supply of New Housing Construction," *Land Economics* (May 1979): 190–199.

Even when the elasticity of supply is measured within urban areas, where land costs rise as the demand for housing services increases, the long-run elasticity of supply is still likely to be large because land costs make up only about one-quarter of total housing costs. In one study of urban housing supply, the price elasticity was found to be 5.3.[13]

The market for rental housing is different, however. The construction of rental housing is often restricted by local zoning laws. Many communities outlaw it entirely, while others limit it to certain areas. Because urban land on which most rental housing is located is restricted and valuable, the long-run elasticity of supply of rental housing is much lower than the elasticity of supply of owner-occupied housing. As the price of rental housing services rises, new high-rise rental units are built, and older units are renovated, which increases the quantity of rental services. With urban land becoming more valuable as housing density increases, and with the cost of construction soaring with the height of buildings, the increased demand causes the input costs of rental housing to rise. In this increasing-cost case, the elasticity of supply can be much less than one; in one study the authors found the supply elasticity to be between 0.3 and 0.7.[14]

8.8 Perfectly Competitive Markets

In this chapter we have focused on the behavior of a perfectly competitive firm, stressing that it takes the market price as given and hence produces at the point where price equals marginal cost. We have also seen how the industry supply curve can be determined by aggregating the marginal cost curves of the individual firms. In the next chapter we will continue the analysis of competitive markets that we began in Chapter 2. At this point, however, it is useful to clarify exactly what we mean by a *perfectly competitive market*.

The theory of perfect competition rests on four basic assumptions. You have encountered these assumptions earlier in the book; here we summarize them.

1. *Price taking.* Each firm sells a sufficiently small proportion of total industry output, so that its decisions have no impact on market price. Hence each firm takes the market price as given. Likewise, each consumer buys such a small proportion of industry output that he or she will have no impact on price, and therefore takes the market price as given. Another way of stating the price-taking assumption is that there are many independent firms and independent consumers in the market. Firms and consumers believe (correctly) that their decisions will not affect price.

---

[13] See Barton A. Smith, "The Supply of Urban Housing," *Journal of Political Economy* 40, no. 3 (Aug. 1976): 389–405.

[14] See Frank deLeeuw and Nkanta Ekanem, "The Supply of Rental Housing," *American Economic Review* 61 (Dec. 1971): 806–817, table 5.2.

2. *Product homogeneity.* All firms produce an identical product. Therefore, consumers consider only price when choosing which firm to buy from, and any firm that tries to raise its price above the market price will lose all sales. This assumption of product homogeneity ensures that there is a single market price, and makes a discussion of market supply and demand meaningful.

3. *Perfect mobility of resources.* Firms can freely enter an industry if they see a profit opportunity and can exit if they are losing money. This means that a firm can hire labor and purchase capital and raw materials as needed, and it can release or relocate these factors of production if it wants to shut down or relocate.

4. *Perfect information.* Consumers have perfect information about their preferences, their income levels, the prices they face, and the quality of the goods they purchase. Likewise, firms have perfect information about their costs, prices, and technology.

If these assumptions hold, firms will earn zero economic profit in the long run, and market demand and supply curves can be used to analyze the behavior of market prices. In most markets, of course, these assumptions are unlikely to hold exactly. Indeed, some students conclude that as a result, the model of perfect competition is not very useful. As we will see, such a conclusion would be mistaken. Some markets, such as those for agricultural products, come close to satisfying the four assumptions that underlie the theory of perfect competition. In these cases, we can take the model of perfect competition more or less at face value. However, even when one or more of these four assumptions fails to hold, and markets are not fully competitive, we will see that much can be learned by making comparisons with the perfectly competitive ideal.

When Is a Market Highly Competitive?

Apart from agriculture, few real-world markets are *perfectly* competitive in the sense that each firm faces a perfectly horizontal demand curve for a homogeneous product, and that firms can freely enter or exit the industry. Nevertheless, many markets are *highly* competitive, in the sense that firms in these markets face highly elastic demand curves, and entry and exit are relatively easy. As a result, firms in these markets will find it profitable to set output, so that the marginal cost of production is approximately equal to price.

A simple rule of thumb to describe whether a market is close to being perfectly competitive would be appealing. Unfortunately, we have no such rule, and it is important to understand why. Consider the most obvious candidate: an industry with many firms (say at least 10 to 20). Unfortunately, the presence of many firms is neither necessary nor sufficient for an industry to approximate perfect competition because firms can implicitly or explicitly collude in setting prices.

The presence of only a few firms in a market also does not rule out competitive behavior. Suppose that five firms are in the market, but market demand for the product is very elastic. Then, the demand curve facing each firm is likely to be nearly horizontal, and the firms will behave *as if* they were operating in a perfectly competitive market. Or even if market demand is not very elastic, these five firms might compete aggressively (as we discuss in Chapter 13).

Contestable Markets

Even when only one firm is in a market, that firm may find it profit-maximizing to act as if it were competitive. The reason is that if it tries to raise price above the competitive level, other firms will enter the market, compete for customers, and force the price back down. Hence, competition among firms *within* a market can be less important than the competition *for a market*. In a *contestable market*, new firms may enter the market under essentially the same cost conditions as a firm that is already in the market. A firm can also exit the market without losing any investment in capital that is specific to that market and valueless elsewhere.[15]

Consider, for example, a neighborhood market for retail gasoline stations. It may be economical for there to be only two stations in the neighborhood, since the presence of three or more would cause all stations to lose profits. Yet this market might be contestable, since the cost of opening a gas station is not *sunk*—i.e., it is not specific to that location. As a result, it is easy for firms to enter or exit the market as economic conditions change.

Most monopolistic or oligopolistic markets are not contestable, because the incumbent firms have sunk costs. These incumbents have a competitive advantage over prospective newcomers and can charge a price higher than marginal cost. Suppose, for example, that a firm has a local monopoly over cable television. Economies of scale make it economical for one firm to provide cable service. But, the market is not fully contestable because some of the cost incurred by the cable company is sunk and cannot be transferred if the company were to move its business elsewhere. The cable itself can be reutilized, but much of the labor involved in moving it would be wasted, and some of the cable and other materials associated with the hookups in each house would be valueless if the company had to exit the business. Because some of the investment is sunk, a new firm competing for the business would have to bid high enough to cover all its costs, whereas the incumbent firm could set a slightly lower price and make a substantial profit above and beyond its variable costs.

The point is that firms may behave competitively in many situations. Unfortunately, no simple indicator signifies when a market approximates perfect competition. Often it is necessary to analyze the number and size of firms and their strategic interactions, as we do in Chapters 12 and 13.

---

15 The theory is developed in William J. Baumol, John C. Panzar, and Robert D. Willig, *Contestable Markets and the Theory of Industry Structure* (New York: Harcourt, Brace, Jovanovich, 1982), and criticized in William G. Shepherd, "Contestability vs. Competition," *American Economic Review* 74 (Sept. 1984): 572–587.

Summary

1. The managers of firms can operate in accordance with a complex set of objectives and under various constraints. However, we can assume that firms act as if they are maximizing their long-run profit.

2. Because a firm in a competitive market has a small share of total industry output, it makes its output choice under the assumption that the demand for its own output is horizontal, in which case the demand curve and the marginal revenue curve are identical.

3. In the short run, a competitive firm maximizes its profit by choosing an output at which price is equal to (short-run) marginal cost, so long as price is greater than or equal to the firm's minimum average variable cost of production.

4. The short-run market supply curve is the horizontal summation of the supply curves of the firms in an industry. It can be characterized by the elasticity of supply—the percentage change in quantity supplied in response to a percentage change in price.

5. The producer surplus for a firm is the difference between revenue of a firm and the minimum cost that would be necessary to produce the profit-maximizing output. In both the short run and the long run, producer surplus is the area under the horizontal price line and above the marginal cost of production for the firm.

6. Economic rent is the payment for a scarce factor of production less the minimum amount necessary to hire that factor. In the long run in a competitive market, producer surplus is equal to the economic rent generated by all scarce factors of production.

7. In the long run, profit-maximizing competitive firms choose the output at which price is equal to long-run marginal cost.

8. A long-run competitive equilibrium occurs when (i) firms maximize profit; (ii) all firms earn zero economic profit, so that there is no incentive to enter or exit the industry; and (iii) the quantity of the product demanded is equal to the quantity supplied.

9. The long-run supply curve for a firm is horizontal when the industry is a constant-cost industry in which the increased demand for inputs to production (associated with an increased demand for the product) has no effect on the market price of the inputs. But the long-run supply curve for a firm is upward sloping in an increasing-cost industry, where the increased demand for inputs causes the market price of some or all inputs to production to rise.

10. Many markets may approximate perfect competition in that one or more firms act as if they face a nearly horizontal demand curve. In general, the number of firms in an industry is not always a good indicator of the extent to which that industry is competitive.

Questions for Review

1. Why would a firm that incurs losses choose to produce rather than shut down?

2. The supply curve for a firm in the short run is the short-run marginal cost curve (above the point of minimum average variable cost). Why is the supply curve in the long run *not* the long-run marginal cost curve (above the point of minimum average total cost)?

3. In long-run equilibrium, all firms in the industry earn zero economic profit. Why is this true?

4. What is the difference between economic profit and producer surplus?

5. Why do firms enter an industry when they know that in the long run economic profit will be zero?

6. At the beginning of the twentieth century, there were many small American automobile manufacturers. At the end of the century, there are only three large ones. Suppose that this situation is not the result of lax federal enforcement of antimonopoly laws. How do you explain the decrease in the number of manufacturers? (*Hint*: What is the inherent cost structure of the automobile industry?)

7. Industry X is characterized by perfect competition, so that every firm in the industry is earning zero economic profit. If the product price falls, no firms can survive. Do you agree or disagree? Discuss.

8. An increase in the demand for video films also increases the salaries of actors and actresses. Is the long-run supply curve for films likely to be horizontal or upward sloping? Explain.

9. True or false: A firm should always produce at an output at which long-run average cost is minimized. Explain.

10. Can there be constant returns to scale in an industry with an upward-sloping supply curve? Explain.

11. What assumptions are necessary for a market to be perfectly competitive? In light of what you have learned in this chapter, why is each of these assumptions important?

12. Suppose a competitive industry faces an increase in demand (i.e., the curve shifts upward). What are the steps by which a competitive market ensures increased output? Does your answer change if the government imposes a price ceiling?

13. The government passes a law that allows a substantial subsidy for every acre of land used to grow tobacco. How does this program affect the long-run supply curve for tobacco?

Exercises

1. From the data in Table 8.2 on the next page, show what happens to the firm's output choice and profit if the price of the product falls from $40 to $35.

2. Again, from the data in Table 8.2, show what happens to the firm's output choice and profit if the fixed cost of production increases from $50 to $100, and then to $150. What general conclusion can you reach about the effects of fixed costs on the firm's output choice?

3. Suppose you are the manager of a watchmaking firm operating in a competitive market. Your cost of production is given by $C = 100 + Q^2$, where Q is the level of output and C is total cost. (The marginal cost of production is $2Q$. The fixed cost of production is $100.)
   a. If the price of watches is $60, how many watches should you produce to maximize profit?
   b. What will the profit level be?
   c. At what minimum price will the firm produce a positive output?

4. Use the same information as in Exercise 1 to answer the following.
   a. Derive the firm's short-run supply curve. (*Hint*: You may want to plot the appropriate cost curves.)
   b. If 100 identical firms are in the market, what is the industry supply curve?

5. A sales tax of $1 per unit of output is placed on one firm whose product sells for $5 in a competitive industry.
   a. How will this tax affect the cost curves for the firm?
   b. What will happen to the firm's price, output, and profit in the short run?
   c. What will happen in the long run?

6. Suppose that a competitive firm's marginal cost of producing output q is given by $MC(q) = 3 + 2q$. Assume that the market price of the firm's product is $9:
   a. What level of output will the firm produce?
   b. What is the firm's producer surplus?

Table 8.2 A Firm's Short-Run Revenues and Costs

Output (units)	Price ($/unit)	Revenue ($)	Total Cost ($)	Profit ($)	Marginal Cost ($)	Marginal Revenue ($)
0	40	0	50	−50	—	—
1	40	40	100	−60	50	40
2	40	80	128	−48	28	40
3	40	120	148	−28	20	40
4	40	160	162	−2	14	40
5	40	200	180	20	18	40
6	40	240	200	40	20	40
7	40	280	222	58	22	40
8	40	320	260	60	38	40
9	40	360	305	55	45	40
10	40	400	360	40	55	40
11	40	440	425	15	65	40

7. Suppose that the average variable cost of the firm in Exercise 6 is given by $AVC(q) = 3 + q$. Suppose that the firm's fixed costs are known to be $3. Will the firm be earning a positive, negative, or zero profit in the short run?

8. A competitive industry is in long-run equilibrium. A sales tax is then placed on all firms in the industry. What do you expect to happen to the price of the product, the number of firms in the industry, and the output of each firm in the long run?

*9. A sales tax of 10 percent is placed on half the firms (the polluters) in a competitive industry. The revenue is paid to the remaining firms (the nonpolluters) as a 10 percent subsidy on the value of output sold.

a. Assuming that all firms have identical constant long-run average costs before the sales tax-subsidy policy, what do you expect to happen to the price of the product, the output of each of the firms, and industry output, in the short run and the long run? (*Hint*: How does price relate to industry input?)

b. Can such a policy *always* be achieved with a balanced budget in which tax revenues are equal to subsidy payments? Why? Explain.

CHAPTER 9

The Analysis of Competitive Markets

In Chapter 2 we saw how supply and demand curves can help us describe and understand the behavior of competitive markets. In Chapters 3 to 8, we saw how these curves are derived and what determines their shapes. With this foundation, we return to supply-demand analysis and show how it can be applied to a wide variety of economic problems—problems that might concern a consumer faced with a purchasing decision, a firm faced with a long-range planning problem, or a government agency that has to design a policy and evaluate its likely impact.

We begin by showing how consumer and producer surplus can be used to study the *welfare effects* of a government policy—in other words, who gains and who loses from the policy, and by how much. We also use consumer and producer surplus to demonstrate the *efficiency* of a competitive market— why the equilibrium price and quantity in a competitive market maximizes the aggregate economic welfare of producers and consumers.

Then we apply supply-demand analysis to a variety of problems. Very few markets in the United States have been untouched by government interventions of one kind or another, so most of the problems that we will study deal with the effects of such interventions. Our objective is not simply to solve these problems, but to show you how to use the tools of economic analysis to deal with others like them on your own. We hope that by working through the examples we provide, you will see how to calculate the response of markets to changing economic conditions or government policies and to evaluate the resulting gains and losses to consumers and producers.

9.1 Evaluating the Gains and Losses from Government Policies—Consumer and Producer Surplus

We saw at the end of Chapter 2 that a price ceiling causes the quantity of a good demanded to rise (consumers want to buy more, given the lower price) and the quantity supplied to fall (producers are not willing to supply as much given the lower price), so that a shortage results. Of course, those consumers who can still buy the good will be better off because they will now pay less. (Presumably, this was the objective of the policy in the first place.) But if we also take into account those who cannot obtain the good, how much better off are consumers *as a whole*? Might they be worse off? And if we lump consumers and producers together, will their total welfare be greater or lower, and by how much? To answer questions like these, we need a way to measure the gains and losses from government interventions and the changes in market price and quantity such interventions cause.

Our method is to calculate the changes in *consumer and producer surplus* that result from an intervention. In Chapter 4 we saw that *consumer surplus* measures the aggregate net benefit that consumers obtain from a competitive market. In Chapter 8 we saw how *producer surplus* measures the aggregate net benefit to producers. Here we will see how consumer and producer surplus can be applied in practice.

Review of Consumer and Producer Surplus

In an unregulated, competitive market, consumers and producers buy and sell at the prevailing market price. But remember, for some consumers the value of the good *exceeds* this market price; they would pay more for the good if they had to. *Consumer surplus* is the total benefit or value that consumers receive beyond what they pay for the good.

For example, suppose the market price is $5 per unit, as in Figure 9.1. Some consumers probably value this good very highly and would pay much more than $5 for it. Consumer A, for example, would pay up to $10 for the good. However, because the market price is only $5, he enjoys a net benefit of $5—the $10 value he places on the good, less the $5 he must pay to obtain it. Consumer B values the good somewhat less highly. She would be willing to pay $7, and thus enjoys a $2 net benefit. Finally, Consumer C values the good

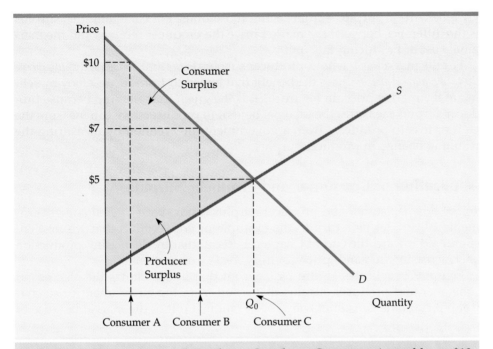

Figure 9.1   Consumer and Producer Surplus   Consumer A would pay $10 for a good whose market price is $5, and therefore enjoys a benefit of $5. Consumer B enjoys a benefit of $2, and Consumer C, who values the good at exactly the market price, enjoys no benefit. Consumer surplus, which measures the total benefit to all consumers, is the yellow-shaded area between the demand curve and the market price. Producer surplus measures the total profits of producers, plus rents to factor inputs. It is the green-shaded area between the supply curve and the market price. Together, consumer and producer surplus measure the welfare benefit of a competitive market.

at exactly the market price, $5. He is indifferent between buying or not buying the good, and if the market price were one cent higher, he would forgo the purchase. Consumer C therefore obtains no net benefit.[1]

For consumers in the aggregate, consumer surplus is the *area between the demand curve and the market price* (i.e., the yellow-shaded area in Figure 9.1). And because consumer surplus measures the total net benefit to consumers, we can measure the gain or loss to consumers from a government intervention by measuring the resulting change in consumer surplus.

Producer surplus is the analogous measure for producers. Some producers are producing units at a cost just equal to the market price. Other units, however, could be produced for less than the market price, and would still be produced and sold even if the market price were lower. Producers therefore en-

---

[1] Of course, some consumers value the good at *less* than $5. These consumers make up the part of the demand curve to the right of the equilibrium quantity Q_0 and will not purchase the good.

joy a benefit—a surplus—from selling those units. For each unit, this surplus is the difference between the market price the producer receives and the marginal cost of producing this unit.

For the market as a whole, producer surplus is *the area above the supply curve up to the market price;* this is the benefit that lower-cost producers enjoy by selling at the market price. In Figure 9.1 it is the green triangle. And because producer surplus measures the total net benefit to producers, we can measure the gain or loss to producers from a government intervention by measuring the resulting change in producer surplus.

Application of Consumer and Producer Surplus

To see how consumer and producer surplus can be used to evaluate government policies, let us return to the example of *price controls* that we first encountered toward the end of Chapter 2. Recall that by decreasing production and increasing demand, price controls create excess demand.

Figure 9.2 replicates Figure 2.22, except that it also shows the changes in consumer and producer surplus that result from the government price control policy. Some consumers have been rationed out of the market because of

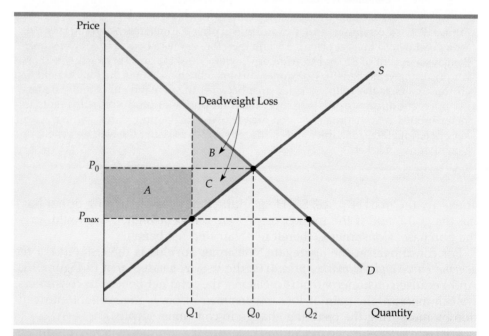

Figure 9.2 Change in Consumer and Producer Surplus from Price Controls The price of a good has been regulated to be no higher than P_{max}, which is below the market-clearing price P_0. The gain to consumers is the difference between rectangle A and triangle B. The loss to producers is the sum of rectangle A and triangle C. Triangles B and C together measure the deadweight loss from price controls.

price controls, and production and sales fall from Q_0 to Q_1. Those consumers who can still purchase the good can now do so at a lower price, so they enjoy an *increase* in consumer surplus, which is given by blue-shaded rectangle A. However, some consumers can no longer buy the good. Their *loss* of consumer surplus is given by the green-shaded triangle B. The net change in consumer surplus is therefore $A - B$. In Figure 9.2, rectangle A is larger than triangle B, so the net change in consumer surplus is positive.

What about the change in producer surplus? Those producers who are still in the market and producing quantity Q_1 are now receiving a lower price. They have lost the producer surplus given by rectangle A. However, total production has also dropped. This represents an additional loss of producer surplus and is given by the purple-shaded triangle C. Therefore, the total change in producer surplus is $-A - C$. Producers clearly lose as a result of price controls.

Is this loss to producers from price controls offset by the gain to consumers? No—as Figure 9.2 shows, price controls result in a net loss of total surplus, which we call a *deadweight loss*. Recall that the change in consumer surplus is $A - B$ and that the change in producer surplus is $-A - C$, so the *total* change in surplus is $(A - B) + (-A - C) = -B - C$. We thus have a deadweight loss,

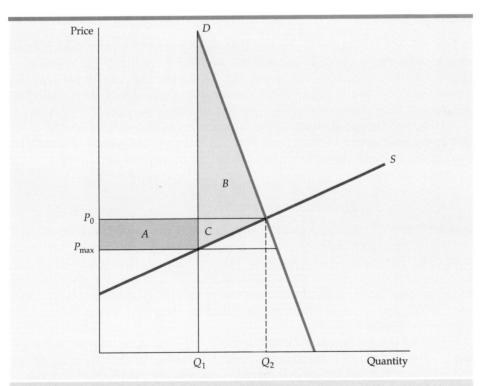

Figure 9.3   Effect of Price Controls When Demand Is Inelastic   If demand is sufficiently inelastic, triangle B can be larger than rectangle A. In this case, consumers suffer a net loss from price controls.

which is given by the two triangles B and C in Figure 9.2. This deadweight loss is an inefficiency caused by price controls; the loss of producer surplus exceeds the gain in consumer surplus.

If politicians value consumer surplus more than producer surplus, this deadweight loss may not carry much political weight. However, if the demand curve is very inelastic, price controls can result in a *net loss of consumer surplus*, as Figure 9.3 shows. In that figure, triangle B, which measures the loss to consumers who have been rationed out of the market, is larger than rectangle A, which measures the gain to consumers able to buy the good. Here, consumers value the good highly, so those who are rationed out suffer a large loss.

The demand for gasoline is very inelastic in the short run (but much more elastic in the long run). During the summer of 1979, gasoline shortages resulted from oil price controls that prevented domestic gasoline prices from increasing to rising world levels. Consumers spent hours waiting in line to buy gasoline. This was a good example of price controls making consumers—the group the policy was presumably intended to protect—worse off.

EXAMPLE 9.1   **Price Controls and Natural Gas Shortages**

In Example 2.8 in Chapter 2, we saw that during the 1970s price controls created a large excess demand for natural gas. But how much did consumers gain from those controls, how much did producers lose, and what was the deadweight loss to the country? We can answer these questions by calculating the resulting changes in consumer and producer surplus.

Again, we base our analysis on the numbers for 1975 and calculate the gains and losses that apply to that year. Refer to Example 2.8, where we showed that the supply and demand curves can be approximated as follows:

$$\text{Supply:} \qquad Q^S = 14 + 2P_G + 0.25P_O$$
$$\text{Demand:} \qquad Q^D = -5P_G + 3.75P_O$$

where Q^S and Q^D are the quantities supplied and demanded, each measured in trillion cubic feet (Tcf), P_G is the price of natural gas in dollars per thousand cubic feet ($/mcf), and P_O is the price of oil in dollars per barrel ($/b). As the reader can verify by setting Q^S equal to Q^D, and using a price of oil of $8 per barrel, the equilibrium free market price and quantity are $2 per mcf and 20 Tcf, respectively. Under the regulations, however, the maximum allowable price was $1 per mcf.

Figure 9.4 shows these supply and demand curves and free market and regulated prices. Rectangle A and triangles B and C measure the changes in consumer and producer surplus resulting from price controls. By calculating the areas of the rectangle and triangles, we can determine the gains and losses from controls.

To do the calculations, first note that 1 Tcf is equal to 1 billion mcf. (We must put the quantities and prices in common units.) Also, by substituting the quantity 18 Tcf into the equation for the demand curve, we can determine

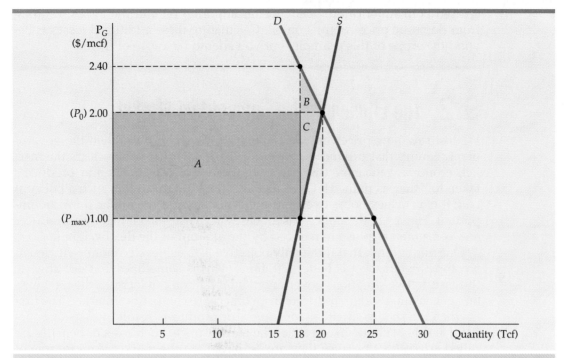

Figure 9.4 Effects of Natural Gas Price Controls   The market-clearing price of natural gas is $2 per mcf, and the maximum allowable price is $1. A shortage of 25 − 18 = 7 Tcf results. The gain to consumers is rectangle A minus triangle B, and the loss to producers is rectangle A plus triangle C.

that the vertical line at 18 Tcf intersects the demand curve at a price of $2.40 per mcf. Then we can calculate the areas as follows:

$$A = (18 \text{ billion mcf}) \times (\$1/\text{mcf}) = \$18 \text{ billion}$$

$$B = (1/2) \times (2 \text{ billion mcf}) \times (\$0.40/\text{mcf}) = \$0.4 \text{ billion}$$

$$C = (1/2) \times (2 \text{ billion mcf}) \times (\$1/\text{mcf}) = \$1 \text{ billion}$$

(The area of a triangle is one-half the product of its altitude and its base.)

   The 1975 change in consumer surplus resulting from price controls was therefore $A - B = 18 - 0.4 = \$17.6$ billion. The change in producer surplus was $-A - C = -18 - 1 = -\$19$ billion. And finally, the deadweight loss for the year was $-B - C = -0.4 - 1 = -\$1.4$ billion.

   Remember that this amount of $1.4 billion per year is in 1975 dollars. In 1996 dollars, the deadweight loss is more than $4 billion per year—a significant loss to society. And this number understates the true loss resulting from natural gas price controls. Our analysis was a *partial equilibrium one*, which means that it ignored the spillover effects that natural gas shortages had on other markets. For example, during the 1970s much of the excess demand for natural gas (25 − 18 = 7 Tcf) wound up as a greater demand for oil and oil products. This increased both American dependence on imported oil and the losses resulting from domestic price controls on oil. Calculating these additional losses is beyond the scope of this example, but you should be aware of them.

9.2 The Efficiency of a Competitive Market

We just saw how price controls create a deadweight loss: When the government requires that producers charge a price below that which clears the market, economic efficiency (the *aggregate* welfare of consumers and producers taken together) is reduced. Of course, this does not mean that such a policy is bad; it may achieve objectives that policymakers and the public think are important. However, the policy has an efficiency cost—taken together, producer and consumer surplus are reduced by the amount of the deadweight loss.

One might think that if the only objective is to achieve economic efficiency, a competitive market is better left alone. This is sometimes, but not always, the case. In two situations government intervention can increase the total welfare of consumers and producers in an otherwise competitive market. The first is when the actions of either consumers or producers result in costs or benefits that do not show up as part of the market price. Such costs or benefits are called *externalities* because they are "external" to the market. An example of an externality is the cost to society of environmental pollution by a producer of industrial chemicals. Without government intervention, such a producer will have no incentive to consider the social cost of this pollution. We examine externalities and the proper government response to them in Chapter 18.

Market failure is the second situation in which government intervention can improve on the outcome of a freely functioning competitive market. Loosely speaking, market failure means that prices fail to provide the proper signals to consumers and producers, so that the market does not operate as we have described it. For example, market failure can occur when consumers lack information about the quality or nature of a product, and therefore cannot make utility-maximizing purchasing decisions. Government intervention (e.g., requiring "truth in labeling") may then be desirable. Market failure and its implications are discussed in Chapters 17 and 18.

Without externalities or market failure, an unregulated competitive market does lead to the economically efficient output level. To see this, let us consider what happens if price is constrained to be something other than the equilibrium market-clearing price.

We have already examined the effects of a price ceiling (i.e., a price held below the market-clearing one). Production falls (from Q_0 to Q_1 in Figure 9.5), and there is a corresponding loss of total surplus (the deadweight loss triangles B and C in the figure). Too little is produced, and consumers and producers in the aggregate are worse off.

Now suppose instead that the government required the price to be *above* the market-clearing one—say, P_2 instead of P_0. As Figure 9.6 shows, produc-

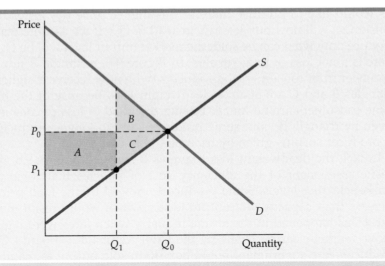

Figure 9.5   Welfare Loss When Price Is Held Below Market-Clearing Level
When price is regulated to be no higher than P_1, the deadweight loss given by triangles B and C results.

Figure 9.6   Welfare Loss When Price Is Held Above Market-Clearing Level
When price is regulated to be no lower than P_2, only Q_3 will be demanded. If Q_3 is produced, the deadweight loss is given by triangles B and C. At price P_2, producers would like to produce more than Q_3. If they do, the deadweight loss will be even larger.

ers would like to produce more at this higher price (Q_2 instead of Q_0), but consumers will now buy less (Q_3 instead of Q_0). If we assume that producers produce only what can be sold, the market output level will be Q_3, and again, there is a net loss of total surplus. In Figure 9.6, rectangle A now represents a transfer from consumers to producers (who now receive a higher price), but triangles B and C are again a deadweight loss. Because of the higher price, some consumers are no longer buying the good (a loss of consumer surplus given by triangle B), and some producers are no longer producing it (a loss of producer surplus given by triangle C).

In fact, the deadweight loss triangles B and C in Figure 9.6 give an optimistic assessment of the efficiency cost of policies that force price above market-clearing levels. Some producers, enticed by the high price P_2, might increase their capacity and output levels, which would result in unsold output. (This happened in the airline industry when fares were regulated to be above market-clearing levels by the Civil Aeronautics Board.) Or to satisfy producers, the government might buy up unsold output to maintain production at Q_2 or close to it. (This is what happens with U.S. agriculture.) In both cases the total welfare loss will significantly exceed triangles B and C.

We will examine minimum prices, price supports, and related policies in some detail in the next few sections. Besides showing how supply-demand analysis can be used to understand and assess these policies, we will see how deviations from the competitive market equilibrium lead to efficiency costs.

EXAMPLE 9.2 The Market for Human Kidneys

Should people have the right to sell parts of their bodies? Congress believes the answer is no. In 1984 it passed the National Organ Transplantation Act, which prohibits the sale of organs for transplantation. Organs may only be donated.

Although the law prohibits their sale, it does not make organs valueless. Instead, it prevents those who supply organs (living persons or the families of the deceased) from reaping their economic value. It also creates a shortage of organs. Each year about 8000 kidneys, 20,000 corneas, and 1200 hearts are transplanted in the United States, but there is considerable excess demand for these organs, and many potential recipients must do without them. Some potential recipients die as a result.

To understand the effects of this law, let's consider the supply and demand for kidneys. First the supply curve. Even at a price of zero (the effective price under the 1984 act), donors supply about 8000 kidneys per year. But many other people who need kidney transplants cannot obtain them because of a lack of donors. It has been estimated that 4000 more kidneys would be supplied if the price were $20,000. This implies the following linear supply curve:[2]

$$Supply: \quad Q^S = 8000 + 0.2P$$

---

[2] The supply curve is of the form $Q = a + bP$. When $P = 0$, $Q = 8000$, so $a = 8000$. If $P = \$20,000$, $Q = 12,000$, so $b = (12,000 - 8000)/20,000 = 0.2$. At a price of $20,000 the elasticity of supply is 0.33.

It is expected that at a price of $20,000 the number of kidneys demanded would be 12,000 per year. Like supply, demand is relatively price inelastic; a reasonable estimate for the elasticity of demand at the $20,000 price is −0.33. This implies the following linear demand curve:

$$\text{Demand:} \quad Q^D = 16,000 - 0.2P$$

These supply and demand curves are plotted in Figure 9.7, which shows the market-clearing price and quantity of $20,000 and 12,000, respectively.

Because the sale of kidneys is prohibited, supply is limited to 8000 (the number of kidneys that people donate). This constrained supply is shown as the vertical line S'. How does this affect the welfare of kidney suppliers and recipients?

First consider suppliers. Those who provide kidneys fail to receive the $20,000 each kidney is worth, a loss of surplus represented by rectangle A,

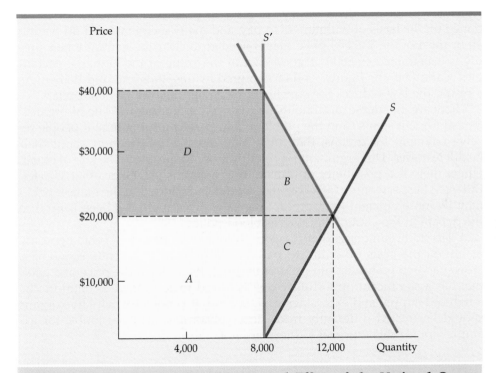

Figure 9.7 The Market for Kidneys, and Effect of the National Organ Transplantation Act   The market-clearing price is $20,000; at this price, about 12,000 kidneys per year would be supplied. The 1984 act effectively makes the price zero. About 8000 kidneys per year are still donated; this constrained supply is shown as S'. The loss to suppliers is given by rectangle A and triangle C. If consumers received kidneys at no cost, their gain would be given by rectangle A less triangle B. In practice, kidneys are often rationed on the basis of willingness to pay, and many recipients pay most or all of the $40,000 price that clears the market when supply is constrained. Rectangles A and D measure the total value of kidneys when supply is constrained.

and equal to (8000)($20,000) = $160 million. Also, some people who would supply kidneys if they were paid for them do not, and they lose an amount of surplus represented by triangle C, equal to (1/2)(4000)($20,000) = $40 million. So the total loss to suppliers is $200 million.

What about recipients? Presumably the law intended to treat the kidney as a gift to the recipient. In this case, those recipients who obtain kidneys *gain* rectangle A ($160 million) because they do not have to pay the $20,000 price. Those who cannot obtain kidneys lose surplus of an amount given by triangle B and equal to $40 million. This implies a net increase in the surplus of recipients of $160 − $40 = $120 million. It also implies a deadweight loss equal to the areas of triangles B and C (i.e., $80 million).

This deadweight loss number underestimates the true efficiency cost of the policy. First, kidneys will not necessarily be allocated to those who value them most highly. Second, with excess demand, there is no way to ensure that recipients will receive their kidneys as gifts. In practice, kidneys are often rationed on the basis of willingness to pay, and many recipients end up paying all or most of the $40,000 price that is needed to clear the market when supply is constrained to 8000. A good part of the value of the kidneys—rectangles A and D in the figure—is then captured by hospitals and middlemen. As a result, the law reduces the surplus of recipients, as well as of suppliers.[3]

There are, of course, arguments in favor of prohibiting the sale of organs.[4] One argument stems from the problem of imperfect information; if people receive payment for organs, they may hide adverse information about their health histories. This argument is probably most applicable to the sale of blood, where there is a possibility of transmitting hepatitis, AIDS, or other viruses. But even here screening (at a cost that would be included in the market price) may be more efficient than prohibiting sales. This issue has been central to the debate in the United States over blood policy.

A second argument is that it is simply unfair to allocate a basic necessity of life on the basis of ability to pay. This argument transcends economics. However, two points should be kept in mind. First, when the price of a good that has a significant opportunity cost is forced to zero, there is bound to be a reduced supply and excess demand. Second, it is not clear why live organs should be treated differently from close substitutes; artificial limbs, for example, are for sale, but real kidneys are not.

---

[3] According to the *New York Times* ("The Body's Value Has Gone Up," Sept. 8, 1986), in 1984–1985 many hospitals were performing nearly 30 percent of kidney transplants on foreigners who were allowed to jump the queue of Americans, and who were charged surgeons' and hospital fees nearly twice those charged Americans. In 1989 Britain passed a similar law banning the sale of human organs, and this has led to the same problems. For further analyses of these efficiency costs, see Dwane L. Barney and R. Larry Reynolds, "An Economic Analysis of Transplant Organs," *Atlantic Economic Journal* 17 (September 1989): 12–20, and David L. Kaserman and A. H. Barnett, "An Economic Analysis of Transplant Organs: A Comment and Extension," *Atlantic Economic Journal* 19 (June 1991): 57–64.

[4] For discussions of the strengths and weaknesses of these arguments, see Susan Rose-Ackerman, "Inalienability and the Theory of Property Rights," *Columbia Law Review* 85 (June 1985): 931–969, and Roger D. Blair and David L. Kaserman, "The Economics and Ethics of Alternative Cadaveric Organ Procurement Policies," *Yale Journal on Regulation* 8 (Summer 1991): 403–452.

Many complex ethical and economic issues are involved in the sale of organs. These issues are important, and this example is not intended to sweep them away. Economics, the dismal science, simply shows us that human organs have economic value that cannot be ignored, and that prohibiting their sale imposes a cost on society that must be weighed against the benefits.

9.3 Minimum Prices

As we have seen, government policy sometimes seeks to *raise* prices above market-clearing levels, rather than lower them. Examples include the former regulation of the airlines by the Civil Aeronautics Board, the minimum wage law, and a variety of agricultural policies. (Most import quotas and tariffs also have this intent, as we will see in Section 9.5.) One way to raise price above the market-clearing level is by direct regulation—simply make it illegal to charge a price lower than a specific minimum level.

Look again at Figure 9.6. If producers correctly anticipate that they can sell only the lower quantity Q_3, the net welfare loss will be given by triangles B and C. But as we explained, producers might not limit their output to Q_3. What happens if producers think they can sell all they want at the higher price, and produce accordingly?

This situation is illustrated in Figure 9.8, where P_{min} denotes a minimum price set by the government. The quantity supplied is now Q_2, and the quan-

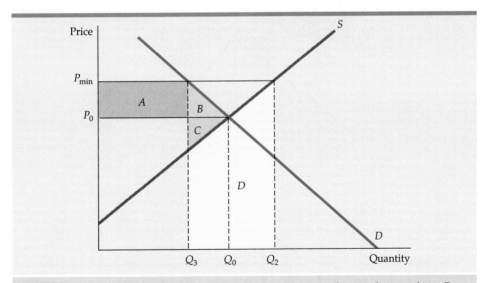

Figure 9.8 Price Minimum Price is regulated to be no lower than P_{min}. Producers would like to supply Q_2, but consumers will buy only Q_3. If producers indeed produce Q_2, the amount $Q_2 - Q_3$ will go unsold and the change in producer surplus will be $A - C - D$. In this case, producers as a group may be worse off.

tity demanded is Q_3, the difference representing an excess, unsold supply. Now let us follow the resulting changes in consumer and producer surplus.

Those consumers who still purchase the good must now pay a higher price and so suffer a loss of surplus, which is given by rectangle A in Figure 9.8. Some consumers have also dropped out of the market because of the higher price, with a corresponding loss of surplus given by triangle B. The total change in consumer surplus is therefore

$$\Delta CS = -A - B$$

Consumers clearly are worse off as a result of this policy.

What about producers? They receive a higher price for the units they sell, which results in an increase of surplus, given by rectangle A. (Rectangle A represents a transfer of money from consumers to producers.) But the drop in sales from Q_0 to Q_3 results in a loss of surplus, which is given by triangle C. Finally, consider the cost to producers of expanding production from Q_0 to Q_2. Because they sell only Q_3, there is no revenue to cover the cost of producing $Q_2 - Q_3$. This cost is the area under the supply curve from Q_3 to Q_2, and is represented

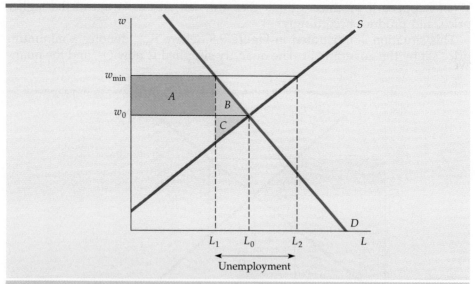

Figure 9.9 **The Minimum Wage** The market-clearing wage is w_0, but firms are not allowed to pay less than w_{min}. This results in unemployment of an amount $L_2 - L_1$, and a deadweight loss given by triangles B and C.

---

5 Remember that the supply curve is the aggregate marginal cost curve for the industry. The supply curve therefore gives us the additional cost of producing each incremental unit, so the area under the supply curve from Q_3 to Q_2 is the cost of producing the quantity $Q_2 - Q_3$.

by the shaded trapezoid D.[5] So unless producers respond to unsold output by cutting production, the total change in producer surplus is

$$\Delta PS = A - C - D$$

Given that trapezoid D can be large, a minimum price can even result in a net loss of surplus to producers alone! As a result, this form of government intervention can reduce producers' profits because of the cost of excess production.

Another example of a government-imposed price minimum is the minimum wage law. This is illustrated in Figure 9.9, which shows the supply of labor and the demand for labor. The wage is set at w_{min}, a level higher than the market-clearing wage w_0. As a result, those workers who can find jobs obtain a higher wage. However, some people who want to work will be unable to. The policy results in unemployment, which in the figure is $L_2 - L_1$. We will examine the minimum wage in more detail in Chapter 14.

EXAMPLE 9.3 Airline Regulation

During 1976–1981 the airline industry in the United States changed dramatically. Until that time fares and routes had been tightly regulated by the Civil Aeronautics Board (CAB). The CAB set most fares well above what would have prevailed in a free market. It also restricted entry, so that many routes were served by only one or two airlines. But in 1976 the CAB started to liberalize fare regulation. In 1977 it approved the first "Super Saver" fares. In 1978 it allowed airlines to set fares as much as 10 percent above or 50 percent below a CAB standard fare, and in 1980 this range was expanded to give airlines unlimited downward flexibility and more upward flexibility over fares. Also, shortly after passage of the Airline Deregulation Act in October 1978, the CAB allowed airlines to serve any routes they wished, and since then many new airlines have begun service. By 1981 the industry had been completely deregulated, and the CAB itself was dissolved in 1982.

Many airline executives feared that deregulation would lead to chaos in the industry, with competitive pressure causing sharply reduced profits and bankruptcies. After all, the original rationale for CAB regulation was to provide "stability" for an industry that was considered vital to the U.S. economy. And one might think that by holding price above its market-clearing level, profits would be higher than they would be in a free market.

Deregulation did lead to major changes in the industry. Some airlines merged or went out of business as new airlines entered the industry. And although prices fell considerably (to the benefit of consumers), profits overall did not fall much because the CAB's minimum prices had caused inefficiencies and artificially high costs. The effect of minimum prices is illustrated in Figure 9.10, where P_0 and Q_0 are the market-clearing price and quantity, P_{min} is the minimum price set by the CAB, and Q_1 is the amount demanded at this higher price. The prob-

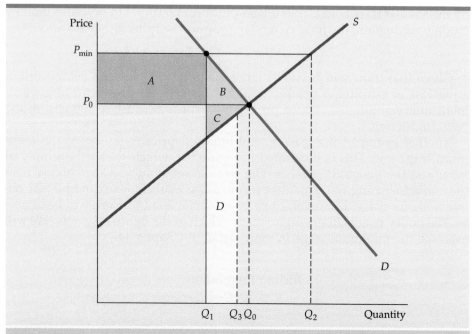

Figure 9.10 Effect of Airline Regulation by the Civil Aeronautics Board
At price P_{min}, airlines would like to supply Q_2, well above the quantity Q_1 that consumers will buy. Here they supply Q_3. Trapezoid D is the cost of unsold output. Airline profits may have been lower as a result of regulation because triangle C and trapezoid D can together exceed rectangle A. In addition, consumers lose $A + B$.

lem was that at price P_{min} airlines wanted to supply a quantity Q_2, much larger than Q_1. And although they did not expand output to Q_2, they did expand it well beyond Q_1—to Q_3 in the figure—hoping to sell this quantity at the expense of competitors. As a result, load factors (the percentage of seats filled) were low, and so were profits. (Trapezoid D measures the cost of unsold output.)

Table 9.1 gives some key numbers that illustrate the evolution of the industry. The number of carriers increased dramatically after deregulation, as did passenger load factors. The passenger-mile rate (the revenue per passenger-mile flown) fell slightly in real (inflation-adjusted) terms from 1975 to 1982, and then fell more rapidly from 1982 to 1993, reflecting increased competition and reductions in fares. And what about costs? The real cost index indicates that even after adjusting for inflation, costs increased by about 25 percent from 1975 to 1982. But this was due to the sharp increase in fuel costs (caused by the increase in oil prices) that occurred during this period, and it had nothing to do with deregulation. The last line in Table 9.1 is the real cost index after adjusting for fuel cost increases. This is what costs would have been had oil prices increased only at the rate of inflation. This index *fell* during the period, although it increased slightly afterwards.

What, then, did airline deregulation do for consumers and producers? As

Table 9.1 Airline Industry Data[6]							
	1970	**1975**	**1980**	**1982**	**1985**	**1990**	**1993**
Number of carriers	35	33	72	89	86	60	52
Passenger load factor (%)	50	54	59	59	61	62	64
Passenger-mile rate (constant 1975 dollars)	.085	.077	.074	.071	.062	.055	.049
Real cost index (1975 = 100)	86	100	120	125	110	102	99
Real cost index corrected for fuel cost increases	95	100	101	96	103	100	104

new airlines entered the industry and fares went down, consumers clearly benefited. (The increase in consumer surplus is given by rectangle *A* and triangle *B* in Figure 9.10.[7]) As for the airlines, they had to learn to live in a more competitive—and therefore more turbulent—environment, and some firms did not survive. But overall, airlines became so much more cost-efficient that producer surplus may have increased. The total welfare gain from deregulation was positive, and quite large.[8]

9.4 Price Supports and Production Quotas

Besides imposing a minimum price, the government can increase the price of a good in other ways. Much of American agricultural policy is based on a system of *price supports*, often combined with incentives to reduce or restrict production. In this section we examine how these policies work and their impact on consumers, producers, and the federal budget.

Price Supports

In the United States, price supports aim to increase the prices of dairy products, tobacco, corn, peanuts, and so on, so that the producers of those goods can receive higher incomes. One way to do this is for the government to set

---

[6] Source: Department of Commerce, *U.S. Statistical Abstract*, 1986, 1989, 1992, 1995.

[7] The benefit to consumers was somewhat smaller than this because *quality* declined as planes became more crowded and delays and cancellations multiplied.

[8] Studies of the effects of deregulation include John M. Trapani and C. Vincent Olson, "An Analysis of the Impact of Open Entry on Price and the Quality of Service in the Airline Industry," *Review of Economics and Statistics* 64 (Feb. 1982): 118–138; David R. Graham, Daniel P. Kaplan, and David S. Sibley, "Efficiency and Competition in the Airline Industry," *Bell Journal of Economics* (Spring 1983): 118–138; S. Morrison and Clifford Whinston, *The Economic Effects of Airline Deregulation* (Washington, D.C.: Brookings Institution, 1986); and Nancy L. Rose, "Profitability and Product Quality: Economic Determinants of Airline Safety Performance," *Journal of Political Economy* 98 (Oct. 1990): 944–964.

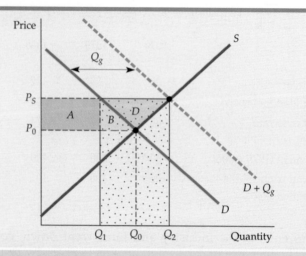

Figure 9.11 **Price Supports** To maintain a price P_s above the market-clearing price P_0, the government buys a quantity Q_g. The gain to producers is $A + B + D$. The loss to consumers is $A + B$. The cost to the government is the speckled rectangle, the area of which is $P_s(Q_2 - Q_1)$.

a support price P_s and then buy up whatever output is needed to keep the market price at this level. Figure 9.11 illustrates this. Let us examine the resulting gains and losses to producers, consumers, and the government.

At price P_s, consumer demand falls to Q_1, but supply increases to Q_2. To maintain this price and avoid having inventories pile up in producer warehouses, the government must buy the quantity $Q_g = Q_2 - Q_1$. In effect the government adds its demand Q_g to the demand of consumers, and producers can sell all they want at price P_s.

Those consumers who purchase the good must pay the higher price P_s instead of P_0, and so they suffer a loss of consumer surplus given by rectangle A. Other consumers no longer buy the good or buy less of it, and their loss of surplus is given by triangle B. So as with the minimum price that we examined above, consumers lose, in this case by an amount

$$\Delta CS = -A - B$$

On the other hand, producers gain (which is why such a policy is implemented). Producers are now selling a larger quantity Q_2 instead of Q_0, and at a higher price P_s. Observe from Figure 9.11 that producer surplus increases by the amount

$$\Delta PS = A + B + D$$

But there is also a cost to the government (which must be paid for by taxes, and so is ultimately a cost to consumers). That cost is $(Q_2 - Q_1)P_s$, which is what the government must pay for the output it purchases. In Figure 9.11 this is the large speckled rectangle. (This cost may be reduced if the government can "dump" some of its purchases—i.e., sell them abroad at a low price. But this hurts the ability of domestic producers to sell in foreign markets, and it is domestic producers that the government is trying to please in the first place.)

What is the total welfare cost of this policy? To find out, we add the change in consumer surplus to the change in producer surplus and then subtract the cost to the government. Hence the total change in welfare is

$$\Delta CS + \Delta PS - \text{Cost to Govt.} = D - (Q_2 - Q_1)P_s$$

In terms of Figure 9.11, society as a whole is worse off by an amount given by the large speckled rectangle, less triangle D.

As we will see in Example 9.4, this welfare loss can be very large. But the most unfortunate part of this policy is that there is a much more efficient way to make farmers better off. If the objective is to give farmers an additional income equal to $A + B + D$, it is far less costly to society to give them this money directly, rather than via price supports. Since consumers are losing $A + B$ anyway with price supports, by paying farmers directly, society saves the large speckled rectangle, less triangle D. Then why doesn't the government make farmers better off by simply giving them money? Perhaps because price supports are a less obvious giveaway, and therefore politically more attractive.[9]

Production Quotas

Besides entering the market and buying up output, thereby increasing total demand, the government can also cause the price of a good to rise by *reducing supply*. It can do this by decree—the government simply sets quotas on how much each firm can produce. By setting the appropriate quotas, the price can then be forced up to any arbitrary level.

This is exactly how many city governments maintain high taxi fares. They limit total supply by requiring each taxicab to have a medallion, and then limit the total number of medallions. Who gains from this? Taxicab companies that own the valuable medallions. Who loses? The consumer, of course.[10]

Another example of such a policy is the control of liquor licenses by state governments. By requiring any bar or restaurant that serves alcohol to have a liquor license and then by limiting the number of licenses, entry by new restaurateurs is limited, which allows those who have the licenses to earn higher prices and profit margins.

In U.S. agricultural policy, output is reduced by incentives rather than out-

[9] In practice, price supports for many agricultural commodities are effected through nonrecourse loans. The loan rate is in effect a price floor. If during the loan period market prices are not sufficiently high, farmers can forfeit their grain to the government (specifically to the Commodity Credit Corporation) as *full payment for the loan*. And, of course, farmers have the incentive to do this unless the market price rises above the support price.

[10] For example, as of 1990 New York City had not issued any new taxi medallions for half a century. Only 11,800 taxis were permitted to cruise the city's streets, the same number as in 1937! As a result, in 1990 a medallion could be sold for about $119,000. It shouldn't be a surprise, then, that the city's taxicab companies have vigorously opposed phasing out medallions in favor of an open system. Washington, D.C., has such an open system: An average taxi ride there costs about half of what it does in New York, and taxis are far more available.

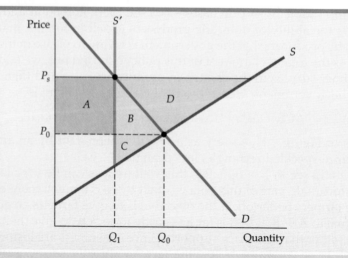

Figure 9.12 Acreage Limitations To maintain a price P_s above the market-clearing price P_0, the government gives producers a financial incentive to reduce output to Q_1. For the incentive to work, it must be at least as large as $B + C + D$, the additional profit earned by planting, given the higher price P_s. The cost to the government is therefore at least $B + C + D$.

right quotas. *Acreage limitation programs* give farmers financial incentives (in the form of direct income transfers) to leave some of their acreage idle. Figure 9.12 shows how prices can be increased by reducing supply in this way. Note that by limiting the acreage planted, the supply curve becomes completely inelastic at the quantity Q_1, and the market price is increased from P_0 to P_s.

Figure 9.12 also shows the changes in consumer and producer surplus resulting from this policy. Again, the change in consumer surplus is

$$\Delta CS = -A - B$$

Farmers now receive a higher price for the production Q_1, which corresponds to a gain in surplus of rectangle A. But because production is reduced from Q_0 to Q_1, there is a loss of producer surplus corresponding to triangle C. Finally, farmers receive money from the government as an incentive to reduce production. Thus, the total change in producer surplus is now

$$\Delta PS = A - C + \text{Payments for not producing}$$

The cost to the government is a payment sufficient to give farmers an incentive to reduce output to Q_1. That incentive must be at least as large as $B + C + D$ because that is the additional profit that could be made by planting, *given the higher price P_s.* (Remember that the higher price P_s gives farmers an incentive to produce *more*, but the government is trying to get them to produce *less*.) So the cost to the government is at least $B + C + D$ and the total change in producer surplus is therefore

$$\Delta PS = A - C + B + C + D = A + B + D$$

This is the same change in producer surplus as with price supports maintained by government purchases of output. (Refer to Figure 9.11.) Farmers, then, should be indifferent between the two policies because they end up gaining the same amount of money from each. Likewise, consumers lose the same amount of money.

But which policy costs the government more? The answer depends on whether the sum of triangles $B + C + D$ in Figure 9.12 is larger or smaller than $(Q_2 - Q_1)P_s$ (the large speckled rectangle) in Figure 9.11. Usually it will be smaller, so that an acreage limitation program costs the government (and society) less than price supports maintained by government purchases.

Still, even an acreage limitation program is more costly to society than simply handing the farmers money. The total change in welfare ($\Delta CS + \Delta PS -$ Cost to Govt.) under the acreage limitation program is

$$\Delta\text{Welfare} = -A - B + A + B + D - B - C - D = -B - C$$

Society would clearly be better off in efficiency terms if the government simply gave the farmers $A + B + D$, leaving price and output alone. Farmers would then gain $A + B + D$, the government would lose $A + B + D$, for a total welfare change of zero, instead of a loss of $B + C$. However, economic efficiency is not always the objective of government policy.

E X A M P L E   9.4   **Supporting the Price of Wheat**

In Example 2.3 of Chapter 2, we began to examine the market for wheat in the United States. Using simple linear demand and supply curves, we found that the market-clearing price of wheat was about $3.46 in 1981, but it fell to about $1.80 by 1985 because of a large drop in export demand, and then rose to $3.27 in 1993. In fact, government price support programs kept the actual price of wheat higher—about $3.70 in 1981, about $3.20 in 1985, and about $3.30 in 1993. How did these programs work, how much did they end up costing consumers, and how much did they add to the federal deficit?

First, let us examine the market in 1981. In that year there were no effective limitations on the production of wheat, and price was increased by government purchases. How much would the government have had to buy to get the price from $3.46 to $3.70? To answer this, first write the equations for supply, and for total (domestic plus export) demand:

1981 Supply: $Q_S = 1800 + 240P$

1981 Demand: $Q_D = 3550 - 266P$

By equating supply and demand, you can check that the market-clearing price is $3.46, and that the quantity produced is 2630 million bushels. Figure 9.13 illustrates this.

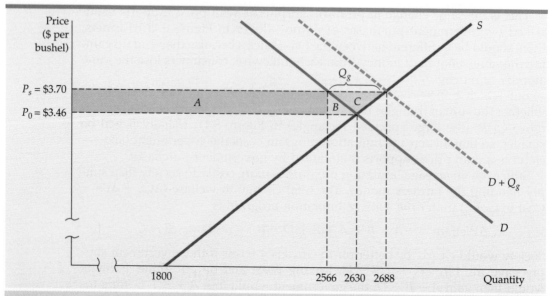

Figure 9.13   The Wheat Market in 1981   By buying 122 million bushels of wheat, the government increased the market-clearing price from $3.46 per bushel to $3.70.

To increase the price to $3.70, the government must buy a quantity of wheat Q_g. *Total* demand (private plus government) will then be

$$1981\ Total\ demand: \quad Q_{DT} = 3550 - 266P + Q_g$$

Now equate supply with this total demand:

$$1800 + 240P = 3550 - 266P + Q_g$$

or

$$Q_g = 506P - 1750$$

This equation can be used to determine the required quantity of government wheat purchases Q_g as a function of the desired support price P. So to achieve a price of $3.70, the government must buy

$$Q_g = (506)(3.70) - 1750 = 122\ million\ bushels$$

Note in Figure 9.13 that these 122 million bushels are the difference between the quantity supplied at the $3.70 price (2688 million bushels) and the quantity of private demand (2566 million bushels). The figure also shows the gains and losses to consumers and producers. Recall that consumers lose rectangle A and triangle B. You can verify that rectangle A is $(3.70 - 3.46)(2566) =$ $616 million, and triangle B is $(1/2)(3.70 - 3.46)(2630 - 2566) =$ $8 million, so the total cost to consumers is $624 million.

The cost to the government is the $3.70 it pays for the wheat times the 122 million bushels it buys, or $452 million. The total cost of the program is then

$624 + $452 = $1076 million. Compare this with the gain to producers, which is rectangle A plus triangles B and C. You can verify that this gain is $638 million.

Price supports for wheat were expensive in 1981. To increase the surplus of farmers by $638 million, consumers and taxpayers had to pay $1076 million. In fact taxpayers paid even more. Wheat producers were also given subsidies of about 30 cents per bushel, which adds up to another $806 million.

In 1985 the situation became even worse because of the drop in export demand. In that year the supply and demand curves were as follows:

1985 Supply: $\qquad Q_S = 1800 + 240P$

1985 Demand: $\qquad Q_D = 2580 - 194P$

You can verify that the market-clearing price and quantity were $1.80 and 2232 million bushels, respectively.

To increase the price to $3.20, the government bought wheat and imposed a production quota of about 2425 million bushels. (Farmers who wanted to take part in the subsidy program—and most did—had to agree to limit their acreage.) Figure 9.14 illustrates this situation. At the quantity 2425 million bushels, the supply curve becomes vertical. Now to determine how much wheat Q_g the government had to buy, set this quantity of 2425 equal to total demand:

$$2425 = 2580 - 194P + Q_g$$

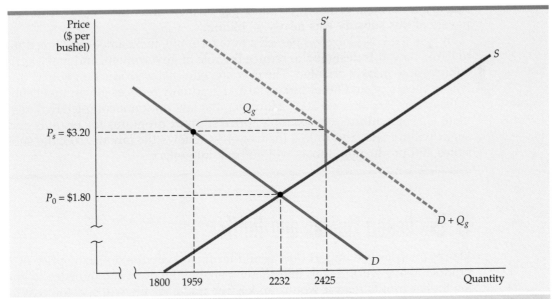

Figure 9.14   The Wheat Market in 1985   In 1985 the demand for wheat was much lower than in 1981, so the market-clearing price was only $1.80. To increase the price to $3.20, the government bought 466 million bushels and also imposed a production quota of 2425 million bushels.

or

$$Q_g = -155 + 194P$$

Substituting $3.20 for P, we see that Q_g must be 466 million bushels. This cost the government ($3.20)(466) = $1491 million.

Again, this is not the whole story. The government also provided a subsidy of 80 cents per bushel, so that producers again received about $4.00 for their wheat. Since 2425 million bushels were produced, that subsidy cost an additional $1940 million. In all, U.S. wheat programs cost taxpayers nearly $3.5 billion in 1985. Of course, there was also a loss of consumer surplus and a gain of producer surplus; you can calculate what they were.

In Example 2.3, we saw that by 1993, export demand had recovered and hence the market-clearing price had rebounded to about $3.27. The supply and demand curves in 1993 were as follows:

$$\text{Demand:} \qquad Q_D = 3385 - 279P$$

$$\text{Supply:} \qquad Q_S = 1728 + 228P$$

We can check that the market-clearing quantity was 2475 million bushels. In 1993 the government imposed a production quota only slightly below that—2465 million bushels. However, the government did not purchase any wheat in 1993. By substituting the quantity of 2465 into the demand curve, we can see that the price to consumers in 1993 was $3.30.

Although the government did not buy wheat in 1993, it again provided a subsidy to farmers of about 80 cents per bushel. Thus the total cost to taxpayers of this subsidy was nearly $2 billion.[11]

In 1996 the U.S. Congress passed a new farm bill, nicknamed the "Freedom to Farm" law. It is designed to reduce the role of government, and make agriculture more market oriented. The new law eliminates production quotas (for wheat, corn, rice, and other products) and gradually reduces government subsidies from 1996 through 2003. However, the law does not completely deregulate U.S. agriculture. For example, price support programs for peanuts and sugar will remain, and unless the Congress renews the law in 2003, the subsidies and production quotas will go back into effect.

9.5 Import Quotas and Tariffs

Many countries use import quotas and tariffs to keep the domestic price of a product above world levels and thereby enable the domestic industry to enjoy higher profits than it would under free trade. As we will see, the cost to

---

[11] In 1990, agricultural programs were estimated to cost American taxpayers more than $20 billion, and to result in a loss of consumer surplus of about $24 billion. See J. Bovard, "Farm Subsidies: Milking Us Dry," *New York Times*, July 20, 1990.

society from this protection can be high, with the loss to consumers exceeding the gain to domestic producers.

Without a quota or tariff, a country will import a good when its world price is below the market price that would prevail if there were no imports. Figure 9.15 shows this. S and D are the domestic supply and demand curves. If there were no imports, the domestic price and quantity would be P_0 and Q_0, which equate supply and demand. But the world price P_w is below P_0, so domestic consumers have an incentive to purchase from abroad, which they will do if imports are not restricted. How much will be imported? The domestic price will fall to the world price P_w, and at this lower price domestic production will fall to Q_s, and domestic consumption will rise to Q_d. Imports are then the difference between domestic consumption and domestic production, $Q_d - Q_s$.

Now suppose the government, bowing to pressure from the domestic industry, eliminates imports by imposing a quota of zero (i.e., forbidding any importation of the good). What are the gains and losses from such a policy?

With no imports allowed, the domestic price will rise to P_0. Consumers who still purchase the good (in quantity Q_0) will pay more and will lose an amount

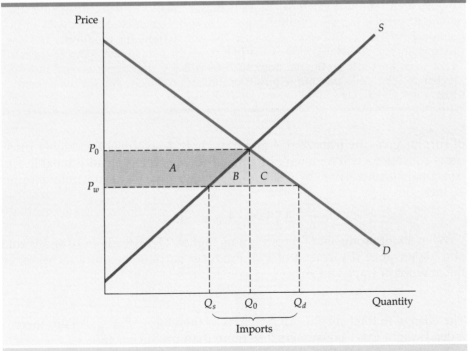

Figure 9.15 Import Tariff or Quota That Eliminates Imports In a free market, the domestic price equals the world price P_w. A total Q_d is consumed, of which Q_s is supplied domestically, and the rest imported. By eliminating imports, the price is increased to P_0. The gain to producers is trapezoid A. The loss to consumers is $A + B + C$, so the deadweight loss is $B + C$.

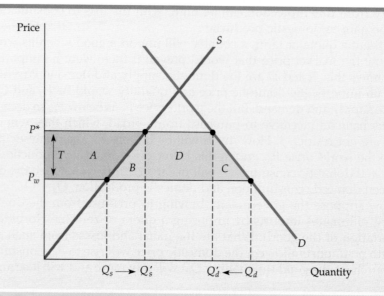

Figure 9.16   Import Tariff or Quota (general case)   By reducing imports, the domestic price is increased from P_w to P^*. This can be achieved by a quota, or by a tariff $T = P^* - P_w$. Trapezoid A is again the gain to domestic producers. The loss to consumers is $A + B + C + D$. If a tariff is used, the government gains D, the revenue from the tariff, so the net domestic loss is $B + C$. If a quota is used instead, rectangle D becomes part of the profits of foreign producers, and the net domestic loss is $B + C + D$.

of surplus given by trapezoid A and triangle B. Also, given this higher price, some consumers will no longer buy the good, so there is an additional loss of consumer surplus, given by triangle C. The total change in consumer surplus is, therefore,

$$\Delta CS = -A - B - C$$

What about producers? Output is now higher (Q_0 instead of Q_d) and is sold at a higher price (P_0 instead of P_w). Producer surplus therefore increases by the amount of trapezoid A:

$$\Delta PS = A$$

The change in total surplus, $\Delta CS + \Delta PS$, is therefore $-B - C$. Again, there is a deadweight loss—consumers lose more than producers gain.

Imports could also be reduced to zero by imposing a large enough tariff. The tariff would have to be equal to or greater than the difference between P_0 and P_w. With a tariff of this size, there will be no imports and, therefore, no government revenue from tariff collections, so the effect on consumers and producers would be the same as with a quota.

More often, government policy is designed to reduce, but not eliminate, imports. Again, this can be done with either a tariff or a quota, as Figure 9.16

shows. With free trade the domestic price will equal the world price P_w, and imports will be $Q_d - Q_s$. Now suppose a tariff of T dollars per unit is imposed on imports. Then the domestic price will rise to P^* (the world price plus the tariff); domestic production will rise; and domestic consumption will fall.

In Figure 9.16 this tariff leads to a change of consumer surplus given by

$$\Delta CS = -A - B - C - D$$

The change in producer surplus is again

$$\Delta PS = A$$

Finally, the government will collect revenue in the amount of the tariff times the quantity of imports, which is rectangle D. The total change in welfare, ΔCS plus ΔPS plus the revenue to the government, is therefore $-A - B - C - D + A + D = -B - C$. Triangles B and C again represent the deadweight loss from restricting imports. (B represents the loss from domestic overproduction, and C the loss from too little consumption.)

Suppose the government uses a quota instead of a tariff to restrict imports: Foreign producers can only ship a specific quantity ($Q'_d - Q'_s$ in Figure 9.16) to the United States. Foreign producers can then charge the higher price P^* for their U.S. sales. The changes in U.S. consumer and producer surplus will be the same as with the tariff, but instead of the U.S. government collecting the revenue given by rectangle D, this money will go to the foreign producers as higher profits. Compared with the tariff, the United States as a whole will be even worse off, losing D as well as the deadweight loss B and C.[12]

This is exactly what happened with automobile imports from Japan in the 1980s. The Reagan administration, under pressure from domestic automobile producers, negotiated "voluntary" import restraints, under which the Japanese agreed to restrict their shipments of cars to the United States. The Japanese could therefore sell those cars that were shipped at a price higher than the world level and capture a higher profit margin on each one. The United States would have been better off by simply imposing a tariff on these imports.

E X A M P L E   9 . 5   **The Sugar Quota**

In recent years the world price of sugar has been as low as 4 cents per pound, while the United States price has been 20 to 25 cents per pound. Why? By restricting imports the U.S. government protects the $3 billion domestic sugar industry, which would virtually be put out of business if it had to compete

---

[12] Alternatively, an import quota can be maintained by rationing imports to U.S. importing firms or trading companies. These middlemen would have the rights to import a fixed amount of the good each year. These rights are valuable because the middleman can buy the product on the world market at price P_w and then sell it at price P^*. The aggregate value of these rights is, therefore, given by rectangle D. If the government *sells* the rights for this amount of money, it can capture the same revenue it would receive with a tariff. But if these rights are given away, as sometimes happens, the money will go instead as a windfall to middlemen.

with low-cost foreign producers. This has been good news for U.S. sugar producers. It has even been good news for some foreign sugar producers—those whose successful lobbying efforts have given them big shares of the quota. But like most policies of this sort, it has been bad news for consumers.

To see just how bad, let's look at the sugar market in 1994. Here are the relevant data for that year:

U.S. production:	15.4 billion pounds
U.S. consumption:	18.4 billion pounds
U.S. price:	22 cents per pound
World price:	12 cents per pound

At these prices and quantities, the price elasticity of U.S. supply is 1.53, and the price elasticity of U.S. demand is −0.3.[13]

We will fit linear supply and demand curves to these data, and then use them to calculate the effects of the quotas. You can verify that the following U.S. supply curve is consistent with a production level of 15.4 billion pounds, a price of 22 cents per pound, and a supply elasticity of 1.53[14]:

$$\text{U.S. supply:} \quad Q_S = -8.19 + 1.07P$$

where quantity is measured in billions of pounds and price in cents per pound. Similarly, the −0.3 demand elasticity together with the data for U.S. consumption and U.S. price give the following linear demand curve:

$$\text{U.S. demand:} \quad Q_D = 23.86 - 0.25P$$

These supply and demand curves are plotted in Figure 9.17. At the 12 cent world price, U.S. production would have been only 4.7 billion pounds, and U.S. consumption would have been about 21 billion pounds, most of this imports. But fortunately for U.S. producers, imports were limited to only 3 billion pounds, which pushed the U.S. price up to 22 cents.

What did this cost U.S. consumers? The lost consumer surplus is given by the sum of trapezoid *A*, triangles *B* and *C*, and rectangle *D*. You should go through the calculations to verify that trapezoid *A* is equal to $1005 million,

---

[13] These elasticity estimates are based on Morris E. Morkre and David G. Tarr, *Effects of Restrictions on United States Imports: Five Case Studies and Theory*, U.S. Federal Trade Commission Staff Report, June 1981; and F. M. Scherer, "The United States Sugar Program," Kennedy School of Government Case Study, Harvard University, 1992. For a general discussion of sugar quotas and other aspects of U.S. agricultural policy, see D. Gale Johnson, *Agricultural Policy and Trade* (New York: New York University Press, 1985); and Gail L. Cramer and Clarence W. Jensen, *Agricultural Economics and Agribusiness* (New York: Wiley, 1985).

[14] See Section 2.5 in Chapter 2 to review how to fit linear supply and demand functions to data of this kind.

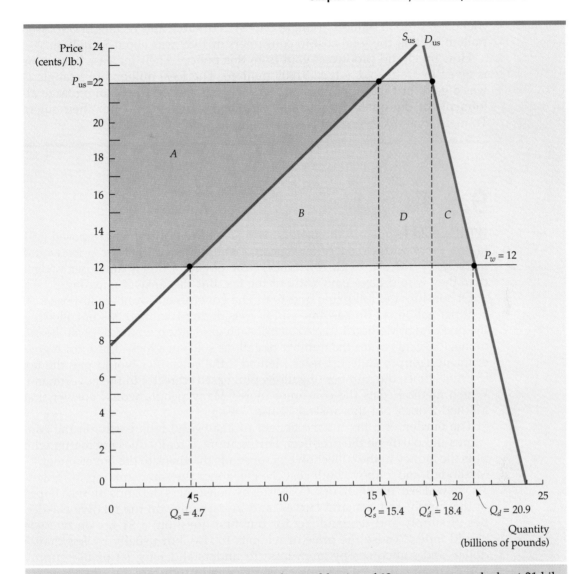

Figure 9.17   Sugar Quota in 1994   At the world price of 12 cents per pound, about 21 billion pounds of sugar would have been consumed in the United States, of which all but 4.7 billion pounds would have been imported. By restricting imports to 3 billion pounds, the U.S. price was increased to 22 cents. The cost to consumers, $A + B + C + D$, was about \$2 billion. The gain to domestic producers was trapezoid A, about \$1 billion. Rectangle D, \$300 million, was a gain to those foreign producers who obtained quota allotments. Triangles B and C represent the deadweight loss of \$660 million.

triangle B to \$535 million, triangle C to \$125 million, and rectangle D to \$300 million, so that the total cost to consumers in 1989 was about \$2 billion.

How much did producers gain from this policy? Their increase in surplus is given by trapezoid A (i.e., \$1005 million). The \$300 million of rectangle D was a gain for those foreign producers who succeeded in obtaining large allotments of the quota because they received a higher price for their sugar. Triangles B and C represent a deadweight loss of \$660 million.

9.6 The Impact of a Tax or Subsidy

What would happen to the price of widgets if the government imposed a \$1 tax on every widget sold? Many people would answer that the price would increase by a dollar, with consumers now paying a dollar more per widget than they would have paid without the tax. But this answer is wrong.

Or consider the following question. The government wants to impose a 50 cent per gallon tax on gasoline and is considering two methods of collecting the tax. Under Method 1, the owner of each gas station would deposit the tax money (50 cents times the number of gallons sold) in a locked box, for a government agent to collect. Under Method 2 the consumer would pay the tax (50 cents times the number of gallons purchased) directly to the government. Which method costs the consumer more? Many people would answer that Method 2 does, but this answer is also wrong.

The burden of a tax (or the benefit of a subsidy) falls partly on the consumer and partly on the producer. Furthermore, it really does not matter who puts the money in the collection box (or sends the check to the government)—Methods 1 and 2 above both cost the consumer the same amount of money. As we will see, the share of a tax borne by consumers depends on the shapes of the supply and demand curves, and in particular on the relative elasticities of supply and demand. As for our first question, a \$1 tax on widgets would indeed cause the price of widgets to rise, but usually by *less* than a dollar, and sometimes by *much* less. To understand why, let us use supply and demand curves to see how consumers and producers are affected when a tax is imposed on a product, and what happens to price and quantity.

For simplicity we will consider a *specific tax*—a tax of a certain amount of money *per unit sold*. This is in contrast to an *ad valorem* (i.e., proportional) tax, such as a state sales tax. (The analysis of an ad valorem tax is roughly the same and yields the same qualitative results.) Examples of specific taxes include federal and state taxes on gasoline and cigarettes.

Suppose the government imposes a tax of t cents per unit on widgets. Assuming everyone obeys the law, the government must then receive t cents for every widget sold. *This means that the price the consumer pays must exceed the net price the seller receives by t cents.* Figure 9.18 illustrates this simple accounting relationship—and its implications. Here, P_0 and Q_0 represent the market price and quantity *before* the tax is imposed. P_b is the price that con-

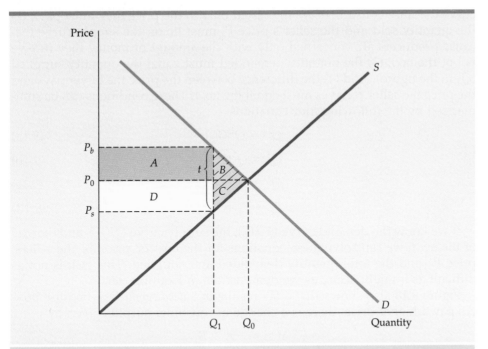

Figure 9.18   Incidence of a Tax P_b is the price (including the tax) paid by buyers. P_s is the price that sellers receive, net of the tax. Here the burden of the tax is split about evenly between buyers and sellers. Buyers lose $A + B$, sellers lose $D + C$, and the government earns $A + D$ in revenue. The deadweight loss is $B + C$.

sumers pay, and P_s is the net price that sellers receive *after* the tax is imposed. Note that $P_b - P_s = t$, so the government is happy.

How do we determine what the market quantity will be after the tax is imposed, and how much of the tax is borne by consumers and how much by producers? First, remember that what consumers care about is the price that they must pay: P_b. The amount that consumers will buy is given by the demand curve; it is the quantity that we read off of the demand curve given a price P_b. Similarly, what producers care about is the net price they receive, P_s. Given P_s, the quantity they will produce is read off the supply curve. Finally, we know that the quantity that producers sell must equal the quantity that consumers buy—a single quantity is bought and sold. The solution, then, is to find the quantity that corresponds to a price of P_b on the demand curve, and a price of P_s on the supply curve, such that the difference $P_b - P_s$ is equal to the tax t. In Figure 9.18 this quantity is shown as Q_1.

Who bears the burden of the tax? In Figure 9.18, this burden is shared roughly equally by consumers and producers. The market price (the price consumers must pay) rises by half of the tax. And the price that producers receive falls by roughly half of the tax.

As Figure 9.18 shows, *four conditions* must be satisfied after the tax is in place: (1) the quantity sold and the buyer's price P_b must lie on the demand curve (because consumers are interested only in the price they must pay); (2) the quantity sold and the seller's price P_s must lie on the supply curve (because producers are concerned only with the amount of money they receive net of the tax); (3) the quantity demanded must equal the quantity supplied (Q_1 in the figure). And (4) the difference between the price the buyer pays and the price the seller receives must equal the tax t. These conditions can be summarized by the following four equations:

$$Q^D = Q^D(P_b) \tag{9.1a}$$

$$Q^S = Q^S(P_s) \tag{9.1b}$$

$$Q^D = Q^S \tag{9.1c}$$

$$P_b - P_s = t \tag{9.1d}$$

If we know the demand curve $Q^D(P_b)$, the supply curve $Q^S(P_s)$, and the size of the tax t, we can solve these equations for the buyers' price P_b, the sellers' price P_s, and the total quantity demanded and supplied. This task is not as difficult as it might seem, as we demonstrate in Example 9.6.

Figure 9.18 also shows that a tax results in a *deadweight loss*. Because buyers pay a higher price, there is a change in consumer surplus given by

$$\Delta CS = -A - B$$

And because sellers now receive a lower price, there is a change in producer surplus given by

$$\Delta PS = -C - D$$

Government tax revenue is tQ_1, the sum of rectangles A and D. The total change in welfare, ΔCS plus ΔPS plus the revenue to the government, is therefore $-A - B - C - D + A + D = -B - C$. Triangles B and C represent the deadweight loss from the tax.

In Figure 9.18 the burden of the tax is shared almost evenly between consumers and producers, but this is not always the case. If demand is relatively inelastic and supply is relatively elastic, the burden of the tax will fall mostly on consumers. Figure 9.19(a) shows why: It takes a relatively large increase in price to get consumers to reduce demand by even a small amount, whereas only a small price decrease is needed to reduce the quantity producers supply. For example, because cigarettes are addictive, the elasticity of demand is small (about -0.3), so federal and state cigarette taxes are borne largely by consumers.[15] Figure 9.19(b) shows the opposite case: If demand is relatively elastic and supply is relatively inelastic, the burden of the tax will fall mostly on producers.

So even if we have only estimates of the elasticities of demand and supply at a point or for a small range of prices and quantities, as opposed to the en-

---

[15] See Daniel A. Sumner and Michael K. Wohlgenant, "Effects of an Increase in the Federal Excise Tax on Cigarettes," *American Journal of Agricultural Economics* 67 (May 1985): 235–242.

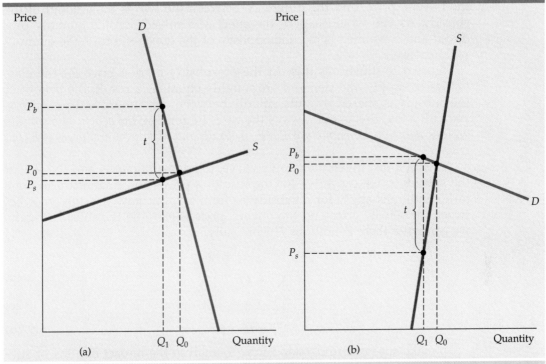

Figure 9.19 Impact of a Tax Depends on Elasticities of Supply and Demand (a) If demand is very inelastic relative to supply, the burden of the tax falls mostly on buyers. (b) If demand is very elastic relative to supply, it falls mostly on sellers.

tire demand and supply curves, we can still roughly determine who will bear the greatest burden of a tax (whether the tax is actually in effect or is only under discussion as a policy option). In general, *a tax falls mostly on the buyer if E_d/E_s is small, and mostly on the seller if E_d/E_s is large.*

In fact, we can calculate the percentage of the tax borne by producers and by consumers, using the following "pass-through" formula:

$$\text{Pass-through fraction} = E_s/(E_s - E_d)$$

This formula tells us what fraction of the tax is passed through to consumers in the form of higher prices.[16] For example, when demand is totally inelastic, so that E_d is zero, the pass-through fraction is 1, and all the tax is borne by consumers. And when demand is totally elastic, the pass-through fraction is zero, and producers bear all the tax.

A *subsidy* can be analyzed in much the same way as a tax—in fact, you can think of a subsidy as a *negative tax*. With a subsidy, the sellers' price *exceeds*

---

[16] The fraction of the tax producers bear is given by: $-E_d/(E_s - E_d)$.

the buyers' price, and the difference between the two is the amount of the subsidy. As you would expect, the effect of a subsidy on the quantity produced and consumed is just the opposite of the effect of a tax—the quantity will increase.

Figure 9.20 illustrates this. At the presubsidy market price P_0, the elasticities of supply and demand are roughly equal; as a result, the benefit of the subsidy is shared roughly equally between consumers and producers. As with a tax, this is not always the case. In general, *the benefit of a subsidy accrues mostly to consumers if E_d/E_s is small, and mostly to producers if E_d/E_s is large.*

As with a tax, given the supply curve, the demand curve, and the size of the subsidy s, we can solve for the resulting prices and quantity. The same four conditions apply for a subsidy as for a tax, but now the difference between the sellers' price and the buyers' price is equal to the subsidy. Again, we can write these conditions algebraically:

$$Q^D = Q^D(P_b) \tag{9.2a}$$

$$Q^S = Q^S(P_s) \tag{9.2b}$$

$$Q^D = Q^S \tag{9.2c}$$

$$P_s - P_b = s \tag{9.2d}$$

To make sure you understand how to analyze the impact of a tax or subsidy, you might find it helpful to work through one or two examples, such as Exercises 2 and 14 at the end of this chapter.

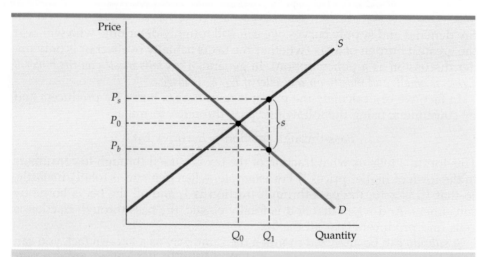

Figure 9.20 Subsidy A subsidy can be thought of as a negative tax. Like a tax, the benefit of a subsidy is split between buyers and sellers, depending on the relative elasticities of supply and demand.

E X A M P L E   9.6   **A Tax on Gasoline**

The idea of a large tax on gasoline, both to raise government revenue and to reduce oil consumption and U.S. dependence on oil imports, has been discussed for many years. Let's see how a 50 cent per gallon tax would affect the price and consumption of gasoline.

We will do this analysis in the setting of market conditions during the early 1990s—when gasoline was selling for about $1 per gallon, and total consumption was about 100 billion gallons per year (bg/yr).[17] We will also use intermediate-run elasticities (i.e., elasticities that would apply to a period of about three to six years after a price change).

A reasonable number for the intermediate-run elasticity of gasoline demand is -0.5 (see Example 2.4 in Chapter 2). We can use this elasticity figure, together with the $1 and 100 bg/yr price and quantity numbers, to calculate a linear demand curve for gasoline. (See Chapter 2, Section 2.5, to review how to do this.) You can verify that the following demand curve fits these data:

$$\text{Gasoline demand:} \quad Q^D = 150 - 50P$$

Gasoline is refined from crude oil, some of which is produced domestically and some imported. (Some gasoline is also imported directly.) The supply curve for gasoline will therefore depend on the world price of oil, on domestic oil supply, and on the cost of refining. The details are beyond the scope of this example, but a reasonable number for the elasticity of supply is 0.4. You should verify that this elasticity, together with the $1 and 100 bg/yr price and quantity, gives the following linear supply curve:

$$\text{Gasoline supply:} \quad Q^S = 60 + 40P$$

You should also verify that these demand and supply curves imply a market price of $1 and quantity of 100 bg/yr.

We can use these linear demand and supply curves to calculate the effect of a 50 cents per gallon tax. First, we write the four conditions that must hold, as given by equations (9.1a–d):

$$Q^D = 150 - 50P_b \qquad \text{(Demand)}$$

$$Q^S = 60 + 40P_s \qquad \text{(Supply)}$$

$$Q^D = Q^S \qquad \text{(Supply must equal demand)}$$

$$P_b - P_s = 0.50 \qquad \text{(Government must receive 50 cents/gallon)}$$

---

[17] Of course, this price varied across regions and grades of gasoline, but we can ignore this here. Quantities of oil and oil products are often measured in barrels; there are 42 gallons in a barrel, so the quantity figure could also be written as 2.4 billion barrels per year.

Now combine the first three equations to equate supply and demand:

$$150 - 50P_b = 60 + 40P_s$$

We can rewrite the last of the four equations as $P_b = P_s + 0.50$, and substitute this for P_b in the above equation:

$$150 - 50(P_s + 0.50) = 60 + 40P_s$$

Now we can rearrange this and solve for P_s:

$$50P_s + 40P_s = 150 - 25 - 60$$

$$90P_s = 65, \text{ or } P_s = .72$$

Remember that $P_b = P_s + 0.50$, so $P_b = 1.22$. Finally, we can determine the total quantity from either the demand or supply curve. Using the demand curve (and the price $P_b = 1.22$), we find that $Q = 150 - (50)(1.22) = 150 - 61$, or $Q = 89$ bg/yr. This represents an 11 percent decline in gasoline consumption. Figure 9.21 illustrates these calculations and the effect of the tax.

The burden of this tax would be split roughly evenly between consumers and producers; consumers would pay about 22 cents per gallon more for the gasoline they bought, and producers would receive about 28 cents per gallon less. It should not be surprising, then, that both consumers and producers

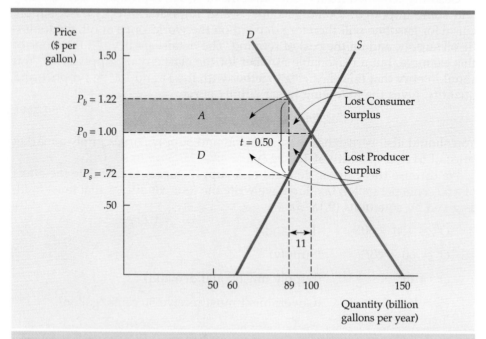

Figure 9.21 Impact of 50 Cent Gasoline Tax The price of gasoline at the pump increases from $1.00 per gallon to $1.22, and the quantity sold falls from 100 to 89 bg/yr. The annual revenue from the tax is $(0.50)(89) = \$44.5$ billion. The two triangles show the deadweight loss of $2.75 billion per year.

opposed such a tax, and politicians representing both groups fought the proposal every time it came up. But note that the tax would raise significant revenue for the government. The annual revenue from the tax would be $tQ =$ (0.50)(89) = $44.5 billion per year.

The cost to consumers and producers, however, will be more than the $44.5 billion in tax revenue. Figure 9.21 shows the deadweight loss from this tax as the two shaded triangles. The two rectangles A and D represent the total tax collected by the government, but the total loss of consumer and producer surplus is larger.

Before deciding whether a gasoline tax is desirable, it is important to know how large the resulting deadweight loss is likely to be. We can easily calculate this from Figure 9.21. Combining the two small triangles into one large one, we see that the area is

$$(1/2) \times (\$0.50/\text{gallon}) \times (11 \text{ billion gallons/year})$$

$$= \$2.75 \text{ billion per year}$$

This deadweight loss is about 6 percent of the government revenue resulting from the tax, and must be balanced against any additional benefits that the tax might bring.

Summary

1. Simple models of supply and demand can be used to analyze a wide variety of government policies. Specific policies that we have examined include price controls, minimum prices, price support programs, production quotas or incentive programs to limit output, import tariffs and quotas, and taxes and subsidies.

2. In each case, consumer and producer surplus are used to evaluate the gains and losses to consumers and producers. Applying the methodology to natural gas price controls, airline regulation, price supports for wheat, and the sugar quota, we found that these gains and losses can be quite large.

3. When government imposes a tax or subsidy, price usually does not rise or fall by the full amount of the tax or subsidy. Also, the incidence of a tax or subsidy is usually split between producers and consumers. The fraction that each group ends up paying or receiving depends on the relative elasticities of supply and demand.

4. Government intervention generally leads to a deadweight loss; even if consumer welfare and producer welfare are weighted equally, there will be a net loss from government policies that shifts welfare from one group to the other. In some cases this deadweight loss will be small, but in other cases—price supports and import quotas are examples—it is large. This deadweight loss is a form of economic inefficiency that must be taken into account when policies are designed and implemented.

5. Government intervention in a competitive market is not always a bad thing. Government—and the society it represents—might have other objectives besides economic efficiency. And there are situations in which government intervention can improve economic efficiency. Examples are externalities and cases of market failure. These situations, and the way government can respond to them, are discussed in Chapters 17 and 18.

Questions for Review

1. What is meant by deadweight loss? Why does a price ceiling usually result in a deadweight loss?

2. Suppose the supply curve for a good was completely inelastic. If the government imposed a price ceiling below the market-clearing level, would a deadweight loss result? Explain.

3. How can a price ceiling make consumers better off? Under what conditions might it make them worse off?

4. Suppose the government regulates the price of a good to be no lower than some minimum level. Can such a minimum price make producers as a whole worse off? Explain.

5. How are production limits used in practice to raise the prices of the following goods or ser-

vices: (a) taxi rides, (b) drinks in a restaurant or bar, (c) wheat or corn?

6. Suppose the government wants to increase farmers' incomes. Why do price supports or acreage limitation programs cost society more than simply giving the farmers money?

7. Suppose the government wants to limit imports of a certain good. Is it preferable to use an import quota or a tariff? Why?

8. The burden of a tax is shared by producers and consumers. Under what conditions will consumers pay most of the tax? Under what conditions will producers pay most of it? What determines the share of a subsidy that benefits consumers?

9. Why does a tax create a deadweight loss? What determines the size of this loss?

Exercises

1. In 1996, the U.S. Congress debated raising the minimum wage from $4.25 per hour to $5.15 per hour. Some people suggested that a government subsidy could help employers finance the higher wage. This exercise examines the economics of a minimum wage and wage subsidies. Suppose the supply of low-skilled labor is given by

$$L^S = 10w$$

where L^S is the quantity of low-skilled labor (in millions of persons employed each year), and w is the wage rate (in dollars per hour). The demand for labor is given by

$$L^D = 80 - 10w$$

a. What will the free-market wage rate and employment level be? Suppose the government sets a minimum wage of $5 per hour. How many people would then be employed?

b. Suppose that instead of a minimum wage, the government paid a subsidy of $1 per

hour for each employee. What will the total level of employment be now? What will the equilibrium wage rate be?

2. Suppose the market for widgets can be described by the following equations:

$$Demand: \quad P = 10 - Q$$

$$Supply: \quad P = Q - 4$$

where P is the price in dollars per unit, and Q is the quantity in thousands of units. Then

a. What is the equilibrium price and quantity?

b. Suppose the government imposes a tax of $1 per unit to reduce widget consumption and raise government revenues. What will the new equilibrium quantity be? What price will the buyer pay? What amount per unit will the seller receive?

c. Suppose the government has a change of heart about the importance of widgets to the happiness of the American public. The tax is removed, and a subsidy of $1 per unit is granted to widget producers. What will the equilibrium quantity be? What price will the buyer pay? What amount per unit (including the subsidy) will the seller receive? What will be the total cost to the government?

3. Japanese rice producers have extremely high production costs, in part due to the high opportunity cost of land and to their inability to take advantage of economies of large-scale production. Analyze two policies intended to maintain Japanese rice production: (1) a per-pound subsidy to farmers for each pound of rice produced, or (2) a per-pound tariff on imported rice. Illustrate with supply-and-demand diagrams the equilibrium price and quantity, domestic rice production, government revenue or deficit, and deadweight loss from each policy. Which policy is the Japanese government likely to prefer? Which policy are Japanese farmers likely to prefer?

4. In 1983 the Reagan administration introduced a new agricultural program called the Payment-in-Kind Program. To examine how the program worked, let's consider the wheat market.
   a. Suppose the demand function is $Q^D = 28 - 2P$ and the supply function is $Q^S = 4 + 4P$, where P is the price of wheat in dollars per bushel, and Q is the quantity in billions of bushels. Find the free-market equilibrium price and quantity.
   b. Now suppose the government wants to lower the supply of wheat by 25 percent from the free-market equilibrium by paying farmers to withdraw land from production. However, the payment is made in wheat rather than in dollars—hence the name of the program. The wheat comes from the government's vast reserves that resulted from previous price support programs. The amount of wheat paid is equal to the amount that could have been harvested on the land withdrawn from production. Farmers are free to sell this wheat on the market. How much is now produced by farmers? How much is indirectly supplied to the market by the government? What is the new market price? How much do farmers gain? Do consumers gain or lose?

   c. Had the government not given the wheat back to the farmers, it would have stored or destroyed it. Do taxpayers gain from the program? What potential problems does the program create?

5. About 100 million pounds of jelly beans are consumed in the United States each year, and the price has been about 50 cents per pound. However, jelly bean producers feel that their incomes are too low, and they have convinced the government that price supports are in order. The government will therefore buy up as many jelly beans as necessary to keep the price at $1 per pound. However, government economists are worried about the impact of this program, because they have no estimates of the elasticities of jelly bean demand or supply.
   a. Could this program cost the government *more* than $50 million per year? Under what conditions? Could it cost *less* than $50 million per year? Under what conditions? Illustrate with a diagram.
   b. Could this program cost consumers (in terms of lost consumer surplus) *more* than $50 million per year? Under what conditions? Could it cost consumers *less* than $50 million per year? Under what conditions? Again, use a diagram to illustrate.

6. A vegetable fiber is traded in a competitive world market, and the world price is $9 per pound. Unlimited quantities are available for import into the United States at this price. The U.S. domestic supply and demand for various price levels are shown below.

Price	U.S. Supply (million pounds)	U.S. Demand (million pounds)
3	2	34
6	4	28
9	6	22
12	8	16
15	10	10
18	12	4

Answer the following about the U.S. market:
   a. What is the equation for demand? What is the equation for supply?

b. What is the price elasticity of demand at a price of $9? A price of $12?

c. What is the price elasticity of supply at a price of $9? A price of $12?

d. If there are no tariffs, quotas, or other trade restrictions in the United States, what will be the U.S. price and level of fiber imports?

e. If the United States imposes a tariff of $9 per pound, what will be the U.S. price and level of imports? How much revenue will the government earn from the tariff? How large is the deadweight loss?

f. If the United States has no tariff but imposes an import quota of 8 million pounds, what will be the U.S. domestic price? What is the cost of this quota for U.S. consumers of the fiber? What is the gain for U.S. producers?

7. A particular metal is traded in a highly competitive world market, and the world price is $9 per ounce. Unlimited quantities are available for import into the United States at this price. The supply of this metal from domestic U.S. mines and mills can be represented by the equation $Q^S = 2/3P$, where Q^S is U.S. output in million ounces, and P is the domestic price. The demand for the metal in the United States is $Q^D = 40 - 2P$, where Q^D is the domestic demand in million ounces.

In recent years the U.S. industry has been protected by a tariff of $9 per ounce. Under pressure from other foreign governments, the United States plans to reduce this tariff to zero. Threatened by this change, the U.S. industry is seeking a Voluntary Restraint Agreement that would limit imports into the United States to 8 million ounces per year.

a. Under the $9 tariff, what was the U.S. domestic price of the metal?

b. If the United States eliminates the tariff and the Voluntary Restraint Agreement is approved, what will be the U.S. domestic price of the metal?

8. Among the tax proposals regularly considered by Congress is an additional tax on distilled liquors. The tax would not apply to beer. The own-price elasticity of supply of liquor is 4.0, and the own-price elasticity of demand is −0.2. The cross-elasticity of demand for beer with respect to the price of liquor is 0.1.

a. If the new tax is imposed, who will bear the greater burden, liquor suppliers or liquor consumers? Why?

b. How will the new tax affect the beer market, assuming that beer supply is infinitely elastic?

9. In Example 9.1 we calculated the gains and losses from price controls on natural gas, and found that there was a deadweight loss of $1.4 billion. This calculation was based on a price of oil of $8 per barrel. If the price of oil had been $12 per barrel, what would the free-market price of gas be? How large a deadweight loss would have resulted if the maximum allowable price of natural gas had been $1.00 per thousand cubic feet?

10. Example 9.5 describes the effects of the sugar quota. In 1994, imports were limited to 3.0 billion pounds, which pushed the domestic price to 22 cents per pound. Suppose imports were expanded to 4.0 billion pounds.

a. What would be the new U.S. domestic price?

b. How much would consumers gain and domestic producers lose?

c. What would be the effect on deadweight loss and foreign producers?

11. Review Example 9.5 on the sugar quota. During the mid-1990s, U.S. sugar producers became more efficient, causing the domestic supply curve to shift to the right. We will examine the implications of this shift. Suppose that the supply curve shifts to the right by 3.0 billion pounds, so that the new supply curve is given by

$$Q_S = -5.19 + 1.07P$$

a. Show that if the demand curve remains the same as in Example 9.5, domestic demand will equal domestic supply at a price of 22 cents per pound. Thus the U.S. price could be maintained at 22 cents with no imports.

b. Suppose that under pressure from foreign sugar producers, the U.S. government allows in imports of 2.5 billion pounds, and requires domestic sugar producers to reduce their production by the same amount.

Draw the supply and demand curves, and calculate the resulting cost to consumers, the benefit to foreign and domestic producers, and the deadweight loss.

12. The domestic supply and demand curves for hula beans are as follows:

    Supply: $P = 50 + Q$

    Demand: $P = 200 - 2Q$

    where P is the price in cents per pound, and Q is the quantity in millions of pounds. We are a small country in the world hula bean market, where the current price (which will not be affected by anything we do), is 60 cents per pound. Congress is considering a tariff of 40 cents per pound. Find the domestic price of hula beans that will result if the tariff is imposed. Also compute the dollar gain or loss to domestic consumers, domestic producers, and government revenue from the tariff.

13. Currently, the social security payroll tax in the United States is evenly divided between employers and employees. Employers must pay the government a tax of 6.2 percent of the wages they pay, and employees must pay 6.2 percent of the wages they receive. Suppose the tax were changed, so that employers pay the full 12.4 percent, and employees pay nothing. Would employees then be better off?

14. You know that if a tax is imposed on a particular product, the burden of the tax is shared by producers and consumers. You also know that the demand for automobiles is characterized by a stock adjustment process. Suppose a special 20 percent sales tax is suddenly imposed on automobiles. Will the share of the tax paid by consumers rise, fall, or stay the same over time? Explain briefly. Repeat for a 50-cents-per-gallon gasoline tax.

PART III
Market Structure and Competitive Strategy

Part III examines a broad range of markets and explains how the pricing, investment, and output decisions of firms depend on market structure and the behavior of competitors.

Chapters 10 and 11 examine market power—the ability to affect price, either by a seller or a buyer. We will see how market power arises, how it differs across firms, how it affects the welfare of consumers and producers, and how it can be limited by government. We will also see how firms can design pricing strategies to take advantage of their market power.

Chapters 12 and 13 deal with markets in which the number of firms is limited. We will examine a variety of such markets, ranging from monopolistic competition, in which many firms sell differentiated products, to cartels, in which a group of firms coordinate their decisions and act as a monopolist. We are particularly concerned with markets in which there are only a few firms. Then, each firm must design its pricing, output, and investment strategies, keeping in mind how its competitors are likely to react. We will develop and apply principles from game theory to analyze such strategies.

Chapter 14 shows how markets for factor inputs such as labor and raw materials operate. We will examine the firm's input decisions, and how those decisions depend on the structure of the input market. Chapter 15 then focuses on the firm's capital investment decisions. We will see how the firm can value the profits it expects an investment to yield in the future, and then compare this value with the cost of the investment to determine whether the investment is worthwhile.

Chapter Outline

List of Examples

Market Power: Monopoly and Monopsony

In a perfectly competitive market, there are enough sellers and buyers of a good, so that no single seller or buyer can affect its price. The market forces of supply and demand determine price. Individual firms take the market price as a given in deciding how much to produce and sell, and consumers take it as a given in deciding how much to buy.

Monopoly and *monopsony*, the subjects of this chapter, are the polar opposites of perfect competition. A *monopoly* is a market that has only one seller, but many buyers. A *monopsony* is just the opposite—a market with many sellers, but only one buyer. Monopoly and monopsony are closely related, which is why we cover them in the same chapter.

We first discuss the behavior of a monopolist. Because a monopolist is the sole producer of a product, the market demand curve relates the price that the monopolist receives to the quantity it offers for sale. We will see how a monopolist can take advantage of its control over price and how the profit-maximizing price and quantity differ from what would prevail in a competitive market.

In general, the monopolist's quantity will be lower and its price higher than the competitive quantity and price. This imposes a cost on society because fewer consumers buy the product, and those who do pay more for it. This is why the antitrust laws forbid firms from monopolizing most markets. When economies of scale make monopoly desirable—for example, with local electric power companies—we will see how the government can then increase efficiency by regulating the monopolist's price.

Pure monopoly is rare, but in many markets only a few firms compete with each other. The interactions of firms in such markets can be complicated and often involve aspects of strategic gaming, a topic covered in Chapters 12 and 13. In any case, the firms may be able to affect price and may find it profitable to charge a price higher than marginal cost. These firms have *monopoly power*. We will discuss the determinants of monopoly power, its measurement, and its implications for pricing.

Next we will turn to *monopsony*. Unlike a competitive buyer, the price that a monopsonist pays depends on the quantity that it purchases. The monopsonist's problem is to choose the quantity that maximizes its net benefit from the purchase—the value derived from the good less the money paid for it. By showing how the choice is made, we will demonstrate the close parallel between monopsony and monopoly.

Pure monopsony is also unusual. But many markets have only a few buyers, who can purchase the good for less than they would pay in a competitive market. These buyers have *monopsony power*. Typically this occurs in markets for inputs to production. For example, the three large U.S. car manufacturers have monopsony power in the markets for tires, car batteries, and other parts. We will discuss the determinants of monopsony power, its measurement, and its implications for pricing.

Monopoly and monopsony power are two forms of *market power*. Market power refers to the ability—by a seller or a buyer—to affect the price of a good.[1] Since sellers or buyers have at least some market power (in most real-world markets), we need to understand how market power works and its implications for firms and consumers.

10.1 Monopoly

As the sole producer of a product, a monopolist is in a unique position. If the monopolist decides to raise the price of the product, it need not worry about competitors who, by charging a lower price, would capture a larger share of the market at the monopolist's expense. The monopolist *is* the market and has complete control over the amount of output offered for sale.

But this does not mean that the monopolist can charge as high a price as it wants—at least not if its objective is to maximize profit. This textbook is a case

---

[1] The courts often use the term "monopoly power" to mean sufficient market power to warrant scrutiny under the antitrust laws. In this book, however, we use "monopoly power" differently, to mean market power on the part of sellers, whether substantial or not.

in point. Prentice Hall, Inc., owns the copyright and is, therefore, a monopoly producer of this book. Then why doesn't it sell the book for $500 a copy? Because few people would buy it, and Prentice Hall would earn a much lower profit.

To maximize profit, the monopolist must first determine the characteristics of market demand, as well as its costs. Knowledge of demand and cost is crucial for a firm's economic decision making. Given this knowledge, the monopolist must then decide how much to produce and sell. The price per unit the monopolist receives then follows directly from the market demand curve. (Equivalently, the monopolist can determine price, and the quantity it will sell at that price follows from the market demand curve.)

Average Revenue and Marginal Revenue

The monopolist's average revenue—the price it receives per unit sold—is just the market demand curve. To choose its profit-maximizing output level, the monopolist also needs to know its *marginal revenue*—that is, the change in revenue that results from a unit change in output. To see the relationship among total, average, and marginal revenue, consider a firm facing the following demand curve: $P = 6 - Q$.

Table 10.1 shows the behavior of total, average, and marginal revenue for this demand curve. Note that revenue is zero when the price is $6 because at that price nothing is sold. However, at a price of $5 one unit is sold, and then total (and marginal) revenue is $5. An increase in quantity sold from 1 to 2 increases revenue from $5 to $8, so that marginal revenue is $3. As quantity sold increases from 2 to 3, marginal revenue falls to $1, and when it increases from 3 to 4, marginal revenue becomes negative. When marginal revenue is positive, revenue is increasing with quantity, but when marginal revenue is negative, revenue is decreasing.

When the demand curve is downward sloping, the price (average revenue) is greater than marginal revenue because all units are sold at the same price.

Table 10.1 Total, Marginal, and Average Revenue

Price P	Quantity Q	Total Revenue R	Marginal Revenue MR	Average Revenue AR
$6	0	$0	—	—
5	1	5	$5	$5
4	2	8	3	4
3	3	9	1	3
2	4	8	−1	2
1	5	5	−3	1

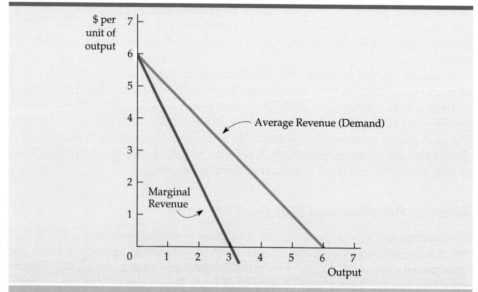

Figure 10.1 Average and Marginal Revenue Average and marginal revenue are shown for the demand curve $P = 6 - Q$.

To increase sales by 1 unit, the price must fall, so that all units sold, not just the additional unit, earn less revenue. Note what happens in Table 10.1 when output is increased from 1 to 2 units, and price is reduced to $4. Marginal revenue is $3: $4 (the revenue from the sale of the additional unit of output) less $1 (the loss of revenue from selling the first unit for $4 instead of $5). Thus, marginal revenue ($3) is less than price ($4).

Figure 10.1 plots average and marginal revenue for the data in Table 10.1. Our demand curve is a straight line, and in this case the marginal revenue curve has twice the slope of the demand curve (and the same intercept).[2]

The Monopolist's Output Decision

What quantity should the monopolist produce? In Chapter 8 we saw that to maximize profit, a firm must set output so that marginal revenue is equal to marginal cost. This is the solution to the monopolist's problem. In Figure 10.2, the market demand curve D is the monopolist's average revenue curve. It specifies the price per unit that the monopolist receives as a function of its output level. Also shown are the corresponding marginal revenue curve MR and the average and marginal cost curves, AC and MC. Marginal revenue and

---

[2] If the demand curve is written so that price is a function of quantity, $P = a - bQ$, total revenue is given by $PQ = aQ - bQ^2$. Marginal revenue (using calculus) is $d(PQ)/dQ = a - 2bQ$. In this example, demand is $P = 6 - Q$ and marginal revenue is $MR = 6 - 2Q$. (This holds only for small changes in Q, and therefore does not exactly match the data in Table 10.1.)

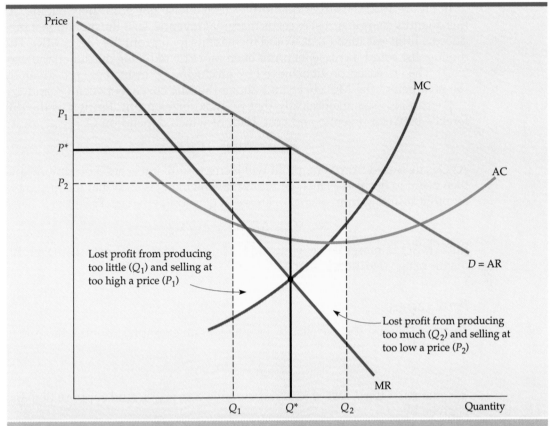

Figure 10.2 Profit Is Maximized When Marginal Revenue Equals Marginal Cost Q^* is the output level at which MR = MC. If the firm produces a smaller output, say Q_1, it sacrifices some profit because the extra revenue that could be earned from producing and selling the units between Q_1 and Q^* exceeds the cost of producing them. Similarly, expanding output from Q^* to Q_2 would reduce profit, because the additional cost would exceed the additional revenue.

marginal cost are equal at quantity Q^*. Then from the demand curve, we find the price P^* that corresponds to this quantity Q^*.

How can we be sure that Q^* is the profit-maximizing quantity? Suppose the monopolist produces a smaller quantity Q_1 and receives the corresponding higher price P_1. As Figure 10.2 shows, marginal revenue would then exceed marginal cost, so if the monopolist produced a little more than Q_1, it would receive extra profit (MR − MC) and thereby increase its total profit. In fact, the monopolist could keep increasing output, adding more to its total profit until output Q^*, at which point the incremental profit earned from producing one more unit is zero. So the smaller quantity Q_1 is not profit maximizing, even though it allows the monopolist to charge a higher price. By producing Q_1 instead of Q^*, the monopolist's total profit would be smaller by an amount equal to the shaded area below the MR curve and above the MC curve, between Q_1 and Q^*.

In Figure 10.2, the larger quantity Q_2 is likewise not profit maximizing. At this quantity marginal cost exceeds marginal revenue, so if the monopolist produced a little less than Q_2, it would increase its total profit (by MC − MR). The monopolist could increase its profit even more by reducing output all the way to Q^*. The increased profit achieved by producing Q^* instead of Q_2 is given by the area below the MC curve and above the MR curve, between Q^* and Q_2.

We can also see algebraically that Q^* maximizes profit. Profit π is the difference between revenue and cost, both of which depend on Q:

$$\pi(Q) = R(Q) - C(Q)$$

As Q is increased from zero, profit will increase until it reaches a maximum, and then begin to decrease. Thus the profit-maximizing Q is such that the incremental profit resulting from a small increase in Q is just zero (i.e., $\Delta\pi/\Delta Q = 0$). Then

$$\Delta\pi/\Delta Q = \Delta R/\Delta Q - \Delta C/\Delta Q = 0$$

But $\Delta R/\Delta Q$ is marginal revenue, and $\Delta C/\Delta Q$ is marginal cost, so the profit-maximizing condition is that MR − MC = 0, or MR = MC.

An Example

To grasp this result more clearly, let's look at an example. Suppose the cost of production is

$$C(Q) = 50 + Q^2$$

(i.e., there is a fixed cost of $50, and variable cost is Q^2). And suppose demand is given by

$$P(Q) = 40 - Q$$

By setting marginal revenue equal to marginal cost, you can verify that profit is maximized when $Q = 10$, which corresponds to a price of $30.[3]

Cost, revenue, and profit are plotted in Figure 10.3(a). When the firm produces little or no output, profit is negative because of the fixed cost. Profit increases as Q increases, until it reaches a maximum of $150 at $Q^* = 10$, and then decreases as Q is increased further. And at the point of maximum profit, the slopes of the revenue and cost curves are the same. (Note that the tangent lines rr' and cc' are parallel.) The slope of the revenue curve is $\Delta R/\Delta Q$, or marginal revenue, and the slope of the cost curve is $\Delta C/\Delta Q$, or marginal cost. Profit is maximized when marginal revenue equals marginal cost, so the slopes are equal.

Figure 10.3(b) shows the corresponding average and marginal revenue curves, and average and marginal cost curves. Marginal revenue and marginal cost intersect at $Q^* = 10$. At this quantity, average cost is $15 per unit, and price is $30 per unit, so average profit is $30 − $15 = $15 per unit. Since 10 units are sold, profit is (10)($15) = $150, the area of the shaded rectangle.

---

[3] Note that average cost is $C(Q)/Q = 50/Q + Q$, and marginal cost is $\Delta C/\Delta Q = 2Q$. Revenue is $R(Q) = P(Q)Q = 40Q - Q^2$, so marginal revenue is MR $= \Delta R/\Delta Q = 40 - 2Q$. Setting marginal revenue equal to marginal cost gives $40 - 2Q = 2Q$, or $Q = 10$.

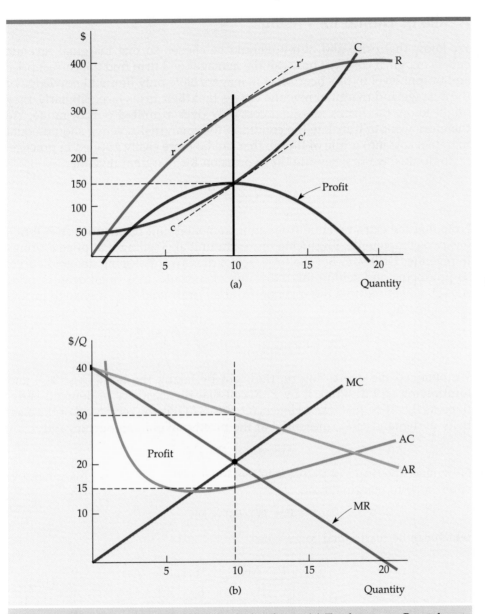

Figure 10.3 Example of Profit Maximization (a) Total revenue R, total cost C, and profit, the difference between the two. (b) Average and marginal revenue and average and marginal cost. Marginal revenue is the slope of the total revenue curve, and marginal cost is the slope of the total cost curve. The profit-maximizing output is $Q^* = 10$, the point where marginal revenue equals marginal cost. At this output level, the slope of the profit curve is zero, and the slopes of the total revenue and total cost curves are equal. The profit per unit is $15, the difference between average revenue and average cost. Because 10 units are produced, total profit is $150.

A Rule of Thumb for Pricing

We know that price and output should be chosen so that marginal revenue equals marginal cost, but how can the manager of a firm find the correct price and output level in practice? Most managers have only limited knowledge of the average and marginal revenue curves that their firms face. Similarly, they might know the firm's marginal cost only over a limited output range. We therefore want to translate the condition that marginal revenue should equal marginal cost into a rule of thumb that can be more easily applied in practice.

To do this, we first rewrite the expression for marginal revenue:

$$MR = \frac{\Delta R}{\Delta Q} = \frac{\Delta(PQ)}{\Delta Q}$$

Note that the extra revenue from an incremental unit of quantity, $\Delta(PQ)/\Delta Q$, has two components. Producing one extra unit and selling it at price P brings in revenue $(1)(P) = P$. But the firm faces a downward-sloping demand curve, so producing and selling this extra unit also results in a small drop in price $\Delta P/\Delta Q$, which reduces the revenue from all units sold (i.e., a change in revenue $Q[\Delta P/\Delta Q]$). Thus,

$$MR = P + Q\frac{\Delta P}{\Delta Q} = P + P\left(\frac{Q}{P}\right)\left(\frac{\Delta P}{\Delta Q}\right)$$

We obtained the expression on the right by taking the term $Q(\Delta P/\Delta Q)$ and multiplying and dividing it by P. Recall that the elasticity of demand is defined as $E_d = (P/Q)(\Delta Q/\Delta P)$. Hence, $(Q/P)(\Delta P/\Delta Q)$ is the reciprocal of the elasticity of demand, $1/E_d$, measured at the profit-maximizing output, and

$$MR = P + P(1/E_d)$$

Now, since the firm's objective is to maximize profit, we can set marginal revenue equal to marginal cost:

$$P + P(1/E_d) = MC$$

which can be rearranged to give us

$$\boxed{\frac{P - MC}{P} = -\frac{1}{E_d}} \tag{10.1}$$

This relationship provides a rule of thumb for pricing. The left-hand side, $(P - MC)/P$, is the markup over marginal cost as a percentage of price. The relationship says that this markup should equal minus the inverse of the elasticity of demand.[4] (This will be a positive number because the elasticity of de-

---

[4] Remember that this markup equation applies at the point of a profit maximum. If both the elasticity of demand and marginal cost vary considerably over the range of outputs under consideration, you may have to know the entire demand and marginal cost curves to determine the optimum output level. On the other hand, this equation can be used to check whether a particular output level and price are optimal.

mand is negative.) Equivalently, we can rearrange this equation to express price directly as a markup over marginal cost:

$$P = \frac{MC}{1 + (1/E_d)} \tag{10.2}$$

For example, if the elasticity of demand is -4 and marginal cost is \$9 per unit, price should be \$9/(1 $-$ 1/4) = \$9/.75 = \$12 per unit.

How does the price set by a monopolist compare with the price under competition? In Chapter 8 we saw that in a perfectly competitive market, price equals marginal cost. A monopolist charges a price that exceeds marginal cost, but by an amount that depends inversely on the elasticity of demand. As the markup equation (10.1) shows, if demand is extremely elastic, E_d is a large negative number, and price will be very close to marginal cost, so that a monopolized market will look much like a competitive one. In fact, when demand is very elastic, there is little benefit to being a monopolist.

Shifts in Demand

In a competitive market, there is a clear relationship between price and the quantity supplied. That relationship is the supply curve, which, as we saw in Chapter 8, represents the marginal cost of production for the industry as a whole. The supply curve tells us how much will be produced at every price.

A monopolistic market has no supply curve. In other words, there is no one-to-one relationship between price and the quantity produced. The reason is that the monopolist's output decision depends not only on marginal cost but also on the shape of the demand curve. As a result, shifts in demand do not trace out a series of prices and quantities as happens with a competitive supply curve. Instead, shifts in demand can lead to changes in price with no change in output, changes in output with no change in price, or changes in both.

This is illustrated in Figure 10.4(a) and (b). In both parts of the figure, the demand curve is initially D_1, the corresponding marginal revenue curve is MR_1, and the monopolist's initial price and quantity are P_1 and Q_1. In Figure 10.4(a) the demand curve is shifted down and rotated; the new demand and marginal revenue curves are shown as D_2 and MR_2. Note that MR_2 intersects the marginal cost curve at the same point that MR_1 does. As a result, the quantity produced stays the same. Price, however, falls to P_2.

In Figure 10.4(b) the demand curve is shifted up and rotated. The new marginal revenue curve MR_2 intersects the marginal cost curve at a larger quantity, Q_2 instead of Q_1. But the shift in the demand curve is such that the price charged is exactly the same.

Shifts in demand usually cause changes in both price and quantity. But the special cases shown in Figure 10.4 illustrate an important distinction between monopoly and competitive supply. A competitive industry supplies a specific quantity at every price. No such relationship exists for a monopolist, which, depending on how demand shifts, might supply several different quantities at the same price, or the same quantity at different prices.

Figure 10.4(a) **Shift in Demand Leads to Change in Price but Same Output** The demand curve D_1 shifts to new demand curve D_2. But the new marginal revenue curve MR_2 intersects marginal cost at the same point that the old marginal revenue curve MR_1 did. The profit-maximizing output therefore remains the same, although price falls from P_1 to P_2.

Figure 10.4(b) **Shift in Demand Leads to Change in Output but Same Price** The new marginal revenue curve MR_2 intersects marginal cost at a higher output level Q_2. But because demand is now more elastic, price remains the same.

The Effect of a Tax

A tax on output can also have a different effect on a monopolist than on a competitive industry. In Chapter 9 we saw that when a specific (i.e., per unit) tax is imposed on a competitive industry, the market price rises by an amount that is less than the tax, and that the burden of the tax is shared by producers and consumers. Under monopoly, however, price can sometimes rise by *more* than the amount of the tax.

Analyzing the effect of a tax on a monopolist is straightforward. Suppose a specific tax of t dollars per unit is levied, so that the monopolist must remit t dollars to the government for every unit it sells. Therefore, the firm's marginal (and average) cost is increased by the amount of the tax t. If MC was the firm's original marginal cost, its optimal production decision is now given by

$$MR = MC + t$$

Graphically, we shift the marginal cost curve upward by an amount t, and find the new intersection with marginal revenue. Figure 10.5 shows this. Here

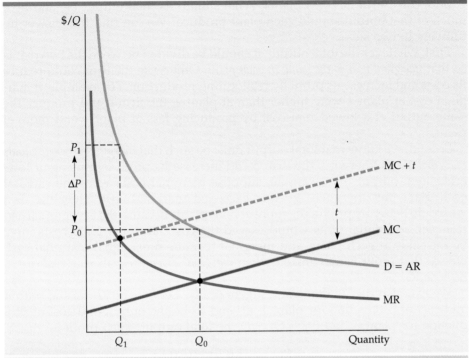

Figure 10.5   Effect of Excise Tax on Monopolist   With a tax t per unit, the firm's effective marginal cost is increased by the amount t to $MC + t$. In this example, the increase in price ΔP is larger than the tax t.

Q_0 and P_0 are the quantity and price before the tax is imposed, and Q_1 and P_1 are the quantity and price after the tax.

Shifting the marginal cost curve upward results in a smaller quantity and higher price. Sometimes price increases by less than the tax, but not always—in Figure 10.5, price increases by *more* than the tax. This would be impossible in a competitive market, but it can happen with a monopolist because the relationship between price and marginal cost depends on the elasticity of demand. Suppose, for example, that a monopolist faces a constant elasticity demand curve, with elasticity -2. Equation (10.2) then tells us that price will equal twice marginal cost. With a tax t, marginal cost increases to $MC + t$, so price increases to $2(MC + t) = 2MC + 2t$; that is, it rises by twice the amount of the tax. (However, the monopolist's profit nonetheless falls with the tax.)

*The Multiplant Firm

We have seen that a firm maximizes profit by setting output where marginal revenue equals marginal cost. For many firms, production takes place in two or more different plants whose operating costs can differ. However, the logic used in choosing output levels is very similar to that for the single-plant firm.

Suppose a firm has two plants. What should its total output be, and how much of that output should each plant produce? We can find the answer intuitively in two steps.

First, whatever the total output, it should be divided between the two plants so that *marginal cost is the same in each plant*. Otherwise the firm could reduce its costs and increase its profit by reallocating production. For example, if marginal cost at plant 1 were higher than at plant 2, the firm could produce the same output at a lower total cost by producing less at plant 1 and more at plant 2.

Second, we know that total output must be such that *marginal revenue equals marginal cost*. Otherwise, the firm could increase its profit by raising or lowering total output. For example, suppose marginal costs were the same at each plant, but marginal revenue exceeded marginal cost. Then the firm would do better by producing more at both plants because the revenue earned from the additional units would exceed the cost. Since marginal costs must be the same at each plant, and marginal revenue must equal marginal cost, we see that profit is maximized when *marginal revenue equals marginal cost at each plant*.

We can also derive this result algebraically. Let Q_1 and C_1 be the output and cost of production for plant 1, Q_2 and C_2 be the output and cost of production for plant 2, and $Q_T = Q_1 + Q_2$ be total output. Then profit is

$$\pi = PQ_T - C_1(Q_1) - C_2(Q_2)$$

The firm should increase output from each plant until the incremental profit from the last unit produced is zero. Setting incremental profit from output at plant 1 to zero:

$$\frac{\Delta \pi}{\Delta Q_1} = \frac{\Delta(PQ_T)}{\Delta Q_1} - \frac{\Delta C_1}{\Delta Q_1} = 0$$

Here $\Delta(PQ_T)/\Delta Q_1$ is the revenue from producing and selling one more unit, i.e., marginal revenue, MR, for all of the firm's output. The next term, $\Delta C_1/\Delta Q_1$, is marginal cost at plant 1, MC_1. We thus have $MR - MC_1 = 0$, or

$$MR = MC_1$$

Similarly, setting incremental profit from output at plant 2 to zero,

$$MR = MC_2$$

Putting these relations together, we see that the firm should produce so that

$$\boxed{MR = MC_1 = MC_2} \tag{10.3}$$

Figure 10.6 illustrates this for a firm with two plants. MC_1 and MC_2 are the marginal cost curves for the two plants. (Note that plant 1 has higher marginal costs than plant 2.) Also shown is a curve labeled MC_T. This is the firm's total marginal cost and is obtained by horizontally summing

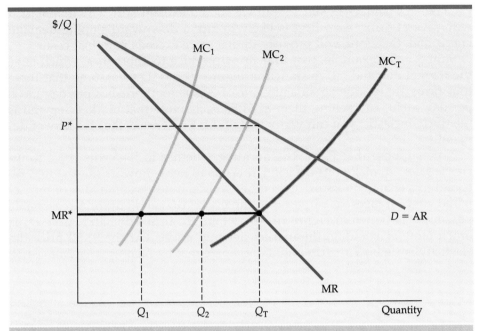

Figure 10.6 Production with Two Plants A firm with two plants maximizes profits by choosing output levels Q_1 and Q_2 so that marginal revenue MR (which depends on *total* output) equals marginal costs for each plant, MC_1 and MC_2.

MC_1 and MC_2.[5] Now we can find the profit-maximizing output levels Q_1, Q_2, and Q_T. First, find the intersection of MC_T with MR; that determines total output Q_T. Next, draw a horizontal line from that point on the marginal revenue curve to the vertical axis; point MR* determines the firm's marginal revenue. The intersections of the marginal revenue line with MC_1 and MC_2 give the outputs Q_1 and Q_2 for the two plants, as shown in Equation (10.3).

Note that total output Q_T determines the firm's marginal revenue (and hence its price P^*), but Q_1 and Q_2 determine marginal costs at each of the two plants. Since MC_T was found by horizontally summing MC_1 and MC_2, we know that $Q_1 + Q_2 = Q_T$. Hence these output levels satisfy the condition that $MR = MC_1 = MC_2$.

10.2 Monopoly Power

Pure monopoly is rare. Markets in which several firms compete with one another are much more common. We say more about the forms this competition

---

[5] Note the similarity to the way we obtained a competitive industry's supply curve in Chapter 8 by horizontally summing the marginal cost curves of the individual firms.

can take in Chapters 12 and 13. But we should explain here why in a market with several firms, each firm is likely to face a downward-sloping demand curve, and, therefore, will produce so that price exceeds marginal cost.

Suppose, for example, that four firms produce toothbrushes, which have the market demand curve shown in Figure 10.7(a). Let's assume that these four firms are producing an aggregate of 20,000 toothbrushes per day (5000 per day each), and selling them at $1.50 each. Note that market demand is relatively inelastic; you can verify that at this $1.50 price, the elasticity of demand is −1.5.

Now suppose that Firm A is deciding whether to lower its price to increase sales. To make this decision, it needs to know how its sales would respond to a change in its price. In other words, it needs some idea of the demand curve it faces, as opposed to the *market* demand curve. A reasonable possibility is shown in Figure 10.7(b), where the firm's demand curve D_A is much more elastic than the market demand curve. (At the $1.50 price the elasticity is −6.0.) The firm might anticipate that by raising price from $1.50

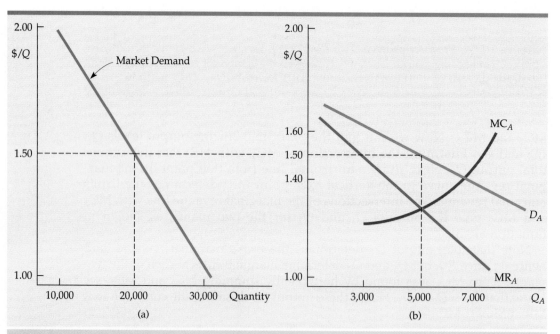

Figure 10.7(a)   Market Demand for Toothbrushes

Figure 10.7(b)   Demand for Toothbrushes as Seen by Firm *A*   At a market price of $1.50, elasticity of market demand is −1.5. Firm A, however, sees a much more elastic demand curve D_A because of competition from other firms. At a price of $1.50, Firm A's demand elasticity is −6. Still, Firm A has some monopoly power. Its profit-maximizing price is $1.50, which exceeds marginal cost.

to $1.60, its sales will drop, say, from 5000 units to 3000, as consumers buy more toothbrushes from the other firms. (If *all* firms raised their prices to $1.60, sales for Firm *A* would fall only to 4500.) But for several reasons, sales won't drop to zero, as they would in a perfectly competitive market. First, Firm *A*'s toothbrushes might be a little different from its competitors, so some consumers will pay a bit more for them. Second, the other firms might also raise their prices. Similarly, Firm *A* might anticipate that by lowering its price from $1.50 to $1.40, it can sell more, perhaps 7000 toothbrushes instead of 5000. But it will not capture the entire market. Some consumers might still prefer the competitors' toothbrushes, and the competitors might also lower their prices.

So Firm *A*'s demand curve depends on how much its product differs from its competitors' products and on how the four firms compete with one another. We will discuss product differentiation and interfirm competition in Chapters 12 and 13. But one important point should be clear: *Firm A is likely to face a demand curve that is more elastic than the market demand curve, but not infinitely elastic like the demand curve facing a perfectly competitive firm.*

Given knowledge of its demand curve, how much should Firm *A* produce? The same principle applies: The profit-maximizing quantity equates marginal revenue and marginal cost. In Figure 10.7(b) that quantity is 5000 units, and the corresponding price is $1.50, which exceeds marginal cost. So although Firm *A* is not a pure monopolist, *it does have monopoly power*—it can profitably charge a price greater than marginal cost. Of course, its monopoly power is less than it would be if it had driven away the competition and monopolized the market, but it might still be substantial.

This raises two questions. First, how can we *measure* monopoly power, so that we can compare one firm with another? (So far we have been talking about monopoly power only in *qualitative* terms.) Second, what are the *sources* of monopoly power, and why do some firms have more monopoly power than others? We address both these questions below, although a more complete answer to the second question will be provided in Chapters 12 and 13.

Measuring Monopoly Power

Remember the important distinction between a perfectly competitive firm and a firm with monopoly power: For the competitive firm, price equals marginal cost; for the firm with monopoly power, price exceeds marginal cost. Therefore, a natural way to measure monopoly power is to examine the extent to which the profit-maximizing price exceeds marginal cost. In particular, we can use the markup ratio of price minus marginal cost to price that we introduced earlier as part of a rule of thumb for pricing. This measure of monopoly power was introduced by economist Abba Lerner in 1934 and is called *Lerner's Degree of Monopoly Power:*

$$L = (P - MC)/P$$

This Lerner index always has a value between zero and one. For a perfectly competitive firm, $P = MC$ so that $L = 0$. The larger L is, the greater the degree of monopoly power.

This index of monopoly power can also be expressed in terms of the elasticity of demand facing the firm. Using equation (10.1), we know that

$$L = (P - MC)/P = -1/E_d \tag{10.4}$$

Remember, however, that E_d is now the elasticity of the *firm's* demand curve, and not the market demand curve. In the toothbrush example discussed above, the elasticity of demand for Firm A is -6.0, and the degree of monopoly power is $1/6 = 0.167.$[6]

Note that considerable monopoly power does not necessarily imply high profits. Profit depends on *average* cost relative to price. Firm A might have more monopoly power than Firm B, but might earn a lower profit because it has much higher average costs.

The Rule of Thumb for Pricing

In the previous section, we used equation (10.2) to compute price as a simple markup over marginal cost:

$$P = \frac{MC}{1 + (1/E_d)}$$

This relationship provides a rule of thumb for *any* firm with monopoly power, if we remember that E_d is the elasticity of demand for the *firm*, not the elasticity of *market* demand.

It is harder to determine the elasticity of demand for the firm than for the market because the firm must consider how its competitors will react to price changes. Essentially, the manager must estimate the percentage change in the firm's unit sales that is likely to result from a 1 percent change in the price the firm charges. This estimate might be based on a formal model or on the manager's intuition and experience.

Given an estimate of the firm's elasticity of demand, the manager can calculate the proper markup. If the firm's elasticity of demand is large, this markup will be small (and we can say that the firm has very little monopoly power). If the firm's elasticity of demand is small, this markup will be large (and the firm will have considerable monopoly power). Figures 10.8(a) and 10.8(b) illustrate these two extremes.

---

[6] There are three problems with applying the Lerner index to the analysis of public policy toward firms. First, because marginal cost is difficult to measure, average variable cost is often used in Lerner index calculations. Second, if the firm prices below its optimal price (possibly to avoid legal scrutiny), its potential monopoly power will not be noted by the index. Third, the index ignores dynamic aspects of pricing such as effects of the learning curve, shifts in demand, etc. See Robert S. Pindyck, "The Measurement of Monopoly Power in Dynamic Markets," *Journal of Law and Economics* 28 (April 1985): 193–222.

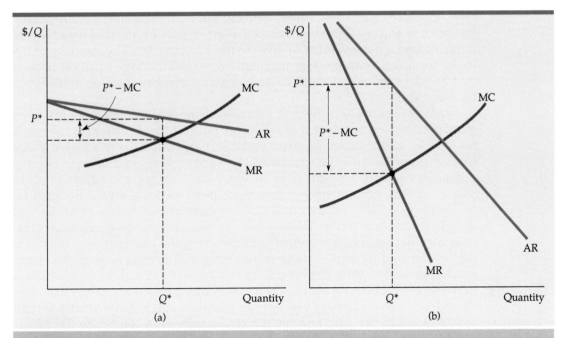

Figure 10.8 **Elasticity of Demand and Price Markup** The markup $(P - \text{MC})/P$ is equal to minus the inverse of the elasticity of demand. If demand is elastic as in (a), the markup is small, and the firm has little monopoly power. The opposite is true if demand is inelastic, as in (b).

EXAMPLE 10.1 **Markup Pricing: Supermarkets to Designer Jeans**

Three examples should help clarify the use of markup pricing. Consider a retail supermarket chain. Although the elasticity of market demand for food is small (about −1), several supermarkets usually serve most areas, so no single supermarket can raise its prices very much without losing many customers to other stores. As a result, the elasticity of demand for any one supermarket is often as large as −10. Substituting this number for E_d in equation (10.2), we find $P = \text{MC}/(1 - 0.1) = \text{MC}/(0.9) = (1.11)\text{MC}$. In other words, the manager of a typical supermarket should set prices about 11 percent above marginal cost. For a reasonably wide range of output levels (over which the size of the store and the number of its employees will remain fixed), marginal cost includes the cost of purchasing the food at wholesale, together with the costs of storing the food, arranging it on the shelves, etc. For most supermarkets the markup is indeed about 10 or 11 percent.

Small convenience stores, which are often open on Sundays or even 24 hours a day, typically charge higher prices than supermarkets. Why? Because a convenience store faces a less elastic demand curve. Its customers are generally less price sensitive. They might need a quart of milk or a loaf of bread late at night, or find it inconvenient to drive to the supermarket. The elasticity of demand for a convenience store is about −5, so the markup equation implies that its prices should be about 25 percent above marginal cost, as indeed they typically are.

The Lerner index, $(P - MC)/P$, tells us that the convenience store has more monopoly power, but does it make larger profits? No. Because its volume is far smaller and its average fixed costs are larger, it usually earns a much smaller profit than a large supermarket, despite its higher markup.

Finally, consider a producer of designer jeans. Many companies produce jeans, but some consumers will pay much more for jeans with a designer label. Just how much more they will pay—or more exactly, how much sales will drop in response to higher prices—is a question that the producer must carefully consider because it is critical in determining the price at which the clothing will be sold (at wholesale to retail stores, which then mark up the price further for sale to their customers). With designer jeans, demand elasticities in the range of −3 to −4 are typical for the major labels. This means that price should be 33 to 50 percent higher than marginal cost. Marginal cost is typically $12 to $18 per pair, and the wholesale price is in the $18 to $27 range.

E X A M P L E   10.2   **The Pricing of Prerecorded Videocassettes**

During the mid-1980s, the number of households owning videocassette recorders (VCRs) grew rapidly, as did the markets for rentals and sales of prerecorded cassettes. Although many more videocassettes are rented through small retail outlets than are sold outright, the market for sales is large and growing. Producers, however, found it difficult to decide what price to charge for their cassettes. As a result, in 1985 popular movies were selling for vastly different prices, as the data for that year show in Table 10.2.

Note that *The Empire Strikes Back* was selling for nearly $80, while *Star Trek*, a film that appealed to the same audience and was about as popular, sold for only about $25. These price differences reflected uncertainty and a wide divergence of views on pricing by producers. The issue was whether lower prices would induce consumers to buy the videocassettes rather than rent them. Because producers do not share in the retailers' revenues from rentals, they should charge a low price for cassettes only if that will induce enough consumers to buy them. Because the market was young, producers had no good estimates of the elasticity of demand, so they based prices on hunches or trial and error.[7]

As the market matured, however, sales data and market research studies put pricing decisions on firmer ground. They strongly indicated that demand

---

[7] "Video Producers Debate the Value of Price Cuts," *New York Times*, Feb. 19, 1985.

Table 10.2 The Prices of Videos in 1985 and 1996			
1985		**1996**	
Title	**Retail Price ($)**	**Title**	**Retail Price ($)**
Purple Rain	$29.98	*Clueless*	$14.95
Raiders of the Lost Ark	24.95	*Jumanji*	19.95
Jane Fonda Workout	59.95	*Babe*	22.95
The Empire Strikes Back	79.98	*Congo*	14.95
An Officer and A Gentleman	24.95	*Twister*	17.95
Star Trek: The Motion Picture	24.95	*Mission Impossible*	14.79
Star Wars	39.98	*Independence Day*	16.95

was elastic and that the profit-maximizing price was in the range of $15 to $30. As one industry analyst said, "People are becoming collectors. . . . As you lower the price you attract households that would not have considered buying at a higher price point."[8] And, indeed, by the early 1990s most producers had lowered prices across the board. As Table 10.2 shows, in 1996 prices of top-selling videos were considerably lower than in 1985. As a result of these price declines, sales of videos were increasing during the 1990s (as were profits from these sales), even though rentals had stopped growing.[9]

10.3 Sources of Monopoly Power

Why do some firms have considerable monopoly power, and other firms have little or none? Remember that monopoly power is the ability to set price above marginal cost, and the amount by which price exceeds marginal cost depends inversely on the firm's elasticity of demand. As equation (10.3) shows, the less elastic its demand curve, the more monopoly power a firm has. The ultimate determinant of monopoly power is therefore the firm's elasticity of demand. The question is, why do some firms (e.g., a supermarket chain) face a demand curve that is more elastic, while others (e.g., a producer of designer clothing) face one that is less elastic?

Three factors determine a firm's elasticity of demand. First is the *elasticity of market demand*. The firm's own demand will be at least as elastic as market demand, so the elasticity of market demand limits the potential for monopoly power. Second is the *number of firms* in the market. If there are many firms, it

---

[8] "Studios Now Stressing Video Sales Over Rentals," *New York Times*, Oct. 17, 1989. For a detailed study of videocassette pricing, see Carl E. Enomoto and Soumendra N. Ghosh, "Pricing in the Home-Video Market" (working paper, New Mexico State University, 1992).

[9] "Video Rentals Are Flat, but Purchases Increase," *New York Times*, September 18, 1995.

is unlikely that any one firm will be able to affect price significantly. Third is the *interaction among firms*. Even if only two or three firms are in the market, each firm will be unable to profitably raise price very much if the rivalry among them is aggressive, with each firm trying to capture as much of the market as it can. Let's examine each of these three determinants of monopoly power.

The Elasticity of Market Demand

If there is only one firm—a pure monopolist—its demand curve is the market demand curve. Then the firm's degree of monopoly power depends completely on the elasticity of market demand. More often, however, several firms compete with one another; then the elasticity of market demand sets a lower limit on the magnitude of the elasticity of demand for each firm. Recall our example of the toothbrush producers that was illustrated in Figure 10.7. The market demand for toothbrushes might not be very elastic, but each firm's demand will be more elastic. How much more depends on how the firms compete with one another. (In Figure 10.7, the elasticity of market demand is −1.5, and the elasticity of demand for each firm is −6.) But no matter how the firms compete, the elasticity of demand for each firm could never become smaller in magnitude than −1.5.

The demand for oil is fairly inelastic (at least in the short run), which is why OPEC could raise oil prices far above marginal production cost during the 1970s and early 1980s. The demands for such commodities as coffee, cocoa, tin, and copper are much more elastic, which is why attempts by producers to cartelize those markets and raise prices have largely failed. In each case, the elasticity of market demand limits the potential monopoly power of individual producers.

The Number of Firms

The second determinant of a firm's demand curve, and hence its monopoly power, is the number of firms in the market. Other things being equal, the monopoly power of each firm will fall as the number of firms increases. As more and more firms compete, each firm will find it harder to raise prices and avoid losing sales to other firms.

What matters, of course, is not just the total number of firms, but the number of "major players" (i.e., firms that have a significant share of the market). For example, if only two large firms account for 90 percent of sales in a market, with another 20 firms accounting for the remaining 10 percent, the two large firms might have considerable monopoly power. When only a few firms account for most of the sales in a market, the market is highly *concentrated*.[10]

It is sometimes said (not always jokingly) that the greatest fear of American business is competition. That may or may not be true. But we would certainly

---

[10] A statistic called the *concentration ratio*, which measures the fraction of sales accounted for by, say, the four largest firms, is often used to describe the concentration of a market. Concentration is one, but not the only, determinant of market power.

expect that when only a few firms are in a market, their managers would prefer that no new firms enter the market. An increase in the number of firms can only reduce the monopoly power of each incumbent firm. An important aspect of competitive strategy (discussed in detail in Chapter 13) is finding ways to create *barriers to entry*—conditions that deter entry by new competitors.

Sometimes there are natural barriers to entry. For example, one firm may have a *patent* on the technology needed to produce a particular product. This makes it impossible for other firms to enter the market, at least until the patent expires.[11] Other legally created rights work in the same way—a *copyright* can limit the sale of a book, music, or a computer software program to a single company, and the need for a government *license* can prevent new firms from entering the market for telephone service, television broadcasting, or interstate trucking. Finally, *economies of scale* may make it too costly for more than a few firms to supply the entire market. In some cases the economies of scale may be so large that it is most efficient for a single firm—*a natural monopoly*— to supply the entire market. We will discuss scale economies and natural monopoly in more detail shortly.

The Interaction Among Firms

How competing firms interact is also an important—and sometimes the most important—determinant of monopoly power. Suppose there are four firms in a market. They might compete aggressively, undercutting one another's prices to capture more market share. This could drive prices down to nearly competitive levels. Each firm will fear that if it raises its price it will be undercut and lose its market share, and thus it will have little monopoly power.

On the other hand, the firms might not compete much. They might even collude (in violation of the antitrust laws), agreeing to limit output and raise prices. Raising prices in concert rather than individually is more likely to be profitable, so collusion can generate substantial monopoly power.

We will discuss the interaction among firms in detail in Chapters 12 and 13. Now we simply want to point out that other things equal, monopoly power is smaller when firms compete aggressively and is larger when they cooperate.

Remember that a firm's monopoly power often changes over time, as its operating conditions (market demand and cost), its behavior, and the behavior of its competitors change. Monopoly power must therefore be thought of in a dynamic context. For example, the market demand curve might be very inelastic in the short run but much more elastic in the long run. (This is the case with oil, which is why OPEC had considerable short-run but less long-run monopoly power.) Furthermore, real or potential monopoly power in the short run can make an industry more competitive in the long run. Large short-run profits can induce new firms to enter an industry, thereby reducing monopoly power over the longer term.

---

[11] Until recently, patents in the United States lasted for 17 years. Under a 1996 World Trade Organization agreement, patent life was extended to 20 years.

10.4 The Social Costs of Monopoly Power

In a competitive market, price equals marginal cost, while monopoly power implies that price exceeds marginal cost. Because monopoly power results in higher prices and lower quantities produced, we would expect it to make consumers worse off and the firm better off. But suppose we value the welfare of consumers the same as that of producers. Does monopoly power make consumers and producers in the aggregate better or worse off?

We can answer this question by comparing the consumer and producer surplus that results when a competitive industry produces a good with the surplus that results when a monopolist supplies the entire market.[12] (We assume that the competitive market and the monopolist have the same cost curves.) Figure 10.9 shows the average and marginal revenue curves and marginal cost curve for the monopolist. To maximize profit, the firm produces at the point where marginal revenue equals marginal cost, so that the price and quantity are P_m and Q_m. In a competitive market, price must equal marginal cost, so the competitive price and quantity, P_c and Q_c, are found at the intersection of the average revenue (demand) curve and the marginal cost curve. Now let's examine how surplus changes if we move from the competitive price and quantity, P_c and Q_c, to the monopoly price and quantity, P_m and Q_m.

Under monopoly the price is higher, and consumers buy less. Because of the higher price, those consumers who buy the good lose surplus of an amount given by rectangle A. Those consumers who do not buy the good at price P_m but will buy at price P_c also lose surplus, of an amount given by triangle B. The total loss of consumer surplus is therefore $A + B$. The producer, however, gains rectangle A by selling at the higher price but loses triangle C, the additional profit it would have earned by selling $Q_c - Q_m$ at price P_c. The total gain in producer surplus is therefore $A - C$. Subtracting the loss of consumer surplus from the gain in producer surplus, we see a net loss of surplus given by $B + C$. This is the *deadweight loss from monopoly power*. Even if the monopolist's profits were taxed away and redistributed to the consumers of its products, there would be an inefficiency because output would be lower than under competition. The deadweight loss is the social cost of this inefficiency.

There may be an additional social cost of monopoly power that goes beyond the deadweight loss in triangles B and C. The firm may spend large amounts of money in a socially unproductive way to acquire, maintain, or exercise its monopoly power. This might involve advertising, lobbying, and legal efforts to avoid government regulation or antitrust scrutiny. Or it might mean installing but not utilizing extra productive capacity to convince potential competitors that they will be unable to sell enough to make entry worthwhile. Roughly speaking, the economic incentive to incur these costs should

---

[12] If there were two or more firms, each with some monopoly power, the analysis would be more complex. However, the basic results would be the same.

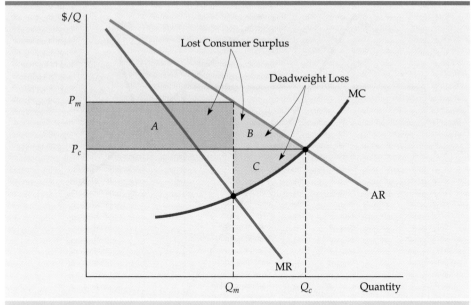

Figure 10.9   Deadweight Loss from Monopoly Power   The shaded rectangle and triangles show changes in consumer and producer surplus when moving from competitive price and quantity, P_c and Q_c, to a monopolist's price and quantity, P_m and Q_m. Because of the higher price, consumers lose $A + B$ and producer gains $A - C$. The deadweight loss is $-B - C$.

bear a direct relation to the gains to the firm from having monopoly power (i.e., rectangle A minus triangle C). Therefore, the larger the transfer from consumers to the firm (rectangle A), the larger the social cost of monopoly.

Price Regulation

Because of its social cost, antitrust laws prevent firms from accumulating excessive amounts of monopoly power. We will say more about the antitrust laws at the end of the chapter. Here, we examine another means by which society can limit monopoly power—price regulation.

We saw in Chapter 9 that in a competitive market, price regulation always results in a deadweight loss. This need not be the case, however, when a firm has monopoly power. On the contrary, price regulation can eliminate the deadweight loss that results from monopoly power.

Figure 10.10 illustrates price regulation. P_m and Q_m are the price and quantity that result without regulation. Now suppose the price is regulated to be no higher than P_1. Because the firm can charge no more than P_1 for output levels up to Q_1, its new average revenue curve is a horizontal line at P_1. For output levels greater than Q_1, the new average revenue curve is identical to the old average revenue curve because at these output levels the firm will charge less than P_1, and so it would be unaffected by the regulation.

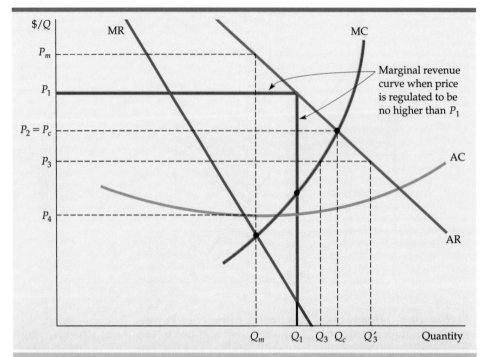

Figure 10.10 **Price Regulation** If left alone, a monopolist produces Q_m and charges P_m. When the government imposes a price ceiling of P_1 the firm's average and marginal revenue are constant and equal to P_1 for output levels up to Q_1. For larger output levels, the original average and marginal revenue curves apply. The new marginal revenue curve is, therefore, the dark line, which intersects the marginal cost curve at Q_1. When price is lowered to P_c, at the point where marginal cost intersects average revenue, output increases to its maximum Q_c. This is the output that would be produced by a competitive industry. Lowering price further, to P_3, reduces output to Q_3 and causes a shortage, $Q_3' - Q_3$.

The firm's new marginal revenue curve corresponds to its new average revenue curve, and is shown by the dark line in the figure. For output levels up to Q_1, marginal revenue equals average revenue. For output levels greater than Q_1, the new marginal revenue curve is identical to the original curve. The firm will produce quantity Q_1 because that is where its marginal revenue curve intersects its marginal cost curve. You can verify that at price P_1 and quantity Q_1 the deadweight loss from monopoly power is reduced.

As the price is lowered further, the quantity produced continues to increase and the deadweight loss to decline. At price P_c, where average revenue and marginal cost intersect, the quantity produced has increased to the competitive level, and the deadweight loss from monopoly power has been eliminated. Reducing the price even more, say to P_3, results in a *reduction* in quantity. This is equivalent to imposing a price ceiling on a competitive industry. A shortage develops, $(Q_3' - Q_3)$, as well as a deadweight loss from regulation. As the price is lowered further, the quantity produced continues to fall,

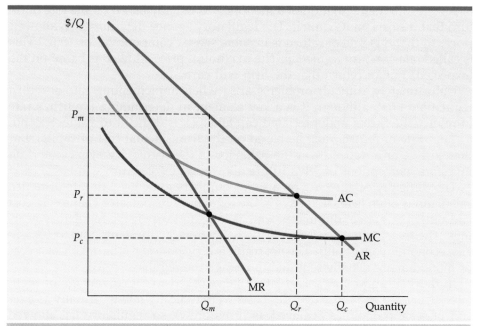

Figure 10.11 **Regulating the Price of a Natural Monopoly** A firm is a natural monopoly because it has economies of scale (declining average and marginal costs) over its entire output range. If price were regulated to be P_c, the firm would lose money and go out of business. Setting the price at P_r yields the largest possible output consistent with the firm's remaining in business; excess profit is zero.

and the shortage grows. Finally, if the price is lowered below P_4, the minimum average cost, the firm loses money and goes out of business.

Price regulation is most often practiced for *natural monopolies*, such as local utility companies. Figure 10.11 illustrates natural monopoly. Note that average cost is declining everywhere, so marginal cost is always below average cost. Unregulated, the firm would produce Q_m at P_m. Ideally, the regulatory agency would like to push the firm's price down to the competitive level P_c, but then the firm could not meet its average cost and would go out of business. The best alternative is therefore to set the price at P_r, where average cost and average revenue intersect. Then the firm earns no monopoly profit, and output is as large as it can be without driving the firm out of business.

Regulation in Practice

Recall that the competitive price (P_c in Figure 10.10) is found where the firm's marginal cost and average revenue (demand) curves intersect. Likewise, for a natural monopoly, the minimum feasible price (P_r in Figure 10.11) is found where average cost and demand intersect. Unfortunately, it is often difficult to determine these prices accurately in practice because the firm's demand and cost curves may shift as market conditions evolve.

As a result, the regulation of a monopoly is usually based on the rate of return that it earns on its capital. The regulatory agency determines an allowed price, so that this rate of return is in some sense "competitive" or "fair." This is called *rate-of-return regulation:* The maximum price allowed is based on the (expected) rate of return that the firm will earn.[13]

Unfortunately, difficult problems arise when implementing rate-of-return regulation. First, although it is a key element in determining the firm's rate of return, the firm's undepreciated capital stock is difficult to value. Second, a "fair" rate of return must be based on the firm's actual cost of capital, but that cost in turn depends on the behavior of the regulatory agency (and on investors' perceptions of what future allowed rates of return will be).

The difficulty of agreeing on a set of numbers to be used in rate-of-return calculations often leads to delays in the regulatory response to changes in cost and other market conditions, as well as long and expensive regulatory hearings. The major beneficiaries are usually lawyers, accountants, and, occasionally, economic consultants. The net result is *regulatory lag*—the delays of a year or more that are usually required to change the regulated price.

In the 1950s and 1960s, regulatory lag worked to the advantage of regulated firms. During those decades costs were typically falling (usually as a result of scale economies achieved as firms grew), so regulatory lag allowed these firms, at least for a while, to enjoy actual rates of return greater than those ultimately deemed "fair" at the end of regulatory proceedings. Beginning in the 1970s, however, the situation changed, and regulatory lag worked to the detriment of regulated firms. For example, when oil prices rose sharply, electric utilities needed to raise their prices. Regulatory lag caused many of them to earn rates of return well below the "fair" rates they had been earning earlier.

10.5 Monopsony

So far our discussion of market power has focused entirely on the seller side of the market. Now we turn to the *buyer* side. We will see that if there are not too many buyers, they can also have market power and use it profitably to affect the price they pay for a product.

First, a few terms. *Monopsony* refers to a market in which there is a single buyer. An *oligopsony* is a market with only a few buyers. With one or only a few buyers, some buyers may have *monopsony power*—a buyer's ability to affect the price of a good. Monopsony power enables the buyer to purchase the good for less than the price that would prevail in a competitive market.

Suppose you are trying to decide how much of a good to purchase. You could apply the basic marginal principle—keep purchasing units of the good

---

[13] Regulatory agencies typically use a formula like the following to determine price:

$$P = AVC + (D + T + sK)/Q$$

where AVC is average variable cost, Q is output, s is the allowed "fair" rate of return, D is depreciation, T is taxes, and K is the firm's current capital stock.

until the last unit purchased gives additional value, or utility, just equal to the cost of that last unit. In other words, on the margin, additional benefit should just be offset by additional cost.

Recall from Chapter 4 that a person's demand curve measures marginal value, or marginal utility, as a function of the quantity purchased. Therefore, your *marginal value* schedule is your *demand* curve for the good. But your marginal cost of buying additional units of the good depends on whether you are a competitive buyer or a buyer with monopsony power.

Suppose you are a competitive buyer, which means that you have no influence over the price of the good. Then the cost of each unit you buy is the same, no matter how many units you purchase—it is the market price of the good. Figure 10.12(a) illustrates this. In that figure the price you pay per unit is your *average expenditure* per unit, and it is the same for all units. But what is your *marginal expenditure* per unit? As a competitive buyer, your marginal expenditure is equal to your average expenditure, which in turn is equal to the market price of the good.

Figure 10.12(a) also shows your marginal value schedule (i.e., your demand curve). How much of the good should you buy? You should buy until the marginal value of the last unit is just equal to the marginal expenditure on that unit. So you should purchase quantity Q^* at the intersection of the marginal expenditure and demand curves.

Figure 10.12   Competitive Buyer Compared to Competitive Seller   The competitive buyer (a) takes market price P^* as given. Therefore, marginal expenditure and average expenditure are constant and equal, and the quantity purchased is found by equating price to marginal value (demand). The competitive seller (b) also takes price as given. Marginal revenue and average revenue are constant and equal, and quantity sold is found by equating price to marginal cost.

We introduced the concepts of marginal and average expenditure because they will make it easier to understand what happens when buyers have monopsony power. But before considering that situation, let's look at the analogy between competitive buyer conditions and competitive seller conditions. Figure 10.12(b) shows how a perfectly competitive seller decides how much to produce and sell. Since the seller takes the market price as given, both average and marginal revenue are equal to the price. The profit-maximizing quantity is at the intersection of the marginal revenue and marginal cost curves.

Now suppose that you are the *only* buyer of the good. You again face a market supply curve, which tells you how much producers are willing to sell as a function of the price you pay. Should the quantity you purchase be at the point where your marginal value curve intersects the market supply curve? No. If you want to maximize your net benefit from purchasing the good, you should purchase a smaller quantity, which you will obtain at a lower price.

To determine how much to buy, set the marginal value from the last unit purchased equal to the marginal expenditure on that unit.[14] But note that the market supply curve is not the marginal expenditure curve. The market supply curve shows how much you must pay *per unit*, as a function of the total number of units you buy. In other words, the supply curve is the *average expenditure* curve. And since this average expenditure curve is upward sloping, the marginal expenditure curve must lie above it because the decision to buy an extra unit raises the price that must be paid for *all* units, not just the extra one.[15]

Figure 10.13 illustrates this. The optimal quantity for the monopsonist to buy, Q_m^*, is found at the intersection of the demand and marginal expenditure curves. And the price that the monopsonist pays is found from the supply curve; it is the price P_m^* that brings forth the supply Q_m^*. Finally, note that this quantity Q_m^* is less, and the price P_m^* is lower, than the quantity and price that would prevail in a competitive market, Q_c and P_c.

Monopsony and Monopoly Compared

Monopsony is easier to understand if you compare it with monopoly. Figures 10.14(a) and 10.14(b) illustrate this comparison. Recall that a monopolist can charge a price above marginal cost because it faces a downward-sloping demand, or average revenue curve, so that marginal revenue is less than average revenue. Equating marginal cost with marginal revenue leads to a quan-

---

[14] Mathematically, we can write the net benefit NB from the purchase as $NB = V - E$, where V is the value to the buyer of the purchase, and E is the expenditure. Net benefit is maximized when $\Delta NB/\Delta Q = 0$. Then

$$\Delta NB/\Delta Q = \Delta V/\Delta Q - \Delta E/\Delta Q = MV - ME = 0$$

so that $MV = ME$.

[15] To obtain the marginal expenditure curve algebraically, write the supply curve with price on the left-hand side: $P = P(Q)$. Then total expenditure E is price times quantity, or $E = P(Q)Q$, and marginal expenditure is

$$ME = \Delta E/\Delta Q = P(Q) + Q(\Delta P/\Delta Q)$$

The supply curve is upward sloping, so $\Delta P/\Delta Q$ is positive, and marginal expenditure is greater than average expenditure.

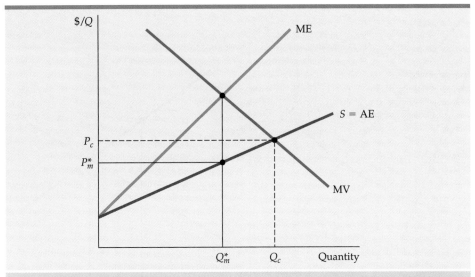

Figure 10.13 Monopsonist Buyer   The market supply curve is the monopsonist's average expenditure curve AE. Average expenditure is rising, so marginal expenditure lies above it. The monopsonist purchases quantity Q_m^* where marginal expenditure and marginal value (demand) intersect. The price paid per unit P_m^* is then found from the average expenditure (supply) curve. In a competitive market, price and quantity, P_c and Q_c, are both higher. They are found at the point where average expenditure (supply) and marginal value (demand) intersect.

tity Q^* that is less than what would be produced in a competitive market, and a price P^* that is higher than the competitive price P_c.

The monopsony situation is exactly analogous. As Figure 10.14(b) illustrates, the monopsonist can purchase a good *at a price below its marginal value* because the supply, or average expenditure curve, it faces is upward sloping, so that marginal expenditure is greater than average expenditure. Equating marginal value with marginal expenditure leads to a quantity Q^* that is less than what would be bought in a competitive market, and a price P^* that is lower than the competitive price P_c.

10.6 Monopsony Power

Much more common than pure monopsony are markets with only a few firms competing among themselves as buyers, so that each firm has some monopsony power. For example, the major U.S. automobile manufacturers compete with one another as buyers of tires. Because each of them accounts for a large share of the tire market, each has some monopsony power in that market. General Motors, the largest, might be able to exert considerable monopsony power when contracting for supplies of tires (and other automotive parts).

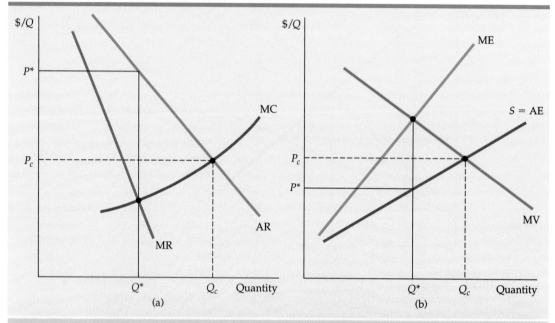

Figure 10.14 **Monopoly and Monopsony** These diagrams show the close analogy between monopoly and monopsony. (a) The monopolist produces where marginal revenue intersects marginal cost. Average revenue exceeds marginal revenue, so that price exceeds marginal cost. (b) The monopsonist purchases up to the point where marginal expenditure intersects marginal value. Marginal expenditure exceeds average expenditure, so that marginal value exceeds price.

In a competitive market, price and marginal value are equal, but a buyer with monopsony power can purchase the good at a price below marginal value. The extent to which price is marked down below marginal value depends on the elasticity of supply facing the buyer.[16] If supply is very elastic (E_s is large), the markdown will be small, and the buyer has little monopsony power. If supply is very inelastic, the markdown will be large, and the buyer has considerable monopsony power. Figures 10.15(a) and 10.15(b) illustrate this.

Sources of Monopsony Power

What determines the degree of monopsony power in a market? Again, we can draw analogies with monopoly and monopoly power. We saw that monopoly power depends on three things: the elasticity of market demand, the number of sellers in the market, and how those sellers interact. Monopsony power depends on three similar things: the elasticity of market supply, the number of buyers in the market, and how those buyers interact.

---

[16] The exact relationship (analogous to equation (10.1)) is given by $(MV - P)/P = 1/E_S$. This follows because $MV = ME$ and $ME = \Delta(PQ)/\Delta Q = P + Q(\Delta P/\Delta Q)$.

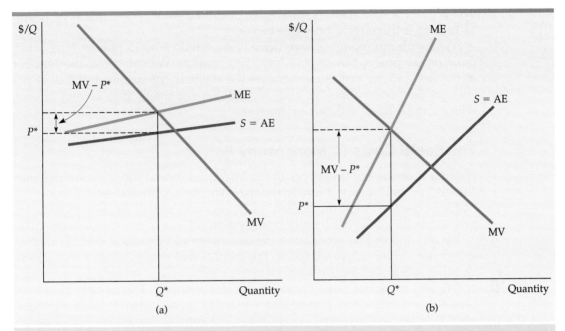

Figure 10.15   Elastic Versus Inelastic Supply, and Monopsony Power   Monopsony power depends on the elasticity of supply. When supply is elastic, as in (a), marginal expenditure and average expenditure do not differ by much, so price is close to what it would be in a competitive market. The opposite is true when supply is inelastic, as in (b).

First consider the *elasticity of market supply*. A monopsonist benefits because it faces an upward-sloping supply curve, so that marginal expenditure exceeds average expenditure. The less elastic the supply curve, the greater is the difference between marginal expenditure and average expenditure, and the more monopsony power the buyer has. If only one buyer is in the market— a pure monopsonist—its monopsony power is completely determined by the elasticity of market supply. If supply is highly elastic, monopsony power is small, and there is little gain in being the only buyer.

Most markets have more than one buyer, and the *number of buyers* is an important determinant of monopsony power. When the number of buyers is very large, no single buyer can have much influence over price. Thus each buyer faces an extremely elastic supply curve, and the market is almost completely competitive. The potential for monopsony power arises when the number of buyers is limited.

Finally, monopsony power is determined by the *interaction among buyers*. Suppose three or four buyers are in the market. If those buyers compete aggressively, they will bid up the price close to their marginal value of the product, and thus they will have little monopsony power. On the other hand, if those buyers compete less aggressively, or even collude, prices will not be bid up very much, and the buyers' degree of monopsony power might be nearly as high as if there were only one buyer.

So as with monopoly power, there is no simple way to predict how much monopsony power buyers will have in a market. We can count the number of buyers, and we can often estimate the elasticity of supply, but that is not enough. Monopsony power also depends on the interaction among buyers, which can be more difficult to ascertain.

The Social Costs of Monopsony Power

Because monopsony power results in lower prices and lower quantities purchased, we would expect it to make the buyer better off and sellers worse off. But suppose we value the welfare of buyers and sellers equally. How is aggregate welfare affected by monopsony power?

We can find out by comparing the consumer and producer surplus that results from a competitive market to the surplus that results when a monopsonist is the sole buyer. Figure 10.16 shows the average and marginal expenditure curves and marginal value curve for the monopsonist. The monopsonist's net benefit is maximized by purchasing a quantity Q_m at a price P_m such that marginal value equals marginal expenditure. In a competitive market, price equals marginal value, so the competitive price and quantity, P_c and Q_c, are found where the average expenditure and marginal value curves intersect. Now let's

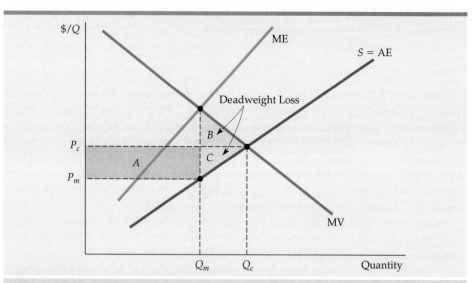

Figure 10.16   Deadweight Loss from Monopsony Power   The shaded rectangle and triangles show changes in consumer and producer surplus when moving from competitive price and quantity, P_c and Q_c, to monopsonist's price and quantity, P_m and Q_m. Because both price and quantity are lower, there is an increase in buyer (consumer) surplus given by $A - B$. Producer surplus falls by $A + C$, so there is a deadweight loss given by triangles B and C.

see how surplus changes if we move from the competitive price and quantity, P_c and Q_c, to the monopsony price and quantity, P_m and Q_m.

With monopsony, the price is lower, and less is sold. Because of the lower price, sellers lose an amount of surplus given by rectangle A. In addition, sellers lose the surplus given by triangle C because of the reduced sales. The total loss of producer (seller) surplus is therefore $A + C$. The buyer gains the surplus given by rectangle A by buying at a lower price. However, the buyer buys less, Q_m instead of Q_c, and so loses the surplus given by triangle B. The total gain in surplus to the buyer is therefore $A - B$. Altogether, there is a net loss of surplus given by $B + C$. This is the *deadweight loss from monopsony power*. Even if the monopsonist's gains were taxed away and redistributed to the producers, there would be an inefficiency because output would be lower than under competition. The deadweight loss is the social cost of this inefficiency.

Bilateral Monopoly

What happens when a monopolist meets a monopsonist? It's hard to say. We call a market with only one seller and only one buyer a *bilateral monopoly*. If you think about such a market, you'll see why it is difficult to predict what the price and quantity will be. Both the buyer and the seller are in a *bargaining situation*. Unfortunately, no simple rule determines which, if either, will get the better part of the bargain. One party might have more time and patience, or might be able to convince the other party that it will walk away if the price is too low or too high.

Bilateral monopoly is rare. Markets in which a few producers have some monopoly power and sell to a few buyers who have some monopsony power are more common. Although bargaining may still be involved, we can apply a rough principle here: Monopsony power and monopoly power will tend to counteract each other. In other words, the monopsony power of buyers will reduce the effective monopoly power of sellers, and vice versa. This does not mean that the market will end up looking perfectly competitive; monopoly power might be large, for example, and monopsony power small, so that the residual monopoly power would still be significant. But in general, monopsony power will push price closer to marginal cost, and monopoly power will push price closer to marginal value.

E X A M P L E   10.3   Monopsony Power in U.S. Manufacturing

Monopoly power, as measured by the price-cost margin $(P - \mathrm{MC})/P$, varies considerably across manufacturing industries in the United States. Some industries have price-cost margins close to zero, while in other industries the price-cost margins are as high as 0.4 or 0.5. These variations are due in part to differences in the determinants of monopoly power—in some industries market demand is more elastic than in others; some industries have more sellers than others; and in some industries sellers compete more aggressively than in others. But something else can help explain these variations in monopoly power—differences in monopsony power among the firms' customers.

The role of monopsony power was investigated in a statistical study of 327 U.S. manufacturing industries.[17] The study sought to determine the extent to which variations in price-cost margins could be attributed to variations in monopsony power by buyers in each industry. Although the degree of buyers' monopsony power could not be measured directly, data were available for variables that help determine monopsony power, such as buyer concentration (the fraction of total sales going to the three or four largest firms) and the average annual size of orders by buyers.

The study found that buyers' monopsony power had an important effect on the price-cost margins of sellers and could significantly reduce any monopoly power that sellers might otherwise have. Take, for example, the concentration of buyers, an important determinant of monopsony power. In industries where only four or five buyers account for all or nearly all sales, the price-cost margins of sellers would on average be as much as 10 percentage points lower than in comparable industries where hundreds of buyers account for the sales.

A good example of monopsony power in manufacturing is the market for automobile parts and components, such as brakes and radiators. There are only three major car producers in the United States. Each typically buys an individual part from at least three, and often as many as a dozen, suppliers. In addition, for a standardized product, such as brakes, each automobile company usually produces part of its needs itself, so that it is not totally reliant on outside firms. This puts GM, Ford, and Chrysler in an excellent bargaining position with respect to their suppliers. Each supplier must compete for sales against five or ten other suppliers, but each can sell to at most three buyers. (For a specialized part, a single auto company may be the *only* buyer.) As a result, the automobile companies have considerable monopsony power.

This monopsony power becomes evident from the conditions under which suppliers must operate. To obtain a sales contract, a supplier must have a track record of reliability, in terms of both the quality of its products and its ability to meet tight delivery schedules. Suppliers are also often required to respond to changes in volume, as auto sales and hence production levels fluctuate. Finally, pricing negotiations are notoriously difficult; a potential supplier will sometimes lose a contract because its bid is a penny per item higher than those of its competitors. Not surprisingly, producers of parts and components usually have little or no monopoly power.[18]

---

17 The study was by Steven H. Lustgarten, "The Impact of Buyer Concentration in Manufacturing Industries," *Review of Economics and Statistics* 57 (May 1975): 125–132.

18 For a detailed discussion of the market for automobile components, see Michael E. Porter, "Note on Supplying the Automobile Industry," Harvard Business School Case No. 9-378-219, July 1981.

10.7 Limiting Market Power: The Antitrust Laws

We have seen that market power—whether of sellers or buyers—harms potential purchasers who could have bought at competitive prices, and this leads to a deadweight loss. Excessive market power also raises problems of equity and fairness; if a firm has significant monopoly power, it will profit at the expense of consumers. In theory, the firm's excess profits could be taxed away and redistributed to the buyers of its products, but such a redistribution is often impractical. It is difficult to determine what portion of a firm's profit is attributable to monopoly power, and it is even more difficult to locate all the buyers and reimburse them in proportion to their purchases. So in addition to the deadweight loss, excessive market power can lead to a socially objectionable transfer of money.

How, then, can society prevent market power from becoming excessive? For a natural monopoly, such as an electric utility company, direct price regulation is the answer. But more generally, the answer is to prevent firms from acquiring excessive market power in the first place. In the United States, this is done via the antitrust laws.

The primary objective of the antitrust laws is to promote a competitive economy by prohibiting actions that restrain, or are likely to restrain, competition, and by restricting the forms of market structure that are allowable.

Monopoly power can arise in a number of ways, each of which is covered by the antitrust laws. Section 1 of the Sherman Act (which was passed in 1890) prohibits contracts, combinations, or conspiracies in restraint of trade. One obvious example of an illegal combination is an explicit agreement among producers to restrict their outputs and/or "fix" price above the competitive level. There have been numerous instances of such illegal combinations.[19] However, *implicit* collusion in the form of *parallel conduct* (the legal term is *conscious parallelism*) can also be construed as violating the law. Firm *A* and Firm *B* need not meet or talk on the telephone to violate the Sherman Act. If Firm *B* consistently follows Firm *A*'s pricing (parallel pricing), and if the firms' conduct is contrary to what one would expect companies to do in the absence of collusion (such as raising prices in the face of decreased demand and oversupply), an implicit understanding may be inferred.[20]

Section 2 of the Sherman Act makes it illegal to monopolize or to attempt to monopolize a market and prohibits conspiracies that result in monopo-

---

[19] For example, in 1983 six companies and six executives were indicted for conspiring to fix the price of copper tubing over a six-year period. In 1993, the four major producers of carbon dioxide were charged with price fixing, and in 1996, three major producers of lysine (an animal feed additive) pleaded guilty to criminal charges of price fixing.

[20] The Sherman Act applies to all firms that do business in the United States (to the extent that a conspiracy to restrain trade could affect U.S. markets). However, foreign governments (or firms operating under their government's control) are not subject to the act, so OPEC need not fear the wrath of the Justice Department. Also, firms *can* collude with respect to *exports*. The *Webb-Pomerene Act* (1918) allows price fixing and related collusion with respect to export markets, *as long as domestic markets are unaffected by such collusion*. Firms operating in this manner must form a "Webb-Pomerene Association" and register it with the government.

lization. The Clayton Act (1914) did much to pinpoint the kinds of practices that are likely to be anticompetitive. For example, the Clayton Act makes it unlawful for a firm with a large market share to require the buyer or lessor of a good not to buy from a competitor. And it makes it illegal to engage in *predatory pricing*—pricing designed to drive current competitors out of business and to discourage new entrants (so that the predatory firm can enjoy higher prices in the future).

Monopoly power can also be achieved by a merger of firms into a larger and more dominant firm, or by one firm acquiring or taking control of another firm by purchasing its stock. The Clayton Act prohibits mergers and acquisitions if they "substantially lessen competition" or "tend to create a monopoly."

The antitrust laws also limit possible anticompetitive conduct by firms in other ways as well. For example, the Clayton Act, as amended by the Robinson-Patman Act (1936), makes it illegal to discriminate by charging buyers of essentially the same product different prices if those price differences are likely to injure competition. Even then, firms are not liable if they can show that the price differences were necessary to meet competition. (As we will see in the next chapter, price discrimination is a common practice. It becomes the target of antitrust action when buyers suffer economic damages and competition is reduced.)

Another important component of the antitrust laws is the *Federal Trade Commission Act* (1914, amended in 1938, 1973, 1975), which created the Federal Trade Commission (FTC). This act supplements the Sherman and Clayton acts by fostering competition through a whole set of prohibitions against unfair and anticompetitive practices, such as deceptive advertising and labeling, agreements with retailers to exclude competing brands, and so on. Because these prohibitions are interpreted and enforced in administrative proceedings before the FTC, the act provides powers that are very broad and reach further than other antitrust laws.

The antitrust laws are actually phrased vaguely in terms of what is and what is not allowed. The laws are intended to provide a general statutory framework to give the Justice Department, the FTC, and the courts wide discretion in interpreting and applying them. This is important because it is difficult to know in advance what might be an impediment to competition, and this ambiguity creates a need for common law (i.e., courts interpreting statutes) and supplemental provisions and rulings (e.g., by the FTC and the Justice Department).

Enforcement of the Antitrust Laws

The antitrust laws are enforced in three ways. The first is through the Antitrust Division of the Department of Justice. As an arm of the executive branch, its enforcement policies closely reflect the view of whatever administration is in power. As the result of an external complaint or an internal study, the department can decide to institute a criminal proceeding, bring a civil suit, or both. The result of a criminal action can be fines for the corporation and fines or jail sentences for individuals. For example, individuals who conspire to fix prices or rig bids can be charged with a *felony*, and if found guilty may be sentenced to jail—something to remember if you are planning to parlay your knowledge of microeconomics into a successful business career! Losing a civil action forces a corporation to cease its anticompetitive practices and often to pay damages.[21]

The second means of enforcement is through the administrative procedures of the Federal Trade Commission. Again, action can result from an external complaint or from the FTC's own initiative. Should the FTC decide that action is required, it can either request a voluntary understanding to comply with the law, or it can decide to seek a formal commission order, requiring compliance.

The last and the most common means of enforcement is via *private proceedings*. Individuals or companies can sue for *treble* (*threefold*) *damages* inflicted on their business or property. The possibility of having to pay treble damages can be a strong deterrent to would-be violators of the laws. Individuals or companies can also ask the courts for an injunction to force a wrongdoer to cease anticompetitive actions.

The U.S. antitrust laws are more stringent and far-reaching than those of most other countries. Some people have argued that the laws have prevented American industry from competing effectively in international markets. The laws certainly constrain American business, and they may at times have put American firms at a disadvantage in world markets. But this must be weighed against their benefits. The laws have been crucial for maintaining competition, and competition is essential for economic efficiency, innovation, and growth.

E X A M P L E 10.4	**A Phone Call About Prices**

In 1981 and early 1982, American Airlines and Braniff Airways were competing fiercely with each other for passengers. A fare war broke out as the firms undercut each other's prices to capture market share. On February 21, 1982, Robert Crandall, president and chief executive officer of American Airlines, made a phone call to Howard Putnam, president and chief executive of Braniff Airways. To Mr. Crandall's later surprise, the call had been taped. It went like this:[22]

---

[21] Most antitrust cases that are filed are either dropped or settled before trial; only a few go through the complete trial process. In 1969, for example, the U.S. Supreme Court upheld a lower court opinion finding the major producers of corrugated containers liable for price fixing in violation of Section 1 of the Sherman Act. The companies had exchanged price information in a manner that was not consistent with the individual self-interest of the firms and that raised prices in the industry. More recently, in 1993, the four major producers of carbon dioxide were charged under civil law with price fixing, having allegedly agreed to restrict competition in the bidding process for carbon dioxide business. The producers settled prior to trial with almost all of the plaintiffs; however, when a small group of purchasers went to trial, the defendants prevailed.

[22] According to the *New York Times*, Feb. 24, 1983.

Mr. Crandall: I think it's dumb as hell for Christ's sake, all right, to sit here and pound the @!#$%&! out of each other and neither one of us making a @!#$%&! dime.

Mr. Putnam: Well . . .

Mr. Crandall: I mean, you know, @!#$%&!, what the hell is the point of it?

Mr. Putnam: But if you're going to overlay every route of American's on top of every route that Braniff has—I just can't sit here and allow you to bury us without giving our best effort.

Mr. Crandall: Oh sure, but Eastern and Delta do the same thing in Atlanta and have for years.

Mr. Putnam: Do you have a suggestion for me?

Mr. Crandall: Yes, I have a suggestion for you. Raise your @!#$%&! fares 20 percent. I'll raise mine the next morning.

Mr. Putnam: Robert, we . . .

Mr. Crandall: You'll make more money and I will, too.

Mr. Putnam: We can't talk about pricing!

Mr. Crandall: Oh @!#$%&!, Howard. We can talk about any @!#$%&! thing we want to talk about.

Mr. Crandall was wrong. Corporate executives cannot talk about anything they want. Talking about prices and agreeing to fix them is a clear violation of Section 1 of the Sherman Act. Mr. Putnam must have known this because he promptly rejected Mr. Crandall's suggestion. After learning about the call, the Justice Department filed a suit accusing Mr. Crandall of violating the antitrust laws by proposing to fix prices.

Proposing to fix prices is not enough to violate Section 1 of the Sherman Act. The two parties must *agree* to collude for the law to be violated. Therefore, because Mr. Putnam had rejected Mr. Crandall's proposal, Section 1 had not been violated. The court later ruled, however, that a proposal to fix prices could be an attempt to monopolize part of the airline industry, and if so would violate Section 2 of the Sherman Act. American Airlines promised the Justice Department never again to engage in such activity.

Summary

1. Market power is the ability of sellers or buyers to affect the price of a good.

2. Market power comes in two forms. When sellers charge a price that is above marginal cost, we say that they have monopoly power, and we measure the amount of monopoly power by the extent to which price exceeds marginal cost. When buyers can obtain a price that is below their marginal value of the good, we say they have monopsony power, and we measure the amount of monopsony power by the extent to which marginal value exceeds price.

3. Monopoly power is determined in part by the number of firms competing in the market. If there is only one firm—a pure monopoly—monopoly power depends entirely on the elasticity of market demand. The less elastic

demand is, the more monopoly power the firm will have. When there are several firms, monopoly power also depends on how the firms interact. The more aggressively they compete, the less monopoly power each firm will have.

4. Monopsony power is determined in part by the number of buyers in the market. If there is only one buyer—a pure monopsony— monopsony power depends on the elasticity of market supply. The less elastic supply is, the more monopsony power the buyer will have. When there are several buyers, monopsony power also depends on how aggressively the buyers compete for supplies.

5. Market power can impose costs on society. Monopoly and monopsony power both cause production to be below the competitive level, so that there is a deadweight loss of consumer and producer surplus.

6. Sometimes, scale economies make pure monopoly desirable. But the government will still want to regulate price to maximize social welfare.

7. More generally, we rely on the antitrust laws to prevent firms from obtaining excessive market power.

Questions for Review

1. A monopolist is producing at a point where its marginal cost exceeds its marginal revenue. How should it adjust its output level to increase its profit?

2. We write the percentage markup of prices over marginal cost as $(P - MC)/P$. For a profit-maximizing monopolist, how does this markup depend on the elasticity of demand? Why can this markup be viewed as a measure of monopoly power?

3. Why is there no market supply curve under monopoly?

4. Why might a firm have monopoly power even if it is not the only producer in the market?

5. What are some of the sources of monopoly power? Give an example of each.

6. What factors determine how much monopoly power an individual firm is likely to have? Explain each one briefly.

7. Why is there a social cost to monopoly power? If the gains to producers from monopoly power could be redistributed to consumers, would the social cost of monopoly power be eliminated? Explain briefly.

8. Why will a monopolist's output increase if the government forces it to lower its price? If the government wants to set a price ceiling that maximizes the monopolist's output, what price should it set?

9. How should a monopsonist decide how much of a product to buy? Will it buy more or less than a competitive buyer? Explain briefly.

10. What is meant by the term "monopsony power"? Why might a firm have monopsony power even if it is not the only buyer in the market?

11. What are some sources of monopsony power? What determines how much monopsony power an individual firm is likely to have?

12. Why is there a social cost to monopsony power? If the gains to buyers from monopsony power could be redistributed to sellers, would the social cost of monopsony power be eliminated? Explain briefly.

13. How do the antitrust laws limit market power in the United States? Give examples of the major provisions of the laws.

14. Explain briefly how the U.S. antitrust laws are actually enforced.

Exercises

1. Will an increase in the demand for a monopolist's product always result in a higher price? Explain. Will an increase in the supply facing a monopsonist buyer always result in a lower price? Explain.

2. Caterpillar Tractor, one of the largest producers of farm tractors in the world, has hired you to advise them on their pricing policy. One of the things the company would like to know is how much a 5 percent increase in price is likely to reduce sales. What would you need to know to help the company with their problem? Explain why these facts are important.

3. A monopolist firm faces a demand with constant elasticity of −2.0. The firm has a marginal cost of $20 per unit and sets a price to maximize profit. If marginal cost should increase by 25 percent, would the price charged also rise by 25 percent?

4. A firm faces the following average revenue (demand) curve:

$$P = 100 - 0.01Q$$

where Q is weekly production and P is price, measured in cents per unit. The firm's cost function is given by $C = 50Q + 30,000$. Assume that the firm maximizes profits.
   a. What is the level of production, price, and total profit per week?
   b. The government decides to levy a tax of 10 cents per unit on this product. What will the new level of production, price, and profit be as a result?

5. The table below shows the demand curve facing a monopolist who produces at a constant marginal cost of $10:

Price	Quantity
27	0
24	2
21	4
18	6
15	8
12	10
9	12
6	14
3	16
0	18

   a. Calculate the firm's marginal revenue curve.
   b. What are the firm's profit-maximizing output and price? What is the firm's profit?
   c. What would the equilibrium price and quantity be in a competitive industry?
   d. What would the social gain be if this monopolist were forced to produce and price at the competitive equilibrium? Who would gain and lose as a result?

6. A firm has two factories, for which costs are given by:

$$\text{Factory \#1: } C_1(Q_1) = 10Q_1^2$$

$$\text{Factory \#2: } C_2(Q_2) = 20Q_2^2$$

The firm faces the following demand curve:

$$P = 700 - 5Q$$

where Q is total output—i.e., $Q = Q_1 + Q_2$.
   a. On a diagram, draw the marginal cost curves for the two factories, the average and marginal revenue curves, and the total marginal cost curve (i.e., the marginal cost of producing $Q = Q_1 + Q_2$). Indicate the profit-maximizing output for each factory, total output, and price.
   b. Calculate the values of Q_1, Q_2, Q, and P that maximize profit.
   c. Suppose labor costs increase in Factory 1 but not in Factory 2. How should the firm

adjust (i.e., raise, lower, or leave un-changed): Output in Factory 1? Output in Factory 2? Total output? Price?

7. A drug company has a monopoly on a new patented medicine. The product can be made in either of two plants. The costs of production for the two plants are $MC_1 = 20 + 2Q_1$, and $MC_2 = 10 + 5Q_2$. The firm's estimate of the demand for the product is $P = 20 - 3(Q_1 + Q_2)$. How much should the firm plan to produce in each plant, and at what price should it plan to sell the product?

8. One of the more important antitrust cases of this century involved the Aluminum Company of America (Alcoa) in 1945. At that time, Alcoa controlled about 90 percent of primary aluminum production in the United States, and the company had been accused of monopolizing the aluminum market. In its defense, Alcoa argued that although it indeed controlled a large fraction of the primary market, secondary aluminum (i.e., aluminum produced from the recycling of scrap) accounted for roughly 30 percent of the total supply of aluminum, and many competitive firms were engaged in recycling. Therefore, Alcoa argued, it did not have much monopoly power.
   a. Provide a clear argument *in favor* of Alcoa's position.
   b. Provide a clear argument *against* Alcoa's position.
   c. The 1945 decision by Judge Learned Hand has been called "one of the most celebrated judicial opinions of our time." Do you know what Judge Hand's ruling was?

9. A monopolist faces the demand curve $P = 11 - Q$, where P is measured in dollars per unit and Q in thousands of units. The monopolist has a constant average cost of $6 per unit.
   a. Draw the average and marginal revenue curves, and the average and marginal cost curves. What are the monopolist's profit-maximizing price and quantity, and what is the resulting profit? Calculate the firm's degree of monopoly power using the Lerner index.
   b. A government regulatory agency sets a price ceiling of $7 per unit. What quantity will be produced, and what will the firm's profit be? What happens to the degree of monopoly power?
   c. What price ceiling yields the largest level of output? What is that level of output? What is the firm's degree of monopoly power at this price?

10. Michelle's Monopoly Mutant Turtles (MMMT) has the exclusive right to sell Mutant Turtle t-shirts in the United States. The demand for these t-shirts is $Q = 10,000/P^2$. The firm's short-run cost is $SRTC = 2000 + 5Q$, and its long-run cost is $LRTC = 6Q$.
   a. What price should MMMT charge to maximize profit in the short run? What quantity does it sell, and how much profit does it make? Would it be better off shutting down in the short run?
   b. What price should MMMT charge in the long run? What quantity does it sell and how much profit does it make? Would it be better off shutting down in the long run?
   c. Can we expect MMMT to have lower marginal cost in the short run than in the long run? Explain why.

*11. You produce widgets that are being sold in a perfectly competitive market at a market price of $10 per widget. The widgets are manufactured in two plants, one in Massachusetts and the other in Connecticut. Because of labor problems in Connecticut, you are forced to raise wages in that plant, so that marginal costs in that plant increase. In response to this, should you shift production and produce more in your Massachusetts plant?

12. The employment of teaching assistants (TAs) by major universities can be characterized as a monopsony. Suppose the demand for TAs is $W = 30,000 - 125n$, where W is the wage (as an annual salary), and n is the number of TAs hired. The supply of TAs is given by $W = 1000 + 75n$.
   a. If the university takes advantage of its monopsonist position, how many TAs will it hire? What wage will it pay?

b. If, instead, the university faced an infinite supply of TAs at the annual wage level of $10,000, how many TAs would it hire?

*13. Dayna's Doorstops, Inc. (DD), is a monopolist in the doorstop industry. Its cost is $C = 100 - 5Q + Q^2$, and demand is $P = 55 - 2Q$.

a. What price should DD set to maximize profit, and what output does the firm produce? How much profit and consumer surplus does DD generate?

b. What would output be if DD acted like a perfect competitor and set $MC = P$? What profit and consumer surplus would then be generated?

c. What is the deadweight loss from monopoly power in part (a)?

d. Suppose the government, concerned about the high price of doorstops, sets a maximum price for doorstops at $27. How does this affect price, quantity, consumer surplus, and DD's profit? What is the resulting deadweight loss?

e. Now suppose the government sets the maximum price at $23. How does this affect price, quantity, consumer surplus, DD's profit, and deadweight loss?

f. Finally, consider a maximum price of $12. What will this do to quantity, consumer surplus, profit, and deadweight loss?

*14. There are 10 households in Lake Wobegon, Minnesota, each with a demand for electricity of $Q = 50 - P$. Lake Wobegon Electric's (LWE) cost of producing electricity is $TC = 500 + Q$.

a. If the regulators of LWE want to make sure that there is no deadweight loss in this market, what price will they force LWE to charge? What will output be in that case? Calculate consumer surplus and LWE's profit with that price.

b. If the regulators want to make sure that LWE doesn't lose money, what is the lowest price they can impose? Calculate output, consumer surplus, and profit in that case. Is there any deadweight loss?

c. Kristina knows that deadweight loss is something that this small town can do without. She suggests that each household be required to pay a fixed amount just to receive any electricity at all, and then a per-unit charge for electricity. Then LWE can break even while charging the price calculated in part (a). What fixed amount would each household have to pay for Kristina's plan to work? Why are you sure that no household will choose instead to refuse the payment and go without electricity?

15. A monopolist faces the following demand curve:

$$Q = 144/P^2$$

where Q is the quantity demanded and P is price. Its *average variable* cost is

$$AVC = Q^{1/2}$$

and its *fixed cost* is 5.

a. What are its profit-maximizing price and quantity? What is the resulting profit?

b. Suppose the government regulates the price to be no greater than $4 per unit. How much will the monopolist produce, and what will its profit be?

c. Suppose the government wants to set a ceiling price that induces the monopolist to produce the largest possible output. What price will do this?

CHAPTER 11

Pricing with Market Power

As we explained in Chapter 10, market power is quite common. Many industries have only a few producers, so that each producer has some monopoly power. And many firms, as buyers of raw materials, labor, or specialized capital goods, have some monopsony power in the markets for these factor inputs. The problem the managers of these firms face is how to use their market power most effectively. They must decide how to set prices, choose quantities of factor inputs, and determine output in both the short and long run to maximize the firm's profit.

Managers of firms with market power have a harder job than those who manage perfectly competitive firms. A firm that is perfectly competitive in output markets has no influence over market price. As a result, its managers need only worry about the cost side of the firm's operations, choosing output so that price is equal to marginal cost. But the managers of a firm with monopoly power must also worry about the characteristics of demand. Even if they set a single price for the firm's output, they must obtain at least a rough estimate of the elasticity of demand to determine what that price (and corresponding output level) should be. Furthermore, firms can often do much better by using a

375

more complicated pricing strategy—for example, charging different prices to different customers. To design such pricing strategies, managers need ingenuity and even more information about demand.

This chapter explains how firms with market power set prices. We begin with the basic objective of every pricing strategy—capturing consumer surplus and converting it into additional profit for the firm. Then we discuss how this can be done using *price discrimination*. Here different prices are charged to different customers, sometimes for the same product, and sometimes for small variations in the product. Because price discrimination is widely practiced in one form or another, it is important to understand how it works.

Next, we discuss the *two-part tariff*. Here customers must pay in advance for the right to purchase units of the good at a later time (and at additional cost). The classic example of this is an amusement park, where customers pay a fee to enter, and then an additional fee for each ride they go on. Although amusement parks may seem like a rather specialized market, there are many other examples of two-part tariffs: the price of a Gillette razor, which gives the owner the opportunity to purchase Gillette razor blades; the price of a Polaroid camera, which gives the owner the opportunity to purchase Polaroid film; or the monthly subscription cost of a mobile telephone, which gives users the opportunity to make phone calls from their automobiles, paying by the message unit as they do so.

We will also discuss *bundling*. This pricing strategy simply involves tying products together and selling them as a package. For example: a personal computer that comes bundled with several software packages; a one-week vacation in Hawaii in which the airfare, rental car, and hotel are bundled and sold at a single package price; or a luxury car, in which the air conditioning, power windows, and stereo are "standard" features.

Finally, we will examine the use of *advertising* by firms with market power. As we will see, deciding how much money to spend on advertising requires information about demand, and it is closely related to the firm's pricing decision. We will derive a simple rule of thumb for determining the profit-maximizing advertising-to-sales ratio.

11.1 Capturing Consumer Surplus

All the pricing strategies that we will examine have one thing in common— they are ways of capturing consumer surplus and transferring it to the producer. You can see this more clearly in Figure 11.1. Suppose the firm sold all its output at a single price. To maximize profit, it would pick a price P^* and corresponding output Q^* at the intersection of its marginal cost and marginal revenue curves. The firm would then be profitable, but its managers might wonder if they could make it even more profitable.

They know that some customers (in region A of the demand curve) would pay more than P^*. But raising price would mean losing some customers, selling less, and earning smaller profits. Similarly, other potential customers are not buying the firm's product because they will not pay a price as high as P^*.

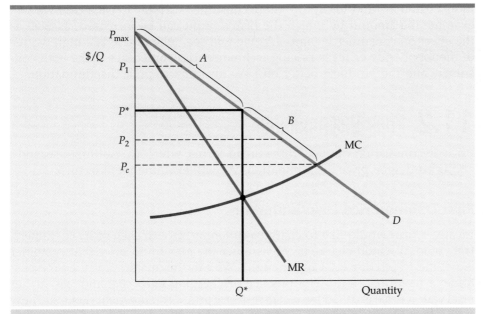

Figure 11.1   Capturing Consumer Surplus   If a firm can charge only one price for all its customers, that price will be P^* and the quantity produced will be Q^*. Ideally, the firm would like to charge a higher price to consumers willing to pay more than P^*, thereby capturing some of the consumer surplus under region A of the demand curve. The firm would also like to sell to consumers willing to pay prices lower than P^* but only if that does not entail lowering the price to other consumers. In that way the firm could also capture some of the surplus under region B of the demand curve.

Many of them, however, would pay prices higher than the firm's marginal cost. (These customers are in region B of the demand curve.) By lowering its price, the firm could sell to some of these customers, but it would then earn less revenue from its existing customers, and again profits would shrink.

How can the firm capture the consumer surplus (or at least part of it) from its customers in region A, and perhaps also sell profitably to some of its potential customers in region B? Charging a single price clearly will not do the trick. However, the firm might charge different prices to different customers, according to where the customers are along the demand curve. For example, some customers in the upper end of region A would be charged the higher price P_1, some in region B would be charged the lower price P_2, and some in between would be charged P^*. This is the basis of *price discrimination*—charging different prices to different customers. The problem, of course, is to identify the different customers, and to get them to pay different prices. We will see how this can be done in the next section.

The other pricing techniques that we will discuss in this chapter—two-part tariffs and bundling—also expand the range of the firm's market to include more customers and to capture more consumer surplus. In each case we will examine the amount by which the firm's profit can be increased, as well as the effect on consumer welfare. (As we will see, when there is a high degree of monopoly power these pricing techniques can sometimes make both consumers and the producer better off.) We turn first to price discrimination.

11.2 Price Discrimination

Price discrimination can take three broad forms, which we call first-, second-, and third-degree price discrimination. We will examine them in turn.

First-Degree Price Discrimination

Ideally, a firm would like to charge a different price to each of its customers. If it could, it would charge each customer the maximum price that customer is willing to pay for each unit bought. We call this maximum price the customer's *reservation price*. The practice of charging each customer his or her reservation price is called perfect *first-degree price discrimination*.[1] Let's see how it affects the firm's profit.

First, we need to know the profit the firm earns when it charges only the single price P^* in Figure 11.2. To find out, we can add the profit on each incremental unit produced and sold, up to the total quantity Q^*. This incremental profit is the marginal revenue less the marginal cost for each unit. In Figure 11.2, this marginal revenue is highest and marginal cost lowest for the first unit. For each additional unit, marginal revenue falls and marginal cost rises, so the firm produces the total output Q^*, where marginal revenue and marginal cost are equal. Total variable profit is simply the sum of the profits on each incremental unit produced, and therefore it is given by the yellow shaded area in Figure 11.2, between the marginal revenue and marginal cost curves.[2] Consumer surplus, which is the area between the average revenue curve and the price P^* that customers pay, is outlined as a black triangle.

Now, what happens if the firm can perfectly price discriminate? Since each consumer is charged exactly what he or she is willing to pay, the marginal revenue curve is no longer relevant to the firm's output decision. Instead, the incremental revenue earned from each additional unit sold is simply the price paid for that unit, and is therefore given by the demand curve.

Since price discrimination does not affect the firm's cost structure, the cost of each additional unit is again given by the firm's marginal cost curve. Therefore, *the profit from producing and selling each incremental unit is now the difference between demand and marginal cost.* As long as demand exceeds mar-

---

[1] We are assuming that each customer buys one unit of the good. If a customer bought more than one unit, the firm would have to charge different prices for each of the units.

[2] Recall that total profit π is the difference between total revenue R and total cost C, so incremental profit is just $\Delta\pi = \Delta R - \Delta C = MR - MC$. Total variable profit is found by summing all the $\Delta\pi$s, and thus it is the area between the MR and MC curves. This ignores fixed costs, which are independent of the firm's output and pricing decisions.

Figure 11.2   Additional Profit from Perfect First-Degree Price Discrimination
The firm charges each consumer his or her reservation price, so it is profitable to expand output to Q^{**}. When only a single price, P^* is charged, the firm's variable profit is the area between the marginal revenue and marginal cost curves. With perfect price discrimination, this profit expands to the area between the demand curve and the marginal cost curve.

ginal cost, the firm can increase its profit by expanding production, and it will do so until it produces a total output Q^{**}. At Q^{**} demand is equal to marginal cost, and producing more reduces profit.

Total profit is now given by the area between the demand and marginal cost curves.[3] Note from Figure 11.2 that total profit is now much larger. (The additional profit resulting from price discrimination is shown by the purple shaded area.) Note also that because every customer is being charged the maximum amount that he or she is willing to pay, all consumer surplus has been captured by the firm.

In practice, perfect first-degree price discrimination is almost never possible. First, it is usually impractical to charge each and every customer a different price (unless there are only a few customers). Second, a firm usually

[3] Incremental profit is again $\Delta\pi = \Delta R - \Delta C$, but ΔR is given by the price to each customer (i.e., the average revenue curve), so $\Delta\pi = AR - MC$. Total profit is the sum of these $\Delta\pi$s and is given by the area between the AR and MC curves.

does not know the reservation price of each customer. Even if the firm could ask how much each customer would be willing to pay, it probably would not receive honest answers. After all, it is in the customers' interest to claim that they would pay very little (because then they would be charged a low price).

Sometimes, however, firms can discriminate imperfectly by charging a few different prices based on estimates of customers' reservation prices. This happens frequently when professionals, such as doctors, lawyers, accountants, or architects, who know their clients reasonably well, are the "firms." Then the client's willingness to pay can be assessed, and fees set accordingly. For example, a doctor may offer a reduced fee to a low-income patient whose willingness to pay or insurance coverage is low, but charge higher fees to upper-income or better-insured patients. And an accountant, having just completed a client's tax returns, is in an excellent position to estimate how much the client is willing to pay for the service.

Another example is a car salesperson, who typically works with a 15 percent profit margin. The salesperson can give part of this away to the customer by making a "deal," or can insist that the customer pay the sticker price for the car. A good salesperson knows how to size up customers and determine whether they will look elsewhere for a car if they don't receive a sizable discount. The customer who is likely to leave and shop around receives a big discount (from the salesperson's point of view, a small profit is better than no sale and no profit), but the customer in a hurry is offered little or no discount. In other words, a successful car salesperson knows how to price discriminate!

Still another example is how colleges and universities charge tuition. Colleges don't charge different tuition rates to different students in the same degree program. Instead, they offer financial aid, in the form of a scholarship or subsidized loan, which reduces the *net* tuition that the student must pay. By requiring those who seek aid to disclose information about family income and wealth, colleges can link the amount of aid to the student's ability (and hence willingness) to pay. Thus students who are financially well off pay more for their education, but students who are less well off pay less.

Figure 11.3 illustrates this kind of imperfect first-degree price discrimination. Here, if only a single price were charged, it would be P_4. Instead, six different prices are charged, the lowest of which, P_6, is at about the point where marginal cost intersects the demand curve. Note that those customers who would not have been willing to pay a price of P_4 or greater are actually better off in this situation—they are now in the market and may be enjoying at least some consumer surplus. In fact, if price discrimination brings enough new customers into the market, consumer welfare can increase, so that both the producer and consumers are better off.

Second-Degree Price Discrimination

In some markets, each consumer purchases many units of the good over any given period, and the consumer's demand declines with the number of units purchased. Examples include water, heating fuel, and electricity. Consumers may each purchase a few hundred kilowatt-hours of electricity a month, but

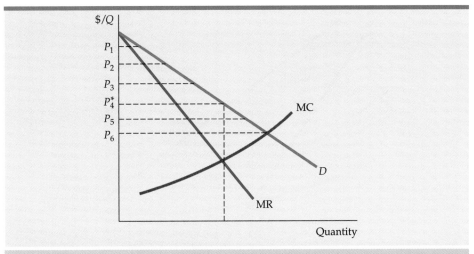

Figure 11.3 First-Degree Price Discrimination in Practice Firms usually don't know the reservation price of every consumer. But sometimes reservation prices can be roughly identified. Here, six different prices are charged. The firm earns higher profits, but some consumers may also benefit. With a single price P_4^*, there are fewer consumers. The consumers who now pay P_5 or P_6 may have a surplus.

their willingness to pay declines with increasing consumption. (The first 100 kilowatt-hours may be worth a lot to the consumer—operating a refrigerator and providing for minimal lighting. Conservation becomes easier with the additional units, and may be worthwhile if the price is high.) In this situation, a firm can discriminate according to the quantity consumed. This is called *second-degree price discrimination*, and it works by charging different prices for different quantities or "blocks" of the same good or service.

An example of second-degree price discrimination is block pricing by electric power companies. If there are scale economies so that average and marginal costs are declining, the state agency that controls the company's rates may encourage block pricing. By expanding output and achieving greater scale economies, consumer welfare can be increased, even allowing for greater profit to the company. The reason is that prices are reduced overall, while the savings from the lower unit costs still permit the power company to make a reasonable profit.

Figure 11.4 illustrates second-degree price discrimination for a firm with declining average and marginal costs. If a single price were charged, it would be P_0, and the quantity produced would be Q_0. Instead, three different prices are charged, based on the quantities purchased. The first block of sales is priced at P_1, the second at P_2, and the third at P_3.

Third-Degree Price Discrimination

A well-known liquor company has what seems to be a strange pricing practice. The company produces a vodka that it advertises as one of the smoothest and best-tasting available. This vodka is called "Three Star Golden Crown,"

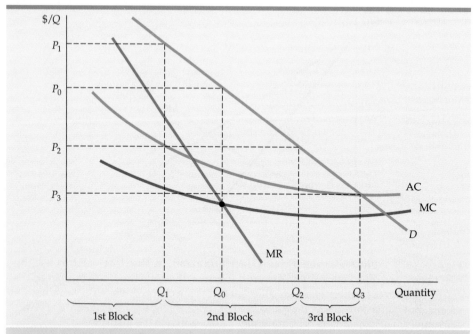

Figure 11.4 Second-Degree Price Discrimination Different prices are charged for different quantities, or "blocks," of the same good. Here, there are three blocks, with corresponding prices P_1, P_2, and P_3. There are also economies of scale, and average and marginal costs are declining. Second-degree price discrimination can then make consumers better off by expanding output and lowering cost.

and it is sold for about $16 a bottle.[4] However, the company also takes some of this same vodka and bottles it under the name "Old Sloshbucket," which is sold for about $8 a bottle. Why does it do this? Has the president of the company been spending too much time near the vats?

Perhaps, but this liquor company is also practicing *third-degree price discrimination*, and it does it because the practice is profitable. This form of price discrimination divides consumers into two or more groups with separate demand curves for each group. This is the most prevalent form of price discrimination, and examples abound: regular versus "special" airline fares; the premium versus nonpremium brand of liquor, canned food or frozen vegetables; discounts to students and senior citizens; and so on.

In each case, some characteristic is used to divide consumers into distinct groups. For example, for many goods, students and senior citizens are usually willing to pay less on average than the rest of the population (because their incomes are lower), and identity can be readily established (via college ID or a driver's license). Likewise, to separate vacationers from business trav-

---

[4] We have changed the names to protect the innocent.

elers (whose companies are usually willing to pay much higher fares), airlines can put restrictions on special low-fare tickets, such as requiring advance purchase. With the liquor company, or the premium versus nonpremium (e.g., supermarket label) brand of food, the label itself divides consumers; many consumers are willing to pay more for a name brand, even though the nonpremium brand is identical or nearly identical (and in fact is sometimes manufactured by the same company that produced the premium brand).

If third-degree price discrimination is feasible, how should the firm decide what price to charge each group of consumers? Let's think about this in two steps. First, we know that however much is produced, total output should be divided between the groups of customers, so that the marginal revenues for each group are equal. Otherwise, the firm would not be maximizing profit. For example, if there are two groups of customers and the marginal revenue for the first group, MR_1, exceeds the marginal revenue for the second group, MR_2, the firm could clearly do better by shifting output from the second group to the first. It would do this by lowering the price to the first group and raising the price to the second group. So whatever the two prices are, they must be such that the marginal revenues for the different groups are equal.

Second, we know that *total* output must be such that the marginal revenue for each group of consumers is equal to the marginal cost of production. Again, if this were not the case, the firm could increase its profit by raising or lowering total output (and lowering or raising its prices to both groups). For example, suppose the marginal revenues were the same for each group of consumers, but marginal revenue exceeded the marginal cost of production. The firm could then make a greater profit by increasing its total output. It would lower its prices to both groups of consumers, so that the marginal revenues for each group fell (but were still equal to each other), and approached marginal cost (which would increase as total output increased).

Let's look at this algebraically. Let P_1 be the price charged to the first group of consumers, P_2 the price charged to the second group, and $C(Q_T)$ the total cost of producing output $Q_T = Q_1 + Q_2$. Then total profit is given by

$$\pi = P_1 Q_1 + P_2 Q_2 - C(Q_T)$$

The firm should increase its sales to each group of consumers, Q_1 and Q_2, until the incremental profit from the last unit sold is zero. First, we set incremental profit for sales to the first group of consumers equal to zero:

$$\frac{\Delta \pi}{\Delta Q_1} = \frac{\Delta(P_1 Q_1)}{\Delta Q_1} - \frac{\Delta C}{\Delta Q_1} = 0$$

Here $\Delta(P_1 Q_1)/\Delta Q_1$ is the incremental revenue from an extra unit of sales to the first group of consumers (i.e., MR_1). The next term, $\Delta C/\Delta Q_1$, is the incremental cost of producing this extra unit, i.e., marginal cost, MC. We thus have

$$MR_1 = MC$$

Similarly, for the second group of consumers, we must have

$$MR_2 = MC$$

Putting these relations together, we see that prices and output must be set so that

$$\boxed{MR_1 = MR_2 = MC} \qquad (11.1)$$

Again, marginal revenue must be equal across groups of consumers and must equal marginal cost.

Managers may find it easier to think in terms of the relative prices that should be charged to each group of consumers, and to relate these prices to the elasticities of demand. Recall that we can write marginal revenue in terms of the elasticity of demand:

$$MR = P(1 + 1/E_d)$$

Then $MR_1 = P_1(1 + 1/E_1)$ and $MR_2 = P_2(1 + 1/E_2)$, where E_1 and E_2 are the elasticities of demand for the firm's sales in the first and second markets, re-

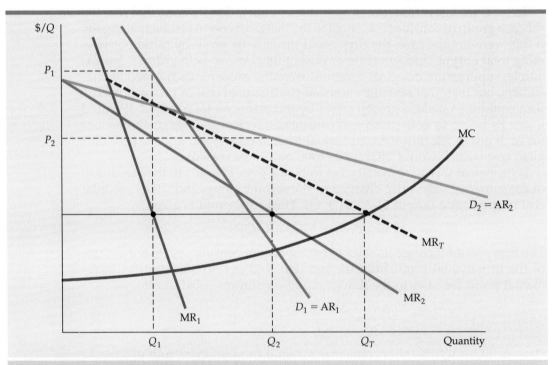

Figure 11.5 **Third-Degree Price Discrimination** Consumers are divided into two groups, with separate demand curves for each group. The optimal prices and quantities are such that the marginal revenue from each group is the same and equal to marginal cost. Here group 1, with demand curve D_1, is charged P_1, and group 2, with the more elastic demand curve D_2, is charged the lower price P_2. Marginal cost depends on the total quantity produced Q_T. Note that Q_1 and Q_2 are chosen so that $MR_1 = MR_2 = MC$.

spectively. Now equating MR_1 and MR_2 gives the following relationship that must hold for the prices:

$$\frac{P_1}{P_2} = \frac{(1 + 1/E_2)}{(1 + 1/E_1)} \qquad (11.2)$$

As you would expect, the higher price will be charged to consumers with the lower demand elasticity. For example, if the elasticity of demand for consumers in group 1 is -2, and the elasticity for consumers in group 2 is -4, we will have $P_1/P_2 = (1 - 1/4)/(1 - 1/2) = (3/4)/(1/2) = 1.5$. In other words, the price charged to the first group of consumers should be 1.5 times as high as the price charged to the second group.

Figure 11.5 illustrates third-degree price discrimination. Note that the demand curve D_1 for the first group of consumers is less elastic than the curve for the second group, and the price charged to the first group is likewise higher. The total quantity produced, $Q_T = Q_1 + Q_2$, is found by summing the marginal revenue curves MR_1 and MR_2 horizontally, which yields the dashed curve MR_T, and finding its intersection with the marginal cost curve. Since MC must equal MR_1 and MR_2, we can draw a horizontal line leftward from this intersection to find the quantities Q_1 and Q_2.

It may not always be worthwhile for the firm to try to sell to more than one group of consumers. In particular, if demand is small for the other group of consumers and marginal cost is rising steeply, the increased cost of producing and selling to this other group may outweigh the increase in revenue. Thus, in Figure 11.6, the firm is better off charging a single price P^* and sell-

Figure 11.6 No Sales to Smaller Market   Even if third-degree price discrimination is feasible, it does not always pay to sell to both groups of consumers if marginal cost is rising. Here, the first group of consumers, with demand D_1, are not willing to pay much for the good. It is unprofitable to sell to them because the price would have to be too low to compensate for the resulting increase in marginal cost.

ing only to the larger group of consumers because the additional cost of serving the smaller market would outweigh the additional revenue that might come from the smaller market.

EXAMPLE 11.1 The Economics of Coupons and Rebates

The producers of processed foods and related consumer goods often issue coupons that let customers buy the product at a discount. These coupons are usually distributed as part of an advertisement for the product, and they may appear in a newspaper or magazine, or as part of a promotional mailing. For example, a coupon for a particular breakfast cereal might be worth 25 cents toward the purchase of a box of the cereal. Why do firms issue these coupons? Why not just lower the price of the product, and thereby save the costs of printing and collecting the coupons?

Coupons provide a means of price discrimination. Studies show that only about 20 to 30 percent of all consumers regularly bother to clip, save, and use coupons when they go shopping. These consumers tend to be more sensitive to price than those who ignore coupons. They generally have more price-elastic demands and lower reservation prices. So by issuing coupons, a cereal company can separate its customers into two groups, and in effect charge the more price-sensitive customers a lower price than the other customers.

Rebate programs work the same way. For example, Kodak ran a program in which a consumer could mail in a form together with the proof of purchase of three rolls of film, and receive a rebate of $1.50. Why not just lower the price of film by 50 cents a roll? Because only those consumers with relatively price-sensitive demands bother to send in the material and request a rebate. Again, the program is a means of price discrimination.

Can consumers really be divided into distinct groups in this way? Table 11.1 shows the results of a statistical study in which, for a variety of products, price elasticities of demand were estimated for users and nonusers of coupons.[5] This study confirms that users of coupons tend to have more price-sensitive demands. It also shows the extent to which the elasticities differ for the two groups of consumers, and how the difference varies from one product to another.

These elasticity estimates by themselves do not tell a firm what price to set and how large a discount to offer through its coupons because they pertain to *market demand*, not the demand for the firm's particular brand. For example, Table 11.1 indicates that the elasticity of demand for cake mix is −0.21 for nonusers of coupons and −0.43 for users. But the elasticity of demand for any of the eight or ten major brands of cake mix on the market will be far larger than either of these numbers—about eight or ten times as large, as a rule of thumb.[6] So for any one brand of cake mix, say, Pillsbury, the elasticity of demand for users of coupons

---

[5] The study is by Chakravarthi Narasimhan, "A Price Discrimination Theory of Coupons," *Marketing Science* (Spring 1984).

[6] This rule of thumb follows if interfirm competition can be described by the Cournot model, which we discuss in Chapter 12.

Table 11.1   Price Elasticities of Demand for Users Versus Nonusers of Coupons

Product	Price Elasticity	
	Nonusers	**Users**
Toilet tissue	−0.60	−0.66
Stuffing/dressing	−0.71	−0.96
Shampoo	−0.84	−1.04
Cooking/salad oil	−1.22	−1.32
Dry mix dinners	−0.88	−1.09
Cake mix	−0.21	−0.43
Cat food	−0.49	−1.13
Frozen entrees	−0.60	−0.95
Gelatin	−0.97	−1.25
Spaghetti sauce	−1.65	−1.81
Creme rinse/conditioner	−0.82	−1.12
Soups	−1.05	−1.22
Hot dogs	−0.59	−0.77

might be about −4, versus about −2 for nonusers. From equation (11.2) we can, therefore, determine that the price to nonusers of coupons should be about 1.5 times the price to users. In other words, if a box of cake mix sells for $1.50, the company should offer coupons that give a 50 cent discount.

EXAMPLE 11.2   How to Set Airline Fares

Travelers are often amazed at the variety of fares available for a round-trip flight from New York to Los Angeles. For example, the first-class fare was recently above $2000; the regular (unrestricted) economy fare was about $1200; and special discount fares (often requiring the purchase of a ticket two weeks in advance and/or a Saturday night stayover) could be bought for as little as $500. Although first-class service is not the same as economy service with a minimum stay requirement, the difference would not seem to warrant a price that is four times as high. Why then do airlines set fares this way?

The reason is that these fares provide a profitable form of price discrimination for airlines. The gains from discriminating are large, because different types of customers, with very different elasticities of demand, purchase these different types of tickets. Table 11.2 shows price (and income) elasticities of

Table 11.2 Elasticities of Demand for Air Travel			
	Fare Category		
Elasticity	**First-Class**	**Unrestricted Coach**	**Discount**
Price	−0.3	−0.4	−0.9
Income	1.2	1.2	1.8

demand for three categories of service within the United States: first-class, unrestricted coach, and discount tickets. (A discounted ticket often has restrictions and may be partly nonrefundable.)

Note that the demand for discounted fares is about two or three times as price elastic as first-class or unrestricted coach service. The reason is that discounted tickets are usually used by families and other leisure travelers, while first-class and unrestricted coach tickets are more often bought by business travelers, who have little choice about when they travel, and whose companies pick up the tab. Of course, these elasticities pertain to market demand, and with several airlines competing for customers, the elasticities of demand for each airline will be larger. But the *relative* sizes of elasticities across the three categories of service should be about the same. When elasticities of demand differ so widely, it should not be surprising that airlines set such different fares for different categories of service.

Price discrimination has become increasingly sophisticated in the United States. A wide variety of fares is available, depending on how far in advance the ticket is bought, the percentage of the fare that is refundable if the trip is changed or cancelled, and whether the trip includes a weekend stay.[7] The objective of the airlines has been to discriminate more finely among travelers with different reservation prices. As American Airlines' vice president of pricing and product planning explained it, "You don't want to sell a seat to a guy for $69 when he is willing to pay $400."[8] At the same time, an airline would rather sell a seat for $69 than leave it empty.

11.3 Intertemporal Price Discrimination and Peak-Load Pricing

Intertemporal price discrimination is an important and widely practiced pricing strategy closely related to third-degree price discrimination. Here consumers

---

[7] Airlines also allocate the number of seats on each flight that will be available for each fare category. This is based on the total demand and mix of passengers expected for each flight. Methods for doing this are discussed in Peter P. Belobaba, "Airline Yield Management: An Overview of Seat Inventory Control," *Transportation Science* 21 (May 1987): 63–73.

[8] "The Art of Devising Air Fares," *New York Times*, March 4, 1987.

are separated into different groups with different demand functions by being charged different prices at different points in time.

To see how intertemporal price discrimination works, think about how an electronics company might price new, technologically advanced equipment, such as videocassette recorders during the 1970s, compact disc players in the early 1980s, and, most recently, digital tape players. In Figure 11.7, D_1 is the (inelastic) demand curve for a small group of consumers who value the product highly and do not want to wait to buy it (e.g., stereo buffs who value high-quality sound and want the latest equipment). D_2 is the demand curve for the broader group of consumers who are more willing to forgo the product if the price is too high. The strategy, then, is to initially offer the product at the high price P_1, selling mostly to consumers on demand curve D_1. Later, after this first group of consumers has bought the product, the price is lowered to P_2, and sales are made to the larger group of consumers on demand curve D_2.[9]

There are other examples of intertemporal price discrimination. One involves charging a high price for a first-run movie, then lowering the price af-

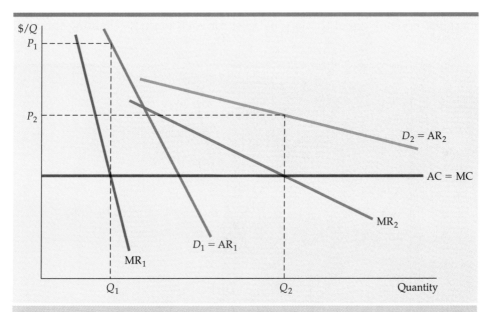

Figure 11.7 Intertemporal Price Discrimination Here, consumers are divided into groups by changing the price over time. Initially, the price is high, and the firm captures surplus from consumers who have a high demand for the good and are unwilling to wait to buy it. Later, the price is reduced to appeal to the mass market.

---

[9] The prices of new electronic products also come down over time because costs fall as producers start to achieve greater scale economies and move down the learning curve. But even if costs did not fall, producers can make more money by first setting a high price and then reducing it over time, thereby discriminating and capturing consumer surplus.

ter the movie has been out a year. Another, practiced almost universally by publishers, is to charge a high price for the hardcover edition of a book, and then to release the paperback version at a much lower price about a year later. Many people think that the lower price of the paperback is due to a much lower cost of production, but this is not true. Once a book has been edited and typeset, the marginal cost of printing an additional copy, whether hardcover or paperback, is quite low, perhaps a dollar or so. The paperback version is sold for much less not because it is much cheaper to print but because high-demand consumers have already purchased the hardbound edition, and the remaining consumers generally have more elastic demands.

Peak-load pricing is another form of intertemporal price discrimination. For some goods and services, demand peaks at particular times—for roads and tunnels during commuter rush hours, for electricity during late summer afternoons, and for ski resorts and amusement parks on weekends. Marginal cost is also high during these peak periods because of capacity constraints. Prices should thus be higher during peak periods.

This is illustrated in Figure 11.8, where D_1 is the demand curve for the peak period, and D_2 is the demand curve for the nonpeak period. The firm sets marginal revenue equal to marginal cost for each period, obtaining the high

Figure 11.8 Peak-Load Pricing Demands for some goods and services increase sharply during particular times of the day or year. Charging a higher price P_1 during the peak periods is more profitable for the firm than charging a single price at all times. It is also more efficient because marginal cost is higher during peak periods.

price P_1 for the peak period, and the lower price P_2 for the nonpeak period, with corresponding quantities Q_1 and Q_2. This increases the firm's profit above what it would be if it charged one price for all periods. It is also more efficient—the sum of producer and consumer surplus is greater because prices are closer to marginal cost.[10]

Note that peak-load pricing is different from third-degree price discrimination. With third-degree price discrimination, marginal revenue has to be equal for each group of consumers and equal to marginal cost. The reason is that the costs of serving the different groups are not independent. For example, with unrestricted versus discounted air fares, increasing the number of seats sold at discounted fares affects the cost of selling unrestricted tickets—marginal cost rises rapidly as the airplane fills up. But this is not so with peak-load pricing (and for that matter, with most instances of intertemporal price discrimination). Selling more tickets for the ski lifts or amusement park on a weekday does not significantly raise the cost of selling tickets on the weekend. Similarly, selling more electricity during the off-peak period will not significantly increase the cost of selling electricity during the peak period. As a result, price and sales in each period can be determined independently by setting marginal cost equal to marginal revenue for each period.

Movie theaters, which charge more for the evening show than for the matinee, are another example of this. For most movie theaters the marginal cost of serving customers during the matinee is independent of the marginal cost during the evening. The owner of a movie theater can determine the optimal prices for the evening and matinee shows independently, using estimates of demand in each period along with estimates of marginal cost.

E X A M P L E 11.3   How to Price a Best-Selling Novel

Publishing both hardbound and paperback editions of a book allows publishers to price discriminate. As they do with most goods, consumers differ considerably in their willingness to pay for books. For example, some consumers want to buy a new best seller as soon as it is released, even if the price is $25. Other consumers, however, will wait a year until the book is available in paperback for $6. But how should a publishing company decide that $25 is the right price for the new hardbound edition and $6 is the right price for the paperback edition? And how long should it wait before bringing out the paperback edition?

The key is to divide consumers into two groups, so that those who are willing to pay a high price do so, and only those unwilling to pay a high price wait and buy the paperback. This means that significant time must be allowed

---

[10] The efficiency gain from peak-load pricing is important. If the firm were a regulated monopolist (e.g., an electric utility), the regulatory agency should set the prices P_1 and P_2 at the points where the *demand* curves, D_1 and D_2, intersect the marginal cost curve, rather than where the marginal revenue curves intersect marginal cost. Consumers then realize the entire efficiency gain.

to pass before the paperback is released. If consumers know that the paperback will be available within a few months, they will have little incentive to buy the hardbound edition.[11] On the other hand, the publisher cannot wait too long to bring out the paperback edition, or else interest in the book will wane, and the market will dry up. As a result, publishers typically wait 12 to 18 months before releasing the paperback edition.

What about price? Setting the price of the hardbound edition is difficult because, except for a few authors whose books always seem to sell, a publisher has little data with which to estimate demand for a book that is about to be published, other than the sales of similar books in the past. But usually only aggregate data are available for each category of book. So most new novels, for example, are released at similar prices. It is clear, however, that those consumers willing to wait for the paperback edition have demands that are far more elastic than those of bibliophiles. It is not surprising, then, that paperback editions sell for so much less than hardbound ones.[12]

11.4 The Two-Part Tariff

The two-part tariff is related to price discrimination and provides another means of extracting consumer surplus. It requires consumers to pay a fee up front for the right to buy a product. Consumers then pay an additional fee for each unit of the product they wish to consume. The classic example of this is an amusement park.[13] You pay an admission fee to enter, and you also pay a certain amount for each ride you go on. The owner of the park has to decide whether to charge a high entrance fee and a low price for the rides, or alternatively, to admit people for free but charge high prices for the rides.

The two-part tariff has been applied in many settings: tennis and golf clubs (you pay an annual membership fee, plus a fee for each use of a court or round of golf); the rental of large mainframe computers (you pay a flat monthly fee plus a fee for each unit of processing time consumed); telephone service (you pay a monthly hook-up fee plus a fee for message units); a Polaroid camera (you pay for the camera, which lets you productively consume the film, which you pay for by the package); and safety razors (you pay for the razor, which lets you consume the blades that fit only that brand of razor).

The problem for the firm is how to set the entry fee (which we denote by T) versus the usage fee (which we denote by P). Assuming that the firm has

---

[11] Some consumers will buy the hardbound edition even if the paperback is already available because it is more durable and more attractive on a bookshelf. This must be taken into account when setting prices, but it is of secondary importance compared with intertemporal price discrimination.

[12] The hardbound and paperback editions are often published by different companies. The author's agent auctions the rights to the two editions, but the contract for the paperback specifies a delay to protect the sales of the hardbound edition. The principle still applies, however. The length of the delay and the prices of the two editions are chosen to intertemporally price discriminate.

[13] See Walter Oi, "A Disneyland Dilemma: Two-Part Tariffs for a Mickey Mouse Monopoly," *Quarterly Journal of Economics* (Feb. 1971): 77–96.

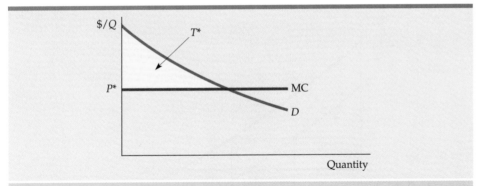

Figure 11.9   Two-Part Tariff with a Single Consumer   The consumer has demand curve D. The firm maximizes profit by setting usage fee P equal to marginal cost and entry fee T equal to the entire surplus of the consumer.

some market power, should it set a high entry fee and low usage fee, or vice versa? To see how a firm can solve this problem, we need to understand the basic principles involved.

Let us begin with an artificial but simple case. Suppose only one consumer is in the market (or many consumers with identical demand curves). Suppose also that the firm knows this consumer's demand curve. Now, remember that the firm wants to capture as much consumer surplus as possible. In this case, the solution is straightforward: Set the usage fee P equal to marginal cost, and the entry fee T equal to the total consumer surplus for each consumer. Thus, in Figure 11.9, the consumer pays T^* (or a bit less) to use the product, and $P^* = MC$ per unit consumed. With the fees set this way, the firm captures *all* the consumer surplus as its profit.

Now, suppose there are two different consumers (or two groups of identical consumers). The firm, however, can set only *one* entry fee and one usage fee. The firm would thus no longer want to set the usage fee equal to marginal cost. If it did, it could make the entry fee no larger than the consumer surplus of the consumer with the smaller demand (or else it would lose that consumer), and this would not give a maximum profit. Instead, the firm should set the usage fee *above* marginal cost, and then set the entry fee equal to the remaining consumer surplus of the consumer with the smaller demand.

Figure 11.10 illustrates this. With the optimal usage fee at P^* greater than MC, the firm's profit is $2T^* + (P^* - MC)(Q_1 + Q_2)$. (There are two consumers, and each pays T^*.) You can verify that this profit is more than twice the area of triangle ABC, the consumer surplus of the consumer with the smaller demand when $P = MC$. To determine the exact values of P^* and T^*, the firm would need to know (in addition to its marginal cost) the demand curves D_1 and D_2. It would then write down its profit as a function of P and T, and choose the two prices that maximize this function. (See Exercise 10 for an example of how to do this.)

Most firms, however, face a variety of consumers with different demands. Unfortunately, there is no simple formula to calculate the optimal two-part

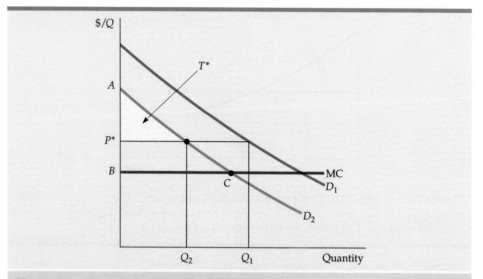

Figure 11.10 **Two-Part Tariff with Two Consumers** The profit-maximizing usage fee P^* will exceed marginal cost. The entry fee T^* is equal to the surplus of the consumer with the smaller demand. The resulting profit is $2T^* + (P^* - MC) \times (Q_1 + Q_2)$. Note that this profit is larger than twice the area of triangle ABC.

tariff in this case, and some trial and error might be required. But there is always a trade-off: A lower entry fee means more entrants and thus more profit from sales of the item. However, as the entry fee becomes smaller and the number of entrants larger, the profit derived from the entry fee will fall. The problem, then, is to pick an entry fee that results in the optimum number of entrants—that is, the fee that allows for maximum profit. In principle, we can do this by starting with a price for sales of the item P, finding the optimum entry fee T, and then estimating the resulting profit. The price P is then changed, and the corresponding entry fee calculated, along with the new profit level. By iterating this way, we can approach the optimal two-part tariff.

Figure 11.11 illustrates this. Here, the firm's profit π is divided into two components, each of which is plotted as a function of the entry fee T, assuming a fixed sales price P. The first component π_a is the profit from the entry fee and is equal to the revenue $n(T)T$, where $n(T)$ is the number of entrants. (Note that a high T implies a small n.) Initially, as T is increased from zero, the revenue $n(T)T$ rises. Eventually, however, further increases in T will make n so small that $n(T)T$ falls. The second component, π_s, is the profit from sales of the item itself at price P, and is equal to $(P - MC)Q$, where Q is the rate at which entrants purchase the item. Q will be larger the larger the number of entrants n. Thus π_s falls when T is increased because a higher T reduces n.

Starting with a number for P, we determine the optimal (profit-maximizing) T^*. We then change P, find a new T^*, and determine whether profit is now higher or lower. This is repeated until profit has been maximized.

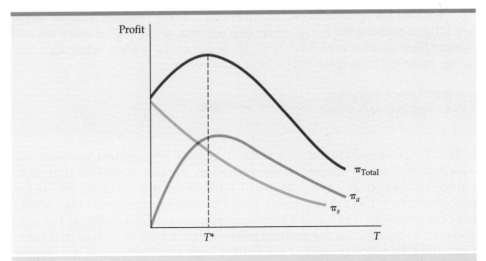

Figure 11.11   Two-Part Tariff with Many Different Consumers   Total profit π is the sum of the profit from the entry fee π_a and the profit from sales π_s. Both π_a and π_s depend on T, the entry fee:

$$\pi = \pi_a + \pi_s = n(T)T + (P - MC)Q(n)$$

where n is the number of entrants, which depends on the entry fee T, and Q is the rate of sales, which is greater the larger is n. Here T^* is the profit-maximizing entry fee, given P. To calculate optimum values for P and T, we can start with a number for P, find the optimum T, and then estimate the resulting profit. P is then changed and the corresponding T is recalculated, along with the new profit level.

Obviously, more data are needed to design an optimal two-part tariff than to choose a single price. Knowing marginal cost and the aggregate demand curve is not enough. It is impossible (in most cases) to determine the demand curve of every consumer, but one would at least like to know by how much individual demands differ from one another. If consumers' demands for your product are fairly similar, you would want to charge a price P that is close to marginal cost, and make the entry fee T large. This is the ideal situation from the firm's point of view because most of the consumer surplus could then be captured. On the other hand, if consumers have different demands for your product, you would probably want to set P substantially above marginal cost, and charge a lower entry fee T. But then the two-part tariff is a much less effective means of capturing consumer surplus; setting a single price may do almost as well.

Firms are perpetually searching for innovative pricing strategies, and a few have devised and introduced a two-part tariff with a "twist"—the entry fee T entitles the customer to a certain number of free units. For example, if you buy a Gillette razor, several blades are usually included in the package. And the monthly lease fee for a large mainframe computer usually includes some free usage before usage is charged. This twist lets the firm set a higher entry fee T without losing as many small consumers. These small consumers might pay little or nothing for usage under this scheme, so the higher entry fee will capture their surplus without driving them out of the market, while also capturing more of the surplus of the large consumers.

EXAMPLE 11.4   Polaroid Cameras

In 1971 Polaroid introduced its new SX-70 camera. This camera was sold, not leased, to individual consumers. Nevertheless, because it sold its film separately, Polaroid could apply a two-part tariff to the pricing of the SX-70. Let us examine how this pricing device gave Polaroid greater profits than would have been possible if its camera had used ordinary roll film, and how Polaroid might have determined the optimal prices for each part of its two-part tariff. Some time later, Kodak entered the market with a competing self-developing film and camera. We will also consider the effect of Kodak's entry into the market on Polaroid's prices and profits.

First, let's make it clear why the pricing of the SX-70 (and Polaroid's other cameras and film as well) involved a two-part tariff. Polaroid had a monopoly on both its camera and the film. (Only Polaroid film could be used in the camera.) Consumers bought the camera and film to take instant pictures: The camera was the "entry fee" that provided access to the consumption of instant pictures, which was what consumers ultimately demanded.[14] In this sense, the price of the camera was like the entry fee at an amusement park. However, while the marginal cost of allowing someone entry into the park is close to zero, the marginal cost of producing a camera was significantly above zero, and thus had to be taken into account when designing the two-part tariff.

It was important that Polaroid have a monopoly on the film as well as the camera. If the camera had used ordinary roll film, competitive forces would have pushed the price of film close to its marginal cost. If all consumers had identical demands, Polaroid could still have captured all the consumer surplus by setting a high price for the camera (equal to the surplus of each consumer). But in practice, consumers were heterogeneous, and the optimal two-part tariff required a price for the film well above marginal cost. (In fact Polaroid got—and still gets—most of its profits from film rather than cameras.) Polaroid needed its monopoly on the film to maintain this high price.

How should Polaroid have selected its prices for the camera and film? It could have begun with some analytical spadework. Its profit is given by

$$\pi = PQ + nT - C_1(Q) - C_2(n)$$

where P is the price of the film, T is the price of the camera, Q is the quantity of film sold, n is the number of cameras sold, and $C_1(Q)$ and $C_2(n)$ are the costs of producing film and cameras, respectively.

---

[14] We are simplifying here. In fact some consumers obtain utility just from owning the camera, even if they take few or no pictures. Adults, like children, enjoy new toys, and can obtain pleasure from the mere possession of a technologically innovative good.

Polaroid wanted to maximize its profit π, taking into account that Q and n depend on P and T. Given a heterogeneous base of potential consumers, this dependence on P and T might only have been guessed at initially, drawing on knowledge of related products. Later, a better understanding of demand and of how Q and n depend on P and T might have been possible as the firm accumulated data from its sales experience. Knowledge of C_1 and C_2 may have been easier to come by, perhaps from engineering and statistical studies (as discussed in Chapter 7).

Given some initial guesses or estimates for $Q(P)$, $n(T)$, $C_1(Q)$, and $C_2(n)$, Polaroid could have calculated the profit-maximizing prices P and T. It could also have determined how sensitive these prices were to uncertainty over demand and cost. This could have provided a guideline for trial-and-error pricing experiments. Over time these experiments would also have told Polaroid more about demand and cost, so that it could refine its two-part tariff.[15]

Did the entry of Kodak with a competing instant camera and film mean that Polaroid lost its ability to use a two-part tariff to extract consumer surplus? No—only Polaroid film could be used in Polaroid cameras, and Polaroid still had some monopoly power to exploit. However, its monopoly power was reduced, the amount of consumer surplus that could potentially be extracted was smaller, and prices had to be changed. With demand now more elastic, Polaroid would have wanted to reduce the price of its cameras significantly (and indeed it did). In 1984 the courts ruled that Kodak's camera and film involved a patent infringement, and Kodak was forced to withdraw from the instant picture market in 1985. Polaroid took advantage of this by introducing new cameras and films to appeal to different consumers. In 1996, Polaroid's One Step cameras sold for about $35 to $60, and used Polaroid 600 film, which was priced at about $14 per pack of 10 pictures. Polaroid's higher-end Spectra cameras sold for above $100 and used Polaroid's Spectra film, which was priced at about $13 per pack. These film prices were well above marginal cost, reflecting the considerable heterogeneity of consumer demands.

*11.5 Bundling

You have probably seen the 1939 film, *Gone with the Wind*. It is a classic that is nearly as popular now as it was then. Yet we would guess that you have not seen *Getting Gertie's Garter*, a flop that the same film company (Loews) also produced in 1939. And we would also guess that you did not know that these two films were priced in what was then an unusual and innovative way.[16]

---

[15] Setting prices for a product such as a Polaroid camera is clearly not a simple matter. We have ignored the *dynamic* behavior of cost and demand: how production costs fall as the firm moves down its learning curve and how demand changes over time as the market begins to saturate.

[16] For those readers who claim to know all this, our final trivia question is: Who played the role of Gertie in *Getting Gertie's Garter*?

Movie theaters that leased *Gone with the Wind* also had to lease *Getting Gertie's Garter*. (Movie theaters pay the film companies or their distributors a daily or weekly fee for the films they lease.) In other words, these two films were *bundled*—i.e., sold as a package. Why would the film company do this?

You might think that the answer is obvious: *Gone with the Wind* was a great film and *Gertie* was a lousy film, so bundling the two forced movie theaters to lease *Gertie*. But this answer doesn't make economic sense. Suppose a theater's reservation price (the maximum price it will pay) for *Gone with the Wind* is $12,000 per week, and its reservation price for *Gertie* is $3000 per week. Then the most it would pay for *both* films is $15,000, whether it takes the films individually or as a package.

Bundling makes sense when *customers have heterogeneous demands*, and when the firm cannot price discriminate. With films, different movie theaters serve different groups of patrons and therefore may well have different demands for films. For example, the theater might appeal to different age groups, who have different relative film preferences.

To see how a film company can use this heterogeneity to its advantage, suppose there are *two* movie theaters, and their reservation prices for our two films are as follows:

	Gone with the Wind	*Getting Gertie's Garter*
Theater *A*	$12,000	$3000
Theater *B*	$10,000	$4000

If the films are rented separately, the maximum price that could be charged for *Wind* is $10,000 because charging more than this would exclude Theater *B*. Similarly, the maximum price that could be charged for *Gertie* is $3000. Charging these two prices would yield $13,000 from each theater, for a total of $26,000 in revenue. But suppose the films are *bundled*. Theater *A* values the *pair* of films at $15,000 ($12,000 + $3000), and Theater *B* values the pair at $14,000 ($10,000 + $4000). So we can charge each theater $14,000 for the pair of films, and earn a total revenue of $28,000. Clearly, we can earn more revenue ($2000 more) by bundling the films.

Why is bundling more profitable than selling the films separately? Because (in this example) the *relative* valuations of the two films are reversed. In other words, although both theaters would pay much more for *Wind* than for *Gertie*, Theater *A* would pay more than Theater *B* for *Wind* ($12,000 vs. $10,000), while Theater *B* would pay more than Theater *A* for *Gertie* ($4000 vs. $3000). In technical terms, we say that the demands are *negatively correlated*—the customer willing to pay the most for *Wind* is willing to pay the least for *Gertie*. To see why this is critical, suppose demands were *positively correlated*—that is, Theater *A* would pay more for *both* films:

	Gone with the Wind	*Getting Gertie's Garter*
Theater *A*	$12,000	$4000
Theater *B*	$10,000	$3000

The most that Theater *A* would pay for the pair of films is now $16,000, but the most that Theater *B* would pay for the pair is only $13,000. So if the films were bundled, the maximum price that could be charged for the package is $13,000, yielding a total revenue of $26,000, the same as by selling the films separately.

Now, suppose a firm is selling two different goods to many consumers. To analyze the possible advantages of bundling, we will use a simple diagram to describe the preferences of the consumers in terms of their reservation prices and their consumption decisions given the prices charged. In Figure 11.12 the horizontal axis is r_1, which is the reservation price of a consumer for good 1, and the vertical axis is r_2, which is the reservation price for good 2. The figure shows the reservation prices for three consumers. Consumer *A* is willing to pay up to $3.25 for good 1 and up to $6 for good 2; consumer *B* is willing to pay $8.25 for good 1 and up to $3.25 for good 2; and consumer *C* is willing to pay up to $10 for each of the goods. In general, the reservation prices for any number of consumers can be plotted this way.

Suppose there are many consumers, and the products are sold separately, at prices P_1 and P_2, respectively. Figure 11.13 shows how consumers can be

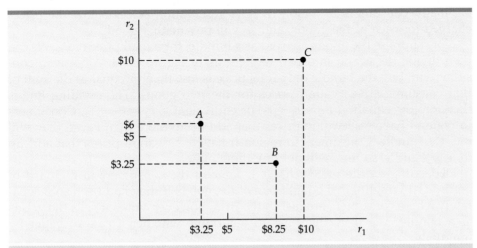

Figure 11.12   Reservation Prices   Reservation prices r_1 and r_2 for two goods are shown for three consumers, labeled *A*, *B*, and *C*. Consumer *A* is willing to pay up to $3.25 for good 1 and up to $6 for good 2.

Figure 11.13 **Consumption Decisions When Products Are Sold Separately**
The reservation prices of consumers in region I exceed the prices P_1 and P_2 for the
two goods, so these consumers buy both goods. Consumers in regions II and IV
buy only one of the goods, and consumers in region III buy neither good.

divided into groups. Consumers in region I of the graph have reservation
prices that are above the prices being charged for each of the goods, and so
will buy both goods. Consumers in region II have a reservation price for good
2 that is above P_2, but a reservation price for good 1 that is below P_1; they
will buy only good 2. Similarly, consumers in region IV will buy only good
1. Finally, consumers in region III have reservation prices below the prices
charged for each of the goods, and so will buy neither good.

Now suppose the goods are sold as a bundle, for a total price of P_B. We can
then divide the graph into two regions, as in Figure 11.14. Any given consumer will buy the bundle only if its price is less than or equal to the sum of
that consumer's reservation prices for the two goods. The dividing line is
therefore the equation $P_B = r_1 + r_2$, or equivalently, $r_2 = P_B - r_1$. Consumers
in region I have reservation prices that add up to more than P_B, so they will
buy the bundle. Consumers in region II have reservation prices that add up
to less than P_B, so they will not buy the bundle.

Depending on the prices charged, some of the consumers in region II of
Figure 11.14 might have bought one of the goods if they had been sold separately. These consumers are lost to the firm, however, when it sells the goods
as a bundle. The firm, then, has to determine whether it can do better by
bundling.

In general, the effectiveness of bundling depends on how negatively correlated demands are. In other words, it works best when consumers who have
a high reservation price for good 1 have a low reservation price for good 2,
and vice versa. Figure 11.15 shows two extremes. In part (a) each point represents the two reservation prices of a consumer. Note that the demands for

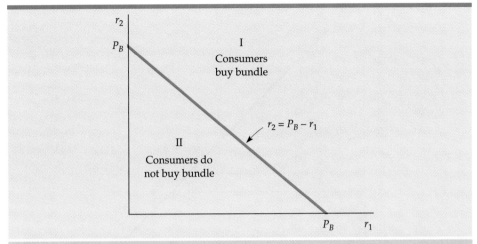

Figure 11.14 Consumption Decisions When Products Are Bundled
Consumers compare the *sum* of their reservation prices, $r_1 + r_2$, with the price of
the bundle P_B. They buy the bundle only if $r_1 + r_2$ is at least as large as P_B.

the two goods are perfectly positively correlated—consumers with a high
reservation price for good 1 also have a high reservation price for good 2. If
the firm bundles and charges a price $P_B = P_1 + P_2$, it will make the same profit
it would if it sold the goods separately at prices P_1 and P_2. In part (b), on the

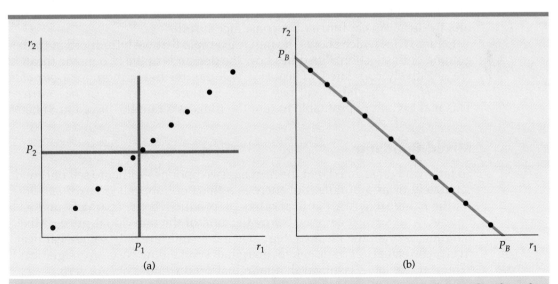

Figure 11.15 Reservation Prices In (a), demands are perfectly positively correlated, so the
firm does not gain by bundling. It would earn the same profit by selling the goods separately. In
(b), demands are perfectly negatively correlated. Bundling is the ideal strategy—all the consumer
surplus can be extracted.

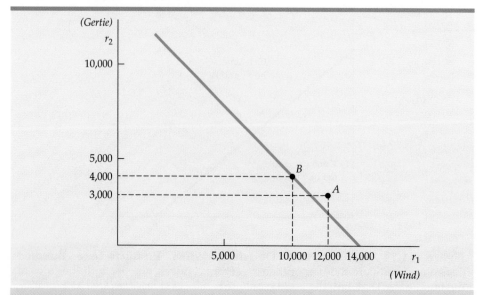

Figure 11.16 Movie Example   Consumers *A* and *B* are two movie theaters. The diagram shows their reservation prices for the films *Gone with the Wind* and *Getting Gertie's Garter*. Since the demands are negatively correlated, bundling pays.

other hand, demands are perfectly negatively correlated—a higher reservation price for good 2 implies a proportionately lower one for good 1. In this case, bundling is the ideal strategy. By charging the price P_B shown in the figure, the firm can capture *all* the consumer surplus.

Figure 11.16, which shows the movie example that we introduced at the beginning of this section, illustrates how the demands of the two movie theaters are negatively correlated. (Theater *A* will pay relatively more for *Gone with the Wind*, but Theater *B* will pay relatively more for *Getting Gertie's Garter*.) This makes it more profitable to rent the films as a bundle, priced at $14,000.

Mixed Bundling

So far, we have assumed that the firm has two options—either to sell the goods separately or as a bundle. But there is a third option, called *mixed bundling*. As the name suggests, the firm offers its products both separately and as a bundle, with a package price below the sum of the individual prices. Mixed bundling is often the ideal strategy when demands are only somewhat negatively correlated, and/or when marginal production costs are significant. (Thus far, we have assumed that marginal production costs are zero.)

In Figure 11.17, mixed bundling is the most profitable strategy. Here, demands are perfectly negatively correlated, but there are significant marginal costs. (The marginal cost of producing good 1 is $20, and the marginal cost of producing good 2 is $30.) Four consumers are shown, labeled *A* through *D*. Now, let's compare three strategies—selling the goods separately at prices

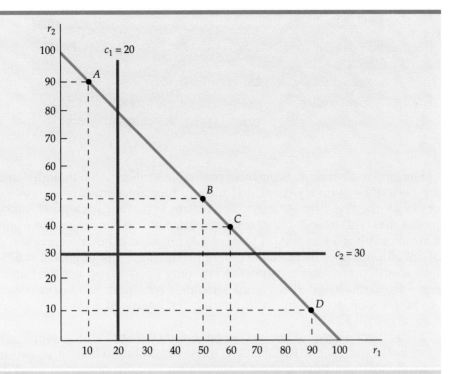

Figure 11.17   Mixed Versus Pure Bundling   With positive marginal costs, mixed bundling may be more profitable than pure bundling, as in this example. Consumer A has a reservation price for good 1 that is below marginal cost c_1, and consumer D has a reservation price for good 2 that is below marginal cost c_2. With mixed bundling, consumer A is induced to buy only good 2, and consumer D is induced to buy only good 1, reducing the firm's cost.

$P_1 = \$50$ and $P_2 = \$90$; selling the goods only as a bundle (a strategy that we will refer to as "pure bundling") at a price of $100; or mixed bundling, where the goods are sold separately at prices $P_1 = P_2 = \$89.95$, or as a bundle at a price of $100.

Table 11.3 shows these three strategies and the resulting profits. (You can try other prices for P_1, P_2, and P_B to verify that those given in the table maximize profit for each strategy.) When the goods are sold separately, only consumers B, C, and D buy good 1, and only consumer A buys good 2, so that the total profit is $3(\$50 - \$20) + 1(\$90 - \$30) = \$150$. With pure bundling, all four consumers buy the bundle for $100, so that total profit is $4(\$100 - \$20 - \$30) = \$200$. As we should expect, pure bundling is better than selling the goods separately because consumers' demands are negatively correlated. But what about mixed bundling? Now consumer D buys only good 1 for $89.95, consumer A buys only good 2 for $89.95, and consumers B and C buy the bundle for $100. Total profit is now $(\$89.95 - \$20) + (\$89.95 - \$30) + 2(\$100 - \$20 - \$30) = \$229.90$.

Table 11.3	Bundling Example			
	P_1	P_2	P_B	**Profit**
Sell separately	$50	$90	—	$150
Pure bundling	—	—	$100	$200
Mixed bundling	$89.95	$89.95	$100	$229.90

Here, mixed bundling is the most profitable strategy, even though demands are perfectly negatively correlated (i.e., all four consumers have reservation prices on the line $r_2 = 100 - r_1$). The reason is that for each good, marginal production cost exceeds the reservation price of one consumer. For example, consumer A has a reservation price of $90 for good 2, but a reservation price of only $10 for good 1. Since the cost of producing a unit of good 1 is $20, the firm would prefer that consumer A buy only good 2, and not the bundle. It can achieve this by offering good 2 separately for a price just below consumer A's reservation price, while also offering the bundle at a price acceptable to consumers B and C.

Mixed bundling would *not* be the preferred strategy in this example if marginal costs were zero, because then there would be no benefit in excluding consumer A from buying good 1 and consumer D from buying good 2. We leave it to you to demonstrate this (see Exercise 12).[17]

If marginal costs are zero, mixed bundling can still be more profitable than pure bundling if consumers' demands are not perfectly negatively correlated. (Recall that in Figure 11.17, the reservation prices of the four consumers are perfectly negatively correlated.) This is illustrated by Figure 11.18, in which we have modified the example of Figure 11.17. In Figure 11.18, marginal costs are zero, but the reservation prices for consumers B and C are now higher. Let us once again compare the three strategies of selling the two goods separately, pure bundling, and mixed bundling.

Table 11.4 shows the optimal prices and the resulting profits for each of the strategies. (Once again, you should try other prices for P_1, P_2, and P_B to verify that those given in the table maximize profit for each strategy.) When the goods are sold separately, only consumers C and D buy good 1, and only consumers A and B buy good 2, so that total profit is $320. With pure bundling, all four consumers buy the bundle for $100, so that total profit is $400. As expected, pure bundling is better than selling the goods separately because consumers' demands are negatively correlated. But mixed bundling is better still. With mixed bundling,

[17] For further discussion of bundling, see William J. Adams and Janet L. Yellin, "Commodity Bundling and the Burden of Monopoly," *Quarterly Journal of Economics* 90 (Aug. 1976): 475–498. Sometimes a firm with monopoly power will find it profitable to bundle its product with the product of another firm; see Richard L. Schmalensee, "Commodity Bundling by Single-Product Monopolies," *Journal of Law and Economics* 25 (April 1982): 67–71. Bundling can also be profitable when the products are substitutes or complements. See Arthur Lewbel, "Bundling of Substitutes or Complements," *International Journal of Industrial Organization* 3 (1985): 101–107.

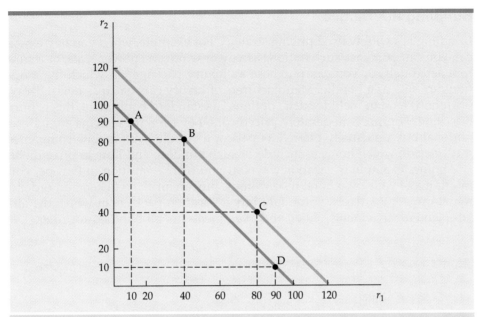

Figure 11.18 Mixed Bundling with Zero Marginal Costs If marginal costs are zero, mixed bundling is still more profitable than pure bundling if consumers' demands are not perfectly negatively correlated. In this example, consumers B and C are willing to pay $20 more for the bundle than are consumers A and D. With pure bundling, the price of the bundle is $100. With mixed bundling, the price of the bundle can be increased to $120, and consumers A and D can still be charged $90 for a single good.

consumer A buys only good 2, consumer D buys only good 1, and consumers B and C buy the bundle at a price of $120. Total profit is now $420.

Why does mixed bundling give higher profits than pure bundling, even though marginal costs are zero? The reason is that demands are not perfectly negatively correlated: The two consumers (B and C) who have high demands for both goods are willing to pay more for the bundle than are consumers A and D. Hence, with mixed bundling, we can increase the price of the bundle (from $100 to $120), sell this bundle to two consumers, and charge the remaining consumers $90 for a single good.

Table 11.4 Mixed Bundling with Zero Marginal Costs				
	P_1	P_2	P_B	**Profit**
Sell separately	$80	$80	—	$320
Pure bundling	—	—	$100	$400
Mixed bundling	$90	$90	$120	$420

Bundling in Practice

Bundling is a widely used pricing strategy. For example, when you buy a new car, you can purchase such options as power windows, power seats, or a sunroof separately, or you can purchase a "luxury package" in which these options are sold as a bundle. Manufacturers of luxury cars (such as Lexis, BMW, or Infiniti) tend to include such "options" as standard equipment; this is pure bundling. For more moderately priced cars, however, these items are indeed optional but are usually offered as part of a bundle. Automobile companies must decide which items to include in such bundles, and how to price them.

Another example is vacation travel. If you plan a vacation to Europe, you might make your own hotel reservations, buy an airplane ticket, and order a rental car. Alternatively, you might buy a vacation package in which the airfare, land arrangements, hotel, and even meals are all bundled together.

Table 11.5 Selected Offerings of Continental Cablevision

Basic Service: $8.99 per month

C-Span 1	WGBH (2) PBS	WGBX (44) PBS
Home Shopping Network	WBZ (4) CBS	WNDS (50) IND
Learning Channel	WCVB (5) ABC	WLVI (56) IND
Home Channel	WHDH (7) NBC	WMFP (62) IND
New England Cable News	WENH (11) PBS	WHSH (66) IND
Sneak Prevue	WFXT (25) FOX	WABU (68) IND
Prevue Guide	WUNI (27) IND	
Story Vision	WSBK (38) IND	

Premium Service (á la carte)

American Movie Classics	$9.95	Movie Channel	$10.95
Bravo	$9.95	New England Sports Network	$9.95
Cinemax	$10.95	Showtime	$10.95
Home Box Office	$10.95	SportsChannel	$10.95
Disney Channel	$10.95		

Premium Packages

American Movie Classics/Bravo Package	$10.95	Sports Package	$15.95
"Take Two" Discount Package	$15.95	Two Premium Package	$19.95
(HBO, Showtime, or Disney only)		Additional Premiums	$7.00

Still another example is cable television. Cable operators typically offer a basic service for a low monthly fee, as well as individual "premium" channels, such as Cinemax, Home Box Office, and the Disney Channel on an individual basis for additional monthly fees. However, they also offer packages in which two or more premium channels are sold as a bundle. This is illustrated in Table 11.5, which shows some of the recent offerings of Continental Cablevision, a Massachusetts operator.

Bundling cable channels is profitable because demands are negatively correlated. How do we know that? Because there are only 24 hours in a day, so that the time a consumer spends watching HBO is time that cannot be spent watching the Disney Channel. Thus consumers with high reservation prices for some channels will have relatively low reservation prices for other channels.

How can a company decide whether to bundle its products, and determine the profit-maximizing prices? Most companies do not know their customers' reservation prices. However, by conducting market surveys, they may be able to estimate the distribution of reservation prices, and then use this information to design a pricing strategy.

This is illustrated in Figure 11.19. The dots in that figure are estimates of reservation prices for a representative sample of consumers (obtained, say, from a

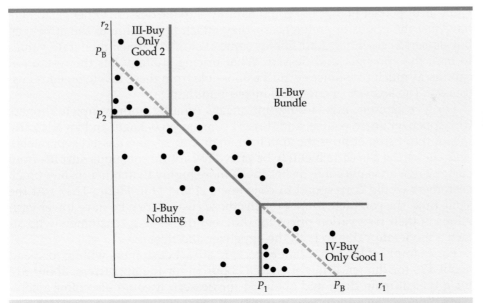

Figure 11.19   Mixed Bundling in Practice   The dots in this figure are estimates of reservation prices for a representative sample of consumers. A company could first choose a price for the bundle, P_B, such that a diagonal line connecting these prices passes roughly midway through the dots. The company could then try individual prices P_1 and P_2. Given P_1, P_2, and P_B, profits can be calculated for this sample of consumers. One can then raise or lower P_1, P_2, and P_B and see whether this leads to higher profits. This is done repeatedly until total profit is roughly maximized.

market survey). The company might first choose a price for the bundle, P_B, such that a diagonal line connecting these prices passes roughly midway through the dots in the figure. The company could then try individual prices P_1 and P_2. Given P_1, P_2, and P_B, we can separate the consumers into four regions, as shown in the figure. Consumers in Region I buy nothing (because $r_1 < P_1$, $r_2 < P_2$, and $r_1 + r_2 < P_B$). Consumers in Region II buy the bundle (because $r_1 + r_2 > P_B$). Consumers in Region III buy only good 2 (because $r_2 > P_2$ but $r_1 < P_B - P_2$). Likewise, consumers in Region IV buy only good 1. Given this distribution, we can calculate the resulting profits. We can then raise or lower P_1, P_2, and P_B and see whether this leads to higher profits. This can be done repeatedly (on a computer), until prices are found that roughly maximize total profit.

E X A M P L E   11.5   **The Complete Dinner Versus à la Carte: A Restaurant's Pricing Problem**

Many restaurants offer complete dinners as well as an à la carte menu. Why? Most customers go out to eat knowing roughly how much they are willing to spend for dinner (and choose the restaurant accordingly). However, the customers that enter a restaurant have different preferences. For example, some value an appetizer highly, but could happily skip the dessert. Other customers have just the opposite preferences—they attach little value to the appetizer, but dessert is essential. And finally, some customers attach moderate values to both the appetizer and dessert. What pricing strategy lets the restaurant capture as much consumer surplus as possible from these heterogeneous customers? The answer, of course, is mixed bundling.

For a restaurant, mixed bundling means offering both complete dinners (the appetizer, main course, and dessert come as a package) and an à la carte menu (the customer buys the appetizer, main course, and dessert separately). This allows the à la carte menu to be priced to capture consumer surplus from customers who value some dishes much more highly than other dishes. (Such customers would correspond to consumers A and D in Figure 11.17.) At the same time, the complete dinner retains those customers who have lower variations in their reservation prices for different dishes (e.g., customers who attach a moderate value to both the appetizer and dessert).

For example, if the restaurant expects to attract customers willing to spend about $20 for dinner, it might charge about $5 for the appetizers, about $14 for a typical main dish, and about $4 for dessert. It could also offer a complete dinner, which includes an appetizer, main course, and dessert, for $20. Then, the customer who loves dessert but couldn't care less about an appetizer will order only the main dish and dessert, and spend $18 (and the restaurant will save the cost of preparing an appetizer). At the same time, another customer who attaches a moderate value (say, $3 or $3.50) to both the appetizer and dessert will buy the complete dinner.

Unfortunately for consumers, perhaps, creative pricing can be more important than creative cooking for the financial success of a restaurant.

Successful restaurateurs know their customers' demand characteristics and use that knowledge to design a pricing strategy that extracts as much consumer surplus as possible.

___

Tying

Tying is a general term that refers to any requirement that products be bought or sold in some combination. Bundling is a common form of tying, but tying can also take other forms. For example, suppose a firm sells a product (such as a copying machine), the use of which requires the consumption of a secondary product (such as paper). The consumer who buys the first product is also required to buy the secondary product from the same company. This requirement is usually imposed through a contract. Note that this is different from the examples of bundling discussed earlier. In those examples, the consumer might have been happy to buy just one of the products. In this case, however, the first product is useless without access to the secondary product.

Why might firms use this kind of pricing practice? One of the main benefits of tying is that it often allows a firm to *meter demand*, and thus to practice price discrimination more effectively. For example, during the 1950s, when Xerox had a monopoly on copying machines but not on paper, customers who leased a Xerox copier also had to buy Xerox paper. This allowed Xerox to meter consumption (customers who used a machine intensively bought more paper), and thereby apply a two-part tariff to the pricing of its machines. Also during the 1950s, IBM required customers who leased its mainframe computers to use paper computer cards made only by IBM. By pricing these cards well above marginal cost, IBM was effectively charging higher prices for computer usage to customers with larger demands.[18]

Tying can also have other uses. An important one is to protect customer goodwill connected with a brand name. This is why franchises are often required to purchase inputs from the franchiser. For example, Mobil Oil requires its service stations to sell only Mobil motor oil, Mobil batteries, and so on. Similarly, until recently, a McDonald's franchisee had to purchase all materials and supplies—from the hamburgers to the paper cups—from McDonald's, thus ensuring product uniformity and protecting the brand name.[19]

*11.6 Advertising

We have seen how firms can utilize their market power when making pricing decisions. Pricing is important for a firm, but most firms with market power have another important decision to make: how much to advertise. In

___

[18] However, antitrust actions forced IBM to discontinue this pricing practice.

[19] In some cases, the courts ruled that tying is not necessary to protect customer goodwill and is anticompetitive, so now a McDonald's franchisee can buy supplies from any McDonald's approved source. For a discussion of some of the antitrust issues involved in franchise tying, see Benjamin Klein and Lester F. Saft, "The Law and Economics of Franchise Tying Contracts," *Journal of Law and Economics* 28 (May 1985): 345–361.

this section we will see how firms with market power can make profit-maximizing advertising decisions, and how those decisions depend on the characteristics of demand for the firm's product.[20]

For simplicity, we will assume that the firm sets only one price for its product. We will also assume that having done sufficient market research, it knows how its quantity demanded depends on both its price P *and* its advertising expenditures in dollars A; that is, it knows $Q(P,A)$. Figure 11.20 shows the firm's demand and cost curves with and without advertising. AR and MR are the firm's average and marginal revenue curves when it does not advertise, and AC and MC are its average and marginal cost curves. It produces a quantity Q_0, where MR = MC, and receives a price P_0. Its profit per unit is the difference between P_0 and average cost, so its total profit π_0 is given by the gray-shaded rectangle.

Now suppose the firm advertises. This causes its demand curve to shift out and to the right; the new average and marginal revenue curves are given by AR' and MR'. Advertising is a fixed cost, so the firm's average cost curve rises (to AC'). Marginal cost, however, remains the same. With advertising, the firm produces Q_1 (where MR' = MC), and receives a price P_1. Its total profit π_1, given by the purple-shaded rectangle, is now much larger.

While the firm in Figure 11.20 is clearly better off advertising, the figure does not help us determine *how much* advertising the firm should do. Our firm must choose its price P and advertising expenditure A to maximize profit, which is now given by:

$$\pi = PQ(P,A) - C(Q) - A$$

Given a price, more advertising will result in more sales, and hence more revenue. But what is the firm's profit-maximizing advertising expenditure? You might be tempted to say that the firm should increase its advertising expenditures until the last dollar of advertising just brings forth an additional dollar of revenue—that is, until the marginal revenue from advertising, $\Delta(P,Q)/\Delta A$, is just equal to 1. But as Figure 11.20 shows, this reasoning omits an important element. Remember that advertising leads to increased output (in the figure, output increased from Q_0 to Q_1). But increased output in turn means increased production costs, and this must be taken into account when comparing the costs and benefits of an extra dollar of advertising.

The correct decision is to increase advertising until the marginal revenue from an additional dollar of advertising, MR_{Ads}, just equals the *full* marginal cost of that advertising. That full marginal cost is the sum of the dollar spent directly on the advertising and the marginal production cost that results from the increased sales that advertising brings about. Thus the firm should advertise up to the point that[21]

---

[20] A perfectly competitive firm has little reason to advertise, since by definition it can sell as much as it produces at a market price that it takes as given. That is why it would be unusual to see a producer of corn or soybeans advertise.

[21] To derive this using calculus, differentiate $\pi(Q,A)$ with respect to A, and set the derivative equal to zero:

$$\partial\pi/\partial A = P(\partial Q)/\partial A) - MC(\partial Q/\partial A) - 1 = 0$$

Rearranging gives equation (11.3).

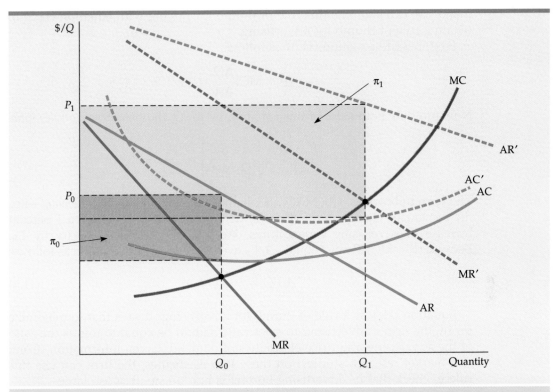

Figure 11.20 Effects of Advertising AR and MR are average and marginal revenue when the firm doesn't advertise, and AC and MC are average and marginal cost. The firm produces Q_0 and receives a price P_0. Its total profit π_0 is given by the gray-shaded rectangle. If the firm advertises, its average and marginal revenue curves shift to the right. Average cost rises (to AC'), but marginal cost remains the same. The firm now produces Q_1 (where MR' = MC), and receives a price P_1. Its total profit, π_1, is now larger.

$$\text{MR}_{\text{Ads}} = P\frac{\Delta Q}{\Delta A} = 1 + \text{MC}\frac{\Delta Q}{\Delta A} \tag{11.3}$$

$$= \textit{full}\text{ marginal cost of advertising}$$

This rule is often ignored by managers, who justify advertising budgets by comparing the expected benefits (i.e., added sales) only with the cost of the advertising. But additional sales mean increased production costs, which must also be taken into account.

A Rule of Thumb for Advertising

Like the rule MR = MC, equation (11.3) is sometimes difficult to apply in practice. In Chapter 10 we saw that MR = MC implies the following rule of thumb for pricing: $(P - \text{MC})/P = -1/E_P$, where E_P is the firm's price elasticity of demand. We can combine this rule of thumb for pricing with equation (11.3) to obtain a rule of thumb for advertising.

First, rewrite equation (11.3) as follows:

$$(P - MC)\frac{\Delta Q}{\Delta A} = 1$$

Now multiply both sides of this equation by A/PQ, the *advertising-to-sales ratio*:

$$\frac{P - MC}{P}\left[\frac{A}{Q}\frac{\Delta Q}{\Delta A}\right] = \frac{A}{PQ}$$

The term in brackets, $(A/Q)(\Delta Q/\Delta A)$, is the *advertising elasticity of demand*—i.e., the percentage change in the quantity demanded that results from a 1 percent increase in advertising expenditures. We will denote this elasticity by E_A. Because $(P - MC)/P$ must equal $-1/E_P$, we can rewrite this equation as follows:

$$\boxed{A/PQ = -(E_A/E_P)} \qquad (11.4)$$

Equation (11.4) is a rule of thumb for advertising. It says that to maximize profit, the firm's advertising-to-sales ratio should be equal to minus the ratio of the advertising and price elasticities of demand. Given information (from, say, market research studies) on these two elasticities, the firm can use this rule to check that its advertising budget is not too small or too large.

To put this rule into perspective, assume that a firm is generating sales revenue of $1 million per year while allocating only $10,000 (1 percent of its revenues) to advertising. The firm knows that its advertising elasticity of demand is .2, so that a doubling of its advertising budget from $10,000 to $20,000 should increase sales by 20 percent. The firm also knows that the price elasticity of demand for its product is −4. Should the firm increase its advertising budget, knowing that with a price elasticity of demand of −4, its markup of price over marginal cost is substantial? The answer is yes; equation (11.4) tells us that the firm's advertising-to-sales ratio should be $-(.2/-4) = 5$ percent, so the firm should increase its advertising budget from $10,000 to $50,000.

This rule makes intuitive sense. It says firms should advertise a lot if (i) demand is very sensitive to advertising (E_A is large), or (ii) demand is not very price elastic (E_P is small). Although (i) is obvious, why should firms advertise more when the price elasticity of demand is small? The reason is that a small elasticity of demand implies a large markup of price over marginal cost, so that the marginal profit from each extra unit sold is high. In this case, if advertising can help sell a few more units, it will be worth its cost.[22]

---

[22] Advertising often affects the price elasticity of demand, and this must be taken into account by the firm. For some products, advertising broadens the market by attracting a large range of customers, or creating a bandwagon effect. This is likely to make demand more price elastic than it would have been otherwise. (But E_A is likely to be large, so that advertising will still be worthwhile.) Sometimes advertising is used to differentiate a product from others (by creating an image, allure, or brand identification), so that its demand is less price elastic than it would be otherwise.

EXAMPLE 11.6 **Advertising in Practice**

In Example 10.1 we looked at the use of markup pricing by supermarkets, convenience stores, and makers of designer jeans, and saw how in each case the markup of price over marginal cost depended on the firm's price elasticity of demand. Now let's see why these firms, and also producers of other goods, advertise as much (or as little) as they do.

First, supermarkets. We said that the price elasticity of demand for a typical supermarket is around -10. To determine the advertising-to-sales ratio, we also need to know the advertising elasticity of demand. This number can vary considerably depending on what part of the country the supermarket is in, and whether it is in a city, suburb, or rural area, but 0.1 to 0.3 would be a reasonable range. Substituting these numbers into equation (11.4), we find that the manager of a typical supermarket should have an advertising budget that is around 1 to 3 percent of sales—which is indeed what many supermarkets spend on advertising.

Convenience stores have lower price elasticities of demand (around -5), but their advertising-to-sales ratios are usually less than those for supermarkets (and are often zero). Why? Because convenience stores mostly serve customers who live nearby and might need a few items late at night, or don't want to drive to the supermarket. These customers already know about the convenience store and are unlikely to change their buying habits if the store advertises. Hence E_A is very small, and advertising is not worthwhile.

Advertising is quite important for makers of designer jeans, who will have advertising-to-sales ratios as high as 10 or 20 percent. We said that price elasticities of demand in the range of -3 to -4 are typical for the major labels, and advertising elasticities of demand can range from .3 to as high as 1. (Advertising is important in making consumers aware of the label and giving it an aura and image.) So, these levels of advertising would seem to make sense.

Laundry detergents have among the very highest advertising-to-sales ratios, sometimes exceeding 30 percent, even though demand for any one brand is at least as price elastic as it is for designer jeans. What justifies all the advertising? The answer is a very large advertising elasticity. The demand for any one brand of laundry detergent depends crucially on advertising; without it, consumers would have little basis for selecting any one brand.[23]

Finally, Table 11.6 shows sales, advertising expenditures, and the ratio of the two for leading brands of over-the-counter drugs. Observe that overall, the ratios are quite high. As with laundry detergents, the advertising elas-

---

[23] For an overview of statistical approaches to estimating the advertising elasticity of demand, see Ernst R. Berndt, *The Practice of Econometrics* (Reading, Mass: Addison-Wesley, 1990), chap. 8.

Table 11.6 1993 Sales and Advertising Expenditures for Leading Brands of Over-the-Counter Drugs (in millions of dollars)			
	Sales	**Advertising**	**Ratio (%)**
Pain Medications			
Tylenol	855	143.8	17
Advil	360	91.7	26
Bayer	170	43.8	26
Excedrin	130	26.7	21
Antacids			
Alka-Seltzer	160	52.2	33
Mylanta	135	32.8	24
Tums	135	27.6	20
Cold Remedies (decongestants)			
Benadryl	130	30.9	24
Sudafed	115	28.6	25
Cough Medicine			
Vicks	350	26.6	8
Robitussin	205	37.7	19
Halls	130	17.4	13

Source: New York Times, September 27, 1994.

ticity for name-brand drugs is very high. Alka-Seltzer, Mylanta, and Tums are all antacids that do much the same thing. Sales depend on consumer identification with a particular brand, which requires advertising.

Summary

1. Firms with market power are in an enviable position because they have the potential to earn large profits, but realizing that potential may depend critically on the firm's pricing strategy. Even if the firm sets a single price, it needs an estimate of the elasticity of demand for its output. More complicated strategies, which can involve setting several different prices, require even more information about demand.

2. A pricing strategy aims to enlarge the customer base that the firm can sell to, and capture as much consumer surplus as possible. There are a number of ways to do this, and they usually involve setting more than a single price.

3. Ideally, the firm would like to perfectly price discriminate—i.e., charge each customer his or her reservation price. In practice this is almost always impossible. On the other hand, various forms of imperfect price discrimination are often used to increase profits.

4. The two-part tariff is another means of capturing consumer surplus. Customers must pay an "entry" fee, which allows them to buy the good at a per-unit price. The two-part tariff is most effective when customer demands are relatively homogeneous.

5. When demands are heterogeneous and negatively correlated, bundling can increase profits. With pure bundling, two or more different goods are sold only as a package. With mixed bundling, the customer can buy the goods individually or as a package. Mixed bundling can be more profitable than pure bundling if marginal costs are significant or if demands are not perfectly negatively correlated.

6. Bundling is a special case of tying, a requirement that products be bought or sold in some combination. Tying can be used to meter demand or to protect customer goodwill associated with a brand name.

7. Advertising can further increase profits. The profit-maximizing advertising-to-sales ratio is equal in magnitude to the ratio of the advertising and price elasticities of demand.

Questions for Review

1. Suppose a firm can practice perfect, first-degree price discrimination. What is the lowest price it will charge, and what will its total output be?

2. How does a car salesperson practice price discrimination? How does the ability to discriminate correctly affect his or her earnings?

3. Electric utilities often practice second-degree price discrimination. Why might this improve consumer welfare?

4. Give some examples of third-degree price discrimination. Can third-degree price discrimination be effective if the different groups of consumers have different levels of demand but the same price elasticities?

5. Show why optimal, third-degree price discrimination requires that marginal revenue for each group of consumers equals marginal cost. Use this condition to explain how a firm should change its prices and total output if the demand curve for one group of consumers shifted outward, so that marginal revenue for that group increased.

6. When pricing automobiles, American car companies typically charge a much higher percen-tage markup over cost for "luxury option" items (such as leather trim, etc.) than for the car itself or for more "basic" options such as power steering and automatic transmission. Explain why.

7. How is peak-load pricing a form of price discrimination? Can it make consumers better off? Give an example.

8. How can a firm determine an optimal two-part tariff if it has two customers with different demand curves? (Assume that it knows the demand curves.)

9. Why is the pricing of a Gillette safety razor a form of a two-part tariff? Must Gillette be a monopoly producer of its blades as well as its razors? Suppose you were advising Gillette on how to determine the two parts of the tariff. What procedure would you suggest?

10. Why did Loews bundle *Gone with the Wind* and *Getting Gertie's Garter*? What characteristic of demands is needed for bundling to increase profits?

11. How does mixed bundling differ from pure bundling? Under what conditions is mixed bundling preferred to pure bundling? Why do many restaurants practice mixed bundling (by offering a complete dinner as well as an à la carte menu) instead of pure bundling?

12. How does tying differ from bundling? Why might a firm want to practice tying?

13. Why is it incorrect to advertise up to the point that the last dollar of advertising expenditures generates another dollar of sales? What is the correct rule for the marginal advertising dollar?

14. How can a firm check that its advertising-to-sales ratio is not too high or too low? What information would it need?

Exercises

1. Price discrimination requires the ability to sort customers and the ability to prevent arbitrage. Explain how the following can function as price discrimination schemes and discuss both sorting and arbitrage:
   a. Requiring airline travelers to spend at least one Saturday night away from home to qualify for a low fare.
   b. Insisting on delivering cement to buyers, and basing prices on buyers' locations.
   c. Selling food processors along with coupons that can be sent to the manufacturer to obtain a $10 rebate.
   d. Offering temporary price cuts on bathroom tissue.
   e. Charging high-income patients more than low-income patients for plastic surgery.

2. If the demand for drive-in movies is more elastic for couples than for single individuals, it will be optimal for theaters to charge one admission fee for the driver of the car and an extra fee for passengers. True or False? Explain.

3. In Example 11.1 we saw how producers of processed foods and related consumer goods use coupons as a means of price discrimination. Although coupons are widely used in the United States, that is not the case in other countries. In Germany, coupons are illegal.
   a. Does prohibiting the use of coupons in Germany make German *consumers* better off or worse off?
   b. Does prohibiting the use of coupons make German *producers* better off or worse off?

4. Suppose that BMW can produce any quantity of cars at a constant marginal cost equal to $15,000 and a fixed cost of $20 million. You are asked to advise the CEO as to what prices and quantities BMW should set for sales in Europe and in the U.S. The demand for BMWs in each market is given by:

$$Q_E = 18{,}000 - 400P_E \text{ and } Q_U = 5500 - 100P_U$$

where the subscript E denotes Europe, the subscript U denotes the United States, and all prices and costs are in thousands of dollars. Assume that BMW can restrict U.S. sales to authorized BMW dealers only.
   a. What quantity of BMWs should the firm sell in each market and what will the price be in each market? What is the total profit?
   b. If BMW were forced to charge the same price in each market, what would be the quantity sold in each market, the equilibrium price, and the company's profit?

5. A monopolist is deciding how to allocate output between two markets. The two markets are separated geographically (East Coast and Midwest). Demand and marginal revenue for the two markets are:

$$P_1 = 15 - Q_1 \qquad MR_1 = 15 - 2Q_1$$

$$P_2 = 25 - 2Q_2 \qquad MR_2 = 25 - 4Q_2$$

The monopolist's total cost is $C = 5 + 3(Q_1 + Q_2)$. What are price, output, profits, marginal revenues, and deadweight loss (i) if the monopolist can price discriminate? (ii) if the law prohibits charging different prices in the two regions?

*6. Elizabeth Airlines (EA) flies only one route: Chicago-Honolulu. The demand for each flight on this route is $Q = 500 - P$. Elizabeth's cost of running each flight is $30,000 plus $100 per passenger.

   a. What is the profit-maximizing price EA will charge? How many people will be on each flight? What is EA's profit for each flight?

   b. Elizabeth learns that the fixed costs per flight are in fact $41,000 instead of $30,000. Will she stay in this business long? Illustrate your answer using a graph of the demand curve that EA faces, EA's average cost curve when fixed costs are $30,000, and EA's average cost curve when fixed costs are $41,000.

   c. Wait! Elizabeth finds out that two different types of people fly to Honolulu. Type A is business people with a demand of $Q_A = 260 - 0.4P$. Type B is students whose total demand is $Q_B = 260 - 0.6P$. The students are easy to spot, so Elizabeth decides to charge them different prices. Graph each of these demand curves and the horizontal sum of them. What price does Elizabeth charge the students? What price does she charge the other customers? How many of each type are on each flight?

   d. What would EA's profit be for each flight? Would she stay in business? Calculate the consumer surplus of each consumer group. What is the total consumer surplus?

   e. Before EA started price discriminating, how much consumer surplus was the Type A demand getting from air travel to Honolulu? Type B? Why did the total surplus decline with price discrimination, even though the total quantity sold was unchanged?

7. Many retail video stores offer two alternative plans for renting films:

   ■ *A two-part tariff:* Pay an annual membership fee (e.g., $40), and then pay a small fee for the daily rental of each film (e.g., $2 per film per day).

   ■ *A straight rental fee:* Pay no membership fee, but pay a higher daily rental fee (e.g., $4 per film per day).

   What is the logic behind the two-part tariff in this case? Why offer the customer a choice of two plans, rather than simply a two-part tariff?

8. Sal's satellite company broadcasts TV to subscribers in Los Angeles and New York. The demand functions for each of these two groups are

$$Q_{NY} = 50 - (1/3)P_{NY}$$

$$Q_{LA} = 80 - (2/3)P_{LA}$$

where Q is in thousands of subscriptions per year, and P is the subscription price per year. The cost of providing Q units of service is given by

$$C = 1000 + 30Q$$

where $Q = Q_{NY} + Q_{LA}$.

   a. What are the profit-maximizing prices and quantities for the New York and Los Angeles markets?

   b. As a consequence of a new satellite that the Pentagon recently deployed, people in Los Angeles receive Sal's New York broadcasts, and people in New York receive Sal's Los Angeles broadcasts. As a result, anyone in New York or Los Angeles can receive Sal's broadcasts by subscribing in either city. Hence Sal can charge only a single price. What price should he charge, and what quantities will he sell in New York and Los Angeles?

   c. In which of the above situations, (a) or (b), is Sal better off? In terms of consumer surplus, which situation do people in New York prefer and which do people in Los Angeles prefer? Why?

*9. You are an executive for Super Computer, Inc. (SC), which rents out super computers. SC receives a fixed rental payment per time period in exchange for the right to unlimited computing at a rate of P cents per second. SC has two types of potential customers of equal number—10 businesses and 10 academic institutions. Each business customer has the demand function $Q = 10 - P$, where Q is in millions of seconds per month; each academic institution has the demand $Q = 8 - P$. The marginal cost to SC of additional computing is 2 cents per second, no matter what the volume.

   a. Suppose that you could separate business and academic customers. What rental fee and usage fee would you charge each group? What are your profits?

b. Suppose you were unable to keep the two types of customers separate, and you charged a zero rental fee. What usage fee maximizes your profits? What are your profits?

c. Suppose you set up one two-part tariff — that is, you set one rental and one usage fee that both business and academic customers face. What usage and rental fees will you set? What are your profits? Explain why price is not equal to marginal cost.

10. As the owner of the only tennis club in an isolated wealthy community, you must decide on membership dues and fees for court time. There are two types of tennis players. "Serious" players have demand

$$Q_1 = 6 - P$$

where Q_1 is court hours per week and P is the fee per hour for each individual player. There are also "occasional" players with demand

$$Q_2 = 3 - (1/2)P$$

Assume that there are 1000 players of each type. You have plenty of courts, so that the marginal cost of court time is zero. You have fixed costs of $5000 per week. Serious and occasional players look alike, so you must charge them the same prices.

a. Suppose that to maintain a "professional" atmosphere, you want to limit membership to serious players. How should you set the *annual* membership dues and court fees (assume 52 weeks per year) to maximize profits, keeping in mind the constraint that only serious players choose to join? What are profits (per week)?

b. A friend tells you that you could make greater profits by encouraging both types of players to join. Is the friend right? What annual dues and court fees would maximize weekly profits? What would these profits be?

c. Suppose that over the years young, upwardly mobile professionals move to your community, all of whom are serious players. You believe there are now 3000 serious players and 1000 occasional players. Is it still profitable to cater to the occasional player? What are the profit-maximizing annual dues and court fees? What are profits per week?

11. Look again at Figure 11.12, which shows the reservation prices of three consumers for two goods. Assuming that marginal production cost is zero for both goods, can the producer make the most money by selling the goods separately, by bundling, or by "mixed" bundling (i.e., offering the goods separately or as a bundle)? What prices should be charged?

12. Look again at Figure 11.17. Suppose the marginal costs c_1 and c_2 were zero. Show that in this case pure bundling is the most profitable pricing strategy, and not mixed bundling. What price should be charged for the bundle, and what will the firm's profit be?

13. On October 22, 1982, an article appeared in the *New York Times* about IBM's pricing policy. The previous day IBM had announced major price cuts on most of its small and medium-sized computers. The article said:

> IBM probably has no choice but to cut prices periodically to get its customers to purchase more and lease less. If they succeed, this could make life more difficult for IBM's major competitors. Outright purchases of computers are needed for ever larger IBM revenues and profits, says Morgan Stanley's Ulric Weil in his new book, *Information Systems in the '80's.* Mr. Weil declares that IBM cannot revert to an emphasis on leasing.

a. Provide a brief but clear argument *in support* of the claim that IBM should try "to get its customers to purchase more and lease less."

b. Provide a brief but clear argument *against* this claim.

c. What factors determine whether leasing or selling is preferable for a company like IBM? Explain briefly.

14. You are selling two goods, 1 and 2, to a market consisting of three consumers with reservation prices as follows:

Reservation Price ($)

Consumer	For 1	For 2
A	10	70
B	40	40
C	70	10

The unit cost of each product is $20.

a. Compute the optimal prices and profits for (i) selling the goods separately, (ii) pure bundling, and (iii) mixed bundling.

b. Which strategy is most profitable? Why?

15. Your firm produces two products, the demands for which are independent. Both products are produced at zero marginal cost. You face four consumers (or groups of consumers) with the following reservation prices:

Consumer	Good 1 ($)	Good 2 ($)
A	30	90
B	40	60
C	60	40
D	90	30

a. Consider three alternative pricing strategies: (i) selling the goods separately; (ii) pure bundling; (iii) mixed bundling. For *each strategy*, determine the optimal prices to be charged and the resulting profits. Which strategy is best?

b. Now suppose the production of each good entails a marginal cost of $35. How does this change your answers to (a)? Why is the optimal strategy now different?

16. A cable TV company offers, in addition to its basic service, two products: a Sports Channel (Product 1) and a Movie Channel (Product 2). Subscribers to the basic service can subscribe to these additional services individually at the monthly prices P_1 and P_2 respectively, or they can buy the two as a bundle for the price P_B, where $P_B < P_1 + P_2$. (Subscribers can also forgo the additional services and simply buy the basic service.) The company's marginal cost for these additional services is *zero*. Through market research, the cable company has estimated the reservation prices for these two services for a representative group of consumers in the company's service area. These reservation prices are plotted (as x's) in Figure 11.21

Figure 11.21 Figure for Exercise 16.

as are the prices P_1, P_2, and P_B that the cable company is currently charging. The graph is divided into regions I, II, III, and IV.

a. Which products, if any, will be purchased by the consumers in region I? In region II? In region III? In region IV? Explain briefly.

b. Note that the reservation prices for the Sports Channel and the Movie Channel, as drawn in the figure, are negatively correlated. Why would you, or why would you not, expect consumers' reservation prices for cable TV channels to be negatively correlated?

c. The company's vice president has said: "Because the marginal cost of providing an additional channel is zero, mixed bundling offers no advantage over pure bundling. Our profits would be just as high if we offered the Sports Channel and the Movie Channel together as a bundle, and only as a bundle." Do you agree or disagree? Explain why.

d. Suppose the cable company continues to use mixed bundling to sell these two services. Based on the distribution of reservation prices shown in Figure 11.21, should the cable company alter any of the prices it is now charging? If so, how?

17. Consider a firm with monopoly power that faces the demand curve

$$P = 100 - 3Q + 4A^{1/2}$$

and has the total cost function

$$C = 4Q^2 + 10Q + A$$

where A is the level of advertising expenditures, and P and Q are price and output.

a. Find the values of A, Q, and P that maximize this firm's profit.

b. Calculate the Lerner index of monopoly power, $L = (P - MC)/P$, for this firm at its profit-maximizing levels of A, Q, and P.

So far we have studied the firm's pricing decision assuming that it sells its output in an *outside market*, i.e., to consumers or to other firms. Many firms, however, are *vertically integrated*—they contain several divisions, with some divisions producing parts and components that other divisions use to produce the finished product.[1] For example, each of the major U.S. automobile companies has "upstream" divisions that produce engines, brakes, radiators, and other components that the "downstream" divisions use to produce the finished products. *Transfer pricing* refers to the valuation of these parts and components within the firm. *Transfer prices* are internal prices at which the parts and components from upstream divisions are "sold" to downstream divisions. Transfer prices must be chosen correctly because they are the signals that divisional managers use to determine output levels.

This appendix shows how a profit-maximizing firm chooses its transfer prices and divisional output levels. We will also examine other issues raised by vertical integration. For example, suppose a computer firm's upstream division produces memory chips that are used by a downstream division to produce the final product. If other firms also produce these chips, should our firm obtain all its chips from the upstream division, or should it also buy some on the outside market? Should the upstream division produce more chips than are needed by the downstream division, selling the excess in the market? And how should the firm coordinate the upstream and downstream divisions? In particular, can we design incentives for the divisions, so that the firm's profit is maximized?

We begin with the simplest case: There is no outside market for the output of the upstream division, i.e., the upstream division produces a good that is neither produced nor used by any other firm. Next we consider what happens when there is an outside market for the upstream division's output.

Transfer Pricing When There Is No Outside Market

Consider a firm that has three divisions: Two upstream divisions produce inputs to a downstream processing division. The two upstream divisions produce quantities Q_1 and Q_2, and have total costs $C_1(Q_1)$ and $C_2(Q_2)$. The downstream division produces a quantity Q using the production function

$$Q = f(K, L, Q_1, Q_2)$$

---

[1] A firm is *horizontally integrated* when it has several divisions that produce the same product or closely related products. Many firms are both vertically and horizontally integrated.

where K and L are capital and labor inputs, and Q_1 and Q_2 are the intermediate inputs from the upstream divisions. Excluding the costs of the inputs Q_1 and Q_2, the downstream division has a total production cost $C_d(Q)$. The total revenue from sales of the final product is $R(Q)$.

We assume there are *no outside markets* for the intermediate inputs Q_1 and Q_2. (They can be used only by the downstream division.) Then the firm has two problems. First, what quantities $Q_1, Q_2,$ and Q maximize its profit? Second, is there an incentive scheme that will decentralize the firm's management? In particular, is there a set of transfer prices P_1 and P_2, so that *if each division maximizes its own divisional profit, the profit of the overall firm will also be maximized?*

To solve these problems, note that the firm's total profit is

$$\pi(Q) = R(Q) - C_d(Q) - C_1(Q_1) - C_2(Q_2) \tag{A11.1}$$

Now, what is the level of Q_1 that maximizes this profit? It is the level at which *the cost of the last unit of Q_1 is just equal to the additional revenue it brings to the firm.* The cost of producing one extra unit of Q_1 is the marginal cost $\Delta C_1/\Delta Q_1 = MC_1$. How much extra revenue results from the unit? An extra unit of Q_1 allows the firm to produce more final output Q of an amount $\Delta Q/\Delta Q_1 = MP_1$, the marginal product of Q_1. An extra unit of final output results in additional revenue $\Delta R/\Delta Q = MR$, but it also results in additional cost to the downstream division, of an amount $\Delta C_d/\Delta Q = MC_d$. Thus the *net marginal revenue* NMR_1 that the firm earns from an extra unit of Q_1 is $(MR - MC_d)MP_1$. Setting this equal to the marginal cost of the unit, we obtain the following rule for profit maximization:[2]

$$\boxed{NMR_1 = (MR - MC_d)MP_1 = MC_1} \tag{A11.2}$$

Going through the same steps for the second intermediate input gives

$$\boxed{NMR_2 = (MR - MC_d)MP_2 = MC_2} \tag{A11.3}$$

Note from equations (A11.2) and (A11.3) that it is *incorrect* to determine the firm's final output level Q by setting marginal revenue equal to marginal cost for the downstream division, i.e., by setting $MR = MC_d$. Doing so ignores the cost of producing the intermediate input. (MR exceeds MC_d because this cost is positive.) Also, note that equations (A11.2) and (A11.3) are standard conditions of marginal analysis—the output of each upstream division should be such that its marginal cost is equal to its marginal contribution to the profit of the overall firm.

Now, what transfer prices P_1 and P_2 should be "charged" to the downstream division for its use of the intermediate inputs? Remember that if each of the three divisions uses these transfer prices to maximize its own divisional

---

[2] Using calculus, we can obtain this by differentiating equation (A11.1) with respect to Q_1:

$$d\pi/dQ_1 = (dR/dQ)(\partial Q/\partial Q_1) - (dC_d/dQ)(\partial Q/\partial Q_1) - dC_1/dQ_1$$
$$= (MR - MC_d)MP_1 - MC_1$$

Setting $d\pi/dQ = 0$ to maximize profit gives equation (A11.2).

profit, the profit of the overall firm should be maximized. The two upstream divisions will maximize their divisional profits, π_1 and π_2, which are given by

$$\pi_1 = P_1 Q_1 - C_1(Q_1)$$

and

$$\pi_2 = P_2 Q_2 - C_2(Q_2)$$

Since the upstream divisions take P_1 and P_2 as given, they will choose Q_1 and Q_2 so that $P_1 = MC_1$ and $P_2 = MC_2$. Similarly, the downstream division will maximize

$$\pi(Q) = R(Q) - C_d(Q) - P_1 Q_1 - P_2 Q_2$$

Since the downstream division also takes P_1 and P_2 as given, it will choose Q_1 and Q_2 so that

$$(MR - MC_d)MP_1 = NMR_1 = P_1 \tag{A11.4}$$

and

$$(MR - MC_d)MP_2 = NMR_2 = P_2 \tag{A11.5}$$

Note that by setting the transfer prices equal to the respective marginal costs ($P_1 = MC_1$ and $P_2 = MC_2$), the profit-maximizing conditions given by equations (A11.2) and (A11.3) will be satisfied. We therefore have a simple solution to the transfer pricing problem: *Set each transfer price equal to the marginal cost of the respective upstream division.* Then when each division is told to maximize its own profit, the quantities Q_1 and Q_2 that the upstream divisions will want to produce will be the same quantities that the downstream division will want to "buy," and they will maximize the total profit of the firm.

We can illustrate this graphically with the following example. Race Car Motors, Inc., has two divisions. The upstream Engine Division produces engines, and the downstream Assembly Division puts together automobiles, using one engine (and a few other parts) in each car. In Figure A11.1, the average revenue curve AR is Race Car Motors' demand curve for cars. (Note that the firm has monopoly power in the automobile market.) MC_A is the marginal cost of assembling automobiles, *given the engines* (i.e., it does not include the cost of the engines). Since the car requires one engine, the marginal product of the engines is one, so that the curve labeled $MR - MC_A$ is also the net marginal revenue curve for engines: $NMR_E = (MR - MC_A)MP_E = MR - MC_A$.

The profit-maximizing number of engines (and number of cars) is given by the intersection of the net marginal revenue curve NMR_E with the marginal cost curve for engines MC_E. Having determined the number of cars it will produce, and knowing its divisional cost functions, the management of Race Car Motors can now set the transfer price P_E that correctly values the engines used to produce its cars. It is this transfer price that should be used to calculate divisional profit (and year-end bonuses for the divisional managers).

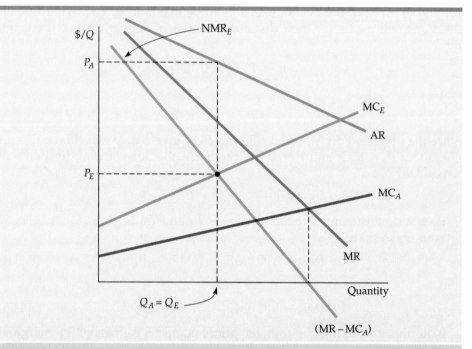

Figure A11.1 Race Car Motors, Inc The firm's upstream division should produce a quantity of engines Q_E that equates its marginal cost of engine production MC_E with the downstream division's net marginal revenue of engines NMR_E. Since the firm uses one engine in every car, NMR_E is the difference between the marginal revenue from selling cars and the marginal cost of assembling them, i.e., $MR - MC_A$. The optimal transfer price for engines P_E equals the marginal cost of producing them. Finished cars are sold at price P_A.

Transfer Pricing with a Competitive Outside Market

Now suppose there is a *competitive* outside market for the intermediate good produced by an upstream division. Since the outside market is competitive, there is a single market price at which one can buy or sell the good. Therefore, *the marginal cost of the intermediate good is simply the market price.* Since the optimal transfer price must equal marginal cost, it must also equal the competitive market price.

To see this, suppose there is a competitive market for the engines that Race Car Motors produces. If the market price is low, Race Car Motors may want to buy some or all of its engines in the market; if it is high, it may want to sell engines in the market. Figure A11.2 illustrates the first case. For quantities below $Q_{E,1}$, the upstream division's marginal cost of producing engines MC_E is below the market price $P_{E,M}$, and for quantities above $Q_{E,1}$ it is above the market price. The firm should obtain engines at least cost, so the marginal cost of engines MC_E^* is the upstream division's marginal cost for quantities up to $Q_{E,1}$

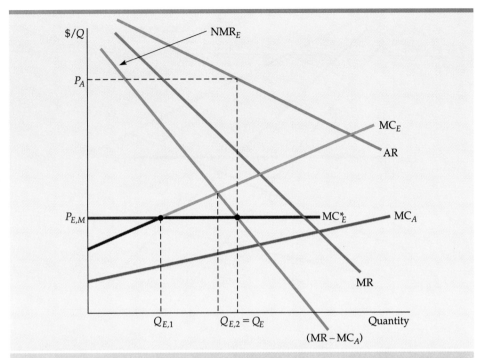

Figure A11.2 Race Car Motors Buys Engines in a Competitive Outside Market The firm's marginal cost of engines MC_E^* is the upstream division's marginal cost for quantities up to $Q_{E,1}$ and the market price $P_{E,M}$ for quantities above $Q_{E,1}$. The downstream division should use a total of $Q_{E,2}$ engines to produce an equal number of cars; then the marginal cost of engines equals net marginal revenue. $Q_{E,2} - Q_{E,1}$ of these engines are bought in the outside market. The upstream division "pays" the downstream division the transfer price $P_{E,M}$ for the remaining $Q_{E,1}$ engines.

and the market price for quantities above $Q_{E,1}$. Note that Race Car Motors uses more engines and produces more cars than it would have had there not been an outside engine market. The downstream division now buys $Q_{E,2}$ engines and produces an equal number of automobiles. However, it "buys" only $Q_{E,1}$ of these engines from the upstream division, and buys the rest on the open market.

It might appear strange that Race Car Motors should have to go into the open market to buy engines, when it can make those engines itself. If it made all its own engines, however, its marginal cost of producing engines would exceed the competitive market price, and although the profit of the upstream division would be higher, *the total profit of the firm would be lower*.

Figure A11.3 shows the case where Race Car Motors *sells* engines in the outside market. Now the competitive market price $P_{E,M}$ is above the transfer price that the firm would have set had there not been an outside market. In this case the upstream Engine Division produces $Q_{E,1}$ engines, but only $Q_{E,2}$ en-

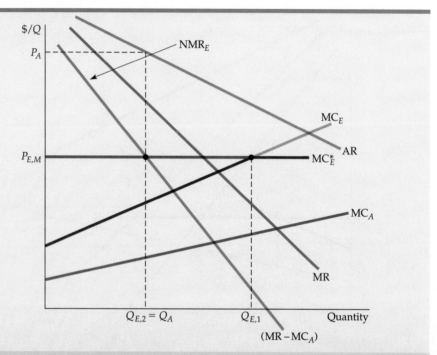

Figure A11.3   Race Car Motors Sells Engines in a Competitive Outside Market   The optimal transfer price is again the market price $P_{E,M}$. This price is above the point at which MC_E intersects NMR_E, so the upstream division sells some of its engines in the outside market. The upstream division produces $Q_{E,1}$ engines, the quantity at which MC_E equals $P_{E,M}$. The downstream division uses only $Q_{E,2}$ of these, the quantity at which NMR_E equals $P_{E,M}$. Compared with Figure A11.1, in which there is no outside market, more engines but fewer cars are produced.

gines are used by the downstream division to produce automobiles. The rest are sold in the outside market at the price $P_{E,M}$.

Note that compared with a situation in which there is no outside engine market, Race Car Motors is producing more engines but fewer cars. Why not produce this larger number of engines but use all of them to produce more cars? Because the engines are too valuable. On the margin, the net revenue that can be earned from selling them in the outside market is higher than the net revenue from using them to build additional cars.

Transfer Pricing with a Noncompetitive Outside Market

Now suppose there is an outside market for the output of the upstream division, but that market is not competitive—the firm has monopoly power. The same principles apply, but we must be careful when measuring net marginal revenue.

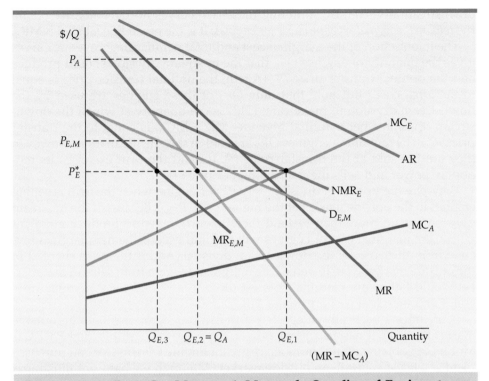

Figure A11.4   Race Car Motors—A Monopoly Supplier of Engines to an Outside Market $D_{E,M}$ is the outside market demand curve for engines, $MR_{E,M}$ is the corresponding marginal revenue curve, and $(MR - MC_A)$ is the net marginal revenue from the use of engines by the downstream division. The *total net marginal revenue curve for engines* NMR_E is the horizontal sum of these two marginal revenues. The optimal transfer price P_E^* and the quantity of engines that the upstream division produces $Q_{E,1}$ are found where $MC_E = NMR_E$. $Q_{E,2}$ of these engines are used by the downstream division, the quantity at which the downstream division's net marginal revenue, $MR - MC_A$, is equal to the transfer price P_E^*. The remaining engines $Q_{E,3}$ are sold in the outside market at the price $P_{E,M}$.

Suppose the engine produced by the upstream Engine Division is a special one that only Race Car Motors can make. There is an outside market for this engine, however, so Race Car Motors can be a monopoly supplier to that market and can also produce engines for its own use. What is the optimal transfer price for use of the engines by the downstream division, and at what price (if any) should engines be sold in the outside market?

We must find the firm's net marginal revenue from the sale of engines. In Figure A11.4, $D_{E,M}$ is the outside market demand curve for engines, and $MR_{E,M}$ is the corresponding marginal revenue curve. Race Car Motors therefore has two sources of marginal revenue from the production and sale of an additional engine—the marginal revenue $MR_{E,M}$ from sales in the outside market and the net marginal revenue $(MR - MC_A)$ from the use of the engines by the downstream division. By summing these two curves horizontally, we obtain the *total net marginal revenue curve for engines;* it is the green line labeled NMR_E.

The intersection of the marginal cost and total net marginal revenue curves gives the quantity of engines $Q_{E,1}$ that the upstream division should produce and the optimal transfer price P_E^*. (Again, the optimal transfer price is equal to marginal cost.) But note that only $Q_{E,2}$ of these engines are used by the downstream division to make cars. (This is the quantity at which the downstream division's net marginal revenue, $\text{MR} - \text{MC}_A$, is equal to the transfer price P_E^*.) The remaining engines $Q_{E,3}$ are sold in the outside market. However, they are not sold at the transfer price P_E^*. Instead the firm exercises its monopoly power and sells them at the higher price $P_{E,M}$.

Why pay the upstream division only P_E^* per engine when the firm is selling engines in the outside market at the higher price $P_{E,M}$? Because if the upstream division is paid more than P_E^* (and thereby encouraged to produce more engines), the marginal cost of engines will rise and exceed the net marginal revenue from their use by the downstream division. And if the price charged in the outside market were lowered, the marginal revenue from sales in that market would fall below marginal cost. At the prices P_E^* and $P_{E,M}$, marginal revenues and marginal cost are equal: $\text{MR}_{E,M} = (\text{MR} - \text{MC}_A) = \text{MC}_E$.

Sometimes a vertically integrated firm can buy components in an outside market in which it has *monopsony* power. Suppose, for example, that Race Car Motors can obtain engines from its upstream Engine Division, or can purchase them *as a monopsonist* in an outside market. Although we have not illustrated this case graphically, you should be able to see that now the transfer price paid to the Engine Division will be *above* the price at which engines are bought in the outside market. Why "pay" the upstream division a price that is higher than that paid in the outside market? The reason is that with monopsony power, purchasing one additional engine in the outside market incurs a *marginal expenditure* that is greater than the actual price per engine paid in that market. (The marginal expenditure is higher because purchasing an additional unit raises the average expenditure paid for *all* units bought in the outside market.)

A Numerical Example

Suppose Race Car Motors has the following demand for its automobiles:

$$P = 20,000 - Q$$

so that its marginal revenue is

$$\text{MR} = 20,000 - 2Q$$

The downstream division's cost of assembling cars is

$$C_A(Q) = 8000Q$$

so that the division's marginal cost is $\text{MC}_A = 8000$. The upstream division's cost of producing engines is

$$C_E(Q_E) = 2Q_E^2$$

so that the division's marginal cost is $MC_E(Q_E) = 4Q_E$.

First, suppose there is *no outside market* for the engines. How many engines and cars should the firm produce, and what should the transfer price for engines be? To solve this problem, we set the net marginal revenue for engines equal to the marginal cost of producing engines. Since each car has one engine, $Q_E = Q$, and the net marginal revenue of engines is

$$NMR_E = MR - MC_A = 12{,}000 - 2Q_E$$

Now set NMR_E equal to MC_E:

$$12{,}000 - 2Q_E = 4Q_E$$

so that $6Q_E = 12{,}000$, and $Q_E = 2000$. The firm should therefore produce 2000 engines and 2000 cars. The optimal transfer price is the marginal cost of these 2000 engines: $P_E = 4Q_E = \$8000$.

Second, suppose that engines can be bought or sold for \$6000 in an *outside competitive market*. This is below the \$8000 transfer price that is optimal when there is no outside market, so the firm should buy some engines outside. Its marginal cost of engines, and the optimal transfer price, is now \$6000. Set this \$6000 marginal cost equal to the net marginal revenue of engines:

$$6000 = NMR_E = 12{,}000 - 2Q_E$$

Thus the total quantity of engines and cars is now 3000. The company now produces more cars (and sells them at a lower price) because its cost of engines is lower. Also, since the transfer price for the engines is now \$6000, the upstream Engine Division supplies only 1500 engines (because $MC_E(1500) = \$6000$). The remaining 1500 engines are bought in the outside market.

Finally, suppose Race Car Motors is the only producer of these engines, but can sell them in an outside market. Demand in the outside market is:

$$P_{E,M} = 10{,}000 - Q_E$$

so that the marginal revenue from sales in the market is:

$$MR_{E,M} = 10{,}000 - 2Q_E$$

To determine the optimal transfer price, we find the *total* net marginal revenue by horizontally summing $MR_{E,M}$ with the net marginal revenue from "sales" to the downstream division, $12{,}000 - 2Q_E$, as in Figure 11A.4. For outputs Q_E greater than 1000, this is:

$$NMR_{E,Total} = 11{,}000 - Q_E$$

Now set this equal to the marginal cost of producing engines:

$$11{,}000 - Q_E = 4Q_E$$

Therefore the total quantity of engines produced should be $Q_E = 2200$.

How many of these engines should go to the downstream division, and how many to the outside market? Note that the marginal cost of producing these 2200 engines, and therefore the optimal transfer price, is $4Q_E = \$8800$. Set this equal to the marginal revenue from sales in the outside market:

$$8800 = 10,000 - 2Q_E$$

or $Q_E = 600$. Therefore 600 engines should be sold in the outside market. Finally, set this $8800 transfer price equal to the net marginal revenue from "sales" to the downstream division:

$$8800 = 12,000 - 2Q_E$$

or $Q_E = 1600$. So 1600 engines should be supplied to the downstream division for use in the production of 1600 cars.

Exercises

1. Review the numerical example about Race Car Motors. Calculate the profit earned by the upstream division, the downstream division, and the firm as a whole in each of the three cases examined: (a) no outside market for engines; (b) a competitive market for engines in which the market price is $6000; and (c) the firm is a monopoly supplier of engines to an outside market. In which case does Race Car Motors earn the most profit? In which case does the upstream division earn the most? The downstream division?

2. Ajax Computer makes a computer for climate control in office buildings. The company uses a microprocessor produced by its upstream division, along with other parts bought in outside competitive markets. The microprocessor is produced at a constant marginal cost of $500, and the marginal cost of assembling the computer (including the cost of the other parts) by the downstream division is a constant $700. The firm has been selling the computer for $2000, and until now there has been no outside market for the microprocessor.

   a. Suppose an outside market for the microprocessor develops and Ajax has monopoly power in that market, selling microprocessors for $1000 each. Assuming that demand for the microprocessor is unrelated to the demand for the Ajax computer, what transfer price should Ajax apply to the microprocessor for its use by the downstream division? Should its produc-

tion of computers be increased, decreased, or left unchanged? Explain briefly.

   b. How would your answer to (a) change if the demands for the computer and the microprocessors were competitive; i.e., some of the people who buy the microprocessors use them to make climate control systems of their own?

3. Reebok produces and sells running shoes. It faces a market demand schedule $P = 11 - 1.5Q_s$, where Q_s is the number of pairs of shoes sold (in thousands) and P is the price in dollars per thousand pairs of shoes. Production of each pair of shoes requires 1 square yard of leather. The leather is shaped and cut by the Form Division of Reebok. The cost function for leather is

$$TC_L = 1 + Q_L + 0.5Q_L^2$$

where Q_L is the quantity of leather (in thousands of square yards) produced. The cost function for running shoes is (excluding the leather)

$$TC_s = 2Q_s$$

   a. What is the optimal transfer price?

   b. Leather can be bought and sold in a competitive market at the price of $P_F = 1.5$. In this case, how much leather should the Form Division supply internally? How much should it supply to the outside market? Will Reebok buy any leather in the outside market? Find the optimal transfer price.

c. Now suppose the leather is unique and of extremely high quality. Therefore the Form Division may act as a monopoly supplier to the outside market as well as a supplier to the downstream division. Suppose the outside demand for leather is given by $P = 32 - Q_L$. What is the optimal transfer price for the use of leather by the downstream division? At what price, if any, should leather be sold to the outside market? What quantity, if any, will be sold to the outside market?

4. The House Products Division of Acme Corporation manufactures and sells digital clock radios. A major component for these is supplied by the electronics division of Acme. The cost functions for the radio and the electronic component divisions are, respectively,

$$TC_r = 30 + 2Q_r$$

$$TC_c = 70 + 6Q_c + Q_c^2$$

(Note that TC_r does not include the cost of the component.) Manufacture of one radio set requires the use of one electronic component. Market studies show that the firm's demand curve for the digital clock radio is given by

$$P_r = 108 - Q_r$$

a. Assuming no outside market for the components, how many of them should be produced to maximize profits for Acme as a whole? What is the optimal transfer price?

b. If other firms are willing to purchase in the outside market the component manufactured by the electronics division (which is the only supplier of this product), what is the optimal transfer price? Why? What price should be charged in the outside market? Why? How many units will the electronics division supply internally and to the outside market? Why? (*Note:* The demand for components in the outside market is $P_c = 72 - 1.5Q_c$.)

CHAPTER 12

Monopolistic Competition and Oligopoly

Chapter Outline

List of Examples

In the last two chapters, we saw how firms with monopoly power can choose prices and output levels to maximize profit. We also saw that monopoly power does not require a firm to be a pure monopolist. In many industries several firms compete, but each firm has at least some monopoly power—it has control over price and will charge a price that exceeds marginal cost.

In this chapter we examine market structures other than pure monopoly that can give rise to monopoly power. We begin with *monopolistic competition*. A monopolistically competitive market is similar to a perfectly competitive market in that there are many firms, and entry by new firms is not restricted. But it differs from perfect competition in that the product is *differentiated*—each firm sells a brand or version of the product that differs in quality, appearance, or reputation, and each firm is the sole producer of its own brand. The amount of monopoly power the firm has depends on its success in differentiating its product from those of other firms. Examples of monopolistically competitive industries abound: toothpaste, laundry detergent, and packaged coffee are a few.

The second form of market structure we will examine is *oligopoly*. In oligopolistic markets, only a few firms compete with one another, and entry by new firms is impeded. The product that the firms produce might be differentiated, as with automobiles, or it might not be, as with steel. Monopoly power and profitability in oligopolistic industries depend in part on how the firms interact. For example, if the interaction is more cooperative than competitive, the firms could charge prices well above marginal cost and earn large profits.

In some oligopolistic industries, firms do cooperate, but in others firms compete aggressively, even though this means lower profits. To see why, we need to consider how oligopolistic firms decide on output and prices. These decisions are complicated because each firm must operate *strategically*—when making a decision, it must weigh the probable reactions of its competitors. To understand oligopolistic markets, we must therefore introduce some basic concepts of gaming and strategy. Later, in Chapter 13, we develop these concepts more fully.

The third form of market structure we examine is a *cartel*. In a cartelized market, some or all of the firms explicitly collude—they coordinate their prices and output levels to maximize their *joint* profits. Cartels can arise in markets that would otherwise be competitive, as with OPEC, or oligopolistic, as with the international bauxite cartel.

At first glance a cartel may seem like a pure monopoly. After all, the firms in a cartel appear to operate as though they were parts of one big company. But a cartel differs from a monopoly in two important respects. First, since cartels rarely control the entire market, they must consider how their pricing decisions will affect noncartel production levels. Second, the members of a cartel are *not* part of one big company, and they may be tempted to "cheat" their partners by undercutting price and grabbing a bigger share of the market. As a result, many cartels tend to be unstable and short-lived.

12.1 Monopolistic Competition

In many industries the products that firms make are differentiated. For one reason or another, consumers view each firm's brand as different from those of other firms. Crest toothpaste, for example, is different from Colgate, Aim, and a dozen other toothpastes. The difference is partly flavor, partly consistency, and partly reputation—the consumer's image (correct or incorrect) of the relative decay-preventing efficacy of Crest. As a result, some consumers (but not all) will pay more for Crest.

Because Procter & Gamble is the sole producer of Crest, it has monopoly power. But its monopoly power is limited because consumers can easily substitute other brands for Crest if its price rises. Although consumers who prefer Crest will pay more for it, most of them will not pay much more. The typical Crest user might pay 25 or even 50 cents a tube more, but probably not a dollar more. For most consumers, toothpaste is toothpaste, and the differences among brands are small. Therefore, the demand curve for Crest toothpaste, though downward sloping, is fairly elastic. (A reasonable estimate of the elasticity of demand for Crest is -7.) Because of its limited monopoly power, Procter & Gamble will charge a price higher, but not much higher, than marginal cost. The situation is similar for Tide detergent or Scott paper towels.

The Makings of Monopolistic Competition

A monopolistically competitive market has two key characteristics: First, firms compete by selling differentiated products, which are highly substitutable for one another but not perfect substitutes. (In other words, the cross-price elasticities of demand are large but not infinite.) Second, there is *free entry and exit*—it is relatively easy for new firms to enter the market with their own brands of the product and for existing firms to leave if their products become unprofitable.

To see why free entry is an important requirement, let's compare the markets for toothpaste and automobiles. The toothpaste market is monopolistically competitive, but the automobile market is better characterized as an oligopoly. It is relatively easy for other firms to introduce new brands of toothpaste that might compete with Crest, Colgate, and so on. This limits the profitability of producing Crest or Colgate. If the profits were large, other firms would spend the necessary money (for development, production, advertising, and promotion) to introduce new brands of their own, which would reduce the market shares and profitability of Crest and Colgate.

The automobile market is also characterized by product differentiation. However, the large-scale economies involved in production make entry by new firms difficult. Hence, until the mid-1970s when Japanese producers became important competitors, the three major U.S. automakers had the market largely to themselves.

There are many other examples of monopolistic competition besides toothpaste. Soap, shampoo, deodorants, shaving cream, cold remedies, and many other items found in a drugstore are sold in monopolistically competitive markets. The markets for bicycles and other sporting goods are likewise monopolistically competitive. So is most retail trade, since goods are sold in many different retail stores that compete with one another by differentiating their services according to location, availability and expertise of salespeople, credit terms, etc. Entry is relatively easy, so if profits are high in a neighborhood because there are only a few stores, new stores will enter.

Equilibrium in the Short Run and the Long Run

As with monopoly, in monopolistic competition firms face downward-sloping demand curves and, therefore, have monopoly power. But this does not mean that monopolistically competitive firms are likely to earn large profits. Monopolistic competition is also similar to perfect competition. There is free entry, so the potential to earn profits will attract new firms with competing brands, driving profits down to zero.

To make this clear, let's examine the equilibrium price and output level for a monopolistically competitive firm in the short and long run. Figure 12.1(a) shows the short-run equilibrium. Because the firm's product differs from its competitors', its demand curve D_{SR} is downward sloping. (This is the *firm's* demand curve, not the market demand curve, which is more steeply sloped.) The profit-maximizing quantity Q_{SR} is found at the intersection of the marginal revenue and marginal cost curves. Since the corresponding price P_{SR} exceeds average cost, the firm earns a profit, as shown by the shaded rectangle in the figure.

In the long run, this profit will induce entry by other firms. As they introduce competing brands, this firm will lose market share and sales; its demand curve will shift down, as in Figure 12.1(b). (In the long run, the average and marginal cost curves may also shift. We have assumed for simplicity that costs do not change.) The long-run demand curve D_{LR} will be just tangent to the firm's average cost curve. Here profit maximization implies the quantity Q_{LR}, the price P_{LR}, and *zero profit* because price is equal to average cost. The firm

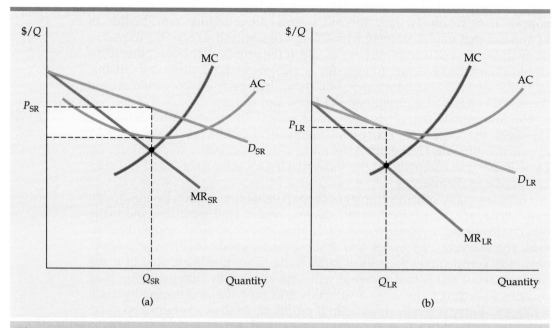

(a)   (b)

Figure 12.1   A Monopolistically Competitive Firm in the Short and Long Run   Because the firm is the only producer of its brand, it faces a downward-sloping demand curve; price exceeds marginal cost, and the firm has monopoly power. In the short run, (a), price also exceeds average cost, and the firm earns profits shown by the yellow-shaded rectangle. In the long run, these profits attract new firms with competing brands into the industry. The firm's market share falls, and its demand curve shifts downward. In long-run equilibrium, (b), price equals average cost, so the firm earns zero profit, even though it has monopoly power.

still has monopoly power; its long-run demand curve is downward sloping because the firm's particular brand is still unique. But the entry and competition of other firms have driven its profit to zero.

More generally, firms may have different costs, and some brands will be more distinctive than others. In this case firms may charge slightly different prices, and some will earn a small profit.

Monopolistic Competition and Economic Efficiency

Perfectly competitive markets are desirable because they are economically efficient—as long as there are no externalities and nothing impedes the workings of the market, the total surplus of consumers and producers is as large as possible. Monopolistic competition is similar to competition in some respects, but is it an efficient market structure? To answer this question, let's compare the long-run equilibrium of a monopolistically competitive industry to the long-run equilibrium of a perfectly competitive industry.

Figure 12.2 shows that there are two sources of inefficiency in a monopolistically competitive industry. First, unlike in perfect competition, the equi-

Figure 12.2 Comparison of Monopolistically Competitive Equilibrium and Perfectly Competitive Equilibrium Under perfect competition, as in (a), price equals marginal cost, but under monopolistic competition, price exceeds marginal cost, so there is a deadweight loss as shown by the yellow-shaded area in (b). In both types of markets, entry occurs until profits are driven to zero. Under perfect competition, the demand curve facing the firm is horizontal, so the zero-profit point occurs at the point of minimum average cost. Under monopolistic competition the demand curve is downward-sloping, so the zero-profit point is to the left of the point of minimum average cost. In evaluating monopolistic competition, these inefficiencies must be balanced against the gains to consumers from product diversity.

librium price exceeds marginal cost. This means that the value to consumers of additional units of output exceeds the cost of producing those units. If output were expanded to the point where the demand curve intersects the marginal cost curve, total surplus could be increased by an amount equal to the yellow-shaded area in Figure 12.2(b). This should not be surprising. We saw in Chapter 10 that monopoly power creates a deadweight loss, and monopoly power exists in monopolistically competitive markets.

Second, note in Figure 12.2 that the monopolistically competitive firm operates with *excess capacity*; its output is below that which minimizes average cost. Entry of new firms drives profits to zero in both perfectly competitive and monopolistically competitive markets. In a perfectly competitive market, each firm faces a horizontal demand curve, so the zero-profit point occurs at minimum average cost, as Figure 12.2(a) shows. In a monopolistically competitive market, however, the demand curve is downward sloping, so the zero-profit point is to the left of minimum average cost. This excess capacity is inefficient because average cost would be lower with fewer firms.

These inefficiencies make consumers worse off. Is monopolistic competition then a socially undesirable market structure that should be regulated? The answer for two reasons is probably not. First, in most monopolistically competitive markets, monopoly power is small. Usually, enough firms compete, with brands that are sufficiently substitutable for one another, so that no single firm will have substantial monopoly power. Any deadweight loss from monopoly power should therefore also be small. And because firms' demand curves will be fairly elastic, the excess capacity will also be small.

Second, whatever inefficiency there is must be balanced against an important benefit that monopolistic competition provides—*product diversity*. Most consumers value the ability to choose among a wide variety of competing products and brands that differ in various ways. The gains from product diversity can be large and may easily outweigh the inefficiency costs resulting from downward-sloping demand curves.

EXAMPLE 12.1 Monopolistic Competition in the Markets for Colas and Coffee

The markets for soft drinks and coffee illustrate the characteristics of monopolistic competition. Each market has a variety of brands that differ slightly but are close substitutes for one another. Each brand of cola, for example, tastes a little different from the next. (Can you tell the difference between Coke and Pepsi? Between Coke and Royal Crown Cola?) And each brand of ground coffee has a slightly different flavor, fragrance, and caffeine content. Most consumers develop their own preferences; you might prefer Maxwell House coffee to the other brands and buy it regularly. However, these brand loyalties are usually limited. If the price of Maxwell House were to rise substantially above those of other brands, you and most

Table 12.1 Elasticities of Demand for Brands of Colas and Coffee		
	Brand	**Elasticity of Demand**
Colas:	Royal Crown	−2.4
	Coke	−5.2 to −5.7
Ground coffee:	Hills Brothers	−7.1
	Maxwell House	−8.9
	Chase & Sanborn	−5.6

other consumers who had been buying Maxwell House would probably switch brands.

Just how much monopoly power does General Foods, the producer of Maxwell House, have with this brand? In other words, how elastic is the demand for Maxwell House? Most large companies carefully study the demands for their product as part of their market research. Company estimates are usually proprietary, but a study of the demands for various brands of colas and ground coffee used a simulated shopping experiment to determine how market shares for each brand would change in response to specific changes in price.[1] Table 12.1 summarizes the results by showing the elasticities of demand for several brands.

First, note that among the colas, Royal Crown is much less price elastic than Coke. Although it has a small share of the cola market, its taste is more distinctive than that of Coke, Pepsi, and other brands, so consumers who buy it have stronger brand loyalty. But because Royal Crown has more monopoly power than Coke does not mean that it is more profitable. Profits depend on fixed costs and volume, as well as price. Even if its average profit is smaller, Coke will generate more profit because it has a much larger share of the market.

Second, note that coffees as a group are more price elastic than colas. There is less brand loyalty among coffees than among colas because the differences among coffees are less perceptible than the differences among colas. Compared with different brands of colas, fewer consumers notice or care about the differences between Hills Brothers and Maxwell House coffees.

With the exception of Royal Crown, all the colas and coffees are very price elastic. With elasticities on the order of −5 to −9, each brand has only limited monopoly power. This is typical of monopolistic competition.

---

[1] The study was by John R. Nevin, "Laboratory Experiments for Estimating Consumer Demand: A Validation Study," *Journal of Marketing Research* 11 (Aug. 1974): 261–268. In simulated shopping trips, consumers had to choose the brands they preferred from a variety of prepriced brands. The trips were repeated several times, with different prices each time.

12.2 Oligopoly

In an oligopolistic market, the product may or may not be differentiated. What matters is that only a few firms account for most or all of total production. In some oligopolistic markets, some or all of the firms earn substantial profits over the long run because *barriers to entry* make it difficult or impossible for new firms to enter the market. Oligopoly is a prevalent form of market structure. Examples of oligopolistic industries include automobiles, steel, aluminum, petrochemicals, electrical equipment, and computers.

Why might barriers to entry arise? We discussed some of the reasons in Chapter 10. Scale economies may make it unprofitable for more than a few firms to coexist in the market; patents or access to a technology may exclude potential competitors; and the need to spend money for name recognition and market reputation may discourage entry by new firms. These are "natural" entry barriers—they are basic to the structure of the particular market. In addition, incumbent firms may take *strategic actions* to deter entry. For example, they might threaten to flood the market and drive prices down if entry occurs, and to make that threat credible, they can construct excess production capacity.

Managing an oligopolistic firm is complicated because pricing, output, advertising, and investment decisions involve important strategic considerations. Because only a few firms are competing, each firm must carefully consider how its actions will affect its rivals, and how its rivals are likely to react.

Suppose that because of sluggish car sales, Ford is considering a 10 percent price cut to stimulate demand. It must think carefully about how GM and Chrysler will react. They might not react at all, or they might cut their prices only slightly, in which case Ford could enjoy a substantial increase in sales, largely at the expense of its competitors. Or they might match Ford's price cut, in which case all three automakers will sell more cars but might make much lower profits because of the lower prices. Another possibility is that GM and Chrysler will cut their prices by even more than Ford did. They might cut price by 15 percent to punish Ford for rocking the boat, and this in turn might lead to a price war and to a drastic fall in profits for all three firms. Ford must carefully weigh all these possibilities. In fact, for almost any major economic decision a firm makes—setting price, determining production levels, undertaking a major promotion campaign, or investing in new production capacity—it must try to determine the most likely response of its competitors.

These strategic considerations can be complex. When making decisions, each firm must weigh its competitors' reactions, knowing that these competitors will also weigh *its* reactions to *their* decisions. Furthermore, decisions, reactions, reactions to reactions, and so forth are dynamic, evolving over time. When the managers of a firm evaluate the potential consequences of their decisions, they must assume that their competitors are as rational and intelligent as they are. Then, they must put themselves in their competitors' place and consider how they would react.

Equilibrium in an Oligopolistic Market

When we study a market, we usually want to determine the price and quantity that will prevail in equilibrium. For example, we saw that in a perfectly competitive market the equilibrium price equates the quantity supplied with the quantity demanded. Then we saw that for a monopoly an equilibrium occurs when marginal revenue equals marginal cost. Finally, when we studied monopolistic competition, we saw how a long-run equilibrium results as the entry of new firms drives profits to zero.

In these markets, each firm could take price or market demand as given, and didn't have to worry much about its competitors. In an oligopolistic market, however, a firm sets price or output based partly on strategic considerations regarding the behavior of its competitors. At the same time, the competitors' decisions depend on the firm's decision. How then can we figure out what the market price and output will be in equilibrium, or whether there will even be an equilibrium? To answer these questions, we need an underlying principle to describe an equilibrium when firms make decisions that explicitly take each other's behavior into account.

Remember how we described an equilibrium in competitive and monopolistic markets: *When a market is in equilibrium, firms are doing the best they can and have no reason to change their price or output.* Hence, a competitive market is in equilibrium when the quantity supplied equals the quantity demanded, because then each firm is doing the best it can—it is selling all that it produces and is maximizing its profit. Likewise, a monopolist is in equilibrium when marginal revenue equals marginal cost, because then it is doing the best it can and is maximizing its profit.

With some modification, we can apply this same principle to an oligopolistic market. Now, however, each firm will want to do the best it can *given what its competitors are doing.* And what should the firm assume that its competitors are doing? Because the firm will do the best it can given what its competitors are doing, *it is natural to assume that these competitors will do the best they can given what the firm is doing.* Each firm, then, takes its competitors into account, and assumes that its competitors are doing likewise.

This may seem a bit abstract at first, but it is logical, and as we will see, it gives us a basis for determining an equilibrium in an oligopolistic market. The concept was first explained clearly by the mathematician John Nash in 1951, so we call the equilibrium it describes a *Nash equilibrium*. It is an important concept that we will use repeatedly:

Nash Equilibrium:	Each firm is doing the best it can given what its competitors are doing.

We discuss this equilibrium concept in more detail in Chapter 13, where we show how it can be applied to a broad range of strategic problems. In this chapter we will apply the concept to the analysis of oligopolistic markets.

The Cournot Model

We will begin with a simple model of *duopoly*—two firms competing with each other—first introduced by the French economist Augustin Cournot in 1838. Suppose the firms produce a homogeneous good and know the market demand curve. *Each firm must decide how much to produce, and the two firms make their decisions at the same time.* When making its production decision, each firm takes its competitor into account. It knows that its competitor is *also* deciding how much to produce, and the price it receives will depend on the *total output* of both firms.

The essence of the Cournot model is that *each firm treats the output level of its competitor as fixed, and then decides how much to produce.* To see how this works, let's consider the output decision of Firm 1. Suppose Firm 1 thinks that Firm 2 will produce nothing. Then Firm 1's demand curve is the market demand curve. In Figure 12.3 this is shown as $D_1(0)$, which means the demand

Figure 12.3   Firm 1's Output Decision   Firm 1's profit-maximizing output depends on how much it thinks Firm 2 will produce. If it thinks Firm 2 will produce nothing, its demand curve, labeled $D_1(0)$, is the market demand curve. The corresponding marginal revenue curve, labeled $MR_1(0)$, intersects Firm 1's marginal cost curve MC_1 at an output of 50 units. If Firm 1 thinks Firm 2 will produce 50 units, its demand curve, $D_1(50)$, is shifted to the left by this amount. Profit maximization now implies an output of 25 units. Finally, if Firm 1 thinks Firm 2 will produce 75 units, Firm 1 will produce only 12.5 units.

curve for Firm 1, assuming Firm 2 produces zero. Figure 12.3 also shows the corresponding marginal revenue curve $MR_1(0)$. We have assumed that Firm 1's marginal cost MC_1 is constant. As shown in the figure, Firm 1's profit-maximizing output is 50 units, the point where $MR_1(0)$ intersects MC_1. So if Firm 2 produces zero, Firm 1 should produce 50.

Suppose, instead, that Firm 1 thinks Firm 2 will produce 50 units. Then Firm 1's demand curve is the market demand curve shifted to the left by 50. In Figure 12.3 this is labeled $D_1(50)$, and the corresponding marginal revenue curve is labeled $MR_1(50)$. Firm 1's profit-maximizing output is now 25 units, the point where $MR_1(50) = MC_1$. Now, suppose Firm 1 thinks Firm 2 will produce 75 units. Then Firm 1's demand curve is the market demand curve shifted to the left by 75. It is labeled $D_1(75)$ in Figure 12.3, and the corresponding marginal revenue curve is labeled $MR_1(75)$. Firm 1's profit-maximizing output is now 12.5 units, the point where $MR_1(75) = MC_1$. Finally, suppose Firm 1 thinks Firm 2 will produce 100 units. Then Firm 1's demand and marginal revenue curves (not shown in the figure) would intersect its marginal cost curve on the vertical axis; if Firm 1 thinks that Firm 2 will produce 100 units or more, it should produce nothing.

To summarize: If Firm 1 thinks Firm 2 will produce nothing, it will produce 50; if it thinks Firm 2 will produce 50, it will produce 25; if it thinks Firm 2 will produce 75, it will produce 12.5; and if it thinks Firm 2 will produce 100, then it will produce nothing. *Firm 1's profit-maximizing output is thus a decreasing schedule of how much it thinks Firm 2 will produce.* We call this schedule Firm 1's *reaction curve* and denote it by $Q_1^*(Q_2)$. This curve is plotted in Figure 12.4, where each of the four output combinations we found above is shown as an x.

We can go through the same kind of analysis for Firm 2 (i.e., determine Firm 2's profit-maximizing quantity given various assumptions about how much Firm 1 will produce). The result will be a reaction curve for Firm 2— i.e., a schedule $Q_2^*(Q_1)$ that relates its output to the output it thinks Firm 1 will produce. If Firm 2's marginal cost curve is different from that of Firm 1, its reaction curve will also differ in form from that of Firm 1. For example, Firm 2's reaction curve might look like the one drawn in Figure 12.4.

How much will each firm produce? Each firm's reaction curve tells it how much to produce, given the output of its competitor. In equilibrium, each firm sets output according to its own reaction curve, so the equilibrium output levels are found at the *intersection* of the two reaction curves. We call the resulting set of output levels a *Cournot equilibrium*. In this equilibrium, each firm correctly assumes how much its competitor will produce, and it maximizes its profit accordingly.

Note that this Cournot equilibrium is an example of a Nash equilibrium.[2] Remember that in a Nash equilibrium, each firm is doing the best it can given what its competitors are doing. As a result, no firm has any incentive to change its behavior. In the Cournot equilibrium, each duopolist is producing an

---

[2] Hence it is sometimes called a *Cournot-Nash equilibrium*.

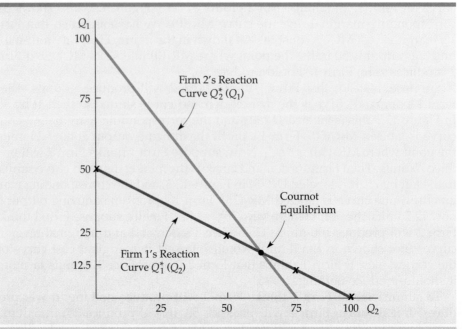

Figure 12.4 **Reaction Curves and Cournot Equilibrium** Firm 1's reaction curve shows how much it will produce as a function of how much it thinks Firm 2 will produce. (The xs, at $Q_2 = 0$, 50, and 75, correspond to the examples shown in Figure 12.3.) Firm 2's reaction curve shows its output as a function of how much it thinks Firm 1 will produce. In Cournot equilibrium, each firm correctly assumes how much its competitor will produce, and thereby maximizes its own profits. Therefore neither firm will move from this equilibrium.

amount that maximizes its profit *given what its competitor is producing,* so neither duopolist has any incentive to change its output.

Suppose the firms are initially producing output levels that differ from the Cournot equilibrium. Will they adjust their outputs until the Cournot equilibrium is reached? Unfortunately, the Cournot model says nothing about the dynamics of the adjustment process. In fact, during any adjustment process, the model's central assumption that each firm can assume that its competitor's output is fixed would not hold. Neither firm's output would be fixed, because both firms would be adjusting their outputs. We need different models to understand dynamic adjustment, and we will examine some in Chapter 13.

When is it rational for each firm to assume that its competitor's output is fixed? It is rational if the two firms are choosing their outputs only once because then their outputs cannot change. It is also rational once they are in the Cournot equilibrium because then neither firm would have any incentive to change its output. When using the Cournot model, we must therefore confine ourselves to the behavior of firms in equilibrium.

The Linear Demand Curve—An Example

Let's work through an example—two identical firms facing a linear market demand curve. This will help clarify the meaning of a Cournot equilibrium and let us compare it with the competitive equilibrium and the equilibrium that results if the firms collude and choose their output levels cooperatively.

Suppose our duopolists face the following market demand curve:

$$P = 30 - Q$$

where Q is the *total* production of both firms (i.e., $Q = Q_1 + Q_2$). Also, suppose both firms have zero marginal cost:

$$MC_1 = MC_2 = 0$$

Then we can determine the reaction curve for Firm 1 as follows. To maximize profit, the firm sets marginal revenue equal to marginal cost. Firm 1's total revenue R_1 is given by

$$R_1 = PQ_1 = (30 - Q)Q_1$$

$$= 30Q_1 - (Q_1 + Q_2)Q_1$$

$$= 30Q_1 - Q_1^2 - Q_2Q_1$$

The firm's marginal revenue MR_1 is just the incremental revenue ΔR_1 resulting from an incremental change in output ΔQ_1:

$$MR_1 = \Delta R_1/\Delta Q_1 = 30 - 2Q_1 - Q_2$$

Now, setting MR_1 equal to zero (the firm's marginal cost) and solving for Q_1, we find:

$$\text{Firm 1's reaction curve:} \quad Q_1 = 15 - \frac{1}{2}Q_2 \qquad (12.1)$$

The same calculation applies to Firm 2:

$$\text{Firm 2's reaction curve:} \quad Q_2 = 15 - \frac{1}{2}Q_1 \qquad (12.2)$$

The equilibrium output levels are the values for Q_1 and Q_2 that are at the intersection of the two reaction curves, i.e., that are the solution to equations (12.1) and (12.2). By replacing Q_2 in equation (12.1) with the expression on the right-hand side of (12.2), you can verify that the equilibrium output levels are

$$\text{Cournot equilibrium:} \quad Q_1 = Q_2 = 10$$

The total quantity produced is therefore $Q = Q_1 + Q_2 = 20$, so the equilibrium market price is $P = 30 - Q = 10$.

Figure 12.5 shows the Cournot reaction curves and this Cournot equilibrium. Note that Firm 1's reaction curve shows its output Q_1 in terms of Firm 2's output Q_2. Similarly, Firm 2's reaction curve shows Q_2 in terms of Q_1. (Since the firms are identical, the two reaction curves have the same form. They look

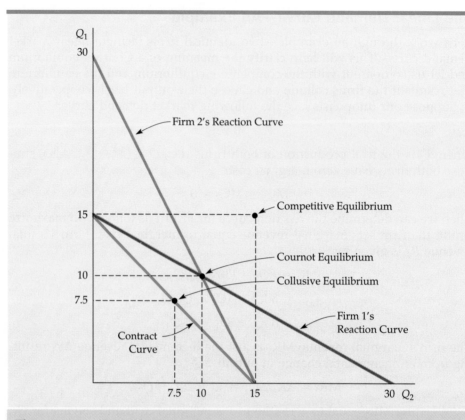

Figure 12.5   Duopoly Example   The demand curve is $P = 30 - Q$, and both firms have zero marginal cost. In Cournot equilibrium, each firm produces 10. The contract curve shows combinations of Q_1 and Q_2 that maximize *total* profits. If the firms collude and share profits equally, they will each produce 7.5. Also shown is the competitive equilibrium, in which price equals marginal cost, and profit is zero.

different because one gives Q_1 in terms of Q_2, and the other gives Q_2 in terms of Q_1.) The Cournot equilibrium is at the intersection of the two curves. At this point each firm is maximizing its own profit, given its competitor's output.

We have assumed that the two firms compete with each other. Suppose, instead, that the antitrust laws were relaxed and the two firms could collude. They would set their outputs to maximize *total profit*, and presumably they would split that profit evenly. Total profit is maximized by choosing total output Q so that marginal revenue equals marginal cost, which in this example is zero. Total revenue for the two firms is

$$R = PQ = (30 - Q)Q = 30Q - Q^2$$

so marginal revenue is

$$MR = \Delta R/\Delta Q = 30 - 2Q$$

Setting MR equal to zero, we see that total profit is maximized when $Q = 15$.

Any combination of outputs Q_1 and Q_2 that add up to 15 maximizes total profit. The curve $Q_1 + Q_2 = 15$, called the *contract curve*, is therefore all pairs of outputs Q_1 and Q_2 that maximize total profit. This curve is also shown in Figure 12.5. If the firms agree to share the profits equally, they will each produce half of the total output:

$$Q_1 = Q_2 = 7.5$$

As you would expect, both firms now produce less—and earn higher profits—than in the Cournot equilibrium. Figure 12.5 shows this collusive equilibrium and the *competitive* output levels found by setting price equal to marginal cost. (You can verify that they are $Q_1 = Q_2 = 15$, which implies that each firm makes zero profit.) Note that the Cournot outcome is much better (for the firms) than perfect competition, but not as good as the outcome from collusion.

12.3 First Mover Advantage— The Stackelberg Model

We have assumed that our two duopolists make their output decisions at the same time. Now let's see what happens if one of the firms can set its output first. There are two questions of interest. First, is it advantageous to go first? Second, how much will each firm now produce?

Continuing with our example, we assume both firms have zero marginal cost, and that the market demand curve is given by $P = 30 - Q$, where Q is the total output. *Suppose Firm 1 sets its output first, and then Firm 2, after observing Firm 1's output, makes its output decision.* In setting output, *Firm 1 must therefore consider how Firm 2 will react.* This is different from the Cournot model, in which neither firm has any opportunity to react.

Let's begin with Firm 2. Because it makes its output decision *after* Firm 1, it takes Firm 1's output as fixed. Therefore Firm 2's profit-maximizing output is given by its Cournot reaction curve, which we found to be

$$\text{Firm 2's reaction curve:} \qquad Q_2 = 15 - \frac{1}{2}Q_1 \qquad (12.2)$$

What about Firm 1? To maximize profit, it chooses Q_1, so that its marginal revenue equals its marginal cost of zero. Recall that Firm 1's revenue is

$$R_1 = PQ_1 = 30Q_1 - Q_1^2 - Q_2Q_1 \qquad (12.3)$$

Because R_1 depends on Q_2, Firm 1 must anticipate how much Firm 2 will produce. Firm 1 knows, however, that Firm 2 will choose Q_2 according to the reaction curve (12.2). Substituting equation (12.2) for Q_2 into equation (12.3), we find that Firm 1's revenue is

$$R_1 = 30Q_1 - Q_1^2 - Q_1\left(15 - \frac{1}{2}Q_1\right)$$

$$= 15Q_1 - \frac{1}{2}Q_1^2$$

so its marginal revenue is

$$MR_1 = \Delta R_1 / \Delta Q_1 = 15 - Q_1 \tag{12.4}$$

Setting $MR_1 = 0$ gives $Q_1 = 15$. And from Firm 2's reaction curve (12.2), we find that $Q_2 = 7.5$. Firm 1 produces twice as much as Firm 2 and makes twice as much profit. *Going first gives Firm 1 an advantage.* This may appear counterintuitive: It seems disadvantageous to announce your output first. Why, then, is going first a strategic advantage?

The reason is that announcing first creates a fait accompli—no matter what your competitor does, your output will be large. To maximize profit, your competitor must take your large output level as given and set a low level of output for itself. (If your competitor produced a large level of output, this would drive price down, and you would both lose money. So unless your competitor views "getting even" as more important than making money, it would be irrational for it to produce a large amount.) This kind of "first mover advantage" occurs in many strategic situations, as we will see in Chapter 13.

The Cournot and Stackelberg models are alternative representations of oligopolistic behavior. Which model is the more appropriate depends on the industry. For an industry composed of roughly similar firms, none of which has a strong operating advantage or leadership position, the Cournot model is probably the more appropriate. On the other hand, some industries are dominated by a large firm that usually takes the lead in introducing new products or setting price; the mainframe computer market is an example, with IBM the leader. Then the Stackelberg model may be more realistic.

12.4 Price Competition

We have assumed that our oligopolistic firms compete by setting quantities. In many oligopolistic industries, however, competition occurs along price dimensions. For example, for GM, Ford, and Chrysler, price is a key strategic variable, and each firm chooses its price with its competitors in mind. In this section we use the Nash equilibrium concept to study price competition, first in an industry that produces a homogeneous good, and then in an industry with some degree of product differentiation.

Price Competition with Homogeneous Products—The Bertrand Model

The Bertrand model was developed in 1883 by another French economist, Joseph Bertrand. As with the Cournot model, firms produce a homogeneous good. Now, however, they choose prices instead of quantities. As we will see, this can dramatically affect the outcome.

Let's return to the duopoly example of the last section, in which the market demand curve is

$$P = 30 - Q$$

where $Q = Q_1 + Q_2$ is again total production of a homogeneous good. This time, we will assume that both firms have a marginal cost of $3:

$$MC_1 = MC_2 = 3$$

As an exercise, you can show that the *Cournot* equilibrium for this duopoly, which results when both firms choose output simultaneously, is $Q_1 = Q_2 = 9$. You can also check that in this equilibrium the market price is \$12, so that each firm makes a profit of \$81.

Now suppose that these two duopolists compete by simultaneously choosing a *price* instead of a quantity. What price will each firm choose, and how much profit will each earn? To answer this, note that because the good is homogeneous, consumers will purchase only from the lowest-price seller. Hence, if the two firms charge different prices, the lower-priced firm will supply the entire market, and the higher-priced firm will sell nothing. If both firms charge the same price, consumers would be indifferent as to which firm they buy from, so we can assume that each firm would then supply half the market.

What is the Nash equilibrium in this case? If you think about this a little, you will see that because of the incentive to cut prices, the Nash equilibrium is the competitive outcome—i.e., both firms set price equal to marginal cost: $P_1 = P_2 = 3. Then industry output is 27 units, of which each firm produces 13.5 units. And since price equals marginal cost, both firms earn zero profit. To check that this is a Nash equilibrium, ask whether either firm would have any incentive to change its price. Suppose Firm 1 raised its price. It would then lose all of its sales to Firm 2, and would therefore be no better off. If instead it lowered its price, it would capture the entire market but would lose money on every unit it produced, and so would be worse off. Hence, Firm 1 (and likewise Firm 2) has no incentive to deviate—it is doing the best it can, given what its competitor is doing.

Why couldn't there be a Nash equilibrium in which the firms charged the same price, but a higher one (say \$5), so that each made some profit? Because in this case, if either firm lowered its price just a little, it could capture the entire market and nearly double its profit. Thus each firm would want to undercut its competitor. This undercutting would continue until the price dropped to \$3.

By changing the strategic choice variable from output to price, we get a dramatically different outcome. In the Cournot model, each firm produces only 9 units, so that the market price is \$12. Now the market price is \$3. In the Cournot model, each firm made a profit; in the Bertrand model, the firms price at marginal cost and make no profit.

The Bertrand model has been criticized on several counts. First, when firms produce a homogeneous good, it is more natural to compete by setting quantities rather than prices. Second, even if the firms do set prices and choose the same price (as the model predicts), what share of total sales will go to each one? We *assumed* that sales would be divided equally among the firms, but there is no reason why this has to be the case. But despite these shortcomings, the Bertrand model is useful because it shows how the equilibrium outcome in an oligopoly can depend crucially on the firms' choice of strategic variable.[3]

---

[3] Also, it has been shown that if firms produce a homogeneous good and compete by first setting output *capacities* and then setting price, the Cournot equilibrium in quantities again results. See David Kreps and Jose Scheinkman, "Quantity Precommitment and Bertrand Competition Yield Cournot Outcomes," *Bell Journal of Economics* 14 (1983):326–338.

Price Competition with Differentiated Products

Oligopolistic markets often have at least some degree of product differentiation.[4] Market shares are determined not just by prices, but also by differences in the design, performance, and durability of each firm's product. Then it is natural for firms to compete by choosing prices rather than quantities. To see how price competition with differentiated products can work, let's go through the following simple example. Suppose each of two duopolists has fixed costs of $20 but zero variable costs, and that they face the same demand curves:

Firm 1's demand: $\qquad Q_1 = 12 - 2P_1 + P_2 \qquad$ (12.5a)

Firm 2's demand: $\qquad Q_2 = 12 - 2P_2 + P_1 \qquad$ (12.5b)

where P_1 and P_2 are the prices that Firms 1 and 2 charge, respectively, and Q_1 and Q_2 are the resulting quantities that they sell. Note that the quantity each firm can sell decreases when the firm raises its own price, but increases when its competitor charges a higher price.

If both firms set their prices at the same time, we can use the Cournot model to determine the resulting equilibrium. Each firm will choose its own price, taking its competitor's price as fixed. Now consider Firm 1. Its profit π_1 is its revenue P_1Q_1 less its fixed cost of $20. Substituting for Q_1 from the demand curve of equation (12.5a), we have

$$\pi_1 = P_1Q_1 - 20 = 12P_1 - 2P_1^2 + P_1P_2 - 20$$

At what price P_1 is this profit maximized? The answer depends on P_2, which Firm 1 assumes is fixed. However, whatever price Firm 2 is charging, Firm 1's profit is maximized when the incremental profit from a very small increase in its own price is just zero. Taking P_2 as fixed, Firm 1's profit-maximizing price is therefore given by

$$\Delta\pi_1/\Delta P_1 = 12 - 4P_1 + P_2 = 0$$

This can be rewritten to give the following pricing rule, or *reaction curve*, for Firm 1:

Firm 1's reaction curve: $\qquad P_1 = 3 + \dfrac{1}{4}P_2$

This tells Firm 1 what price to set, given the price P_2 that Firm 2 is setting. We can similarly find the following pricing rule for Firm 2:

Firm 2's reaction curve: $\qquad P_2 = 3 + \dfrac{1}{4}P_1$

These reaction curves are drawn in Figure 12.6. The Nash equilibrium is at the point where the two reaction curves cross; you can verify that each firm

---

[4] Product differentiation can exist even for a seemingly homogeneous product. Consider gasoline, for example. Although gasoline itself is a homogeneous good, service stations differ in terms of location and services provided. As a result, gasoline prices may differ from one service station to another.

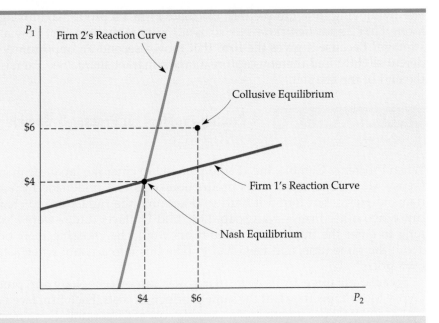

Figure 12.6 Nash Equilibrium in Prices Here two firms sell a differentiated product, and each firm's demand depends on its own price and its competitor's price. The two firms choose their prices at the same time, and each takes its competitor's price as given. Firm 1's reaction curve gives its profit-maximizing price as a function of the price that Firm 2 sets, and similarly for Firm 2. The Nash equilibrium is at the intersection of the two reaction curves; when each firm charges a price of $4, it is doing the best it can given its competitor's price, and it has no incentive to change price. Also shown is the collusive equilibrium. If the firms cooperatively set price, they would choose $6.

is then charging a price of $4, and earning a profit of $12. *At this point, because each firm is doing the best it can given the price its competitor has set, neither firm has an incentive to change its price.*

Now, suppose the two firms colluded. Instead of choosing their prices independently, they both decide to charge the same price, which will be the price that maximizes both of their profits. You can verify that the firms would then charge $6, and that they would be better off colluding because each would now earn a profit of $16.[5] Figure 12.6 shows this collusive equilibrium.

Finally, suppose Firm 1 set its price first, and after observing Firm 1's price, Firm 2 made its pricing decision. Unlike the Stackelberg model in which the firms set their quantities, in this case Firm 1 would be at a distinct *disadvan-*

---

[5] The firms have the same costs, so they will charge the same price P. Total profit is given by
$$\pi_T = \pi_1 + \pi_2 = 24P - 4P^2 + 2P^2 - 40 = 24P - 2P^2 - 40.$$
This is maximized when $\Delta \pi_T / \Delta P = 0$. $\Delta \pi_T / \Delta P = 24 - 4P$, so the joint profit-maximizing price is $P = 6$. Each firm's profit is then
$$\pi_1 = \pi_2 = 12P - P^2 - 20 = 72 - 36 - 20 = \$16$$

tage by moving first. (To see this, calculate Firm 1's profit-maximizing price, *taking Firm 2's reaction curve into account*.) Why is moving first now a disadvantage? Because it gives the firm that moves second an opportunity to undercut slightly, and thereby capture a larger market share. (See Exercise 10 at the end of the chapter.)

EXAMPLE 12.2 **A Pricing Problem for Procter & Gamble**

When Procter & Gamble, Inc. (P&G) planned to enter the Japanese market for Gypsy Moth Tape, it knew its production costs and understood the market demand curve, but found it hard to determine the right price to charge because two other firms—Kao Soap, Ltd., and Unilever, Ltd.—were also planning to enter the market. All three firms would be choosing their prices at about the same time, and P&G had to take this into account when setting its own price.[6]

Because all three firms were using the same technology for producing Gypsy Moth Tape, they had the same production costs. Each firm faced a fixed cost of $480,000 per month and a variable cost of $1 per unit. From market research, P&G ascertained that its demand curve for monthly sales was

$$Q = 3375 P^{-3.5}(P_U)^{.25}(P_K)^{.25}$$

where Q is monthly sales in thousands of units, and P, P_U, and P_K are P&G's, Unilever's, and Kao's prices, respectively. Now, put yourself in P&G's position. Assuming that Unilever and Kao face the same demand conditions, *with what price should you enter the market, and how much profit should you expect to earn?*

You might begin by calculating the profit you would earn as a function of the price you charge, under alternative assumptions about the prices that Unilever and Kao will charge. Using the demand curve and cost numbers given above, we have done these calculations and tabulated the results in Table 12.2. Each entry shows your profit, in thousands of dollars per month, for a particular combination of prices (but in each case assumes that Unilever and Kao set the same price). For example, if you charge $1.30 and Unilever and Kao both charge $1.50, you will earn a profit of $15,000 per month.

Remember that in all likelihood, the managers of Unilever and Kao are making the same calculations that you are and probably have their own versions of Table 12.2. Now suppose your competitors charge $1.50 or more. As the table shows, you would want to charge only $1.40 because that gives you the highest profit. (For example, if they charged $1.50, you would make $29,000 per month by charging $1.40, but only $20,000 by charging $1.50, and $15,000 by charging $1.30.) So you would not want to charge $1.50 (or more).

---

[6] This example is based on classroom material developed by Professor John Hauser of MIT. To protect P&G's proprietary interests, some of the facts about the product and the market have been altered. The fundamental description of P&G's problem, however, is accurate.

Assuming that your competitors have gone through the same reasoning, you should not expect them to charge $1.50 (or more) either.

What if your competitors charge $1.30? Then you will lose money, but you will lose the least amount of money ($6,000 per month) by charging $1.40. Your competitors would therefore not expect you to charge $1.30, and by the same reasoning, you should not expect them to charge a price this low. What price lets you do the best you can, given your competitors' prices? It is $1.40. This is also the price at which your competitors are doing the best *they* can, so it is a Nash equilibrium.[7] As the table shows, in this equilibrium you and your competitors each make a profit of $12,000 per month.

If you could *collude* with your competitors, you could make a larger profit. You would all agree to charge $1.50, and each of you would earn $20,000. But this collusive agreement might be hard to enforce—you could increase your profit further at your competitors' expense by dropping your price below theirs, and your competitors might think about doing the same to you.

Table 12.2 P&G's Profit (in thousands of $ per month)

P&G's Price ($)	Competitors' (Equal) Prices ($)							
	1.10	1.20	1.30	1.40	1.50	1.60	1.70	1.80
1.10	−226	−215	−204	−194	−183	−174	−165	−155
1.20	−106	−89	−73	−58	−43	−28	−15	−2
1.30	−56	−37	−19	2	15	31	47	62
1.40	−44	−25	−6	12	29	46	62	78
1.50	−52	−32	−15	3	20	36	52	68
1.60	−70	−51	−34	−18	−1	14	30	44
1.70	−93	−76	−59	−44	−28	−13	1	15
1.80	−118	−102	−87	−72	−57	−44	−30	−17

12.5 Competition Versus Collusion: The Prisoners' Dilemma

A Nash equilibrium is a *noncooperative* equilibrium—each firm makes the decisions that give it the highest possible profit, given the actions of its competitors. As we have seen, the resulting profit earned by each firm is higher

---

[7] This Nash equilibrium can also be derived algebraically from the demand curve and cost data above. We leave this to you as an exercise.

than it would be under perfect competition, but lower than if the firms colluded.

Collusion is, however, illegal, and most managers prefer to stay out of jail and not pay stiff fines. But if cooperation can lead to higher profits, why don't firms cooperate *without* explicitly colluding? In particular, if you and your competitor can both figure out the profit-maximizing price you would agree to charge *if* you were to collude, *why not just set that price and hope your competitor will do the same?* If your competitor *does* do the same, you will both make more money.

The problem is that your competitor *probably won't* choose to set price at the collusive level. Why not? *Because your competitor would do better by choosing a lower price, even if it knew that you were going to set price at the collusive level.*

To understand this, let's go back to our example of price competition from the last section. The firms in that example each have a fixed cost of $20, have zero variable cost, and face the following demand curves:

$$\textit{Firm 1's demand:} \qquad Q_1 = 12 - 2P_1 + P_2 \qquad (12.6a)$$

$$\textit{Firm 2's demand:} \qquad Q_2 = 12 - 2P_2 + P_1 \qquad (12.6b)$$

We found that in the Nash equilibrium each firm will charge a price of $4 and earn a profit of $12, whereas if the firms collude they will charge a price of $6 and earn a profit of $16. Now suppose the firms do not collude, but that Firm 1 charges the $6 collusive price, hoping that Firm 2 will do the same. If Firm 2 *does* do the same, it will earn a profit of $16. But what if it charges the $4 price instead? Then, Firm 2 would earn a profit of

$$\pi_2 = P_2 Q_2 - 20 = (4)[12 - (2)(4) + 6] - 20 = \$20$$

Firm 1, on the other hand, will earn a profit of

$$\pi_1 = P_1 Q_1 - 20 = (6)[12 - (2)(6) + 4] - 20 = \$4$$

So if Firm 1 charges $6 but Firm 2 charges only $4, Firm 2's profit will increase to $20. And it will do so at the expense of Firm 1's profit, which will fall to $4. Clearly, Firm 2 does best by charging only $4. And similarly, Firm 1 does best by charging only $4. If Firm 2 charges $6 and Firm 1 charges $4, Firm 1 will earn a $20 profit, and Firm 2 will earn only $4.

Table 12.3 summarizes the results of these different pricing possibilities. In deciding what price to set, the two firms are playing a *noncooperative game*—each firm independently does the best it can, taking its competitor into account. Table 12.3 is called the *payoff matrix* for this game because it shows the profit (or payoff) to each firm given its decision and the decision of its competitor. For example, the upper left-hand corner of the payoff matrix tells us that if both firms charge $4, each firm will make a $12 profit. The upper right-hand corner tells us that if Firm 1 charges $4 and Firm 2 charges $6, Firm 1 will make $20, and Firm 2 will make $4.

This payoff matrix can clarify the answer to our original question: Why

Table 12.3 Payoff Matrix for Pricing Game

		Firm 2	
		Charge $4	Charge $6
Firm 1	Charge $4	$12, $12	$20, $4
	Charge $6	$4, $20	$16, $16

don't firms behave cooperatively, and thereby earn higher profits, even if they can't collude? In this case, cooperating means *both* firms charging $6 instead of $4, and thereby earning $16 instead of $12. The problem is that each firm always makes more money by charging $4, *no matter what its competitor does.* As the payoff matrix shows, if Firm 2 charges $4, Firm 1 does best by charging $4. And if Firm 2 charges $6, Firm 1 still does best by charging $4. Similarly, Firm 2 always does best by charging $4, no matter what Firm 1 does. As a result, unless the two firms can sign an enforceable agreement to charge $6, neither firm can expect its competitor to charge $6, and both will charge $4.

A classic example in game theory, called the *Prisoners' Dilemma*, illustrates the problem oligopolistic firms face. It goes as follows: Two prisoners have been accused of collaborating in a crime. They are in separate jail cells and cannot communicate with each other. Each has been asked to confess to the crime. If both prisoners confess, each will receive a prison term of five years. If neither confesses, the prosecution's case will be difficult to make, so the prisoners can expect to plea bargain and receive a term of two years. On the other hand, if one prisoner confesses and the other does not, the one who confesses will receive a term of only one year, while the other will go to prison for ten years. If you were one of these prisoners, what would you do—confess or not confess?

The payoff matrix in Table 12.4 summarizes the possible outcomes. (Note that the "payoffs" are negative; the entry in the lower right-hand corner of the payoff matrix means a two-year sentence for each prisoner.) As the table shows, these prisoners face a dilemma. If they could only both agree not to confess (in a way that would be binding), then each would go to jail for only

Table 12.4 Payoff Matrix for Prisoners' Dilemma

		Prisoner B	
		Confess	Don't confess
Prisoner A	Confess	−5, −5	−1, −10
	Don't confess	−10, −1	−2, −2

two years. But they can't talk to each other, and even if they could, can they trust each other? If Prisoner A does not confess, he risks being taken advantage of by his former accomplice. After all, *no matter what Prisoner A does, Prisoner B comes out ahead by confessing*. Similarly, Prisoner A always comes out ahead by confessing, so Prisoner B must worry that by not confessing, she will be taken advantage of. Therefore, both prisoners will probably confess and go to jail for five years.

Oligopolistic firms often find themselves in a Prisoners' Dilemma. They must decide whether to compete aggressively, attempting to capture a larger share of the market at their competitor's expense, or to "cooperate" and compete more passively, coexisting with their competitors and settling for the market share they currently hold, and perhaps even implicitly colluding. If the firms compete passively, setting high prices and limiting output, they will make higher profits than if they compete aggressively.

Like our prisoners, however, each firm has an incentive to "fink" and undercut its competitors, and each knows that its competitors have the same incentive. As desirable as cooperation is, each firm worries—with good reason—that if it competes passively, its competitor might compete aggressively, taking the lion's share of the market. In the pricing problem illustrated in Table 12.3, both firms do better by "cooperating" and charging a high price. But the firms are in a Prisoners' Dilemma, where neither firm can trust or expect its competitor to set a high price.

EXAMPLE 12.3 **Procter & Gamble in a Prisoners' Dilemma[8]**

In Example 12.2, we examined the problem that arose when P&G, Unilever, and Kao Soap were all planning to enter the Japanese market for Gypsy Moth Tape at the same time. They all faced the same cost and demand conditions, and each firm had to decide on a price that took its competitors into account. In Table 12.2, we tabulated the profits to P&G corresponding to alternative prices that it and its competitors might charge. We argued that P&G should expect its competitors to charge a price of $1.40, and should do the same.

P&G would be better off if it *and its competitors* all charged a price of $1.50. This is clear from the payoff matrix in Table 12.5. (This payoff matrix is the portion of Table 12.2 corresponding to prices of $1.40 and $1.50, with the payoffs to P&G's competitors also tabulated.) If all the firms charge $1.50, they will each make a profit of $20,000 per month, instead of the $12,000 per month they make by charging $1.40. Then why don't they charge $1.50?

Because these firms are in a Prisoners' Dilemma. No matter what Unilever and Kao do, P&G makes more money by charging $1.40. For example, if Unilever and Kao charge $1.50, P&G can make $29,000 per month by charging $1.40, versus $20,000 by charging $1.50. This is also true for Unilever and

---

[8] As in Example 12.2, some of the facts about the product and the market have been altered to protect P&G's proprietary interests.

Table 12.5 Payoff Matrix for Pricing Problem

		Unilever and Kao[9]	
		Charge $1.40	Charge $1.50
P&G	Charge $1.40	$12, $12	$29, $11
	Charge $1.50	$3, $21	$20, $20

for Kao. For example, if P&G charges $1.50 and Unilever and Kao both charge $1.40, they will each make $21,000, instead of $20,000.[10] As a result, P&G knows that if it sets a price of $1.50, its competitors will have a strong incentive to undercut and charge $1.40. P&G will then have only a small share of the market and will make only $3000 per month profit. Should P&G make a leap of faith and charge $1.50? If you were faced with this dilemma, what would you do?

12.6 Implications of the Prisoners' Dilemma for Oligopolistic Pricing

Does the Prisoners' Dilemma doom oligopolistic firms to aggressive competition and low profits? Not necessarily. Although our imaginary prisoners have only one opportunity to confess, most firms set output and price over and over again, continually observing their competitors' behavior and adjusting their own accordingly. This allows firms to develop reputations from which trust can arise. As a result, oligopolistic coordination and cooperation can sometimes prevail.

Take, for example, an industry made up of three or four firms that have coexisted for a long time. Over the years, the managers of those firms might grow tired of losing money because of price wars, and an implicit understanding might arise in which all the firms maintain high prices, and no firm attempts to take market share from its competitors. Although each firm might be tempted to undercut its competitors, the managers know that the gains from this will be short lived. They know their competitors will retaliate, and the result will be renewed warfare and lower profits over the long run.

This resolution of the Prisoners' Dilemma occurs in some industries, but not in others. Sometimes managers are not content with the moderately high profits resulting from implicit collusion and prefer to compete aggressively

---

[9] Assumes that Unilever and Kao both charge the same price. Entries represent profits in thousands of dollars per month.

[10] If P&G and Kao both charged $1.50 and *only* Unilever undercut and charged $1.40, Unilever would make $29,000 per month. It is especially profitable to be the only firm charging the low price.

to try and capture most of the market. Sometimes implicit understandings are difficult to reach. For example, firms with different costs and different assessments of market demand might disagree about what the "correct" collusive price is. Firm A might think the "correct" price is $10, while Firm B thinks it is $9. When it sets a $9 price, Firm A might view this as an attempt to undercut, and might retaliate by lowering its price to $8, so a price war begins.

As a result, in many industries implicit collusion is short lived. There is often a fundamental layer of mistrust, so warfare erupts as soon as one firm is perceived by its competitors to be "rocking the boat" by changing its price or doing too much advertising.

Price Rigidity

Because implicit collusion tends to be fragile, oligopolistic firms often have a strong desire for stability, particularly with respect to price. This is why *price rigidity* can be a characteristic of oligopolistic industries. Even if costs or demand change, firms are reluctant to change price. If costs fall or market demand declines, firms are reluctant to lower price because that might send the wrong message to their competitors, and thereby set off a round of price warfare. And if costs or demand rises, firms are reluctant to raise price because they are afraid that their competitors might not also raise their prices.

This price rigidity is the basis of the well-known "kinked demand curve" model of oligopoly. According to this model, each firm faces a demand curve kinked at the currently prevailing price P^*. (See Figure 12.7.) At prices above P^*, the demand curve is very elastic. The reason is that the firm believes that if it raises its price above P^*, other firms will not follow suit, and it will therefore lose sales and much of its market share. On the other hand, the firm believes that if it lowers its price below P^*, other firms will follow suit because they will not want to lose *their* shares of the market, so that sales will expand only to the extent that a lower market price increases the total market demand.

Because the firm's demand curve is kinked, its marginal revenue curve is discontinuous. (The bottom part of the marginal revenue curve corresponds to the less elastic part of the demand curve, as shown by the solid portions of each curve.) As a result, the firm's costs can change without resulting in a change in price. As shown in the figure, marginal cost could increase, but it would still equal marginal revenue at the same output level, so that price stays the same.

The kinked demand curve model is attractively simple, but it does not really explain oligopolistic pricing. It says nothing about how firms arrived at price P^* in the first place, and why they didn't arrive at some different price. It is useful mainly as a description of price rigidity, rather than an

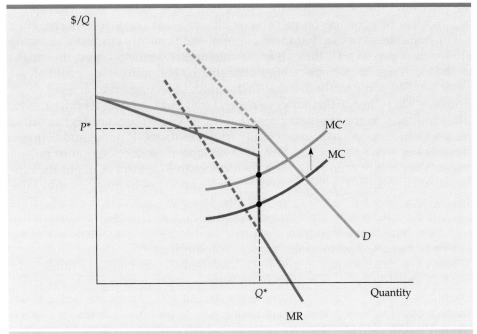

Figure 12.7 The Kinked Demand Curve Each firm believes that if it raises its price above the current price P^*, none of its competitors will follow suit, so it will lose most of its sales. Each firm also believes that if it lowers price, everyone will follow suit, and its sales will increase only to the extent that market demand increases. As a result, the firm's demand curve D is kinked at price P^*, and its marginal revenue curve MR is discontinuous at that point. If marginal cost increases from MC to MC', the firm will still produce the same output level Q^* and charge the same price P^*.

explanation of it.[11] The explanation for price rigidity comes from the Prisoners' Dilemma and from firms' desires to avoid mutually destructive price competition.

Price Signaling and Price Leadership

One of the main impediments to implicitly collusive pricing is that it is difficult for firms to agree (without talking to each other) on what the price should be. Agreement becomes particularly problematic when cost and demand conditions are changing, and thus the "correct" price is also changing. *Price signaling* is a form of implicit collusion that sometimes gets around this problem. For example, a firm might announce that it has raised its price (perhaps through a press release) and hope that its competitors will take this as a signal that they should also raise their prices. If the competitors go along with this, a pattern of *price leadership* might be established. Here the first firm sets

---

[11] Also, the model has not stood up well to empirical tests; there is evidence that rival firms do match price increases as well as decreases.

the price, and the other firms, the "price followers," follow suit. This solves the problem of agreeing on price—just charge what the leader is charging.

For example, suppose that three oligopolistic firms are currently charging $10 for their product. (If they all know the market demand curve, this might be the Nash equilibrium price.) Suppose that by colluding, they could all set a price of $20 and greatly increase their profits. Meeting and agreeing to set a price of $20 is illegal. But suppose instead that Firm A raises its price to $15, and announces to the business press that it is doing so because higher prices are needed to restore economic vitality to the industry. Firms B and C might view this as a clear message—Firm A is seeking their cooperation in raising prices. They might then raise their own prices to $15. Firm A might then increase price further, say to $18, and Firms B and C might go along and raise their prices as well. Whether or not the profit-maximizing price of $20 is reached (or surpassed), a pattern of coordination and implicit collusion has now been established that from the firms' point of view may be nearly as effective as meeting and formally agreeing on a price.[12]

This example of signaling and price leadership is extreme, and might lead to an antitrust lawsuit. But in some industries, a large firm might naturally emerge as a leader, with the other firms deciding that they are best off just matching the leader's prices, rather than trying to undercut the leader or each other. An example is the U.S. automobile industry, where General Motors has traditionally been the price leader.

Price leadership can also serve as a way for oligopolistic firms to deal with their reluctance to change prices, a reluctance that arises out of fear of being undercut or "rocking the boat." As cost and demand conditions change, firms may find it increasingly necessary to change prices that for some time had remained rigid. Then the firms might look to a price leader to signal when and by how much the price should change. Sometimes a large firm will naturally act as leader, and sometimes different firms will be the leader from time to time. The example of commercial banking that follows illustrates this.

E X A M P L E 1 2 . 4 **Price Leadership and Price Rigidity in Commercial Banking**

Commercial banks borrow money from individuals and companies that deposit funds in checking accounts, savings accounts, and certificates of deposit. They then use this money to make loans to household and corporate borrowers. By lending at an interest rate higher than the rate they pay on their deposits, they earn a profit.

The largest commercial banks in the United States—BankAmerica, Bankers Trust, Chase Manhattan, Citicorp, and First Chicago Corp, among others—compete with each other to make loans to large corporate clients.

---

[12] For a formal model of how price leadership of this sort can facilitate collusion, see Julio J. Rotemberg and Garth Saloner, "Collusive Price Leadership," *Journal of Industrial Economics*, 1990.

The main form of competition is over price, in this case the interest rate these banks charge corporate clients for loans. If competition becomes aggressive, the interest rates they charge fall, and so do their profits. The incentive to avoid aggressive competition leads to price stickiness, and a form of price leadership.

The interest rate that banks charge large corporate clients is called the *prime rate*. This rate is widely cited in newspapers, and so is a convenient focal point for price leadership. Most large banks charge the same or nearly the same prime rate, and they avoid making frequent changes in the rate that might be destabilizing and lead to competitive warfare. The prime rate changes only when money market conditions have changed enough so that other interest rates have risen or fallen substantially. When that happens, one of the major banks announces a change in its rate, and the other banks quickly follow suit. Different banks act as leader from time to time, but when one bank announces a change, the other banks follow within two or three days.

Table 12.6 shows the evolution of the prime rate from March 1994 through January 1996. Note that when the prime rate changed, several large banks raised or lowered their rates at about the same time, and other banks quickly followed suit. In most cases, all banks changed their rates within the same day. The table also shows that changes in the prime rate were relatively infrequent. Other market interest rates were fluctuating considerably during this period, but the prime rate changed only after other rates had changed sub-

Table 12.6 The Prime Rate		
Date	**Bank**	**Rate Change**
March 23, 1994	Major commercial banks	$6 \rightarrow 6\frac{1}{4}$
April 18, 1994	Banc One, Citicorp, Chemical Bank, Bank of New York	$6\frac{1}{4} \rightarrow 6\frac{3}{4}$
May 17, 1994	Citicorp, First Chicago, Bank of New York	$6\frac{3}{4} \rightarrow 7\frac{1}{4}$
August 16, 1994	Citicorp, BankAmerica, Chemical Bank, Chase Manhattan, Norwest	$7\frac{1}{4} \rightarrow 7\frac{3}{4}$
November 15, 1994	First Chicago	$7\frac{3}{4} \rightarrow 8\frac{1}{2}$
February 1, 1995	Major commercial banks	$8\frac{1}{2} \rightarrow 9$
July 6, 1995	Banc One, Bank of America	$9 \rightarrow 8\frac{3}{4}$
December 20, 1995	Banc One	$8\frac{3}{4} \rightarrow 8\frac{1}{2}$
January 31, 1996	Citicorp, NationsBank, Chase Manhattan	$8\frac{1}{2} \rightarrow 8\frac{1}{4}$

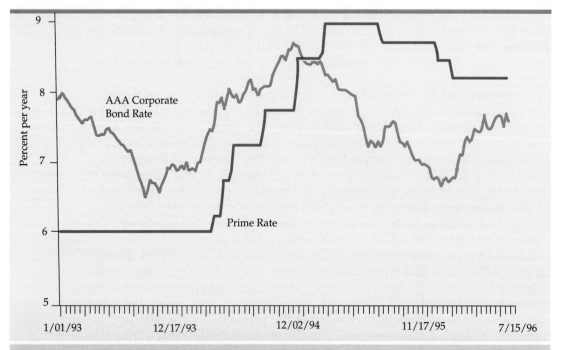

Figure 12.8 **Prime Rate Versus Corporate Bond Rate** The prime rate is the rate that major banks charge large corporate customers for short-term loans. It changes only infrequently because banks are reluctant to undercut one another. When a change does occur, it begins with one bank, and other banks quickly follow suit. The corporate bond rate is the return on long-term corporate bonds. Because these bonds are widely traded, this rate fluctuates with market conditions.

stantially. Figure 12.8 shows this by comparing the prime rate with the interest rate on high-grade (AAA) long-term corporate bonds during the same period. Observe that the corporate bond rate was fluctuating continually, but there were extended periods during which prime rate did not change.

The Dominant Firm Model

In some oligopolistic markets, one large firm has a major share of total sales, and a group of smaller firms supplies the remainder of the market. The large firm might then act as a *dominant firm*, setting a price that maximizes its own profits. The other firms, which individually could have little influence over price anyway, would then act as perfect competitors; they take the price set by the dominant firm as given and produce accordingly. But what price should the dominant firm set? To maximize profit, it must take into account how the output of the other firms depends on the price it sets.

Figure 12.9 shows how a dominant firm sets its price. Here, D is the market demand curve, and S_F is the supply curve (i.e., the aggregate marginal cost curve of the smaller fringe firms). The dominant firm must determine *its* demand curve D_D. As the figure shows, this is just the difference between market demand and the supply of fringe firms. For example, at price P_1 the supply of fringe firms is just equal to market demand, so the dominant firm can sell nothing at this price. At a price P_2 or less, fringe firms will not supply any of the good, so the dominant firm faces the market demand curve. At prices between P_1 and P_2, the dominant firm faces the demand curve D_D.

Corresponding to D_D is the dominant firm's marginal revenue curve MR_D. MC_D is the dominant firm's marginal cost curve. To maximize its profit, the dominant firm produces quantity Q_D at the intersection of MR_D and MC_D. From the demand curve D_D, we find price P^*. At this price, fringe firms sell a quantity Q_F, so that the total quantity sold is $Q_T = Q_D + Q_F$.

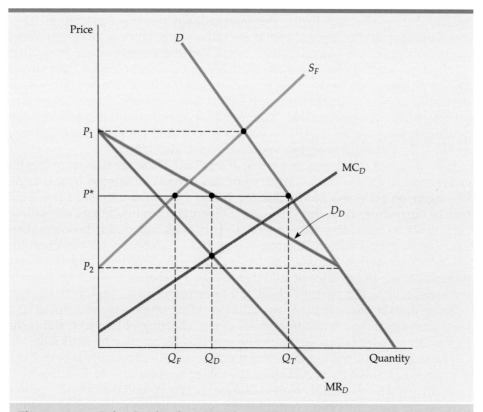

Figure 12.9   Price Setting by a Dominant Firm   The dominant firm sets price, and the other firms sell as much as they want at that price. The dominant firm's demand curve, D_D, is the difference between market demand D and the supply of fringe firms S_F. The dominant firm produces a quantity Q_D at the point where its marginal revenue MR_D is equal to its marginal cost MC_D. The corresponding price is P^*. At this price, fringe firms sell Q_F, so that total sales is Q_T.

12.7 Cartels

Producers in a cartel explicitly agree to cooperate in setting prices and output levels. Not all the producers in an industry need to join the cartel, and most cartels involve only a subset of producers. But if enough producers adhere to the cartel's agreements, and if market demand is sufficiently inelastic, the cartel may drive prices well above competitive levels.

Cartels are often international. The U.S. antitrust laws prohibit American companies from colluding, but the antitrust laws of other countries are much weaker and are sometimes poorly enforced. Furthermore, nothing prevents countries, or companies owned or controlled by foreign governments, from forming a cartel. For example, the OPEC cartel is an international agreement among oil-producing countries, which for over a decade succeeded in raising world oil prices far above what they would have been otherwise.

Other international cartels have also succeeded in raising prices. For example, during the mid-1970s, the International Bauxite Association (IBA) quadrupled bauxite prices, and a secretive international uranium cartel pushed up uranium prices. Some cartels had longer successes: From 1928 through the early 1970s, a cartel called Mercurio Europeo kept the price of mercury close to monopoly levels, and an international cartel monopolized the iodine market from 1878 through 1939. However, most cartels have failed to raise prices. An international copper cartel operates to this day, but it has never had a significant impact on copper prices. And cartel attempts to drive up the prices of tin, coffee, tea, and cocoa have also failed.[13]

Why do some cartels succeed while others fail? There are two requisites for cartel success. First, a stable cartel organization must be formed whose members agree on price and production levels and then adhere to that agreement. Unlike our prisoners in the Prisoners' Dilemma, cartel members can talk to each other to formalize an agreement. This does not mean, however, that agreeing is easy. Different members may have different costs, different assessments of market demand, and even different objectives, and they may therefore want to set price at different levels. Furthermore, each member of the cartel will be tempted to "cheat" by lowering its price slightly to capture a larger market share than it was allotted. Most often, only the threat of a long-term return to competitive prices deters cheating of this sort. But if the profits from cartelization are large enough, that threat may be sufficient.

The second requisite for success is the potential for monopoly power. Even if a cartel can solve its organizational problems, there will be little room to raise price if it faces a highly elastic demand curve. Potential monopoly power may be the most important condition for success; if the potential gains from cooperation are large, cartel members will have more incentive to solve their organizational problems.

---

[13] See Robert S. Pindyck, "The Cartelization of World Commodity Markets," *American Economic Review* 69 (May 1979): 154–158; and Jeffrey K. MacKie-Mason and Robert S. Pindyck, "Cartel Theory and Cartel Experience in International Minerals Markets," in *Energy: Markets and Regulation* (Cambridge, Mass.: MIT Press, 1986).

The Analysis of Cartel Pricing

Only rarely do *all* the producers of a good combine to form a cartel. A cartel usually accounts for only a portion of total production and must take the supply response of competitive (noncartel) producers into account when setting price. Cartel pricing can thus be analyzed by using the dominant firm model discussed earlier. We will apply this model to two cartels, the OPEC oil cartel and the CIPEC copper cartel.[14] This will help us understand why OPEC was successful in raising price, while CIPEC was not.

Figure 12.10 illustrates the case of OPEC. Total Demand TD is the total world demand curve for crude oil, and S_c is the competitive (non-OPEC) supply curve. The demand for OPEC oil D_{OPEC} is the difference between total demand and competitive supply, and MR_{OPEC} is the corresponding marginal

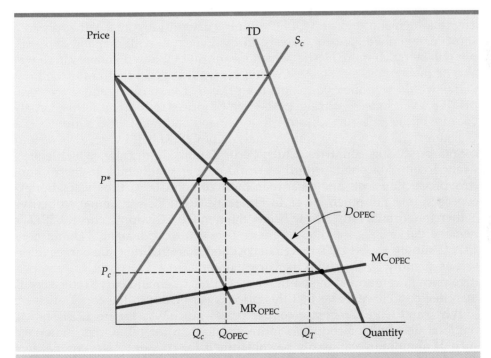

Figure 12.10   The OPEC Oil Cartel   TD is the total world demand curve for oil, and S_c is the competitive (non-OPEC) supply curve. OPEC's demand D_{OPEC} is the difference between the two. Because both total demand and competitive supply are inelastic, OPEC's demand is inelastic. OPEC's profit-maximizing quantity Q_{OPEC} is found at the intersection of its marginal revenue and marginal cost curves; at this quantity, OPEC charges price P^*. If OPEC producers had not cartelized, price would be P_c, where OPEC's demand and marginal cost curves intersect.

---

14 CIPEC is the French acronym for International Council of Copper Exporting Countries.

revenue curve. MC_{OPEC} is OPEC's marginal cost curve; OPEC has much lower production costs than do non-OPEC producers. OPEC's marginal revenue and marginal cost are equal at quantity Q_{OPEC}, which is the quantity that OPEC will produce. We see from OPEC's demand curve that the price will be P^* at which competitive supply is Q_c.

Suppose petroleum-exporting countries had not formed a cartel and instead had produced competitively. Price would then have equaled marginal cost. We can therefore determine the competitive price from the point where OPEC's demand curve intersects its marginal cost curve. That price, labeled P_c, is much lower than the cartel price P^*. Because both total demand and non-OPEC supply are inelastic, the demand for OPEC oil is also fairly inelastic; thus the cartel has substantial monopoly power. It used that power to drive prices well above competitive levels.

In Chapter 2 we stressed the importance of distinguishing between short-run and long-run supply and demand, and that distinction is important here. The total demand and non-OPEC supply curves in Figure 12.10 apply to a short- or intermediate-run analysis. In the long run, both demand and supply will be much more elastic, which means that OPEC's demand curve will also be much more elastic. As a result, we would expect that in the long run OPEC would be unable to maintain a price that is so much above the competitive level. Indeed, during 1982–1989, oil prices fell in real terms, largely because of the long-run adjustment of demand and non-OPEC supply.

Figure 12.11 provides a similar analysis of CIPEC. CIPEC consists of four copper-producing countries: Chile, Peru, Zambia, and Zaire, which collectively account for about a third of world copper production. In these countries production costs are lower than those of non-CIPEC producers, but except for Chile, not much lower. In Figure 12.11 CIPEC's marginal cost curve is therefore drawn only a little below the non-CIPEC supply curve. CIPEC's demand curve D_{CIPEC} is the difference between total demand TD and non-CIPEC supply S_c. CIPEC's marginal cost and marginal revenue curves intersect at quantity Q_{CIPEC}, with the corresponding price P^*. Again, the competitive price P_c is found at the point where CIPEC's demand curve intersects its marginal cost curve. Note that this price is very close to the cartel price P^*.

Why can't CIPEC increase copper prices much? As Figure 12.11 shows, the total demand for copper is more elastic than for oil. (Other materials, such as aluminum, can easily be substituted for copper.) Also, competitive supply is much more elastic. Even in the short run, non-CIPEC producers can easily expand supply if prices should rise (in part because of the availability of supply from scrap metal). Thus CIPEC's potential monopoly power is small.

As the examples of OPEC and CIPEC illustrate, successful cartelization requires two things. First, the total demand for the good must not be very price elastic. Second, either the cartel must control nearly all the world's supply, or if it does not, the supply of noncartel producers must not be price elastic. Most international commodity cartels have failed because few world markets meet both conditions.

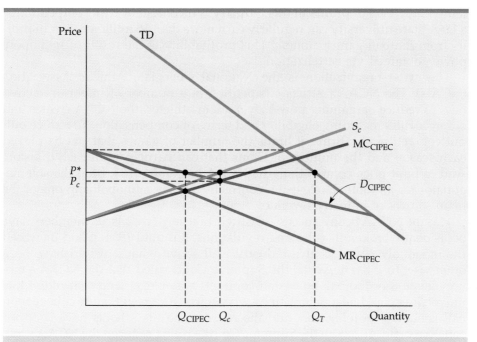

Figure 12.11 The CIPEC Copper Cartel TD is the total demand for copper, and S_c is the competitive (non-CIPEC) supply. CIPEC's demand D_{CIPEC} is the difference between the two. Both total demand and competitive supply are relatively elastic, so CIPEC's demand curve is elastic, and CIPEC has very little monopoly power. Note that CIPEC's optimal price P^* is close to the competitive price P_c.

E X A M P L E   1 2 . 5   The Cartelization of Intercollegiate Athletics

Many people think of intercollegiate athletics as an extracurricular activity for college students and a diversion for fans. They assume that universities support athletics avidly because it gives amateur athletes a chance to develop their skills and play football or basketball before a large audience, and also provides entertainment and promotes school spirit and alumni support. Although it does these things, intercollegiate athletics is also a big—and an extremely profitable—industry.

Like any industry, intercollegiate athletics has firms and consumers. The "firms" are the universities that support and finance teams. The inputs to production are the coaches, student athletes, and capital in the form of stadiums and playing fields. The consumers, many of whom are current or former college students, are the fans who buy tickets to games, and the TV and radio networks that pay to broadcast the games. There are many firms and consumers, which suggests that the industry is competitive. But the persistently high level of profits in this industry is inconsistent with competition—a large state university can regularly earn more than $6 million a year in profits from football games alone.[15] This profitability is the result of monopoly power, obtained via cartelization.

The cartel organization is the National Collegiate Athletic Association (NCAA). The NCAA restricts competition in a number of important activities. To reduce bargaining power by student athletes, the NCAA creates and enforces rules regarding eligibility and terms of compensation. To reduce output competition by firms, it limits the number of games that can be played each season and the number of teams that can participate in each division. And to limit price competition, the NCAA has, until 1984, been the sole negotiator for all football television contracts, thereby monopolizing one of the main sources of industry revenues.[16]

Has the NCAA been a successful cartel? Like most cartels, its members have occasionally broken its rules and regulations. But until 1984, it had increased the monopoly power of this industry well above what it would have been otherwise. In 1984, however, the Supreme Court ruled that the NCAA's monopolization of football television contracts was illegal, and that individual universities could negotiate their own contracts. As a result, more college football is shown on television, and the revenues to the schools have dropped somewhat. But although the Supreme Court's ruling reduced the NCAA's monopoly power, it did not eliminate it. Intercollegiate athletics remains very profitable, thanks to the cartel.

Summary

1. In a monopolistically competitive market, firms compete by selling differentiated products, which are highly substitutable. New firms can enter or exit easily. Firms have only a small amount of monopoly power. In the long run, entry will occur until profits are driven to zero. Firms then produce with excess capacity (i.e., at output levels below those that minimize average cost).

2. In an oligopolistic market, only a few firms account for most or all of production. Barriers to entry allow some firms to earn substantial profits, even over the long run. Economic decisions involve strategic considerations—each firm must consider how its actions will affect its rivals, and how they are likely to react.

3. In the Cournot model of oligopoly, firms make their output decisions at the same time, each taking the other's output as fixed. In equilibrium, each firm is maximizing its profit, given the output of its competitor, so no firm has an incentive to change its output. The firms are therefore in a Nash equilibrium. Each firm's profit is higher than under per-

---

[15] See "In Big-Time College Athletics, the Real Score Is in Dollars," *New York Times*, March 1, 1987.

[16] See James V. Koch, "The Intercollegiate Athletics Industry," in Walter Adams, *The Structure of American Industry*, 7th ed. (New York: Macmillan, 1986). Koch provides a detailed and informative discussion of the nature of this industry and the behavior of the NCAA cartel.

fect competition, but less than what it would earn by colluding.

4. In the Stackelberg model, one firm sets its output first. That firm has a strategic advantage and earns a higher profit. It knows it can choose a large output, and its competitors will have to choose small outputs if they want to maximize profits.

5. The Nash equilibrium concept can also be applied to markets in which firms produce substitute goods and compete by setting price. In equilibrium, each firm maximizes its profit, given the prices of its competitors, and so has no incentive to change price.

6. Firms would earn higher profits by collusively agreeing to raise prices, but the antitrust laws usually prohibit this. They might all set a high price without colluding, each hoping its competitors will do the same, but

they are in a Prisoners' Dilemma, which makes this unlikely. Each firm has an incentive to cheat by lowering its price and capturing sales from its competitors.

7. The Prisoners' Dilemma creates price rigidity in oligopolistic markets. Firms are reluctant to change prices for fear of setting off a round of price warfare.

8. Price leadership is a form of implicit collusion that sometimes gets around the Prisoners' Dilemma. One firm sets price, and the other firms follow with the same price.

9. In a cartel, producers explicitly collude in setting prices and output levels. Successful cartelization requires that the total demand not be very price elastic, and that either the cartel control most supply or else the supply of noncartel producers be inelastic.

Questions for Review

1. What are the characteristics of a monopolistically competitive market? What happens to the equilibrium price and quantity in such a market if one firm introduces a new, improved product?

2. Why is the firm's demand curve flatter than the total market demand curve in monopolistic competition? Suppose a monopolistically competitive firm is making a profit in the short run. What will happen to its demand curve in the long run?

3. Some experts have argued that too many brands of breakfast cereal are on the market. Give an argument to support this view. Give an argument against it.

4. Why is the Cournot equilibrium stable (i.e., why don't firms have any incentive to change their output levels once in equilibrium)? Even if they can't collude, why don't firms set their outputs at the joint profit-maximizing levels (i.e., the levels they would have chosen had they colluded)?

5. In the Stackelberg model, the firm that sets output first has an advantage. Explain why.

6. Explain the meaning of a Nash equilibrium when firms are competing with respect to price. Why is the equilibrium stable? Why don't the firms raise their prices to the level that maximizes joint profits?

7. The kinked demand curve describes price rigidity. Explain how the model works. What are its limitations? Why does price rigidity arise in oligopolistic markets?

8. Why does price leadership sometimes evolve in oligopolistic markets? Explain how the price leader determines a profit-maximizing price.

9. Why has the OPEC oil cartel succeeded in raising prices substantially, while the CIPEC copper cartel has not? What conditions are necessary for successful cartelization? What organizational problems must a cartel overcome?

Exercises

1. Suppose all firms in a monopolistically competitive industry were merged into one large firm. Would that new firm produce as many different brands? Would it produce only a single brand? Explain.

2. Consider the following duopoly. Demand is given by $P = 10 - Q$, where $Q = Q_1 + Q_2$. The firms' cost functions are $C_1(Q_1) = 4 + 2Q_1$ and $C_2(Q_2) = 3 + 3Q_2$.
   a. Suppose both firms have entered the industry. What is the joint profit-maximizing level of output? How much will each firm produce? How would your answer change if the firms have not yet entered the industry?
   b. What is each firm's equilibrium output and profit if they behave noncooperatively? Use the Cournot model. Draw the firms' reaction curves, and show the equilibrium.
   c. How much should Firm 1 be willing to pay to purchase Firm 2 if collusion is illegal, but the takeover is not?

3. A monopolist can produce at a constant average (and marginal) cost of $AC = MC = 5$. The firm faces a market demand curve given by $Q = 53 - P$.
   a. Calculate the profit-maximizing price and quantity for this monopolist. Also calculate the monopolist's profits.
   b. Suppose a second firm enters the market. Let Q_1 be the output of the first firm and Q_2 be the output of the second. Market demand is now given by
   $$Q_1 + Q_2 = 53 - P$$
   Assuming that this second firm has the same costs as the first, write the profits of each firm as functions of Q_1 and Q_2.
   c. Suppose (as in the Cournot model) each firm chooses its profit-maximizing level of output under the assumption that its competitor's output is fixed. Find each firm's "reaction curve" (i.e., the rule that gives its desired output in terms of its competitor's output).

   d. Calculate the Cournot equilibrium (i.e., the values of Q_1 and Q_2 for which both firms are doing as well as they can given their competitor's output). What are the resulting market price and profits of each firm?
   *e. Suppose there are N firms in the industry, all with the same constant marginal cost, $MC = 5$. Find the Cournot equilibrium. How much will each firm produce, what will be the market price, and how much profit will each firm earn? Also, show that as N becomes large, the market price approaches the price that would prevail under perfect competition.

4. This exercise is a continuation of Exercise 3. We return to two firms with the same constant average and marginal cost, $AC = MC = 5$, facing the market demand curve $Q_1 + Q_2 = 53 - P$. Now we will use the Stackelberg model to analyze what will happen if one of the firms makes its output decision ahead of the other one.
   a. Suppose Firm 1 is the Stackelberg leader (i.e., makes its output decisions ahead of Firm 2). Find the reaction curves that tell each firm how much to produce in terms of the output of its competitor.
   b. How much will each firm produce, and what will its profit be?

5. Two firms compete in selling identical widgets. They choose their output levels Q_1 and Q_2 simultaneously, and face the demand curve
   $$P = 30 - Q$$
   where $Q = Q_1 + Q_2$. Until recently both firms had *zero marginal costs*. Recent environmental regulations have increased Firm 2's marginal cost to $15. Firm 1's marginal cost remains constant at zero. True or false: As a result, the market price will rise to the *monopoly* level.

6. Suppose that two identical firms produce widgets and that they are the only firms in the market. Their costs are given by $C_1 =$

$30Q_1$ and $C_2 = 30Q_2$, where Q_1 is the output of Firm 1, and Q_2 is the output of Firm 2. Price is determined by the following demand curve:

$$P = 150 - Q$$

where $Q = Q_1 + Q_2$.

a. Find the Cournot–Nash equilibrium. Calculate the profit of each firm at this equilibrium.
b. Suppose the two firms form a cartel to maximize joint profits. How many widgets will be produced? Calculate each firm's profit.
c. Suppose Firm 1 were the only firm in the industry. How would the market output and Firm 1's profit differ from that found in part (b) above?
d. Returning to the duopoly of part (b), suppose Firm 1 abides by the agreement, but Firm 2 cheats by increasing production. How many widgets will Firm 2 produce? What will be each firm's profits?

7. Suppose the airline industry consisted of only two firms: American and Texas Air Corp. Let the two firms have identical cost functions, $C(q) = 40q$. Assume the demand curve for the industry is given by $P = 100 - Q$, and that each firm expects the other to behave as a Cournot competitor.
a. Calculate the (Cournot-Nash) equilibrium for each firm, assuming that each chooses the output level that maximizes its profits taking its rival's output as given. What are the profits of each firm?
b. What would be equilibrium quantity if Texas Air had constant marginal and average costs of 25, and American had constant marginal and average costs of 40?
c. Assuming that both firms have the original cost function, $C(q) = 40q$, how much should Texas Air be willing to invest to lower its marginal cost from 40 to 25, assuming that American will not follow suit? How much should American be willing to spend to reduce its marginal cost to 25, assuming that Texas Air will have marginal costs of 25 regardless of American's actions?

*8. Demand for light bulbs can be characterized by $Q = 100 - P$, where Q is in millions of boxes of lights sold, and P is the price per box. There are two producers of lights, Everglow and Dimlit. They have identical cost functions:

$$C_i = 10Q_i + \tfrac{1}{2}Q_i^2 \ (i = E, D)$$
$$Q = Q_E + Q_D$$

a. Unable to recognize the potential for collusion, the two firms act as short-run perfect competitors. What are the equilibrium values of Q_E, Q_D, and P? What are each firm's profits?
b. Top management in both firms is replaced. Each new manager independently recognizes the oligopolistic nature of the light bulb industry and plays Cournot. What are the equilibrium values of Q_E, Q_D, and P? What are each firm's profits?
c. Suppose the Everglow manager guesses correctly that Dimlit has a Cournot conjectural variation, so Everglow plays Stackelberg. What are the equilibrium values of Q_E, Q_D, and P? What are each firm's profits?
d. If the managers of the two companies collude, what are the equilibrium values of Q_E, Q_D, and P? What are each firm's profits?

9. Two firms produce luxury sheepskin auto seat covers: Western Where (WW) and B.B.B. Sheep (BBBS). Each firm has a cost function given by

$$C(q) = 20q + q^2$$

The market demand for these seat covers is represented by the inverse demand equation

$$P = 200 - 2Q$$

where $Q = q_1 + q_2$, total output.
a. If each firm acts to maximize its profits, taking its rival's output as given (i.e., the firms behave as Cournot oligopolists), what will be the equilibrium quantities selected by each firm? What is total output, and what is the market price? What are the profits for each firm?
b. It occurs to the managers of WW and BBBS that they could do a lot better by colluding. If the two firms collude, what will be

the profit-maximizing choice of output? What is the industry price? What is the output and the profit for each firm in this case?

c. The managers of these firms realize that explicit agreements to collude are illegal. Each firm must decide on its own whether to produce the Cournot quantity or the cartel quantity. To aid in making the decision, the manager of WW constructs a payoff matrix like the one below. Fill in each box with the profit of WW and the profit of BBBS. Given this payoff matrix, what output strategy is each firm likely to pursue?

Profit Payoff Matrix (WW profit, BBBS profit)		BBBS	
		Produce Cournot q	Produce Cartel q
WW	Produce Cournot q		
	Produce Cartel q		

d. Suppose WW can set its output level *before* BBBS does. How much will WW choose to produce in this case? How much will BBBS produce? What is the market price, and what is the profit for each firm? Is WW better off by choosing its output first? Explain why or why not.

*10. Two firms compete by choosing price. Their demand functions are

$$Q_1 = 20 - P_1 + P_2$$

and

$$Q_2 = 20 + P_1 - P_2$$

where P_1 and P_2 are the prices charged by each firm, respectively, and Q_1 and Q_2 are the resulting demands. (Note that the demand for each good depends only on the difference in prices; if the two firms colluded and set the same price, they could make that price as high as they wanted, and earn infinite profits.) Marginal costs are zero.

a. Suppose the two firms set their prices at the *same time*. Find the resulting Nash equilibrium. What price will each firm

charge, how much will it sell, and what will its profit be? (*Hint:* Maximize the profit of each firm with respect to its price.)

b. Suppose Firm 1 sets its price *first*, and then Firm 2 sets its price. What price will each firm charge, how much will it sell, and what will its profit be?

c. Suppose you are one of these firms, and there are three ways you could play the game: (i) Both firms set price at the same time. (ii) You set price first. (iii) Your competitor sets price first. If you could choose among these, which would you prefer? Explain why.

*11. The dominant firm model can help us understand the behavior of some cartels. Let us apply this model to the OPEC oil cartel. We will use isoelastic curves to describe world demand W and noncartel (competitive) supply S. Reasonable numbers for the price elasticities of world demand and noncartel supply are $-1/2$ and $1/2$, respectively. Then, expressing W and S in millions of barrels per day (mb/d), we could write

$$W = 160P^{-1/2}$$

and

$$S = (3\tfrac{1}{3})P^{1/2}$$

Note that OPEC's net demand is $D = W - S$.

a. Sketch the world demand curve W, the non-OPEC supply curve S, OPEC's net demand curve D, and OPEC's marginal revenue curve. For purposes of approximation, assume OPEC's production cost is zero. Indicate OPEC's optimal price, OPEC's optimal production, and non-OPEC production on the diagram. Now, show on the diagram how the various curves will shift, and how OPEC's optimal price will change if non-OPEC supply becomes more expensive because reserves of oil start running out.

b. Calculate OPEC's optimal (profit-maximizing) price. (*Hint:* Because OPEC's cost is zero, just write the expression for OPEC revenue and find the price that maximizes it.)

c. Suppose the oil-consuming countries were to unite and form a "buyers' cartel" to gain monopsony power. What can we say, and what can't we say, about the impact this would have on price?

*12. A lemon-growing cartel consists of four orchards. Their total cost functions are

$$TC_1 = 20 + 5Q_1^2$$
$$TC_2 = 25 + 3Q_2^2$$
$$TC_3 = 15 + 4Q_3^2$$
$$TC_4 = 20 + 6Q_4^2$$

(TC is in hundreds of dollars, Q is in cartons per month picked and shipped.)

a. Tabulate total, average, and marginal costs for each firm for output levels between 1 and 5 cartons per month (i.e., for 1, 2, 3, 4, and 5 cartons).

b. If the cartel decided to ship 10 cartons per month and set a price of $25 per carton, how should output be allocated among the firms?

c. At this shipping level, which firm has the most incentive to cheat? Does any firm *not* have an incentive to cheat?

Chapter Outline

List of Examples

CHAPTER 13

Game Theory and Competitive Strategy

In Chapter 12 we began to explore some of the strategic output and pricing decisions that firms must often make. We saw how a firm can take into account the likely responses of its competitors when it makes these decisions. However, there are many questions about market structure and firm behavior that we have not yet addressed. For example, why do firms tend to collude in some markets and compete aggressively in others? How do some firms manage to deter entry by potential competitors? And how should firms make pricing decisions when demand or cost conditions are changing, or new competitors are entering the market?

To answer these questions, we will use game theory to extend our analysis of strategic decision making by firms. The application of game theory has been an important development in microeconomics. This chapter explains some of this theory and shows how it can be used to understand how markets evolve and operate, and how managers should think about the strategic decisions they continually face. We will see, for example, what happens when oligopolistic firms must set and adjust prices strategically over time, so that the Prisoners' Dilemma, which we discussed in Chapter 12, is repeated over and over. We will discuss how firms can make strategic moves that give them an advantage over their competitors or the edge in a bargaining situation. And we will see how firms can use threats, promises, or more concrete actions to deter entry by potential competitors.

13.1 Gaming and Strategic Decisions

First, we should clarify what gaming and strategic decision making are all about. In essence, we are concerned with the following question: *If I believe that my competitors are rational and act to maximize their own profits, how should I take their behavior into account when making my own profit-maximizing decisions?*

As we will see, this question can be difficult to answer, even under conditions of complete symmetry and perfect information (i.e., my competitors and I have the same cost structure and are fully informed about each others' costs, about demand, etc.). Moreover, we will be concerned with more complex situations in which firms have different costs, different types of information, and various degrees and forms of competitive "advantage" and "disadvantage."

Noncooperative versus Cooperative Games

The economic games that firms play can be either *cooperative* or *noncooperative*. A game is *cooperative* if the players can negotiate binding contracts that allow them to plan joint strategies. A game is *noncooperative* if negotiation and enforcement of a binding contract are not possible.

An example of a cooperative game is the bargaining between a buyer and a seller over the price of a rug. If the rug costs $100 to produce and the buyer values the rug at $200, a cooperative solution to the game is possible because an agreement to sell the rug at any price between $101 and $199 will maximize the sum of the buyer's consumer surplus and the seller's profit, while making both parties better off. Another cooperative game would involve two firms in an industry, which negotiate a joint investment to develop a new technology (where neither firm would have enough know-how to succeed on its own). If the firms can sign a binding contract to divide the profits from their joint investment, a cooperative outcome that makes both parties better off is possible.[1] An example of a noncooperative game is a situation in which two competing firms take each other's likely behavior into account and independently determine a pricing or advertising strategy to win market share.

Note that the fundamental difference between cooperative and noncooperative games lies in the contracting possibilities. In cooperative games binding contracts are possible; in noncooperative games they are not.

---

[1] Bargaining over a rug is called a *constant sum* game because no matter what the selling price, the sum of consumer surplus and profit will be the same. Negotiating over a joint venture is a *nonconstant sum* game: the total profit that results from the venture will depend on the outcome of the negotiations, e.g., the resources that each firm devotes to the venture.

We will be concerned mostly with noncooperative games. In any game, however, the most important aspect of strategy design is *understanding your opponent's point of view, and (assuming your opponent is rational) deducing how he or she is likely to respond to your actions.* This may seem obvious—of course, one must understand an opponent's point of view. Yet even in simple gaming situations, people often ignore or misjudge their opponents' positions and the rational responses those positions imply.

An example of this is the following game devised by Martin Shubik.[2] A dollar bill is auctioned, but in an unusual way. The highest bidder receives the dollar in return for the amount bid. However, the second-highest bidder must also hand over the amount he or she bid—and get nothing in return. *If you were playing this game, how much would you bid for the dollar bill?*

Classroom experience shows that students often end up bidding more than a dollar for the dollar. In a typical scenario, one player bids 20 cents, and another 30 cents. The lower bidder now stands to lose 20 cents, but figures he can earn a dollar by raising his bid, and so bids 40 cents. The escalation continues until two players carry the bidding to a dollar against 90 cents. Now the 90-cent bidder has to choose between bidding $1.10 for the dollar, or paying 90 cents to get nothing. Most often, he raises his bid, and the bidding escalates further. In some experiments, the "winning" student has ended up paying more than $3 for the dollar!

How could intelligent students put themselves in this position? By failing to think through the likely response of the other players, and the sequence of events it implies. How much would you bid for the dollar? We hope nothing.

In the rest of this chapter, we will examine simple games that involve pricing, advertising, and investment decisions. The games are simple in that, *given some behavioral assumption,* we can determine the best strategy for each firm. But even for these simple games, we will find that the correct behavioral assumptions are not always easy to make, and will depend on how the game is played (e.g., how long the firms stay in business, their reputations, etc.). Therefore, when reading this chapter, you should try to understand the basic issues involved in making strategic decisions. You should also keep in mind the importance of carefully assessing your opponent's position and rational response to your actions, as Example 13.1 illustrates.

EXAMPLE 13.1   Acquiring a Company

You represent Company *A* (the acquirer), which is considering acquiring Company *T* (the target).[3] You plan to offer cash for all of Company *T*'s shares, but you are unsure what price to offer. The complication is this: The value of Company *T*—indeed, its viability—depends on the outcome of a major oil exploration project that it is currently undertaking. If the project

---

[2] Martin Shubik, *Game Theory in the Social Sciences* (Cambridge, Mass.: MIT Press, 1982).

[3] This is a revised version of an example designed by Max Bazerman for a course at MIT.

fails, Company *T* under current management will be worth nothing. But if it succeeds, Company *T*'s value under current management could be as high as $100/share. All share values between $0 and $100 are considered equally likely.

It is well known, however, that Company *T* will be worth much more under the progressive management of Company *A* than under current management. In fact, whatever the ultimate value under current management, *Company T will be worth 50 percent more under the management of Company A.* If the project fails, Company *T* is worth $0/share under either management. If the exploration project generates a $50/share value under current management, the value under Company *A* will be $75/share. Similarly, a $100/share value under Company *T* implies a $150/share value under Company *A*, and so on.

You must determine what price Company *A* should offer for Company *T*'s shares. This offer must be made *now, before* the outcome of the exploration project is known. From all indications, Company *T* would be happy to be acquired by Company *A*, *for the right price.* You expect Company *T* to delay a decision on your bid until the exploration results are in and then accept or reject your offer before news of the drilling results reaches the press.

Thus, *you (Company A) will not know the results of the exploration project when submitting your price offer, but Company T will know the results when deciding whether to accept your offer. Also, Company T will accept any offer by Company A that is greater than the (per share) value of the company under current management.* As the representative of Company *A*, you are considering price offers in the range $0/share (i.e., making no offer at all) to $150/share. *What price per share should you offer for Company T's stock?*

Note: The typical response—to offer between $50 and $75 per share—is wrong. The correct answer to this problem appears at the end of this chapter, but we urge you to try to answer it on your own.

13.2 Dominant Strategies

How can we decide on the best strategy for playing a game? How can we determine a game's likely outcome? We need something to help us determine how the rational behavior of each player will lead to an equilibrium solution. Some strategies may be successful if competitors make certain choices but will fail if they make other choices. Other strategies, however, may be successful whatever competitors choose to do. We begin with the concept of a *dominant strategy—one that is optimal for a player no matter what an opponent does.*

The following example illustrates this in a duopoly setting. Suppose Firms *A* and *B* sell competing products and are deciding whether to undertake advertising campaigns. Each firm, however, will be affected by its competitor's decision. The possible outcomes of the game are illustrated by

Table 13.1 Payoff Matrix for Advertising Game

		Firm B	
		Advertise	Don't advertise
Firm A	Advertise	10, 5	15, 0
	Don't advertise	6, 8	10, 2

the payoff matrix in Table 13.1. (Recall that the payoff matrix summarizes the possible outcomes of the game; the first number in each cell is the payoff to *A* and the second is the payoff to *B*.) Observe from this payoff matrix that if both firms decide to advertise, Firm *A* will make a profit of 10, and Firm *B* will make a profit of 5. If Firm *A* advertises and Firm *B* doesn't, Firm *A* will earn 15, and Firm *B* will earn zero. And similarly for the other two possibilities.

What strategy should each firm choose? First, consider Firm *A*. It should clearly advertise because no matter what Firm *B* does, Firm *A* does best by advertising. (If Firm *B* advertises, *A* earns a profit of 10 if it advertises, but only 6 if it doesn't. And if *B* does not advertise, *A* earns 15 if it advertises, but only 10 if it doesn't.) Thus advertising is a dominant strategy for Firm *A*. The same is true for Firm *B*; no matter what Firm *A* does, Firm *B* does best by advertising. Therefore, assuming that both firms are rational, we know that the outcome for this game is that both *firms will advertise*. This outcome is easy to determine because both firms have dominant strategies.

However, not every game has a dominant strategy for each player. To see this, let's change our advertising example slightly. The payoff matrix in Table 13.2 is the same as in Table 13.1, except for the bottom right-hand corner—if neither firm advertises, Firm *B* will again earn a profit of 2, but Firm *A* will earn a profit of 20 (perhaps because Firm *A*'s ads are largely defensive, designed to refute Firm *B*'s claims, and expensive; so by not advertising, Firm *A* can reduce its expenses considerably).

Now Firm *A* has no dominant strategy. *Its optimal decision depends on what Firm B does.* If Firm *B* advertises, then Firm *A* does best by advertising; but if Firm *B* does not advertise, Firm *A* also does best by not advertising. Now suppose both firms must make their decisions at the same time. What should Firm *A* do?

Table 13.2 Modified Advertising Game

		Firm B	
		Advertise	Don't advertise
Firm A	Advertise	10, 5	15, 0
	Don't advertise	6, 8	20, 2

To answer this, Firm *A* must put itself in Firm *B*'s shoes. What decision is best from Firm *B*'s point of view, and what is Firm *B* likely to do? The answer is clear: Firm *B* has a dominant strategy—advertise, no matter what Firm *A* does. (If Firm *A* advertises, *B* earns 5 by advertising and 0 by not advertising. If *A* doesn't advertise, *B* earns 8 if it advertises and 2 if it doesn't.) Therefore, Firm *A* can conclude that Firm *B* will advertise. This means that Firm *A* should itself advertise (and thereby earn 10 instead of 6). The equilibrium is that both firms will advertise. It is the logical outcome of the game because Firm *A* is doing the best it can, given Firm *B*'s decision; and Firm *B* is doing the best it can, given Firm *A*'s decision.

13.3 The Nash Equilibrium Revisited

To determine the likely outcome of a game, we have been seeking "self-enforcing," or "stable," strategies. Dominant strategies are stable, but in many games, one or more players do not have a dominant strategy. We therefore need a more general equilibrium concept. In Chapter 12 we introduced the concept of a *Nash equilibrium* and saw that it is widely applicable and intuitively appealing.[4]

Recall that a Nash equilibrium is a set of strategies (or actions) such that *each player is doing the best it can given the actions of its opponents*. Since each player has no incentive to deviate from its Nash strategy, the strategies are stable. In the example shown in Table 13.2, the Nash equilibrium is that both firms advertise. It is a Nash equilibrium because, given the decision of its competitor, each firm is satisfied that it has made the best decision possible, and has no incentive to change its decision.

In Chapter 12 we used the Nash equilibrium to study output and pricing by oligopolistic firms. In the Cournot model, for example, each firm sets its own output while taking the outputs of its competitors as fixed. We saw that in a Cournot equilibrium, no firm has an incentive to change its output unilaterally because each firm is doing the best it can given the decisions of its competitors. Hence a Cournot equilibrium is a Nash equilibrium.[5] We also examined models in which firms choose price, taking the prices of their competitors as fixed. Again, in the Nash equilibrium, each firm is earning the largest profit it can given the prices of its competitors, and thus has no incentive to change its price.

---

[4] Our discussion of the Nash equilibrium, and of game theory in general, is at an introductory level. For a more in-depth discussion of game theory and its applications, see James W. Friedman, *Game Theory with Applications to Economics* (New York: Oxford University Press, 1990); David M. Kreps, *A Course in Microeconomic Theory* (Princeton, N.J.: Princeton University Press, 1990); and Drew Fudenberg and Jean Tirole, *Game Theory* (Cambridge, Mass.: MIT Press, 1991).

[5] A Stackelberg equilibrium is also a Nash equilibrium. In the Stackelberg model, the rules of the game are different: One firm makes its output decision before its competitor does. Under these rules, each firm is doing the best it can given the decision of its competitor.

It is helpful to compare the concept of a Nash equilibrium with that of an equilibrium in dominant strategies:

Dominant Strategies:	I'm doing the best I can *no matter what you do.* You're doing the best you can *no matter what I do.*
Nash Equilibrium:	I'm doing the best I can *given what you are doing.* You're doing the best you can *given what I am doing.*

Note that a dominant strategy equilibrium is a special case of a Nash equilibrium.

In the advertising game of Table 13.2 there is a single Nash equilibrium—both firms advertise. In general, a game does not have to have a single Nash equilibrium. Sometimes there is no Nash equilibrium, and sometimes there are several (i.e., several sets of strategies are stable and self-enforcing). A few more examples will help to clarify this.[6]

Consider the following "product choice" problem. Two breakfast cereal companies face a market in which two new variations of cereal can be successfully introduced—provided each variation is introduced by only one firm. There is a market for a new "crispy" cereal and for a new "sweet" cereal, but each firm has the resources to introduce only one new product. Then the payoff matrix for the two firms might look like the one in Table 13.3.

In this game each firm is indifferent about which product it produces, so long as it does not introduce the same product as its competitor. If coordination were possible, the firms would probably agree to divide the market. But what will happen if the firms must behave *noncooperatively*? Suppose that somehow—perhaps through a news release—Firm 1 indicates it is about to introduce the sweet cereal, and Firm 2 (after hearing this) indicates it will introduce the crispy one. Now, given the action it believes its opponent is taking, neither firm has an incentive to deviate from its proposed action. If it takes the proposed action, its payoff is 10, but if it deviates—given that its opponent's action remains unchanged—its payoff will be −5. Therefore, the strategy set given by the bottom left-hand corner of the payoff matrix is stable and

Table 13.3 Product Choice Problem

		Firm 2	
		Crispy	Sweet
Firm 1	Crispy	−5, −5	10, 10
	Sweet	10, 10	−5, −5

---

[6] Several of these examples were developed by Garth Saloner.

constitutes a Nash equilibrium: Given the strategy of its opponent, each firm is doing the best it can and has no incentive to deviate.

Note that the upper right-hand corner of the payoff matrix is also a Nash equilibrium, which might occur if Firm 1 indicated it was about to produce the crispy cereal. Each Nash equilibrium is stable because *once the strategies are chosen*, no player will unilaterally deviate from them. However, without more information, we have no way of knowing which equilibrium (crispy/sweet vs. sweet/crispy) is likely to result—or if *either* will result. Of course, both firms have a strong incentive to reach *one* of the two Nash equilibria—if they both introduce the same type of cereal, they will both lose money. The fact that the two firms are not allowed to collude does not mean that they will not reach a Nash equilibrium. As an industry develops, understandings often evolve as firms "signal" each other about the paths the industry is to take.

As another example of a Nash equilibrium, suppose that you (Y) and a competitor (C) are planning to sell soft drinks on a beach this summer. The beach is 200 yards long, and sunbathers are spread evenly across its length. You and your competitor sell the same soft drinks at the same prices, so customers will walk to whichever vendor is closest. Where on the beach will you locate, and where do you think your competitor will locate?

If you think about this for a minute, you will see that the only Nash equilibrium is the one where both you and your competitor locate at the same spot in the center of the beach (see Figure 13.1). To see why, suppose your competitor located at some other point *A*, which in the figure is three quarters of the way to the end of the beach. In that case you would no longer want to locate in the center; you would locate near your competitor, just to her left. You would thus capture nearly three-fourths of the sales, and your competitor would get only the remaining fourth. This is not an equilibrium

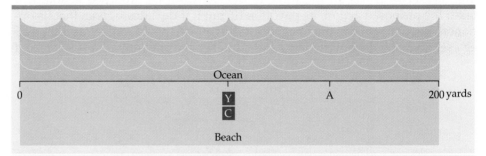

Figure 13.1 Beach Location Game You (*Y*) and a competitor (*C*) plan to sell soft drinks on a beach. If sunbathers are spread evenly across the beach and will walk to whichever vendor is closest, the two of you will locate next to each other at the center of the beach. This is the only Nash equilibrium. If your competitor located at point *A*, you would want to move, so that you were just to her left, and thereby capture three-fourths of the sales. But your competitor would then want to move back to the center, and you would do the same.

because your competitor would then want to move to the center of the beach, as would you.

This "beach location game" can help us understand a variety of phenomena. Have you ever noticed how, along a two- or three-mile stretch of road, two or three gas stations, or several car dealerships, will be close to each other? Likewise, as a presidential election approaches, the Democratic and Republican candidates typically move close to the center as they define their political positions.

Maximin Strategies

The concept of a Nash equilibrium relies heavily on individual rationality. Each player's choice of strategy depends not only on its own rationality, but also on that of its opponent. This can be a limitation, as the example in Table 13.4 shows.

In this game, playing "right" is a dominant strategy for Player 2 because by using this strategy, Player 2 will do better (earning 1 rather than 0), no matter what Player 1 does. Thus Player 1 should expect Player 2 to play the "right" strategy. In this case Player 1 would do better by playing "bottom" (and earning 2) than by playing "top" (and earning 1). Clearly the outcome (bottom, right) is a Nash equilibrium for this game, and you can verify that it is the only Nash equilibrium. But note that Player 1 had better be sure that Player 2 understands the game and is rational. If Player 2 should happen to make a mistake and play "left," it would be extremely costly to Player 1.

If you were Player 1, what would you do? If you tend to be cautious, and you are concerned that Player 2 might not be fully informed or rational, you might choose to play "top," in which case you will be assured of earning 1, and you will have no chance of losing 1000. Such a strategy is called a *maximin strategy* because it *maximizes the minimum gain that can be earned.* If both players used maximin strategies, the outcome would be "top, right." A maximin strategy is conservative, but not profit maximizing (since Player 1 earns a profit of 1 rather than 2). Note that if Player 1 *knew for certain* that Player 2 was using a maximin strategy, it would prefer to play "bottom" (and earn 2), instead of following the maximin strategy of playing "top."

What is the Nash equilibrium for the Prisoners' Dilemma discussed in Chapter 12? Table 13.5 shows the payoff matrix for the Prisoners' Dilemma. For the two

Table 13.4 Maximin Strategy

		Player 2	
		Left	Right
Player 1	Top	1, 0	1, 1
	Bottom	−1000, 0	2, 1

Table 13.5 Prisoners' Dilemma			
		Prisoner B	
		Confess	Don't confess
Prisoner A	Confess	−5, −5	−1, −10
	Don't confess	−10, −1	−2, −2

prisoners, the ideal outcome is one in which neither confessed, so that they both get two years in prison. However, confessing is a *dominant strategy* for each prisoner—it yields a higher payoff regardless of the strategy of the other prisoner. Dominant strategies are also maximin strategies. Therefore the outcome in which both prisoners confess is both a Nash equilibrium and a maximin solution. Thus, in a very strong sense, it is rational for each prisoner to confess.

*Mixed Strategies

In all of the games that we examined so far, we have considered strategies in which players make a specific choice or take a specific action: advertise or don't advertise, set a price of $4 or a price of $6, and so on. Strategies of this kind are called *pure strategies*. There are games, however, in which pure strategies are not the best way to play.

An example is the game of "Matching Pennies." In this game, each player chooses heads or tails, and the two players reveal their coins at the same time. If the coins match (i.e., both are heads or both are tails), Player *A* wins and receives a dollar from Player *B*. If the coins do not match, Player *B* wins and receives a dollar from Player *A*. The payoff matrix is shown in Table 13.6.

Note that there is no Nash equilibrium in pure strategies for this game. Suppose, for example, that Player *A* chose the strategy of playing heads. Then Player *B* would want to play tails. But if Player *B* plays tails, Player *A* would also want to play tails. No combination of heads or tails leaves both players satisfied, so that neither would want to change strategies.

Although there is no Nash equilibrium in pure strategies, there is a Nash equilibrium in *mixed strategies*. A mixed strategy is a strategy in which the player *makes a random choice among two or more possible actions, based on a set of chosen*

Table 13.6 Matching Pennies			
		Player B	
		Heads	Tails
Player A	Heads	1, −1	−1, 1
	Tails	−1, 1	1, −1

probabilities. In this game, for example, Player *A* might simply flip the coin, thereby playing heads with probability 1/2 and playing tails with probability 1/2. In fact, if Player *A* follows this strategy and Player *B* does the same, we will have a Nash equilibrium; both players will be doing the best they can given what the opponent is doing. Note that the outcome of the game is random, but the *expected payoff* is 0 for each player.

It may seem strange to play a game by choosing actions randomly. But put yourself in the position of Player *A* and think what would happen if you followed a strategy *other* than just flipping the coin. Suppose, for example, you decided to play heads. If Player *B* knows this, she would play tails, and you would lose. Even if Player *B* didn't know your strategy, if the game were played over and over again, she could eventually discern your pattern of play and choose a strategy that countered it. Of course, you would then want to change your strategy—which is why this would not be a Nash equilibrium. Only if you and your opponent both choose heads or tails randomly with probability 1/2, would neither of you have any incentive to change strategies.[7]

One reason to consider mixed strategies is that some games (such as "Matching Pennies") do not have any Nash equilibria in pure strategies. It can be shown, however, that *every* game has at least one Nash equilibrium, once we allow for mixed strategies.[8] Hence, mixed strategies provide solutions to games when pure strategies fail. Of course, whether solutions involving mixed strategies are reasonable will depend on the particular game and players. Mixed strategies are likely to be very reasonable for "Matching Pennies," poker, and other such games. A firm, on the other hand, might not find it reasonable to believe that its competitor will set its price randomly.

Some games have Nash equilibria both in pure strategies and in mixed strategies. An example is "The Battle of the Sexes," a game that you might find familiar. It goes like this. Jim and Joan would like to spend Saturday night together, but have different tastes in entertainment. Joan would like to go to the opera, but Jim prefers mud wrestling. (Feel free to reverse these preferences.) As the payoff matrix in Table 13.7 shows, Joan would most prefer to

Table 13.7 The Battle of the Sexes			
		Joan	
		Wrestling	Opera
Jim	Wrestling	2, 1	0, 0
	Opera	0, 0	1, 2

---

[7] You can check that the use of different probabilities, say 3/4 for heads and 1/4 for tails, does not generate a Nash equilibrium.

[8] More precisely, every game with a finite number of players and a finite number of actions has at least one Nash equilibrium. For a proof, see David M. Kreps, *A Course in Microeconomic Theory* (Princeton, N.J.: Princeton University Press, 1990), p. 409.

go to the opera with Jim, but prefers watching mud wrestling with Jim to going to the opera alone, and similarly for Jim.

First, note that there are two Nash equilibria in pure strategies for this game—the one in which Jim and Joan both watch mud wrestling, and the one in which they both go to the opera. Jim, of course, would prefer the first of these outcomes and Joan the second, but both outcomes are equilibria—neither Jim nor Joan would want to change his or her decision, given the decision of the other.

This game also has an equilibrium in mixed strategies: Jim chooses wrestling with probability 2/3 and opera with probability 1/3, and Joan chooses wrestling with probability 1/3 and opera with probability 2/3. You can check that if Joan uses this strategy, Jim cannot do better with any other strategy, and vice versa.[9] The outcome is random, and Jim and Joan will each have an expected payoff of 2/3.

Should we expect Jim and Joan to use these mixed strategies? Unless they're very risk loving or in some other way a strange couple, probably not. By agreeing to either form of entertainment, each will have a payoff of at least 1, which exceeds the expected payoff of 2/3 from randomizing. In this game as in many others, mixed strategies provide another solution, but not a very realistic one. Hence for the remainder of this chapter we will focus on pure strategies.

13.4 Repeated Games

We saw in Chapter 12 that in oligopolistic markets, firms often find themselves in a Prisoners' Dilemma when making output or pricing decisions. Can firms find a way out of this dilemma, so that oligopolistic coordination and cooperation (whether explicit or implicit) could prevail?

To answer this question, we must recognize that the Prisoners' Dilemma, as we have described it so far, is static and thus limited. Although some prisoners may have only one opportunity in life to confess or not, most firms set output and price over and over again. In real life, firms play a *repeated game*. With each repetition of the Prisoners' Dilemma, firms can develop reputations about their behavior and study the behavior of their competitors.

How does repetition change the likely outcome of the game? Suppose you are Firm 1 in the Prisoners' Dilemma illustrated by the payoff matrix in Table 13.8. If you and your competitor both charge a high price, you will both make a higher profit than if you both charged a low price. However, you are afraid to charge a high price because if your competitor charges a low price, you will lose money and, to add insult to injury, your competitor will get rich. But suppose this game is repeated over and over

---

[9] Suppose Jim randomizes, letting p be the probability of wrestling, and $(1 - p)$ the probability of opera. Since Joan is using probabilities of 1/3 for wrestling and 2/3 for opera, the probability that both will choose wrestling is (1/3)p, and the probability that both will choose opera is (2/3)(1 − p). Hence Jim's expected payoff is $2(\frac{1}{3})p + 1(\frac{2}{3})(1 - p) = (\frac{2}{3})p + \frac{2}{3} - (\frac{2}{3})p = \frac{2}{3}$. This is independent of p, so Jim cannot do better in terms of expected payoff no matter what he chooses.

Table 13.8   Pricing Problem

		Firm 2	
		Low price	High price
Firm 1	Low price	10, 10	100, −50
	High price	−50, 100	50, 50

again—for example, you and your competitor simultaneously announce your prices on the first day of every month. Should you then play the game differently, perhaps changing your price over time in response to your competitor's behavior?

In an interesting study, Robert Axelrod asked game theorists to come up with the best strategy they could think of to play this game in a repeated manner.[10] (A possible strategy might be: "I'll start off with a high price, then lower my price, but then if my competitor lowers its price, I'll raise mine for a while before lowering it again, etc.") Then, in a computer simulation, Axelrod played these strategies off against one another to see which worked best.

As you would expect, any given strategy would work better against some strategies than it would against others. The objective, however, was to find the strategy that was most robust, i.e., would work best on average against *all*, or almost all, other strategies. The result was surprising. The strategy that worked best was extremely simple—it was a *"tit-for-tat"* strategy: I start out with a high price, which I maintain so long as you continue to "cooperate" and also charge a high price. As soon as you lower your price, however, I follow suit and lower mine. If you later decide to cooperate and raise your price again, I'll immediately raise my price as well.

Why does this tit-for-tat strategy work best? In particular, can I expect that using the tit-for-tat strategy will induce my competitor to behave cooperatively (and charge a high price)?

Suppose the game is *infinitely repeated*. In other words, my competitor and I repeatedly set price month after month, *forever*. Cooperative behavior (i.e., charging a high price) is then the rational response to a tit-for-tat strategy. (This assumes that my competitor knows, or can figure out, that I am using a tit-for-tat strategy.) To see why, suppose that in one month my competitor sets a low price and undercuts me. In that month it will make a large profit. But the competitor knows that the following month I will set a low price, so that its profit will fall and will remain low as long as we both continue to charge a low price. Since the game is infinitely repeated, the cumulative loss of profits that results must outweigh any short-term gain that accrued during the first month of undercutting. Thus, it is not rational to undercut.

---

[10] See Robert Axelrod, *The Evolution of Cooperation* (New York: Basic Books, 1984).

In fact, with an infinitely repeated game, my competitor does not even have to be sure that I am playing tit-for-tat to make cooperation the rational strategy for it to follow. Even if the competitor believes there is only some chance that I am playing tit-for-tat, it will still be rational for it to start by charging a high price, and maintain the high price as long as I do. The reason is that with infinite repetition of the game, the *expected* gains from cooperation will outweigh those from undercutting. This will be true even if the probability that I am playing tit-for-tat (and so will continue cooperating) is small.

Now suppose the game is repeated a *finite* number of times—say N months. (N can be large as long as it is finite.) If my competitor (Firm 2) is rational, *and believes that I am rational*, it would reason as follows: "Because Firm 1 is playing tit-for-tat, I (Firm 2) cannot undercut—that is, *until the last month*. I *should* undercut in the last month because then I can make a large profit that month, and afterward the game is over, so that Firm 1 cannot retaliate. Therefore," figures Firm 2, "I will charge a high price until the last month, and then I will charge a low price."

However, since I (Firm 1) have also figured this out, I also plan to charge a low price in the last month. Of course, Firm 2 can figure this out as well, and therefore *knows* I will charge a low price in the last month. But then what about the next-to-last month? Firm 2 figures that it should undercut and charge a low price in the next-to-last month, because there will be no cooperation anyway in the last month. But, of course, I have figured this out too, so I *also* plan to charge a low price in the next-to-last month. And because the same reasoning applies to each preceding month, the only rational outcome is for both of us to charge a low price every month.

Since most of us do not expect to live forever, the tit-for-tat strategy seems of little value; once again we are stuck in the Prisoners' Dilemma without a way out. However, there *is* a way out if my competitor *has even a slight doubt about my "rationality."*

Suppose my competitor thinks (it need not be certain) that I am playing tit-for-tat. It also thinks that *perhaps* I am playing tit-for-tat "blindly," or with limited rationality, in the sense that I have failed to work out the logical implications of a finite time horizon as discussed above. My competitor thinks, for example, that perhaps I have not figured out that it will undercut me in the last month, so that I should also charge a low price in the last month, so that it should charge a low price in the next-to-last month, and so on. "*Perhaps*," thinks my competitor, "Firm 1 will play tit-for-tat blindly, charging a high price as long as I charge a high price." Then (if the time horizon is long enough), it is rational for my competitor to maintain a high price until the last month (when it will undercut me).

Note that we have stressed the word "perhaps." My competitor need not be sure that I am playing tit-for-tat "blindly," or even that I am playing tit-for-tat at all. Just the *possibility* of this can make cooperative behavior a good strategy (until near the end) if the time horizon is long enough. Although my competitor's conjecture about how I am playing the game might be wrong, cooperative behavior is profitable *in expected value terms*. With a long time horizon, the sum of current and future profits, weighted by the probability that the conjecture is correct, can exceed the sum of profits from warfare, even if the competitor is the first to undercut.[11]

Most managers don't know how long they and their firms will be competing with their rivals, and this also serves to make cooperative behavior a good strategy. Although the number of months that the firms compete is probably finite, managers are unlikely to know just what that number is. As a result, the unravelling argument that begins with a clear expectation of undercutting in the last month no longer applies. As with an infinitely repeated game, it will be rational to play tit-for-tat.

Thus, in a repeated game, the Prisoners' Dilemma can have a cooperative outcome. In most markets the game is in fact repeated over a long and uncertain length of time, and managers have doubts about how "perfectly rationally" they and their competitors operate. As a result, in some industries, particularly those in which only a few firms compete over a long period under stable demand and cost conditions, cooperation prevails, even though no contractual arrangements are made. (The water meter industry, discussed below, is an example of this.) In many other industries, however, there is little or no cooperative behavior.

Sometimes cooperation breaks down or never begins because there are too many firms. More often, the failure to cooperate is the result of rapidly shifting demand or cost conditions. Uncertainties about demand or costs make it difficult for the firms in the industry to reach an implicit understanding of what cooperation should entail. (Remember that an *explicit* understanding, arrived at through meetings and discussions, could lead to an antitrust conviction.) Suppose, for example, that cost differences or different beliefs about demand lead one firm to conclude that cooperation means charging $50, but lead a second firm to think it means charging $40. If the second firm charges $40, the first firm might view that as a grab for market share and respond in tit-for-tat fashion with a $35 price. A price war could then develop.

EXAMPLE 13.2 | **Oligopolistic Cooperation in the Water Meter Industry**

For more than 30 years, almost all the water meters sold in the United States have been produced by four American companies: Rockwell International, Badger Meter, Neptune Water Meter Company, and Hersey Products. Rockwell has had about a 35 percent share of the market, and the other three firms have together had about a 50 to 55 percent share.[12]

---

[11] After all, if I am wrong and my competitor charges a low price, I can shift my strategy at the cost of only one period's profit, a minor cost in light of the substantial profit that I can make if we both choose to set a high price. These results on the repeated Prisoners' Dilemma were first developed by David Kreps, Paul Milgrom, John Roberts, and Robert Wilson, "Rational Cooperation in the Finitely Repeated Prisoners' Dilemma," *Journal of Economic Theory* 27 (1982): 245–252.

[12] This example is based in part on Nancy Taubenslag, "Rockwell International," Harvard Business School Case No. 9–383–019, July 1983. In 1979, Neptune Water Meter Company was acquired by Wheelabrator-Frye. Hersey Products is a small privately held company.

Most buyers of water meters are municipal water utilities, who install the meters in residential and commercial establishments so that they can measure water consumption and bill consumers accordingly. Since the cost of the water meters is a small part of the total cost of providing water, the utilities are concerned mainly that the meters be accurate and reliable. The price of the meters is thus not a primary issue, and demand is very price inelastic. Demand is also very stable; every residence or commercial establishment must have a water meter, so demand grows slowly along with the population.

In addition, utilities tend to have long-standing relationships with suppliers and are reluctant to shift from one supplier to another. This creates a barrier to entry because any new entrant will find it difficult to lure customers from existing firms. Substantial economies of scale create a second barrier to entry: To capture a significant share of the market, a new entrant would have to invest in a large factory. This virtually precludes entry by new firms.

With inelastic and stable demand and little threat of entry by new firms, the existing four firms could earn substantial monopoly profits if they set prices cooperatively. If, on the other hand, they compete aggressively, with each firm cutting price to try and increase its own share of the market, profits would fall to nearly competitive levels. The firms are thus in a Prisoners' Dilemma. Can cooperation prevail?

It can and *has* prevailed since the 1960s. Remember that the same four firms have been playing a *repeated game* for decades. Demand has been stable and predictable, and over the years the firms have been able to assess their own and each other's costs. In this situation, tit-for-tat strategies work well; it pays each firm to cooperate, as long as its competitors are cooperating.

So, the firms operate as though they were members of a country club. There is rarely an attempt to undercut price, and each firm appears satisfied with its share of the market. And while the business may appear dull, it is certainly profitable. All four firms have been earning returns on their investments that far exceed those in more competitive industries.

EXAMPLE 13.3 **Competition and Collusion in the Airline Industry**

In March 1983, American Airlines, whose president, Robert Crandall, had become notable for his use of the telephone (see Example 10.4), proposed that all airlines adopt a uniform fare schedule based on mileage. The rate per mile would depend on the length of the trip, with the lowest rate of 15 cents per mile for trips over 2500 miles, higher rates for shorter trips, and the highest rate, 53 cents per mile, for trips under 250 miles. For example, a one-way coach ticket from Boston to Chicago, a distance of 932 miles, would cost $233 (based on a rate of 25 cents per mile for trips between 751 and 1000 miles).

This proposal would do away with the many different fares (some heavily discounted) then available. The cost of a ticket from one city to another would depend only on the number of miles between those cities. As a senior vice-president of American Airlines said, "The new streamlined fare structure will help reduce fare confusion." Most other major airlines reacted favorably to the plan and began to adopt it. A vice-president of TWA said, "It's a good move. It's very businesslike." United Airlines quickly announced that it would adopt the plan on routes where it competes with American, which includes most of its system, and TWA and Continental said that they would adopt it for all of their routes.[13]

Why did American Airlines propose this fare structure, and what made it so attractive to the other airlines? Was it really to "help reduce fare confusion"? No, the aim was to reduce price competition and achieve a collusive pricing arrangement. Prices had been driven down by competitive undercutting, as airlines competed for market share. And as Robert Crandall had learned less than a year earlier, fixing prices over the telephone is illegal. Instead, the companies would implicitly fix prices by agreeing to use the same formula for fares.

The plan failed, a victim of the Prisoners' Dilemma. Only two weeks after the plan was announced and adopted by most airlines, Pan Am, which was dissatisfied with its small share of the U.S. market, dropped its fares. American, United, and TWA, afraid of losing their own shares of the market, quickly dropped their fares to match Pan Am. The price-cutting continued, and fortunately for consumers, the plan was soon dead.

This episode exemplifies the problem of oligopolistic pricing. One economist summarized it accurately: "You can't blame American Airlines for trying. After all, it is the American Way to try to cartelize prices with a simple formula. But it is also in the great tradition of open competition in this country to frustrate any such establishment of cartel prices by competitive chiseling."[14]

American Airlines introduced another simplified, four-tier fare structure in April 1992, which was quickly adopted by most major carriers. But it, too, soon fell victim to competitive discounts. In May 1992, Northwest Airlines announced a "kids fly free" program, and American responded with a summer half-price sale, which other carriers matched. As a result, the airline industry lost billions of dollars in 1992.

13.5 Sequential Games

In most of the games we have discussed so far, both players move at the same time. For example, in the Cournot model of duopoly, both firms set output at the same time. In *sequential games*, the players move in turn. The Stackelberg model discussed in Chapter 12 is an example of a sequential game; one firm sets output before the other does. There are many other examples: an adver-

---

13 "American to Base Fares on Mileage," *New York Times*, March 15, 1983; "Most Big Airlines Back American's Fare Plan," *New York Times*, March 17, 1983.

14 Paul W. MacAvoy, "A Plan That Won't Endure Competition," *New York Times*, April 3, 1983.

Table 13.9 Modified Product Choice Problem

		Firm 2	
		Crispy	Sweet
Firm 1	Crispy	−5, −5	10, 20
	Sweet	20, 10	−5, −5

tising decision by one firm and the response by its competitor, entry-deterring investment by an incumbent firm and the decision whether to enter the market by a potential competitor, or a new government regulatory policy and the investment and output response of the firms being regulated.

We will look at a variety of sequential games in the remainder of this chapter. As we will see, they are often easier to analyze than games in which the players move at the same time. In a sequential game, the key is to think through the possible actions and rational reactions of each player.

As a simple example, let's return to the product choice problem first discussed in Section 13.3. This involves two companies who face a market in which two new variations of breakfast cereal can be successfully introduced, as long as each firm introduces only one variation. This time, let's change the payoff matrix slightly. As Table 13.9 shows, the new sweet cereal will inevitably be a better seller than the new crispy cereal, earning a profit of 20 rather than 10 (perhaps because consumers prefer sweet things to crispy things). Both new cereals will still be profitable, however, as long as each is introduced by only one firm. (Compare Table 13.9 with Table 13.3.)

Suppose that both firms, in ignorance of each other's intentions, must announce their decisions independently and simultaneously. Both will then probably introduce the sweet cereal—and both will lose money.

Now suppose that Firm 1 can introduce its new cereal first. (Perhaps it can gear up its production faster.) We now have a sequential game: Firm 1 introduces a new cereal, and then Firm 2 introduces one. What will be the outcome of this game? When making its decision, Firm 1 must consider the rational response of its competitor. It knows that whichever cereal it introduces, Firm 2 will introduce the other kind. Hence it will introduce the sweet cereal, knowing that Firm 2 will respond by introducing the crispy one.

The Extensive Form of a Game

This outcome can be deduced from the payoff matrix in Table 13.9, but sometimes sequential games are easier to visualize if we represent the possible moves in the form of a decision tree. This is called the *extensive form* of the game, and is shown in Figure 13.2. The figure shows the possible choices of Firm 1 (introduce a crispy or a sweet cereal), and then the possible responses

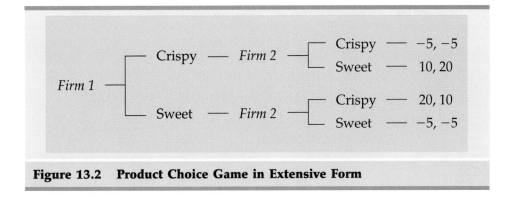

Figure 13.2 **Product Choice Game in Extensive Form**

of Firm 2 for each of those choices. The resulting payoffs are given at the end of each branch. For example, if Firm 1 produces a crispy cereal and Firm 2 responds by also producing a crispy cereal, each firm will have a payoff of −5.

To find the solution to the extensive form game, work backward from the end. For Firm 1, the best sequence of moves is the one in which it earns 20, and Firm 2 earns 10. Thus it can deduce that it should produce the sweet cereal, because then Firm 2's best response is to produce the crispy cereal.

The Advantage of Moving First

In this product-choice game, there is a clear advantage to moving first; by introducing the sweet cereal, Firm 1 creates a fait accompli that leaves Firm 2 little choice but to introduce the crispy one. This is much like the first mover advantage that we saw in the Stackelberg model in Chapter 12. In that model the firm that moves first can choose a large level of output, thereby giving its competitor little choice but to choose a small level of output.

To clarify the nature of this first mover advantage, it would be useful to review the Stackelberg model and compare it to the Cournot model in which both firms choose their outputs simultaneously. As in Chapter 12, we will use the example in which two duopolists face the market demand curve

$$P = 30 - Q$$

where Q is total production, i.e., $Q = Q_1 + Q_2$. We will also assume, as before, that both firms have zero marginal cost. Recall that the Cournot equilibrium is then $Q_1 = Q_2 = 10$, so that $P = 10$, and each firm earns a profit of 100. Recall also that if the two firms colluded, they would set $Q_1 = Q_2 = 7.5$, so that $P = 15$, and each firm earns a profit of 112.50. Finally, recall from Section 12.3 that in the Stackelberg model in which Firm 1 moves first, the outcome is $Q_1 = 15$ and $Q_2 = 7.5$, so that $P = 7.50$, and the firms' profits are 112.50 and 56.25, respectively.

These and a few other possible outcomes are summarized in the payoff matrix of Table 13.10. If both firms move simultaneously, the only solution to the game is that both firms produce 10 and earn 100. In this Cournot equilibrium

Table 13.10	Choosing Output		
		Firm 2	
		7.5	10	15
	7.5	112.50, 112.50	93.75, 125	56.25, 112.50
Firm 1	10	125, 93.75	100, 100	50, 75
	15	112.50, 56.25	75, 50	0, 0

each firm is doing the best it can given what its competitor is doing. If Firm 1 moves first, however, it knows its decision will constrain Firm 2's choice. Observe from the payoff matrix that if Firm 1 sets $Q_1 = 7.5$, Firm 2's best response will be to set $Q_2 = 10$, which will give Firm 1 a profit of 93.75 and Firm 2 a profit of 125. If Firm 1 sets $Q_1 = 10$, Firm 2 will set $Q_2 = 10$, and both firms will earn 100. But if Firm 1 sets $Q_1 = 15$, Firm 2 will set $Q_2 = 7.5$, so that Firm 1 earns 112.50, and Firm 2 earns 56.25. Thus the most Firm 1 can earn is 112.50, and it does this by setting $Q_1 = 15$. Compared to the Cournot outcome, when Firm 1 moves first, it does better—and Firm 2 does much worse.

13.6 Threats, Commitments, and Credibility

The product choice problem and the Stackelberg model are two examples of how a firm that moves first can create a fait accompli that gives it an advantage over its competitor. In this section we'll take a broader look at the advantage a firm can have by moving first, and also consider what determines *which* firm goes first. We will focus on the following question: *What actions can a firm take to gain advantage in the marketplace?* For example, how might a firm deter entry by potential competitors, or induce existing competitors to raise prices, reduce output, or leave the market altogether? Or how might a firm reach an implicit agreement with its competitors that is heavily weighted in its own favor?

An action that gives a firm this kind of advantage is called a *strategic move.* A good definition of a strategic move was given by Thomas Schelling, who first explained the concept and its implications: "A strategic move is one that influences the other person's choice in a manner favorable to one's self, by affecting the other person's expectations of how one's self will behave. One constrains the partner's choice by constraining one's own behavior."[15]

The idea of constraining your own behavior to gain an advantage may seem paradoxical, but we'll soon see that it is not. Let's consider a few examples.

---

[15] Thomas C. Schelling, *The Strategy of Conflict* (New York: Oxford University Press, 1960), p. 160 (1980 edition published by Harvard University Press). For a general discussion of strategic moves in business planning, see Michael E. Porter, *Competitive Strategy* (New York: Free Press, 1980).

First, let's return once more to the product-choice problem shown in Table 13.9. The firm that introduces its new breakfast cereal first will do best. *But which firm will introduce its cereal first?* Even if both firms require the same amount of time to gear up production, each has an incentive to *commit itself first to the sweet cereal.* The key word is "commit." If Firm 1 simply announces it will produce the sweet cereal, Firm 2 will have little reason to believe it. After all, Firm 2, knowing the incentives, can make the same announcement louder and more vociferously. Firm 1 must constrain its own behavior—Firm 2 must be convinced that Firm 1 has *no choice* but to produce the sweet cereal. Such an action by Firm 1 might include an expensive advertising campaign describing the new sweet cereal well before its introduction, thereby putting Firm 1's reputation on the line. Firm 1 might also sign a contract for the forward delivery of a large quantity of sugar (and make the contract public, or at least send a copy to Firm 2). The idea is for Firm 1 to *commit itself* to produce the sweet cereal. Commitment is a strategic move that will induce Firm 2 to make the decision Firm 1 wants it to make—to produce the crispy cereal.

Why can't Firm 1 simply *threaten* Firm 2, vowing to produce the sweet cereal even if Firm 2 does the same? Because Firm 2 has little reason to believe the threat and can make the same threat itself. A threat is useful only if it is credible. The following example should help make this clear.

Empty Threats

Suppose Firm 1 produces personal computers that can be used both as word processors and to do other tasks. Firm 2 produces only dedicated word processors. As the payoff matrix in Table 13.11 shows, as long as Firm 1 charges a high price for its computers, both firms can make a good deal of money. Even if Firm 2 charges a low price for its word processors, many people will still buy Firm 1's computers (because they can do so many other things), although some will be induced by the price differential to buy the dedicated word processor instead. However, if Firm 1 charges a low price for its computers, Firm 2 will also have to charge a low price (or else make zero profit), and the profit of both firms will be significantly reduced.

Firm 1 would prefer the outcome in the upper left-hand corner of the matrix. For Firm 2, however, charging a low price is clearly a dominant strategy.

Table 13.11 Pricing of Computers and Word Processors

		Firm 2	
		High price	Low price
Firm 1	High price	100, 80	80, 100
	Low price	20, 0	10, 20

Thus the outcome in the upper right-hand corner will prevail (no matter which firm sets its price first).

Firm 1 would probably be viewed as the "dominant" firm in this industry because its pricing actions will have the greatest impact on overall industry profits. Then, can't Firm 1 induce Firm 2 to charge a high price by *threatening* to charge a low price itself if Firm 2 charges a low price? No, as the payoff matrix in Table 13.11 makes clear. *Whatever* Firm 2 does, Firm 1 will be much worse off if it charges a low price. As a result, its threat is not credible.

Commitment and Credibility

Sometimes firms can make a threat credible. To see how, consider the following example. Race Car Motors, Inc., produces cars, and Far Out Engines, Ltd., produces specialty car engines. Far Out Engines sells most of its engines to Race Car Motors, and a few to a limited outside market. Nonetheless, it depends heavily on Race Car Motors, and makes its production decisions in response to the production plans of Race Car Motors.

We thus have a sequential game in which Race Car Motors is the "leader." It will decide what kind of cars to build, and Far Out Engines will then decide what kind of engines to produce. The payoff matrix in Table 13.12(a) shows the possible outcomes of this game. (Profits are in millions of dollars.) Observe that Race Car Motors will do best by deciding to produce small cars. It knows that in response to this, Far Out Engines will produce small engines, most of which Race Car Motors will then buy for its new cars. As a result, Far Out Engines will make $3 million, and Race Car Motors will earn $6 million.

Far Out Engines, however, would much prefer the outcome in the lower right-hand corner of the payoff matrix. If it could produce big engines, *and* Race Car Motors produced big cars and therefore bought the big engines, it would make $8 million. (Race Car Motors, however, would make only $3 million.) Can Far Out Engines induce Race Car Motors to produce big cars instead of small ones?

Suppose Far Out Engines *threatens* to produce big engines no matter what Race Car Motors does, and no other engine producer can easily satisfy the needs of Race Car Motors. If Race Car Motors believed this, it would produce big cars, since it would have trouble finding engines for its small cars, and

Table 13.12(a) Production Choice Problem			
		Race Car Motors	
		Small cars	Big cars
Far Out Engines	Small engines	3, 6	3, 0
	Big engines	1, 1	8, 3

would earn only $1 million instead of $3 million. But the threat is not credible. Once Race Car Motors announced its intentions to produce small cars, Far Out Engines would have no incentive to carry out its threat.

Far Out Engines can make its threat credible by visibly and irreversibly reducing some of its own payoffs in the matrix, so that its choices become constrained. In particular, Far Out Engines must reduce its profits from small engines (the payoffs in the top row of the matrix). It might do this by *shutting down or destroying some of its small engine production capacity*. This would result in the payoff matrix shown in Table 13.12(b). Now Race Car Motors *knows* that whatever kind of car it produces, Far Out Engines will produce big engines. (If Race Car Motors produces the small cars, Far Out Engines will sell the big engines as best it can to other car producers and will make only $1 million. But this is better than making no profits by producing small engines. Race Car Motors will also have to look elsewhere for its engines, so its profit will also be lower, at $1 million.) Now it is clearly in Race Car Motors' interest to produce the large cars. By making a strategic move that *seemingly puts itself at a disadvantage*, Far Out Engines has improved the outcome of the game.

Strategic commitments of this kind can be effective, but they are risky and depend heavily on the committing firm's having accurate knowledge of the payoff matrix and the industry. Suppose, for example, that Far Out Engines commits itself to producing big engines but is surprised to find that another firm can produce small engines at a low cost. The commitment may then lead Far Out Engines to bankruptcy rather than to continued high profits.

Developing the right kind of *reputation* can also give one a strategic advantage. Again, consider Far Out Engines' desire to produce big engines for Race Car Motors' big cars. Suppose the managers of Far Out Engines develop a reputation for being irrational—perhaps downright crazy. They threaten to produce big engines no matter what Race Car Motors does. (Refer to Table 13.12a.) Now the threat might be credible without any further action; after all, you can't be sure that an irrational manager will always make a profit-maximizing decision. In gaming situations, the party that is known (or thought) to be a little crazy can have a significant advantage. The game of "chicken" (two cars careen toward each other, and the first driver to swerve to the side is the loser) is a dramatic example of this.

Developing a reputation can be an especially important strategy in a repeated game. A firm might find it advantageous to behave irrationally for sev-

Table 13.12(b) Modified Production Choice Problem			
		Race Car Motors	
		Small cars	Big cars
Far Out Engines	Small engines	0, 6	0, 0
	Big engines	1, 1	8, 3

eral plays of the game. This might give it a reputation that will allow it to increase its long-run profits substantially.

| EXAMPLE 13.4 | **Wal-Mart Stores' Preemptive Investment Strategy** |

Wal-Mart Stores, Inc., is an enormously successful chain of discount retail stores started by Sam Walton in 1969.[16] Its success was unusual in the industry. During the 1960s and 1970s, rapid expansion by existing firms and the entry and expansion of new firms made discount retailing increasingly competitive. During the 1970s and 1980s, industrywide profits fell, and large discount chains—including such giants as King's, Korvette's, Mammoth Mart, W. T. Grant, and Woolco—went bankrupt. Wal-Mart Stores, however, kept on growing (from 153 stores in 1976 to 1009 in 1986) and became even more profitable. By the end of 1985, Sam Walton was one of the richest people in the United States.

How did Wal-Mart Stores succeed where others failed? The key is in Wal-Mart's expansion strategy. To charge less than ordinary department stores and small retail stores, discount stores rely on size, no frills, and high inventory turnover. Through the 1960s, the conventional wisdom held that a discount store could succeed only in a city with a population of 100,000 or more. Sam Walton disagreed and decided to open his stores in small Southwestern towns; by 1970 there were 30 Wal-Mart stores in small towns in Arkansas, Missouri, and Oklahoma. The stores succeeded because Wal-Mart had created 30 "local monopolies." Discount stores that had opened in larger towns and cities were competing with other discount stores, which drove prices and profit margins down. These small towns, however, had room for only one discount operation. Wal-Mart could undercut the nondiscount retailers but never had to worry that another discount store would open and compete with it.

By the mid-1970s, other discount chains realized that Wal-Mart had a profitable strategy: Open a store in a small town that could support only one discount store and enjoy a local monopoly. There are a lot of small towns in the United States, so the issue became who would get to each town first. Wal-Mart now found itself in a *preemption game* of the sort illustrated by the payoff matrix in Table 13.13. As the matrix shows, if Wal-Mart enters a town, but Company X doesn't, Wal-Mart will make 20, and Company X will make 0. Similarly, if Wal-Mart doesn't enter, but Company X does, Wal-Mart makes 0, and Company X makes 20. But if Wal-Mart and Company X *both* enter, *they will both lose 10.*

This game has two Nash equilibria—the lower left-hand corner and the upper right-hand corner. Which equilibrium results depends on *who moves first.* If Wal-Mart moves first, it can enter, knowing that the rational response of Company X will be not to enter, so that Wal-Mart will be assured of earning

---

[16] This example is based in part on information in Pankaj Ghemawat, "Wal-Mart Stores' Discount Operations," Harvard Business School, 1986.

Table 13.13 The Discount Store Preemption Game			
		Company X	
		Enter	Don't enter
Wal-Mart	Enter	−10, −10	20, 0
	Don't enter	0, 20	0, 0

20. *The trick is, therefore, to preempt*—to set up stores in other small towns quickly, before Company X (or Company Y or Z) can do so. That is exactly what Wal-Mart did. By 1986 it had 1009 stores in operation and was earning an annual profit of $450 million. And while other discount chains were going under, Wal-Mart continued to grow. By 1993 it had over 1800 stores and was earning an annual profit of over $1.5 billion, and by 1996 the number of stores had surpassed 2000, and annual profits were $2.7 billion.

13.7 Entry Deterrence

Barriers to entry, which are an important source of monopoly power and profits, sometimes arise naturally. For example, economies of scale, patents and licenses, or access to critical inputs can create entry barriers. However, firms themselves can sometimes deter entry by potential competitors.

To deter entry, *the incumbent firm must convince any potential competitor that entry will be unprofitable.* To see how this might be done, put yourself in the position of an incumbent monopolist facing a prospective entrant, Firm X. Suppose that to enter the industry, Firm X will have to pay a (sunk) cost of $40 million to build a plant. You, of course, would like to induce Firm X to stay out of the industry. If X stays out, you can continue to charge a high price and enjoy monopoly profits. As shown in the upper right-hand corner of the payoff matrix in Table 13.14(a), you would then earn $100 million in profits.

If Firm X does enter the market, you must make a decision. You can be "accommodating," maintaining a high price in the hope that X will do the same. You will then earn only $50 million in profit because you will have to share the market. The new entrant X will earn a *net* profit of $10 million: $50 million less the $40 million cost of constructing a plant. (This outcome is shown in the upper left-hand corner of the payoff matrix.) Alternatively, you can increase your production capacity, produce more, and force price down. Increasing production capacity is costly, however, and lower prices will mean lower revenues. Warfare will therefore mean lower profits for both you and Firm X. As Table 13.14(a) shows, your profit will fall to $30 million, and Firm X will have a net loss of $10 million: the $30 million that it earns from sales less the $40 million for the cost of its plant.

Table 13.14(a) Entry Possibilities		Potential Entrant	
		Enter	Stay out
Incumbent	High price (accommodation)	50, 10	100, 0
	Low price (warfare)	30, −10	40, 0

If Firm X thinks you will be accommodating and maintain a high price after entry, it will find it profitable to enter and will do so. Suppose you threaten to expand output and fight a price war to keep X out. If X believed the threat, it would not enter the market because it would expect to lose $10 million. However, the threat is not credible. As Table 13.14(a) shows (and as the potential competitor knows), *once entry has occurred, it will be in your best interest to accommodate and maintain a high price.* Firm X's rational move is to enter the market; the outcome will be the upper left-hand corner of the matrix.

But what if you can make an irrevocable commitment that would alter your incentives once entry occurred—a commitment that would give you little choice but to charge a low price if entry occurred? In particular, suppose you invest *now*, rather than later, in the extra capacity needed to increase output and engage in competitive warfare should entry occur. We'll assume that this extra capacity will cost $30 million to build, maintain, and operate. Of course, if you later maintain a high price (whether or not X enters), this added cost will reduce your payoffs.

We now have a new payoff matrix, as shown in Table 13.14(b). Now your threat to engage in competitive warfare if entry occurs is *completely credible*, as a result of your decision to invest in additional capacity. Because you have the additional capacity, you will do better in competitive warfare, if entry occurs, than you would by maintaining a high price. The potential competitor now knows that entry will result in warfare, so it is rational for it to stay out of the market. You can therefore maintain a high price, and earn a profit of $70 million, having deterred entry.[17]

Table 13.14(b) Entry Deterrence		Potential Entrant	
		Enter	Stay out
Incumbent	High price (accommodation)	20, 10	70, 0
	Low price (warfare)	30, −10	40, 0

---

[17] This use of investment to deter entry is discussed in more detail in Jean Tirole, *The Theory of Industrial Organization* (Cambridge, Mass.: MIT Press, 1988), and Marvin B. Lieberman, "Strategies for Capacity Expansion," *Sloan Management Review* (Summer 1987): 19–27.

Might an incumbent monopolist deter entry without making the costly move of installing additional production capacity? Earlier we saw that a reputation for irrationality can bestow a strategic advantage. Suppose the incumbent firm has such a reputation. Suppose also that with vicious price-cutting this firm has eventually driven out every entrant in the past, even though it incurred (rationally unwarranted) losses in doing so. Its threat might then indeed be credible. In this case the incumbent's irrationality suggests to the potential competitor that it might be better off staying away.

Of course, if the game described above were to be *indefinitely repeated*, then the incumbent might have a *rational* incentive to carry out the threat of warfare whenever entry actually occurs. The reason is that short-term losses from warfare might be outweighed by longer-term gains from preventing entry. Furthermore, the potential competitor, making the same calculations, might find the incumbent's threat of warfare credible and decide to stay out of the market. Now the incumbent relies on its reputation for being rational—and in particular for being far-sighted—to provide the credibility needed to deter entry. But whether this works depends on the time horizon and the relative gains and losses associated with accommodation and warfare.

We have seen that the attractiveness of entry depends largely on how incumbents can be expected to react. In general, incumbents cannot be expected to maintain output at the preentry level once entry has occurred. Eventually, incumbents may back off and reduce output, raising price to a new joint profit-maximizing level. Because potential entrants know this, incumbent firms must create a credible threat of warfare to deter entry. A reputation for irrationality can help do this. Indeed, this seems to be the basis for much of the entry-preventing behavior that goes on in actual markets. The potential entrant must consider that *rational* industry discipline can break down after entry occurs. By fostering an image of irrationality and belligerence, an incumbent firm might convince potential entrants that the risk of warfare is too high.[18]

Strategic Trade Policy and International Competition

We have seen how a preemptive investment can give a firm an advantage by creating a credible threat to potential competitors. In some situations a preemptive investment—subsidized or otherwise encouraged by the government—can give a *country* an advantage in international markets, and be an important instrument of trade policy.

---

[18] There is an analogy here to *nuclear deterrence*. Consider the use of a nuclear threat to deter the former Soviet Union from invading Western Europe during the Cold War. If they invaded, would the United States actually react with nuclear weapons, knowing that the Soviets would then respond in kind? It is not rational for the United States to react this way, so a nuclear threat might not seem credible. But this assumes that everyone is rational; there is a reason to fear an *irrational* response by the United States. Even if an irrational response is viewed as very improbable, it can be a deterrent, given the costliness of an error. The United States can thus gain by promoting the idea that it might act irrationally, or that events might get out of control once an invasion occurs. This is the "rationality of irrationality." See Schelling, *The Strategy of Conflict*.

Does this conflict with what you have learned about the benefits of free trade? In Chapter 9, for example, we saw how trade restrictions such as tariffs or quotas lead to deadweight losses. In Chapter 16 we go further and show how, in a general way, free trade between people (or between countries) is mutually beneficial. Given the virtues of free trade, how could government intervention in an international market ever be warranted? An emerging literature in international trade theory suggests that in certain situations a country can benefit by adopting policies that give its domestic industries a competitive advantage.[19]

To see how this might occur, consider an industry with substantial economies of scale, so that a few large firms can produce much more efficiently than many small ones. Suppose that by granting subsidies or tax breaks, the government can encourage domestic firms to expand faster than they would otherwise. This might prevent firms in other countries from entering the world market, so that the domestic industry can enjoy higher prices and greater sales. Such a policy would work by creating a credible threat to potential entrants; large domestic firms, taking advantage of scale economies, would be able to satisfy world demand at a low price, so that if other firms entered price would be driven below the point at which they could make a profit.

For example, consider the international market for commercial aircraft. The development and production of a new line of aircraft are subject to substantial economies of scale; it would not pay to develop a new aircraft unless a firm expected to sell many of them. Suppose that Boeing and Airbus (a European consortium that includes France, Germany, Britain, and Spain) are each considering developing a new aircraft (as indeed they were in the late 1970s and early 1980s). The ultimate payoff to each firm depends in part on what the other firm does. Suppose it is only economical for one firm to produce the new aircraft. Then the payoffs might look like those in Table 13.15(a).[20]

Table 13.15(a) Development of a New Aircraft			
		Airbus	
		Produce	Don't produce
Boeing	Produce	−10, −10	100, 0
	Don't produce	0, 100	0, 0

---

[19] For a good overview of this literature, see Paul R. Krugman, "Is Free Trade Passé?" *Journal of Economic Perspectives* 1 (Fall 1987): 131–144; and Elhanan Helpman and Paul R. Krugman, *Trade Policy and Market Structure* (Cambridge, Mass.: MIT Press, 1989).

[20] This example is drawn from Krugman, "Is Free Trade Passé?"

If Boeing has a head start in the development process, the outcome of the game is the upper right-hand corner of the payoff matrix. Boeing will produce a new aircraft, and Airbus, realizing that it would lose money if it did the same, will not. Boeing will then earn a profit of 100.

European governments, of course, would prefer that Airbus produce the new aircraft. Could they change the outcome of this game? Suppose they commit to subsidizing Airbus, and make this commitment before Boeing has committed itself to produce. If the European governments committed to pay a subsidy of 20 to Airbus if it produces the plane, *regardless of what Boeing does*, the payoff matrix would change to the one in Table 13.15(b).

Now Airbus will make money from a new aircraft whether or not Boeing produces one. Hence, Boeing knows that even if it commits to producing, Airbus will produce as well, and Boeing will lose money. Thus Boeing will decide not to produce, and the outcome will be the one in the lower left-hand corner. A subsidy of 20, then, changes the outcome from one in which Airbus does not produce and earns 0 to one in which it does produce and earns 120. Of this, 100 is a transfer of profit from the United States to Europe. Thus, from the European point of view, subsidizing Airbus yields a high return.

European governments *did* commit to subsidizing Airbus, and during the 1980s, Airbus successfully introduced several new airplanes. The result, however, was not quite the one in our stylized example. Boeing also introduced new airplanes (the 757 and 767 models) that were extremely profitable. As commercial air travel grew, it became clear that both companies could profitably develop and sell a new generation of airplanes. Nonetheless, Boeing's market share would have been much larger without the European subsidies to Airbus. One study estimated that those subsidies totalled $25.9 billion during the 1980s and found that Airbus would not have entered the market without them.[21]

The example of Boeing and Airbus shows how strategic trade policy can transfer profits from one country to another. The story, however, is not complete. A country that uses such a policy may provoke retaliation from its trad-

Table 13.15(b) Development of Aircraft After European Subsidy

		Airbus	
		Produce	Don't produce
Boeing	Produce	−10, 10	100, 0
	Don't produce	0, 120	0, 0

---

[21] "Aid to Airbus Called Unfair in U.S. Study," *New York Times*, September 8, 1990.

ing partners. If a trade war results, all countries could end up much worse off. The possibility of such an outcome must be considered before adopting a strategic trade policy.

EXAMPLE 13.5 **Du Pont Deters Entry in the Titanium Dioxide Industry**

Titanium dioxide is a whitener used in paints, paper, and other products. In the early 1970s, Du Pont and National Lead each accounted for about a third of U.S. titanium dioxide sales; another seven firms produced the remainder. In 1972, Du Pont was weighing whether to expand its capacity. The industry was changing, and with the right strategy, those changes might enable Du Pont to capture more of the market and dominate the industry.[22]

Three factors had to be considered. First, although the future demand for titanium dioxide was uncertain, it was expected to grow substantially. Second, the government had announced that new environmental regulations would be imposed. And third, the prices of raw materials used to make titanium dioxide were rising. The new regulations and the higher input prices would have a major effect on production cost, and give Du Pont a cost advantage, both because its production technology was less sensitive to the change in input prices and because its plants were in areas that made disposal of corrosive wastes much less difficult than it would be for other producers. Because of these cost changes, Du Pont anticipated that National Lead and some of the other producers would have to shut down part of their capacity. Du Pont's competitors would in effect have to "reenter" the market by building new plants. Could Du Pont deter them from doing this?

In 1972, Du Pont's Executive Committee considered the following strategy: invest nearly $400 million in increased production capacity to try to capture 64 percent of the market by 1985. The production capacity that would be put on line would be much more than what was actually needed. The idea was to *deter Du Pont's competitors from investing*. Scale economies and movement down the learning curve would give Du Pont a cost advantage. This would make it hard for other firms to compete, and would make credible the implicit threat that Du Pont would fight in the future, rather than accommodate.

The strategy was sensible, and it seemed to work for a few years. By 1975, however, things began to go awry. First, demand grew much less than expected, so that there was excess capacity industrywide. Second, the environmental regulations were only weakly enforced, so that Du Pont's competitors did not have to shut down capacity as expected. And finally, Du Pont's strat-

---

[22] This example is based on Pankaj Ghemawat, "Capacity Expansion in the Titanium Dioxide Industry," *Journal of Industrial Economics* 33 (Dec. 1984): 145–163; and P. Ghemawat, "Du Pont in Titanium Dioxide," Harvard Business School, Case No. 9–385–140, June 1986.

egy led to antitrust action by the Federal Trade Commission in 1978. (The FTC claimed that Du Pont was attempting to monopolize the market. Du Pont won the case, but the decline in demand made its victory moot.)

E X A M P L E   13.6   Diaper Wars

For more than a decade, the disposable diaper industry in the United States has been dominated by just two firms: Procter & Gamble, with an approximately 50–60 percent market share, and Kimberly-Clark, with another 30 percent.[23] How do these firms compete? And why haven't other firms been able to enter and take a significant share of this $4 billion per year market?

Even though there are only two major firms, competition is intense. The competition occurs mostly in the form of *cost-reducing innovation*. The key to success is to perfect the manufacturing process, so that a plant can manufacture diapers in high volume and at low cost. This is not as simple as it might seem. Packing cellulose fluff for absorbency, adding an elastic gatherer, and binding, folding, and packaging the diapers—at a rate of about 3000 diapers per minute and at a cost of about 6 to 8 cents per diaper—requires an innovative, carefully designed, and finely tuned process. Furthermore, small technological improvements in the manufacturing process can result in a significant competitive advantage. If a firm can shave its production cost even slightly, it can reduce price and capture market share. As a result, both firms are forced to spend heavily on research and development (R&D) in a race to reduce cost.[24]

The payoff matrix in Table 13.16 illustrates this. If both firms spend aggressively on R&D, they can expect to maintain their current market shares. P&G will then earn a profit of 40, and Kimberly-Clark (with a smaller market share) will earn 20. If neither firm spends money on R&D, their costs and prices

Table 13.16	Competing Through R&D		
		Kimberly-Clark	
		R&D	No R&D
P&G	R&D	40, 20	80, −20
	No R&D	−20, 60	60, 40

---

[23] Procter & Gamble makes Pampers, Ultra Pampers, and Luvs. Kimberly-Clark has only one major brand, Huggies.

[24] See Michael E. Porter, "The Disposable Diaper Industry," Harvard Business School Case 9–380–175, July 1981; "Innovation Key to Diaper War," *New York Times*, Nov. 25, 1986; and "P&G Moves to Revamp Its Pampers," *Wall Street Journal*, August 9, 1989. P&G developed a superabsorbent chemical to replace the cellulose fluff, allowing for a thinner and lighter diaper.

would remain constant, and the money saved would become part of profits. P&G's profit would increase to 60, and Kimberly-Clark's to 40. However, if one firm continues to do R&D and the other doesn't, the innovating firm will eventually capture most of its competitor's market share. (For example, if Kimberly-Clark does R&D and P&G doesn't, P&G can expect to lose 20, while Kimberly-Clark's profit increases to 60.) The two firms are therefore in a Prisoners' Dilemma; spending money on R&D is a dominant strategy for each firm.

Why hasn't cooperative behavior evolved? After all, the two firms have been competing in this market for years, and the demand for diapers is fairly stable. For several reasons, a Prisoners' Dilemma involving R&D is particularly hard to resolve. First, it is difficult for a firm to monitor its competitor's R&D activities the way it can monitor price. Second, it can take several years to complete an R&D program that leads to a major product improvement. As a result, tit-for-tat strategies, in which both firms cooperate until one of them "cheats," are less likely to work. A firm may not find out that its competitor has been secretly doing R&D until the competitor announces a new and improved product, and by then it may be too late for the firm to gear up an R&D program of its own.

The ongoing R&D expenditures by P&G and Kimberly-Clark also serve to deter entry. In addition to brand name recognition, these two firms have accumulated so much technological know-how and manufacturing proficiency that they would have a substantial cost advantage over any firm just entering the market. Besides building new factories, an entrant would have to spend a considerable amount on R&D to capture even a small share of the market. After it began producing, a new firm would have to continue to spend heavily on R&D to reduce its costs over time. Entry would be profitable only if P&G and Kimberly-Clark stop doing R&D, so that the entrant could catch up and eventually gain a cost advantage. But as we have seen, no rational firm would expect this to happen.[25]

13.8 Bargaining Strategy

In looking at the Prisoners' Dilemma and related problems, we have assumed that collusion was limited by an inability to make an enforceable agreement. Clearly, alternative outcomes are possible (and likely) if firms or individuals can make promises that can be enforced. The Prisoners' Dilemma illustrated by the pricing problem shown in Table 13.8 is a good example of this. If there were no antitrust laws and both firms could make an enforceable agreement about pricing, they would both charge a high price and make profits of 50. Here, the bargaining problem is simple.

Other bargaining situations are more complicated, however, and the outcome can depend on the ability of either side to make a strategic move that alters its relative bargaining position. For example, consider two firms that are each planning to introduce one of two products, which happen to be com-

---

[25] Example 15.3 in Chapter 15 examines in more detail the profitability of capital investment by a new entrant in the diaper market.

Table 13.17 Production Decision

		Firm 2	
		Produce A	Produce B
Firm 1	Produce A	40, 5	50, 50
	Produce B	60, 40	5, 45

plementary goods. As the payoff matrix of Table 13.17 shows, Firm 1 has an advantage in producing A, so that if both firms produce A, Firm 1 will be able to maintain a lower price and will make much higher profits. Similarly, Firm 2 has an advantage in producing product B. As should be clear from the payoff matrix, if the two firms could agree about who will produce what, the only rational outcome would be that in the upper right-hand corner. Firm 1 produces A, Firm 2 produces B, and both firms make profits of 50. Indeed, even *without cooperation* this outcome will result, whether Firm 1 or Firm 2 moves first or both firms move simultaneously. The reason is that producing B is a dominant strategy for Firm 2, so (A, B) is the only Nash equilibrium.

Firm 1 would, of course, prefer the outcome in the lower left-hand corner of the payoff matrix. But in the context of this limited set of decisions, it cannot achieve that outcome. Suppose, however, that Firms 1 and 2 are also bargaining over a second issue—whether to join a research consortium that a third firm is trying to form. Table 13.18 shows the payoff matrix for this decision problem. Clearly, the dominant strategy is for both firms to enter the consortium, thereby obtaining increased profits of 40.

Now suppose that Firm 1 *links the two bargaining problems* by announcing that it will join the consortium *only* if Firm 2 agrees to produce product A. (How can Firm 1 make this threat credible?) In this case it is indeed in Firm 2's interest to agree to produce A (with Firm 1 producing B), in return for Firm 1's participation in the consortium. This example illustrates how a strategic move can be used in bargaining, and why combining issues in a bargaining agenda can sometimes benefit one side at the other's expense.

Two people bargaining over the price of a house is another example of this. Suppose I, as a potential buyer, do not want to pay more than $200,000 for a house that is actually worth $250,000 to me. The seller is willing to part with

Table 13.18 Decision to Join Consortium

		Firm 2	
		Work alone	Enter consortium
Firm 1	Work alone	10, 10	10, 20
	Enter consortium	20, 10	40, 40

the house at any price above $180,000 but would like to receive the highest price she can. If I am the only bidder for the house, how can I make the seller think I will walk away rather than pay more than $200,000?

I might declare that I will never, ever pay more than $200,000 for that house. But is such a promise credible? It is if the seller knows that I have a *strong reputation* for toughness and steadfastness and that I have never broken my word on a promise of this sort. But suppose I have no such reputation. Then the seller knows that I have every incentive to make the promise (making it costs nothing), but little incentive to keep it (since this will probably be our only business transaction together). As a result, this promise by itself is not likely to improve my bargaining position.

The promise can work, however, if it is combined with a strategic move that gives it credibility. Such a strategic move must reduce my flexibility—limit my options—so that I have no choice but to keep the promise. A possible move would be to make an enforceable bet with a third party—for example, "If I pay more than $200,000 for that house, I'll pay you $60,000." Alternatively, if I am buying the house on behalf of my company, the company might insist on authorization by the Board of Directors for a price above $200,000, and announce that the board will not meet again for several months. In both cases, my promise becomes credible because I have destroyed my ability to break it. The result is less flexibility—and more bargaining power.

Summary

1. A game is cooperative if the players can communicate and arrange binding contracts; otherwise it is noncooperative. In either kind of game, the most important aspect of strategy design is understanding your opponent's position, and (if your opponent is rational) correctly deducing the likely response to your actions. Misjudging an opponent's position is a common mistake, as Example 13.1, "Acquiring a Company," illustrates.[26]

2. A Nash equilibrium is a set of strategies such that all players are doing their best, given the strategies of the other players. An equilibrium in dominant strategies is a special case of a Nash equilibrium; a dominant strategy is optimal no matter what the other players do. A Nash equilibrium relies on the rationality of each player. A maximin strategy is more conservative because it maximizes the minimum possible outcome.

3. Some games have no Nash equilibria in pure strategies, but have one or more equilibria in mixed strategies. A mixed strategy is one in which the player makes a random choice

---

[26] Here is the solution to Company A's problem: *It should offer nothing for Company T's stock.* Remember that Company T will accept an offer only if it is greater than the per share value under current management. Suppose you offer $50. Thus Company T will accept this offer only if the outcome of the exploration project results in a per share value under current management of $50 or less. Any values between $0 and $100 are equally likely. Therefore the *expected value* of Company T's stock, *given that it accepts the offer*—i.e., given that the outcome of the exploration project leads to a value less than $50—is $25, so that under the management of Company A the value would be $(1.5)(\$25) = \$37.5$, which is less than $50. In fact, for any price P, if the offer is accepted, Company A can expect a value of only $(3/4)P$.

among two or more possible actions, based on a set of chosen probabilities.

4. Strategies that are not optimal for a one-shot game may be optimal for a repeated game. Depending on the number of repetitions, a "tit-for-tat" strategy, in which one plays cooperatively as long as one's competitor does the same, may be optimal for the repeated Prisoners' Dilemma.

5. In a sequential game, the players move in turn. In some cases, the player who moves first has an advantage. Players may then have an incentive to try to precommit themselves to particular actions before their competitors can do the same.

6. An empty threat is a threat that one would have no incentive to carry out. If one's competitors are rational, empty threats are of no value. To make a threat credible, it is sometimes necessary to make a strategic move by constraining one's later behavior, so that there would be an incentive to carry out the threat.

7. To deter entry, an incumbent firm must convince any potential competitor that entry will be unprofitable. This may be done by investing, and thereby giving credibility to the threat that entry will be met by price warfare. Strategic trade policies by governments sometimes have this objective.

8. Bargaining situations are examples of cooperative games. Just as with noncooperative games, in bargaining players can sometimes gain a strategic advantage by limiting their flexibility.

Questions for Review

1. What is the difference between a cooperative and a noncooperative game? Give an example of each.

2. What is a dominant strategy? Why is an equilibrium stable in dominant strategies?

3. Explain the meaning of a Nash equilibrium. How does it differ from an equilibrium in dominant strategies?

4. How does a Nash equilibrium differ from a game's maximin solution? In what situations is a maximin solution a more likely outcome than a Nash equilibrium?

5. What is a "tit-for-tat" strategy? Why is it a rational strategy for the infinitely repeated Prisoners' Dilemma?

6. Consider a game in which the Prisoners' Dilemma is repeated 10 times, and both players are rational and fully informed. Is a tit-for-tat strategy optimal in this case? Under what conditions would such a strategy be optimal?

7. Suppose you and your competitor are playing the pricing game shown in Table 13.8. Both of you must announce your prices at the same time. Might you improve your outcome by promising your competitor that you will announce a high price?

8. What is meant by "first mover advantage"? Give an example of a gaming situation with a first mover advantage.

9. What is a "strategic move"? How can the development of a certain kind of reputation be a strategic move?

10. Can the threat of a price war deter entry by potential competitors? What actions might a firm take to make this threat credible?

11. A strategic move limits one's flexibility and yet gives one an advantage. Why? How might a strategic move give one an advantage in bargaining?

Exercises

1. In many oligopolistic industries, the same firms compete over a long period of time, setting prices and observing each other's behavior repeatedly. Given that the number of repetitions is large, why don't collusive outcomes typically result?

2. Many industries are often plagued by overcapacity—firms simultaneously make major investments in capacity expansion, so that total capacity far exceeds demand. This happens in industries in which demand is highly volatile and unpredictable, but also in industries in which demand is fairly stable. What factors lead to overcapacity? Explain each briefly.

3. Two computer firms, A and B, are planning to market network systems for office information management. Each firm can develop either a fast, high-quality system (H), or a slower, low-quality system (L). Market research indicates that the resulting profits to each firm for the alternative strategies are given by the following payoff matrix:

		Firm B	
		H	L
Firm A	H	30, 30	50, 35
	L	40, 60	20, 20

a. If both firms make their decisions at the same time and follow *maximin* (low-risk) strategies, what will the outcome be?

b. Suppose both firms try to maximize profits, but Firm A has a head start in planning and can commit first. Now what will the outcome be? What will the outcome be if Firm B has the head start in planning and can commit first?

c. Getting a head start costs money (you have to gear up a large engineering team). Now consider the *two-stage* game in which *first*, each firm decides how much money to spend to speed up its planning, and *second*, it announces which product (H or L) it will produce. Which firm will spend more to speed up its planning? How much

will it spend? Should the other firm spend *anything* to speed up its planning? Explain.

4. Two firms are in the chocolate market. Each can choose to go for the high end of the market (high quality) or the low end (low quality). Resulting profits are given by the following payoff matrix:

		Firm 2	
		Low	High
Firm 1	Low	−20, −30	900, 600
	High	100, 800	50, 50

a. What outcomes, if any, are Nash equilibria?

b. If the manager of each firm is conservative and each follows a maximin strategy, what will be the outcome?

c. What is the cooperative outcome?

d. Which firm benefits most from the cooperative outcome? How much would that firm need to offer the other to persuade it to collude?

5. Two major networks are competing for viewer ratings in the 8:00–9:00 P.M. and 9:00–10:00 P.M. slots on a given weeknight. Each has two shows to fill this time period and is juggling its lineup. Each can choose to put its "bigger" show first or to place it second in the 9:00–10:00 P.M. slot. The combination of decisions leads to the following "ratings points" results:

		Network 2	
		First	Second
Network 1	First	18, 18	23, 20
	Second	4, 23	16, 16

a. Find the Nash equilibria for this game, assuming that both networks make their decisions at the same time.

b. If each network is risk averse and uses a maximin strategy, what will be the resulting equilibrium?

c. What will be the equilibrium if Network 1 makes its selection first? If Network 2 goes first?

d. Suppose the network managers meet to coordinate schedules, and Network 1 promises to schedule its big show first. Is this promise credible, and what would be the likely outcome?

6. Two competing firms are each planning to introduce a new product. Each firm will decide whether to produce Product *A*, Product *B*, or Product *C*. They will make their choices at the same time. The resulting payoffs are shown below.

Firm 2

		A	B	C
	A	−10, −10	0, 10	10, 20
Firm 1	B	10, 0	−20, −20	−5, 15
	C	20, 10	15, −5	−30, −30

a. Are there any Nash equilibria in pure strategies? If so, what are they?
b. If both firms use maximin strategies, what outcome will result?
c. If Firm 1 uses a maximin strategy, and Firm 2 knows this, what will Firm 2 do?

7. We can think of U.S. and Japanese trade policies as a Prisoners' Dilemma. The two countries are considering policies to open or close their import markets. The payoff matrix is shown below.

Japan

		Open	Close
U.S.	Open	10, 10	5, 5
	Close	−100, 5	1, 1

a. Assume that each country knows the payoff matrix and believes that the other country will act in its own interest. Does either country have a dominant strategy? What will be the equilibrium policies if each country acts rationally to maximize its welfare?
b. Now assume that Japan is not certain that the United States will behave rationally. In particular, Japan is concerned that U.S. politicians may want to penalize Japan even if that does not maximize U.S. welfare. How might this affect Japan's choice of strategy? How might this change the equilibrium?

8. You are a duopolist producer of a homogeneous good. Both you and your competitor have zero marginal costs. The market demand curve is

$$P = 30 - Q$$

where $Q = Q_1 + Q_2$. Q_1 is your output, and Q_2 is your competitor's output. Your competitor has also read this book.

a. Suppose you are to play this game only once. If you and your competitor must announce your outputs at the same time, how much will you choose to produce? What do you expect your profit to be? Explain.
b. Suppose you are told that you must announce your output before your competitor does. How much will you produce in this case, and how much do you think your competitor will produce? What do you expect your profit to be? Is announcing first an advantage or a disadvantage? Explain briefly. *How much would you pay* to be given the option of announcing either first or second?
c. Suppose instead that you are to play the first round of a *series of 10 rounds* (with the same competitor). In each round you and your competitor announce your outputs at the same time. You want to maximize the sum of your profits over the 10 rounds. How much will you produce *in the first round*? How much would you expect to produce in the tenth round? The ninth round? Explain briefly.
d. Once again you will play a series of 10 rounds. This time, however, in each round your competitor will announce its output before you announce yours. How will your answers to (c) change in this case?

9. You play the following bargaining game. Player *A* moves first, and makes Player *B* an offer for the division of $100. (For example, Player *A* could suggest that she take $60 and Player *B* take $40). Player *B* can accept or reject the offer. If he rejects, the amount of money available drops to $90, and he then makes an offer for the division of this amount. If Player *A* rejects this offer, the amount of money drops to $80, and Player *A* makes an offer for its division. If Player *B* rejects this of-

fer, the amount of money drops to 0. Both players are rational, fully informed, and want to maximize their payoffs. Which player will do best in this game?

*10. Defendo has decided to introduce a revolutionary video game, and as the first firm in the market, it will have a monopoly position for at least some time. In deciding what type of manufacturing plant to build, it has the choice of two technologies. Technology A is publicly available, and will result in annual costs of

$$C^A(q) = 10 + 8q$$

Technology B is a proprietary technology developed in Defendo's research labs. It involves higher fixed cost of production, but lower marginal costs:

$$C^B(q) = 60 + 2q$$

Defendo's CEO must decide which technology to adopt. Market demand for the new product is $P = 20 - Q$, where Q is total industry output.

a. Suppose Defendo were certain that it would maintain its monopoly position in the market for the entire product lifespan (about five years) without threat of entry. Which technology would you advise the CEO to adopt? What would be Defendo's profit given this choice?

b. Suppose Defendo expects its archrival, Offendo, to consider entering the market shortly after Defendo introduces its new product. Offendo will have access only to Technology A. If Offendo does enter the market, the two firms will play a Cournot game (in quantities) and arrive at the Cournot–Nash equilibrium.

i. If Defendo adopts Technology A and Offendo enters the market, what will be the profits of both firms? Would Offendo choose to enter the market given these profits?

ii. If Defendo adopts Technology B and Offendo enters the market, what will be the profit of each firm? Would Offendo choose to enter the market given these profits?

iii. Which technology would you advise the CEO of Defendo to adopt given the threat of possible entry? What will be Defendo's profit given this choice? What will be consumer surplus given this choice?

c. What happens to social welfare (the sum of consumer surplus and producer profit) as a result of the threat of entry in this market? What happens to equilibrium price? What might this imply about the role of *potential* competition in limiting market power?

11. Three contestants, A, B, and C, each have a balloon and a pistol. From fixed positions, they fire at each other's balloon. When a balloon is hit, its owner is out. When only one balloon remains, its owner is the winner, and receives a $1000 prize. At the outset, the players decide by lot the order in which they will fire, and each player can choose any remaining balloon as his target. Everyone knows that A is the best shot and always hits the target, that B hits the target with probability .9, and that C hits the target with probability .8. Which contestant has the highest probability of winning the $1000? Explain why.

CHAPTER 14

Markets for Factor Inputs

So far we have concentrated on *output markets*—markets for goods and services that firms sell and consumers purchase. In this chapter we discuss *factor markets*—markets for labor, raw materials, and other inputs to production. Much of our material will be familiar because the same forces that shape supply and demand in output markets also affect factor markets.

We have seen that some output markets are perfectly or almost perfectly competitive, while in others producers have market power. The same is true for factor markets. We will examine three different factor market structures: (1) perfectly competitive factor markets, (2) markets in which buyers of factors have monopsony power, and (3) markets in which sellers of factors have monopoly power. We will also point out instances in which equilibrium in the factor market depends on how much market power there is in *output* markets.

14.1 Competitive Factor Markets

A competitive factor market is one in which there are a large number of sellers and buyers of the factor of production. Because no single seller or buyer can affect the price of the factor, each is a price taker. For example, if individual firms that buy lumber to construct homes purchase a small share of the total volume of lumber available, their purchasing decision will have no effect on price. Similarly, if suppliers of lumber each control a small share of the market, their supply decisions will not affect the price of the lumber they sell.

We begin by analyzing the demands for a factor by individual firms. These demands are added to get market demand. We then shift to the supply side of the market and show how market price and input levels are determined.

Demand for a Factor Input When Only One Input Is Variable

Demand curves for factors of production are downward sloping, just like demand curves for the final goods that result from the production process. Unlike consumers' demands for goods and services, however, factor demands are *derived demands*—they depend on, and are derived from, the firm's level of output and the costs of inputs. For example, the demand of Microsoft Corporation for computer programmers is a derived demand that depends not only on the current salaries of programmers, but also on how much software Microsoft expects to sell.

To analyze factor demands, we will use the material from Chapter 7 that shows how a firm chooses its production inputs. We will assume that the firm produces its output using two inputs, capital K and labor L, that can be purchased at the prices r (the rental cost of capital) and w (the wage rate), respectively.[1] We will also assume that the firm has its plant and equipment in place (as in a short-run analysis), and must decide how much labor to hire.

Suppose that the firm has hired a certain number of workers and wants to know whether it is profitable to hire one additional worker. This will be profitable if the additional revenue from the output of the worker's labor is greater than the cost of this labor. The additional revenue from an incremental unit of labor, the *marginal revenue product of labor*, is denoted MRP_L. We know that the firm should hire more labor if the MRP_L is at least as large as the wage rate w.

How do we measure the MRP_L? It's the additional output obtained from the additional unit of this labor, multiplied by the additional revenue from an extra unit of output. The additional output is given by the marginal product of labor MP_L, and the additional revenue by the marginal revenue MR. Thus[2]

---

[1] We implicitly assume that all inputs to production are identical in quality. Differences in workers' skills and abilities are discussed in Chapter 17.

[2] The marginal revenue product is $\Delta R/\Delta L$, where L is the number of units of labor input and R is revenue. Note that $MP_L = \Delta Q/\Delta L$, and $MR = \Delta R/\Delta Q$, where Q is output. Therefore, $MRP_L = \Delta R/\Delta L = (\Delta R/\Delta Q)(\Delta Q/\Delta L) = (MR)(MP_L)$.

$$\text{MRP}_L = (\text{MP}_L)(\text{MR}) \tag{14.1}$$

This important result holds for any competitive factor market, whether the output market is competitive or not. However, to examine the characteristics of the MRP_L, let's begin with the case of a perfectly competitive output (and input) market. In a competitive output market, a firm will sell all its output at the market price P. The marginal revenue from the sale of an additional unit of output is then equal to P. In this case the marginal revenue product of labor is equal to the marginal product of labor times the price of the product:

$$\text{MRP}_L = (\text{MP}_L)(P) \tag{14.2}$$

The higher of the two curves in Figure 14.1 represents the MRP_L curve for a firm in a competitive output market. Note that the marginal product of labor falls as the number of hours of labor increases because there are diminishing returns to labor. The marginal revenue product curve thus slopes downward, even though the price of the product is constant.

The lower curve in Figure 14.1 is the MRP_L curve when the firm has monopoly power in the output market. When firms have monopoly power, they must lower the price of all units of the product to sell more of it. As a result, marginal revenue is always less than price (MR < P), and marginal revenue

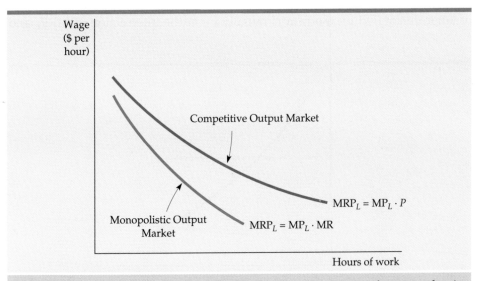

Figure 14.1 Marginal Revenue Product In a competitive factor market in which the producer of the product is a price taker, the buyer's demand for an input is given by the marginal revenue product curve. The MRP curve falls because the marginal product of labor falls as hours of work increases. When the producer of the product has monopoly power, the demand for the input is also given by the MRP curve, but the MRP curve falls because both the marginal product of labor and marginal revenue fall.

falls as output increases. Thus the marginal revenue product curve slopes downward in this case because the marginal revenue curve *and* the marginal product curve slope downward.

Note that the marginal revenue product tells us how much the firm should be willing to pay to hire an additional unit of labor. As long as the MRP_L is greater than the wage rate, the firm should hire an additional unit of labor. If the marginal revenue product is less than the wage rate, the firm should lay off workers. Only when the marginal revenue product is equal to the wage rate will the firm have hired the profit-maximizing amount of labor. So the profit-maximizing condition is

$$\boxed{MRP_L = w} \tag{14.3}$$

Figure 14.2 illustrates this condition. The demand for labor curve D_L is the MRP_L. Note that the quantity of labor demanded increases as the wage rate falls. Since the labor market is perfectly competitive, the firm can hire as many workers as it wants at the market wage w^*, so that the supply of labor curve facing the firm, S_L, is a horizontal line. The profit-maximizing amount of labor that the firm hires, L^*, is at the intersection of the supply and demand curves.

Figure 14.3 shows how the quantity of labor demanded changes in response to a drop in the market wage rate from w_1 to w_2. The wage rate might decrease if more people entering the labor force are looking for jobs for the first time (as happened, for example, when all the baby boomers came of age). The quantity of labor demanded by the firm is initially L_1, at the intersection of MRP_L and

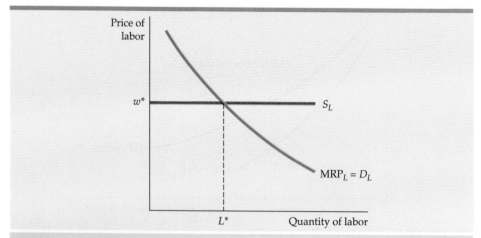

Figure 14.2   Hiring by a Firm in the Labor Market (with Capital Fixed)
In a competitive labor market, a firm faces a perfectly elastic supply of labor S_L, and can hire as many workers as it wants at a wage rate w^*. The firm's demand for labor D_L is given by its marginal revenue product of labor MRP_L. The profit-maximizing firm will hire L^* units of labor at the point where the marginal revenue product of labor is equal to the wage rate.

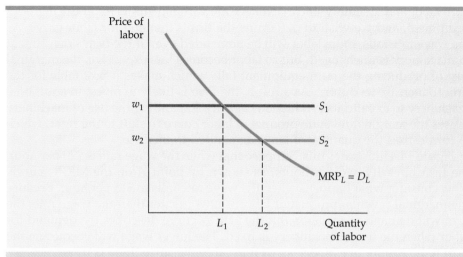

Figure 14.3   A Shift in the Supply of Labor   When the supply of labor facing the firm is S_1, the firm hires L_1 units of labor at wage w_1. But when the market
wage rate decreases and the supply of labor shifts to S_2, the firm maximizes its
profit by moving along the demand for labor curve until the new wage rate w_2 is
equal to the marginal revenue product of labor, and L_2 units of labor are hired.

S_1. However, when the supply of labor curve shifts from S_1 to S_2, the wage falls
from w_1 to w_2, and the quantity of labor demanded increases from L_1 to L_2.

Factor markets are similar to output markets in many ways. For example,
the factor market profit-maximizing condition that the marginal revenue
product of labor be equal to the wage rate is analogous to the output market
condition that marginal revenue be equal to marginal cost. To see why this is
true, recall that $MRP_L = (MP_L)(MR)$ and divide both sides of equation (14.3)
by the marginal product of labor. Then,

$$MR = w/MP_L \tag{14.4}$$

Since MP_L measures the additional output per unit of input, the right-
hand side of equation (14.4) measures the cost of an additional unit of output (the wage rate multiplied by the labor needed to produce one unit of
output), i.e., the marginal cost of production. Equation (14.4) shows that *both
the hiring and output choices of the firm follow the same rule—inputs or outputs
are chosen so that the marginal revenue (from the sale of output) is equal to marginal cost (from the purchase of inputs).* This holds in both competitive and
noncompetitive markets.

Demand for a Factor Input When Several Inputs Are Variable

When the firm simultaneously chooses quantities of two or more variable inputs, the hiring problem becomes more difficult because a change in the price
of one input will change the demand for others. Suppose, for example, that

both labor and assembly-line machinery are variable inputs to producing farm equipment, and we wish to determine the firm's demand for labor curve. As the wage rate falls, more labor will be demanded even if the firm's investment in machinery is unchanged. But as labor becomes less expensive, the marginal cost of producing the farm equipment falls, which makes it profitable for the firm to increase its output. As a result, the firm is likely to invest in additional machinery to expand its production capacity. Expanding the use of machinery causes the marginal revenue product of labor curve to shift to the right, which in turn causes the quantity of labor demanded to increase.

Figure 14.4 illustrates this. Suppose that when the wage rate is $20 per hour, the firm hires 100 worker-hours, as shown by point A on the MRP_{L1} curve. Now consider what happens when the wage rate falls to $15 per hour. Because the marginal revenue product of labor is now greater than the wage rate, the firm will demand more labor. But the MRP_{L1} curve describes the demand for labor when the use of machinery is fixed. The lower wage will encourage the firm to hire more machinery as well as labor. Because there is more machinery, the marginal product of labor will increase (with more machinery, workers can be more productive), and the marginal revenue product curve will shift to the right (to MRP_{L2}). Thus, when the wage rate falls, the firm will use 140 hours of labor as shown by point C, rather than 120 hours as given by B.

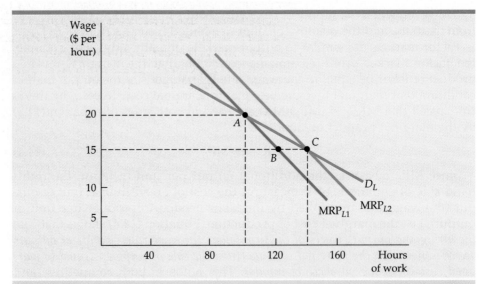

Figure 14.4 Firm's Demand Curve for Labor (with Variable Capital)
When two or more inputs are variable, a firm's demand for one input depends on the marginal revenue product of both inputs. When the wage rate is $20, A represents one point on the firm's demand for labor curve. When the wage rate falls to $15, the MRP curve shifts from MRP_{L1} to MRP_{L2}, generating a new point C on the firm's demand for labor curve. Thus A and C are on the demand for labor curve, but B is not.

A and C are two points on the firm's demand for labor curve (with machinery variable) D_L. Note that as constructed, the demand for labor curve is more elastic than either of the two marginal product of labor curves (which presume no change in the amount of machinery). Thus, when capital inputs are variable in the long run, there is a greater elasticity of demand because firms can substitute capital for labor in the production process.

The Market Demand Curve

When we aggregated the individual demand curves of consumers to obtain the market demand curve for a product, we were concerned with a single industry. However, a factor input like skilled labor is demanded by firms in many different industries. To obtain the total market demand for labor curve, we must therefore first determine each industry's demand for labor, then add the industry demand curves horizontally. The second step is straightforward. Adding industry demand curves for labor to obtain a market demand curve for labor is just like adding individual product demand curves to obtain the market demand curve for that product. So let's concentrate our attention on the more difficult first step.

The first step—determining industry demand—takes into account that the level of output produced by the firm and its product price both change as the prices of the inputs to production change. It is easiest to determine market demand when there is a single producer of the product. Then, the marginal revenue product curve is the industry demand curve for the input. With many firms, however, the analysis is more complex because of the possible interaction among the firms. To illustrate, consider the demand for labor when output markets are perfectly competitive. Then, the marginal revenue product of labor is the product of the price of the good and of the marginal product of labor (see equation 14.2), as shown by the curve MRP_{L1} in Figure 14.5.

Suppose initially that the wage rate for labor is $15 per hour, and the firm demands 100 worker-hours of labor. Now the wage rate for this firm falls to $10 per hour. If no other firms could hire workers at the lower wage, then our firm would hire 150 worker-hours of labor (by finding the point on the MRP_{L1} curve that corresponds to the $10-per-hour wage rate). But if the wage rate falls for all firms in an industry, the industry as a whole will hire more labor. This will lead to more output from the industry, a shift to the right of the industry supply curve, and a lower market price for the product.

In Figure 14.5(a), when the product price falls, the original marginal revenue product curve shifts downward, from MRP_{L1} to MRP_{L2}. This leads to a smaller firm demand for labor than we originally expected—120 worker-hours rather than 150. Consequently, industry demand for labor will be lower than if only one firm were able to hire workers at the lower wage. Figure 14.5(b) illustrates this. The lighter line shows the horizontal sum of the individual firms' demands for labor that would result if the product price did not change as the wage falls. The darker line shows the industry demand curve for labor, which takes into account that the product price will fall as all firms expand their output in response to the lower wage rate. The industry demand for labor is L_0 worker-hours when the wage rate is $15 per hour. When the wage falls to $10

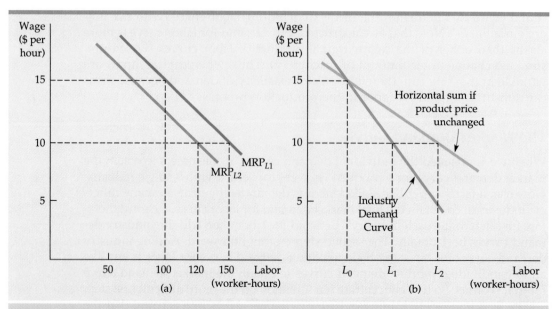

Figure 14.5 **The Industry Demand for Labor** The demand curve for labor of a competitive firm, MRP_{L1} in (a), assumes that the product price is given. But as the wage rate falls from $15 to $10 per hour, the product price also falls, and the firm's demand curve shifts downward to MRP_{L2}. As a result, the industry demand curve, shown in (b), is more inelastic than the demand curve that would be obtained if the product price were assumed to be unchanged.

per hour, the industry demand increases to L_1, a smaller increase than L_2, which would occur if the product price were fixed. The aggregation of industry demand curves into the market demand curve for labor is the final step—to complete it we simply add the labor demanded in all industries.

The derivation of the market demand curve for labor (or any other input) is essentially the same when the output market is noncompetitive. The only difference is that it is more difficult to predict the change in product price in response to a change in the wage rate because each firm in the market is likely to be pricing strategically, rather than taking product price as given.

EXAMPLE 14.1 **The Demand for Jet Fuel**

Throughout the 1970s and the early 1980s, fuel costs for U.S. airlines increased rapidly, in tandem with rising world oil prices. For example, whereas fuel costs made up 12.4 percent of total operating costs in 1971, fuel's share of operating costs rose to about 30 percent in 1980. As we would expect, the amount of jet fuel used by airlines during this period fell as its price rose. Thus the output of the airline industry, as measured by the number of ton-miles (one ton-mile is short for one ton of passengers, baggage, or freight transported one mile), rose by 29.6 percent, while the amount of jet fuel consumed increased by only 8.8 percent. Jet fuel's share of operating costs fell during the late 1980s as oil prices fell, but it remained significant—it was over 15 percent in the early 1990s.

Understanding the demand for jet fuel is important to managers of oil refineries, who must decide how much jet fuel to produce, and to managers of airlines, who must project how their fuel purchases and costs will change when fuel prices rise.[3]

The effect of the increase in fuel costs on the airline industry depends on the ability of airlines either to cut fuel usage by reducing weight (by carrying less excess fuel) and flying slower (reducing drag and increasing engine efficiency) or to pass on their higher costs in prices to customers. Thus the price elasticity of demand for jet fuel depends both on the ability to conserve fuel and on the elasticities of demand and supply of travel.

To measure the short-run elasticity of demand for jet fuel, we use as the quantity of fuel demanded the number of gallons of fuel used by an airline in all markets within its domestic route network. The price of jet fuel is measured in dollars per gallon. A statistical analysis of demand must control for factors other than price that can explain why some firms demand more fuel than others. One factor is that some airlines are using more fuel-efficient jet aircraft, while others are not. A second factor is the length of the flights. The shorter the flight, the more fuel consumed per mile of travel. Both these factors were included in a statistical analysis that relates the quantity of fuel demanded to its price.[4] Table 14.1 shows some short-run price elasticities. (They do not account for the introduction of new types of aircraft.)

The jet fuel price elasticities for the airlines range in value from 0 (for Pan Am) to −.15 (for Delta). Overall, the results show that the demand for jet fuel as an input to the production of airline flight-miles is very inelastic. This is

Table 14.1 Short-Run Price Elasticity of Demand for Jet Fuel

Airline	Elasticity	Airline	Elasticity
American	−.06	Braniff	−.10
Continental	−.09	Delta	−.15
Eastern	−.07	National	−.03
Northwest	−.07	Pan American	.00
TWA	−.10	United	−.10

---

[3] This example is drawn in part from Joseph M. Cigliano, "The Demand for Jet Fuel by the U.S. Domestic Trunk Airlines," *Business Economics* (Sept. 1982): 32–36.

[4] The study controls for the number of trips taken, so that the elasticities measured do not reflect the possibility that higher fuel prices may lead to fewer trips.

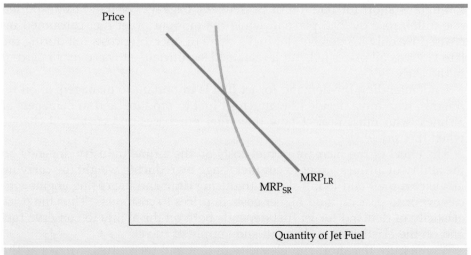

Figure 14.6 **The Short- and Long-Run Demand for Jet Fuel** The short-run demand for jet fuel MRP$_{SR}$ is more inelastic than the long-run demand MRP$_{LR}$. In the short run, airlines cannot reduce fuel consumption much when fuel prices increase. In the long run, however, the airlines can take longer, more fuel-efficient routes and put more fuel-efficient planes into service.

not surprising—in the short run, there is no good substitute for jet fuel. The long-run elasticity of demand is higher, however, because airlines can eventually introduce more energy-efficient airplanes.

Figure 14.6 shows the short- and long-run demands for jet fuel. The short-run demand curve, MRP$_{SR}$, is much less elastic than the long-run demand curve because it takes time to substitute newer, more fuel-efficient airplanes for other planes when the price of fuel goes up.

The Supply of Inputs to a Firm

When the market for a factor input is perfectly competitive, a firm can purchase as much of that input as it wants at a fixed price. The input supply curve facing a firm is then perfectly elastic, as in Figures 14.2 and 14.7(b). In Figure 14.7(b) a firm is buying fabric at $10 per yard to sew into clothing. Because the firm is only a small part of the fabric market, it can buy all it wants without affecting the price.

The supply curve AE facing the firm in Figure 14.7(b) is an *average expenditure curve* (just as the demand curve facing a firm is an average revenue curve) because it represents the expenditure that the firm must make per unit of input that it purchases. The *marginal expenditure curve* ME, on the other hand, represents the expenditure of the firm for each *additional* unit of input it buys. (The marginal expenditure curve in a factor market is analogous to

Figure 14.7   A Firm's Input Supply in a Competitive Factor Market   In a competitive factor market, a firm can buy any amount of the input it wants without affecting the price. Therefore the firm faces a perfectly elastic supply curve for that input. As a result, the quantity of the input purchased by the producer of the product is determined by the intersection of the input demand and supply curves. In (a) the industry quantity demanded and quantity supplied of fabric are equated at a price of $10 per yard. In (b) the firm faces a horizontal marginal expenditure curve at a price of $10 per yard of fabric, and chooses to buy 50 yards.

the marginal revenue curve in the output market.) When the factor market is competitive, the average expenditure and marginal expenditure curves are identical horizontal curves, just as the marginal and average revenue curves are identical (and horizontal) for a competitive firm in the output market.

How much of the input should a firm facing a competitive factor market purchase? As long as the marginal revenue product curve lies above the marginal expenditure curve, profit can be increased by purchasing more of the input because the benefit of an additional unit (MRP) exceeds the cost (ME). However, when the marginal revenue product curve lies below the marginal expenditure curve, some units yield benefits that are less than cost. Therefore, profit maximization requires that *marginal revenue product be equal to marginal expenditure:*

$$\boxed{\text{ME} = \text{MRP}}$$ (14.5)

When we considered the special case of a competitive output market, we saw that the firm bought inputs, such as labor, up to the point at which the marginal revenue product is equal to the price of the input w, as in equation

(14.3). Thus, in the competitive case, the condition for profit maximization is that the price of the input be equal to marginal expenditure:

$$\boxed{ME = w} \tag{14.6}$$

In our example, the price of the fabric ($10 per yard) is determined in the competitive fabric market shown in Figure 14.7(a) at the intersection of the demand and supply curves. Figure 14.7(b) shows the amount of fabric purchased by a firm at the intersection of the marginal expenditure and marginal revenue product curves. When 50 yards of fabric are purchased, the marginal expenditure of $10 is equal to the marginal revenue from the sale of clothing made possible by the increased use of fabric in the production process. If less than 50 yards of fabric were purchased, the firm would be forgoing an opportunity to make additional profit from clothing sales. If more than 50 yards were purchased, the cost of the fabric would be greater than the additional revenue that the firm would receive when it sold the extra clothing.

The Market Supply of Inputs

The market supply curve for a factor is usually upward sloping. We saw in Chapter 8 that the market supply of a good sold in a competitive market is upward sloping when the marginal cost of production is increasing. The same argument applies to inputs such as fabric, which are usually produced with increasing marginal cost as well.

When the factor input is labor, however, people rather than firms are making supply decisions. Then, utility maximization rather than profit maximization becomes the operative goal. In the discussion that follows, we use the analysis of income and substitution effects from Chapter 4 to show that the market supply curve for labor can be upward sloping, but that it may also, as in Figure 14.8, be *backward bending*, i.e., a higher wage rate can lead to *less* labor being supplied.

To see why a labor supply curve may be backward bending, divide the day into hours of work and hours of leisure. Leisure is a generic term that describes nonwork activities, including sleeping and eating. Leisure is assumed to be enjoyable, but work benefits the worker only through the income that is earned. We also assume that a worker has the flexibility to choose how many hours per day to work.

The wage rate measures the price that the worker places on leisure time because the wage is the amount of money that the worker gives up to enjoy leisure. As the wage rate increases, the price of leisure also increases. This price change brings about both a substitution effect (a change in relative price with utility held constant) and an income effect (a change in utility with relative prices unchanged). There is a substitution effect because the higher price of leisure encourages workers to substitute work for leisure. An income effect occurs because the higher wage rate increases the worker's purchasing power. With this higher income, the worker can buy more of many goods, one of which is leisure. If more leisure is chosen, then the income effect encourages

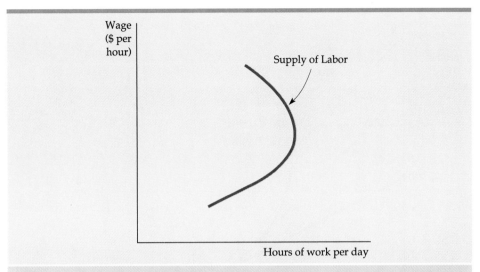

Figure 14.8 Backward-Bending Supply of Labor When the wage rate increases, the hours of work supplied increase initially but eventually decrease as individuals choose to enjoy more leisure and to work less. The backward-bending portion of the labor supply curve arises when the income effect associated with the higher wage (which encourages more leisure) is greater than the substitution effect (which encourages more work).

the laborer to work fewer hours. Income effects can be very large because wages are the primary determinant of most people's income. When the income effect outweighs the substitution effect, the result is the backward-bending supply curve.

Figure 14.9 shows the work-leisure decision that leads to the backward-bending supply curve for labor. The horizontal axis shows hours of leisure per day, the vertical axis income generated by work. (We assume there are no other sources of income.) Initially the wage rate is $10 per hour, and the budget line is given by PQ. Point P, for example, shows that the individual who works a 24-hour day earns an income of $240.

The worker maximizes utility by choosing point A and by enjoying 16 hours of leisure per day (with 8 hours of work) and earning $80. When the wage rate increases to $20 per hour, the budget line rotates about the horizontal intercept to line RQ. (Only 24 hours of leisure are possible.) Now the worker maximizes utility at B by choosing 20 hours of leisure per day (with 4 hours of work), while earning $80. Were only the substitution effect to arise, the higher wage rate would encourage the worker to work 12 hours (at C) instead of 8. However, the income effect works in the opposite direction. It overcomes the substitution effect and lowers the work day from 8 hours to 4.

In real life, a backward-bending labor supply curve might apply to a college student working during the summer to earn living expenses for the school year. As soon as a target level of earnings is reached, the student stops work-

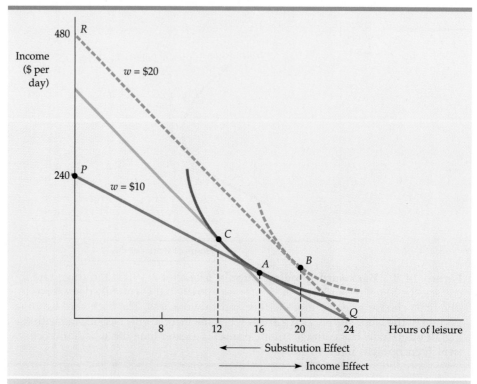

Figure 14.9 Substitution and Income Effects of a Wage Increase When the wage rate increases from $10 to $20 per hour, the worker's budget line shifts from *PQ* to *RQ*. In response, the worker moves from *A* to *B*, while decreasing work hours from 8 to 4. The reduction in hours worked arises because the income effect outweighs the substitution effect. Then, the supply of labor curve is backward bending.

ing and allocates more time to leisure activities. An increase in the wage rate will then lead to fewer hours worked because it enables the student to reach the target level of earnings faster.

EXAMPLE 14.2 **Labor Supply for One- and Two-Earner Households**

One of the most dramatic changes in the labor market in the twentieth century has been the increase in women's participation in the labor force. Women made up 29 percent of the labor force in 1950 and over 60 percent in 1996. Married women account for a substantial portion of this increase. The increased role of women in the labor market has also had a major impact on housing markets: Where to live and work has increasingly become a joint husband-and-wife decision. The complex nature of the work choice was analyzed in a study that compared the work decisions of 94 unmarried females with the work decisions of heads of households and spouses in 397 families.[5]

One way to describe the work decisions of the various family groups is to calculate labor supply elasticities. Each elasticity relates the numbers of hours worked to the wage that the head of household was paid, and also to the wage of the other member of two-earner households. Table 14.2 summarizes the results.

When a higher wage rate leads to fewer hours worked, the labor supply curve is backward bending because the income effect, which encourages more leisure, outweighs the substitution effect, which encourages more work. The elasticity of labor supply is then negative. Table 14.2 shows that heads of one-earner families with children and two-earner families (with or without children) all have backward-bending labor supply curves, with elasticities ranging from −.002 to −.078. Most single-earner heads of households are on the upward-sloping portion of their labor supply curve, with the largest elasticity of .106 associated with single women with children. Married women (listed as spouses of heads of households) are also on the backward-bending portion of the labor supply curve, with elasticities of −.028 and −.086. This suggests that higher wages for women in two-earner

Table 14.2 Elasticities of Labor Supply (Hours Worked)			
Group	Head's Hours with Respect to Head's Wage	Spouse's Hours with Respect to Spouse's Wage	Head's Hours with Respect to Spouse's Wage
Unmarried males (no children)	.026		
Unmarried females (with children)	.106		
Unmarried females (no children)	.011		
One-earner family (with children)	−.078		
One-earner family (no children)	.007		
Two-earner family (with children)	−.002	−.086	−.004
Two-earner family (no children)	−.107	−.028	−.059

---

[5] See Janet E. Kohlhase, "Labor Supply and Housing Demand for One- and Two-Earner Households," *Review of Economics and Statistics* 68 (1986): 48–56.

families will discourage, rather than encourage, more work. The work decision of the head of the household is also responsive to the wage of the spouse: The household head works fewer hours when the spouse earns a higher wage.

14.2 Equilibrium in a Competitive Factor Market

A competitive factor market is in equilibrium when the price of the input equates the quantity demanded to the quantity supplied. Figure 14.10(a) shows such an equilibrium for a labor market. At point A, the equilibrium wage rate is w_C, and the equilibrium quantity supplied is L_C. Since they are well informed, all workers receive the identical wage and generate the identical marginal revenue product of labor wherever they are employed. If any

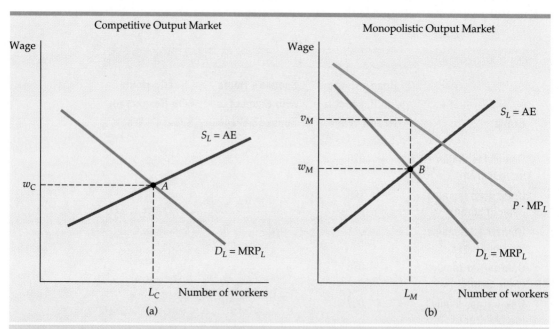

Figure 14.10   Labor Market Equilibrium   In a competitive labor market in which the output market is competitive, the equilibrium wage w_C is given by the intersection of the demand for labor (marginal revenue product) curve and the supply of labor (average expenditure) curve. This is point A in part (a) of the figure. Part (b) shows that when the producer of the product has monopoly power, the marginal value of a worker v_M is greater than the wage w_M, so that not enough workers are employed. (Point B determines the quantity of labor that the firm hires and the wage rate paid.)

worker had a wage lower than his or her marginal product, a firm would find it profitable to offer that worker a higher wage.[6]

If the output market is also perfectly competitive, the demand curve for an input measures the benefit that consumers of the product place on the additional use of the input in the production process. The wage rate also reflects the cost to the firm and to society of using an additional unit of the input. Thus, at A in Figure 14.10(a), the marginal benefit of an hour of labor (its marginal revenue product MRP_L) is equal to its marginal cost (the wage rate w).

When output and input markets are both perfectly competitive, resources are used efficiently because the difference between total benefits and total costs is maximized. Efficiency requires that the additional revenue received by the firm from employing an additional unit of labor (the marginal product of labor, MRP_L) equal the social benefit of the additional output, given by the price of the product times the marginal product of labor, $(P)(MP_L)$.

When the output market is not perfectly competitive, the condition $MRP_L = (P)(MP_L)$ no longer holds. Note in Figure 14.10(b) that the curve representing the product price multiplied by the marginal product of labor $[(P)(MP_L)]$ lies above the marginal revenue product curve $[(MR)(MP_L)]$. Point B is the equilibrium wage w_M and the equilibrium labor supply L_M. But $(P)(MP_L)$ is the value that consumers place on additional inputs of labor. Therefore, when L_M laborers are employed, the marginal cost to the firm w_M is less than the marginal benefit to society v_M. The firm is maximizing its profit, but because its output is below the efficient level, it uses less than the efficient level of the input.

Economic Rent

The concept of economic rent helps explain how factor markets work. When discussing output markets in Chapter 8, we defined economic rent as the payments received by a firm over and above the minimum cost of producing its output. For a factor market, *economic rent is the difference between the payments made to a factor of production and the minimum amount that must be spent to obtain the use of that factor.* Figure 14.11 illustrates the concept of economic rent as applied to a competitive labor market. The equilibrium price of labor is w^*, and the quantity of labor supplied is L^*. The supply of labor curve is the upward-sloping average expenditure curve, and the demand for labor is the downward-sloping marginal revenue product curve. Because the supply curve tells us how much labor will be supplied at each wage rate, the minimum expenditure needed to employ L^* units of labor is given by the tan-

---

[6] As discussed in Chapter 17, however, when information is limited, employers can discriminate against workers.

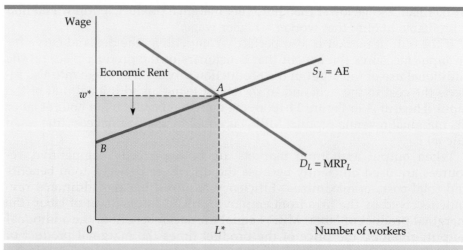

Figure 14.11 Economic Rent The economic rent associated with the employment of labor is the excess of wages paid above the minimum amount needed to hire workers. The equilibrium wage is given by A, at the intersection of the labor supply and labor demand curves. Because the supply curve (AE) is upward sloping, some workers would have accepted jobs for a wage less than w^*. The green-shaded area ABw^* is the economic rent received by all workers.

shaded region AL^*0B, the area below the supply curve to the left of the equilibrium labor supply L^*.

In perfectly competitive markets, all workers are paid the wage w^*. This wage is required to get the last "marginal" worker to supply his or her labor, but all other "inframarginal" workers earn rents because their wage is greater than the wage that would be needed to get them to work. Since total wage payments are equal to the rectangle $0w^*AL^*$, the economic rent earned by labor is given by the area Abw^*.

Note that if the supply curve were perfectly elastic, economic rent would be zero. Rents arise only when supply is somewhat inelastic. And when supply is perfectly inelastic, all payments to a factor of production are economic rents because the factor will be supplied no matter what price is paid.

One example of an inelastically supplied factor is land, as Figure 14.12 shows. The supply curve is perfectly inelastic because land for housing (or for agriculture) is fixed, at least in the short run. With land inelastically supplied, its price is determined entirely by demand. In the figure, the demand for land is given by D_1, and its price per unit is s_1. Total land rent is given by the green-shaded rectangle. But when the demand for land increases to D_2, the rental value per unit of land increases to s_2, and the total land rent includes the blue-shaded area as well. Thus, an increase in the demand for land (a shift to the right in the demand curve) leads to a higher price per acre, and a higher economic rent.

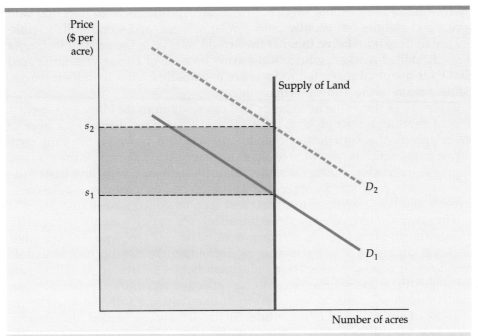

Figure 14.12 Land Rent When the supply of land is perfectly inelastic, the market price of land is determined at the point of intersection with the demand curve, and the entire value of the land is an economic rent. When demand is given by D_1, the economic rent per acre is given by s_1, and when demand increases to D_2, rent increases to s_2.

E X A M P L E 14.3 Pay in the Military

The U.S. Army has had a personnel problem for many years. During the Civil War, roughly 90 percent of the armed forces were unskilled workers involved in ground combat. But since then the nature of warfare has evolved, so that ground combat forces now make up only 16 percent of the armed forces. Meanwhile, changes in technology have led to a severe shortage in skilled technicians, trained pilots, computer analysts, mechanics, and others needed to operate sophisticated military equipment. Why has such a shortage developed, and why has the military been unable to keep its skilled personnel? An economic study provides some answers.[7]

The rank structure of the army has remained essentially unchanged over the years. Among the officer ranks, pay increases are determined primarily

---

[7] Walter Y. Oi, "Paying Soldiers: On a Wage Structure for a Large Internal Labor Market" (unpublished, undated paper).

by the number of years of service. Consequently, officers with differing skill levels and abilities are usually paid similar salaries, and some skilled workers are underpaid relative to what they could receive in the private sector. As a result, skilled workers who join the army because of attractive salaries find that their marginal revenue products are eventually higher than their wages. Some remain in the army, but many leave.

Figure 14.13 shows the inefficiency that can result from the army's pay policy. The equilibrium wage rate w^* is the wage that equates the demand for labor to the supply. Because of inflexibility in its pay structure, however, the army pays the wage w_0, which is below the equilibrium wage. At w_0, demand is greater than supply, and there is a shortage of skilled labor. By contrast, competitive labor markets pay more productive workers higher wages than their less productive counterparts. But how can the army attract and keep its skilled labor force?

The army's choice of wage structure affects the nation's ability to maintain an effective fighting force. In response to its personnel problems, the army has begun to change its salary structure by expanding the number and size of its reenlistment bonuses. Selective reenlistment bonuses targeted at skilled jobs for which there are shortages can be an effective recruiting device. The immediate bonuses create more of an incentive than the somewhat uncertain promise of higher wages in the future. As the demand for skilled military jobs increases, we can expect the army to make greater use of these reenlistment bonuses and other market-based incentives.

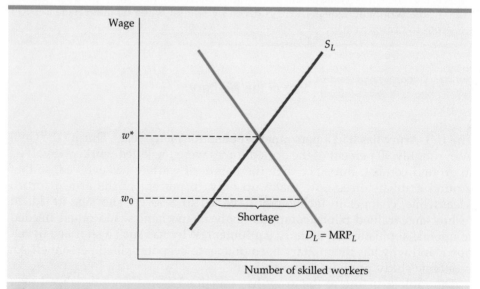

Figure 14.13   The Shortage of Skilled Military Personnel   When the wage w^* is paid to military personnel, the labor market is in equilibrium. When the wage is kept below w^*, at w_0, however, there is a shortage of personnel because the quantity of labor demanded is greater than the quantity supplied.

14.3 Factor Markets with Monopsony Power

In some factor markets, individual buyers of factors have monopsony power. For example, we saw in Chapter 10 that U.S. automobile companies have considerable monopsony power as buyers of parts and components. GM, Ford, and Chrysler buy large quantities of brakes, radiators, tires, and other parts and can negotiate lower prices than smaller purchasers might pay. Similarly, IBM has monopsony power in the market for disk drives because it purchases so many drives for its computers.

Throughout this section we will assume that the output market is perfectly competitive. Also, because a single buyer is easier to visualize than several buyers who all have some monopsony power, we will restrict our attention to pure monopsony.

Marginal and Average Expenditure

When a firm buys a factor input in a competitive market, the marginal and average expenditure curves are identical. But when the firm is a monopsonist, the marginal and average expenditure curves are not the same, as Figure 14.14 shows.

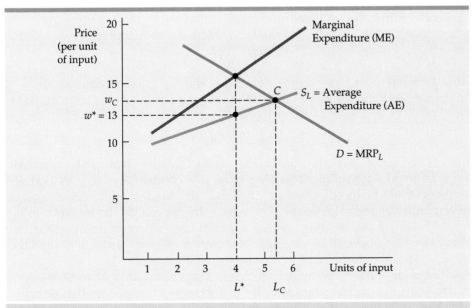

Figure 14.14   Marginal and Average Expenditure   When the buyer of an input has monopsony power, the marginal expenditure curve lies above the average expenditure curve because the firm raises the input price as more of the input is bought. The number of units of input purchased is given by L^*, at the intersection of the marginal revenue product and marginal expenditure curves. The corresponding wage rate w^* is lower than the competitive wage w_C.

The factor supply curve facing the monopsonist is the market supply curve. (It shows how much of the factor suppliers are willing to sell as the price of the factor increases.) Because the monopsonist pays the same price for each unit, the supply curve is its *average expenditure curve*. The average expenditure curve is upward sloping because the monopsonist must pay a higher price if it wants to buy more of the factor. For a profit-maximizing firm, however, it is the *marginal expenditure curve* that is relevant in deciding how much of the factor to buy. Recall from Chapter 10 that the marginal expenditure curve lies above the average expenditure curve because when the firm increases the price of the factor to hire more units, the firm must pay *all* units that higher price, not just the last unit hired.

The Input Purchasing Decision of the Firm

How much of the input should the firm buy? It should buy up to the point where marginal expenditure equals marginal revenue product. Here the benefit from the last unit bought (MRP) is just equal to the cost (ME). Figure 14.14 illustrates this for a labor market. Note that the monopsonist hires L^* units of labor; at that point $ME = MRP_L$. The wage rate w^* that workers are paid is given by finding the point on the average expenditure or supply curve associated with L^* units of labor.

As we showed in Chapter 10, a buyer with monopsony power maximizes net benefit (utility less expenditure) from a purchase by buying up to the point where marginal value (MV) is equal to marginal expenditure:

$$MV = ME$$

For a firm buying a factor input, MV is just the marginal revenue product of the factor MRP. So we have (as in the case of a competitive factor market):

$$\boxed{ME = MRP} \tag{14.7}$$

Note from Figure 14.14 that the monopsonist hires less labor than a firm or group of firms with no monopsony power. In a competitive labor market, L_C workers would be hired because at that level the quantity of labor demanded (given by the marginal revenue product curve) is equal to the quantity of labor supplied (given by the average expenditure curve). Note also that the monopsonistic firm will be paying its workers a wage w^* that is less than the wage w_C that would be paid in a competitive market.

Monopsony power can arise in different ways. One source can be the specialized nature of a firm's business. If the firm buys a component that no other firm buys, it is likely to be a monopsonist in the market for that component. Another source of monopsony power in labor markets can be the business's location—it may be the only major employer within an area. Monopsony power can also arise when the buyers of a factor form a cartel to limit purchases of the factor, so they can buy it at less than the competitive price.

Few firms in our economy are pure monopsonists. But firms (or individuals) often have some monopsony power either because their purchases represent a substantial portion of the market, or because they have some advantage over other potential purchasers of the product. The government is a monopsonist when it hires volunteer soldiers or buys missiles, aircraft, and other specialized equipment for the army. A mining firm or other company that is the only major employer in a community also has monopsony power in the local labor market. Even in these cases, however, monopsony power may be limited because the government competes to some extent with other firms that offer similar jobs, and the mining firm competes to some extent with companies in nearby communities.

E X A M P L E   14.4   **Monopsony Power in the Market for Baseball Players**

In the United States, major league baseball is exempt from the antitrust laws, the result of a Supreme Court decision and the policy of Congress not to apply the antitrust laws to labor markets.[8] This antitrust exemption allowed baseball team owners (before 1975) to operate a monopsonistic cartel. Like all cartels, this one depended on an agreement among owners. This agreement involved an annual draft of players and a *reserve clause* that effectively tied each player to one team for life, thereby eliminating most interteam competition for players. Under the reserve clause, once a player was drafted by a team, he could not play for another team unless rights were sold to that team. As a result, baseball owners had monopsony power in negotiating new contracts with their players—the only alternative to signing an agreement was to give up the game or play it outside the United States.

During the 1960s and early 1970s, baseball players' salaries were far below the market value of their marginal products (determined in part by the incremental attention that better hitting or pitching might achieve). For example, players receiving a salary of about $42,000 in 1969 would have received a salary of $300,000 were the players' market perfectly competitive.

Fortunately for the players, and unfortunately for the owners, there was a strike in 1972 followed by a lawsuit by one player (Curt Flood of the St. Louis Cardinals) and an arbitrated labor–management agreement. This process eventually led in 1975 to an agreement by which baseball players could become free agents after playing for a team for six years. The reserve clause was no longer in effect, and a highly monopsonistic labor market became much more competitive.

The result was an interesting experiment in labor market economics. Between 1975 and 1980, the market for baseball players adjusted to a new post-reserve clause equilibrium. Whereas before 1975, expenditures on players' contracts made up approximately 25 percent of all team expenditures, by 1980 those expenditures had increased to 40 percent. Moreover, the average

---

[8] This example builds on a recent analysis of the structure of baseball players' salaries by Roger Noll, who has kindly supplied us with the relevant data. See also G. W. Scully, "Pay and Performance in Major League Baseball," *American Economic Review* 64 (Dec. 1974): 915–930.

player's salary doubled in real terms. By 1992, the average baseball player was earning $1,014,942, an incredible increase from the monopsonistic wages of the late 1960s. (In 1969, for example, the average baseball salary was approximately $42,000. When adjusted for inflation, this comes to approximately $160,000 in 1992.)

EXAMPLE 14.5 Teenage Labor Markets and the Minimum Wage

Recent increases in the national minimum wage rate (from $4.50 in early 1996 to $5.15 in 1997) have been controversial, raising the question of whether the cost of any unemployment that might be generated will be outweighed by the benefit of higher incomes to those whose wage has been increased.[9] A recent study of the effects of the minimum wage on employment in fast-food restaurants in New Jersey has created even more controversy about this policy.[10]

Some states have minimum wages above the Federal level. In April 1992 the New Jersey minimum wage was increased from $4.25 to $5.05 per hour. Using a survey of 410 fast-food restaurants, David Card and Alan Krueger found that employment had actually *increased* by 13 percent after the minimum wage went up. What is the explanation for this surprising result? One possibility is that restaurants responded to the higher minimum wage by reducing fringe benefits, which usually take the form of free and reduced-price meals for employees. A related explanation is that employers responded by providing less on-the-job training and by offering lower wages for those with experience who had been paid more than the minimum wage. Neither explanation could account for the New Jersey experience, however.

An alternative explanation for the increased New Jersey employment is that the labor market for teenage (and other) unskilled workers is not highly competitive, and the analysis of Chapter 9 does not apply. If the unskilled fast-food labor market were monopsonistic, for example, we would expect a different effect from the increased minimum wage. To see this, suppose that the wage of $4.25 was the wage that fast-food employers with monopsony power in the labor market would offer their workers even if there were no wage minimum. Suppose also that $5.10 would be the wage enjoyed by workers if the labor market were fully competitive. Then, as Figure 14.14 shows, the increase in the minimum wage will not only raise the wage, but will also increase the employment level (from L^* to L_C in the figure).

Does the fast-food study show that employers have monopsony power in this labor market? The evidence suggests that the answer is no. If firms do

---

[9] See Example 1.2 for an initial discussion of the minimum wage, and Section 9.3 for an analysis of its effects on employment.

[10] David Card and Alan Krueger, "Minimum Wages and Employment: A Case Study of the Fast Food Industry in New Jersey and Pennsylvania," National Bureau of Economic Research Working Paper No. 4509, October 1993.

have monopsony power but the fast-food market is competitive, then the increase in the minimum wage should have no effect on the price of fast food. (Because the market for fast food is so competitive, firms paying the higher minimum wage would be forced to absorb the higher wage cost themselves.) However, the study suggests that prices did increase after the introduction of the higher minimum wage. The conclusion: The fast-food labor market cannot be accurately described as either monopsonistic or perfectly competitive.

Perhaps a better characterization of this labor market requires a more sophisticated theory (e.g., the efficiency wage theory discussed in Chapter 17), or perhaps the New Jersey survey generated misleading or unusual results. Hopefully, new empirical analyses will shed more light on the working of this labor market, and on the impact of the minimum wage.

14.4 Factor Markets with Monopoly Power

Just as buyers of inputs can have monopsony power, sellers of inputs can have monopoly power. In the extreme, the seller of an input may be a monopolist, as when a firm has a patent to produce a computer chip that no other firm can duplicate. There are relatively few pure monopolies in factor markets, but in many industries firms have some monopoly power in the sale of products that other firms will use as factors of production. Because the most important example of monopoly power in factor markets involves labor unions, we will concentrate most of our attention there. In the subsections that follow, we briefly describe how a labor union, which is a monopolist in the sale of labor services, might increase the well-being of its members and substantially affect nonunionized workers.

Monopoly Power over the Wage Rate

Figure 14.15 shows a demand for labor curve in a market with no monopsony power—it aggregates the marginal revenue products of firms that compete to buy labor. The labor supply curve describes how union members would supply labor *if* the union exerted no monopoly power. Then the labor market would be competitive, and L^* workers would be hired at a wage of w^*.

Because of its monopoly power, however, the union can choose any wage rate and the corresponding quantity of labor supplied (just as a monopolist seller of output chooses price and the corresponding quantity of output). If the union wanted to maximize the number of workers hired, it would choose the competitive outcome at A. However, if the union wished to obtain a higher than competitive wage, it could restrict its membership to L_1 workers. As a result, the firm would pay a wage rate of w_1. The union members who work would be better off, while those who cannot obtain jobs would be worse off.

Is a policy of restrictive union membership worthwhile? Yes, if the union wishes to maximize the economic rent that its workers receive. By restricting membership, the union would be acting like a monopolist that restricts out-

put to maximize profit. Profit to a firm is the revenue it receives less its opportunity costs. Rent to a union represents the wages its members earn in excess of their opportunity cost. To maximize rent, the union must choose the
number of workers hired so that the marginal revenue to the union (the additional wages earned) is equal to the extra cost of inducing the worker to
work. In Figure 14.15 this involves choosing the quantity of labor at which
the marginal revenue curve MR crosses the supply curve (because the supply
curve represents the opportunity cost of workers being employed). We have
chosen the wage-employment combination of w_1 and L_1 with this in mind.
The shaded area below the demand for labor curve, above the supply of labor curve and to the left of L_1, represents the economic rent that workers receive.

A rent-maximizing policy might benefit nonunion workers if they can find
nonunion jobs. However, if these jobs are not available, rent maximization
could create too sharp a distinction between winners and losers. An alternative objective is to maximize the aggregate wages that all workers receive. To
achieve this goal, in the example in Figure 14.15, the number of workers hired

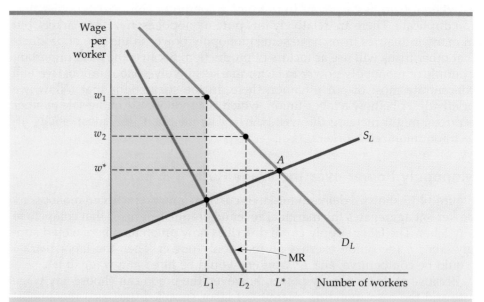

Figure 14.15   Monopoly Power of Sellers of Labor   When a labor union is
a monopolist, it chooses among points on the buyer's demand for labor curve D_L.
The seller can maximize the number of workers hired, at L^*, by agreeing that workers will work at wage w^*. The quantity of labor L_1 that maximizes the rent that employees earn is determined by the intersection of the marginal revenue and supply
of labor curves; union members will receive a wage rate of w_1. Finally, if the union
wishes to maximize total wages paid to workers, it should allow L_2 union members to be employed at a wage rate of w_2 because the marginal revenue to the union
will then be zero.

is increased from L_1 until the marginal revenue to the union is equal to zero. Because any further employment decreases total wage payments, aggregate wages are maximized when the wage is equal to w_2 and the number of workers is equal to L_2.

A Two-Sector Model of Labor Employment

When the union uses its monopoly power to increase its members' wages, fewer unionized workers are hired. Because these workers either move to the nonunion sector or choose not to join the union initially, it is important to understand what happens in the nonunionized part of the economy.

Assume that the total supply of unionized and nonunionized workers is fixed. In Figure 14.16 the market supply of labor in both sectors is given by S_L. The demand for labor by firms in the unionized sector is given by D_U, and the demand in the nonunionized sector by D_{NU}. The total market demand is the horizontal sum of the demands in the two sectors and is given by D_L.

Suppose the union chooses to increase the wage of its workers above the competitive wage w^*, to w_U. At that wage rate, the number of workers hired in the unionized sector falls by an amount ΔL_U, as shown on the horizontal axis. As these workers find employment in the nonunionized sector, the wage rate in the nonunionized sector adjusts until the labor market is in equilib-

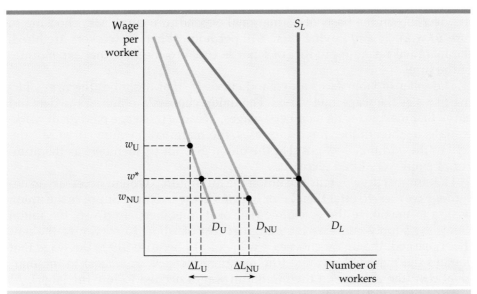

Figure 14.16   Wage Determination in Unionized and Nonunionized Sectors
When a monopolistic union raises the wage in the unionized sector of the economy from w^* to w_U, employment in that sector falls, as shown by the movement along the demand curve D_U. For the total supply of labor, given by S_L, to remain unchanged, the wage in the nonunionized sector must fall from w^* to w_{NU}, as shown by the movement along the demand curve D_{NU}.

rium. The new wage rate in the nonunionized sector, w_{NU}, was chosen so that the additional number of workers hired in the nonunionized sector, ΔL_{NU}, is equal to the number of workers who left the unionized sector.

Figure 14.16 shows an adverse consequence of a union strategy directed toward raising union wages—nonunionized wages fall. Unionization can improve working conditions and provide useful information to workers and management. But when the demand for labor is not perfectly inelastic, union workers are helped at the expense of nonunion workers.

Bilateral Monopoly in the Labor Market

The adverse effects of union wage policies by a monopolistic union depend to some extent on our assumption that the input market is otherwise competitive. To see this, we now consider the consequences of union wage policies when the buyers of labor also have monopsony power.

As we discussed in Chapter 10, *bilateral monopoly* is a market in which a monopolist sells to a monopsonist. In a labor market, bilateral monopoly might arise when representatives from a union and companies that hire a certain type of worker meet to negotiate wages. Figure 14.17 shows a typical bilateral bargaining situation. The S_L curve represents the supply curve for skilled labor, and the firm's demand curve for labor is given by the marginal revenue product curve D_L.

If the union had no monopoly power, the monopsonist would make its hiring decision on the basis of its marginal expenditure curve ME, choosing to hire 20 workers and paying them $10 per hour. When 20 workers are hired, the marginal revenue product of labor is equal to the marginal expenditure of the firm.

The seller of labor faces a demand curve D_L that describes the firm's hiring plans as the wage rate varies. The union chooses a point on the demand curve that maximizes its members' wages. Because the wage paid to all workers falls as the number hired increases, the marginal revenue curve MR describes the additional wages that the union gets for its members as the number of employees hired increases.

The supply curve S_L tells the union the minimum payment necessary to encourage workers to offer their labor to firms in the industry. Suppose the union wishes to maximize the economic rent of its members. To do so, the union views the supply curve as the marginal cost of labor. To maximize the rent that is earned, the union chooses a wage of $19 because $19 is the wage that equates the marginal revenue (the marginal increase in wages) to the marginal cost (the increase in the minimum wages needed to hire the labor). At $19, the firms would hire 25 workers.

In summary, firms are willing to pay a wage of $10 and hire 20 workers, but the union is demanding a wage of $19 and wants the firm to hire 25 workers. What happens in this case? The result depends on the bargaining strategies of the two parties. If the union can make a credible threat to strike, it might secure a wage closer to $19 than to $10. If the firms can make a credible threat to hire nonunion labor, they might secure a wage closer to $10. If

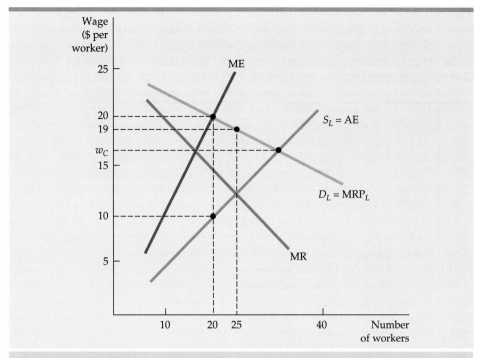

Figure 14.17   Bilateral Monopoly   When the seller of labor is a monopolist and the buyer of labor a monopsonist, the wage rate that is negotiated will be between a high of $19 (determined by the intersection of the marginal revenue and average expenditure curves) and a low of $10 (determined by the intersection of the marginal revenue product curve and marginal expenditure curves).

both parties can make credible threats, the resulting agreement might be close to the competitive outcome (wage w_C) of about $15 in Figure 14.17.[11]

EXAMPLE   14.6   **The Decline of Private Sector Unionism**

For several decades, both the membership and bargaining power of labor unions have been declining.[12] A decline in union monopoly power can lead to different responses by union negotiators and can also affect the wage rate and level of employment. During the 1970s most of the effect was on union

[11] There is no guarantee that monopoly power and monopsony power will cancel, nor that the total number of workers hired will be near the competitive level because both the monopolist and the monopsonist want to limit the number of workers hired. In "Unions and Monopoly Profits," *Review of Economics and Statistics* 67 (1985): 34–42, Thomas Karier shows that unions reduce profits in highly concentrated industries but have little or no effect on profits in more competitive industries.

[12] This example is based on Richard Edwards and Paul Swaim, "Union-Nonunion Earnings Differentials and the Decline of Private-Sector Unionism," *American Economic Review* 76 (May 1986): 97–102.

wages: Levels of employment did not change much, but the differential between union and nonunion wages decreased substantially. We would have expected the same pattern to occur in the 1980s because of the heavily publicized wage freezes and the rapid growth of two-tier wage provisions, in which newer union members are paid less than their more experienced counterparts.

Surprisingly, however, the union-management bargaining process changed during this period. From 1979 to 1984, the level of unionized employment fell from 27.8 percent to 19.0 percent. Yet the union-nonunion wage differential remained relatively stable and in fact grew wider in some industries. For example, the union wage rate in mining, forestry, and fisheries declined only from 25 percent higher than the nonunion wage in 1979 to 24 percent higher in 1984. On the other hand, the union wage rate in manufacturing increased slightly from approximately 14 percent higher than the nonunion wage in 1979 to 16 percent in 1984. This same pattern has continued into the 1990s. As Figure 14.18 shows, by 1995 unionized employment had fallen to below 15 percent of total employment. The union-nonunion wage differential remained essentially unchanged.

One explanation for this pattern of wage-employment responses is a change in union strategy—a move to maximize the individual wage rate rather than the total wages paid to all union members. However, the demand for unionized employees has probably become increasingly elastic over time as firms find it easier to substitute capital for skilled labor in the production process. Faced with an elastic demand for its services, the union would have little choice but to maintain the wage rate of its members and allow employment levels to fall. Of course, the substitution of nonunion for union workers may cause further losses in the bargaining power of labor unions. How this will affect the differential between union and nonunion wages remains to be seen.

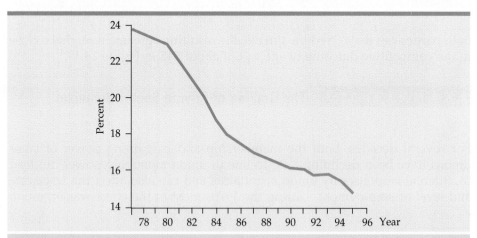

Figure 14.18   Union Workers as a Percentage of Total   The percentage of workers that are unionized has been declining steadily over the past two decades.

SOURCE: Bureau of Labor Statistics, "Employment and Earnings," January issues.

Summary

1. In a competitive input market, the demand for an input is given by the marginal revenue product, the product of the firm's marginal revenue, and the marginal product of the input.

2. A firm in a competitive labor market will hire workers to the point at which the marginal revenue product of labor is equal to the wage rate. This is analogous to the profit-maximizing output condition that production be increased to the point at which marginal revenue is equal to marginal cost.

3. The market demand for an input is the horizontal sum of the industry demands for the input. But industry demand is not the horizontal sum of the demands of all the firms in the industry. To determine industry demand one must take into account that the market price of the product will change in response to the change in the price of an input.

4. When factor markets are competitive, the buyer of an input assumes that its purchases will have no effect on the price of the input. As a result, the marginal expenditure and average expenditure curves that the firm faces are both perfectly elastic.

5. The market supply of a factor such as labor need not be upward sloping. A backward-bending labor supply curve can result if the income effect associated with a higher wage rate (more leisure is demanded because leisure is a normal good) is greater than the substitution effect (less leisure is demanded because the price of leisure has gone up).

6. Economic rent is the difference between the payments to factors of production and the minimum payment that would be needed to employ those factors. In a labor market, rent is measured by the area below the wage level and above the marginal expenditure curve.

7. When a buyer of an input has monopsony power, the marginal expenditure curve lies above the average expenditure curve, which reflects that the monopsonist must pay a higher price to attract more of the input into employment.

8. When the input seller is a monopolist such as a labor union, the seller chooses the point on the marginal revenue product curve that best suits its objective. Maximization of employment, economic rent, and wages are three plausible objectives for labor unions.

9. When a monopolistic union bargains with a monopsonistic employer, the wage rate depends on the nature of the bargaining process. There is little reason to believe that the competitive outcome will be achieved.

Questions for Review

1. Why is a firm's demand for labor curve more inelastic when the firm has monopoly power in the output market than when the firm is producing competitively?

2. Why might a labor supply curve be backward bending?

3. How is a computer company's demand for computer programmers a derived demand?

4. Compare the hiring choices of a monopsonistic and a competitive employer of workers. Which will hire more workers, and which will pay the higher wage? Explain.

5. Rock musicians sometimes earn several million dollars per year. Can you explain this large income in terms of economic rent?

6. What happens to the demand for one input when the use of a complementary input increases?

7. For a monopsonist, what is the relationship between the supply of an input and the marginal expenditure on that input?

8. Currently the National Football League has a system for drafting college players by which each player is picked by only one team and must sign with that team or not play in the league. What would happen to the wages of newly drafted and more experienced football players if the draft system were repealed, so that all teams could compete for college players?

9. Why are wages and employment levels indeterminate when the union has monopoly power and the firm has monopsony power?

Exercises

1. Workers whose incomes are less than $10,000 currently pay no federal income taxes. Suppose a new government program guarantees each worker $5000, whether or not he or she earns any income. For all earned income up to $10,000, the worker must pay a 50 percent tax to the government. Draw the budget line facing the worker under this new program. How is the program likely to affect the labor supply curve of workers?

2. Using your knowledge of marginal revenue product, explain the following:
   a. A famous tennis star is paid $200,000 for appearing in a 30-second television commercial. The actor who plays his doubles partner is paid $500.
   b. The president of an ailing savings and loan is paid *not* to hold office for the last two years of his contract.
   c. A jumbo jet carrying 400 passengers is priced higher than a 250-passenger model even though both aircraft cost the same to manufacture.

3. The demands for the factors of production listed below have increased. What can you conclude about changes in the demands for the related consumer goods? If demands for the consumer goods remain unchanged, what other explanation is there for an increase in derived demands for these items?
   a. Computer memory chips
   b. Jet fuel for passenger planes
   c. Paper used for newsprint
   d. Aluminum used for beverage cans

4. Suppose there are two groups of workers, unionized and nonunionized. Congress passes a law that requires all workers to join the union. What do you expect to happen to the wage rates of formerly nonunionized workers and those workers who were originally unionized? What have you assumed about the union's behavior?

5. Suppose a firm's production function is given by $Q = 12L - L^2$, for $L = 0$ to 6, where L is labor input per day, and Q is output per day. Derive and draw the firm's demand for labor curve if the output sells for $10 in a competitive market. How many workers will the firm hire when the wage rate is $30 per day? $60 per day? (*Hint:* The marginal product of labor is $12 - 2L$.)

6. The only legal employer of military soldiers in the United States is the federal government. If the government uses its knowledge of its monopsonistic position, what criteria will it employ when figuring how many soldiers to recruit? What happens if a mandatory draft is implemented?

7. The demand for labor by an industry is given by the curve $L = 1200 - 10w$, where L is the labor demanded per day, and w is the wage rate. The supply curve is given by $L = 20w$. What is the equilibrium wage rate and quantity of labor hired? What is the economic rent earned by workers?

8. Using the same information in Exercise 7, suppose now that the only labor available is controlled by a monopolistic labor union that wishes to maximize the rent that union members earn. What will be the quantity of labor employed and the wage rate? How does your answer compare with your answer to Exercise 7? Discuss. (*Hint:* The union's marginal revenue curve is given by $L = 600 - 5w$.)

CHAPTER 15

Investment, Time, and Capital Markets

In Chapter 14 we saw that in competitive markets, firms compare the marginal revenue product of each factor to its cost to decide how much to purchase each month. The decisions of all firms determine the market demand for each factor, and the market price is the one that equates the quantity demanded with the quantity supplied. For factor inputs such as labor and raw materials, this picture is reasonably complete, but not so for capital. The reason is that capital is *durable*—it can last and contribute to production for years after it is purchased.

Firms sometimes rent capital much the way they hire workers. For example, a firm might rent office space for a monthly fee, just as it hires a worker for a monthly wage. But more often, capital expenditures involve the purchases of factories and equipment that are expected to last for years. This introduces the element of *time*. When a firm decides whether to build a factory or purchase machines, it must compare the outlays it would have to make *now* with the additional profit the new capital will generate *in the future*. To make this comparison, the firm must address the following question: *How much are future profits worth today?* This problem does not arise when hiring labor or purchasing raw materials. To make those choices, the firm need only compare its *current* expenditure on the factor—e.g., the wage or the price of steel—with the factor's *current* marginal revenue product.

In this chapter we will learn how to calculate the current value of future flows of money. This is the basis for our study of the firm's investment decisions. Most of these decisions involve comparing an outlay today with profits that will be received in the future; we will see how firms can make this comparison and determine whether the outlay is warranted. Often, the future profits resulting from a capital investment may be higher or lower than anticipated. We will see how firms can take this kind of uncertainty into account.

We will also examine other intertemporal decisions that firms sometimes face. For example, producing a depletable resource, such as coal or oil, now means that less will be available to produce in the future. How should a producer take this into account? And how long should a timber company let the trees on its land grow before harvesting them for lumber?

The answers to these investment and production decisions depend in part on the *interest rate* that one pays or receives when borrowing or lending money. We will discuss what determines interest rates, and why interest rates on government bonds, corporate bonds, and savings accounts differ.

15.1 Stocks Versus Flows

Before proceeding, we must be clear about how to measure capital and other factor inputs that firms purchase. Capital is measured as a *stock*, i.e., a quantity of plant and equipment that the firm owns. For example, if a firm owns an electric motor factory worth $10 million, we say that it has a *capital stock* worth $10 million. Inputs of labor and raw materials, on the other hand, are measured as *flows*, as is the output of the firm. For example, this same firm might use 20,000 worker-hours of labor and 50,000 pounds of copper *per month* to produce 8000 electric motors *per month*. (The choice of monthly units is arbitrary; we could just as well have expressed these quantities in weekly or annual terms, for example, 240,000 worker-hours of labor per year, 600,000 pounds of copper per year, and 96,000 motors per year.)

Let's look at this producer of electric motors in more detail. Both variable cost and the rate of output are flows. Suppose the wage rate is $15 per hour, and the price of copper is 80 cents per pound. Then variable cost is $(20,000)(\$15) + (50,000)(\$0.80) = \$340,000$ *per month*. Average variable cost, on the other hand, is a cost *per unit*: ($340,000 per month)/(8000 units per month) = $42.50 per unit.

Suppose the firm sells its electric motors for $52.50 each. Then its average profit is $52.50 − $42.50 = $10.00 per unit, and its total profit is $80,000 *per month*. (Note that this is also a flow.) To make and sell these motors, however, the firm needs capital—the factory that it built for $10 million. *Thus the firm's $10 million capital stock allows it to earn a flow of profit of $80,000 per month.*

Was the $10 million investment in this factory a sound decision? To answer this question, we need to translate the $80,000 per month profit flow into a number that we can compare with the factory's $10 million cost. Suppose the factory is expected to last for 20 years. Then, simply put, the problem is: What is the value today of $80,000 per month for the next 20 years? If that value is greater than $10 million, the investment was a good one.

A profit of $80,000 per month for 20 years comes to ($80,000)(20)(12) = $19.2 million. That would make the factory seem like an excellent investment. But is $80,000 five years—or 20 years—from now worth $80,000 today? No, because money today can be invested—in a bank account, a bond, or other interest-bearing assets—to yield more money in the future. As a result, $19.2 million received over the next 20 years is worth *less* than $19.2 million today.

15.2 Present Discounted Value

We will return to the $10 million electric motor factory in Section 15.4, but first we must address a basic problem: *How much is $1 paid in the future worth today?* The answer depends on the *interest rate*, the rate at which one can borrow or lend money.

Suppose the interest rate is R. (Don't worry about which interest rate this actually is; later, we'll discuss how to choose among the various types of interest rates.) Then $1 today can be invested to yield $(1 + R)$ dollars a year from now. Therefore, $1 + R$ dollars is the *future value* of $1 today. Now, what is the value today, i.e., the *present discounted value* (PDV), of $1 paid one year from now? The answer is easy, once we see that $1 + R$ dollars one year from now is worth $(1 + R)/(1 + R) = \$1$ today. Therefore, *$1 a year from now is worth $\$1/(1 + R)$ today.* This is the amount of money that will yield $1 after one year if invested at the rate R.

What is the value today of $1 paid *two* years from now? If $1 were invested today at the interest rate R, it would be worth $1 + R$ dollars after one year, and $(1 + R)(1 + R) = (1 + R)^2$ dollars at the end of two years. Since $(1 + R)^2$ dollars two years from now is worth $1 today, $1 two years from now is worth $\$1/(1 + R)^2$ today. Similarly, $1 paid three years from now is worth $\$1/(1 + R)^3$ today, and $1 paid n years from now is worth $\$1/(1 + R)^n$ today.[1]

---

[1] We are assuming that the annual rate of interest R is constant from year to year. Suppose the annual interest rate were expected to change, so that R_1 is the rate in year 1, R_2 is the rate in year 2, and so forth. After two years, $1 invested today would be worth $(1 + R_1)(1 + R_2)$, so that the PDV of $1 received two years from now is $\$1/(1 + R_1)(1 + R_2)$. Similarly, the PDV of $1 received n years from now is $\$1/(1 + R_1)(1 + R_2)(1 + R_3) \ldots (1 + R_n)$.

We can summarize this as follows:

$$\text{PDV of \$1 paid after 1 year} = \frac{\$1}{(1 + R)}$$

$$\text{PDV of \$1 paid after 2 years} = \frac{\$1}{(1 + R)^2}$$

$$\text{PDV of \$1 paid after 3 years} = \frac{\$1}{(1 + R)^3}$$

$$\vdots$$

$$\text{PDV of \$1 paid after } n \text{ years} = \frac{\$1}{(1 + R)^n}$$

Table 15.1 shows, for different interest rates, the present value of $1 paid after 1, 2, 5, 10, 20, and 30 years. Note that for interest rates above 6 or 7 percent, $1 paid 20 or 30 years from now is worth very little today; but this is not the case for low interest rates. For example, if R is 3 percent, the PDV of $1 paid 20 years from now is about 55 cents. Put another way, if 55 cents were invested now at the rate of 3 percent, it would yield about $1 after 20 years.

Table 15.1   PDV of $1 Paid in the Future

Interest Rate	1 Year	2 Years	5 Years	10 Years	20 Years	30 Years
0.01	$0.990	$0.980	$0.951	$0.905	$0.820	$0.742
0.02	0.980	0.961	0.906	0.820	0.673	0.552
0.03	0.971	0.943	0.863	0.744	0.554	0.412
0.04	0.962	0.925	0.822	0.676	0.456	0.308
0.05	0.952	0.907	0.784	0.614	0.377	0.231
0.06	0.943	0.890	0.747	0.558	0.312	0.174
0.07	0.935	0.873	0.713	0.508	0.258	0.131
0.08	0.926	0.857	0.681	0.463	0.215	0.099
0.09	0.917	0.842	0.650	0.422	0.178	0.075
0.10	0.909	0.826	0.621	0.386	0.149	0.057
0.15	0.870	0.756	0.497	0.247	0.061	0.015
0.20	0.833	0.694	0.402	0.162	0.026	0.004

Table 15.2 Two Payment Streams			
	Today	**1 Year**	**2 Years**
Payment Stream *A*:	$100	$100	0
Payment Stream *B*:	$ 20	$100	$100

Valuing Payment Streams

We can now determine the present value of a stream of payments over time. For example, consider the two payment streams in Table 15.2. Stream *A* comes to $200: $100 paid now and $100 a year from now. Stream *B* comes to $220: $20 paid now, $100 a year from now, and $100 two years from now. Which payment stream would you prefer to receive? The answer depends on the interest rate.

To calculate the present discounted value of these two streams, we compute and add the present values of each year's payment:

$$\text{PDV of Stream } A = \frac{\$100}{(1 + R)}$$

$$\text{PDV of Stream } B = \frac{\$100}{(1 + R)} + \frac{\$100}{(1 + R)^2}$$

Table 15.3 shows the present values of the two streams for interest rates of 5, 10, 15, and 20 percent. As the table shows, which stream is preferred depends on the interest rate. For interest rates of 10 percent or less, Stream *B* is worth more; for interest rates of 15 percent or more, Stream *A* is worth more. The reason is that less is paid out in Stream *A*, but it is paid out sooner.

Table 15.3 PDV of Payment Streams				
	R = .05	**R = .10**	**R = .15**	**R = .20**
PDV of Stream *A*:	$195.24	$190.90	$186.96	$183.33
PDV of Stream *B*:	205.94	193.54	182.57	172.77

E X A M P L E   15.1   The Value of Lost Earnings

In legal cases involving accidents, victims or their heirs (if the victim is killed) sue the injuring party (or an insurance company) to recover damages. In addition to compensating for pain and suffering, those damages include the future income that the injured or deceased person would have earned had the accident not occurred. To see how the present value of these lost earnings can be calculated, let's examine an actual 1986 accident case. (The names and some of the data have been changed to preserve anonymity.)

Harold Jennings died in an automobile accident on January 1, 1986, at the age of 53. His family sued the driver of the other car for negligence. A major part of the damages they asked to be awarded was the present value of the earnings that Jennings would have received from his job as an airline pilot had he not been killed. The calculation of present value was typical of cases like this.

Had he worked in 1986, Jennings' salary would have been $85,000, and the normal age of retirement for an airline pilot is age 60. To calculate the present value of Jennings' lost earnings, we need to take several things into account. First, Jennings' salary would probably have increased over the years. Second, we cannot be sure that he would have lived to retirement had the accident not occurred; he might have died from some other cause. The PDV of his lost earnings until retirement at the end of 1993 is, therefore,

$$PDV = W_0 + \frac{W_0(1 + g)(1 - m_1)}{(1 + R)} + \frac{W_0(1 + g)^2(1 - m_2)}{(1 + R)^2}$$

$$+ \cdots + \frac{W_0(1 + g)^7(1 - m_7)}{(1 + R)^7}$$

where W_0 is his salary in 1986, g is the annual percentage rate at which his salary is likely to have grown (so that $W_0(1 + g)$ would be his salary in 1987, $W_0(1 + g)^2$ would be his salary in 1988, etc.), and $m_1, m_2, \ldots, m_7$ are *mortality rates*, i.e., the probabilities that he would have died from some other cause by 1987, 1988, ..., 1993.

To calculate this PDV, we need to know the mortality rates $m_1, \ldots, m_7$, the expected rate of growth of Jennings' salary g, and the interest rate R. Mortality data are available from insurance tables that provide death rates for men of similar age and race.[2] As a value for g, we can use 8 percent, the average rate of growth of wages for airline pilots over the past decade. Finally, for the interest rate we can use the rate on government bonds, which in 1986 was about 9 percent. (We will say more about how one chooses the correct interest rate to discount future cash flows in Sections 15.4 and 15.5.) Table 15.4 shows the details of the present value calculation.

By summing the last column we obtain a PDV of $650,252. If Jennings' family were successful in proving that the defendant was at fault, and there were no other damage issues involved in the case, they could recover this amount as compensation.[3]

---

[2] See, for example, the *Statistical Abstract of the United States*, 1992, Table 107.

[3] Actually, this sum should be reduced by the amount of Mr. Jennings' wages that would have been spent on his own consumption, and therefore would not have benefitted his wife or children.

Table 15.4	Calculating Lost Wages			
Year	$W_0(1 + g)^t$	$(1 - m_t)$	$1/(1 + R)^t$	$W_0(1 + g)^t(1 - m_t)/(1 + R)^t$
1986	$ 85,000	.991	1.000	$84,235
1987	91,800	.990	.917	83,339
1988	99,144	.989	.842	82,561
1989	107,076	.988	.772	81,671
1990	115,642	.987	.708	80,810
1991	124,893	.986	.650	80,043
1992	134,884	.985	.596	79,185
1993	145,675	.984	.547	78,408

15.3 The Value of a Bond

A bond is a contract in which a borrower agrees to pay the bondholder (the lender) a stream of money. For example, a corporate bond (a bond issued by a corporation) might make "coupon" payments of $100 per year for the next ten years, and then a principal payment of $1000 at the end of ten years.[4] How much would you pay for such a bond? To find out how much the bond is worth, we simply compute the present value of the payment stream:

$$\text{PDV} = \frac{\$100}{(1 + R)} + \frac{\$100}{(1 + R)^2} + \cdots + \frac{\$100}{(1 + R)^{10}} + \frac{\$1000}{(1 + R)^{10}} \quad (15.1)$$

Again, the present value depends on the interest rate. Figure 15.1 shows the value of the bond—the present value of its payment stream—for interest rates up to 20 percent. Note that the higher the interest rate, the lower the value of the bond. At an interest rate of 5 percent, the bond is worth about $1386, but at an interest rate of 15 percent, its value is only $749.

Perpetuities

A *perpetuity* is a bond that pays out a fixed amount of money each year, *forever*. How much is a perpetuity that pays $100 per year worth? The present value of the payment stream is given by the infinite summation:

---

[4] In the United States, the coupon payments on most corporate bonds are made in semiannual installments. To keep the arithmetic simple, we will assume that the payments are made annually.

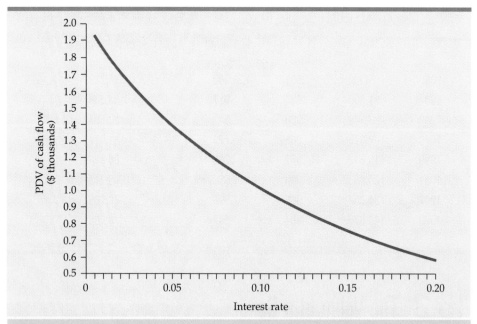

Figure 15.1 Present Value of the Cash Flow from a Bond Because most of the bond's payments occur in the future, the present discounted value declines as the interest rate increases. For example, when the interest rate is 5 percent, the PDV of a 10-year bond paying $100 per year on a principal of $1000 is $1386.

$$PDV = \frac{\$100}{(1 + R)} + \frac{\$100}{(1 + R)^2} + \frac{\$100}{(1 + R)^3} + \frac{\$100}{(1 + R)^4} + \cdots$$

Fortunately, it isn't necessary to calculate and add up all these terms to find the value of this perpetuity; the summation can be expressed in terms of a simple formula:[5]

$$PDV = \$100/R \qquad (15.2)$$

So if the interest rate is 5 percent, the perpetuity is worth $100/(.05) = $2000, but if the interest rate is 20 percent, the perpetuity is worth only $500.

The Effective Yield on a Bond

Many corporate and most government bonds are traded in the *bond market*. The value of a traded bond can be determined directly by looking at its mar-

---

[5] Let x be the PDV of $1 per year in perpetuity, so $x = 1/(1 + R) + 1/(1 + R)^2 + \dots$. Then $x(1 + R) = 1 + 1/(1 + R) + 1/(1 + R)^2 + \dots$, so $x(1 + R) = 1 + x$, $xR = 1$, and $x = 1/R$.

ket price, since this is what buyers and sellers agree that the bond is worth.[6] Thus we usually know the value of a bond, but to compare the bond with other investment opportunities, we would like to determine the interest rate consistent with that value.

Equations (15.1) and (15.2) show how the values of two different bonds depend on the interest rate used to discount future payments. These equations can be "turned around" to relate the interest rate to the bond's value. This is particularly easy to do for the perpetuity. Suppose the market price—and hence the value—of the perpetuity is P. Then from equation (15.2), $P = \$100/R$, and $R = \$100/P$. So if the price of the perpetuity is $1000, we know that the interest rate is $R = \$100/\$1000 = 0.10$, or 10 percent. This interest rate is called the *effective yield*, or *rate of return*. It is the percentage return that one receives by investing in the perpetuity.

For the ten-year coupon bond in equation (15.1), calculating the effective yield is a bit more complicated. If the price of the bond is P, we write equation (15.1) as

$$P = \frac{\$100}{(1 + R)} + \frac{\$100}{(1 + R)^2} + \frac{\$100}{(1 + R)^3} + \cdots + \frac{\$100}{(1 + R)^{10}} + \frac{\$1000}{(1 + R)^{10}}$$

Given the price P, this equation must be solved for R. Although there is no simple formula to express R in terms of P in this case, there are methods (sometimes available on hand-held calculators) for calculating R numerically. Figure 15.2, which plots the same curve that is in Figure 15.1, shows how R depends on P for this ten-year coupon bond. Note that if the price of the bond is $1000, the effective yield is 10 percent. If the price rises to $1300, the figure shows that the effective yield drops to about 6 percent. If the price falls to $700, the effective yield rises to over 16 percent.

Yields can differ considerably among different bonds. Corporate bonds generally yield more than government bonds, and as Example 15.2 shows, the bonds of some corporations yield much more than the bonds of others. One of the most important reasons for this is that different bonds carry different degrees of risk. The U.S. government is less likely to *default* (fail to make interest or principal payments) on its bonds than is a private corporation. And some corporations are financially stronger and therefore less likely to default on their bonds than others. As we saw in Chapter 5, the more risky an investment is, the greater the return that an investor demands. As a result, riskier bonds have higher yields.

---

[6] The prices of actively traded corporate and U.S. government bonds are shown daily in newspapers, such as the *Wall Street Journal* and *New York Times*.

Figure 15.2   Effective Yield on a Bond   The effective yield is the interest rate that equates the present value of the bond's payment stream with the bond's market price. The figure shows the present value of the payment stream as a function of the interest rate, so the effective yield can be found by drawing a horizontal line at the level of the bond's price. For example, if the price of this bond were $1000, its effective yield would be about 10 percent. If the price were $1300, the effective yield would be about 6 percent, and if the price were $700, it would be 16.2 percent.

E X A M P L E   15.2   The Yields on Corporate Bonds

To see how corporate bond yields are calculated, and how they can differ from one corporation to another, let's examine the yields for two coupon bonds—one issued by IBM and the other by the Time Warner Corporation. Each has a *face value* of $100, which means that when the bond matures, the holder receives a principal payment of that amount. Each bond makes a "coupon" (i.e., interest) payment every six months.

We calculate the bond yields using the closing prices on July 29, 1996. The following information on the bonds appeared on the bond page of the newspapers on July 30:

For IBM:

IBM	7 1/4 02	7.2	35	101	−1

For Time Warner:

TimeWar	7 1/4 05	8.0	65	96 5/8	−1/4

What do these numbers mean? For IBM, 7 1/4 refers to the coupon payments *over one year*. This bond pays $3.625 every six months, for a total of $7.25 per year. The number 02 means that the bond matures in 2002 (at which time the holder will receive $100 in principle). The next number, 7.2, is the annual coupon divided by the bond's closing price (i.e., 7.25/101). The number 35 refers to the number of these IBM bonds traded that day. The number 101 refers to the closing price for the bond. Finally, the −1 means that the closing price was one point lower than the preceding day's close.[7]

What is the yield on this bond? For simplicity, we'll assume that the coupon payments are made annually instead of every six months. (The error that this introduces is small.) Because the bond matures in 2002, payments will be made for 2002 − 1996 = 6 years. The yield is given by the following equation:

$$101 = \frac{7.25}{(1 + R)} + \frac{7.25}{(1 + R)^2} + \frac{7.25}{(1 + R)^3} + \cdots + \frac{7.25}{(1 + R)^6} + \frac{100}{(1 + R)^6}$$

This equation must be solved for R. You can check (by substituting and seeing whether the equation is satisfied) that the solution is $R^* = 7.0$ percent.

The yield on the Time Warner bond is found in the same way. This bond makes coupon payments of $7.75 per year, matures in the year 2005, and had a closing price of 96 5/8. Since the bond has nine years to mature, the equation for its yield is

$$96.625 = \frac{7.75}{(1 + R)} + \frac{7.75}{(1 + R)^2} + \frac{7.75}{(1 + R)^3} + \cdots + \frac{7.75}{(1 + R)^9} + \frac{100}{(1 + R)^9}$$

The solution to this equation is $R^* = 8.3$ percent.

Why was the yield on the Time Warner bond higher than that on the IBM bond? Because it was riskier. In 1996 Time Warner had yet to earn profits and was burdened by considerable debt. Given Time Warner's more uncertain financial situation, investors required a higher return before they would hold its bonds.

15.4 The Net Present Value Criterion for Capital Investment Decisions

One of the most common and important decisions that firms make is to invest in new capital. Millions of dollars may be invested in a factory or machines that will last—and affect the firm's profits—for many years. The future cash flows that the investment will generate are often uncertain. And once the factory has been built, the firm usually cannot disassemble and resell it to recoup its investment—it becomes a sunk cost.

---

[7] These bonds actually have a face value of $1000, not $100. The prices and coupon payments are listed as though the face value were $100 to save space. To get the actual prices and payments, just multiply the numbers that appear in the newspaper by 10.

How should a firm decide whether a particular capital investment is worthwhile? It should calculate the present value of the future cash flows that it expects to receive from the investment, and compare it with the cost of the investment. This is the *net present value (NPV) criterion*.

> *NPV criterion: Invest if the present value of the expected future cash flows from an investment is larger than the cost of the investment.*

Suppose a capital investment costs C and is expected to generate profits over the next 10 years of amounts $\pi_1, \pi_2, \ldots, \pi_{10}$. We then write the net present value as

$$\text{NPV} = -C + \frac{\pi_1}{(1 + R)} + \frac{\pi_2}{(1 + R)^2} + \cdots + \frac{\pi_{10}}{(1 + R)^{10}} \qquad (15.3)$$

where R is the *discount rate* that we use to discount the future stream of profits. (R might be a market interest rate, or it might be some other rate; we will discuss how to choose it shortly.) Equation (15.3) describes the net benefit to the firm from the investment. The firm should make the investment only if that net benefit is positive, i.e., *only if NPV > 0*.

What discount rate should the firm use? The answer depends on the alternative ways that the firm could use its money. For example, instead of this investment, the firm might invest in another piece of capital that generates a different stream of profits. Or it might invest in a bond that yields a different return. As a result, we can think of R as the *firm's opportunity cost of capital*. Had the firm not invested in this project, it could have earned a return by investing in something else. *The correct value for R is therefore the return that the firm could earn on a "similar" investment.*

By "similar" investment, we mean one with the same *risk*. As we saw in Chapter 5, the more risky an investment, the greater the return one expects to receive from it. Therefore the opportunity cost of investing in this project is the return that one could earn from another project or asset of similar riskiness.

We'll see how to evaluate the riskiness of an investment in the next section. For now, let's assume that this project has *no risk* (i.e., the firm is sure that the future profit flows will be π_1, π_2, etc.). Then the opportunity cost of the investment is the *risk-free* return—e.g., the return one could earn on a government bond. If the project is expected to last for 10 years, the firm could use the annual interest rate on a 10-year government bond to compute the NPV of the project, as in equation (15.3).[8] If the NPV is zero, the benefit from the investment would just equal the opportunity cost, so the firm should be indifferent between investing and not investing. If the NPV is greater than zero, the benefit exceeds the opportunity cost, so the investment should be made.[9]

---

[8] This is an approximation. To be precise, the firm should use the rate on a one-year bond to discount π_1, the rate on a two-year bond to discount π_2, etc.

[9] This NPV rule is incorrect when the investment is irreversible, subject to uncertainty, and can be delayed. For a treatment of irreversible investment, see Avinash Dixit and Robert Pindyck, *Investment Under Uncertainty* (Princeton, NJ: Princeton University Press, 1994).

The Electric Motor Factory

In Section 15.1, we discussed a decision to invest $10 million in a factory to produce electric motors. This factory would enable the firm to use labor and copper to produce 8000 motors per month for 20 years, at a cost of $42.50 each. The motors could be sold for $52.50 each, for a profit of $10 per unit, or $80,000 per month. We will assume that after 20 years the factory will be obsolete, but it can be sold for scrap for $1 million. Is this a good investment? To find out, we must calculate its net present value.

We will assume for now that the $42.50 production cost and the $52.50 price at which the motors can be sold are certain, so that the firm is sure it will receive $80,000 per month, or $960,000 per year, in profit. We also assume that the $1 million scrap value of the factory is certain. The firm should therefore use a risk-free interest rate to discount future profits. Writing the cash flows in millions of dollars, the NPV is

$$\text{NPV} = -10 + \frac{.96}{(1 + R)} + \frac{.96}{(1 + R)^2} + \frac{.96}{(1 + R)^3}$$
$$+ \cdots + \frac{.96}{(1 + R)^{20}} + \frac{1}{(1 + R)^{20}} \tag{15.4}$$

Figure 15.3 shows the NPV as a function of the discount rate R. Note that at the rate R^*, which is about 7.5 percent, the NPV is equal to zero.[10] For discount rates below 7.5 percent, the NPV is positive, so the firm should invest in the factory. For discount rates above 7.5 percent, the NPV is negative, and the firm should not invest.

Real Versus Nominal Discount Rates

In the example above, we assumed that future cash flows are certain, so that the discount rate R should be a risk-free interest rate, such as the rate on U.S. government bonds. Suppose that rate happened to be 9 percent. Does that mean the NPV is negative, and the firm should not invest?

To answer this question, we must distinguish between real and nominal discount rates, and between real and nominal cash flows. Let's begin with the cash flows. In Chapter 1 we discussed real versus nominal prices, and we explained that the real price is *net of inflation*, whereas the nominal price includes inflation. In our example, we assumed that the electric motors coming out of the factory could be sold for $52.50 each over the next 20 years. We said nothing, however, about the effect of inflation. Is the $52.50 a real price, net of inflation, or does it include inflation? As we will see, the answer to this question can be critical.

Let's assume that the $52.50 price—and the $42.50 production cost—are in real terms. (This means that if we expect a 5 percent annual rate of inflation, the nominal price of the motors will increase from $52.50 in the first year to

---

[10] The rate R^* is sometimes referred to as the *internal rate of return* on the investment.

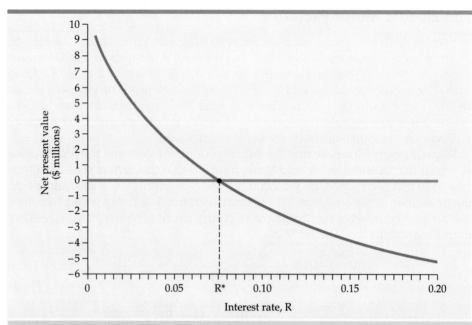

Figure 15.3 **Net Present Value of a Factory** The NPV of a factory is the present discounted value of all the cash flows involved in building and operating it. Here it is the PDV of the flow of future profits less the current cost of construction. The NPV declines as the interest rate increases. At the interest rate R^*, the NPV is zero.

(1.05)(52.50) = \$55.13 in the second year, to (1.05)(55.13) = \$57.88 in the third year, and so on.) Therefore, our profit of \$960,000 per year is also in real terms.

Now let's turn to the discount rate. *If the cash flows are in real terms, the discount rate must also be in real terms.* The reason is that the discount rate is the opportunity cost of the investment. If inflation is not included in the cash flows, it should not be included in the opportunity cost either.

In our example, the discount rate should therefore be the real interest rate on government bonds. The nominal interest rate (9 percent) is the rate that we see in the newspapers; it includes inflation. *The real interest rate is the nominal rate minus the expected rate of inflation.*[11] If we expect inflation to be 5 percent per year on average, the real interest rate would be $9 - 5 = 4$ percent. This is the discount rate that should be used to calculate the NPV of the investment in the electric motor factory. Note from Figure 15.3 that at this rate the NPV is clearly positive, so the investment should be undertaken.

When using the NPV rule to evaluate investments, the numbers in the calculations may be in real or in nominal terms, as long as they are consistent. If cash flows are in real terms, the discount rate should also be in real terms.

---

[11] People may have different views about future inflation and may therefore have different estimates of the real interest rate.

If a nominal discount rate is used, the effect of future inflation must also be included in the cash flows.

Negative Future Cash Flows

Factories and other production facilities can take several years to build and equip. Then, the cost of the investment will also be spread out over several years, instead of occurring only at the outset. In addition, some investments are expected to result in *losses*, rather than profits, for the first few years. (For example, demand may be low until consumers learn about the product, or costs may start high and fall only when managers and workers have moved down the learning curve.) Negative future cash flows create no problem for the NPV rule; they are simply discounted just like positive cash flows.

For example, suppose that our electric motor factory will take a year to build: $5 million is spent right away, and another $5 million is spent next year. Also, suppose the factory is expected to *lose* $1 million in its first year of operation and $0.5 million in its second year. Afterward, it will earn $0.96 million a year until year 20, when it will be scrapped for $1 million, as before. (All these cash flows are in real terms.) Now the net present value is

$$\text{NPV} = -5 - \frac{5}{(1+R)} - \frac{1}{(1+R)^2} - \frac{.5}{(1+R)^3} + \frac{.96}{(1+R)^4} + \frac{.96}{(1+R)^5}$$

$$+ \cdots + \frac{.96}{(1+R)^{20}} + \frac{1}{(1+R)^{20}} \tag{15.5}$$

Suppose the real interest rate is 4 percent. Should the firm build this factory? You can confirm that the NPV is positive, so this project is a good investment.

15.5 Adjustments for Risk

We have seen that a risk-free interest rate is an appropriate discount rate for future cash flows that are certain. For most projects, however, future cash flows are far from certain. For example, for our electric motor factory, we would expect uncertainty over future copper prices, over the future demand and hence the price of motors, and even over future wage rates. Thus the firm cannot know what its profits from the factory will be over the next 20 years. Its best estimate of profits might be $960,000 per year, but actual profits may turn out to be higher or lower than this. How should the firm take this uncertainty into account when calculating the net present value of the project?

A common practice is to increase the discount rate by adding a *risk premium* to the risk-free rate. The idea is that the owners of the firm are risk averse, which makes future cash flows that are risky worth less than those that are certain. Increasing the discount rate takes this into account by reducing the present value of those future cash flows. But how large should the risk premium be? As we will see, the answer depends on the nature of the risk.

Diversifiable Versus Nondiversifiable Risk

Adding a risk premium to the discount rate must be done with care. If the firm's managers are operating in the stockholders' interests, they must distinguish between two kinds of risk—*diversifiable* and *nondiversifiable risk*.[12] Diversifiable risk can be eliminated by investing in many projects or by holding the stocks of many companies. Nondiversifiable risk cannot be eliminated in this way. *Only nondiversifiable risk affects the opportunity cost of capital, and should enter into the risk premium.*

To understand this, recall from Chapter 5 that diversifying can eliminate many risks. For example, I cannot know whether the result of a coin flip will be heads or tails. But I can be reasonably sure that of a thousand coin flips, roughly half will be heads. Similarly, an insurance company that sells me life insurance cannot know how long I will live. But by selling life insurance to thousands of people, it can be reasonably sure about the fraction of those people who will die each year.

Much the same is true about capital investment decisions. Although the profit flow from a single investment may be very risky, if the firm invests in dozens of projects (as most large firms do), its overall risk will be much less. Furthermore, even if the company invests in only one project, the stockholders can easily diversify by holding the stocks of a dozen or more different companies, or by holding a mutual fund that invests in many stocks. So the stockholders, i.e., the owners of the firm, can eliminate diversifiable risk.

Because investors can eliminate diversifiable risk, they cannot expect to earn a return higher than the risk-free rate by bearing it. (No one will pay you for bearing a risk that there is no need to bear.) And indeed, assets that have only diversifiable risk tend on average to earn a return close to the risk-free rate. Now, remember that the discount rate for a project is the opportunity cost of investing in that project, rather than in some other project or asset with similar risk characteristics. Therefore, if the project's only risk is diversifiable, the opportunity cost is the risk-free rate, *and no risk premium should be added to the discount rate.*

What about nondiversifiable risk? First, let's be clear about how it can arise. For a life insurance company, the possibility of a major war poses nondiversifiable risk. A war may increase mortality rates sharply, and the company could not expect that an "average" number of its customers would die each year, no matter how many customers it had. As a result, most insurance policies, whether for life, health, or property, do not cover losses resulting from acts of war.

For capital investments, nondiversifiable risk arises because firms' profits tend to depend on the overall economy. When economic growth is strong, corporate profits tend to be higher. (For our electric motor factory, the demand

---

[12] Diversifiable risk is also called *nonsystematic* risk and nondiversifiable risk is called *systematic* risk. Adding a simple risk premium to the discount rate may not always be the correct way of dealing with risk. See, for example, Richard Brealey and Stewart Myers, *Principles of Corporate Finance* (New York: McGraw-Hill, 1996).

for motors is likely to be strong, so profits increase.) On the other hand, profits tend to fall in a recession. Because future economic growth is uncertain, diversification cannot eliminate all risk. Investors should (and indeed can) earn a higher return by bearing this risk.

To the extent that a project has nondiversifiable risk, the opportunity cost of investing in that project is higher than the risk-free rate, and a risk premium must be included in the discount rate. Let's see how the size of that risk premium can be determined.

The Capital Asset Pricing Model

The *Capital Asset Pricing Model* (CAPM) measures the risk premium for a capital investment by comparing the expected return on that investment with the expected return on the entire stock market. To understand the model, suppose, first, that you invest in the entire stock market (say, through a mutual fund). Then your investment would be completely diversified, and you would bear no diversifiable risk. You would, however, bear nondiversifiable risk because the stock market tends to move with the overall economy. (The stock market reflects expected future profits, which depend in part on the economy.) As a result, the expected return on the stock market is higher than the risk-free rate. Denoting the expected return on the stock market by r_m and the risk-free rate by r_f, the risk premium on the market is $r_m - r_f$. This is the additional expected return you can expect to earn by bearing the nondiversifiable risk associated with the stock market.

Now consider the nondiversifiable risk associated with one asset, such as a company's stock. We can measure that risk in terms of the extent to which the return on the asset tends to be *correlated* with (move in the same direction as) the return on the stock market as a whole. For example, one company's stock might have almost no correlation with the market as a whole. On average, the price of that stock would move independently of changes in the market, so it would have little or no nondiversifiable risk. The return on that stock should therefore be about the same as the risk-free rate. Another stock, however, might be highly correlated with the market. Its price changes might even amplify changes in the market as a whole. That stock would have substantial nondiversifiable risk, perhaps more than the stock market as a whole, in which case its return on average will exceed the market return r_m.

The CAPM summarizes this relationship between expected returns and the risk premium by the following equation:

$$r_i - r_f = \beta(r_m - r_f)$$ (15.6)

where r_i is the expected return on an asset. The equation says that the risk premium on the asset (its expected return less the risk-free rate) is proportional to the risk premium on the market. The constant of proportionality, β, is called the *asset beta*. It measures how sensitive the asset's return is to market movements and therefore the asset's nondiversifiable risk. If a 1 percent rise in the market tends to result in a 2 percent rise in price of the asset, the beta is 2. If a 1 percent rise in the market tends to result in a 1 percent rise in the price of the asset, the beta is 1. And if a 1 percent rise in the market tends to result in no change in the price of the asset, the beta is zero. As equation (15.6) shows, the larger beta is, the greater is the expected return on the asset because the greater is the asset's nondiversifiable risk.

Given beta, we can determine the correct discount rate to use in computing an asset's net present value. That discount rate is the expected return on the asset or on another asset with the same risk. It is therefore the risk-free rate plus a risk premium to reflect nondiversifiable risk:

$$\text{Discount rate} = r_f + \beta(r_m - r_f) \tag{15.7}$$

Over the past 60 years, the risk premium on the stock market, $(r_m - r_f)$, has been about 8 percent on average. If the real risk-free rate were 4 percent and beta were 0.6, the correct discount rate would thus be $0.04 + 0.6(0.08) = 0.09$, or 9 percent.

If the asset is a stock, its beta can usually be estimated statistically.[13] When the asset is a new factory, however, determining its beta is more difficult. Many firms therefore use a company cost of capital as a (nominal) discount rate. The company cost of capital is a weighted average of the expected return on the company's stock (which depends on the beta of the stock) and the interest rate it pays for debt. This approach is correct as long as the capital investment in question is typical for the company as a whole. It can be misleading, however, if the capital investment has much more or much less nondiversifiable risk than the company as a whole. In that case it may be better to make a reasoned guess as to how much the revenues from the investment are likely to depend on the overall economy.

EXAMPLE 15.3	Capital Investment in the Disposable Diaper Industry

In Example 13.6, we discussed the disposable diaper industry, which has been dominated by Procter & Gamble, with about a 60 percent market share, and Kimberly-Clark, with another 30 percent. We explained that their continuing R&D (research and development) expenditures have given these firms a cost advantage that deters entry. Now we'll examine the capital investment decision of a potential entrant.

Suppose you are considering entering this industry. To take advantage of scale economies, both in production and in advertising and distribution, you would need to build three plants at a cost of $60 million each, which, when operating at capacity, would produce 2.5 billion diapers per year. These would be sold at wholesale for about 16 cents per diaper, yielding revenues of about

---

[13] You can estimate beta by running a linear regression of the return on the stock against the excess return on the market, $r_m - r_f$. You would find, for example, that the beta for Digital Equipment is about 1.4, the beta for Eastman Kodak is about 0.8, and the beta for General Motors is about 0.5.

$400 million per year. You can expect your variable production costs to be about $290 million per year, for a net revenue of $110 million per year.

You will have other expenses, however. Using the experience of P&G and Kimberly-Clark as a guide, you can expect to spend about $60 million in R&D before start-up to design an efficient manufacturing process, and another $20 million in R&D during each year of production to maintain and improve that process. Finally, once you are operating at full capacity, you can expect to spend another $50 million per year for a sales force, advertising, and marketing, for a net operating profit of $40 million per year. The plants will last for 15 years and will then be obsolete.[14]

Is the investment a good idea? To find out, let's calculate its net present value. Table 15.5 shows the relevant numbers. We assume that production begins at 33 percent of capacity when the plant is completed in 1993, takes two years to reach full capacity, and continues through the year 2008. Given the net cash flows, the NPV is calculated as

$$\text{NPV} = -120 - \frac{93.4}{(1+R)} - \frac{56.6}{(1+R)^2} + \frac{40}{(1+R)^3}$$
$$+ \frac{40}{(1+R)^4} + \cdots + \frac{40}{(1+R)^{15}}$$

The table shows the NPV for discount rates of 5, 10, and 15 percent.

Table 15.5 Data for NPV Calculation ($ millions)						
	Pre-1993	**1993**	**1994**	**1995**	**...**	**2008**
Sales		133.3	266.7	400.0	...	400.0
LESS						
Variable cost		96.7	193.3	290.0	...	290.0
Ongoing R&D		20.0	20.0	20.0	...	20.0
Sales force, ads, and promotion		50.0	50.0	50.0	...	50.0
Operating profit		−33.4	3.4	40.0	...	40.0
LESS						
Construction cost	60.0	60.0	60.0			
Initial R&D	60.0					
NET CASH FLOW	−120.0	−93.4	−56.6	40.0	...	40.0
	Discount Rate:	0.05	0.10	0.15		
	NPV:	80.5	−16.9	−75.1		

---

[14] These numbers are from Michael E. Porter, "The Disposable Diaper Industry," Harvard Business School Case 9–380–175, July 1981, and articles from the *New York Times* and *Wall Street Journal*.

Note that the NPV is positive for a discount rate of 5 percent, but it is negative for discount rates of 10 or 15 percent. What is the correct discount rate? First, we have ignored inflation, so the discount rate should be in *real* terms. Second, the cash flows are risky—we don't know how efficient our plants will be, how effective our advertising and promotion will be, or even what the future demand for disposable diapers will be. Some of this risk is nondiversifiable. To calculate the risk premium, we will use a beta of 1, which is typical for a producer of consumer products of this sort. Using 4 percent for the real risk-free interest rate and 8 percent for the risk premium on the stock market, our discount rate should be

$$R = 0.04 + 1(0.08) = 0.12$$

At this discount rate, the NPV is clearly negative, so the investment does not make sense. We will not enter the industry; P&G and Kimberly-Clark can breathe a sigh of relief. You should not be surprised, however, that these firms can make money in this market while we cannot. Their experience, years of earlier R&D, and brand name recognition give them a competitive advantage that a new entrant would find hard to overcome. (For example, they would not need to spend $60 million on R&D before building new plants.)

15.6 Investment Decisions by Consumers

We have seen how firms value future cash flows and thereby decide whether to invest in long-lived capital. Consumers face similar decisions when they purchase a durable good, such as a car or major appliance. Unlike the decision to purchase food, entertainment, or clothing, buying a durable good involves comparing a flow of *future* benefits with the *current* purchase cost.

Suppose you are deciding whether to buy a new car. If you keep the car for six or seven years, most of the benefits (and costs of operation) will occur in the future. You must therefore compare the future flow of net benefits from owning the car (the benefit of having transportation less the cost of insurance, maintenance, and gasoline to operate the car) with the purchase price. Likewise, when deciding whether to buy a new air conditioner, you must compare its price with the present value of the flow of net benefits (the benefit of a cool room less the cost of electricity to operate the unit).

These problems are analogous to the problem of a firm, which must compare a future flow of profits with the current cost of plant and equipment when making a capital investment decision. We can therefore analyze these problems just as we analyzed the firm's investment problem. Let's do this for a consumer's decision to buy a car.

The main benefit from owning a car is the flow of transportation services it provides. The value of those services differs from consumer to consumer. Let's assume our consumer values the service at S dollars per year. Let's also assume that the total operating expense (insurance, maintenance, and gasoline) is E dollars per year, that the car costs $10,000, and that after six years its resale value will be $2000. The decision to buy the car can then be framed in net present value terms:

$$NPV = -10,000 + (S - E) + \frac{(S - E)}{(1 + R)} + \frac{(S - E)}{(1 + R)^2}$$

$$+ \cdots + \frac{(S - E)}{(1 + R)^6} + \frac{2000}{(1 + R)^6} \tag{15.8}$$

What discount rate R should the consumer use? The consumer should apply the same principle that the firm does—the discount rate is the opportunity cost of money. If the consumer already has $10,000 and does not need a loan, the correct discount rate is the return that could be earned by investing the money in another asset, say, a savings account or a government bond. On the other hand, if the consumer is in debt, the discount rate would be the borrowing rate that he or she is already paying. This rate is likely to be much higher than the interest rate on a bond or savings account, so the NPV of the investment will be smaller.

E X A M P L E   15.4   **Choosing an Air Conditioner**

Buying a new air conditioner involves making a trade-off. Some air conditioners cost less but are less efficient—they consume a lot of electricity relative to their cooling power. Other air conditioners cost more but are also more efficient. Should you buy an inefficient air conditioner that costs less now but will cost more in the future to operate, or an efficient one that costs more now but will cost less to operate?

Let's assume you are comparing air conditioners of equivalent cooling power, so that they yield the same flow of benefits. We can then compare the present discounted values of their costs. Assuming an eight-year lifetime and no resale, the PDV of the costs of buying and operating air conditioner i is

$$PDV = C_i + OC_i + \frac{OC_i}{(1 + R)} + \frac{OC_i}{(1 + R)^2} + \cdots + \frac{OC_i}{(1 + R)^8}$$

where C_i is the purchase price of air conditioner i and OC_i is its average annual operating cost.

Which air conditioner is best depends on your discount rate. If you have little free cash and must borrow, you should use a high discount rate. This would make the present value of the future operating costs smaller, so you would probably choose a less expensive but relatively inefficient unit. If you have plenty of free cash, so that your opportunity cost of money (and hence your discount rate) is low, you would probably buy the more expensive unit.

An econometric study of household purchases of air conditioners shows that consumers tend to trade off capital costs and expected future operating costs in just this way, although the discount rates that people use are high—

about 20 percent for the population as a whole.[15] (American consumers seem to behave myopically by overdiscounting future savings.) The study also shows that consumers' discount rates vary inversely with their incomes. (For example, people whose 1978 annual income was between $25,000 and $35,000 used discount rates of about 9 percent, while those with incomes under $10,000 used discount rates of 39 percent or more.) We would expect this because higher-income people are likely to have more free cash available and therefore have a lower opportunity cost of money.

*15.7 Intertemporal Production Decisions— Depletable Resources

Firms' production decisions often have *intertemporal* aspects—production today affects sales or costs in the future. The learning curve, which we discussed in Chapter 7, is an example of this. By producing today, the firm gains experience that lowers its future costs. In this case production today is partly an investment in future cost reduction, and the value of this must be taken into account when comparing costs and benefits. Another example is the production of a depletable resource. When the owner of an oil well pumps oil today, less oil is available for future production. This must be taken into account when deciding how much to produce.

Production decisions in cases like these involve comparisons between costs and benefits today with costs and benefits in the future. We can make those comparisons using the concept of present discounted value. We'll look in detail at the case of a depletable resource, although the same principles apply to other intertemporal production decisions.

The Production Decision of an Individual Resource Producer

Suppose your rich uncle gives you an oil well. The well contains 1000 barrels of oil that can be produced at a constant average and marginal cost of $10 per barrel. Should you produce all the oil today, or should you save it for the future?[16]

You might think that the answer depends on the profit you can earn if you remove the oil from the ground. After all, why not remove the oil if its price is greater than the cost of extraction? However, this ignores the opportunity cost of using up the oil today so that it is not available for the future.

---

[15] See Jerry A. Hausman, "Individual Discount Rates and the Purchase and Utilization of Energy-Using Durables," *Bell Journal of Economics* 10 (Spring 1979): 33–54.

[16] For most real oil wells, marginal and average cost are not constant, and it would be extremely costly to extract all the oil in a short time. We will ignore this complication.

The correct answer, then, depends not on the current profit level but on how fast you expect the price of oil to rise. Oil in the ground is like money in the bank, and you should keep it in the ground only if it earns a return at least as high as the market interest rate. So if you expect the price of oil to remain constant or rise very slowly, you would be better off extracting and selling all of it now and investing the proceeds. But if you expect the price of oil to rise rapidly, you should leave it in the ground.

How fast must the price rise for you to keep the oil in the ground? The value of each barrel of oil in your well is equal to the price of oil, less the $10 cost of extracting it. (This is the profit you can obtain by extracting and selling each barrel.) This value must rise at least as fast as the rate of interest for you to keep the oil. Your production decision rule is therefore: *Keep all your oil if you expect its price less its extraction cost to rise faster than the rate of interest. Extract and sell all of it if you expect price less cost to rise at less than the rate of interest.* And what if you expect price less cost to rise at exactly the rate of interest? Then you would be indifferent between extracting the oil and leaving it in the ground. Letting P_t be the price of oil this year, P_{t+1} be the price next year, and c the cost of extraction, we can write this production rule as follows:

If $(P_{t+1} - c) > (1 + R)(P_t - c)$, keep the oil in the ground.

If $(P_{t+1} - c) < (1 + R)(P_t - c)$, sell all the oil now.

If $(P_{t+1} - c) = (1 + R)(P_t - c)$, makes no difference.

Given our expectation about the growth rate of oil prices, we can use this rule to determine production. But how fast should we expect the market price of oil to rise?

The Behavior of Market Price

Suppose there were no OPEC cartel, and the oil market consisted of many competitive producers with oil wells like our own. We could then determine how fast oil prices are likely to rise by considering the production decisions of other producers. If other producers want to earn the highest possible return, they will follow the production rule we stated above. This means that *price less marginal cost must rise at exactly the rate of interest.*[17] To see why, suppose price less cost were to rise faster than the rate of interest. Then no one would sell any oil. Inevitably, this would drive the current price of oil up. If, on the other hand, price less cost were to rise at a rate less than the rate of interest, everyone would try to sell all of their oil immediately, which would drive the current price down.

Figure 15.4 illustrates how the market price must rise. The marginal cost of extraction is c, and the price and total quantity produced are initially P_0 and Q_0.

---

[17] This result is called the Hotelling rule because it was first demonstrated by Harold Hotelling in "The Economics of Exhaustible Resources," *Journal of Political Economy* 39 (April 1931): 137–175.

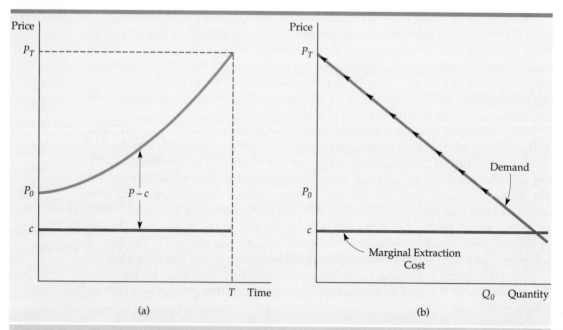

Figure 15.4 **Price of an Exhaustible Resource** In (a), the price is shown rising over time. Units of a resource in the ground must earn a return commensurate with that on other assets. Therefore, in a competitive market, price less marginal production cost will rise at the rate of interest. Part (b) shows the movement up the demand curve as price rises.

Part (a) shows the net price, $P - c$, rising at the rate of interest. Part (b) shows that as price rises, the quantity demanded falls. This continues until time T, when all the oil has been used up, and the price P_T is such that demand is just zero.

User Cost

We saw in Chapter 8 that a competitive firm always produces up to the point where price is equal to marginal cost. However, in a competitive market for an exhaustible resource, price *exceeds* marginal cost (and the difference between price and marginal cost rises over time). Does this conflict with what we learned in Chapter 8?

No, once we recognize that the *total* marginal cost of producing an exhaustible resource is greater than the marginal cost of extracting it from the ground. There is an additional opportunity cost because producing and selling a unit today makes it unavailable for production and sale in the future. We call this opportunity cost the *user cost* of production. In Figure 15.4, user cost is the difference between price and marginal production cost. It rises over time because as the resource remaining in the ground becomes scarcer, the opportunity cost of depleting another unit becomes higher.

Resource Production by a Monopolist

What if the resource is produced by a *monopolist* rather than a competitive industry? Should price less marginal cost still rise at the rate of interest?

Suppose a monopolist is deciding between keeping an incremental unit of a resource in the ground, or producing and selling it. The value of that unit is the *marginal revenue* less the marginal cost. The unit should be left in the ground if its value is expected to rise faster than the rate of interest; it should be produced and sold if its value is expected to rise at *less* than the rate of interest. Since the monopolist controls total output, it will produce so that marginal revenue less marginal cost—i.e., the value of an incremental unit of resource—rises at exactly the rate of interest:

$$(MR_{t+1} - c) = (1 + R)(MR_t - c)$$

Note that this rule also holds for a competitive firm, but for a competitive firm, marginal revenue equals the market price p.

For a monopolist facing a downward-sloping demand curve, price is greater than marginal revenue. Hence, if marginal revenue less marginal cost rises at the rate of interest, *price* less marginal cost will rise at less than the rate of interest. We thus have the interesting result that a monopolist is *more conservationist* than a competitive industry. In exercising monopoly power, the monopolist starts out charging a higher price and depletes the resource more slowly.

E X A M P L E   15.5   **How Depletable Are Depletable Resources?**

Resources like oil, natural gas, coal, uranium, copper, iron, lead, zinc, nickel, and helium are all depletable—there is a finite amount of each in the earth's crust, so that ultimately the production and consumption of each will cease. Nonetheless, some resources are more depletable than others.

For oil, natural gas, and helium, known and potentially discoverable inground reserves are equal to only 50 to 100 years of current consumption. For these resources, the user cost of depletion can be a significant component of the market price. Other resources, such as coal and iron, have a proved and potential reserve base equal to several hundred or even thousands of years of current consumption. For these resources, the user cost is very small.

The user cost for a resource can be estimated from geological information about existing and potentially discoverable reserves, and from knowledge of the demand curve and the rate at which that curve is likely to shift out over time in response to economic growth. Or if the market is competitive, user cost can be determined from the economic rent earned by the owners of resource-bearing lands.

Table 15.6 User Cost as a Fraction of Competitive Price	
Resource	**User Cost/Competitive Price**
Crude oil	.4 to .5
Natural gas	.4 to .5
Uranium	.1 to .2
Copper	.2
Bauxite	.05 to .1
Nickel	.1 to .2

Table 15.6 shows estimates of user cost as a fraction of the competitive price for crude oil, natural gas, uranium, copper, bauxite, and nickel.[18] Note that only for crude oil and natural gas is user cost a substantial component of price. For the other resources, it is small and in some cases almost negligible. Moreover, although most of these resources have experienced sharp price fluctuations, user cost had almost nothing to do with those fluctuations. For example, oil prices changed because of OPEC and political turmoil in the Persian Gulf, natural gas prices because of changes in government price controls, uranium and bauxite because of cartelization during the 1970s, and copper because of major changes in demand.

Resource depletion, then, has not been very important as a determinant of resource prices over the past few decades. Much more important have been market structure and changes in market demand. But the role of depletion should not be ignored. Over the long term it will be the ultimate determinant of resource prices.

15.8 How Are Interest Rates Determined?

We have seen how market interest rates are used to help make capital investment and intertemporal production decisions. But what determines how high interest rates will be and why they fluctuate over time? To answer these questions, remember that an interest rate is the price that borrowers pay lenders to use their funds. Like any market price, interest rates are determined by supply and demand—in this case the supply and demand for loanable funds.

---

[18] These numbers are based on Robert S. Pindyck, "Gains to Producers from the Cartelization of Exhaustible Resources," *Review of Economics and Statistics* 60 (1978): 238–251; Michael J. Mueller, "Scarcity and Ricardian Rents for Crude Oil," *Economic Inquiry* 23 (1985): 703–724; Kenneth R. Stollery, "Mineral Depletion with Cost as the Extraction Limit: A Model Applied to the Behavior of Prices in the Nickel Industry," *Journal of Environmental Economics and Management* 10 (1983): 151–165; and Robert S. Pindyck, "On Monopoly Power in Extractive Resource Markets," *Journal of Environmental Economics and Management* 14 (1987): 128–142.

The *supply of loanable funds* comes from households that wish to save part of their incomes in order to consume more in the future (or make bequests to their heirs). For example, some households have high incomes now but expect to earn less in the future after retirement. Saving lets them spread their consumption more evenly over time. Also, because they receive interest on the money they lend, they can consume more in the future in return for consuming less now. As a result, the higher the interest rate, the greater the incentive to save. The supply of loanable funds is therefore an upward-sloping curve, labeled *S* in Figure 15.5.

The *demand for loanable funds* has two components. First, some households want to consume more than their current incomes, either because their incomes are low now but are expected to grow, or because they want to make a large purchase (e.g., a house) that has to be paid for out of future income. These households are willing to pay interest in return for not having to wait to consume. However, the higher the interest rate, the greater the cost of consuming rather than waiting, so the less willing these households will be to borrow. The household demand for loanable funds is therefore a declining function of the interest rate. In Figure 15.5, it is the curve labeled D_H.

The second source of demand for loanable funds is firms that want to make capital investments. Remember that firms will invest in projects with NPVs that are positive because a positive NPV means that the expected return on

Figure 15.5   Supply and Demand for Loanable Funds   Market interest rates are determined by the demand and supply of loanable funds. Households supply funds to consume more in the future; the higher the interest rate, the more they supply. Households and firms both demand funds, but they demand less the higher the interest rate is. Shifts in demand or supply cause changes in interest rates.

the project exceeds the opportunity cost of funds. That opportunity cost—the discount rate used to calculate the NPV—is the interest rate, perhaps adjusted for risk. Often firms borrow to invest because the flow of profits from an investment comes in the future, while the cost of an investment must usually be paid now. Firms' desires to invest are thus an important source of demand for loanable funds.

As we saw earlier, however, the higher the interest rate, the lower the NPV of a project. If interest rates rise, some investment projects that had positive NPVs will now have negative NPVs, and will therefore be cancelled. Overall, because firms' willingness to invest falls when interest rates rise, their demand for loanable funds also falls. The demand for loanable funds by firms is thus a downward-sloping curve; in Figure 15.5 it is labeled D_F.

The total demand for loanable funds is the sum of the household demand and the firm demand; in Figure 15.5 it is the curve D_T. This total demand curve together with the supply curve determine the equilibrium interest rate. In Figure 15.5, that rate is R^*.

Figure 15.5 can also help us understand why interest rates change. Suppose the economy goes into a recession. Firms will then expect lower sales and lower future profits from new capital investments. The NPVs of projects will fall, and firms' willingness to invest will decline, as will their demand for loanable funds. D_F, and therefore D_T, will shift to the left, and the equilibrium interest rate will fall. Or suppose the federal government spends much more money than it takes through taxes, i.e., that it runs large deficits, as it has done since the 1980s. It will have to borrow to finance these deficits, shifting the total demand for loanable funds D_T to the right, so that R increases. The monetary policies of the Federal Reserve are another important determinant of interest rates. The Federal Reserve can create money, shifting the supply of loanable funds to the right and reducing R.

A Variety of Interest Rates

Figure 15.5 aggregates individual demands and supplies as though there were a single market interest rate. In fact, households, firms, and the government lend and borrow under a variety of terms and conditions. As a result, there is a wide range of "market" interest rates. Here we briefly describe some of the more important interest rates that are quoted in the newspapers, and sometimes used for capital investment decisions.

Treasury Bill Rate   A Treasury bill is a short-term (one year or less) bond issued by the U.S. government. It is a pure *discount bond*—i.e., it makes no coupon payments but instead is sold at a price less than its redemption value at maturity. For example, a three-month Treasury bill might be sold for $98. In three months it can be redeemed for $100; it thus has an effective three-month yield of about 2 percent and an effective annual yield of about 8 percent.[19] The Treasury bill rate can be viewed as a short-term, risk-free rate.

---

[19] To be exact, the three-month yield is $(100/98) - 1 = 0.0204$, and the annual yield is $(100/98)^4 - 1 = 0.0842$, or 8.42 percent.

Treasury Bond Rate A Treasury bond is a longer-term bond (more than one year, and typically 10 to 30 years) issued by the U.S. government. Rates vary, depending on the maturity of the bond.

Discount Rate Commercial banks sometimes borrow for short periods from the Federal Reserve. These loans are called *discounts,* and the rate that the Federal Reserve charges on them is the discount rate.

Commercial Paper Rate Commercial paper refers to short-term (six months or less) discount bonds issued by high-quality corporate borrowers. Because commercial paper is only slightly riskier than a Treasury bill, the commercial paper rate is usually less than 1 percent higher than the Treasury bill rate.

Prime Rate This is the rate (sometimes called the *reference rate*) that large banks post as a reference point for short-term loans to their biggest corporate borrowers. As we saw in Example 12.4, this rate does not fluctuate from day to day as other rates do.

Corporate Bond Rate Newspapers and government publications report the average annual yields on long-term (typically 20-year) corporate bonds in different risk categories (e.g., high-grade bonds, medium-grade bonds, etc.). These average yields indicate how much corporations are paying for long-term debt. However, as we saw in Example 15.2, the yields on corporate bonds can vary considerably, depending on the financial strength of the corporation and the time to maturity for the bond.

Summary

1. A firm's holding of capital is measured as a stock, but inputs of labor and raw materials are flows. Its stock of capital enables a firm to earn a flow of profits over time.

2. When a firm makes a capital investment, it spends money now, so that it can earn profits in the future. To decide whether the investment is worthwhile, the firm must determine the present value of future profits by discounting them.

3. The present discounted value (PDV) of $1 paid one year from now is $\$1/(1 + R)$, where R is the interest rate. The PDV of $1 paid n years from now is $\$1/(1 + R)^n$.

4. A bond is a contract in which a lender agrees to pay the bondholder a stream of money. The value of the bond is the PDV of that stream. The effective yield on a bond is the interest rate that equates that value with the bond's market price. Bond yields differ because of differences in riskiness and time to maturity.

5. Firms can decide whether to undertake a capital investment by applying the net present value (NPV) criterion: Invest if the present value of the expected future cash flows from an investment is larger than the cost of the investment.

6. The discount rate that a firm uses to calculate the NPV for an investment should be the op-

portunity cost of capital—i.e., the return the firm could earn on a similar investment.

7. When calculating NPVs, if cash flows are in nominal terms (i.e., include inflation), the discount rate should also be nominal, but if cash flows are in real terms (i.e., are net of inflation), a real discount rate should be used.

8. An adjustment for risk can be made by adding a risk premium to the discount rate. However, the risk premium should reflect only nondiversifiable risk. Using the Capital Asset Pricing Model (CAPM), the risk premium is the "asset beta" for the project multiplied by the risk premium on the stock market as a whole. The "asset beta" measures the sensitivity of the project's return to movements in the market.

9. Consumers are also faced with investment decisions that require the same kind of analysis as those of firms. When deciding whether to buy a durable good like a car or a major appliance, the consumer must consider the present value of future operating costs.

10. An exhaustible resource in the ground is like money in the bank and must earn a comparable return. Therefore, if the market is competitive, price less marginal extraction cost will grow at the rate of interest. The difference between price and marginal cost is called *user cost*—it is the opportunity cost of depleting a unit of the resource.

11. Market interest rates are determined by the demand and supply of loanable funds. Households supply funds so they can consume more in the future. Households, firms, and the government demand funds. Changes in demand or supply cause changes in interest rates.

Questions for Review

1. A firm uses cloth and labor to produce shirts in a factory that it bought for $10 million. Which of its factor inputs are measured as flows and which as stocks? How would your answer change if the firm had leased a factory instead of buying one? Is its output measured as a flow or a stock? Its profit?

2. Suppose the interest rate is 10 percent. If $100 is invested at this rate today, how much will it be worth after one year? After two years? After five years? What is the value today of $100 paid one year from now? Paid two years from now? Paid five years from now?

3. You are offered the choice of two payment streams: (a) $100 paid one year from now and $100 paid two years from now; (b) $80 paid one year from now and $130 paid two years from now. Which payment stream would you prefer if the interest rate is 5 percent? If it is 15 percent?

4. How do investors calculate the present value of a bond? If the interest rate is 5 percent, what is the present value of a perpetuity that pays $1000 per year forever?

5. What is the *effective yield* on a bond? How does one calculate it? Why do some corporate bonds have effective yields that are higher than others?

6. What is the net present value (NPV) criterion for investment decisions? How does one calculate the NPV of an investment project? If all the cash flows for the project are certain, what discount rate should be used to calculate the NPV?

7. What is the difference between a real discount rate and a nominal discount rate? When should a real discount rate be used in an NPV calculation, and when should a nominal rate be used?

8. How is a risk premium used to account for risk in NPV calculations? What is the difference between diversifiable and nondiversifiable risk? Why should only nondiversifiable risk enter into the risk premium?

9. What is meant by the "market return" in the Capital Asset Pricing Model (CAPM)? Why is the market return greater than the risk-free interest rate? What does an asset's "beta" measure in the CAPM? Why should high-beta assets have a higher expected return than low-beta assets?

10. Suppose you are deciding whether to invest $100 million in a steel mill. You know the expected cash flows for the project, but they are risky—steel prices could rise or fall in the future. How would the CAPM help you select a discount rate for an NPV calculation?

11. How does a consumer trade off current and future costs when selecting an air conditioner or other major appliance? How could this selection be aided by an NPV calculation?

12. What is meant by the "user cost" of producing an exhaustible resource? Why does price minus extraction cost rise at the rate of interest in a competitive exhaustible resource market?

13. What determines the supply of loanable funds? The demand for loanable funds? What might cause the supply or demand for loanable funds to shift, and how would that affect interest rates?

Exercises

1. Suppose the interest rate is 10 percent. What is the value of a coupon bond that pays $80 per year for each of the next five years, and then makes a principal repayment of $1000 in the sixth year? Repeat for an interest rate of 15 percent.

2. A bond has two years to mature. It makes a coupon payment of $100 after one year, and both a coupon payment of $100 and a principal repayment of $1000 after two years. The bond is selling for $966. What is its effective yield?

3. Equation (15.5) shows the net present value of an investment in an electric motor factory, where half of the $10 million cost is paid initially and the other half after a year, and where the factory is expected to lose money during its first two years of operation. If the discount rate is 4 percent, what is the NPV? Is the investment worthwhile?

4. The market interest rate is 10 percent and is expected to stay at that level. Consumers can borrow and lend all they want at this rate. Explain your choice in each of the following situations:
   a. Would you prefer a $500 gift today or a $540 gift next year?
   b. Would you prefer a $100 gift now or a $500 loan without interest for four years?

   c. Would you prefer a $250 rebate on an $8000 car or one year of financing for the full price of the car at 5 percent interest?
   d. You have just won a million dollars in the lottery and will receive $50,000 a year for the next 20 years. How much is this worth to you today?
   e. You win the "honest million" jackpot. You can have $1 million today or $50,000 per year for eternity (this right can be passed on to your heirs). Which do you prefer?
   f. Until recently, adult children had to pay taxes on gifts of over $10,000 from their parents, but parents could loan money to their children interest-free. Why did some people call this unfair? To whom were the rules unfair?

5. Ralph is trying to decide whether to go to graduate school. If he spends two years in graduate school, paying $10,000 tuition each year, he will get a job that will pay $50,000 per year for the rest of his working life. If he does not go to school, he will go into the work force immediately. He will then make $20,000 per year for the next three years, $30,000 for the following three years, and $50,000 per year every year after that. If the interest rate is 10 percent, is graduate school a good financial investment?

6. Suppose your uncle gave you an oil well like the one described in Section 15.7. (Marginal production cost is constant at $10.) The price of oil is currently $20 but is controlled by a cartel that accounts for a large fraction of total production. Should you produce and sell all your oil now or wait to produce? Explain your answer.

*7. You are planning to invest in fine wine. Each case costs $100, and you know from experience that the value of a case of wine held for t years is $(100)t^{12}$. One hundred cases of wine are available for sale, and the interest rate is 10 percent.

   a. How many cases should you buy, how long should you wait to sell them, and how much money will you receive at the time of their sale?

   b. Suppose that at the time of purchase, someone offers you $130 per case immediately. Should you take the offer?

   c. How would your answers change if the interest rate were only 5 percent?

8. Reexamine the capital investment decision in the disposable diaper industry (Example 15.3) from the point of view of an incumbent firm. If P&G or Kimberly-Clark were to expand capacity by building three new plants, they would not need to spend $60 million on R&D before start-up. How does this affect the NPV calculations in Table 15.5? Is the investment profitable at a discount rate of 12 percent?

PART IV
Information, Market Failure, and the Role of Government

Much of the analysis of the first three parts of this book has focused on positive questions—how consumers and firms behave, and how that behavior affects different market structures. Part IV takes a more normative approach—by describing the goal of economic efficiency, and discussing when markets generate efficient outcomes, and when they fail and thus require government intervention.

Chapter 16 discusses general equilibrium analysis, in which the interactions among related markets are taken into account. This chapter also analyzes the conditions that are required for an economy to be efficient and shows why a perfectly competitive market is efficient. Chapter 17 examines an important source of market failure, incomplete information. We show that when some economic actors have better information than others, markets may fail to allocate goods efficiently or may not even exist. We also show how sellers of products can avoid problems of asymmetric information by giving potential buyers signals about the quality of their product. Finally, Chapter 18 discusses two additional sources of market failure: externalities and public goods. We show how these failures can sometimes be resolved through private bargaining, but other times require government intervention. We also discuss a number of remedies for these market failures, such as pollution taxes and tradeable emission permits.

CHAPTER 16

General Equilibrium and Economic Efficiency

For the most part, we have studied individual markets in isolation. Yet markets are often interdependent—conditions in one can affect prices and outputs in others either because one good is an input to the production of another good or because two goods are substitutes or complements. In this chapter we see how a *general equilibrium analysis* can be used to take these interrelationships into account.

We also expand the concept of economic efficiency that we introduced in Chapter 9, and we discuss the benefits of a competitive market economy. To do this, we first analyze economic efficiency, beginning with the exchange of goods among people or countries. We then use this analysis of exchange to discuss whether the outcomes generated by an economy are equitable. To the extent that these outcomes are deemed to be inequitable, government can help redistribute income.

We then go on to describe the conditions that an economy must satisfy if it is to produce and distribute goods efficiently. We explain why a perfectly competitive market system satisfies those conditions. We also show why free international trade can expand the production possibilities of a country and make its consumers better off. Most markets, however, are not perfectly competitive, and many deviate substantially from that ideal. In the final section of the chapter (as a preview to our detailed discussion of market failure in Chapters 17 and 18), we discuss why markets may fail to work efficiently.

16.1 General Equilibrium Analysis

So far our discussions of market behavior have been largely based on *partial equilibrium analysis*. When determining the equilibrium prices and quantities in a market, we presumed that the activity in that market had little or no effect on other markets. For example, in Chapters 2 and 9, we presumed that the wheat market was largely independent of the markets for related products, such as corn and soybeans.

Often a partial equilibrium analysis of this sort is sufficient to understand market behavior. However, market interrelationships can be important. For example, in Chapter 2 we saw how a change in the price of one good can affect the demand for another if they are complements or substitutes, and in Chapter 8 we saw that an increase in a firm's input demand can cause both the market price of the input and the product price to rise.

Unlike partial equilibrium analysis, *general equilibrium analysis determines the prices and quantities in all markets simultaneously*, and it explicitly takes feedback effects into account. A *feedback effect* is a price or quantity adjustment in one market caused by price and quantity adjustments in related markets. Suppose, for example, that the U.S. government taxes oil imports. This would immediately shift the supply curve for oil to the left (because foreign oil is more expensive) and raise the price of oil. But the effect of the tax would not end there. The higher price of oil would increase the demand for and then the price of natural gas. The higher natural gas price would in turn cause oil demand to rise (shift to the right) and increase the oil price even more. The oil and the natural gas markets would continue to interact until eventually an equilibrium would be reached in which the quantity demanded and quantity supplied were equated in both markets.

In practice, a complete general equilibrium analysis, which evaluates the effects of a change in one market on *all* other markets, is not feasible. Instead, we confine ourselves to two or three markets that are closely related. For example, when looking at a tax on oil, we might also look at markets for natural gas, coal, and electricity.

Two Interdependent Markets—Moving to General Equilibrium

To study the interdependence of markets, let's examine the competitive markets for videocassette rentals and movie theater tickets. The two markets are closely related because the widespread ownership of videocassette recorders

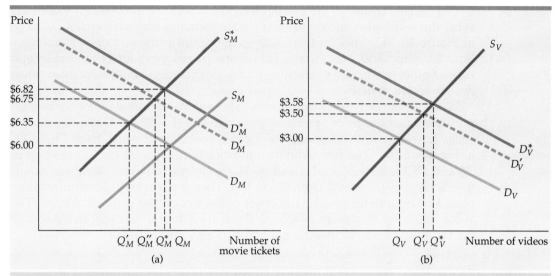

Figure 16.1 Two Interdependent Markets: (a) Movie Tickets and (b) Videocassette Rentals When markets are interdependent, the prices of all products must be simultaneously determined. Here a tax on movie tickets shifts the supply of movies upward from S_M to S_M^*, shown in (a). The higher price of movie tickets ($6.35 rather than $6.00) initially shifts the demand for videocassettes upward (from D_V to D_V'), causing the price of videos to rise (from $3.00 to $3.50), shown in (b). The higher video price feeds back into the movie ticket market, causing demand to shift from D_M to D_M' and the price of movies to increase from $6.35 to $6.75. This continues until a general equilibrium is reached, shown as the intersection of D_M^* and S_M^* in (a), with a movie ticket price of $6.82, and the intersection of D_V^* and S_V in (b), with a video price of $3.58.

has given most consumers the option of watching movies at home as well as at the theater. Changes in pricing policies that affect one market are likely to affect the other market, which in turn causes feedback effects in the first market.

Figure 16.1 shows the supply and demand curves for videos and movies. In part (a) the price of movie tickets is initially $6.00, and the market is in equilibrium at the intersection of D_M and S_M. In part (b) the video market is also in equilibrium with a price of $3.00.

Now suppose that the government places a tax of $1 on each movie ticket purchased. The effect of this tax is determined on a partial equilibrium basis by shifting the supply curve for movies upward by $1, from S_M to S_M^* in Figure 16.1(a). Initially, this causes the price of movies to increase to $6.35 and the quantity of movie tickets sold to fall from Q_M to Q_M'. This is as far as a partial equilibrium analysis takes us. But we can go further with a general equilibrium analysis by (1) looking at the effects of the movie tax on the market for videos, and (2) seeing whether there are any feedback effects from the video market to the movie market.

The movie tax affects the market for videos because movies and videos are substitutes. A higher movie price shifts the demand for videos from D_V to D_V' in Figure 16.1(b). This, in turn, causes the rental price of videos to increase from $3.00 to $3.50. Note that a tax on one product can affect the prices and sales of other products—something that policymakers should remember when designing tax policies.

What about the market for movies? The original demand curve for movies presumed that the price of videos was unchanged at $3.00. That price is now $3.50, however, so the demand for movies will shift upward, from D_M to D_M' in Figure 16.1(a). The new equilibrium price of movies (at the intersection of S_M^* and D_M') is now $6.75, instead of $6.35, and the quantity of movie tickets purchased has increased from Q_M' to Q_M''. Thus a partial equilibrium analysis would have underestimated the effect of the tax on the price of movies. The video market is so closely related to the market for movies that to determine the tax's full effect, we need a general equilibrium analysis.

The Attainment of General Equilibrium

This analysis is not yet complete. The change in the market price of movies will generate a feedback effect on the price of videos, which in turn will affect the price of movies, and so on. In the end, we must determine the equilibrium prices and quantities of *both* movies and videos simultaneously. The equilibrium movie price of $6.82 is given in Figure 16.1(a) by the intersection of the equilibrium supply and demand curves for movie tickets (S_M^* and D_M^*), and the equilibrium video price of $3.58 is given in Figure 16.1(b) by the intersection of the equilibrium supply and demand curves for videos (S_V and D_V^*). These are the correct general equilibrium prices because the video market supply and demand curves have been drawn on the assumption that the price of movie tickets is $6.82, and the movie ticket curves have been drawn on the assumption that the price of videos is $3.58. In other words, both sets of curves are consistent with the prices in related markets, and we have no reason to expect that the supply and demand curves in either market will shift further.[1]

Note that even if we were only interested in the market for movies, it would be important to account for the videocassette market when determining the impact of a movie tax. A partial equilibrium analysis would *understate* the effect on the tax, leading us to conclude that the tax will increase the price of movie tickets from $6.00 to $6.35. A general equilibrium analysis, however, shows us that the impact of the tax on the price of movie tickets is greater—the price would increase to $6.82.

Movies and videocassettes are substitute goods. By drawing diagrams analogous to those in Figure 16.1, you should be able to convince yourself that if

[1] To find the general equilibrium prices (and quantities) in practice, we must simultaneously find two prices that equate quantity demanded and quantity supplied in all related markets. For our two markets, this would mean finding the solution to four equations (supply of movie tickets, demand for movie tickets, supply of videos, and demand for videos) in four unknowns.

the goods in question are *complements*, a partial equilibrium analysis will *overstate* the impact of a tax. (Think about gasoline and automobiles. A tax on gasoline will cause its price to go up, but this will reduce demand for automobiles, which in turn reduces the demand for gasoline, causing its price to fall somewhat.)

EXAMPLE 16.1 The Interdependence of International Markets

Because Brazil and the United States compete in the world soybean market, Brazilian regulation of its own soybean market can significantly affect the U.S. soybean market, which in turn can have feedback effects on the Brazilian market. This led to unexpected results when Brazil adopted a regulatory policy aimed at increasing short-run domestic supplies and long-run exports of soybeans.[2]

During the late 1960s and early 1970s, the Brazilian government limited the export of soybeans, causing the price in Brazil to fall. It hoped that making soybeans cheaper in Brazil would encourage the domestic sale of soybeans and stimulate the domestic demand for soybean products. Eventually the export controls were to be removed, and Brazilian exports were expected to increase.

This expectation was based on a partial equilibrium analysis of the Brazilian soybean market. In fact, the reduction in Brazilian exports increased the price and production of soybeans in the United States, as well as U.S. exports. This made it more difficult for Brazil to export soybeans, even after the controls were removed.

Figure 16.2 shows the consequences of the program. The bottom two lines show Brazilian soybean exports, and the top two lines refer to U.S exports. Actual exports are shown as purple and blue lines, and the estimated levels of U.S. and Brazilian exports *had the Brazilian government regulations not gone into effect* are shown as red and green lines, respectively. (The lines diverge from approximately 1970 forward because that is when the major export controls were put into effect.) The figure shows that soybean exports from Brazil would have been higher, and exports from the United States lower, without the regulatory program. In 1977, for example, Brazilian soybean exports were 73 percent lower than they would have been had the government not intervened. However, between 1973 and 1978, U.S. soybean exports were over 30 percent higher than they would otherwise have been.

Thus Brazilian soybean policy was misguided, and hurt Brazil in the long run. Policymakers failed to take into account the effect of this policy on the U.S. production and export of soybeans.

---

[2] This example presents a simplified version of the analysis in Gary W. Williams and Robert L. Thompson, "Brazilian Soybean Policy: The International Effects of Intervention," *American Journal of Agricultural Economics* 66 (1984): 488–498.

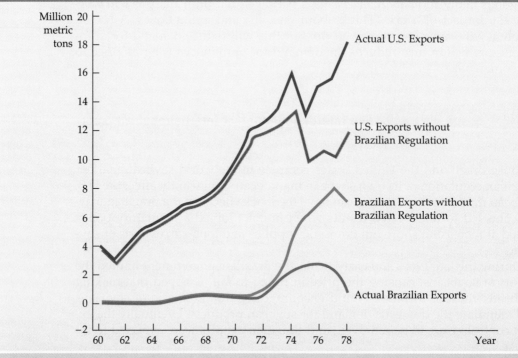

Figure 16.2 **Soybean Exports—Brazil and the United States** World competition in the soybean market makes the Brazilian and U.S. export markets highly interactive. As a result of the general equilibrium nature of these markets, regulations to stimulate Brazil's market were counterproductive in the long run. Brazil's actual exports of soybeans were lower (and U.S. exports higher) than they would have been without the regulatory policy.

16.2 Efficiency in Exchange

In Chapter 9 we saw that an unregulated competitive market is efficient because it maximizes consumer and producer surplus. To examine the concept of economic efficiency in more detail, we begin with an *exchange economy*, analyzing the behavior of two consumers who can trade either of two goods between themselves. (The analysis also applies to trade between two countries.) Suppose the two goods are initially allocated so that both consumers can make themselves better off by trading with each other. This means that the initial allocation of goods is economically *inefficient. In an efficient allocation of goods, no one can be made better off without making someone else worse off.* In the subsections that follow, we show why mutually beneficial trades result in an efficient allocation of goods.

The Advantages of Trade

As a rule, voluntary trade between two people or two countries is mutually beneficial.[3] To see how trade makes people better off, let's look at a two-person exchange in detail. Our analysis is based on two important assumptions:

1. Both people know each other's preferences.
2. Exchanging goods involves zero *transaction costs.*

Suppose James and Karen have 10 units of food and 6 units of clothing between them. Table 16.1 shows that initially James has 7 units of food and 1 unit of clothing, and Karen has 3 units of food and 5 units of clothing. To decide whether a trade between James and Karen would be advantageous, we need to know their preferences for food and clothing. Suppose that because Karen has a lot of clothing and little food, her marginal rate of substitution (MRS) of food for clothing is 3. (To get 1 unit of food, she will give up 3 units of clothing.) However, James's MRS of food for clothing is only 1/2. (He will give up only 1/2 a unit of clothing to get 1 unit of food.)

There is thus room for mutually advantageous trade because James values clothing more highly than Karen does, whereas Karen values food more highly than James does. To get another unit of food, Karen would be willing to trade up to 3 units of clothing. But James will give up 1 unit of food for 1/2 unit of clothing. The actual terms of the trade depend on the bargaining process. Among the possible outcomes are a trade of 1 unit of food (by James) for anywhere between 1/2 and 3 units of clothing (from Karen).

Suppose Karen offers James 1 unit of clothing for 1 unit of food, and James agrees. Both will be better off. James will have more clothing, which he values more than food, and Karen will have more food, which she values more than clothing. Whenever two consumers' MRSs are different, there is room for mutually beneficial trade because the allocation of resources is inefficient—trading will make both consumers better off. Conversely, to achieve economic efficiency, the two consumers' MRSs must be equal.

Table 16.1	The Advantage of Trade		
Individual	**Initial Allocation**	**Trade**	**Final Allocation**
James	7F, 1C	−1F, +1C	6F, 2C
Karen	3F, 5C	+1F, −1C	4F, 4C

---

[3] There are several situations in which trade may not be advantageous. First, limited information may lead people to believe that trade will make them better off when in fact it will not. Second, people may be coerced into making trades, either by physical threats or by the threat of future economic reprisals. Third, as we saw in Chapter 13, barriers to free trade can sometimes provide a strategic advantage to a country.

This important result also holds when there are many goods and consumers: *An allocation of goods is efficient only if the goods are distributed so that the marginal rate of substitution between any two pairs of goods is the same for all consumers.*

The Edgeworth Box Diagram

If trade is beneficial, which trades can occur? Which of those trades will allocate goods efficiently among customers, and how much better off will consumers then be? We can answer these questions for any two-person, two-good example by using a diagram called an Edgeworth box.[4]

Figure 16.3 shows an Edgeworth box in which the horizontal axis describes the number of units of food, and the vertical axis the units of clothing. The length of the box is 10 units of food, the total quantity of food available, and its height is 6 units of clothing, the total quantity of clothing available.

In the Edgeworth box each point describes the market baskets of *both* consumers. James's holdings are read from the origin at O_J, and Karen's holdings

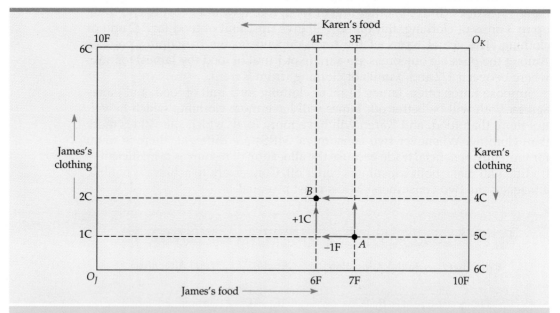

Figure 16.3   Exchange in an Edgeworth Box   Each point in the Edgeworth box simultaneously represents James's and Karen's market baskets of food and clothing. At *A*, for example, James has 7 units of food and 1 unit of clothing, and Karen has 3 units of food and 5 units of clothing.

---

[4] The Edgeworth box is named after political economist F. Y. Edgeworth, who suggested its use in his 1881 book *Mathematical Psychics: An Essay on the Application of Mathematics to the Moral Sciences* (New York: August M. Kelley, 1953).

are read in reverse direction from the origin at O_K. For example, point A represents the initial allocation of food and clothing. Reading on the horizontal axis from left to right at the bottom of the box, we see that James has 7 units of food, and reading upward along the vertical axis on the left of the diagram, 1 unit of clothing. Thus, for James, A represents 7F and 1C. This leaves 3F and 5C for Karen. Karen's allocation of food (3F) is read from right to left at the top of the box diagram beginning at O_K, and her allocation of clothing (5C) from top to bottom at the right of the box diagram.

We can also see the effect of the trade between Karen and James. James gives up 1F in exchange for 1C, moving from A to B. Karen gives up 1C and obtains 1F, also moving from A to B. Point B thus represents the market baskets of both James and Karen after the mutually beneficial trade.

Efficient Allocations

A trade from A to B thus made both Karen and James better off. But is B an efficient allocation? The answer depends on whether James's and Karen's MRSs are the same at B, which in turn depends on the shape of their indifference curves. Figure 16.4 shows several indifference curves for both James and Karen. James's indifference curves are drawn in the usual way, because his allocations are measured from the origin O_J. But for Karen, we have rotated the indifference curves 180 degrees, so that the origin is at the upper

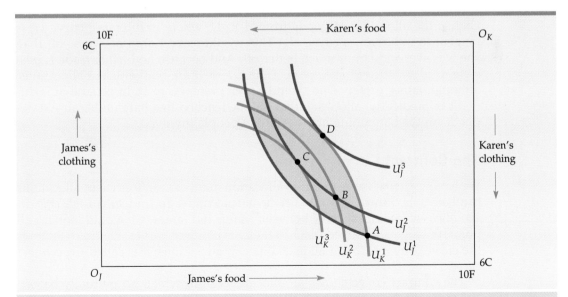

Figure 16.4   Efficiency in Exchange   The Edgeworth box illustrates the possibilities for both consumers to increase their satisfaction by trading goods. If A gives the initial allocation of resources, the shaded area describes all mutually beneficial trades.

right-hand corner of the box. Karen's indifference curves are convex, just like James's—we simply see them from a different perspective.

Now that we are familiar with the two sets of indifference curves, let's examine the curves labeled U_J^1 and U_K^1 that pass through the initial allocation at A. Both James's and Karen's MRSs give the slope of their indifference curves at A. James's is equal to 1/2, Karen's to 3. The shaded area between these two indifference curves represents all possible allocations of food and clothing that would make both James and Karen better off than at A. In other words, it describes all possible mutually beneficial trades.

Starting at A, any trade that moved the allocation of goods outside the shaded area would make one of the two consumers worse off, and should not occur. The move from A to B was mutually beneficial. But in Figure 16.4, B is not an efficient point, because indifference curves U_J^2 and U_K^2 intersect. This means that James's and Karen's MRSs are not the same, and that the allocation is not efficient. This illustrates an important point: *Even if a trade from an inefficient allocation makes both people better off, the new allocation is not necessarily efficient.*

Suppose that from B an additional trade is made, with James giving up another unit of food to obtain another unit of clothing and Karen giving up a unit of clothing for a unit of food. Point C in Figure 16.4 gives the new allocation. At C, the MRSs of both people are identical, which is why the indifference curves are tangent there. When the indifference curves are tangent, one person cannot be made better off without making the other person worse off. As a result, C represents an efficient allocation.

Of course, C is not the only possible efficient outcome of a bargain between James and Karen. For example, if James is an effective bargainer, a trade might change the allocation of goods from A to D, where indifference curve U_J^3 is tangent to indifference curve U_K^1. This would leave Karen no worse off than she was at A and James much better off. And because no further trade is possible, D is an efficient allocation. Thus C and D are both efficient allocations, although James prefers D to C, and Karen prefers C to D. In general, it is difficult to predict the allocation that will be reached in a bargain because it depends on the bargaining abilities of the people involved.

The Contract Curve

We have seen that from an initial allocation many possible efficient allocations can be reached through mutually beneficial trade. To find *all possible efficient allocations of food and clothing* between Karen and James, we would look for all points of tangency between each of their indifference curves. Figure 16.5 shows the curve drawn through all such efficient allocations; it is called the *contract curve*.

The contract curve shows all allocations from which no mutually beneficial trade can be made. These allocations are sometimes called *Pareto efficient* allocations, after Italian economist Vilfredo Pareto (1848–1923), who developed the concept of efficiency in exchange: *An allocation is Pareto efficient if goods cannot be reallocated to make someone better off without making someone else worse off.*

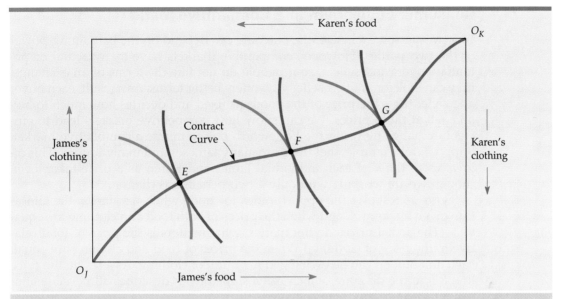

Figure 16.5 **The Contract Curve** The contract curve contains all allocations for which consumers' indifference curves are tangent. Every point on the curve is efficient because one person cannot be made better off without making the other person worse off.

In Figure 16.5 three allocations labeled *E*, *F*, and *G* are Pareto efficient, although each involves a different distribution of food and clothing, because one person could not be made better off without making someone else worse off.

Several properties of the contract curve may help us understand the concept of efficiency in exchange. Once a point on a contract curve, such as *E*, has been chosen, there is no way to move to another point on the contract curve, say *F*, without making one person worse off (in this case, Karen). Without making further comparison between James's and Karen's preferences, we cannot compare allocations *E* and *F*—we simply know that both are efficient. In this sense Pareto efficiency is a modest goal: It says that we should make all mutually beneficial exchanges, but it does not say which exchanges are best. Pareto efficiency can be a powerful concept, however. If a change would improve efficiency, it is in *everyone's* self-interest to support it.

We can frequently improve efficiency even when one aspect of a proposed change makes someone worse off. We need only include a second change, so that the *combined* set of changes leaves someone better off and no one worse off than before. Suppose, for example, that we propose to eliminate a quota on automobile imports into the United States. U.S. consumers would then enjoy lower prices and a greater selection of cars, but some U.S. autoworkers would lose their jobs. But if eliminating the quota were combined with federal tax breaks and job relocation subsidies for autoworkers, so that U.S. consumers would be better off (after accounting for the cost of the job subsidies) and U.S. autoworkers no worse off, the result would increase efficiency.

Consumer Equilibrium in a Competitive Market

In a two-person exchange, the outcome can depend on the bargaining power of the two parties. However, competitive markets have many actual or potential buyers and sellers, so if people do not like the terms of an exchange, they can look for another seller who offers better terms. As a result, each buyer and seller takes the price of the goods as fixed and decides how much to buy and sell at those prices. We can show how competitive markets lead to efficient exchange by using the Edgeworth box to mimic a competitive market. Suppose, for example, that there are many Jameses and many Karens. This allows us to think of each individual James and Karen as a price taker, even though we are working with only a two-person box diagram.

Figure 16.6 shows the opportunities for trade when we start at the allocation given by point A, and when the prices of both food and clothing are equal to 1. (The actual prices do not matter; what matters is the price of food relative to the price of clothing.) When the prices of food and clothing are equal, each unit of food can be exchanged for 1 unit of clothing. As a result, the price line PP' in the diagram, which has a slope of -1, describes all possible allocations that exchange can achieve.

Suppose each James decides to buy 2 units of clothing and sell 2 units of food in exchange. This would move each from A to C and increase satisfaction from indifference curve U_J^1 to U_J^2. Meanwhile, each Karen buys 2 units of

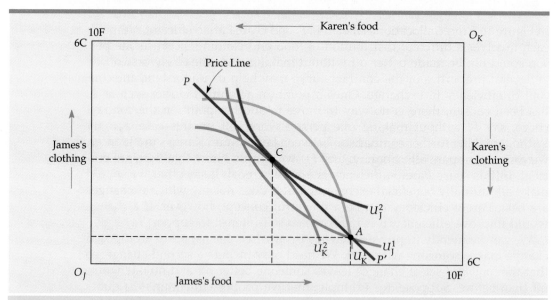

Figure 16.6   Competitive Equilibrium   In a competitive market the prices of the two goods determine the terms of exchange among consumers. If A is the initial allocation of goods, and the price line PP' represents the ratio of prices, the competitive market will lead to an equilibrium at C, the point of tangency of both indifference curves. As a result, the competitive equilibrium is efficient.

food and sells 2 units of clothing. This would move each from A to C as well, increasing satisfaction from indifference curve U_K^1 to U_K^2.

We choose prices for the two goods so that the quantity of food demanded by each Karen is equal to the quantity of food that each James wishes to sell, and the quantity of clothing demanded by each James is equal to the quantity of food that each Karen wishes to sell. As a result, the markets for food and clothing are in equilibrium. An *equilibrium is a set of prices at which the quantity demanded equals the quantity supplied in every market*. This is also a *competitive equilibrium* because all suppliers and demanders are price takers.

Not all prices are consistent with an equilibrium. For example, if the price of food is 1 and the price of clothing is 3, food must be exchanged for clothing on a 3-to-1 basis. But then each James will be unwilling to trade any food to get additional clothing because his MRS of clothing for food is only 1/2. Each Karen, on the other hand, would be happy to sell clothing to get more food, but has no one to trade with. The market is therefore in *disequilibrium* because the quantity demanded is not equal to the quantity supplied.

This disequilibrium should only be temporary. In a competitive market, prices will adjust if there is *excess demand* in some markets (the quantity demanded of one good is greater than the quantity supplied) and *excess supply* in others (the quantity supplied is greater than the quantity demanded). In our example, each Karen's quantity demanded for food is greater than each James's willingness to sell it, whereas each Karen's willingness to trade clothing is greater than each James's quantity demanded. As a result of this excess quantity demanded for food and excess quantity supplied of clothing, we would expect the price of food to increase relative to the price of clothing. And as the price changed, so would the quantities demanded by all those in the market. Eventually, the prices would adjust until an equilibrium was reached. In our example, the price of both food and clothing might be 2; we know from the previous analysis that when the price of clothing is equal to the price of food, the market will be in competitive equilibrium. (Recall that only relative prices matter; prices of 2 for clothing and food are equivalent to prices of 1 for each.)

Note the important difference between exchange with two people and an economy with many people. When only two people are involved, bargaining leaves an indeterminate outcome. However, when many people are involved, the prices of the goods are determined by the combined choices of demanders and suppliers of goods.

The Economic Efficiency of Competitive Markets

We can now understand one of the fundamental results of microeconomic analysis. We can see from point C in Figure 16.6 that *the allocation in a competitive equilibrium is economically efficient*. The central reason why this is so is that C must occur at the tangency of two indifference curves. If it does not, then one of the Jameses or one of the Karens will not be achieving maximum satisfaction; he or she will be willing to trade to achieve a higher level of utility.

This result holds in an exchange framework and in a general equilibrium setting in which all markets are perfectly competitive. It is the most direct way of illustrating the workings of Adam Smith's famous *invisible hand*, because it tells us that the economy will automatically allocate resources efficiently without the need for governmental regulatory control. It is the independent actions of consumers and producers, who take prices as given, that allows markets to function in an economically efficient manner. Not surprisingly, the invisible-hand result is often used as the norm against which the workings of all real-world markets are compared. For some, the invisible hand supports the normative argument for less government, on the grounds that markets are highly competitive. For others, the invisible hand supports a more expansive role for government, on the grounds that government intervention is needed to make markets more competitive.

Whatever one's view of government, most economists consider this invisible-hand result important. In fact, the result that a competitive equilibrium is economically efficient is often described as the *first theorem of welfare economics*. (Welfare economics involves the normative evaluation of markets and economic policy.) Formally, the first theorem states the following:

> If everyone trades in the competitive marketplace, all mutually beneficial trades will be completed, and the resulting equilibrium allocation of resources will be economically efficient.

Let's summarize what we know about a competitive equilibrium from the consumer's perspective. First, because the indifference curves are tangent, all marginal rates of substitution between consumers are equal. Second, because each indifference curve is tangent to the price line, each person's MRS of clothing for food is equal to the ratio of the prices of the two goods. Formally, if P_C and P_F are the two prices

$$\boxed{\text{MRS}^J_{FC} = P_C/P_F = \text{MRS}^K_{FC}} \tag{16.1}$$

To achieve an efficient allocation when there are many consumers (and many producers) is not easy. It can be done if all markets are perfectly competitive. But efficient outcomes can also be achieved by other means—for example, through a centralized system in which the government allocates all goods and services. The competitive solution is often preferred because it allocates resources with a minimum of information. All consumers must know their own preferences and the prices they face, but consumers do not need to know what is being produced, or the demands of other consumers. Other allocation methods need more information, and as a result they become difficult and cumbersome to manage.

16.3 Equity and Efficiency

We have shown that different efficient allocations of goods are possible, and we have seen how a perfectly competitive economy generates an efficient allocation. But are efficient allocations *equitable*? That is a difficult question—

economists and others disagree both about how to define equity and how to quantify it. Any such view would involve subjective comparisons of utility, and reasonable people could disagree about how to make these comparisons. In this section we discuss this general point and then illustrate it in a particular case by showing that there is no reason to believe that the allocation associated with a competitive equilibrium will be equitable.

The Utility Possibilities Frontier

Recall that every point on the contract curve in our two-person exchange economy shows the levels of utility that James and Karen can achieve. In Figure 16.7 we put the information from the Edgeworth box in a different form. James's utility is measured on the horizontal axis and Karen's on the vertical axis. Any point in the Edgeworth box corresponds to a point in Figure 16.7 because every allocation generates utility for both people. Every movement to the right in Figure 16.7 represents an increase in James's utility, and every upward movement an increase in Karen's.

The *utility possibilities frontier represents all allocations that are efficient.* Point O_J is one extreme in which James has no goods and therefore zero utility, while point O_K is the opposite extreme where Karen has no goods. All other points on the frontier, such as E, F, and G, correspond to points on the contract curve, so that one person cannot be made better off without making the other worse off. Point H, however, represents an inefficient allocation because any trade within the shaded area makes one or both parties better off. At L both people

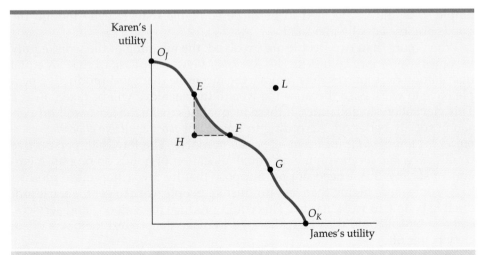

Figure 16.7 Utility Possibilities Frontier The utility possibilities frontier shows the levels of satisfaction that each of two people achieve when they have traded to an efficient outcome on the contract curve. Points E, F, and G correspond to points on the contract curve and are efficient. Point H is inefficient because any trade within the shaded area will make one or both people better off.

would be better off, but *L* is not attainable because there is not enough of both goods to generate the levels of utility that the point represents.

It might seem reasonable to conclude that an allocation must be efficient to be equitable. Compare point *H* with *F* and *E*. Both *F* and *E* are efficient, and (relative to *H*) each makes one person better off without making the other worse off. We might agree, therefore, that it is inequitable to James or Karen or both for an economy to yield allocation *H*, as opposed to *F* or *E*.

But suppose *H* and *G* are the only possible allocations. Is *G* more equitable than *H*? Not necessarily. Compared with *H*, *G* yields more utility for James and less for Karen. Some people may feel that *H* is more equitable than *G*; others may feel the opposite. We can conclude, therefore, that *one inefficient allocation of resources may be more equitable than another efficient allocation.*

The problem is how to define an equitable allocation. Even if we restrict ourselves to all points on the utility possibilities frontier, which point is the most equitable? *The answer depends on what one thinks equity entails*, and, therefore, on the interpersonal comparisons of utility that one is willing to make.

In economics, we often use a *social welfare function* to describe the particular weights that are applied to each individual's utility in determining what is socially desirable. One social welfare function, the *utilitarian*, weights everyone's utility equally and consequently maximizes the total utility of all members of society.[5] Each social welfare function can be associated with a particular view about equity. But some views do not explicitly weight individual utilities and cannot therefore be represented by a social welfare function. For example, a market-oriented view argues that the outcome of the competitive market process is equitable because it rewards those who are most able and who work the hardest.[6] If *E* is the competitive equilibrium allocation, for example, *E* would be deemed to be more equitable than *F*, even though the goods are less equally allocated.

When more than two people are involved, the meaning of the word equity becomes even more complex. The *Rawlsian* view[7] emphasizes that an equal distribution of resources may remove the incentive that most productive people have to work hard (because the wealth they achieve will be taxed away). This view allows inequalities, if these inequalities make the least-well-off person in society better off. According to Rawls, *the most equitable allocation maximizes the utility of the least-well-off person in society.* The Rawlsian perspective could be *egalitarian*, involving an equal allocation of goods among all members of society, but it need not be. Suppose that by rewarding more productive people more highly than less productive people, we can get the most productive people to work harder. This could produce more goods and services, some of which could then be reallocated to make the poorest members of society better off.

---

[5] One of the important developers of utilitarian thought was Jeremy Bentham (1748–1832). See *An Introduction to the Principle of Morals and Legislation* (London: Oxford University Press, 1907).

[6] See Robert Nozick, *Anarchy, State, and Utopia* (New York: Basic Books, 1974).

[7] See John Rawls, *A Theory of Justice* (New York: Oxford University Press, 1971).

Table 16.2 Four Views of Equity
1. Egalitarian—all members of society receive equal amounts of goods
2. Rawlsian—maximize the utility of the least-well-off person
3. Utilitarian—maximize the total utility of all members of society
4. Market-oriented—the market outcome is the most equitable

The four views of equity in Table 16.2 move roughly from most to least egalitarian. The egalitarian view explicitly requires equal allocations, while the Rawlsian puts a heavy weight on equality (otherwise some would be much worse off than others). The utilitarian is likely to require some difference between the best- and worst-off members of society. Finally, the market-oriented view may lead to substantial inequality in the allocations of goods and services.

Equity and Perfect Competition

A competitive equilibrium leads to a Pareto efficient outcome that may or may not be equitable. In fact, a competitive equilibrium could occur at any point on the contract curve, depending on the initial allocation. Imagine, for example, that the initial allocation gave all food and clothing to Karen. This would be at O_J in Figure 16.7, and Karen would have no reason to trade. Point O_J would then be a competitive equilibrium, as would point O_K and all intermediate points on the contract curve.

Because efficient allocations are not necessarily equitable, society must rely to some extent on government to redistribute income or goods among households to achieve equity goals. These goals can be reached through the tax system—a progressive income tax whose funds are used for programs that benefit households proportionally to income will redistribute income from the wealthy to the poor, for example. The government can also provide public services, such as medical aid to the poor (Medicaid), or it can transfer funds through programs, such as Food Stamps.

The result that a competitive equilibrium can sustain every point on the contract curve is a fundamental result in microeconomics. It is important because it suggests an answer to a basic normative question: Is there a trade-off between equity and efficiency; that is, must a society that wishes to achieve a more equitable allocation of resources necessarily operate in an economically inefficient manner? The answer, which is given by the *second theorem of welfare economics*, tells us that redistribution need not conflict with economic efficiency. Formally, the second theorem states the following:

> *If individual preferences are convex, then every efficient allocation (every point on the contract curve) is a competitive equilibrium for some initial allocation of goods.*

Literally, this theorem tells us that any equilibrium deemed to be equitable can be achieved by a suitable distribution of resources among individuals, and that such a distribution need not in itself generate inefficiencies. Unfortunately, all programs that redistribute income in our society are economically costly. Taxes may encourage individuals to work less or cause firms to devote resources to avoiding taxes rather than to producing output. So in effect, there is a trade-off between the goals of equity and efficiency, and hard choices must be made.[8] Welfare economics, which builds on the first and second theorems, provides a useful framework for debating the normative issues that surround the equity and efficiency aspects of public policy.

16.4 Efficiency in Production

Having described the conditions required to achieve an efficient allocation in the exchange of two goods, we now consider the efficient use of inputs in the production process. We assume there are fixed total supplies of two inputs, labor and capital, that are needed to produce the same two products, food and clothing. Instead of only two people, however, we now assume that many consumers own the inputs to production (including labor) and earn income by selling them. This income, in turn, is allocated between the two goods.

This framework links together the various supply and demand elements of the economy. People supply inputs to production and then use the income this brings to demand and consume goods and services. When the price of one input increases, the individuals who supply a lot of that input earn more income and consume more of one of the two goods. This in turn increases the demand for the inputs needed to produce the good and has a feedback effect on the price of those inputs. Only a general equilibrium analysis can find the prices that equate supply and demand in every market.

Production in the Edgeworth Box

We will continue to use the Edgeworth box diagram, but rather than measure goods on each axis as we did before, we will now measure inputs to the production process. Figure 16.8 shows a box diagram in which labor input is measured along the horizontal axis, and capital input on the vertical axis. Fifty hours of labor and 30 hours of capital are available for the production process. In our earlier analysis of exchange, each origin represented an individual; now each origin represents an output. The food origin is O_F, and O_C is the clothing origin. The only difference between the production analysis and the exchange analysis is that now we measure inputs rather than outputs in the diagram, and we focus on two outputs rather than two consumers.

Each point in the diagram represents the labor and capital inputs to the production of food and clothing. For example, A represents the input of 35 hours of labor and 5 hours of capital in the production of food, and the input

---

[8] This tradeoff between equity and efficiency is stated clearly by Arthur Okun in *Equality and Efficiency: The Big Tradeoff* (Washington: Brookings Institution, 1975).

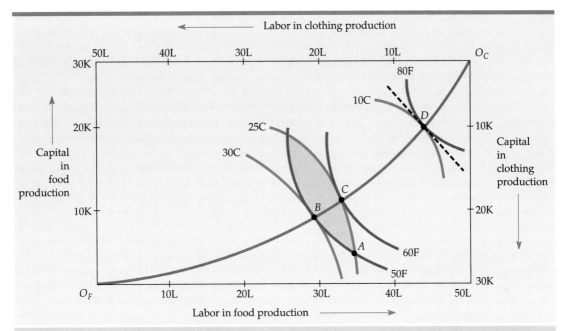

Figure 16.8 Efficiency in Production In an Edgeworth production box with two fixed inputs and two goods, an efficient use of inputs occurs when the isoquants for the two goods are tangent. If production initially uses the inputs described by A, the shaded area shows the region in which more of both outputs can be produced by rearranging input use. Points B, C, and D are on the production contract curve and involve efficient input use.

of 15 hours of labor and 25 hours of capital in the production of clothing. Every way in which labor and capital can be combined to produce the two goods is represented by a point in the diagram.

A series of production isoquants shows the levels of output produced with the various input combinations. Each isoquant represents the total production of a good that can be obtained, without distinguishing the firm or firms that produced it. We have drawn three food isoquants representing 50, 60, and 80 units of food output. The isoquants for food look just like the isoquants we worked with in Chapter 6, but we have rotated the clothing isoquants by 180 degrees, so that they can be read from the point of view of the origin O_C. For example, the isoquant 50F represents all combinations of labor and capital that combine to produce 50 units of food, while 25C represents all combinations of labor and capital that combine to produce 25 units of clothing.

We have also drawn three isoquants representing 10, 25, and 30 units of clothing. These isoquants increase in output as we move from upper right to lower left, again because one or both inputs have increased. Now we can see that A simultaneously represents 50 units of food and 25 units of clothing, each associated with a different combination of production inputs.

Input Efficiency

To see how inputs can be combined efficiently, we must find the various combinations of inputs that can be used to produce each of the two outputs. A particular allocation of inputs into the production process is *technically efficient* if the output of one good cannot be increased without decreasing the output of another good. Efficiency in production is not a new concept; in Chapter 6 we saw that a production function represents the maximum output that can be achieved with a given set of inputs. Here we are extending the concept to the production of two goods rather than one.

Figure 16.8 shows that inputs are allocated inefficiently if reallocating them generates more of one or both goods. For example, an inefficient allocation, such as that shown at point *A*, might arise if a labor union market has effectively enforced inefficient work rules. The allocation at *A* is clearly inefficient because any input combination in the shaded area generates more of both food and clothing. Thus, we can move from *A* to *B* by switching some labor from the production of food to the production of clothing, and some capital from the production of clothing to the production of food. This generates the same amount of food (50 units), but a larger amount of clothing (from 25 to 30 units).

Points *B* and *C* in Figure 16.8 are both efficient allocations, as are all points lying on the curve that connects O_F to O_C. Each of these points is a point of tangency of two isoquants, just as every point on the exchange contract curve represents a point of tangency of two indifference curves. The *production contract curve* represents all technically efficient combinations of inputs. Every point that does not lie on this production contract curve is inefficient because the two isoquants that pass through the point intersect. When two isoquants intersect, as at point *A*, labor and capital can be reallocated to increase the output of at least one of the two goods. From *A*, we have seen that any allocation within the shaded area increases the production of both goods—so *A* is technically inefficient.

Producer Equilibrium in a Competitive Input Market

If input markets are competitive, a point of efficient production will be achieved. Let's see why. If the labor and capital markets are perfectly competitive, then the wage rate *w* will be the same in all industries. Likewise, the rental price of capital *r* will be the same whether capital is used in the food or clothing industry. We know from Chapter 7 that if producers of food and clothing minimize production costs, they will use combinations of labor and capital so that the ratio of the marginal products of the two inputs is equal to the ratio of the input prices:

$$\mathrm{MP}_L/\mathrm{MP}_K = w/r$$

But we also showed that the ratio of the marginal products of the two inputs is equal to the marginal rate of technical substitution of labor for capital MRTS_{LK}. As a result,

$$\text{MRTS}_{LK} = w/r \qquad\qquad (16.2)$$

Since the MRTS is the slope of the firm's isoquant, for a competitive equilibrium to occur in the input market, each producer must use labor and capital so that the slopes of the isoquants are equal to one another and to the ratio of the prices of the two inputs. As a result, *the competitive equilibrium lies on the production contract curve, and the competitive equilibrium is efficient in production.*

Where we end up on the production contract curve depends on consumers' demands for the two goods. For example, suppose consumers tend to prefer food rather than clothing. One possible competitive equilibrium occurs at *D* in Figure 16.8. Here, the food producer minimizes the cost of producing 80 units of food by employing 43 units of labor and 20 units of capital. The clothing producer generates 10 units of clothing with 7 units of labor and 10 units of capital. The wage rate is equal to the rental price of capital, so the isocost lines have a slope of −1 in the diagram. At these prices neither producer will wish to purchase additional production inputs.

It is easy to check that if we begin at a point off the production contract curve, both producers will find it advantageous to hire labor or rent capital so that they can reallocate their inputs to minimize costs. It is also clear from the diagram in Figure 16.8 that the input market has no unique competitive equilibrium. Efficiency in the use of inputs can involve the production of much food and little clothing, or vice versa.

The Production Possibilities Frontier

The *production possibilities frontier* shows the various combinations of food and clothing that can be produced with fixed inputs of labor and capital. The frontier in Figure 16.9 is derived from the production contract curve in Figure 16.8. Each point on both the contract curve and the production possibilities frontier describes an efficiently produced level of both food and clothing.

We have labeled the points on the frontier to correspond to the points on the production contract curve. Point O_F represents one extreme, in which only clothing is produced, and O_C represents the other extreme, in which only food is produced. Points *B, C,* and *D* are the three other labeled points from the contract curve of Figure 16.8.

Point *A*, representing an inefficient allocation, lies inside the production possibilities frontier. All points within the triangle *ABC* involve the complete utilization of labor and capital in the production process. However, a distortion in the labor market has caused the economy as a whole to be productively inefficient.

The production possibilities frontier is downward sloping because to produce more food efficiently, one must switch inputs from the production of clothing, which in turn lowers the clothing production level. Because all points lying within the frontier are inefficient, they are off the production contract curve.

The production possibilities frontier is concave (bowed in)—i.e., its slope increases in magnitude as more food is produced. To describe this, we define

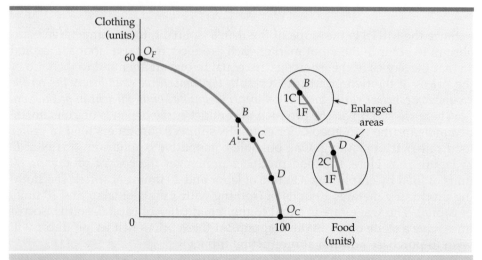

Figure 16.9 **Production Possibilities Frontier** The production possibilities frontier shows all efficient combinations of outputs. Points *B*, *C*, and *D* are taken from comparable points on the production contract curve in Figure 16.8. The production possibilities frontier is concave because its slope (the marginal rate of transformation) increases as the level of production of food increases.

the *marginal rate of transformation of food for clothing* (MRT) as the magnitude of the slope of the frontier at each point. The MRT measures how much clothing must be given up to produce one additional unit of food. For example, the enlarged areas of Figure 16.9 show that at *B* on the frontier, the MRT is 1 because 1 unit of clothing must be given up to obtain one additional unit of food. At *D*, however, the MRT is 2 because 2 units of clothing must be given up to obtain one more unit of food.

Note that as we increase the production of food by moving along the production possibilities frontier, the MRT increases.[9] This happens because the productivity of labor and capital differs depending on whether the inputs are used to produce more food or clothing. Suppose we begin at O_F, where only clothing is produced. Now we remove some labor and capital from clothing production, where their marginal products are relatively low, and put them into food production, where their marginal products are high. Then, to obtain the first unit of food, very little clothing production is lost (the MRT is much less than 1). But as we move along the frontier and produce less clothing, the productivities of labor and capital in clothing production rise and the productivities of labor and capital in food production fall. At *B*, the productivities are equal, and the MRT is 1. Continuing along the frontier, we note that

---

[9] The production possibilities frontier need not have a continually increasing MRT. Suppose, for example, that there were strongly decreasing returns to scale in the production of food. Then as inputs were moved from clothing to food production the amount of clothing that must be given up to obtain one more unit of food would decline.

the input productivities in clothing rise more, and the productivities in food decrease, so the MRT becomes greater than 1.

We could also have described the shape of the production possibilities frontier in terms of the costs of production. At O_F, where very little clothing output is lost to produce additional food, the marginal cost of producing food is very low (a lot of output is produced with very little input), and the marginal cost of producing clothing is very high (it takes a lot of both inputs to produce another unit of clothing). Thus, when the MRT is low, so is the ratio of the marginal cost of producing food MC_F to the marginal cost of producing clothing MC_C. In fact, *the slope of the production possibilities frontier measures the marginal cost of producing one good relative to the marginal cost of producing the other*. The curvature of the production possibilities frontier follows directly from the fact that the marginal cost of producing food relative to the marginal cost of producing clothing is increasing. At every point along the frontier, the following condition holds:

$$MRT = MC_F/MC_C \qquad (16.3)$$

At B, for example, the MRT is equal to 1. Here, when inputs are switched from clothing to food production, 1 unit of output is lost and 1 is gained. If the input cost of producing 1 unit of either good is $100, the ratio of the marginal costs would be $100/$100, or 1. Equation (16.3) also holds at D (and at every other point on the frontier). Suppose the inputs needed to produce 1 unit of food cost $160. Then, the marginal cost of food would be $160, but the marginal cost of clothing would be only $80 ($160/2 units of clothing). As a result, the ratio of the marginal costs, 2, is equal to the MRT.

Output Efficiency

For an economy to be efficient, goods must not only be produced at minimum cost; *goods must also be produced in combinations that match people's willingness to pay for them*. To understand this, recall from Chapter 3 that the marginal rate of substitution of clothing for food (MRS) measures the consumer's willingness to pay for an additional unit of food by consuming less clothing. But the marginal rate of transformation measures the cost of an additional unit of food in terms of producing less clothing. An economy produces output efficiently only if, for each consumer,

$$MRS = MRT \qquad (16.4)$$

To see why this condition is necessary for efficiency, suppose the MRT equals 1, but the MRS equals 2. Then consumers are willing to give up 2 units of clothing to get 1 unit of food, but the cost of getting the additional food is only 1 unit of lost clothing. Clearly, too little food is being produced. To achieve efficiency, food production must be increased, so that the MRS falls and the MRT increases until the two are equal. The outcome is efficient only when MRS = MRT for all pairs of goods.

Figure 16.10 shows this important efficiency condition graphically. Here, we have superimposed one consumer's indifference curve on the production

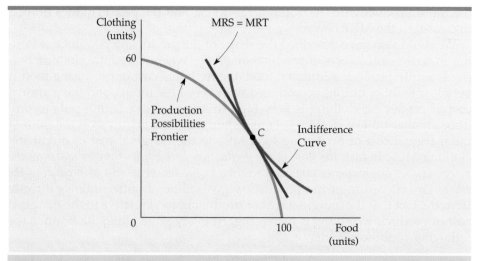

Figure 16.10 **Output Efficiency** The efficient combination of outputs is produced when the marginal rate of transformation between the two goods (which measures the cost of producing one good relative to the other) is equal to the consumer's marginal rate of substitution (which measures the marginal benefit of consuming one good relative to the other).

possibilities frontier from Figure 16.9. Note that C is the only point on the production possibilities frontier that maximizes the consumer's satisfaction. Although all points on the production frontier are technically efficient, they do not all involve the most efficient production of goods from the consumer's perspective. At the point of tangency of the indifference curve and the production frontier, the MRS (the slope of the indifference curve) and the MRT (the slope of the production frontier) are equal.

If you were a planner in charge of managing an economy, you would face a difficult problem. To achieve efficiency you must equate the marginal rate of transformation with the marginal rate of substitution of the consumer. But if different consumers have different preferences for food and clothing, how can you decide what levels of food and clothing to produce and what amount of each to give to every consumer, so that all consumers have the same MRS? The informational and logistical costs of doing this are enormous. (That is one reason why centrally planned economies, like that of the former Soviet Union, performed so poorly.) Fortunately, a well-functioning competitive market system can achieve the same efficient outcome.

Efficiency in Output Markets

When output markets are perfectly competitive, all consumers allocate their budgets so their marginal rates of substitution between two goods are equal to the price ratio. For our two goods, food and clothing,

$$\mathrm{MRS} = P_F/P_C$$

At the same time, each profit-maximizing firm will produce its output up to the point at which price is equal to marginal cost. Again, for our two goods,

$$P_F = \mathrm{MC}_F \text{ and } P_C = \mathrm{MC}_C$$

Because the marginal rate of transformation is equal to the ratio of the marginal costs of production, it follows that

$$\mathrm{MRT} = \mathrm{MC}_F/\mathrm{MC}_C = P_F/P_C = \mathrm{MRS} \tag{16.5}$$

When output and input markets are competitive, production will be efficient in that the MRT is equal to the MRS. This condition is just another version of the marginal benefit–marginal cost rule discussed in Chapter 4. There we saw that consumers buy additional units of a good to the point at which the marginal benefit of consumption is equal to the marginal cost. Here the production of food and clothing is chosen so that the marginal benefit of consuming another unit of food is equal to the marginal cost of producing food, and the same is true for the consumption and production of clothing.

Figure 16.11 shows that efficient competitive output markets are achieved when production and consumption choices are separated. Suppose the market generates a price ratio of P_F^1/P_C^1. If producers are using inputs efficiently, they will produce food and clothing at A, where the price ratio is equal to the

Figure 16.11 Competition and Output Efficiency   In a competitive output market, people consume to the point where their marginal rate of substitution is equal to the price ratio. Producers choose outputs so that the marginal rate of transformation is equal to the price ratio. Because the MRS equals the MRT, the competitive output market is efficient. Any other price ratio will lead to an excess demand for one good and an excess supply of the other.

MRT, the slope of the production possibilities frontier. When faced with this budget constraint, however, consumers will consume at B, where they maximize their level of satisfaction (on indifference curve U_2). Because the producer wants to produce F_1 units of food, but consumers want to buy F_2, there will be an excess demand for food. Correspondingly, because consumers wish to buy C_2 units of clothing, but producers wish to sell C_1, there will be an excess supply of clothing. Prices in the market will then adjust—the price of food will rise and that of clothing will fall. As price ratio P_F/P_C increases, the price line will move along the production frontier.

An equilibrium results when the price ratio is P_F^*/P_C^* at C. Here, producers want to sell F* units of food and C* units of clothing, and consumers want to buy the same amounts. At this equilibrium, the MRT and the MRS are equal, so again the competitive equilibrium is efficient.

16.5 The Gains from Free Trade

That there are gains from international trade in an exchange economy is clear—we have seen that two persons or two countries can benefit by trading to reach a point on the contract curve. However, there are additional gains from trade when the economies of two countries differ so that one country has a *comparative advantage* in producing one good, while a second country has a comparative advantage in producing another.

Comparative Advantage

Country 1 has a comparative advantage over country 2 in producing a good if the cost of producing that good, relative to the cost of producing other goods, in 1, is lower than the cost of producing the good in 2, relative to the cost of producing other goods in 2. Note that comparative advantage is not the same as *absolute* advantage. A country has an absolute advantage in producing a good if its cost is lower than the cost in another country. A comparative advantage, on the other hand, implies that a country's cost, *relative to the costs of other goods it produces*, is lower than the other country's.

When each of two countries has a comparative advantage, they are better off producing what they are best at, and purchasing the rest. To see this, suppose that the first country, Holland, has an *absolute* advantage in producing both cheese and wine. A worker there can produce a pound of cheese in 1 hour, and a gallon of wine in 2 hours. In Italy, on the other hand, it takes a worker 6 hours to produce a pound of cheese and 3 hours to produce a gallon of wine. The production relationships are summarized in Table 16.3.[10]

Holland has a *comparative* advantage over Italy in producing cheese, since Holland's cost of cheese production (in terms of hours of labor used) is half its cost of producing wine, whereas Italy's cost of producing cheese is twice

---

[10] This example is based on "World Trade: Jousting for Advantage," *The Economist* (Sept. 22, 1990): 5–40.

Table 16.3 Hours of Labor Required to Produce		
	Cheese **(1 lb.)**	**Wine** **(1 gal.)**
Holland	1	2
Italy	6	3

its cost of producing wine. Likewise, Italy has a comparative advantage in producing wine, which it can produce at half the cost of producing cheese.

The comparative advantage of each country determines what happens when there is trade between the two countries. The outcome will depend on the price of each good relative to the other when trade occurs. To see how this might work, suppose that with trade one gallon of wine sells for the same price as one pound of cheese in both Holland and Italy.

Without trade, with 24 hours of labor input, Holland could produce 24 pounds of cheese, 12 gallons of wine, or a combination of the two, such as 18 pounds of cheese and 3 gallons of wine. But Holland can do better. For every hour of labor Holland can produce 1 pound of cheese, which it can trade for 1 gallon of wine; if the wine were produced at home, 2 hours of labor would be required. It is, therefore, in Holland's interest to specialize in the production of cheese, which it will export to Italy in exchange for wine. If, for example, Holland produced 24 pounds of cheese and traded 6, it would be able to consume 18 pounds of cheese and 6 gallons of wine, a definite improvement over the 18 pounds of cheese and 3 gallons of wine available in the absence of trade.

Italy is also better off with trade. Note that without trade, with the same 24 hours of labor input, Italy can produce 4 pounds of cheese, 8 gallons of wine, or a combination of the two, such as 3 pounds of cheese and 2 gallons of wine. On the other hand, with every hour of labor Italy can produce one-third of a gallon of wine, which it can trade for one-third of a pound of cheese. If it produced cheese at home, twice as much time would be involved, so specialization in wine production is advantageous for Italy. Suppose that Italy produced 8 gallons of wine and traded 6; then it would be able to consume 6 pounds of cheese and 2 gallons of wine, likewise an improvement over the 3 pounds of cheese and 2 gallons of wine available without trade.

An Expanded Production Possibilities Frontier

When there is comparative advantage, international trade has the effect of allowing a country to consume outside its production possibilities frontier. This can be seen graphically in Figure 16.12, which shows a production possibilities frontier for Holland. Suppose initially that Holland has been prevented from trading with Italy because of a protectionist trade barrier. The outcome

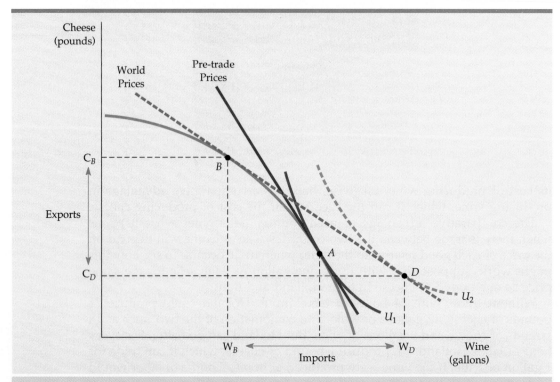

Figure 16.12   The Gains from Trade   Without trade, production and consumption are at point A, corresponding to a relative price of cheese to wine of 2 to 1. With trade at a relative price of 1 cheese to 1 wine, domestic production is now at B, while domestic consumption is at D. Free trade has allowed utility to increase from U_1 to U_2.

of the competitive process in Holland is that production is at point A, on in-difference curve U_1, where the MRT and the pre-trade relative price of wine and cheese is 2. If Holland were able to trade, it would want to export 2 pounds of cheese in exchange for 1 gallon of wine.

Suppose now that the trade barrier is dropped, and Holland and Italy are both open to trade; suppose also that as a result of differences in demand and costs in the two countries, trade occurs on a one-to-one basis. Holland will find it advantageous to produce at point B, the point of tangency of the 1/1 price line and Holland's production possibilities frontier.

That is not the end of the story, however. Point B represents the production decision in Holland (Holland will produce less wine and more cheese do-mestically once the trade barrier has been removed). But, with trade, con-sumption will occur at point D, at which the higher indifference curve U_2 is tangent to the trade price line. Thus trade has the effect of expanding Holland's consumption choices beyond its production possibilities frontier. Holland will import $W_D - W_B$ units of wine and export $C_B - C_D$ units of cheese.

With trade each country will undergo a number of important adjustments. As Holland imports wine, the production of domestic wine will fall as will employment in the wine industry. Cheese production will increase, however, as will the number of jobs in that industry. Workers with job-specific skills may find it difficult to change the nature of their employment. Thus not everyone in Holland will gain as the result of free trade. Consumers will clearly be better off, but producers of wine and workers in the wine industry are likely to be worse off, at least temporarily.

EXAMPLE 16.2 **The Effects of Automobile Import Quotas**

Governments can use quotas and tariffs to discourage imports and stimulate domestic production. But these devices can restrict or alter consumer choices and thereby generate substantial output inefficiencies. One recent example is the U.S. imposition of quotas on imports of Japanese automobiles.

During the past three decades, the U.S. automobile industry has faced increasing world competition. In 1965, for example, imports were only 6.1 percent of total domestic sales. This percentage increased, however, to 28.8 percent in 1980, when the industry earned a negative profit rate of −9.3 percent on its investment. Part of the industry's difficulty was due to higher-quality, lower-priced Japanese cars. To deal with these problems, the automobile industry convinced the government to negotiate a voluntary export restraint (VER) agreement with the Japanese in 1981. The VER limited Japanese exports to the United States to 1.68 million cars per year as compared with the 2.5 million cars imported in 1980. It was argued that the quotas would give U.S. automobile manufacturers time to retool their machines and restructure their union agreements to compete effectively in the world market.

How did these quotas affect the world market? Did they help or hurt American consumers and producers? Answers to these questions require a general equilibrium analysis of the Japanese and U.S. automobile industries, as well as the markets for labor, materials, and other inputs to the production process.

The evidence suggests that the quotas did little to help the industry retool; U.S. manufacturers had already begun to restructure their production toward smaller and more fuel-efficient cars during the late 1970s. (Real investment expenditures increased by 88 percent from 1975–1976 to 1979–1980, for example.) The quotas initially forced the Japanese to sell fewer cars, but Japanese prices rose nearly $1000 per car in 1981–82 and in later years, causing a $2 billion per year increase in revenues. In turn, the higher Japanese prices increased the demand for U.S. cars, which allowed the U.S. auto industry to increase its prices, wages, and profits. The increased profits were between $900 million and $1.4 billion, substantially less than the Japanese revenue gain. Finally, U.S. consumers were made worse off by the policy because U.S. automobile prices were approximately $350 to $400 per car higher than they would have been without the export restrictions.[11]

The quotas initially benefitted U.S. automobile workers. Without quotas, domestic sales would have been about 500,000 units lower in the early 1980s, which translates into about 26,000 jobs. But the higher prices cost consumers well over $4.3 billion dollars, which means that each job that was retained cost approximately $160,000 ($4.3 billion/26,000). The VER was thus an extremely inefficient way to increase domestic employment.

In the early 1990s, the voluntary quota program had little effect on automobile imports. In 1991, for example, Japan exported 1.8 million cars to the United States, even though the voluntary quota was 2.3 million. By March 1992 Japan opted to voluntarily lower the limit to 1.65 million and by April 1992 the program was eliminated. Yet, despite the reduction in imported cars, Japan's share of the U.S. automobile market increased from 20.5 percent in 1981 to 30.3 percent in 1991, and has stabilized at around 30 percent for some time. The explanation for the increase in market share is simple: The production of Japanese automobiles in U.S. plants has increased substantially over the past decade. Today, Japanese automobiles are being produced in several states, including Tennessee and California.

E X A M P L E   16.3   **The Costs and Benefits of Special Protection**

The demands for protectionist policies increased steadily during the 1980s and into the 1990s. They remain a subject of debate, whether out of concern for trade with various Asian countries, or in relation to the North American Free Trade Agreement (NAFTA). Protectionism can take many forms; they include tariffs and quotas of the kind that we analyzed in Chapter 9, regulatory hurdles, subsidies to domestic producers, and controls on the use of foreign exchange. Table 16.4 highlights the findings of one recent study of U.S.-imposed trade restrictions.[12]

Since one of the major purposes of protectionism is to protect jobs in particular industries, it is not surprising that these policies create gains to producers. The costs, however, involve losses to consumers, and a substantial reduction in economic efficiency. These efficiency losses are the sum of the loss of producer surplus resulting from inefficient excess domestic production and the loss of consumer surplus resulting from higher domestic prices and lower consumption.

---

[11] See Robert W. Crandall, "Import Quotas and the Automobile Industry: The Costs of Protectionism," *The Brookings Review* (Summer 1984): 8–16.

[12] This example is based on Cletus Coughlin, K. Alec Chrystal, and Geoffrey E. Wood, "Protectionist Trade Policies: A Survey of Theory, Evidence and Rationale," *Federal Reserve Bank of St. Louis* (January/February 1988): 12–30. The data in the table are taken from Gary Clyde Hufbauer, Diane T. Berliner, and Kimberly Ann Elliott, "Trade Protection in the United States: 31 Case Studies," *Institute for International Economics* (1986).

Table 16.4 Quantifying the Costs of Protection			
Industry	**Producer Gains[13] ($ millions)**	**Consumer Losses[14] ($ millions)**	**Efficiency Losses[15] ($ millions)**
Book manufacturing	305	500	29
Orange juice	390	525	130
Textiles and apparel	22,000	27,000	4,850
Carbon steel	3,800	6,800	330
Color televisions	190	420	7
Sugar	550	930	130
Dairy products	5,000	5,500	1,370
Meat	1,600	1,800	145

As the table shows, the textiles and apparel industry is the largest source of efficiency losses. Although there were substantial gains to producers, consumer losses are larger in each case. In addition, efficiency losses from excess (inefficient) domestic production of textiles and reduced domestic consumption of imported textile products were also large—an estimated $4.85 billion. The second largest source of inefficiency was the dairy industry, where losses amounted to $1.37 billion.

Finally, note that the efficiency cost of helping domestic producers varies considerably across industries. In textiles the ratio of efficiency costs to producer gains is 22 percent, and in dairy products it is 27 percent; only orange juice is higher (33.3 percent). However, much lower ratios apply to color televisions (3.7 percent), carbon steel (8.7 percent), and book manufacturing (9.5 percent).

16.6 An Overview—The Efficiency of Competitive Markets

Our analysis of general equilibrium and economic efficiency is now complete. In the process we have obtained two remarkable results. First, we have shown that for any initial allocation of resources, a competitive process of exchange among individuals, whether through exchange, input markets, or output markets, will lead to an economically efficient outcome. The first theorem of welfare economics tells us that a competitive system, building on the self-interested goals of consumers and producers and on the ability of market

---

[13] Producer gains in this tariff case are defined as the area of trapezoid *A* in Figure 9.16.

[14] Consumer losses are the sum of areas *A, B, C,* and *D* in Figure 9.16.

[15] These are given by triangles *B* and *C* in Figure 9.16.

prices to convey information to both parties, will, by the invisible hand of Adam Smith, achieve an efficient allocation of resources.

Second, we have shown that with consumer preferences that are convex, any efficient allocation of resources can be achieved by a competitive process with a suitable redistribution of those resources. The second theorem of welfare economics tells us that under certain, admittedly ideal conditions, issues of equity and efficiency can be treated distinctly from one another.

Both theorems of welfare economics depend crucially on the assumption that markets are competitive. Unfortunately, neither of these results necessarily holds when for some reason markets are no longer competitive. In the next two chapters, we will discuss ways in which markets fail, and what the government can do about it. Before proceeding, however, it is essential to review our understanding of the workings of the competitive process. To do so, we list the conditions that are required for economic efficiency in exchange, in input markets, and in output markets. These conditions are important; in each of these three cases, you should review the explanation of the conditions in this chapter and the underlying building blocks in prior chapters.

1. *Efficiency in Exchange.* All allocations must lie on the exchange contract curve, so that every consumer's marginal rate of substitution of food for clothing is the same:

$$MRS_{FC}^J = MRS_{FC}^K$$

A competitive market achieves this efficient outcome because (recall from Chapter 3) for consumers the tangency of the budget line and the highest attainable indifference curve assure that

$$MRS_{FC}^J = P_F/P_C = MRS_{FC}^K$$

2. *Efficiency in the Use of Inputs in Production.* All input combinations must lie on the production contract curve, so that every producer's marginal rate of technical substitution of labor for capital is equal in the production of both goods:

$$MRTS_{LK}^F = MRTS_{LK}^C$$

A competitive market achieves this efficient outcome because (recall from Chapter 7) each producer maximizes profit by choosing labor and capital inputs so that the ratio of the input prices is equal to the marginal rate of technical substitution:

$$MRTS_{LK}^F = w/r = MRTS_{LK}^C$$

3. *Efficiency in the Output Market.* The mix of outputs must be chosen so that the marginal rate of transformation between outputs is equal to consumers' marginal rates of substitution:

$$MRT_{FC} = MRS_{FC} \text{ (for all consumers)}$$

A competitive market achieves this efficient outcome because (recall from Chapter 8) profit-maximizing producers increase their output to the point at which marginal cost equals price:

$$P_F = MC_F, \ P_C = MC_C$$

As a result,

$$MRT_{FC} = MC_F/MC_C = P_F/P_C$$

But consumers maximize their satisfaction in competitive markets only if

$$P_F/P_C = MRS_{FC} \ \text{(for all consumers)}$$

Therefore,

$$MRS_{FC} = MRT_{FC}$$

and the output efficiency conditions are satisfied. Thus efficiency requires that goods are produced in combinations and at costs that match people's willingness to pay for them.

16.7 Why Markets Fail

We can give two different interpretations of the conditions required for efficiency. The first stresses that competitive markets work, and that we ought to ensure that the prerequisites for competition hold, so that resources can be efficiently allocated. The second stresses that the prerequisites for competition are unlikely to hold, and that we ought to concentrate on how to deal with market failures. Thus far we have focused on the first interpretation. For the remainder of the book, we concentrate on the second.

Competitive markets fail for four basic reasons: *market power, incomplete information, externalities,* and *public goods*. We will discuss each in turn.

Market Power

We saw in Chapters 10 and 14 that inefficiency arises when a producer or supplier of a factor input has market power. Suppose, for example, that the producer of food in our Edgeworth box diagram has monopoly power. It therefore chooses the output quantity at which marginal revenue (rather than price) is equal to marginal cost, and sells less output at a price higher than in a competitive market. The lower output will mean a lower marginal cost of food production. Meanwhile, the freed-up production inputs will be allocated to produce clothing, whose marginal cost will increase. As a result, the marginal rate of transformation will decrease, because $MRT_{FC} = MC_F/MC_C$. We might end up, for example, at A on the production possibilities frontier in Figure 16.11. Producing too little food and too much clothing is an output inefficiency because firms with market power use a different price in their output decisions than consumers use in their consumption decisions.

A similar argument would apply to market power in an input market. Suppose that unions gave workers market power over the supply of their labor in the production of food. Too little labor would then be supplied to the food industry at too high a wage (w_F), and too much labor to the clothing industry at too low a wage (w_C). In the clothing industry, the input efficiency conditions would be satisfied because $\text{MRTS}_{LK}^C = w_C/r$. But in the food industry, the wage paid would be greater than the wage in the clothing industry. Therefore, $\text{MRTS}_{LK}^F = w_F/r > w_C/r = \text{MRTS}_{LK}^C$. The result is input inefficiency because efficiency requires that the marginal rates of technical substitution be equal in the production of all goods.

Incomplete Information

If consumers do not have accurate information about market prices or product quality, the market system will not operate efficiently. This lack of information may give producers an incentive to supply too much of some products and too little of others. In other cases, some consumers may not buy a product even though they would benefit from doing so, while other consumers buy products that leave them worse off. For example, consumers may buy pills that guarantee weight loss, only to find that the pills have no medical value. Finally, a lack of information may prevent some markets from ever developing. It may, for example, be impossible to purchase certain kinds of insurance because suppliers of insurance lack adequate information about who is likely to be at risk.

Each of these informational problems can lead to competitive market inefficiency. We will describe informational inefficiencies in detail in Chapter 17, and see whether government intervention might cure them.

Externalities

The price system works efficiently because market prices convey information to both producers and consumers. Sometimes, however, market prices do not reflect the activities of either producers or consumers. There is an *externality* when a consumption or production activity has an indirect effect on other consumption or production activities that is not reflected directly in market prices. As we explained in Section 9.2, the word "externality" is used because the effects on others (whether benefits or costs) are external to the market.

Suppose, for example, that a steel plant dumps effluent in a river, which makes a recreation site downstream unsuitable for swimming or fishing. There is an externality because the steel production does not bear the true cost of waste water and hence uses too much waste water to produce its steel. This causes an input inefficiency. If this externality prevails throughout the industry, the price of steel (which is equal to the marginal cost of production) will be lower than if the cost of production reflected the effluent cost. As a result, too much steel will be produced, and there will be an output inefficiency.

We will discuss externalities and ways to deal with them in Chapter 18.

Public Goods

The last source of market failure arises when the market fails to supply goods that many consumers value. A *public good* is a good that can be made available cheaply to many consumers, but once the good is provided to some consumers, it is very difficult to prevent others from consuming it. For example, suppose a firm is considering whether to undertake research on a new technology for which it cannot obtain a patent. Once the invention is made public, others can duplicate it. As long as it is difficult to exclude other firms from selling the product, the research will be unprofitable.

Thus, markets undersupply public goods. We will see in Chapter 18 that the government can sometimes resolve this problem either by supplying the good itself or by altering the incentives for private firms to produce it.

Summary

1. Partial equilibrium analyses of markets assume that related markets are unaffected. General equilibrium analyses examine all markets simultaneously, taking into account feedback effects of other markets on the market being studied.

2. An allocation is efficient when no consumer can be made better off by trade without making someone else worse off. When consumers make all mutually advantageous trades, the outcome is Pareto efficient and lies on the contract curve.

3. A competitive equilibrium describes a set of prices and quantities, so that when each consumer chooses his or her most preferred allocation, the quantity demanded is equal to the quantity supplied in every market. All competitive equilibrium allocations lie on the exchange contract curve and are Pareto efficient.

4. The utility possibilities frontier measures all efficient allocations in terms of the levels of utility that each person achieves. Although both individuals prefer some allocations to an inefficient allocation, not *every* efficient allocation must be so preferred. Thus an inefficient allocation can be more equitable than an efficient one.

5. Because a competitive equilibrium need not be equitable, the government may wish to help redistribute wealth from rich to poor. Because such redistribution is costly, there is some conflict between equity and efficiency.

6. An allocation of production inputs is technically efficient if the output of one good cannot be increased without decreasing the output of some other good. All points of technical efficiency lie on the production contract curve and represent points of tangency of the isoquants for the two goods.

7. A competitive equilibrium in input markets occurs when the marginal rate of technical substitution between pairs of inputs is equal to the ratio of the prices of the inputs.

8. The production possibilities frontier measures all efficient allocations in terms of the levels of output that can be produced with a given combination of inputs. The marginal rate of transformation of food for clothing increases as more food and less clothing are produced. The marginal rate of transformation is equal to the ratio of the marginal cost of producing food to the marginal cost of producing clothing.

9. Efficiency in the allocation of goods to consumers is achieved only when the marginal rate of substitution of one good for another in consumption (which is the same for all consumers) is equal to the marginal rate of transformation of one good for another in production.

10. When input and output markets are perfectly competitive, the marginal rate of substitution (which equals the ratio of the prices of the goods) will equal the marginal rate of transformation (which equals the ratio of the marginal costs of producing the goods).

11. Free international trade expands a country's production possibilities frontier. As a result, consumers will be better off.

12. Competitive markets may be inefficient for four reasons. First, firms or consumers may have market power in input or output mar- kets. Second, consumers or producers may have incomplete information and may there- fore err in their consumption and production decisions. Third, externalities may be present. Fourth, some socially desirable public goods may not be produced.

Questions for Review

1. Why can feedback effects make a general equilibrium analysis substantially different from a partial equilibrium analysis?

2. In the Edgeworth box diagram, explain how one point can simultaneously represent the market baskets owned by two consumers.

3. In the analysis of exchange using the Edgeworth box diagram, explain why both consumers' marginal rates of substitution are equal at every point on the contract curve.

4. "Since all points on a contract curve are effi- cient, they are all equally desirable from a so- cial point of view." Do you agree with this statement? Explain.

5. How does the utility possibilities frontier re- late to the contract curve?

6. In the Edgeworth production box diagram, what conditions must hold for an allocation to be on the production contract curve? Why is a competitive equilibrium on the contract curve?

7. How is the production possibilities frontier related to the production contract curve?

8. What is the marginal rate of transformation (MRT)? Explain why the MRT of one good for another is equal to the ratio of the marginal costs of producing the two goods.

9. Explain why goods will not be distributed ef- ficiently among consumers if the MRT is not equal to the consumers' marginal rate of sub- stitution.

10. Why can free trade between two countries make consumers of both countries better off?

11. What are the four major sources of market failure? In each case, explain briefly why the competitive market does not operate effi- ciently.

Exercises

1. In the analysis of an exchange between two people, suppose both people have identical preferences. Will the contract curve be a straight line? Explain. (Can you think of a counterexample?)

2. Give an example of conditions when the pro- duction possibilities frontier might not be concave.

3. A monopsonist buys labor for less than the competitive wage. What type of inefficiency will this use of monopsony power cause? How would your answer change if the monopsonist in the labor market were also a monopolist in the output market?

4. Jane has 8 liters of soft drinks and 2 sand- wiches. Bob, on the other hand, has 2 liters of

soft drinks and 4 sandwiches. With these endowments, Jane's marginal rate of substitution (MRS) of soft drinks for sandwiches is three, and Bob's MRS is equal to one. Draw an Edgeworth box diagram to show whether this allocation of resources is efficient. If it is, explain why. If it is not, what exchanges will make both parties better off?

5. The Acme Corporation produces x and y units of goods Alpha and Beta, respectively.
   a. Use a production possibility frontier to explain how the willingness to produce more or less Alpha depends on the marginal rate of transformation of Alpha for Beta.
   b. Consider two cases of production extremes: (i) Acme produces zero units of Alpha initially, or (ii) Acme produces zero units of Beta initially. If Acme always tries to stay on its production possibility frontier, describe the initial positions of cases (i) and (ii). What happens as the Acme Corporation begins to produce *both* goods?

6. In the context of our analysis of the Edgeworth production box, suppose a new invention causes a constant-returns-to-scale production process for food to become a sharply increasing-returns process. How does this change affect the production contract curve?

7. Suppose gold (G) and silver (S) are substitutes for each other because both serve as hedges against inflation. Suppose also that the supplies of both are fixed in the short run ($Q_G = 50$, and $Q_S = 200$), and that the demands for gold and silver are given by the following equations:

$$P_G = 850 - Q_G + 0.5P_S$$
$$P_S = 540 - Q_S + 0.2P_G$$

   a. What are the equilibrium prices of gold and silver?
   b. Suppose a new discovery of gold increases the quantity supplied by 85 units. How will this discovery affect the prices of both gold and silver?

CHAPTER 17

Markets with Asymmetric Information

For most of this book, we have assumed that consumers and producers have complete information about the economic variables that are relevant for the choices they face. Now we will see what happens when some parties know more than others—i.e., when there is *asymmetric information*.

Asymmetric information is characteristic of many business situations. Frequently, a seller of a product knows more about its quality than the buyer does. Workers usually know their own skills and abilities better than employers. And business managers know more about their firm's costs, competitive position, and investment opportunities than do the owners of the firm.

Asymmetric information explains many institutional arrangements in our society. It is a reason why automobile companies offer warranties on parts and service for new cars; why firms and employees sign contracts that include incentives and rewards; and why the shareholders of corporations need to monitor the behavior of the firm's managers.

We begin by examining a situation in which the sellers of a product have better information about its quality than buyers have. We will see how this kind of asymmetric information can lead to market failure. In the second section, we see how sellers can avoid some of the problems associated with asymmetric information by giving potential buyers signals about the quality of their product. Product warranties provide a type of insurance that can be helpful when buyers have less information than sellers. But as the third section shows, the purchase of insurance entails difficulties of its own when buyers have better information than sellers.

In the fourth section, we show that managers may pursue goals other than profit maximization when it is costly for the owners of private corporations to monitor the managers' behavior. (In other words, managers have better information than owners.) We also show how firms can give managers an incentive to maximize profits even when monitoring their behavior is costly. Finally, we show that labor markets may operate inefficiently when employees have better information about their productivity than employers have.

17.1 Quality Uncertainty and the Market for Lemons

Suppose you bought a new car for $10,000, drove it 100 miles, and then decided you really didn't want it. There was nothing wrong with the car—it performed beautifully and met all your expectations. You simply felt that you could do just as well without it and would be better off saving the money for other things. So you decide to sell the car. How much should you expect to get for it? Probably not more than $8000—even though the car is brand new, has been driven only 100 miles, and has a warranty that is transferable to a new owner. And if you were a prospective buyer, you probably wouldn't pay much more than $8000 yourself.

Why does the mere fact that the car is second-hand reduce its value so much? To answer this question, think about your own concerns as a prospective buyer. Why, you would wonder, is this car for sale? Did the owner really change his or her mind about the car just like that, or is there something wrong with it? Perhaps this car is a "lemon."

Used cars sell for much less than new cars because *there is asymmetric information about their quality:* The seller of a used car knows much more about the car than the prospective buyer does. The buyer can hire a mechanic to check the car, but the seller has had experience with it, and will know more about it. Furthermore, the very fact that the car is for sale indicates that it may be a "lemon"—why sell a reliable car? As a result, the prospective buyer of a used car will always be suspicious of its quality—and with good reason.

The implications of asymmetric information about product quality were first analyzed by George Akerlof in a classic paper.[1] Akerlof's analysis goes

---

[1] George A. Akerlof, "The Market for 'Lemons': Quality Uncertainty and the Market Mechanism," *Quarterly Journal of Economics* (Aug. 1970): 488–500.

far beyond the market for used cars. The markets for insurance, financial credit, and even employment are also characterized by asymmetric quality information. To understand its implications, we will start with the market for used cars and then see how the same principles apply to other markets.

The Market for Used Cars

Suppose two kinds of used cars are available—high-quality cars and low-quality cars. Also, *suppose that both sellers and buyers can tell which kind of car is which*. There will then be two markets, as illustrated in Figure 17.1. In part (a), S_H is the supply curve for high-quality cars, and D_H is the demand curve. Similarly, S_L and D_L in part (b) are the supply and demand curves for low-quality cars. For any given price, S_H lies to the left of S_L because owners of high-quality cars are more reluctant to part with them and must receive a

(a) High-quality cars   (b) Low-quality cars

Figure 17.1 The Lemons Problem When sellers of products have better information about product quality than buyers, a lemons market may develop in which low-quality goods drive out high-quality goods. In (a) the demand curve for high-quality cars is D_H. However, as buyers lower their expectations about the average quality of cars on the market, their perceived demand shifts to D_M. Likewise, in (b) the perceived demand curve for low-quality cars shifts from D_L to D_M. As a result, the quantity of high-quality cars sold falls from 50,000 to 25,000, and the quantity of low-quality cars sold increases from 50,000 to 75,000. Eventually, only low-quality cars are sold.

higher price to do so. Similarly, D_H is higher than D_L because buyers are willing to pay more to get a high-quality car. As the figure shows, the market price for high-quality cars is $10,000, for low-quality cars $5000, and 50,000 cars of each type are sold.

In reality, the seller of a used car knows much more about its quality than a buyer does. Consider what happens, then, if sellers know the quality of cars, but buyers do not. (Buyers discover the quality only after they buy a car and drive it for a while.) Initially, buyers might think that the odds are 50-50 that a car they buy will be high quality. (The reason is that when both sellers *and* buyers knew the quality, 50,000 cars of each type were sold.) When making a purchase, buyers would therefore view all cars as being of "medium" quality. (Of course, after buying the car, they will learn its true quality.) The demand for cars perceived to be medium-quality, denoted by D_M in Figure 17.1, is below D_H but above D_L. As the figure shows, *fewer high-quality cars (25,000) and more low-quality cars (75,000) will now be sold.*

As consumers begin to realize that most cars sold (about three-fourths of the total) are low quality, their perceived demand shifts. As Figure 17.1 shows, the new perceived demand curve might be D_{LM}, which means that on average cars are thought to be of low to medium quality. However, the mix of cars then shifts even more heavily to low quality. As a result, the perceived demand curve shifts further to the left, pushing the mix of cars even further to low quality. *This shifting continues until only low-quality cars are sold.* At that point the market price would be too low to bring forth any high-quality cars for sale, so consumers correctly assume that any car they buy will be low quality, and the only relevant demand curve will be D_L.

The situation in Figure 17.1 is extreme. The market may come into equilibrium at a price that brings forth at least some high-quality cars. *But the fraction of high-quality cars will be smaller than it would be if consumers could identify quality before making the purchase.* That is why I should expect to sell my brand new car, which I *know* is in perfect condition, for much less than I paid for it. Because of asymmetric information, low-quality goods drive high-quality goods out of the market.

Implications of Asymmetric Information

Our used cars example shows how asymmetric information can result in market failure. In an ideal world of fully functioning markets, consumers would be able to choose between low-quality and high-quality cars. Some would choose low-quality cars because they cost less, while others would prefer to pay more for high-quality cars. Unfortunately, consumers cannot in fact easily determine the quality of a used car until after they purchase it, so the price of used cars falls, and high-quality cars are driven out of the market.

The market failure arises, therefore, because there are owners of high-quality cars who value their cars less than potential buyers of high-quality cars. As a result, both parties can enjoy gains from trade. Unfortunately, the lemons problem prevents this mutually beneficial trade from occurring.

Used cars are just a stylized example to illustrate an important problem that affects many markets—the problem of adverse selection. *Adverse selection* arises when products of different qualities are sold at a single price because buyers or sellers are not sufficiently informed to determine the true quality at the time of purchase. As a result, too much of the low-quality product and too little of the high-quality product are sold in the marketplace. Now let's look at some other examples of asymmetric information and adverse selection, and then see how the government or private firms might react.

Insurance

Why do people over age 65 have difficulty buying medical insurance at almost any price? Older people do have a much higher risk of serious illness, but why doesn't the price of insurance rise to reflect that higher risk? The reason is asymmetric information. People who buy insurance know much more about their general health than any insurance company can hope to know, even if it insists on a medical examination. As a result, there is *adverse selection*, much as with used cars. Because unhealthy people are more likely to want insurance, the proportion of unhealthy people in the pool of insured people increases. This forces the price of insurance to rise, so that more healthy people, realizing their low risks, elect not to be insured. This further increases the proportion of unhealthy people, which forces the price of insurance up more, and so on, until nearly all people who want to buy insurance are unhealthy. At that point selling insurance becomes unprofitable.

Adverse selection can make the operation of insurance markets problematic in other ways. Suppose an insurance company wants to offer a policy for a particular event, such as an auto accident that results in property damage. It selects a target population—say, men under age 25—to whom it plans to market this policy, and it estimates the frequency of accidents within this group. For some of these people, the probability of being in an accident is low, much less than .01; for others it is high, much more than .01. If the insurance company cannot distinguish between high- and low-risk men, it will base the premium for all men on the average experience, i.e., an accident probability of .01. With better information some people (those with low probabilities of an accident) will choose not to insure, while others (those with high probabilities of an accident) will purchase the insurance. This in turn raises the accident probability of those who are insured above .01, forcing the insurance company to raise its premium. In the extreme, only those who are likely to suffer a loss will choose to insure, making it impractical to sell insurance.

These kinds of market failure create a role for government. For health insurance, it provides an argument in favor of Medicare or related forms of government health insurance for the elderly. By providing insurance for *all* people over age 65, the government eliminates the problem of adverse selection.[2]

---

[2] The same general argument applies to all age groups. That is one reason that insurance companies avoid adverse selection by offering group health insurance policies at places of employment.

The Market for Credit

By using a credit card, many of us borrow money without providing any collateral. Most credit cards allow the holder to run a debit of several thousand dollars, and many people hold several credit cards. Credit card companies earn money by charging interest on the debit balance. But how can a credit card company or bank distinguish high-quality borrowers (who pay their debts) from low-quality borrowers (who don't)? Clearly, borrowers know more about whether they will pay than the company does. Again, the lemons problem arises. Credit card companies and banks must charge the same interest rate to *all* borrowers, which attracts more low-quality borrowers, which forces the interest rate up, which increases the number of low-quality borrowers, which forces the interest rate up further, and so on.

In fact, credit card companies and banks *can*, to some extent, use computerized credit histories, which they often share with one another, to distinguish "low-quality" from "high-quality" borrowers. Many people think that computerized credit histories are an invasion of privacy. Should companies be allowed to keep these credit histories and share them with other companies? We can't answer this question for you, but we can point out that credit histories perform an important function. They eliminate, or at least greatly reduce, the problem of asymmetric information and adverse selection, which might otherwise prevent credit markets from operating. Without these histories, even the creditworthy would find it extremely costly to borrow money.

The Importance of Reputation and Standardization

Asymmetric information is also present in many other markets. Here are just a few examples: *retail stores* (Will the store repair or allow you to return a defective product? The store knows more about its policy than you do.); *dealers of rare stamps, coins, books, and paintings* (Are the items real or counterfeit? The dealer knows much more about their authenticity than you do.); *roofers, plumbers, and electricians* (When a roofer repairs or renovates the roof of your house, do you climb up to check the quality of the work?); *restaurants* (How often do you go into the kitchen to check if the chef is using fresh ingredients and obeying the health laws?).

In all these cases, the seller knows much more about the quality of the product than the buyer does. Unless sellers can provide information about quality to buyers, low-quality goods and services will drive out high-quality ones, and there will be market failure. Sellers of high-quality goods and services, therefore, have a big incentive to convince consumers that their quality is indeed high. In the examples cited above, this is done largely by *reputation*. You shop at a particular store because it has a reputation for servicing its products; you hire a particular roofer and plumber because they have a reputation for doing good work; and you go to a particular restaurant because it has a reputation for using fresh ingredients, and nobody you know became sick after eating there.

Sometimes it is impossible for a business to develop a reputation. For example, most of the customers of a diner or a motel on a highway go there only once, or infrequently, while on a trip, so that the business has no opportunity to develop a reputation. How, then, can these diners and motels deal with the "lemons" problem? One way is by *standardization*. In your hometown, you may not prefer to eat regularly at McDonald's. But a McDonald's may look more attractive when you are driving along a highway and want to stop for lunch. The reason is that McDonald's provides a standardized product; the same ingredients are used and the same food is served in every McDonald's anywhere in the country. Who knows? Joe's Diner might serve better food, but at least you *know* exactly what you will be buying at McDonald's.

E X A M P L E   17.1   **Lemons in Major League Baseball**

How can we test for the presence of a lemons market? One way is to compare the performance of products that are resold with similar products that are seldom put up for resale. In a lemons market, purchasers of second-hand products will have limited information, and resold products should be lower in quality than products that rarely appear on the market. One such "second-hand" market has been created in recent years by a change in the rules governing contracts in major league baseball.[3]

Before 1976, major league baseball teams had the exclusive right to renew their players' contracts. After a 1976 ruling declared this system illegal, a new contracting arrangement was created. After six years of major league service, players can now sign new contracts with their original team or become free agents and sign with new teams. Having many free agents creates a second-hand market in baseball players. The original team can make an offer that will either retain a player or lose him to the free-agent market.

Asymmetric information is prominent in the free-agent market. One potential purchaser, the player's original team, has better information about the player's abilities than other teams have. If we were looking at used cars, we could test for the existence of asymmetric information by comparing their repair records. In baseball we can compare player disability records. If players are working hard and following rigorous conditioning programs, we would expect a low probability of injury and a high probability that they will be able to perform if injured. In other words, more motivated players will spend less time on the bench owing to disabilities. If a lemons market exists, we would expect free agents to have higher disability rates than players who are renewed. Players may also have preexisting physical conditions that their original teams know about that make them less desirable candidates for contract

---

[3] This example is based on Kenneth Lehn's study of the free-agent market. See "Information Asymmetries in Baseball's Free-Agent Market," *Economic Inquiry* (1984): 37–44.

Table 17.1 Player Disability			
	Days Spent on Disabled List per Season		
	Precontract	Postcontract	Percentage Change
All players	4.73	12.55	165.4
Renewed players	4.76	9.68	103.4
Free agents	4.67	17.23	268.9

renewal. Because more such players would become free agents, free agents would experience higher disability rates for health reasons.

Table 17.1, which lists the postcontract performance of all players who have signed multiyear contracts, makes two points. First, both free agents and renewed players have increased disability rates after signing contracts. The disabled days per season increase from an average of 4.73 to an average of 12.55. Second, the postcontract disability rates of renewed and not-renewed players are significantly different. On average, renewed players are disabled 9.68 days, free agents 17.23 days.

These two findings suggest a lemons market in free agents that exists because baseball teams know their own players better than the other teams with which they compete.

17.2 Market Signaling

We have seen that asymmetric information can sometimes lead to a "lemons problem": Because sellers know more about the quality of a good than buyers do, buyers may assume that quality is low, so that price falls, and only low-quality goods are sold. We also saw how government intervention (in the market for health insurance, for example) or the development of a reputation (in service industries, for example) can alleviate this problem. Now we will examine another important mechanism through which sellers and buyers deal with the problem of asymmetric information: *market signaling*. The concept of market signaling was first developed by Michael Spence, who showed that in some markets sellers send buyers *signals* that convey information about a product's quality.[4]

To see how market signaling works, let's look at a *labor market*, which is a good example of a market with asymmetric information. Suppose a firm is thinking about hiring some new people. The new workers (the "sellers" of labor) know much more about the quality of the labor they can provide than

---

[4] Michael Spence, *Market Signaling* (Cambridge, MA: Harvard University Press, 1974).

the firm (the buyer of labor). For example, they know how hard they tend to work, how responsible they are, what their skills are, and so forth. The firm will find these things out only after workers have been hired and have been working for some time. At the time they are hired, the firm knows little about how productive they will turn out to be.

Why don't firms simply hire workers, see how well they work, and then fire those with low productivity? Because this is often very costly. In many countries, and in many firms in the United States, it is difficult to fire someone who has been working more than a few months. (The firm may have to show just cause or pay severance pay.) Also, in many jobs workers do not become fully productive for at least six months. Before that time, considerable on-the-job training may be required, for which the firm must invest substantial resources. Thus the firm might not learn how good workers are for six months to a year. As a result, firms would be much better off if they knew how productive potential employees were *before* they hired them.

What characteristics can a firm examine to obtain information about people's productivity before it hires them? Can potential employees convey information about their productivity? Dressing well for the job interview might convey some information, but even unproductive people sometimes dress well to get a job. Dressing well is thus a weak signal—it doesn't do much to distinguish high-productivity from low-productivity people. *To be strong, a signal must be easier for high-productivity people to give than for low-productivity people to give, so that high-productivity people are more likely to give it.*

For example, *education* is a strong signal in labor markets. A person's educational level can be measured by several things—the number of years of schooling, degrees obtained, the reputation of the university or college that granted the degrees, the person's grade point average, and so on. Of course, education can directly and indirectly improve a person's productivity by providing information, skills, and general knowledge that are helpful in work. But even if education did *not* improve productivity, it would still be a useful *signal* of productivity because more productive people will find it easier to attain a high level of education. (Productive people tend to be more intelligent, more motivated, and more energetic and hard-working—characteristics that are also helpful in school.) More productive people are therefore more likely to attain a high level of education *to signal their productivity to firms and thereby obtain better-paying jobs.* And firms are correct in considering education a signal of productivity.

A Simple Model of Job Market Signaling

To understand how signaling works, it will be useful to discuss a simple model.[5] Let's assume there are only low-productivity workers (Group I), whose average and marginal product is 1, and high-productivity workers

---

[5] This is essentially the model developed in Spence, *Market Signaling.*

(Group II), whose average and marginal product is 2. Workers will be employed by competitive firms whose products sell for $10,000, and who expect an average of 10 years of work from each employee. We also assume that half the workers in the population are in Group I and the other half in Group II, so that the *average* productivity of all workers is 1.5. Note that the revenue expected to be generated from Group I workers is $100,000 ($10,000/year × 10 years) and from Group II workers is $200,000 ($20,000/year × 10 years).

If firms could identify people by their productivity, they would offer them a wage equal to their marginal revenue product. Group I people would be paid $10,000 per year, Group II people $20,000. On the other hand, if firms could not identify people's productivity before they hired them, they would pay all workers an annual wage equal to the average productivity, $15,000. Group I people would then earn more ($15,000 instead of $10,000), at the expense of Group II people (who would earn $15,000 instead of $20,000).

Now let's consider what can happen with signaling via education. Suppose all the attributes of an education (degrees earned, grade point average, etc.) can be summarized by a single index y that represents years of higher education. All education involves a cost, and the higher the educational level y, the higher the cost. This cost includes tuition and books, the opportunity cost of foregone wages, and the psychic cost of having to work hard to obtain high grades. What is important is that *the cost of education is greater for the low-productivity group than for the high-productivity group.* We might expect this for two reasons. First, low-productivity workers may simply be less studious. Second, low-productivity workers may progress more slowly through degree programs in which they enroll. In particular, suppose that for Group I people the cost of attaining educational level y is given by

$$C_I(y) = \$40,000y$$

and for Group II people it is

$$C_{II}(y) = \$20,000y$$

Now suppose (to keep things simple and to dramatize the importance of signaling) that *education does nothing to increase one's productivity; its only value is as a signal.* Let's see if we can find a market equilibrium in which different people obtain different levels of education, and firms look at education as a signal of productivity.

Consider the following possible equilibrium. Suppose firms use this decision rule: *Anyone with an education level of y^* or more is a Group II person and is offered a wage of $20,000, and anyone with an education level below y^* is a Group I person and is offered a wage of $10,000.* The particular level y^* that the firms choose is arbitrary, but for this decision rule to be part of an equilibrium, firms must have identified people correctly, or else the firms will want to change the rule. Will this rule work?

To answer this, we must determine how much education the people in each group will obtain, *given that firms are using this decision rule.* To do this, remember that education allows one to get a better-paying job. The benefit of

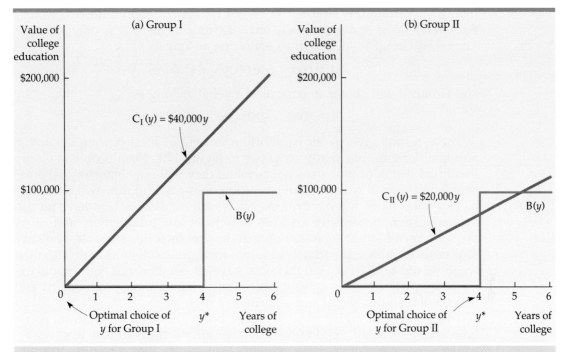

Figure 17.2   Signaling   Education can be a useful signal of the high productivity of a group of workers if education is easier to obtain for this group than for the low-productivity group. In (a) the low-productivity group will choose an education level of $y = 0$ because the cost of education is greater than the increased earnings. However, in (b), the high-productivity group will choose an education level of $y^* = 4$ because the gain in earnings is greater than the cost.

education $B(y)$ is the *increase* in the wage associated with each level of education, as shown in Figure 17.2. Observe that $B(y)$ is 0 initially, which represents the $100,000 base 10-year earnings that are earned without any college education. But when the education level reaches y^* or greater, $B(y)$ jumps to $100,000.

How much education should a person obtain? Clearly the choice is between *no* education (i.e., $y = 0$) and an education level of y^*. The reason is that any level of education less than y^* results in the same base earnings of $100,000, so there is no benefit from obtaining an education at a level above 0, but below y^*. Similarly, there is no benefit from obtaining an educational level above y^* because y^* is sufficient to allow one to enjoy the higher total earnings of $200,000.

In deciding how much education to obtain, people compare the benefit of education with the cost. People in each group make the following cost-benefit calculation: *Obtain the education level y^* if the benefit (i.e., the increase in earnings) is at least as large as the cost of this education.* For both groups, the benefit (the increase in earnings) is $100,000. The costs, however, differ for the two groups. For Group I, the cost is $40,000$y$, but for Group II the cost is only $20,000$y$. Therefore, Group I will obtain *no* education as long as

$$\$100{,}000 < \$40{,}000y^* \text{ or } y^* > 2.5$$

and Group II will obtain an education level y^* as long as

$$\$100{,}000 > \$20{,}000y^* \text{ or } y^* < 5$$

These results give us an equilibrium *as long as y^* is between 2.5 and 5.* Suppose, for example, that y^* is 4.0, as in Figure 17.2. Then people in Group I will find that education does not pay, and they will not obtain any, whereas people in Group II will find that education does pay, and they will obtain the level $y = 4.0$. Now, when a firm interviews job candidates who have no college education, it correctly assumes they have low productivity and offers them a wage of $10,000. Similarly, when the firm interviews people who have four years of college, it correctly assumes their productivity is high, and their wage should be $20,000. We therefore have an equilibrium; high-productivity people will obtain a college education to signal their productivity, and firms will read this signal and offer them a high wage.

This is a simple, highly stylized model, but it illustrates a significant point: Education can be an important signal that allows firms to sort workers according to productivity. Some workers (those with high productivity) will want to obtain a college education, *even if that education does nothing to increase their productivity*. These workers simply want to identify themselves as being highly productive, so they obtain the education to send a signal.

Of course, in the real world, education *does* provide useful knowledge and does increase one's ultimate productivity. (We wouldn't have written this book if we didn't believe that.) But education also serves a signaling function. For example, many firms insist that a prospective manager have an MBA. One reason for this is that MBAs learn economics, finance, and other useful subjects. But there is a second reason—to complete an MBA program takes intelligence, discipline, and hard work, and people with those qualities tend to be very productive.

Guarantees and Warranties

We have stressed the role of signaling in labor markets, but signaling can also play an important role in many other markets in which there is asymmetric information. Consider the markets for such durable goods as televisions, stereos, cameras, and refrigerators. Many firms produce these items, but some brands are more dependable than others. If consumers could not tell which brands tend to be more dependable, the better brands could not be sold for higher prices. Firms that produce a higher-quality, more dependable product would therefore like to make consumers aware of this, but how can they do it in a convincing way? The answer is through *guarantees and warranties*.

Guarantees and warranties effectively signal product quality because an extensive warranty is more costly for the producer of a low-quality item than for the producer of a high-quality item. (The low-quality item is more likely to require servicing under the warranty, which the producer will have to pay for.) As a result, in their own self-interest, producers of low-quality items will not offer an extensive warranty. Consumers can therefore correctly view an extensive warranty as a signal of high quality, and they will pay more for products that offer one.

17.3 Moral Hazard

When one party is fully insured and cannot be accurately monitored by an insurance company with limited information, the insured party may take an action that increases the likelihood that an accident or an injury will occur. The possibility that an individual's behavior may change because that person has insurance is an example of the problem of *moral hazard*. The concept of moral hazard applies generally, not only to problems of insurance, but also to problems of workers who perform below their capabilities when employers cannot monitor their behavior ("job shirking"). In general, *moral hazard occurs when the party to be insured can affect the probability or magnitude of the event that triggers payment.* For example, if I have complete medical insurance coverage, I may visit the doctor more often than I would if my coverage were limited. If the insurance provider can monitor its insurees' behavior, it can charge higher fees for those who make more claims. But if the company cannot monitor behavior, it may find its payments to be larger than expected. With moral hazard, insurance companies may be forced to increase their premiums or even to refuse to sell insurance at all.

Consider, for example, the decisions faced by the owners of a warehouse worth $100,000 and by their insurance company. Suppose that if the owners run a $50 fire prevention program for their employees, the probability of a fire is .005. Without this program, the probability of a fire increases to .01. Knowing this, the insurance company faces a dilemma if it cannot monitor whether there will be a fire prevention program. The policy that the insurance company offers cannot include a clause stating that payments will be made only if there is a fire prevention program. If the program were in place, the company could insure the warehouse for a premium equal to the expected loss from a fire, which is $500 (.005 × $100,000). Once the insurance policy is purchased, however, the owners no longer have an incentive to run the program. If there is a fire, they will be fully compensated for their financial loss. Thus, if the insurance company sells a policy for $500, it will incur losses because the expected loss from fire will be $1000 (.01 × $100,000).

Moral hazard is not only a problem for insurance companies. It also alters the ability of markets to allocate resources efficiently. In Figure 17.3, for example, D gives the demand for automobile driving in miles per week. The demand curve, which measures the marginal benefits of driving, is downward sloping because some people switch to alternative transportation as the cost of driving increases. Suppose initially that the cost of driving includes

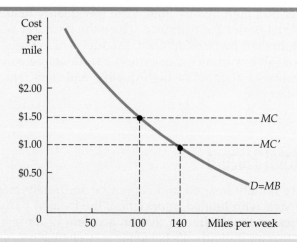

Figure 17.3 The Effects of Moral Hazard Moral hazard alters the ability of markets to allocate resources efficiently. D gives the demand for automobile driving. With no moral hazard, the marginal cost of transportation MC is $1.50 per mile, and the driver drives 100 miles, which is the efficient amount. With moral hazard, the driver perceives the cost per mile to be MC' = $1.00 and drives 140 miles.

the insurance cost, and that insurance companies can accurately measure miles driven. In this case, there is no moral hazard and the marginal cost of driving is given by MC. Drivers know that more driving will increase their insurance premium and hence increase their total cost of driving (the cost per mile is assumed to be constant). For example, if the cost of driving is $1.50 per mile (50 cents of which is insurance cost), the driver will go 100 miles per week.

A moral hazard problem arises because it is difficult for insurance companies to monitor individual driving habits; the insurance premium does not depend on miles driven. As a result, drivers assume that any additional accident costs that they incur will be spread over a large group, with only a negligible portion accruing to each of them individually. Since their insurance premium does not vary with the number of miles that they drive, an additional mile of transportation will cost $1.00 as shown by the marginal cost curve MC', rather than $1.50. The number of miles driven will increase from 100 to the socially inefficient level of 140.

Moral hazard not only alters behavior; it also creates economic inefficiency. The inefficiency arises because with insurance the individual's perception of either the cost or the benefit of the activity differs from the true social cost or benefit. For example, in the driving example of Figure 17.3, the efficiency level of driving is given by the intersection of the marginal benefit (MB) and marginal cost (MC) curves. However, with moral hazard, the individual's perceived marginal cost (MC') is less than actual cost, and the number of miles driven per week (140) is higher than the efficient level at which marginal benefit is equal to marginal cost (100).

EXAMPLE 17.2 **Reducing Moral Hazard—Warranties of Animal Health**

For buyers of livestock, information about the animals' health is very important.[6] Unhealthy animals gain weight more slowly than healthy animals, and are less likely to reproduce. Because of asymmetric information in the livestock market (sellers know the health of an animal better than buyers do), most states require warranties on the sale of livestock. Under these laws sellers promise (warrant) that their animals are free from hidden diseases and are responsible for all costs arising from any diseased animals.

Although warranties solve the problem of the seller's having better information than the buyer, they also create a form of moral hazard. Guaranteeing reimbursement to the buyer for all costs associated with diseased animals means that insurance rates are not tied to the level of care that buyers or their agents take to protect their livestock against disease. As a result of these warranties, livestock buyers tend to avoid early diagnosis of diseased livestock, and losses increase.

In response to the moral hazard problem, half the states have modified their animal warranty laws by requiring sellers to tell buyers whether livestock are diseased at the time of sale. Some states also require sellers to comply with state and federal animal health regulations, thereby reducing disease. Beyond this, however, warranties that animals are free from hidden disease must be an explicit written or oral guarantee to buyers.

EXAMPLE 17.3 **Crisis in the Savings and Loan Industry**

In 1934, during the Great Depression, the U.S. government introduced a broad-based system of financial insurance. The Federal Deposit Insurance Corporation provided insurance for deposits at commercial banks, and the Federal Savings and Loan Insurance Corporation did the same (up to $100,000 per account) for deposits at savings and loans. These insurance programs created the seeds of moral hazard on the part of depositors, since a depositor could lend money to any financial institution, no matter how risky that institution's loans, without bearing any risk.

Later, depositor moral hazard was coupled with moral hazard by owners of savings and loans. Beginning in 1982, new participants in the business found that they could attract large sums of government-insured capital and invest the money virtually without restriction in highly speculative investments. Because the deposits were insured, they had little incentive to evaluate the risks involved.

---

[6] This example is based on Terence J. Centner and Michael E. Wetzstein, "Reducing Moral Hazard Associated with Implied Warranties of Animal Health," *American Journal of Agricultural Economics* 69 (1987): 143–150.

Essentially, deposit insurance enabled savings and loans to make riskier loans on a larger scale than they would otherwise. The adverse incentives created by moral hazard coupled with the collapse of the real estate boom in the sun belt and energy-producing states led to the failure of many savings and loans.

In 1990 the cost of bailing out depositors whose money was lost when over 1000 savings and loans failed was estimated conservatively to be over $200 billion.[7] The biggest losses were in Texas, where over $42 billion had been spent by October 1990. The total outlays by the agencies responsible for deposit insurance were nearly $100 billion just through 1990.

While the prospects for the future are not bright, there are some hopeful signs. Aware of the adverse incentives that were created by moral hazard, the government has modified its insurance system. Today, the Federal Deposit Insurance Corporation regulates the savings and loan and banking industries, and savings and loans now face stiff capital requirements that force managers to bear a stake in the outcome of their investment policies. With a good deal of their own money at risk, managers are less inclined to invest speculatively.

A number of additional reforms could help to remove the moral hazard problem on the part of depositors and savings and loan owners. Proposals that would affect depositors include (1) lowering the amount of insurance coverage; (2) making the maximum coverage apply to each individual, no matter how many accounts that individual has; and (3) allowing for coinsurance, whereby the deposit insurance reimburses losses on less than a dollar-for-dollar basis. Proposals directed towards owners include (1) charging savings and loans insurance premiums that are based on the riskiness of the savings and loan portfolio—the greater the risk, the higher the premium; and (2) restricting the investment opportunities available to savings and loan owners.

17.4 The Principal–Agent Problem

If monitoring the productivity of workers were costless, the owners of a business could ensure that their managers and workers were working effectively. In most firms, however, owners can't monitor everything that employees do—employees are better informed than owners. This information asymmetry creates a *principal–agent* problem.

An *agency relationship* exists whenever there is an arrangement in which one person's welfare depends on what another person does.[8] The *agent* is the person who acts, and the *principal* is the party whom the action affects. In our example, the manager and the workers are agents, and the owner is the princi-

---

[7] *American Banker*, October 9, 1990.

[8] For more discussion of agency costs, see Richard Jensen and William Meckling, "Theory of the Firm: Managerial Behavior, Agency Costs, and Ownership Structure," *Journal of Financial Economics* 11 (1976): 305–360; and Eugene Fama, "Agency Problems and the Theory of the Firm," *Journal of Political Economy* 88 (1980): 288–307. See also Oliver Williamson, *The Economic Institutions of Capitalism* (New York: Free Press, 1985).

pal. *The principal–agent problem is that managers may pursue their own goals, even at the cost of obtaining lower profits for owners.*

Agency relationships are widespread in our society. For example, doctors serve as agents for hospitals, and as such, may select patients and do procedures consistent with their personal preferences, but not necessarily with the objectives of the hospital. Similarly, managers of housing properties may not maintain the property the way that the owners would like. And sometimes insured parties may be seen as agents and insurance companies as principals.

How does incomplete information and costly monitoring affect how agents act? And what mechanisms can give managers the incentive to operate in the owner's interest? These questions are central to any principal–agent analysis. In this section we study the principal–agent problem from several perspectives. First, we look at the owner–manager problem within private and public enterprises. Second, we discuss how owners can use contractual relationships with their employees to deal with the principal–agent problems.

The Principal–Agent Problem in Private Enterprises

An individual family or financial institution owns more than 10 percent of the shares of only 16 of the 100 largest industrial corporations.[9] Clearly, most large firms are controlled by management. The fact that most stockholders have only a small percentage of the firm's total equity makes it difficult for them to obtain information about how well the firm's managers are performing. One function of owners (or their representatives) is to monitor the behavior of managers. But monitoring is costly, and information is expensive to gather and use, especially for an individual.[10]

Managers of private enterprises can thus pursue their own objectives. But what are these objectives? One view is that managers are more concerned with growth than with profit per se; more rapid growth and larger market share provide more cash flow, which in turn allows managers to enjoy more perks. Another view deemphasizes growth but does emphasize the utility that managers get from their jobs, not only from profit but also from the respect of their peers, the power to control the corporation, the fringe benefits and other perks, and a long tenure on the job.

However, there are important limitations to managers' ability to deviate from the objectives of owners. First, stockholders can complain loudly when they feel that managers are behaving improperly, and in exceptional cases they can oust the current management (perhaps with the help of the board of directors of the corporation, whose job it is to monitor managerial behavior). Second, a vigorous market for corporate control can develop. If a takeover bid becomes more likely when the firm is poorly managed, managers will have a strong incentive to pursue the goal of profit maximization. Third, there can

---

[9] See Merritt B. Fox, *Finance and Industrial Performance in a Dynamic Economy* (New York: Columbia University Press, 1987).

[10] There are economies of scale in gathering information but there is no obvious way in which the information can be sold.

be a highly developed market for managers. If managers who maximize profit are in great demand, they will earn high wages, which in turn will give other managers an incentive to pursue the same goal.

Unfortunately, the means by which stockholders control managers' behavior are limited and imperfect. Corporate takeovers may be motivated by personal and economic power, for example, instead of economic efficiency. The managers' labor market may also not work perfectly, given that top managers are frequently near retirement and have long-term contracts. As a result, it is important to look for solutions to the principal–agent problem in which owners alter the incentives that managers face, without resort to government intervention. We consider some of these solutions in the next section.

The Principal–Agent Problem in Public Enterprises

The principal–agent framework can also help us understand the behavior of the managers of public organizations. There managers may be interested in power and perquisites, both of which can be obtained by expanding their organization beyond its "efficient" level. Because it is also costly to monitor the behavior of public managers, there are no guarantees that they will produce the efficient output. Legislative checks on a government agency are not likely to be effective as long as the agency has better information about its costs than the legislature has.

Although the public sector lacks some of the market forces that keep private managers in line, government agencies can still be effectively monitored. First, managers of government agencies care about more than just the size of their agency. Indeed, many choose lower-paying public jobs because they are concerned about the "public interest." Second, public managers are subject to the rigors of the managerial job market, much the way private managers are. If public managers are perceived to be pursuing improper objectives, their ability to obtain high salaries in the future might be impaired. Third, the legislature and other government agencies perform an oversight function. For example, the Government Accounting Office and the Office of Management and Budget spend much of their energy monitoring other agencies.

At the local rather than the federal level, public managers are subject to even more checks. Suppose, for example, that a city transit agency has expanded bus service beyond the efficient level. The citizens can vote the transit managers out of office, or, if all else fails, use alternative transportation or move. Competition among agencies can be as effective as competition among private firms in constraining the non-profit-maximizing behavior of managers.

E X A M P L E   17.4 **The Managers of Nonprofit Hospitals as Agents**

Do the managers of nonprofit organizations have the same goals as those of for-profit organizations? Are nonprofit organizations more or less efficient than for-profit firms? We can get some insight into these issues by looking at the provision of health care. In a study of 725 hospitals, from 14 major hospital chains, the return on investment and average costs of nonprofit and for-profit were compared to determine if they performed differently.[11]

The study found that for 1977 and 1981 the rate of returns between the two types of hospitals did indeed differ. For example, in 1977 for-profits earned an 11.6 percent return, while nonprofits earned 8.8 percent. In 1981, for-profits earned 12.7 percent and nonprofits only 7.4 percent. A straight comparison of returns and costs of these hospitals is not appropriate, however, because the hospitals perform different functions. For example, 24 percent of the nonprofit hospitals provide medical residency programs as compared with only 6 percent of the for-profit hospitals. Similar differences can be found in the provision of speciality care, where 10 percent of the nonprofits have open-heart units as compared with 5 percent of the for-profits. In addition, 43 percent of nonprofits had premature infant units, while only 29 percent of the for-profits had the equivalent units.

Using a statistical regression analysis, which controls for differences in the services performed, one can determine whether differences in services account for the higher costs. The study found that after adjusting for services performed, the average cost of a patient day in nonprofit hospitals was 8 percent higher than in for-profit hospitals. This implies that the profit status of the hospital affects its performance in the way principal–agent theory predicts: Without the competitive forces faced by for-profit hospitals, nonprofit hospitals may be less cost-conscious and therefore less likely to serve appropriately as agents for their principals, society at large.

Of course, nonprofit hospitals provide services that society may well wish to subsidize. But the added cost of running a nonprofit hospital should be considered when determining whether it should be granted tax-exempt status.

Incentives in the Principal–Agent Framework

We have seen why managers' and owners' objectives are likely to differ within the principal–agent framework. How, therefore, can owners design reward systems so that managers and workers can come as close as possible to meeting the owners' goals? To answer this question, let's study a specific problem.[12]

A small manufacturer uses labor and machinery to produce watches. The owners want to maximize their profit. They must rely on a machine repairperson whose effort will influence the likelihood that the machines break down, and thus affect the firm's level of profit. Revenue also depends on other random factors, such as the quality of parts and the reliability of other labor.

---

[11] Regina E. Herzlinger and William S. Krasker, "Who Profits from Nonprofits?" *Harvard Business Review* 65 (Jan.–Feb. 1987): 93–106.

[12] This discussion was motivated in part by Bengt Holmstrom, "Moral Hazard and Observability," *Bell Journal of Economics* 10 (1979): 74–91.

Table 17.2 **Revenue from Making Watches**		
	Poor Luck	**Good Luck**
Low effort ($a = 0$)	$10,000	$20,000
High effort ($a = 1$)	$20,000	$40,000

As a result of high monitoring costs, the owners can neither measure the effort of the repairperson directly nor be sure that the same effort will always generate the same profit level. Table 17.2 describes these circumstances.

The table shows that the repairperson can work with either a low or high amount of effort. Low effort ($a = 0$) generates either $10,000 or $20,000 revenue (with equal probability), depending on the random factors that we mentioned. We've labeled the lower of the two revenue levels "poor luck," and the higher revenue level "good luck." When the repairperson makes a high effort ($a = 1$), revenue will be either $20,000 (poor luck) or $40,000 (good luck). These numbers highlight the problem of incomplete information, because the owners cannot know whether the repairperson has made a low or high effort when the firm's revenue is $20,000.

Suppose the repairperson's goal is to maximize the wage payment that he receives, net of the cost of lost leisure and unpleasant work time associated with any effort that he makes. To simplify, we'll suppose that the cost of effort is 0 for low effort and $10,000 for high effort. (Formally, $c = $10,000a$.)

Now we can state the principal–agent problem from the owners' perspective. The owners' goal is to maximize expected profit, given the uncertainty of outcomes and given that the repairperson's behavior cannot be monitored. The owners can contract to pay the repairperson for his work, but the payment scheme must be based entirely on the measurable output of the manufacturing process, not on the repairperson's effort. To signify this link, we describe the payment scheme as $w(R)$, stressing that payments can depend only on measured revenue.

What is the best payment scheme? And can that scheme be as effective as one based on effort rather than output? We can only begin to study the answers here. The best payment scheme depends on the nature of production, the degree of uncertainty, and the objectives of both owners and managers. The arrangement will not always be as effective as an ideal scheme that is directly tied to effort. A lack of information can lower economic efficiency because both the owners' revenue and the repairperson's payment may fall at the same time.

Let's see how to design a payment scheme when the repairperson wishes to maximize his payment received net of the cost of effort made.[13] Suppose

---

[13] We assume that the repairperson is risk neutral, so that no efficiency is lost. If, however, the repairperson were risk averse, there would be an efficiency loss.

first that the owners offer a fixed wage payment to the repairperson. Any wage will do, but we can see things most clearly if we assume that the wage is 0. (Here, 0 could represent a wage no higher than the wage rate paid in other comparable jobs.) Facing a wage of 0, the repairperson has no incentive to make a high level of effort. The reason is simple: The repairperson does not share in any of the gains that the owners enjoy from the increased effort. It follows, therefore, that a fixed payment will lead to an inefficient outcome. When $a = 0$, and $w = 0$, the owner will earn an expected revenue of $15,000, and the repairperson a net wage of 0.

Both the owners and the repairperson will be better off if the repairperson is rewarded for his productive effort. Suppose, for example, that the owners offer the repairperson the following payment scheme:

$$\text{If } R = \$10,000 \text{ or } \$20,000, w = 0 \qquad (17.1)$$

$$\text{If } R = \$40,000, w = \$24,000$$

Under this bonus arrangement, a low effort generates no payment. A high effort, however, generates an expected payment of $12,000, and a payment net of the cost of effort of $2000. Now, the repairperson will choose to make a high level of effort. This makes the owners better off than before because they get an expected revenue of $30,000, and a profit of $18,000.

This is not the only payment scheme that will work for the owners, however. Suppose they contract to have the worker participate in the following revenue-sharing arrangement. When revenues are greater than $18,000:

$$w = R - \$18,000 \qquad (17.2)$$

(Otherwise the wage is zero.) Now if the repairperson offers low effort, he receives an expected payment of $1000. But if he offers a high level of effort, his expected payment is $12,000, and his expected payment net of the cost of effort is $2000. (The owners' profit is $18,000 as before.)

Thus, in our example, a revenue-sharing arrangement achieves the same outcome as a bonus payment system. In more complex situations, the incentive effects of the two types of arrangements will differ. However, the basic idea illustrated here applies to all principal-agent problems. When it is impossible to measure effort directly, an incentive structure that rewards the outcome of high levels of effort can induce agents to aim for the goals that the owners set.

*17.5 Managerial Incentives in an Integrated Firm

We have seen that owners and managers of firms can have asymmetric information about demand, cost, and other variables. We've also seen how owners can design a reward structure to encourage managers to make the appropriate effort. Now we focus our attention on firms that are *integrated*— that consist of several divisions, each with its own managers. Some firms are *horizontally integrated*—several plants produce the same or related products. Others are also *vertically integrated*—upstream divisions produce materials, parts, and components that downstream divisions use to produce final products. Integration creates organizational problems. We addressed some of these problems in the Appendix to Chapter 11, where we discussed *transfer pricing* in the vertically integrated firm, that is, how the firm sets prices for parts and components that upstream divisions supply to downstream ones. Here we will examine problems that stem from asymmetric information.

Asymmetric Information and Incentive Design in the Integrated Firm

In an integrated firm, the managers of the different divisions are likely to have better information about their operating costs and production potential than central management has. This asymmetric information causes two problems.

First, how can central management elicit accurate information about divisional operating costs and production potential from the divisional managers? This is important because the inputs to some divisions may be the outputs of other divisions, because deliveries must be scheduled to customers, and because prices cannot be set without knowing overall production capacity and costs. Second, what reward or incentive structure should central management use to encourage the divisional managers to produce as efficiently as possible? Should the divisional managers be given a bonus based on how much they produce, and if so, how should it be structured?

To understand these problems, consider a firm with several plants that all produce the same product. Each plant's manager has much better information about its production capacity than central management has. The firm's central management wants to learn more about how much each plant can produce, so that it can avoid bottlenecks and schedule deliveries reliably. It also wants each plant to produce as much as possible. Let's examine how central management can obtain the information it wants and also encourage the plant managers to run the plants as efficiently as possible.

One way is to give the plant managers a bonus based on either the total output of their plant or its operating profit. While this would encourage the plant managers to maximize their plant's output, it would penalize managers whose plants have higher costs and lower capacity. (Even if these plants produced efficiently, their output and operating profit—and hence their bonus—would be lower than that of plants with lower costs and higher capacities.) The plant managers would also have no incentive to obtain and reveal accurate information about cost and capacity.

A second way is to ask the plant managers about their costs and capacities, and *then* to base their bonus on how well they do relative to their answer. For example, each manager might be asked how much his or her plant can produce each year. Then at the end of the year, the manager would receive a bonus based on how close the plant's output was to this target. For example, if the manager's estimate of the feasible production level is Q_f, the annual bonus in dollars, B, might be

$$B = 10,000 - .5(Q_f - Q) \tag{17.3}$$

where Q is the plant's actual output, 10,000 is the bonus when output is at capacity, and .5 is a factor chosen to reduce the bonus if Q is below Q_f.

With this scheme, however, the plant managers would have an incentive to *underestimate* the capacity of their plant. By claiming a capacity below what they know to be true, they can more easily earn a large bonus, even if they do not operate efficiently. For example, if a manager estimates the capacity of her plant to be 18,000 rather than 20,000, and the plant actually produces only 16,000, her bonus increases from $8000 to $9000. Thus this scheme fails to elicit accurate information about capacity, and does not ensure that the plants will be run as efficiently as possible.

Now let's modify this scheme. We will still ask the plant managers how much their plants can feasibly produce and tie their bonuses to this estimate. However, we will use a slightly more complicated formula than (17.3) to calculate the bonus:

$$\begin{aligned} \text{If } Q > Q_f, \quad B &= .3Q_f + .2(Q - Q_f) \\ \text{If } Q \le Q_f, \quad B &= .3Q_f - .5(Q_f - Q) \end{aligned} \tag{17.4}$$

The parameters (.3, .2, and .5) have been chosen so that each plant manager has the incentive to reveal the *true* feasible production level, *and* to make Q, the actual output of the plant, as large as possible.

To see that this scheme does the job, look at Figure 17.4. Assume that the true production limit is $Q^* = 20,000$ units per year. The bonus that the manager will receive if she states the feasible capacity to be the true production limit is given by the line $Q_f = 20,000$. The line is continued for outputs beyond 20,000 to illustrate the bonus scheme, but dashed to signify the infeasibility of such production. Note that the manager's bonus is maximized when the firm produces at its limit of 20,000 units; the bonus is then $6000.

Suppose, however, that the manager reports a feasible capacity of only 10,000. Then the bonus she receives is given by the line $Q_f = 10,000$. The maximum bonus is now $5000, which is obtained by producing an output of 20,000. But note that this is less than the bonus the manager would receive if she correctly stated the feasible capacity to be 20,000.

The same line of argument applies when the manager exaggerates available capacity. If the manager states the feasible capacity to be 30,000 units per year, the bonus is given by the line $Q_f = 30,000$. The maximum bonus of $4000, which is achieved at an output of 20,000, is less than the bonus she could have received had she reported feasible capacity correctly.[14]

---

[14] Any bonus of the form $B = \beta Q_f + \alpha(Q - Q_f)$ for $Q > Q_f$, and $B = \beta Q_f - \gamma(Q_f - Q)$ for $Q \le Q_f$, with $\gamma > \beta > \alpha > 0$ will work. See Martin L. Weitzman, "The New Soviet Incentive Model," *Bell Journal of Economics* VII (Spring 1976): 251–256. There is a dynamic problem with this scheme that we have ignored: Managers must weigh a large bonus for good performance this year against being assigned more ambitious targets in the future. This is discussed in Martin Weitzman, "The 'Ratchet Principle' and Performance Incentives," *Bell Journal of Economics* 11 (Spring 1980): 302–308.

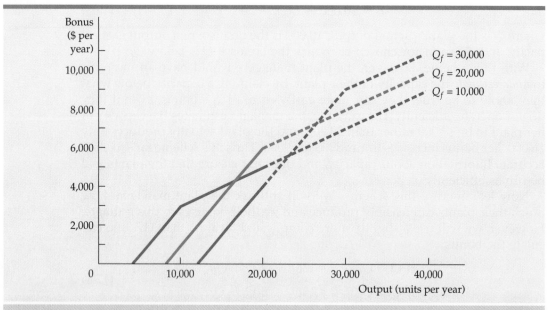

Figure 17.4 **Incentive Design in an Integrated Firm** A bonus scheme can be designed that gives a manager the incentive to estimate accurately the size of the plant. If the manager reports a feasible capacity of 20,000 units per year, equal to the actual capacity, then the bonus received is maximized (at $6000).

Applications

This problem of asymmetric information and incentive design comes up often in managerial settings, so incentive schemes like the one described above arise in many contexts. One example is how to encourage salespeople to set and reveal realistic sales targets, and then work as hard as possible to meet them.

Most salespeople cover specific territories. A salesperson assigned to an urban and densely populated territory can usually sell more product each month than a salesperson assigned to a sparsely populated area. The company, however, wants to reward all its salespeople equitably. It also wants to give them the incentive to work as hard as possible and to report realistic sales targets, so that it can plan production and delivery schedules. Companies have always used bonuses and commissions to reward salespeople, but the incentive schemes have often been poorly designed. Typically, salespeople's commissions were proportional to their sales. This elicited neither accurate information about feasible sales targets nor maximum performance.

Now companies are learning that bonus schemes of the sort given by equation (17.4) provide better results. The salesperson can be given a matrix of numbers that shows the bonus as a function of both the sales target (chosen by the salesperson) and the actual level of sales. (The numbers would be calculated from equation 17.4 or some similar formula.) Salespeople will quickly figure out that they do best by reporting a feasible sales target, and then work-ing as hard as possible to meet it.[15]

17.6 Asymmetric Information in Labor Markets: Efficiency Wage Theory

When the labor market is competitive, all who wish to work will find jobs for a wage equal to their marginal product. Yet most countries have substantial unemployment even though many people are aggressively seeking work. Many of the unemployed would presumably work even for a lower wage rate than that being received by employed people. Why don't we see firms cut-ting wage rates, increasing employment levels, and thereby increasing their profit? Can our models of competitive equilibrium explain persistent unem-ployment?

In this section we show how the *efficiency wage theory* can explain the pres-ence of unemployment and wage discrimination.[16] We have thus far deter-mined labor productivity according to workers' abilities and firms' invest-ment in capital. Efficiency wage models recognize that labor productivity also depends on what wage rate is paid. There are various explanations for this relationship. In developing countries, economists have suggested that the pro-ductivity of workers depends on the wage rate for nutritional reasons. Better-paid workers can afford to buy more and better food and are therefore health-ier and can work harder.

A better explanation for the United States is found in the *shirking model*. Because monitoring workers is costly or impossible, firms have imperfect in-formation about worker productivity, and there is a principal–agent problem. In its simplest form, the shirking model assumes perfectly competitive mar-kets, so all workers are equally productive and earn the same wage. Once hired, workers can either work productively or slack off (shirk). But because information about their performance is limited, workers may not get fired for shirking.

The model works as follows. If a firm pays its workers the market clearing wage w^*, they have an incentive to shirk. Even if they get caught and are fired (and they might not be), they can immediately get hired somewhere else for the same wage. In this situation, the threat of being fired does not impose a cost on workers, so they have no incentive to be productive. As an incentive not to shirk, a firm must offer workers a higher wage. At this higher wage, workers who are fired for shirking will have to face a decrease in wages if they get hired by another firm at w^*. If the difference in wages is large enough,

---

[15] See Jacob Gonik, "Tie Salesmen's Bonuses to Their Forecasts," *Harvard Business Review* (May–June 1978): 116–123.

[16] See Janet L. Yellen, "Efficiency Wage Models of Unemployment," *American Economic Review* 74 (May 1984): 200–205. The graphical analysis relies on Joseph E. Stiglitz, "The Causes and Consequences of the Dependence of Quality on Price," *Journal of Economic Literature* 25 (March 1987): 1–48.

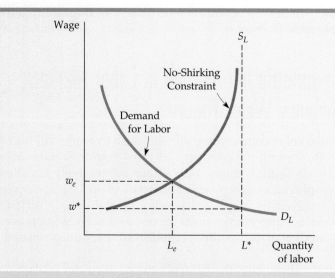

Figure 17.5   Unemployment in a Shirking Model   Unemployment can arise in otherwise competitive labor markets when employers cannot accurately monitor workers. Here the "no shirking constraint" gives the wage necessary to keep workers from shirking on the job. The firm hires L_e workers (at a higher than competitive efficiency wage w_e), creating $L^* - L_e$ of unemployment.

workers will be induced to be productive, and this firm will not have a problem with shirking. The wage at which no shirking occurs is the *efficiency wage*.

Up to this point, we have looked at only one firm. But all firms face the problem of shirking. This means that all firms will offer wages greater than the market clearing wage w^*, say, w_e (efficiency wage). Does this remove the incentive for workers not to shirk because they will be hired at the higher wage by other firms if they get fired? No; because all firms are offering wages greater than w^*, the demand for labor is less than the market-clearing quantity, and there is unemployment. This means that workers fired for shirking will face a spell of unemployment before earning w_e at another firm.

Figure 17.5 shows shirking in the labor market. The demand for labor D_L is downward-sloping for the traditional reasons. If there were no shirking, the intersection of D_L with the supply of labor (S_L) would set the market wage at w^*, and full employment would result (L^*). With shirking, however, individual firms are unwilling to pay w^*. Rather, for every level of unemployment in the labor market, firms need to pay some wage greater than w^* to induce workers to be productive. This wage is shown as the no-shirking constraint (NSC) curve. This curve shows the minimum wage workers need earn in order not to shirk, for each level of unemployment. Note that the greater the level of unemployment, the smaller the difference between the efficiency wage and w^*. This is because with high levels of unemployment, people who shirk

risk long periods of unemployment and therefore don't need much induce-
ment to be productive.

In Figure 17.5, the equilibrium wage will be at the intersection of the NSC
curve and D_L curves, with L_e workers earning w_e. This is because the NSC
curve gives the lowest wage that firms can pay and still avoid shirking. Firms
do not need to pay more than this to get the number of workers they need,
and they will not pay less than this because of shirking. Note that the NSC
curve never crosses the labor supply curve. This means that there will always
be some unemployment in equilibrium.

EXAMPLE 17.5 **Efficiency Wages at Ford Motor Company**

One of the early examples of the payment of efficiency wages can be found
in the history of Ford, one of America's major automobile producers.[17] Before
1913 automobile production had depended heavily on skilled workers. But
the introduction of the assembly line drastically changed the workplace. Now
jobs demanded much less skill, and production depended on maintaining the
assembly-line equipment. As the automobile plants changed, workers became
increasingly disenchanted. In 1913, turnover at Ford was 380 percent. The following year, it rose to 1000 percent, and profit margins fell sharply.

Ford needed to maintain a stable work force, and Henry Ford (and his business partner James Couzens) provided it. In 1914, when the going wage for a
day's work in industry averaged between $2 and $3, Ford Motor Company
introduced a pay policy of $5 a day for its workers. Improved labor efficiency
(not generosity) was behind this policy. The goal was to attract better workers who would stay with their jobs, and eventually to increase profits.

Although Henry Ford was attacked for it, this policy succeeded. The workforce did become more stable, and the publicity helped Ford's sales. And because Henry Ford had his pick of workers, he could hire a group that was on
average more productive. Ford stated that the wage increase did in fact increase the loyalty and personal efficiency of his workers, and quantitative estimates support his statements. According to calculations by Ford's chief of
labor relations, productivity increased by 51 percent. Another study found
that absenteeism had been halved, and discharges for cause had declined
sharply. So the productivity increase more than offset the increase in wages.
As a result, Ford's profitability rose from $30 million in 1914 to $60 million in
1916.

---

[17] See J.R. Lee, "So-Called Profit Sharing System in the Ford Plant," *Annals of the American Academy
of Political and Social Science* (May 1915): 297–310; David Halberstam, *The Reckoning* (New York:
William Morrow, 1986), pp. 91–92; and Daniel M.G. Raff and Lawrence H. Summers, "Did Henry
Ford Pay Efficiency Wages?" *Journal of Labor Economics* (1987): 557–586.

Summary

1. The seller of a product often has better information about its quality than the buyer. Asymmetric information of this type creates a market failure in which bad products tend to drive good products out of the market. The market failure can be eliminated if sellers offer standardized products, provide guarantees or warranties, or find other ways to maintain a good reputation for their product.

2. Insurance markets frequently involve asymmetric information because the insuring party has better information about the risk involved than the insurance company. This can lead to adverse selection, in which the poorer risks choose to insure, and the good risks do not. Another problem for insurance markets is moral hazard, in which the insuring party takes less care to avoid losses after insuring than before.

3. Sellers can deal with the problem of asymmetric information by sending buyers signals about the quality of their product. For example, workers can signal their high productivity by obtaining a high level of education.

4. Asymmetric information may make it costly for the owners of firms (the principal) to monitor accurately the behavior of the firm's manager (the agent). Managers may seek higher fringe benefits for themselves, or a goal of sales maximization, even though the shareholders would prefer to maximize profit.

5. Owners can avoid some of the principal–agent problems by designing contracts that give their agents the incentive to perform productively.

6. Asymmetric information can explain why labor markets have substantial unemployment when some workers are actively seeking work. According to efficiency wage theory, a wage higher than the competitive wage (the efficiency wage) increases worker productivity by discouraging workers from shirking on the job.

Questions for Review

1. Why can asymmetric information between buyers and sellers lead to market failure when a market is otherwise perfectly competitive?

2. If the used car market is a "lemons" market, how would you expect the repair record of used cars that are sold to compare with the repair record of those not sold?

3. Explain the difference between adverse selection and moral hazard in insurance markets. Can one exist without the other?

4. Describe several ways in which sellers can convince buyers that their products are of high quality. Which methods apply to the following products: Maytag washing machines, Burger King hamburgers, large diamonds?

5. Why might a seller find it advantageous to signal the quality of her product? How are guarantees and warranties a form of market signaling?

6. Why might managers of firms be able to achieve objectives other than profit maximization, the goal of the firm's shareholders?

7. How can the principal–agent model be used to explain why public enterprises, such as post offices, might pursue goals other than profit maximization?

8. Why are bonus and profit-sharing payment schemes likely to resolve principal–agent problems, whereas a fixed wage payment will not?

9. What is an efficiency wage? Why is it profitable for the firm to pay an efficiency wage when workers have better information about their productivity than firms do?

Exercises

1. Many consumers view a well-known brand name as a signal of quality and will pay more for a brand-name product (e.g., Bayer aspirin instead of generic aspirin, or Birds Eye frozen vegetables instead of the supermarket's own brand). Can a brand name provide a useful signal of quality? Why or why not?

2. Gary is a recent college graduate. After six months at his new job, he has finally saved enough to buy his first car.
   a. Gary knows very little about the differences between makes and models of cars. How could he use market signals, reputation, or standardization to make comparisons?
   b. You are a loan officer in a bank. After selecting a car, Gary comes to you seeking a loan. Since he has only recently graduated, he does not have a long credit history. Despite this, the bank has a long history of financing cars of recent college graduates. Is this information useful in Gary's case? If so, how?

3. A major university bans the assignment of D or F grades. It defends its action by claiming that students tend to perform above average when they are free from the pressures of flunking out. The university states that it wants all its students to get As and Bs. If the goal is to raise overall grades to the B level or above, is this a good policy? Discuss with respect to the problem of moral hazard.

4. Professor Jones has just been hired by the economics department at a major private university. The president of the board of regents has stated that the university is committed to providing top-quality education for its undergraduates. Two months into the semester, Professor Jones fails to show up for his classes. It seems he is devoting all his time to economic research rather than to teaching. Professor Jones argues that his research will bring additional prestige to the department and the university. Should he be allowed to continue exclusively with research? Discuss with reference to the principal–agent problem.

5. Faced with a reputation for producing automobiles with poor repair records, a number of American automobile companies have offered extensive guarantees to car purchasers (e.g., a seven-year warranty on all parts and labor associated with mechanical problems).
   a. In light of your knowledge of the lemons market, why is this a reasonable policy?
   b. Is the policy likely to create a moral hazard problem? Explain.

6. To promote competition and consumer welfare, the Federal Trade Commission requires firms to advertise truthfully. How does truth in advertising promote competition? Why would a market be less competitive if firms advertised deceptively?

7. An insurance company is considering issuing three types of fire insurance policies: (i) complete insurance coverage, (ii) complete coverage above and beyond a $10,000 deductible, and (iii) 90 percent coverage of all losses. Which policy is more likely to create moral hazard problems?

8. You have seen how asymmetric information can reduce the average quality of the products sold in a market, as low-quality products drive out the high-quality ones. For those markets where asymmetric information is prevalent, would you agree or disagree with each of the following? Explain briefly:
   a. The government should subsidize *Consumer Reports*.
   b. The government should impose quality standards—e.g., firms should not be allowed to sell low-quality items.
   c. The producer of a high-quality good will probably want to offer an extensive warranty.
   d. The government should require *all* firms to offer extensive warranties.

9. Two used car dealerships compete side by side on a main road. The first, Harry's Cars, sells high-quality cars that it carefully inspects and, if necessary, services. It costs Harry's, on average, $8000 to buy and service

each car that it sells. The second dealership, Lew's Motors, sells lower-quality cars. It costs Lew's on average only $5000 for each car that it sells. If consumers knew the quality of the used cars they were buying, they would gladly pay $10,000 on average for cars Harry's sells and pay only $7000 on average for the cars Lew's sells.

Unfortunately, the dealerships are too new to have established reputations, so consumers do not know the quality of each dealership's cars. Consumers shopping at these dealerships figure that they have a 50–50 chance of ending up with a high-quality car, no matter which dealership they go to, and hence are willing to pay $8500 on average for a car.

Harry's has an idea—it will offer a bumper-to-bumper warranty for all the cars it sells. It knows that a warranty lasting Y years will cost $500Y$ on average, and it also knows that if Lew's tries to offer the same warranty, it will cost Lew's $1000Y$ on average.

a. Suppose Harry's offers a one-year warranty on all the cars it sells. Will this generate a credible signal of quality? Will Lew's match the offer, or will it fail to match it so that consumers can correctly assume that because of the warranty, Harry's cars are high quality and hence worth $10,000 on average?

b. What if Harry's offers a two-year warranty on its cars? Will this generate a credible signal of quality? What about a three-year warranty?

c. If you were advising Harry's, how long a warranty would you urge it to offer? Explain why.

10. A firm's short-run revenue is given by $R = 10e - e^2$, where e is the level of effort by a typical worker (all workers are assumed to be identical). A worker chooses his level of effort to maximize his wage net of effort $w - e$ (the per-unit cost of effort is assumed to be 1). Determine the level of effort and the level of profit (revenue less wage paid) for each of the following wage arrangements. Explain why these different principal–agent relationships generate different outcomes.

a. $w = 2$ for $e \geq 1$; otherwise $w = 0$.

b. $w = R/2$.

c. $w = R - 12.5$.

CHAPTER 18

Externalities and Public Goods

In this chapter we study *externalities*—the effects of production and consumption activities not directly reflected in the market—and *public goods*—goods that benefit all consumers, but that the market either undersupplies or does not supply at all. Externalities and public goods are important sources of market failure and thus raise serious public policy questions. For example, how much effluent, if any, should firms be allowed to dump into rivers and streams? How strict should automobile emission standards be? How much money should the government spend on national defense? Education? Basic research? Public television?

When externalities are present, the price of a good need not reflect its social value. As a result, firms may produce too much or too little, so that the market outcome is inefficient. We begin by describing externalities and showing exactly how they create market inefficiencies. We then evaluate remedies; some remedies involve government regulation, while others rely primarily on bargaining among individuals or on the legal right of those adversely affected to sue those who create the externality.

Next, we analyze public goods. The marginal cost of providing a public good to an additional consumer is zero, and people cannot be excluded from consuming it. We distinguish between those goods that are difficult to provide privately and those that could have been provided by the market. We conclude by describing the problem policymakers face when trying to decide how much of a public good to provide.

18.1 Externalities

Externalities can arise between producers, between customers, or between consumers and producers. Externalities can be *negative*—when the action of one party imposes costs on another party—or *positive*—when the action of one party benefits another party.

A negative externality occurs, for example, when a steel plant dumps its waste in a river that fishermen downstream depend on for their daily catch. The more waste the steel plant dumps in the river, the fewer fish will be supported. The firm, however, has no incentive to account for the external costs that it imposes on fishermen when making its production decision. A positive externality occurs when a home owner repaints her house and plants an attractive garden. All the neighbors benefit from this activity, yet the home owner's decision to repaint and landscape probably did not take these benefits into account.

Negative Externalities and Inefficiency

Because externalities are not reflected in market prices, they can be a source of economic inefficiency. To see why, let's take our example of a steel plant dumping waste in a river. Figure 18.1(a) shows the production decision of the steel plant in a competitive market, and Figure 18.1(b) shows the market demand and supply curves, assuming that all steel plants generate similar externalities. We assume that the firm has a fixed-proportions production function, so that it cannot alter its input combinations; effluent can be reduced only by lowering output. We will analyze the nature of the externality in two steps: first when only one steel plant pollutes, and then when all steel plants pollute in the same way.

The price of steel is P_1, at the intersection of the demand and supply curves in Figure 18.1(b). The MC curve in (a) gives a typical steel firm's marginal cost of production. The firm maximizes profit by producing output q_1, at which marginal cost is equal to price (which equals marginal revenue because the firm takes price as given). As the firm's output changes, however, the external cost imposed on fishermen downstream also changes. This external cost is given by the *marginal external cost (MEC) curve* in Figure 18.1(a). The curve is upward sloping for most forms of pollution because as the firm produces additional output and dumps additional effluent in the river, the incremental harm to the fish industry increases.

From a social point of view, the firm produces too much output. The efficient output is the level at which the price of the product is equal to the *mar-*

Figure 18.1 **External Cost** When there are negative externalities, the marginal social cost MSC is higher than the marginal private cost MC. The difference is the marginal external cost MEC. In (a), a profit-maximizing firm produces at q_1, where price is equal to MC. The efficient output is q^*, at which price equals MSC. In (b), the industry competitive output is Q_1, at the intersection of industry supply MC^I and demand D. However, the efficient output Q^* is lower, at the intersection of demand and marginal social cost MSC^I.

ginal social cost of production—the marginal cost of production *plus* the marginal external cost of dumping effluent. In Figure 18.1(a), the marginal social cost curve is obtained by adding marginal cost and marginal external cost for each level of output (i.e., MSC = MC + MEC). The marginal social cost curve MSC intersects the price line at the output q^*. Because only one plant is dumping effluent into the river in this case, the market price of the product is unchanged. However, the firm is producing too much output (q_1 instead of q^*) and generating too much effluent.

Now consider what happens when all steel plants dump their effluent into rivers. In Figure 18.1(b), the MC^I curve is the industry supply curve. The marginal external cost associated with the industry output, MEC^I, is obtained by summing the marginal cost of every person harmed at each level of output. The MSC^I curve represents the sum of the marginal cost of production and the marginal external cost *for all steel firms*. As a result, $MSC^I = MC^I + MEC^I$.

Is industry output efficient when there are externalities? As Figure 18.1(b) shows, the efficient industry output level is the one at which the marginal benefit of an additional unit of output is equal to the marginal social cost. Because the demand curve measures the marginal benefit to consumers, the efficient output is Q^*, at the intersection of the marginal social cost MSC^I and demand D curves. The competitive industry output, however, is at Q_1, the intersection of the demand curve and the supply curve, MC^I. Clearly, industry output is too high.

In our example, each unit of output results in some effluent being dumped. Therefore, whether we are looking at one firm's pollution or the entire industry's, the economic efficiency is the excess production that causes too much effluent to be dumped in the river. The source of the inefficiency is the incorrect pricing of the product. The market price P_1 in Figure 18.1(b) is too low—it reflects the firms' marginal private cost of production, but not the marginal *social* cost. Only at the higher price P^* will steel firms produce the efficient level of output.

What is the cost to society of this inefficiency? For each unit produced above Q^*, the social cost is given by the difference between the marginal social cost and the marginal benefit (the demand curve). As a result, the aggregate social cost is shown in Figure 18.1(b) as the shaded triangle between MSC^I, D, and output Q_1.

Externalities generate long-run as well as short-run inefficiencies. In Chapter 8 we saw that firms enter a competitive industry whenever the price of the product is above the *average cost* of production, and exit whenever price is below average cost. In long-run equilibrium, price is equal to (long-run) average cost. When there are negative externalities, the average private cost of production is less than the average social cost. As a result, some firms remain in the industry even when it would be efficient for them to leave. Thus negative externalities encourage too many firms to remain in the industry.

Positive Externalities and Inefficiency

Externalities can also result in too little production, as the example of home repair and landscaping shows. In Figure 18.2, the horizontal axis measures the home owner's investment (in dollars) in repairs and landscaping. The marginal cost curve for home repair shows the cost of repairs as more work is done on the house; it is horizontal because this cost is unaffected by the amount of repairs. The demand curve D measures the marginal private benefit of the repairs to the home owner. The home owner will choose to invest q_1 in repairs, at the intersection of her demand and marginal cost curves. But repairs generate external benefits to the neighbors, as the *marginal external benefit* curve, MEB, shows. This curve is downward sloping in this example because the marginal benefit is large for a small amount of repair but falls as the repair work becomes extensive.

The marginal social benefit curve MSB is calculated by adding the marginal private benefit and the marginal external benefit at every level of output. In short, $MSB = D + MEB$. The efficient level of output q^*, at which the marginal social benefit of additional repairs is equal to the marginal cost of those repairs, is found at the intersection of the MSB and MC curves. The inefficiency arises because the home owner doesn't capture all the benefits of her investment in repairs and landscaping. As a result, the price P_1 is too high to encourage her to invest in the socially desirable level of house repair. A lower price P^* is required to encourage the efficient level of supply, q^*.

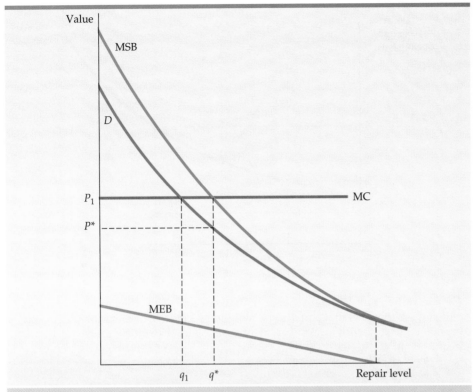

Figure 18.2   External Benefits   When there are positive externalities, marginal social benefits MSB are higher than marginal benefits D. The difference is the marginal external benefit MEB. A self-interested home owner invests q_1 in repairs, determined by the intersection of the marginal benefit curve D and the marginal cost curve MC. The efficient level of repair q^* is higher, and is given by the intersection of the marginal social benefit and marginal cost curves.

Another example of a positive externality is the money that firms spend on research and development (R&D). Often the innovations resulting from research cannot be protected from other firms. Suppose, for example, that a firm designs a new product. If that design can be patented, the firm might earn a large profit by manufacturing and marketing the new product. If the new design can be closely imitated by other firms, however, those firms can compete away some of the developing firm's profit. There is then little reward for doing R&D, and the market is likely to underfund it.

18.2 Ways of Correcting Market Failure

How can the inefficiency resulting from an externality be remedied? If the firm that generates the externality has a fixed-proportions production technology, the externality can be reduced only by encouraging the firm to produce

Figure 18.3 **The Efficient Level of Emissions** The efficient level of factory emissions is the level that equates the marginal social cost of emissions MSC to the benefit associated with lower abatement costs MCA. The efficient level of 12 units is E^*.

less. This can be achieved through an output tax, as we saw in Chapter 8. Fortunately, most firms can substitute among inputs in the production process by altering their choice of technology. For example, a manufacturer can add a scrubber to its smokestack to reduce its emissions.

Consider a firm that sells its output in a competitive market. The firm emits pollutants that damage air quality in a neighborhood. The firm can reduce its emissions, but only at a cost. Figure 18.3 illustrates this. The horizontal axis represents the level of factory emissions and the vertical axis the cost per unit of emissions. To simplify, we assume that the firm's output decision and its emissions decision are independent, and that the firm has already chosen its profit-maximizing output level. The firm is therefore ready to choose its preferred level of emissions. The curve labeled MSC represents the *marginal social cost of emissions*. This social cost curve represents the increased harm associated with the emissions of the factory and is therefore equivalent to the MEC curve described earlier. The MSC curve slopes upward because the *marginal* cost of the externality is higher the more extensive it is. (Evidence from studies of the effects of air and water pollution suggests that small levels of pollutants generate little harm. However, the harm increases substantially as the level of pollutants increases.)

The curve labeled MCA is the *marginal cost of abating emissions*. It measures the additional cost to the firm of installing pollution control equipment. The MCA curve is downward sloping because the marginal cost of reducing emissions is low when the reduction has been slight, and high when it has been substantial. (A slight reduction is inexpensive—the firm can reschedule production so the greatest emissions occur at night, when few people are outside—but substantial reductions require costly changes in the production process.)

Because emissions reduction is costly and offers no direct benefit to the firm, the firm's profit-maximizing level of emissions is 26, the level at which the marginal cost of abatement is zero. The efficient level of emissions, 12 units, is at point E^*, where the marginal social cost of emissions, \$3, is equal to the marginal cost of abating emissions. At E^*, the sum of the firm's abatement costs and of the social costs is minimized. Note that if emissions are lower than E^*, say, E_0, the marginal cost of abating emissions, \$7, is greater than the marginal social cost, \$2, so emissions are too low. However, if the level of emissions is E_1, the marginal social cost, \$4, is greater than the marginal benefit, \$1, so emissions are too high.

We can encourage the firm to reduce emissions to E^* in three ways: emissions standards, emissions fees, and transferable emissions permits.

An Emissions Standard

An *emissions standard* is a legal limit on how much pollutant a firm can emit. If the firm exceeds the limit, it can face monetary and even criminal penalties. In Figure 18.4, the efficient emission standard is 12 units, at point E^*. The firm will be heavily penalized for emissions greater than this.

The standard ensures that the firm produces efficiently. The firm meets the standard by installing pollution abatement equipment. The increased abatement expenditure will cause the firm's average cost curve to rise (by the average cost of abatement). Firms will find it profitable to enter the industry only if the price of the product is greater than the average cost of production plus abatement—the efficient condition for the industry.[1]

An Emissions Fee

An *emissions fee* is a charge levied on each unit of a firm's emissions. A \$3 emissions fee will generate efficient behavior by our factory, as Figure 18.4 shows. With this fee, the firm minimizes its costs by reducing emissions from 26 to 12 units. To see why, note that the first unit of emissions can be reduced (from 26 to 25 units of emissions) at very little cost (the marginal cost of additional abatement is close to zero). Therefore, for very little cost, the firm can avoid paying the \$3 per unit fee. In fact, for all levels of emission above 12 units, the marginal cost of abatement is less than the emissions fee, so it pays to reduce emissions. Below 12 units, however, the marginal cost of abatement is greater than the fee, so the firm will prefer to pay the fee rather than reduce

---

[1] This assumes that the social costs of emissions do not change over time. If they do, the efficient standard will also change.

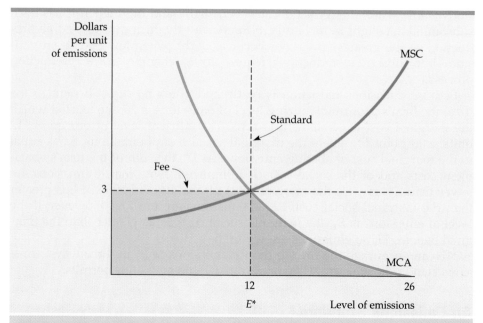

Figure 18.4 **Standards and Fees** The efficient level of emissions at E^* can be achieved either through an emissions fee or an emissions standard. Facing a fee of $3 per unit of emissions, a firm reduces emissions to the point at which the fee is equal to the marginal benefit. The same level of emissions reduction can be achieved with a standard that limits emissions to 12 units.

emissions further. The firm will therefore pay a total fee given by the gray-shaded rectangle and will incur a total abatement cost given by the blue-shaded triangle under the MCA curve to the right of $E = 12$. This cost is less than the fee the firm would pay if it did not reduce its emissions at all.

Standards Versus Fees

The United States has historically relied on standards to regulate emissions. However, other countries, such as Germany, have used fees successfully. Which method is better?

There are important differences between standards and fees when the policymaker has incomplete information and when it is costly to regulate firms' emissions. To understand these differences, let's suppose that because of administrative costs the agency that regulates emissions must charge the same fee or set the same standard for all firms.

First, let's examine the case for fees. Consider two firms that are located so that the marginal social cost of emissions is the same no matter which firm reduces its emissions. Because the firms have different abatement costs, however, their marginal cost of abatement curves are not the same. Figure 18.5 shows why emissions fees are preferable to standards in this case. MCA_1 and

MCA_2 represent the marginal cost of abatement curves for the two firms. Each firm initially generates 14 units of emissions. Suppose we want to reduce total emissions by 14 units. Figure 18.5 shows that the cheapest way to do this is to have Firm 1 reduce emissions by 6 units and Firm 2 reduce emissions by 8 units. With these reductions, both firms have marginal costs of abatement of $3. But consider what happens if the regulatory agency asks both firms to reduce their emissions by 7 units. Then the marginal cost of abatement of Firm 1 increases from $3 to $3.75, and the marginal cost of abatement of Firm 2 decreases from $3 to $2.50. This cannot be cost-minimizing because the second firm can reduce emissions more cheaply than the first. Only when the marginal cost of abatement is equal for both firms will emissions be reduced by 14 units at minimum cost.

Now we can see why an emissions fee ($3) might be preferable to an emissions standard (7 units). With a $3 emissions fee, Firm 1 will reduce emissions by 6 units and Firm 2 by 8 units, the efficient outcome. By contrast, with the emissions standard, Firm 1 incurs additional abatement costs given by the green-shaded area between 7 and 8 units of emission. But Firm 2 enjoys reduced abatement costs given by the purple-shaded area between 6 and 7 units of emission. Clearly, the added abatement costs to Firm 1 are larger than the

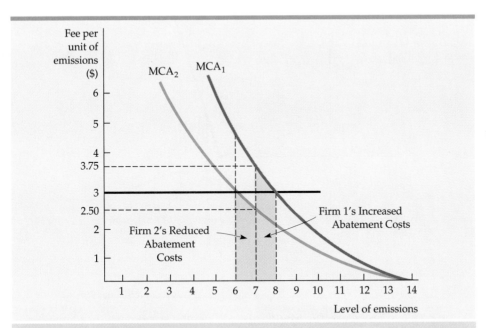

Figure 18.5 **The Case for Fees** With limited information, a policymaker may be faced with the choice of either a single emissions fee or a single emissions standard for all firms. The fee of $3 achieves a total emissions level of 14 units more cheaply than a 7-unit-per-firm emissions standard. With the fee, the firm with a lower abatement cost curve (Firm 2) reduces emissions more than the firm with a higher cost curve (Firm 1).

reduced costs to Firm 2. The emissions fee thus achieves the same level of emissions at a lower cost than the equal per-firm emissions standard.

In general, fees can be preferable to standards for several reasons. First, when standards must be assessed equally for all firms, fees achieve the same emissions reduction at a lower cost. Second, fees give a firm a strong incentive to install new equipment that would allow it to reduce emissions *even further*. Suppose the standard requires that each firm reduce its emission by 6 units, from 14 to 8. Firm 1 is considering installing new emissions devices that would lower its marginal cost of abatement from MCA_1 to MCA_2. If the equipment is relatively inexpensive, the firm will install it because this equipment would lower the cost of meeting the standard. However, a $3 emission fee would provide a greater incentive for the firm to reduce emissions. With the fee, not only will the firm's cost of abatement be lower on the first 6 units of reduction, it will also be cheaper to reduce emissions by 2 more units (because the emissions fee is greater than the marginal abatement cost for emissions levels between 6 and 8).

Now let's examine the case for standards by looking at Figure 18.6. The marginal social cost curve is very steep, while the marginal cost of abatement

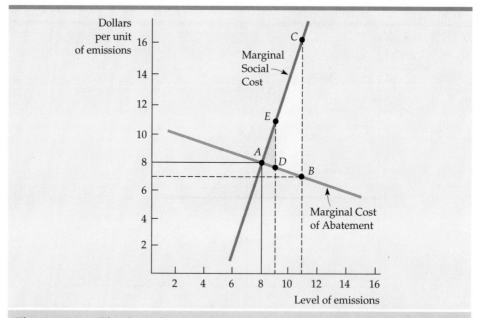

Figure 18.6   The Case for Standards   When the government has limited information about the costs and benefits of pollution abatement, either a standard or a fee may be preferable. The standard is preferable when the marginal social cost curve is steep and the marginal abatement cost curve is relatively flat. Here a 12.5 percent error in setting the standard leads to extra social costs of triangle *ADE*. The same percentage error in setting a fee would result in excess costs of *ABC*.

is relatively flat. The efficient emissions fee is $8. But suppose that because of limited information a lower fee of $7 is charged (this amounts to a 1/8 or 12.5 percent reduction). Because the MCA curve is flat, the firm's emissions will be increased from 8 to 11 units. This lowers the firm's abatement costs somewhat, but because the MSC curve is steep, there will be substantial additional social costs. The increase in social costs, less the savings in abatement costs, is given by the entire shaded (light and dark) triangle *ABC*.

What happens if a comparable error is made in setting the standard? The efficient standard is 8 units of emissions. But suppose the standard is relaxed by 12.5 percent, from 8 to 9 units. This will lead to an increase in social costs and a decrease in abatement costs as before. But the net increase in social costs, given by the small triangle *ADE*, is much smaller than before.

This example illustrates the difference between standards and fees. When the marginal social cost curve is relatively steep and the marginal cost of abatement curve relatively flat, the cost of not reducing emissions is high, and a standard is preferable to a fee. With incomplete information, standards offer more certainty about emissions levels but leave the costs of abatement uncertain. Fees, on the other hand, offer certainty about the costs of abatement but leave the reduction of emissions levels uncertain. Which policy is preferable depends, therefore, on the nature of uncertainty and on the shapes of the cost curves.

Transferable Emissions Permits

Suppose we want to reduce emissions, but because of uncertainty, we don't want to rely on an emissions fee. We also want to avoid imposing high costs on the firms that reduce their emissions the most. We can reach these goals by using *transferable emissions permits*. Under this system, each firm must have a permit to generate emissions. Each permit specifies exactly how much the firm is allowed to emit. Any firm that generates emissions that are not allowed by permit is subject to substantial monetary sanctions. Permits are allocated among firms, with the number of permits chosen to achieve the desired maximum level of emissions. The permits are marketable—they can be bought and sold.

Under the transferable emissions permit system, the firms least able to reduce emissions are those that purchase permits. Thus, suppose the two firms in Figure 18.5 were given permits to emit up to 7 units. Firm 1, facing a relatively high marginal cost of abatement, would pay up to $3.75 to buy a permit for one unit of emissions, but the value of that permit is only $2.50 to Firm 2. Firm 2 should therefore sell its permit to Firm 1 for a price between $2.50 and $3.75.

If there are enough firms and permits, a competitive market for the permits will develop. In market equilibrium, the price of a permit equals the marginal cost of abatement for all firms; otherwise a firm will find it advantageous to buy more permits. The level of emissions chosen by the government will be achieved at minimum cost. Those firms with relatively low marginal cost of abatement curves will be reducing emissions the most, and those firms with relatively high marginal cost of abatement curves will be buying more permits and reducing emissions the least.

Marketable emissions permits create a market for externalities. This market approach is appealing because it combines some of the advantageous features of a system of standards with the cost advantages of a fee system. The agency that administers the system determines the total number of permits and therefore the total amount of emissions, just as a system of standards would do. But the marketability of the permits allows pollution abatement to be achieved at minimum cost, just as a system of fees would do.[2]

EXAMPLE 18.1 **The Costs and Benefits of Reduced Sulfur Dioxide Emissions**

In 1968 Philadelphia imposed air quality regulations that limited the maximum allowable sulfur content in fuel oil to 1.0 percent or less. This regulation decreased sulfur dioxide levels in the air substantially—from 0.10 parts per million (ppm) in 1968 to below 0.025 ppm in 1973. This improved air quality led to better human health, less damage to materials, and higher property values. But these improvements had a cost: Industrial, manufacturing, commercial, and residential fuel users had to alter their fuel choices and to install pollution-control equipment to abate the pollution. Was the benefit—the reduction in social cost due to the abatement—worth the additional abatement cost? A cost–benefit study of reductions in sulfur dioxide emissions provides some answers.[3]

In Philadelphia the emissions reductions necessitated increased costs of converting from coal and oil to gas to comply with the air quality regulation. Emissions control equipment also had to be added to manufacturing processes to ensure that fuels were used efficiently. Figure 18.7 shows the marginal social cost and the marginal cost to the firm of reduced emissions. Note that the marginal abatement cost jumps whenever new capital-intensive pollution control equipment is needed to improve fuel efficiency.

The benefits of reduced sulfur dioxide emissions can be divided into three parts: (1) reductions in illness and death from diseases like cancer, bronchitis, pneumonia, emphysema, asthma, and the common cold; (2) reductions in materials costs caused by corrosion of metals, stone, and paint; and (3) improvements in visibility and other aesthetic values.

---

[2] With limited information and costly monitoring, a marketable permit system is not always ideal. For example, if the total number of permits is chosen incorrectly and the marginal cost of abatement rises sharply for some firms, a permit system could drive those firms out of business by imposing high abatement costs. (This would also be a problem for fees.) For further discussion of fees, standards, and transferable pollution permits, see William J. Baumol and Wallace E. Oates, *Economics, Environmental Policy, and the Quality of Life* (Englewood Cliffs, N.J.: Prentice-Hall, 1979).

[3] The study is by Thomas R. Irvin, "A Cost-Benefit Analysis of Sulfur Dioxide Abatement Regulations in Philadelphia," *Business Economics* (Sept. 1977): 12–20.

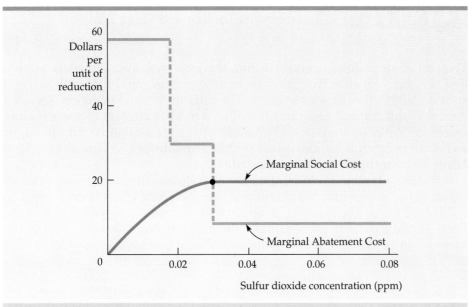

Figure 18.7   Sulfur Dioxide Emissions Reductions   The efficient sulfur dioxide concentration equates the marginal abatement cost to the marginal social cost. Here the marginal abatement cost curve is a series of steps, each representing the use of a different abatement technology.

Because benefits are the negative of social costs, we can obtain information about the marginal social cost curve by asking how each of these three types of benefits decreases in value when sulfur dioxide concentrations are increased. For very low concentrations, evidence suggests little health, material, or aesthetic effects. But for moderate concentrations of sulfur dioxide, studies of respiratory diseases, corrosion of materials, and lost visibility suggest that marginal social costs are positive and relatively constant. Thus the marginal social cost curve is shown to rise initially and then become horizontal.

The efficient level of reduced sulfur dioxide emissions is given by the number of ppm of sulfur dioxide at which the marginal cost of reduced emissions is equal to the marginal social cost. We can see from Figure 18.7 that this level is approximately 0.0275 ppm. The marginal social cost and marginal abatement cost curves intersect at a point where the marginal abatement cost curve is sharply decreasing owing to the introduction of expensive desulfurization equipment. Because 0.0275 ppm is slightly below the emissions level achieved in 1973 by the regulation, we can conclude that the regulation improved economic efficiency. In fact, given that sulfur dioxide levels were above 0.0275 ppm for most of the period, it appears that the regulations were not stringent enough to achieve the most efficient outcome.

EXAMPLE 18.2 **Emissions Trading and Clean Air**

The cost of air pollution control during the 1980s was approximately $18 billion per year.[4] An effective emissions trading system could reduce those costs substantially in the decades to come. The Environmental Protection Agency's "bubble" and "offset" programs provided a modest attempt to use a trading system to lower cleanup costs. A bubble allows an individual firm to adjust its pollution controls for individual sources of pollutants, as long as a *total pollutant limit* for the firm is not exceeded.

In theory a bubble could be used to set pollutant limits for many firms or for an entire geographic region; in practice, however, it has been applied to individual firms. The result is, in effect, that "permits" are traded within the firm—if one part of the firm could reduce its emissions, another part of the firm would be allowed to emit more. Abatement cost savings associated with the EPA's program of 42 bubbles have been approximately $300 million since 1979.

Under the offset program, new sources of emissions may be located in regions in which air quality standards have not been met, but only if they offset their new emissions by reducing emissions from existing sources at least as much. Offsets can be obtained by internal trading, but external trading among firms is also allowed. Over 2000 offset transactions have occurred since 1976.

Because of their limited natures, the bubble and offset programs substantially understate the potential gain from a broad-based emissions trading program. In one study, the cost of achieving an 85 percent reduction in hydrocarbon emissions in all of the DuPont plants in the United States was estimated under three alternative policies: (1) each source at each plant must reduce emissions by 85 percent; (2) each plant must reduce its overall emissions by 85 percent; only internal trading is possible; and (3) total emissions at all plants must be reduced by 85 percent, and both internal and external trading are possible.[5] When no trading was allowed, the cost of emissions reduction was $105.7 million. Internal trading reduced the cost to $42.6 million. Allowing for both external and internal trading reduced the cost further to $14.6 million.

Clearly, the potential cost savings from an effective transferable emissions program can be substantial. This may explain why Congress focused on transferable permits as a way of dealing with "acid rain" in the 1990 Clean Air Act. Acid rain is created when sulfur dioxide and nitrogen oxide pollution travels through the atmosphere and returns to earth as sulfuric and nitric acids. These acids can be extremely harmful to people, animals, vegetation, and buildings.

---

[4] See Robert W. Hahn and Gordon L. Hester, "The Market for Bads: EPA's Experience with Emissions Trading," *Regulation* (1987): 48–53.

[5] M.T. Maloney and Bruce Yandle, "Bubbles and Efficiency: Cleaner Air at Lower Cost," *Regulation* (May/June 1980): 49–52.

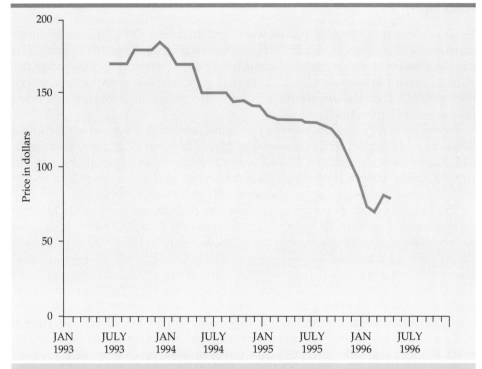

Figure 18.8   Price of Tradeable Emissions Permits   The price of tradeable permits for sulfur dioxide emissions declined from 1993 to 1996 due in part to the reduced cost of emissions reductions.

The government has authorized a permit system to reduce sulfur dioxide emissions by 10 million tons and nitrogen oxide emissions by 2.5 million tons by the year 2000.

Under the plan, each tradeable permit allows a maximum of one ton of sulfur dioxide to be released into the air. Electric utilities and other polluting entities are allocated permits in proportion to their current level of emissions. Companies can make the capital investments necessary to reduce emissions, perhaps selling their excess permits, or they can buy permits and avoid having to make these costly emission-reducing investments.

In the early 1990s, economists expected these permits to trade for $300 or more each. In fact, during 1993, prices were below $200, and, as Figure 18.8 shows, by 1996 they fell to below $100. The reason is that reducing sulfur dioxide emissions has turned out to be less costly than anticipated. The price of low-sulfur coal has dropped considerably, and many electric utilities have taken advantage of this to reduce emissions.

Recycling

To the extent that the disposal of waste products involves no cost to either consumers or producers, society will dispose of too much waste material. The overutilization of virgin materials and the underutilization of recycled materials will result in a market failure that may require government intervention. Fortunately, given the appropriate incentive to recycle products, this market failure can be corrected.[6]

To see how recycling incentives can work, consider a typical household's decision with respect to the disposal of glass containers. In many communities, households are charged a fixed annual fee for trash disposal. As a result, these households can dispose of glass and other garbage at very low cost—only the time and effort to put the materials in a trash receptacle.

The low cost of disposal creates a divergence between the private and the social cost of disposal. The marginal private cost of disposal, which is the cost to the household of throwing out the glass, is likely to be constant (independent of the amount of disposal) for low to moderate levels of disposal, and then to increase for large disposal levels involving additional shipping and dump charges. In contrast, the social cost of disposal includes the harm to the environment from littering as well as the injuries caused by sharp glass objects. Marginal social cost is likely to increase, in part because the marginal private cost is increasing, and in part because the environmental and aesthetic costs of littering are likely to increase sharply as the level of disposal increases.

Both cost curves are shown in Figure 18.9. In the figure, the horizontal axis measures, from left to right, the amount of scrap material m that the household disposes, up to a maximum of 12 pounds per week. Consequently, the amount recycled can be read from right to left. As the amount of scrap disposal increases, the marginal private cost, MC, increases, but at a much lower rate than the marginal social cost MSC.

Recycling of containers can be accomplished by a municipality or a private firm that arranges for collection, consolidation, and processing of materials. The marginal cost of recycling is likely to increase as the amount of recycling grows, in part because collection, separation, and cleaning costs grow at an increasing rate. The marginal cost of recycling curve, MCR, in Figure 18.9 is best read from right to left. Thus, when there is 12 pounds of disposed material, there is no recycling and the marginal cost is zero. As the amount of disposal decreases, the amount of recycling increases, and the marginal cost of recycling increases.

The efficient amount of recycling occurs at the point at which the marginal cost of recycling, MCR, is equal to the marginal *social* cost of disposal, MSC. As Figure 18.9 shows, the efficient amount of scrap for disposal m^* is less than the amount that will arise in a private market, m_1.

Why not utilize a disposal fee, a disposal standard, or even transferable disposal permits to resolve this externality? Any of these policies can help in

---

[6] Even without market intervention, some recycling will occur if the price of virgin material is sufficiently high. For example, recall from Chapter 2 that when the price of copper is high, there is more recycling of scrap copper.

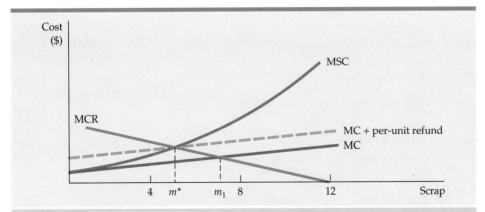

Figure 18.9   The Efficient Amount of Recycling   The efficient amount of recycling of scrap material is the amount that equates the marginal social cost of scrap disposal, MSC, to the marginal cost of recycling, MCR. The efficient amount of scrap for disposal m^* is less than the amount that will arise in a private market, m_1.

theory, but they are not easy to put into practice and are rarely used. For example, a disposal fee is difficult to implement because it would be very costly for a community to sort through trash to separate and then to collect glass materials. Pricing and billing for the scrap disposal would also be expensive, since the weight and composition of materials would affect the social cost of the scrap and, therefore, the appropriate price to be charged.

One policy solution that has been used with some success to encourage recycling is the *refundable deposit*.[7] Under a refundable deposit system an initial deposit is paid to the store owner when the glass container product is purchased. The deposit is refunded if and when the container is returned to the store or to a recycling center. Refundable deposits create a desirable incentive: the per-unit refund can be chosen so that households (or firms) recycle more material.

From an individual's point of view, the refundable deposit creates an additional private cost of disposal—the opportunity cost of failing to obtain a refund. As shown in Figure 18.9, with the higher cost of disposal, the individual will reduce disposal and increase recycling to the optimal social level m^*.

A similar analysis applies at the industry level. Figure 18.10 shows a downward sloping market demand for glass containers, D. The supply of virgin glass containers is given by S_v and the supply of recycled glass by S_r. The market supply S is the horizontal sum of these two curves. As a result, the market price of glass is P, and the equilibrium supply of recycled glass is M_1.

---

[7] See Tom Tietenberg, *Environmental and Natural Resource Economics* (Chicago: Scott, Foresman, 1988), chap. 8, for a general discussion of recycling, and Richard Porter, "A Social Benefit-Cost Analysis of Mandatory Deposits on Beverage Containers," *Journal of Environmental Economics and Management* (1978): 351–366, for an analysis of mandatory deposit systems.

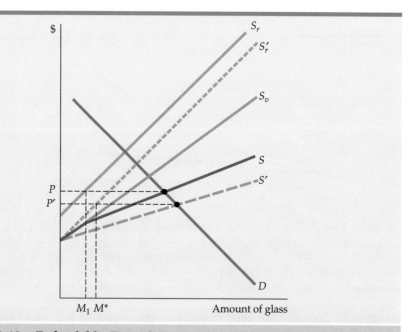

Figure 18.10   Refundable Deposits   Initially equilibrium in the market for glass containers involves a price P and a supply of recycled glass M_1. By raising the relative cost of disposal and encouraging recycling, the refundable deposit increases the supply of recycled glass from S_r to S_r' and the aggregate supply of glass from S to S'. The price of glass then falls to P', the quantity of recycled glass increases to M^*, and the amount of disposed glass decreases.

By raising the relative cost of disposal and encouraging recycling, the refundable deposit increases the supply of recycled glass from S_r to S_r', the aggregate supply increases from S to S', and the price of glass falls to P'. As a result, the quantity of recycled glass increases to M^*, which means a decrease in the amount of disposed glass.

The refundable deposit scheme has another advantage—a market for recycled products is created. In many communities public or private firms as well as private individuals specialize in collecting and returning recyclable materials. As this market becomes larger and more efficient, the demand for recycled rather than virgin materials increases, therefore increasing the benefit to the environment.

E X A M P L E   1 8 . 3   **Regulating Municipal Solid Wastes**

By 1990 the average resident of Los Angeles was generating about 6.4 pounds of solid waste per day, and residents of other large American cities were not far behind. By contrast, residents of Tokyo, Paris, Hong Kong, and Rome generated 3 pounds, 2.4 pounds, 1.9 pounds, and 1.5 pounds, respectively.[8] Some of these differences are due to variations in consumption levels, but most are due to the efforts that many other countries have made to encourage recycling. In the United States, only about 25 percent of aluminum, 23 percent of paper, and 8.5 percent of glass scrap are recycled.

A number of policy proposals have been introduced to encourage recycling in the United States. The first is the refundable deposit described above. A second policy is a *curbside charge*, in which communities charge individuals a fee for refuse disposal that is proportional to the weight (or the volume) of the refuse. To encourage separation of recyclable materials, all separable glass materials are collected for free. Curbside charges encourage recycling, but they fail to discourage consumption of products that might require recycling.

A third alternative is to require the *mandatory separation* of recyclable materials such as glass. Random spot checks with substantial penalties for violations are required to make the system effective. Mandatory separation is perhaps the least desirable of the three alternatives, not only because it is difficult to implement, but also because individuals, if the cost of separation is sufficiently high, may be encouraged to shift to alternative containers such as plastic, which are environmentally damaging and which cannot readily be recycled.

The potential effectiveness of these three policies is illustrated by a recent analysis that focused on the mix between glass and plastic. Consumers were assumed to have varying preferences, with half preferring glass and half preferring plastic, for products that are otherwise identical in price, quantity, and quality. Without any incentive to recycle, a 50-50 percent division between glass and plastic would result. From a social perspective, however, greater use of recyclable glass would be preferred.

Mandatory separation fails as a policy in this case—the cost of separation is so high that the percentage of glass container materials purchased actually falls to 40 percent. A curbside charge does much better—it leads to a 72.5 percent use of recyclable glass. Finally, a refundable deposit system does best, with 78.9 percent of consumers purchasing recyclable glass containers.

A recent case in Perkasie, Pennsylvania, shows that recycling programs can indeed be effective. Prior to implementation of a program combining all three of the economic incentives just described, the total amount of unseparated solid waste was 2573 tons per year. When the program was implemented this amount fell to within 1038 tons, a 59 percent reduction. As a result, the town saved $90,000 per year in disposal costs.

18.3 Externalities and Property Rights

We have seen how government regulation can deal with the inefficiencies that arise from externalities. Emissions fees and transferable emissions permits work because they change a firm's incentives—forcing it to take into account

---

[8] This example is based on Peter S. Menell, "Beyond the Throwaway Society: An Incentive Approach to Regulating Municipal Solid Waste," *Ecology Law Quarterly* (1990): 655–739.

the external costs that it imposes. But government regulation is not the only way to deal with externalities. In this section we show that in some circumstances inefficiencies can be eliminated through private bargaining among the affected parties, or by a legal system in which parties can sue to recover the damages they suffer.

Property Rights

Property rights are the legal rules that describe what people or firms may do with their property. When people have property rights to land, for example, they may build on it or sell it and are protected from interference by others.

To see why property rights are important, let's return to our example of the firm that dumps effluent into the river. We assumed that it had a property right to use the river to dispose of its waste, and that the fishermen did not have a property right to "effluent-free" water. As a result, the firm had no incentive to include the cost of effluent in its production calculations. In other words, the firm externalized the costs generated by the effluent. Suppose the fishermen owned the river, i.e., had a property right to clean water. Then they could demand that the firm pay them for the right to dump effluent. The firm would either cease production or pay the costs associated with the effluent. These costs would be internalized, and an efficient allocation of resources could be achieved.

Bargaining and Economic Efficiency

Economic efficiency can be achieved without government intervention when the externality affects relatively few parties and when property rights are well specified. To see how this might arise, let's consider a numerical version of the effluent example. Suppose the steel factory's effluent reduces the fishermen's profit. As Table 18.1 shows, the factory can install a filter system to reduce its effluent, or the fishermen can pay for the installation of a water treatment plant.[9]

The efficient solution maximizes the joint profit of the factory and the fishermen. This occurs when the factory installs a filter and the fishermen do not

Table 18.1 Profits Under Alternative Emissions Choices (Daily)			
	Factory's Profit ($)	**Fishermen's Profit ($)**	**Total Profit ($)**
No filter, no treatment plant	500	100	600
Filter, no treatment plant	300	500	800
No filter, treatment plant	500	200	700
Filter, treatment plant	300	300	600

---

[9] For a more extensive discussion of a variant of this example, see Robert Cooter and Thomas Ulen, *Law and Economics* (Glenview, IL: Scott-Foresman, 1997), chap. 4.

Table 18.2 Bargaining with Alternative Property Rights		
	Right to Dump	**Right to Clean Water**
No cooperation		
Profit of factory	$500	$300
Profit of fishermen	$200	$500
Cooperation		
Profit of factory	$550	$300
Profit of fishermen	$250	$500

build a treatment plant. Let's see how alternative property rights lead these two parties to negotiate different solutions.

Suppose the factory has the property right to dump effluent into the river. Initially, the fishermen's profit is $100, and the factory's is $500. By installing a treatment plant, the fishermen can increase their profit to $200, so that the joint profit without cooperation is $700 ($500 + $200). Moreover, the fishermen are willing to pay the factory up to $300 to install a filter ($300 is the difference between the $500 profit with a filter and the $200 profit without cooperation). Because the factory loses only $200 in profit by installing a filter, it will be willing to do so if it is more than compensated for its loss. The gain to both parties by cooperating is equal to $100 in this case (the $300 gain to the fishermen less the $200 cost of a filter).

Suppose the factory and the fishermen agree to split this gain equally by having the fishermen pay the factory $250 to install the filter. As Table 18.2 shows, this bargaining solution achieves the efficient outcome. Under the column "Right to Dump," we see that without cooperation the fishermen earn a profit of $200 and the factory $500. With cooperation, the profit of both increases by $50.

Now suppose the fishermen are given the property right to clean water, which requires the factory to install the filter. The factory earns a profit of $300 and the fishermen $500. Because neither party can be made better off by bargaining, the initial outcome is efficient.

This analysis applies to all situations in which property rights are well specified. *When parties can bargain without cost and to their mutual advantage, the resulting outcome will be efficient, regardless of how the property rights are specified.* The italicized proposition is called the *Coase theorem*, in honor of Ronald Coase, who did much to develop it.[10]

Costly Bargaining—The Role of Strategic Behavior

Bargaining can be time consuming and costly, especially when property rights are not clearly specified. Then neither party is sure how hard to bargain before the other party will agree to a settlement. In our example, both parties knew

---

[10] See Ronald Coase, "The Problem of Social Cost," *Journal of Law and Economics* 3 (1960): 1–44.

that the bargaining process had to settle on a payment between $200 and $300. If the parties were unsure of the property rights, however, the fishermen might be willing to pay only $100, and the bargaining process would break down.

Bargaining can also break down even when communication and monitoring are costless, if both parties believe they can obtain larger gains. One party makes a demand for a large share and refuses to bargain, assuming incorrectly that the other party will eventually concede. This *strategic behavior* can lead to an inefficient, noncooperative outcome. Suppose the factory has the right to emit effluent and claims that it will not install a filter unless it receives $300, and its offer is final. The fishermen offer to pay at most $250, however, believing that eventually the factory will agree to the "fair" solution. In this situation, an agreement may never be reached, especially if one or both parties want to earn a reputation for tough bargaining.

A Legal Solution—Suing for Damages

In many situations involving externalities, a party that is harmed (the victim) by another has the legal right to sue. If successful, the victim can recover monetary damages equal to the harm it has been caused. A suit for damages is different from an emissions or effluent fee because the victim, not the government, is paid.

To see how the potential for a lawsuit can lead to an efficient outcome, let's reexamine our fishermen–factory example. Suppose first that the fishermen are given the right to clean water (meaning that the factory is responsible for harm to the fishermen *if* the factory does not install a filter). The harm to the fishermen in this case is $400 (the difference between the profit that the fishermen make when there is no effluent [$500] and their profit when there is effluent [$100]). The factory has the following options:

1. Do not install filter, pay damages: Profit = $100 ($500 − $400)
2. Install filter, avoid damages: Profit = $300 ($500 − $200)

The factory will find it advantageous to install a filter, which is substantially cheaper than paying damages, and the efficient outcome will be achieved.

An efficient outcome (with a different division of profits) will also be achieved if the factory is given the property right to emit effluent. Under the law, the fishermen would have the legal right to require the factory to install the filter, but they would have to pay the factory for its $200 lost profit (not for the cost of the filter). This leaves the fishermen three options:

1. Put in a treatment plant: Profit = $200
2. Have factory put in a filter, but pay damages: Profit = $300 ($500 − $200)
3. Do not put in treatment plant or require a filter: Profit = $100

The fishermen earn the highest profit if they take the second option; they will require the factory to put in a filter but compensate the factory $200 for its lost profit. Just as in the situation in which the fishermen had the right to clean water, this outcome is efficient because the filter has been installed. Note, however, that the $300 profit is substantially less than the $500 profit that the fishermen get when they have a right to clean water.

This example shows that a suit for damages eliminates the need for bargaining because it specifies the consequences of the choices that the parties have to make. Giving the party that is harmed the right to recover damages from the injuring party ensures an efficient outcome.[11]

EXAMPLE 18.4   **The Coase Theorem at Work**

The Coase theorem applies to governments as well as to people, as a September 1987 cooperative agreement between New York City and New Jersey illustrates.

For many years garbage spilling from waterfront trash facilities from New York harbor had adversely affected the quality of water along the New Jersey shore and occasionally littered the beaches. One of the worst instances occurred on August 13–15, 1987, when more than 200 tons of garbage, including syringes and crack-cocaine vials, formed a 50-mile-long slick off the New Jersey shore.

In this situation New Jersey had the right to clean beaches and could have sued New York City to recover damages associated with garbage spills. New Jersey could have also asked the court to grant an injunction that would have required New York City to stop using its trash facilities until the problem was removed.

But New Jersey wanted cleaner beaches, not simply the recovery of damages. And New York wanted to be able to operate its trash facility. As a result, there was room for mutually beneficial exchange. After two weeks of negotiations, New York and New Jersey reached a settlement. New Jersey agreed not to bring a lawsuit against the city. New York City agreed to use special boats and other floatation devices to contain spills that might arise from Staten Island and Brooklyn. It also agreed to create a monitoring team to survey all trash facilities and shut down those that failed to comply. At the same time, New Jersey officials were allowed unlimited access to New York City's trash facilities to monitor the effectiveness of the program.

18.4 Common Property Resources

Occasionally externalities arise when resources can be used without payment. *Common property resources* are those to which anyone has free access. As a result, they are likely to be overutilized. Air and water are the two most common

---

[11] When information is imperfect, however, suing for damages may lead to inefficient outcomes.

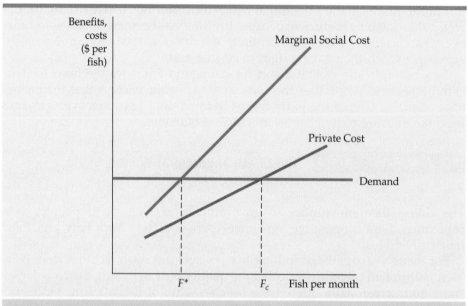

Figure 18.11 **Common Property Resources** When a common property re-source, such as a fishery, is accessible to all, the resource is used up to the point F_c at which the private cost is equal to the additional revenue generated. This usage exceeds the efficient level F^* at which the marginal social cost of using the resource is equal to the marginal benefit (as given by the demand curve).

examples of these resources. Other examples include fish, animal populations, mineral exploration, and extraction. Let's look at some of the inefficiencies that can occur when resources are common property rather than privately owned.

Consider a large lake with trout, to which an unlimited number of fisher-men have access. Each fisherman fishes up to the point at which the marginal revenue from fishing (or the marginal value, if fishing is for sport instead of profit) is equal to the cost. But the lake is a common property resource, and no fisherman has the incentive to take into account how his fishing affects the opportunities of others. As a result, the fisherman's private cost understates the true cost to society because more fishing reduces the stock of fish, mak-ing less available for others.[12] This leads to an inefficiency—too many fish are caught.

Figure 18.11 illustrates this. Suppose that the fish catch is sufficiently small relative to demand, so that fishermen take the price of fish as given. Suppose also that someone can control the number of fishermen that have access to the lake. The efficient level of fish per month F^* is determined at the point at which the marginal benefit from fish caught is equal to the marginal social cost. The marginal benefit is the price taken from the demand curve. The mar-

---

[12] We made a similar argument in our discussion of depletable resources in Section 15.7.

ginal social cost is shown in the diagram to include not only the private operating costs but also the social cost of depleting the stock of fish.

Now compare the efficient outcome with what happens when the lake is common property. Then, the marginal external costs are not taken into account, and each fisherman fishes until there is no longer any profit to be made. When only F^* fish are caught, the revenue from fishing is greater than the cost, and there is a profit to be earned by fishing more. Entry into the fishing business occurs until the point at which the price is equal to the marginal cost, point F_c in Figure 18.11. But, at F_c, too many fish will be caught.

There is a relatively simple solution to the common property resource problem—let a single owner manage the resource. The owner will set a fee for use of the resource that is equal to the marginal cost of depleting the stock of fish. Facing the payment of this fee, fishermen in the aggregate will no longer find it profitable to catch more than F^* fish. Unfortunately, most common property resources are vast, and single ownership may not be practical. Then, government ownership or direct government regulation may be needed.

EXAMPLE 18.5 Crawfish Fishing in Louisiana

In recent years, crawfish has become a popular restaurant item. In 1950, for example, the annual crawfish harvest in the Atchafalaya river basin in Louisiana was just over 1 million pounds. By 1990 it had grown to nearly 30 million pounds. Because most crawfish grow in ponds to which fishermen have unlimited access, a common property resource problem has arisen—too many crawfish have been trapped, causing the crawfish population to fall far below the efficient level.

How serious is the problem? Specifically, what is the social cost of unlimited access to fishermen? The answer can be found by estimating the private cost of trapping crawfish, the marginal social cost, and the demand for crawfish. Figure 18.12 shows portions of the relevant curves.[13] Private cost is upward-sloping because as the catch increases, so does the additional effort that must be made to obtain it. The demand curve is downward sloping but elastic because other shellfish are close substitutes for crawfish.

We can find the efficient crawfish catch graphically or algebraically. To do so, let F represent the catch of crawfish in millions of pounds per year (shown on the horizontal axis), and let C represent cost in dollars per pound (shown on the vertical axis). In the region where the various curves intersect, the three curves in the graph are as follows:

Demand:	$C = 0.401 - 0.0064F$
Marginal social cost:	$C = -5.645 + 0.6509F$
Private cost:	$C = -0.357 + 0.0573F$

---

[13] This example was based on Frederick W. Bell, "Mitigating the Tragedy of the Commons," *Southern Economic Journal* 52 (1986): 653–664.

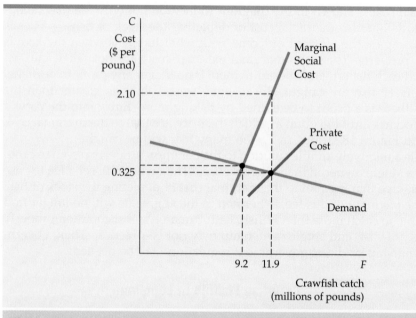

Figure 18.12   Crawfish as a Common Property Resource   Because crawfish are reared in ponds to which fishermen have unlimited access, they are a common property resource. The efficient level of fishing occurs when the marginal benefit is equal to the marginal social cost. However, the actual level of fishing occurs at the point at which the price for crawfish is equal to the private cost of fishing. The shaded area represents the social cost of the common property resource.

The efficient crawfish catch of 9.2 million pounds, which equates demand to marginal social cost, is shown as the intersection of the two curves. The actual catch, 11.9 million pounds, is determined by equating demand to private cost and is shown as the intersection of those two curves. The yellow-shaded triangle in the figure measures the social cost of free access. This represents the excess of social cost above the private benefit of fishing summed from the efficient level (where demand is equal to marginal social cost) to the actual level (where demand is equal to private cost). In this case, the social cost is approximated by the area of a triangle with a base of 2.7 million pounds (11.9 − 9.2), and a height of $1.775 ($2.10 − $0.325), or $2,396,000. Note that by regulating the ponds—limiting access or limiting the size of the catch—this social cost could be avoided.

18.5 Public Goods

We have seen that externalities, including common property resources, create market inefficiencies that sometimes warrant government regulation. When, if ever, should governments replace private firms as the producer of goods and services? In this section we describe a set of conditions under which the private market either may not provide a good at all or may not price it properly once it is available.

Public goods have two characteristics: They are *nonrival* and *nonexclusive*. A good is *nonrival* if for any given level of production, the marginal cost of providing it to an additional consumer is zero. For most goods that are provided privately, the marginal cost of producing more of the good is positive. But for some goods, additional consumers do not add to cost. Consider the use of a highway during a period of low traffic volume. Because the highway already exists and there is no congestion, the additional cost of driving on it is zero. Or consider the use of a lighthouse by a ship. Once the lighthouse is built and functioning, its use by an additional ship adds nothing to its running costs. Finally, consider public television. Clearly, the cost of one more viewer is zero.

Most goods are rival in consumption. For example, when you buy furniture, you have ruled out the possibility that someone else can buy it. Goods that are rival must be allocated among individuals. Goods that are nonrival can be made available to everyone without affecting any individual's opportunity for consuming them.

A good is *nonexclusive* if people cannot be excluded from consuming it. As a consequence, it is difficult or impossible to charge people for using nonexclusive goods—the goods can be enjoyed without direct payment. One example of a nonexclusive good is national defense. Once a nation has provided for its national defense, all citizens enjoy its benefits. A lighthouse and public television are also examples of nonexclusive goods.

Nonexclusive goods need not be national in character. If a state or city eradicates an agricultural pest, all farmers and consumers benefit. It would be virtually impossible to exclude a particular farmer from the benefits of the program. Automobiles are exclusive (as well as rival). If a dealer sells a new car to one consumer, then the dealer has excluded other individuals from buying the car.

Some goods are exclusive but nonrival. For example, in periods of low traffic, travel on a bridge is nonrival because an additional car on the bridge does not lower the speed of other cars. But bridge travel is exclusive because bridge authorities can keep people from using it. A television signal is another example. Once a signal is broadcast, the marginal cost of making the broadcast available to another user is zero, so the good is nonrival. But broadcast signals can be made exclusive by scrambling the signal and charging for the code that allows it to be unscrambled.

Some goods are nonexclusive but rival. Air is nonexclusive but can be rival if the emissions of one firm adversely affect the quality of the air and the ability of others to enjoy it. An ocean or large lake is nonexclusive, but fishing is rival because it imposes costs on others—the more fish caught, the fewer fish available to others.

Public goods, which are both nonrival and nonexclusive, provide benefits to people at zero marginal cost, and no one can be excluded from enjoying them. The classic example of a public good is national defense. Defense is nonexclusive, as we have seen, but it is also nonrival because the marginal cost of providing defense to an additional person is zero. The lighthouse mentioned earlier is also a public good, because it is nonrival and nonexclusive, i.e., it would be difficult to charge ships for the benefits they receive from it.[14]

The list of public goods is much smaller than the list of goods that governments provide. Many publicly provided goods are either rival in consumption, exclusive, or both. For example, high school education is rival in consumption. There is a positive marginal cost of providing education to one more child because other children get less attention as class sizes increase. Likewise, charging tuition can exclude some children from enjoying education. Public education is provided by local government because it entails positive externalities, not because it is a public good.

Finally, consider the management of a national park. Part of the public can be excluded from using the park by raising entrance and camping fees. Use of the park is also rival—because of crowded conditions, the entrance of an additional car into a park can reduce the benefits that others receive from it.

Efficiency and Public Goods

The efficient level of provision of a private good is determined by comparing the marginal benefit of an additional unit to the marginal cost of producing the unit. Efficiency is achieved when the marginal benefit and the marginal cost are equal. The same principle applies to public goods, but the analysis is different. With private goods, the marginal benefit is measured by the benefit the consumer receives. With a public good, we must ask how much each person values an additional unit of output. The marginal benefit is obtained by adding these values for all people who enjoy the good. Then to determine the efficient level of provision of a public good, we must equate the sum of these marginal benefits to the marginal cost of production.

Figure 18.13 illustrates the efficient level of producing a public good. D_1 represents the demand for the public good by one consumer, and D_2 the demand by a second consumer. Each demand curve tells us the marginal benefit that the consumer gets from consuming every level of output. For example, when there are 2 units of the public good, the first consumer is willing to pay $1.50 for the good, and $1.50 is the marginal benefit. Similarly, the second consumer has a marginal benefit of $4.00.

To calculate the sum of the marginal benefits to both people, we must add each of the demand curves *vertically*. For example, when the output is 2 units, we add the marginal benefit of $1.50 to the marginal benefit of $4.00 to obtain a marginal social benefit of $5.50. When this is calculated for every level of public output, we obtain the aggregate demand curve for the public good D.

The efficient amount of output is the one at which the marginal benefit to society is equal to the marginal cost. This occurs at the intersection of the de-

---

[14] Lighthouses need not be provided by the government. See Ronald Coase, "The Lighthouse in Economics," *Journal of Law and Economics* 17 (1974): 357–376, for a description of how lighthouses were privately provided in nineteenth-century England.

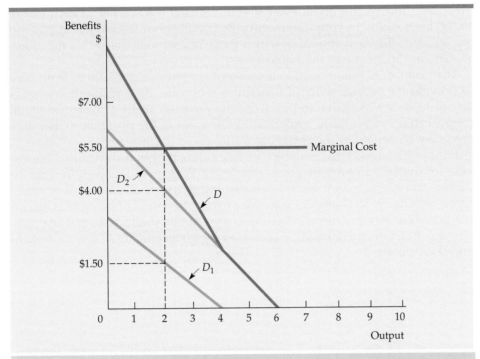

Figure 18.13   Efficient Public Good Provision   When a good is nonrival, the social marginal benefit of consumption, given by the demand curve D, is determined by vertically summing the individual demand curves for the good, D_1 and D_2. At the efficient output, the demand and the marginal cost curves intersect.

mand and the marginal cost curves. In our example, the marginal cost of production is $5.50, so 2 is the efficient output level.

To see why 2 is efficient, note what happens if only 1 unit of output is provided: The marginal cost remains at $5.50, but the marginal benefit is approximately $7.00. Because the marginal benefit is greater than the marginal cost, too little of the good has been provided. Similarly, suppose 3 units of the public good have been produced. Now the marginal benefit of approximately $4.00 is less than the marginal cost of $5.50, and too much of the good has been provided. Only when the marginal social benefit is equal to the marginal cost is the public good provided efficiently.[15]

Public Goods and Market Failure

Suppose you are considering providing a mosquito abatement program for your community. You know that the program is worth more to the community than the $50,000 it will cost. Can you make a profit by providing the program

---

[15] We have shown that nonexclusive, nonrival goods are inefficiently provided. A similar argument would apply to nonrival but exclusive goods.

privately? You would break even if you assessed a $5.00 fee to each of the 10,000 households in your community. But you cannot force them to pay the fee, let alone devise a system in which those households that value mosquito abatement the most pay the highest fees.

The problem is that mosquito abatement is nonexclusive—there is no way to provide the service without benefiting everyone. As a result, households do not have the incentive to pay what the program really is worth to them. People can act as *free riders*, understating the value of the program so that they can enjoy its benefit without paying for it.

With public goods, the presence of free riders makes it difficult or impossible for markets to provide goods efficiently. Perhaps if few people were involved and the program were relatively inexpensive, all households might agree voluntarily to share its costs. However, when many households are involved, voluntary private arrangements are usually ineffective, and the public good must be subsidized or provided by governments if it is to be produced efficiently.

EXAMPLE 18.6 **The Demand for Clean Air**

In Example 4.5 we used the demand curve for clean air to calculate the benefits of a cleaner environment. Now let's examine the public good characteristics of clean air. Many factors, including the weather, driving patterns, and industrial emissions determine air quality in a region. Any effort to clean up the air will generally improve air quality throughout the region. As a result, clean air is nonexclusive—it is difficult to stop any one person from enjoying it. Clean air is also nonrival—my enjoyment does not inhibit yours.

Because clean air is a public good, there is no market and no observable price at which people are willing to trade clean air for other commodities. Fortunately, we can infer people's willingness to pay for clean air from the housing market—households will pay more for a home located in an area with good air quality than for an otherwise identical home in an area with poor air quality.

Let's look at the estimates of the demand for clean air obtained from a statistical analysis of housing data for the Boston metropolitan area.[16] The statistical analysis correlates housing prices with the quality of air and other characteristics of the houses and their neighborhoods. Figure 18.14 shows three demand curves in which the value put on clean air depends on the level of nitrogen oxides and on income. The horizontal axis measures the level of air pollution in terms of parts per hundred million (pphm) of nitrogen oxides in the air, and the vertical axis measures each household's willingness to pay for a one-part-per-hundred million reduction in the nitrogen oxide level.

---

[16] See David Harrison, Jr., and Daniel L. Rubinfeld, "Hedonic Housing Prices and the Demand for Clean Air," *Journal of Environmental Economics and Management* 5 (1978): 81–102.

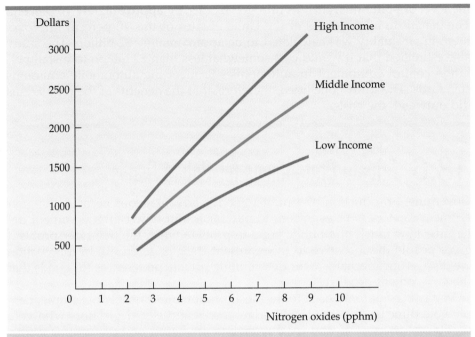

Figure 18.14   The Demand for Clean Air   The three curves describe the willingness to pay for clean air (a reduction in the level of nitrogen oxides) for each of three different households (low income, middle income, and high income). In general, higher-income households have greater demands for clean air than lower-income households. Also, each household is less willing to pay for clean air as the level of air quality increases.

The demand curves are upward sloping because we are measuring pollution rather than clean air on the horizontal axis. As we would expect, the cleaner the air, the lower the willingness to pay for more of the good. These differences in the willingness to pay for clean air vary substantially. In Boston, for example, nitrogen oxide levels ranged from 3 to 9 pphm. A middle-income household would be willing to pay $800 for a 1 pphm reduction in nitrogen oxide levels when the level is 3 pphm, but the figure would jump to $2200 for a 1 pphm reduction when the level is 9 pphm.

Note that higher-income households are willing to pay more to obtain a small improvement in air quality than lower-income households. At low nitrogen oxide levels (3 pphm), the differential between low- and middle-income households is only $200, but at high levels (9 pphm), the differential increases to about $700.

With the quantitative information about the demand for clean air and separate estimates of the costs of improving air quality, we can determine whether the benefits of environmental regulations outweigh the costs. A study by the National Academy of Sciences of the regulations on automobile emissions did just this. The study found that automobile emissions controls would lower the level of pollutants, such as nitrogen oxides, by approximately 10 percent. The benefit to all residents of the United States of this 10 percent improvement in air quality was calculated to be approximately $2 billion. The study also estimated that it would cost somewhat less than $2 billion to install pollution control equipment in automobiles to meet the automobile emissions standards. The study concluded, therefore, that the benefits of the regulations did outweigh the costs.[17]

18.6 Private Preferences for Public Goods

Government production of a public good is advantageous because the government can assess taxes or fees to pay for it. But how can government determine how much of a public good to provide when the free rider problem gives people the incentive to misrepresent their preferences? In this section we discuss one mechanism for determining private preferences for goods that the government produces.

Voting is commonly used to decide allocation questions. For example, people vote directly on some local budget issues and elect legislators who vote on others. Many state and local referenda are based on *majority rule voting*: Each person has one vote, and the candidate or the issue that receives more than 50 percent of the votes wins. Let's see how majority rule voting determines the provision of public education. Figure 18.15 describes the preferences for spending on education (on a per-pupil basis) of three citizens who are representative of three interest groups in the school district.

Curve W_1 gives the first citizen's willingness to pay for education, net of any required tax payments. The willingness to pay for each spending level is the maximum amount of money the citizen will pay to enjoy that spending level rather than no spending at all.[18] In general, the benefit from increased spending on education increases as spending increases. But the tax payments required to pay for that education increase as well. The willingness-to-pay curve, which represents the net benefit of educational spending, initially slopes upward because the citizen places great value on low spending levels. When spending increases beyond $600 per pupil, however, the value that the household puts on education increases at a diminishing rate, so the net benefit actually declines. Eventually, the spending level becomes so great (at $2400 per pupil) that the citizen is indifferent between this level of spending and no spending at all.

Curve W_2, which represents the second citizen's willingness to pay (net of taxes) is similarly shaped but reaches its maximum at a spending level of $1200 per pupil. Finally, W_3, the willingness to pay of the third citizen, peaks at $1800 per pupil.

---

[17] See U.S. Senate, Committee on Public Works, *Air Quality and Automobile Emission Control*, vol. 4 (Washington: Government Printing Office, Sept. 1974).

[18] In other words, the willingness to pay measures the consumer surplus that the citizen enjoys when a particular level of spending is chosen.

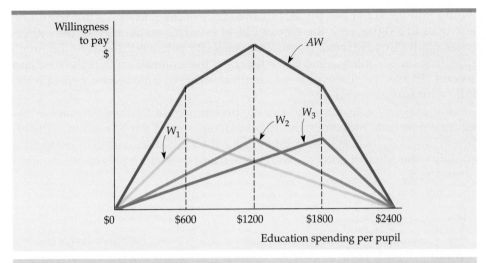

Figure 18.15   Determining the Level of Educational Spending   The efficient level of educational spending is determined by summing the willingness to pay for education (net of tax payments) of each of three citizens. Curves W_1, W_2, and W_3 represent their willingness to pay, and curve AW represents the aggregate willingness to pay. The efficient level of spending is $1200 per pupil. The level of spending actually provided is the level demanded by the median voter. In this particular case, the median voter's preference (given by the peak of the W_2 curve) is also the efficient level.

The dark line labeled AW represents the aggregate willingness to pay for education—the vertical summation of the W_1, W_2, and W_3 curves. The AW curve provides a measure of the maximum amount that all three citizens are willing to pay to enjoy each spending level. As Figure 18.15 shows, the aggregate willingness to pay is maximized when $1200 per pupil is spent. Because the AW curve measures the benefit of spending net of the tax payments required to pay for that spending, the maximum point, $1200 per pupil, also represents the efficient level of spending.

Will majority rule voting achieve the efficient outcome in this case? Suppose the public must vote whether to spend $1200 or $600 per pupil. The first citizen will vote for $600, but the other two citizens will vote for $1200, which will then have been chosen by majority rule. In fact, $1200 per pupil will beat any other alternative in a majority rule vote. Thus $1200 represents the most preferred alternative of the *median voter*—the citizen with the median or middle preference. (The first citizen prefers $600 and the third $1800.) *Under majority rule voting, the preferred spending level of the median voter will always win an election against any other alternative.*

But will the preference of the median voter be the efficient level of spending? In this case yes, because $1200 is efficient. But the preference of the median voter is often *not* the efficient spending level. Suppose the third citizen's preferences were the same as the second's. Then, the median voter's choice would still be $1200 per pupil, but the efficient level of spending would be less than $1200 (because the efficient level involves an average of the preferences of all three citizens). In this case, majority rule would lead to too much spending on education. And if we reversed the example so that the first and second citizens' preferences were identical, majority rule would generate too little educational spending.

Thus majority rule voting allows the preferences of the median voter to determine referenda outcomes, but these outcomes need not be economically efficient. Majority rule is inefficient because it weighs each citizen's preference equally—the efficient outcome weighs each citizen's vote by his or her strength of preference.

Summary

1. There is an externality when a producer or a consumer affects the production or consumption activities of others in a manner that is not directly reflected in the market. Externalities cause market inefficiencies because they inhibit the ability of market prices to convey accurate information about how much to produce and how much to buy.

2. Pollution is a common example of an externality that leads to market failure. It can be corrected by emissions standards, emissions fees, marketable emissions permits, or by encouraging recycling. When there is uncertainty about costs and benefits, any one of these mechanisms can be preferable, depending on the shapes of the marginal social cost and marginal benefit curves.

3. Inefficiencies due to market failure may be eliminated through private bargaining among the affected parties. According to the Coase theorem, the bargaining solution will be efficient when property rights are clearly specified, when transactions costs are zero, and when there is no strategic behavior. But bargaining is unlikely to generate an efficient outcome because parties frequently behave strategically.

4. Common property resources are not controlled by a single person and can be used without a price being paid. As a result of the free usage, an externality is created in which the current overuse of the resource harms those who might use it in the future.

5. Goods that private markets are not likely to produce efficiently are either nonrival or nonexclusive. Public goods are both. A good is nonrival if for any given level of production, the marginal cost of providing it to an additional consumer is zero. A good is nonexclusive if it is expensive or impossible to exclude people from consuming it.

6. A public good is provided efficiently when the vertical sum of the individual demands for the public good is equal to the marginal cost of producing it.

7. Majority rule voting is one way for citizens to voice their preference for public goods. Under majority rule, the level of spending provided will be that preferred by the median voter. This need not be the efficient outcome.

Questions for Review

1. Which of the following describes an externality and which does not? Explain the difference.

a. A policy of restricted coffee exports in Brazil causes the U.S. price of coffee to rise, which in turn also causes the price of tea to increase.

b. An advertising blimp distracts a motorist who then hits a telephone pole.

2. Compare and contrast the following three mechanisms for treating pollution externalities when the costs and benefits of abatement are uncertain: (a) an emissions fee, (b) an emissions standard, and (c) a system of transferable emissions permits.

3. When do externalities require government intervention, and when is such intervention unlikely to be necessary?

4. An emissions fee is paid to the government, whereas an injurer who is sued and is held liable pays damages directly to the party harmed by an externality. What differences in the behavior of victims might you expect to arise under these two arrangements?

5. Why does free access to a common property resource generate an inefficient outcome?

6. Public goods are both nonrival and nonexclusive. Explain each of these terms and state clearly how they differ from each other.

7. Public television is funded in part by private donations, even though anyone with a television set can watch for free. Can you explain this phenomenon in light of the free rider problem?

8. Explain why the median voter outcome need not be efficient when majority rule voting determines the level of public spending.

Exercises

1. A number of firms have located in the western portion of a town, after single-family residences took up the eastern portion. Each firm produces the same product and in the process emits noxious fumes that adversely affect the residents of the community.
   a. Why is there an externality created by the firms?
   b. Do you think that private bargaining can resolve the problem with the externality? Explain.
   c. How might the community determine the efficient level of air quality?

2. A computer programmer lobbies against copyrighting software. He argues that everyone should benefit from innovative programs written for personal computers, and that exposure to a wide variety of computer programs will inspire young programmers to create even more innovative programs. Considering the marginal social benefits possibly gained by his proposal, do you agree with the programmer's position?

3. Four firms located at different points on a river dump various quantities of effluent into it. The effluent adversely affects the quality of swimming for homeowners who live downstream. These people can build swimming pools to avoid swimming in the river, and the firms can purchase filters that eliminate harmful chemicals in the material that is dumped in the river. As a policy adviser for a regional planning organization, how would you compare and contrast the following options for dealing with the harmful effect of the effluent:
   a. An equal rate effluent fee on firms located on the river.
   b. An equal standard per firm on the level of effluent each firm can dump.
   c. A transferable effluent permit system, in which the aggregate level of effluent is fixed and all firms receive identical permits.

4. Recent social trends point to growing intolerance of smoking in public areas. Medical research has shown the negative health effects of "secondhand" smoke. If you are a smoker and you wish to continue smoking despite tougher antismoking laws, describe the effect of the following legislative proposals on your behavior. As a result of these programs, do you, the individual smoker, benefit? Does society benefit as a whole?
   a. A bill is proposed that would lower tar and nicotine levels in all cigarettes.
   b. A tax is levied on each pack of cigarettes

b. A tax is levied on each pack of cigarettes sold.

c. Smokers would be required to carry smoking permits at all times. These permits would be sold by the government.

5. A beekeeper lives adjacent to an apple orchard. The orchard owner benefits from the bees because each hive pollinates about one acre of apple trees. The orchard owner pays nothing for this service, however, because the bees come to the orchard without his having to do anything. There are not enough bees to pollinate the entire orchard, and the orchard owner must complete the pollination by artificial means, at a cost of $10 per acre of trees.

Beekeeping has a marginal cost $MC = 10 + 2Q$, where Q is the number of beehives. Each hive yields $20 worth of honey.

a. How many beehives will the beekeeper maintain?

b. Is this the economically efficient number of hives?

c. What changes would lead to the more efficient operation?

6. There are three groups in a community. Their demand curves for public television in hours of programming , T, are given respectively by

$$W_1 = \$150 - T$$

$$W_2 = \$200 - 2T$$

$$W_3 = \$250 - T$$

Suppose public television is a pure public good that can be produced at a constant marginal cost of $200 per hour.

a. What is the efficient number of hours of public television?

b. How much public television would a competitive private market provide?

7. Reconsider the common resource problem given in Example 18.5. Suppose that crawfish popularity continues to increase, and that the demand curve shifts from $C = 0.401 - 0.0064F$ to $C = 0.50 - 0.0064F$. How does this shift in demand affect the actual crawfish catch, the efficient catch, and the social cost of common access? (*Hint:* Use the marginal social cost and private cost curves given in the example.)

8. The Georges Bank, a highly productive fishing area off New England, can be divided into two zones in terms of fish population. Zone 1 has the higher population per square mile but is subject to severe diminishing returns to fishing effort. The daily fish catch (in tons) in Zone 1 is

$$F_1 = 200(X_1) - 2(X_1)^2$$

where X_1 is the number of boats fishing there. Zone 2 has fewer fish per mile but is larger, and diminishing returns are less of a problem. Its daily fish catch is

$$F_2 = 100(X_2) - (X_2)^2$$

where X_2 is the number of boats fishing in Zone 2. The marginal fish catch MFC in each zone can be represented as

$$MFC_1 = 200 - 4(X_1)$$

$$MFC_2 = 100 - 2(X_2)$$

There are 100 boats now licensed by the U.S. government to fish in these two zones. The fish are sold at $100 per ton. The total cost (capital and operating) per boat is constant at $1000 per day. Answer the following questions about this situation.

a. If the boats are allowed to fish where they want, with no government restriction, how many will fish in each zone? What will be the gross value of the catch?

b. If the U.S. government can restrict the boats, how many should be allocated to each zone? What will the gross value of the catch be? Assume the total number of boats remains at 100.

c. If additional fishermen want to buy boats and join the fishing fleet, should a government wishing to maximize the net value of the fish catch grant them licenses to do so? Why or why not?

APPENDIX

The Basics of Regression

This appendix explains the basics of multiple regression analysis, using an example to illustrate its application in economics.[1] Multiple regression is a means of fitting economic relationships to data. It lets us quantify economic relationships and test hypotheses about them.

In a *linear regression*, the relationships that we fit to the data are of the following form:

$$Y = b_0 + b_1 X_1 + b_2 X_2 + \cdots + b_k X_k + e \tag{A.1}$$

Equation (A.1) relates a *dependent* variable Y to several *independent* (or *explanatory*) variables, $X_1, X_2, \ldots$. For example, in an equation with two independent variables, Y might be the demand for a good, X_1 its price, and X_2 income. The equation also includes an *error term e* that represents the collective influence of any omitted variables that may also affect Y (for example, prices of other goods, the weather, unexplainable shifts in consumers' tastes, etc.). Data are available for Y and the Xs, but the error term is assumed to be unobservable.

Note that Equation (A.1) must be linear in the *parameters*, but it need not be linear in the variables. For example, if Equation (A.1) represented a demand function, Y might be the *logarithm* of quantity (log Q), X_1 the logarithm of price (log P), and X_2 the logarithm of income (log I):

$$\log Q = b_0 + b_1 \log P + b_2 \log I + e \tag{A.2}$$

Our objective is to obtain *estimates* of the parameters $b_0, b_1, \ldots, b_k$ that provide a "best fit" to the data. We explain how this is done below.

An Example

Suppose we wish to explain and then forecast quarterly automobile sales in the United States. Let's start with a simplified case in which sales S (in billions of dollars) is the dependent variable that will be explained, and the only explanatory variable is the price of new automobiles P (measured by a new car price index scaled so that 1967 = 100). We could write this simple model as

$$S = b_0 + b_1 P + e \tag{A.3}$$

---

[1] For a textbook treatment of applied econometrics, see R. S. Pindyck and D. L. Rubinfeld, *Econometric Models and Economic Forecasts*, 4th ed. (New York: McGraw-Hill, 1998).

In Equation (A.3), b_0 and b_1 are the parameters to be determined from the data, and e is the random error term. The parameter b_0 is the intercept, while b_1 is the slope—it measures the effect of a change in the new car price index on automobile sales.

Were no error term present, the relationship between S and P would be a straight line that describes the systematic relationship between the two variables. However, not all the actual observations fall on the line, so the error term e is required to account for omitted factors.

Estimation

Some criterion for a "best fit" is needed to choose values for the regression parameters. The criterion most often used is to *minimize the sum of squared residuals* between the actual values of Y and the *fitted* values for Y obtained after equation (A.1) has been estimated. This is called the *least-squares criterion*. If we denote the estimated parameters (or *coefficients*) for the model in (A.1) by $\hat{b}_0, \hat{b}_1, \ldots, \hat{b}_k$, then the *fitted* values for Y are given by

$$\hat{Y} = \hat{b}_0 + \hat{b}_1 X_1 + \cdots + \hat{b}_k X_k \tag{A.4}$$

Figure A.1 illustrates this for our example in which there is a single independent variable. The data are shown as a scatter of points with sales on the vertical axis and price on the horizontal. The fitted regression line is drawn through the data points. The fitted value for sales associated with any particular value for the price values P_i is given by $\hat{S}_i = \hat{b}_0 + \hat{b}_1 P_i$ (at point B).

For each data point, the regression *residual* is the difference between the actual and fitted value of the dependent variable. The residual $\hat{e}_i$, associated with

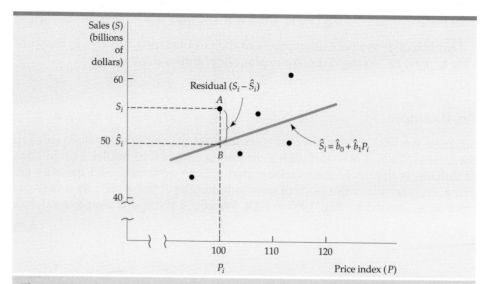

Figure A.1 **Least-Squares** The regression line is chosen to minimize the sum of squared residuals. The residual associated with price P_i is given by line AB.

data point A in the figure, is given by $\hat{e}_i = S_i - \hat{S}_i$. The parameter values are chosen so that when all the residuals are squared and then added, the resulting sum is minimized. In this way positive errors and negative errors are treated symmetrically, and large errors are given a more-than-proportional weight. This criterion lets us do some simple statistical tests to help interpret the regression, as we will see shortly.

As an example of estimation, let's return to the two-variable model of auto sales given by equation (A.3). The result of fitting this equation to the data using the least-squares criterion is

$$\hat{S} = -25.5 + 0.57P \tag{A.5}$$

In equation (A.5) the intercept -25.5 indicates that if the price index were zero, sales would be $\$-25.5$ billion. The slope parameter indicates that a 1-unit increase in the price index for new cars leads to a $\$0.57$ billion increase in auto sales. This rather surprising result—an upward-sloping demand curve—is inconsistent with economic theory and should make us question the validity of our model.

Let's expand the model to consider the possible effects of two additional explanatory variables, personal income I (in billions of dollars) and the rate of interest R (the three-month Treasury bill rate). The estimated regression when there are three explanatory variables is

$$\hat{S} = 51.1 - 0.42P + 0.046I - 0.84R \tag{A.6}$$

The importance of including all relevant variables in the model is suggested by the change in the regression results after the income and interest rate variables are added. Note that the coefficient of the P variable has changed substantially, from 0.57 to -0.42. The coefficient -0.42 measures the effect of an increase in price on sales, *with the effect of interest rates and income held constant*. The negative price coefficient is consistent with a downward-sloping demand curve. Clearly, the failure to control for interest rates and income leads to the false conclusion that sales and price are positively related.

The income coefficient, 0.046, tells us that for every $\$1$ billion increase in personal income in the United States, automobile sales are likely to increase by $\$46$ million (or $\$0.046$ billion). The interest rate coefficient reflects that for every one percentage point increase in the rate of interest, automobile sales are likely to fall by $\$840$ million. Clearly, automobile sales are very sensitive to the cost of borrowing.

Statistical Tests

Our estimates of the true (but unknown) parameters are numbers that depend on the set of observations that we started with, that is, with our *sample*. With a different sample we would obtain different estimates.[2] If we continue to col-

---

[2] The least-squares formula that generates these estimates is called the *least-squares estimator*, and its values vary from sample to sample.

lect more and more samples and generate additional estimates, the estimates of each parameter will follow a probability distribution. This can be summarized by a *mean* and a measure of dispersion around that mean, a standard deviation that we refer to as the *standard error of the coefficient*.

Least-squares has several desirable properties. First, least-squares is *unbiased*. Intuitively, this means that if we could run our regression over and over again with different samples, the average of the many estimates we obtained for each coefficient would be the true parameter. Second, least-squares is *consistent*, i.e., if our sample were very large, we would obtain estimates that came very close to the true parameters.

In econometric work we often assume that the error term and therefore the estimated parameters are normally distributed. The normal distribution has the property that the area within 1.96 standard errors of its mean is equal to 95 percent of the total area. With this information, we can ask the following question: Can we construct an interval around $\hat{b}$ such that there is a 95 percent probability that the true parameter lies within that interval? The answer is yes, and this 95 percent *confidence interval* is given by

$$\hat{b} \pm 1.96 \text{ (standard error of } \hat{b}) \tag{A.7}$$

Thus when working with an estimated regression equation, we must not only look at the *point* estimates but also examine the standard errors of the coefficients to determine bounds for the true parameters.[3]

If a 95 percent confidence interval contains 0, then the true parameter b may actually be zero (even if our estimate $\hat{b}$ is not), which implies that the corresponding independent variable may *not* really affect the dependent variable, even if we thought it did. We can test the hypothesis that a true parameter is actually equal to 0 by looking at its *t-statistic*, which is defined as

$$t = \frac{\hat{b}}{\text{Standard error of } \hat{b}} \tag{A.8}$$

If the *t*-statistic is less than 1.96 in magnitude, the 95 percent confidence interval around $\hat{b}$ must include 0. Because this means that we cannot reject the hypothesis that the true parameter b equals 0, we therefore say that our estimate, whatever it may be, is *not statistically significant*. Conversely, if the *t*-statistic is greater than 1.96 in absolute value, we reject the hypothesis that $b = 0$ and call our estimate *statistically significant*.

Equation (A.9) shows the multiple regression for the auto sales model (equation A.6) with a set of standard errors and *t*-statistics added:

$$
\begin{array}{cccc}
\hat{S} = 51.1 & -0.42P & +0.046I & -0.84R \\
(9.4) & (0.13) & (0.006) & (0.32) \\
t = 5.44 & -3.23 & 8.23 & -2.63
\end{array} \tag{A.9}
$$

The standard error of each estimated parameter is given in parentheses just below the estimate, and the corresponding *t*-statistics appear below that.

---

[3] When there are fewer than 100 observations, we multiply the standard error by a number somewhat larger than 1.96.

Let's begin by considering the price variable. The standard error of 0.13 is small relative to the coefficient −0.42. In fact, we can be 95 percent certain that the *true* value of the price coefficient is −0.42 plus or minus 1.96 standard deviations (i.e., −0.42 plus or minus [1.96][0.13] = −0.42 ± 0.25). This puts the true value of the coefficient between −0.16 and −0.68. Because this range does not include zero, the effect of price is both significantly different from zero and negative. We can also see this from the *t*-statistic. The *t* of −3.23 reported in equation (A.9) for the price variable is equal to −0.42 divided by 0.13. Because this *t*-statistic exceeds 1.96 in absolute value, we conclude that price is a significant determinant of auto sales.

Note that the income and interest rate variables are also significantly different from zero. The regression results tell us that an increase in income is likely to have a statistically significant positive effect on auto sales, whereas an increase in interest rates will have a significant negative effect.

Goodness of Fit

Reported regression results usually contain information that tells us how closely the regression line fits the data. One statistic, the *standard error of the regression* (SER) is an estimate of the standard deviation of the regression error term *e*. Whenever all the data points lie on the regression line the SER is zero. Other things being equal, the larger the standard error of the regression, the poorer the fit of the data to the regression line. To decide whether the SER is large or small, we compare it in magnitude with the mean of the dependent variable. This comparison provides a measure of the *relative* size of the SER, a more meaningful statistic than its absolute size.

R-squared (R^2), the percentage of the variation in the dependent variable[4] that is accounted for by all the explanatory variables, measures the overall goodness-of-fit of the multiple regression equation.[5] Its value ranges from 0 to 1. An R^2 of 0 means that the independent variables explain none of the variation of the dependent variable, while an R^2 of 1 means that the independent variables explain the variation perfectly. The R^2 for the sales equation (A.9) is 0.94. This tells us that the three independent variables explain 94 percent of the variation in sales.

Note that a high R^2 does not by itself mean that the variables actually included in the model are the appropriate ones. First, the R^2 varies with the types of data being studied. Time series data with substantial upward growth usually generate much higher R^2s than do cross-section data. Second, the underlying economic theory provides a vital check. If a regression of auto sales on the price of wheat happened to yield a high R^2, we would question the model's reliability.

The overall reliability of a regression result depends on the formulation of the model. When studying an estimated regression, we should consider

---

[4] The variation in Y is the sum of the squared deviations of Y from its mean.

[5] R^2 and SER provide similar information about goodness of fit, because $R^2 = 1 − \text{SER}^2/\text{Variance}\ (Y)$.

things that might make the reported results suspicious. First, have variables that should appear in the relationship been omitted? That is, is the *specification* of the equation wrong? Second, is the functional form of the equation correct? For instance, should variables be in logarithms? Third, is there another relationship that relates one of the explanatory variables (say X) to the dependent variable Y? If so, X and Y are jointly determined, and we must deal with a two-equation model, not one with a single equation. Finally, does adding or removing one or two data points result in a major change in the estimated coefficients—i.e., is the equation *robust?* If not, we should be very careful not to overstate the importance or reliability of the results.

Economic Forecasting

A forecast is a prediction about the values of the dependent variable, given information about the explanatory variables. Often, we use regression models to generate *ex ante* forecasts, in which we predict values of the dependent variable beyond the time period over which the model has been estimated. (If we know the values of the explanatory variables, the forecast is *unconditional;* if they must be predicted as well, the forecast is *conditional* on these predictions.) Sometimes *ex post* forecasts, in which we predict what the value of the dependent variable would have been had the values of the independent variables been different, can be useful. An *ex post* forecast has a forecast period such that all values of the dependent and explanatory variables are known. Thus *ex post* forecasts can be checked against existing data and provide a direct means of evaluating a model.

For example, reconsider the auto sales regression discussed above. In general, the forecasted value for auto sales is given by

$$\hat{S} = \hat{b}_0 + \hat{b}_1 P + \hat{b}_2 I + \hat{b}_3 R + \hat{e} \tag{A.10}$$

where $\hat{e}$ is our prediction for the error term. Without additional information, we usually take $\hat{e}$ to be zero.

Then, to calculate the forecast we use the estimated sales equation:

$$\hat{S} = 51.1 - 0.42P + 0.046I - 0.84R \tag{A.11}$$

We can use (A.11) to predict sales when, for example, $P = 100$, $I = \$1$ trillion, and $R = 8$ percent. Then,

$$\hat{S} = 51.1 - 0.42(100) + 0.046(1000 \text{ billion}) - 0.84(8\%) = \$48.4 \text{ billion}$$

Note that $48.4 billion is an *ex post* forecast for a time when $P = 100$, $I = \$1$ trillion, and $R = 8$ percent.

To determine the reliability of *ex ante* and *ex post* forecasts, we use the *standard error of forecast* (SEF). The SEF measures the standard deviation of the forecast error within a sample in which the explanatory variables are known with certainty. Two sources of error are implicit in the SEF. The first is the error term itself, because $\hat{e}$ may not equal 0 in the forecast period. The second source arises because the estimated parameters of the regression model may not be exactly equal to the true parameters.

As an application, consider the SEF of $7.0 billion associated with equation (A.11). If the sample size is large enough, the probability is roughly 95 percent that the predicted sales will be within 1.96 standard errors of the forecasted value. In this case, the 95 percent confidence interval is $48.4 billion $\pm$ $14.0 billion, i.e., from $34.4 billion to $62.4 billion.

Now suppose we wish to forecast automobile sales for some date in the future, such as 2000. To do so, the forecast must be conditional because we need to predict the values for the independent variables before calculating the forecast for automobile sales. Assume, for example, that our predictions of these variables are as follows: $\hat{P} = 200$, $\hat{I} = \$5$ trillion, and $\hat{R} = 10$ percent. Then, the forecast is given by $\hat{P} = 51.1 - 0.42(200) + 0.046(5000 \text{ billion}) - 0.84(10) = \$188.7$ billion. Here $190.8 billion is an *ex ante* conditional forecast.

Because we are predicting the future, and the explanatory variables do not lie close to the means of the variables throughout our period of study, the SEF is equal to $8.2 billion, which is somewhat greater than the SEF that we calculated previously.[6] The 95 percent confidence interval associated with our forecast is the interval from $174.4 billion to $207.2 billion.

Suppose we want to estimate the demand for bituminous coal (given by sales in tons per year, COAL), and then use the relationship to forecast future coal sales. We would expect the quantity demanded to depend on the price of coal (given by the Producer Price Index for coal, PCOAL) and on the price of a close substitute for coal (given by the Producer Price Index for natural gas, PGAS). Because coal is used to produce steel and electricity, we would also expect the level of steel production (given by the Federal Reserve Board Index of iron and steel production, FIS), and electricity production (given by the Federal Reserve Board Index of electric utility production, FEU) to be important demand determinants.

Our model of coal demand is therefore given by the following equation:

$$\text{COAL} = b_0 + b_1 \text{ PCOAL} + b_2 \text{ PGAS} + b_3 \text{ FIS} + b_4 \text{ FEU} + e$$

From our theory, we would expect b_1 to be negative because the demand curve for coal is downward sloping. We would also expect b_2 to be positive because a higher price of natural gas should lead industrial consumers of energy to substitute coal for natural gas. Finally, we would expect both b_3 and b_4 to be positive because the greater the production of steel and electricity, the greater the demand for coal.

---

[6] For more on SEF, see Pindyck and Rubinfeld, *Econometric Models and Economic Forecasts*, Chapter 8.

This model was estimated using monthly time-series data covering eight years. The results (with t-statistics in parentheses) are:

$$\text{COAL} = 12{,}262 + 92.34 \text{ FIS} + 118.57 \text{ FEU} - 48.90 \text{ PCOAL} + 118.91 \text{ PGAS}$$
$$\quad\quad\ (3.51) \quad\ (6.46) \quad\quad\ (7.14) \quad\quad (-3.82) \quad\quad\quad\quad (3.18)$$

$$R^2 = 0.692 \quad \text{SER} = 120{,}000$$

All the estimated coefficients have the signs that econometric theory would predict. Each coefficient is also statistically significantly different from zero because the t-statistics are all greater than 1.96 in absolute value. The R^2 of 0.692 says that the model explains more than two-thirds of the variation in coal sales. The standard error of the regression SER is equal to 120,000 tons of coal. Because the mean level of coal production was 3.9 million tons, SER represents approximately 3 percent of the mean value of the dependent variable. This suggests a reasonably good model fit.

Now suppose we want to use the estimated coal demand equation to forecast coal sales up to one year into the future. To do so, we substitute values for each of the explanatory values for the 12-month forecasting period into the estimated equation. We also estimate the standard error of forecast (the estimate is 0.17 million tons) and use it to calculate 95 percent confidence intervals for the forecasted values of coal demand. Some representative forecasts and confidence intervals are given in Table A.1.

Table A.1 Forecasting Coal Demand		
	Forecast	Confidence Interval
1-month forecast (tons)	5.2 million	4.9–5.5 million
6-month forecast (tons)	4.7 million	4.4–5.0 million
12-month forecast (tons)	5.0 million	4.7–5.3 million

Summary

1. Multiple regression is a means of fitting economic relationships to data.

2. The linear regression model, which relates one dependent variable to one or more independent variables, is usually estimated by choosing the intercept and slope parameters that minimize the sum of the squared residuals between the actual and predicted values of the dependent variable.

3. In a multiple-regression model, each slope coefficient measures the effect on the dependent variable of a change in the corresponding independent variable, holding the effects of all other interdependent variables constant.

4. A t-test can be used to test the hypothesis that a particular slope coefficient is different from zero.

5. The overall fit of the regression equation can be evaluated using the standard error of the regression (SER) (a value close to zero means a good fit), or R^2 (a value close to one means a good fit).

6. Regression models can be used to forecast future values of the dependent variable. The standard error of forecast (SEF) measures the accuracy of the forecast.

Glossary

A

Accounting Cost *(page 206)* Actual expenses plus depreciation charges for capital equipment. (These charges are determined by the Internal Revenue Service.)

Adverse Selection *(page 621)* A form of market failure resulting from asymmetric information: If insurance companies must charge a single premium because they cannot distinguish between high-risk and low-risk individuals, more high-risk individuals will insure, making it unprofitable to sell insurance.

Agent *(page 632)* An individual employed by a principal to implement the objective of the principal.

Antitrust Laws *(page 367)* Regulations intended to promote a competitive economy by prohibiting actions that restrain competition.

Arbitrage *(page 9)* Buying a product at a low price in one location and selling it at a higher price somewhere else.

Arc Elasticity of Demand *(page 119)* Used when dealing with a relatively large price change, the arc elasticity is equal to $(\Delta Q/\Delta P)(\overline{P}/\overline{Q})$ where $\overline{P}$ and $\overline{Q}$ are the averages of the prices and quantities before and after the price change.

Asymmetric Information *(page 617)* A situation in which a buyer and a seller have different information about a transaction.

Average Cost *(page 209)* Production cost per unit of output.

Average Expenditure *(page 359)* The price per unit paid by a buyer.

Average Product *(page 180)* Total output per unit of a particular input.

Average Revenue *(page 335)* Revenue divided by the number of units sold, i.e., price per unit.

B

Backward-Bending Labor Supply Curve *(page 524)* The portion of the labor supply curve at which the wage rate increases and the hours of work supplied decrease, giving the curve a negative slope.

Bandwagon Effect *(page 127)* A positive network externality in which an individual demands a good in part because many other people have the good.

Barrier to Entry *(page 440)* Anything that makes it prohibitive for new firms to enter a market; it is necessary if incumbent firms are to maintain monopoly power.

Bilateral Monopoly *(page 365)* A market with one buyer and one seller.

Bond *(page 551)* A contract in which a borrower agrees to pay the bond holder (the lender) a stream of money.

Budget Line *(page 73)* All combinations of goods that can be purchased with an individual's income.

Bundling *(page 376)* A pricing strategy that involves selling two or more products as a package.

C

Capital *(page 176)* Buildings, equipment, and inventories which can be utilized (along with labor and raw materials) to produce output.

CAPM (Capital Asset Pricing Model) *(page 561)* A model in which the risk premium for a capital investment depends on the correlation of the investment's return with the return on the entire stock market.

Cardinal Ranking *(page 67)* A quantitative measure of the value of a good in terms of a basic unit of utility.

Cartel *(page 434)* A group of firms that explicitly agree to set prices and/or to limit output.

Ceiling Price *(page 54)* A maximum price that firms are allowed by the government to charge for a good.

Clayton Act *(page 368)* As amended by the Robinson-Patman Act, a law that makes it illegal to discriminate by charging buyers of essentially the same product different prices.

Coase Theorem *(page 667)* When parties can bargain without cost and to their mutual advantage, the resulting outcome will be efficient, regardless of how the property rights are specified.

Common Property Resource *(page 669)* A resource, such as air and water, to which anyone has free access.

Comparative Advantage *(page 604)* A country A has a comparative advantage over another country B in producing a good if the cost of producing the good in A, relative to the cost of producing other goods in A, is lower than the cost of producing the good in B, relative to the cost of producing other goods in B.

Competitive Markets *(page 10)* Markets in which buyers and sellers individually have little or no ability to affect prices.

Complements *(page 34)* Goods that tend to be used together, so that an increase in the price of one good tends to decrease the demand for its complement.

Constant Cost Industry *(page 276)* An industry whose long-run supply curve is horizontal.

Constant Returns to Scale *(page 198)* When a doubling of inputs causes output to double.

Consumer Price Index *(page 12)* A Laspeyres cost-of-living index, calculated by the U.S. Bureau of Labor Statistics as the ratio of the cost of buying a typical bundle of consumer goods and services today in comparison to the cost of buying that bundle in a base period.

Consumer Surplus *(page 122)* The difference between the amount consumers are willing to pay for a good and the amount they actually pay.

Contestable Market *(page 285)* A market that firms can freely enter or exit without incurring sunk costs.

Contract Curve *(page 588)* A curve that includes all efficient allocations of two goods between two consumers, or two inputs between two production functions, in an Edgeworth box.

Cooperative Game *(page 476)* A game in which players can negotiate binding contracts that allow them to plan joint strategies.

Cost Function *(page 235)* A relationship between the cost of production and the level of output of a firm or firms.

Cournot Equilibrium *(page 443)* The Nash equilibrium that occurs when firms simultaneously choose the quantities they will produce.

Cournot Model *(page 442)* An oligopoly model in which firms assume that their competitors' outputs are fixed, and simultaneously decide how much to produce.

Cross-Price Elasticity of Demand *(page 34)* The percentage change in the quantity demanded of a good that results from a 1 percent increase in the price of another good.

D

Deadweight Loss *(page 320)* A measure of efficiency loss, given by the sum of lost consumer and producer surplus, less revenues to the government.

Decreasing Cost Industry *(page 279)* An industry whose long-run supply curve is downward sloping.

Decreasing Returns to Scale *(page 198)* When a doubling of inputs causes output to increase by less than a factor of two.

Demand Curve *(page 21)* The amount of a good consumers are willing to purchase as a function of its price.

Depletable Resource *(page 566)* A natural resource, such as oil or copper, which if produced today is unavailable for future production.

Depreciation *(page 206)* The decline in value of a capital asset as it is used over time.

Discount Rate *(page 557)* A rate used to compare the value of a dollar received in the future to a dollar received today.

Diseconomies of Scale *(page 223)* When a firm's costs more than double in response to a doubling of output.

Diseconomies of Scope *(page 227)* When one firm produces less of two outputs than two separate specialized firms could produce.

Diversifiable Risk (also Nonsystematic Risk) *(page 560)* Risk that can be eliminated by diversifying, e.g., by investing in many projects or by holding the stocks of many companies.

Dominant Firm Model *(page 462)* A model of oligopoly in which one firm sets price, knowing that other firms will produce as much as they want at that price.

Dominant Strategy *(page 478)* A strategy that is optimal regardless of how one's competitors behave.

Duality in Consumer Theory *(page 143)* The optimum allocation of income between two goods may be determined by choosing the highest indifference curve that is tangent to the budget line, or by choosing the lowest budget line that touches a given indifference curve.

Durable Good *(page 35)* A consumption or capital good bought to provide services for a long time.

E

Economic Profit *(page 271)* The difference between a firm's revenues and costs, including any opportunity costs.

Economic Rent *(page 274)* The difference between the payments made to a factor of production and the minimum amount that must be spent to obtain the use of that factor.

Economies of Scale *(page 223)* When a firm's costs less than double in response to a doubling of output.

Economies of Scope *(page 227)* When one firm produces more of two outputs than two specialized firms could produce.

Edgeworth Box Diagram *(page 586)* A diagram that shows all possible allocations of two goods between two people, or of two inputs between two production processes.

Effective Yield *(page 553)* The interest rate that equates the price of a bond with the present discounted value of its expected future payments. Also called the *rate of return* on the bond.

Efficiency Wage *(page 641)* The wage a firm will pay to an employee as an incentive not to shirk.

Elastic Demand *(page 33)* When the percentage change in quantity demanded of a good in response to a 1 percent change in price is greater than one in magnitude.

Elasticity *(page 32)* A measure of the percentage change in one variable resulting from a 1 percent increase in the other variable.

Emissions Fee *(page 653)* A charge per unit of emissions imposed on a polluter.

Emissions Standard *(page 653)* A legal limit on how much pollutant a firm may emit.

Engel Curve *(page 107)* The quantity of a good consumed as a function of income.

Equal Marginal Principle *(page 91)* A rule for optimization when two or more options are available, i.e., to maximize utility, a consumer should equalize the marginal utility of each dollar spent on each good consumed.

Equilibrium Price (also Market-Clearing Price) *(page 21)* The price at which the quantity supplied and quantity demanded are equal.

Excess Demand *(page 54)* Demand that results when the quantity demanded exceeds the quantity supplied because a price ceiling keeps the price of a good below its equilibrium price.

Expansion Path *(page 220)* A curve that describes the combinations of labor and capital a firm will choose to minimize costs for every level of output.

Expected Value *(page 149)* The average value of a set of uncertain outcomes.

Explicit Cost *(page 206)* The actual outlays by a firm, including wages, salaries, costs of materials, and property rentals.

Extent of a Market *(page 11)* The boundaries of a market, both geographic, and in terms of the range of products to be included.

Externality *(page 296)* An action by either a producer or a consumer that affects other producers or consumers, yet is not accounted for in the market price.

F

Feedback Effect *(page 580)* A price or quantity adjustment in one market that is caused by price and quantity adjustments in related markets.

First-Degree Price Discrimination *(page 378)* Charging each person her reservation price for a good.

First Theorem of Welfare Economics *(page 592)* If everyone trades in the competitive marketplace, all mutually beneficial trades will be completed and the resulting equilibrium allocation of resources will be economically efficient.

Fixed Cost *(page 208)* A cost that does not vary with the level of production, such as plant maintenance and insurance.

Fixed Inputs *(page 179)* Factors that cannot be changed in the short run.

Fixed-Proportions Production Function *(page 194)* When the production isoquants are L-shaped, so that only one combination of labor and capital can be used to produce each level of output.

Free Entry (Exit) *(page 436)* When firms may enter (exit) an industry without incurring a sunk cost.

Free Rider *(page 676)* A consumer or producer that does not pay for a nonexclusive good in the expectation that others will.

G

General Equilibrium Analysis *(page 580)* A method of analysis that simultaneously determines the prices and quantities in several markets.

Giffen Good *(page 113)* A good whose demand curve slopes upward as a result of a large income effect.

I

Ideal Cost-of-Living Index *(page 95)* The cost of attaining a given level of utility at current prices divided by the cost of attaining the same utility at base year prices.

Income-Consumption Curve *(page 105)* A curve that includes the utility-maximizing combinations of goods associated with every income level.

Income Effect *(page 112)* The increase in consumption brought about by an increase in income, when the prices of goods are held constant.

Income Elasticity of Demand *(page 33)* The percentage change in the quantity demanded of a good resulting from a 1 percent increase in income.

Increasing Cost Industry *(page 277)* An industry whose long-run supply curve is upward sloping.

Increasing Returns to Scale *(page 197)* When a doubling of inputs causes output to more than double.

Indifference Curve *(page 64)* A graphical representation of all combinations of market baskets that provide the same level of satisfaction.

Indifference Map *(page 66)* A set of indifference curves that describes the consumer's preferences among various combinations of market baskets.

Industry *(page 9)* A collection of firms that sell the same or closely related products.

Inelastic Demand *(page 32)* When the percentage change in the quantity demanded of a good in response to a 1 percent change in price is less than one in magnitude.

Inferior Good *(page 106)* A good for which consumption falls as an individual's income rises.

Interest Rate *(page 546)* The rate at which one can borrow or lend money. There is a wide range of "market" interest rates; see pages 572–573 for descriptions of some of the more important ones.

Intertemporal Price Discrimination *(page 388)* Separating consumers into groups with varying demand functions and charging them different prices at different points in time.

Isocost Line *(page 215)* A line that includes all possible combinations of inputs that can be purchased for a given amount of money.

Isoquant *(page 177)* A curve that shows all the possible combinations of inputs that yield the same output.

Isoquant Map *(page 179)* A set of isoquants, each of which shows the maximum output that can be achieved for any set of inputs.

K

Kinked Demand Curve *(page 458)* The demand curve oligopolistic firms face due to the rigidity of prices, where the price elasticity of demand is higher for price increases than for decreases.

L

Labor Productivity *(page 187)* The average product of labor as applied to an industry or to the economy as a whole.

Laspeyres Index *(page 95)* A cost-of-living index that calculates the amount of money at current year prices that an individual requires to purchase the bundle of goods and services that was *chosen in the base year*, divided by the cost of purchasing the same bundle at base year prices.

Law of Diminishing Returns *(page 183)* As the use of an input increases (while other inputs remain constant), the additional output produced will eventually decrease.

Learning Curve *(page 230)* The relationship between a firm's cumulative output and the (declining) amount of inputs needed to produce a unit of output.

Lerner Index *(page 348)* A measure of monopoly power calculated as the excess of price over marginal cost as a fraction of marginal cost.

M

Marginal Cost (or Incremental Cost) *(page 209)* The increase in cost from producing one additional unit of output.

Marginal Expenditure *(page 359)* The incremental cost of purchasing one additional unit of a good.

Marginal External Cost *(page 648)* The increase in cost imposed externally as a firm (or firms) increases its output by one unit.

Marginal Product of Inputs *(page 180)* The additional output produced as the input is increased by one unit.

Marginal Rate of Substitution *(page 68)* The amount of one good an individual will give up to gain one more unit of another good.

Marginal Rate of Technical Substitution *(page 192)* The amount by which one input can be reduced when one extra unit of another input is used, so that output remains constant.

Marginal Rate of Transformation *(page 60)* A measure of how much of one good must be given up to produce an additional unit of another good.

Marginal Revenue *(page 253)* The change in revenue resulting from a one-unit increase in output.

Marginal Revenue Product *(page 514)* The additional revenue resulting from the sale of output created by the use of one additional unit of an input.

Marginal Social Cost *(page 649)* The sum of marginal cost and marginal external cost (for each level of output).

Marginal Utility *(page 90)* A measure of the additional satisfaction obtained from consuming one additional unit of a good.

Market *(page 9)* The collection of buyers and sellers that, through their actual or potential interactions, determine the price of a product or set of products.

Market Definition *(page 9)* The identification of those buyers and sellers that should be included in a particular market. This involves determining the *extent* of the market—i.e., its *boundaries*, both geographic and in terms of the range of products to be included in it.

Market Demand Curve *(page 116)* The horizontal summation of all individual consumers' demand curves.

Market Power *(page 334)* The ability to profitably affect price. Refers to either monopoly or monopsony power.

Market Signaling *(page 624)* The process by which sellers send buyers information about a product's quality.

Markup Pricing *(page 348)* Increasing the production cost of a good by a fixed percentage to determine a sales price.

Maximin Strategy *(page 483)* A gaming strategy that maximizes the minimum gain that can result.

Median Voter *(page 679)* The individual with the median preferred outcome among all voters.

Mixed Bundling *(page 402)* When two or more goods are sold both as a package and individually.

Mixed Strategy *(page 484)* A gaming strategy in which a player makes a random choice among two or more possible actions, based on a set of chosen probabilities.

Model *(page 4)* A mathematical representation, based on theory, of a firm, a market, or some other economic entity.

Monopolistic Competition *(page 433)* A market in which firms compete by selling differentiated products that are highly substitutable for one another, and there is free entry and exit.

Monopoly *(page 333)* A market with only one seller.

Monopoly Power *(page 334)* The ability of a firm to profitably charge a price higher than marginal cost.

Monopsony *(page 333)* A market with only one buyer.

Monopsony Power *(page 334)* The ability of a buyer to purchase a good at a price below its marginal value.

Moral Hazard *(page 629)* When an insured party can affect the probability or magnitude of an event against the occurrence of which it is insured.

N

Nash Equilibrium *(page 441)* A set of strategies or actions in which each player is doing the best it can, given the actions of its opponents.

Natural Monopoly *(page 357)* An industry in which economies of scale are so great that the efficient level of production for one firm satisfies the entire market demand.

Net Present Value *(page 556)* The present discounted value of expected future cash flows from an investment, less the cost of the investment.

Network Externality *(page 126)* The dependence of an individual's demand on the consumption levels of other people.

Nominal Discount Rate *(page 556)* A discount rate that includes the effects of inflation.

Nominal Price *(page 12)* The price actually quoted for a good at a given point in time; also called the "current dollar" price.

Noncooperative Game *(page 476)* A game in which negotiation and enforcement of a binding contract are not possible.

Nonexclusive Good *(page 673)* A good that people cannot be excluded from consuming, and for the use of which it is difficult to charge them.

Nonrival Good *(page 673)* A good for which the marginal cost of provision to an additional consumer is zero.

Normal Good *(page 106)* A good for which consumption increases when income rises.

Normative Analysis *(page 5)* An analysis leading to a recommendation or a prescription.

O

Oligopoly *(page 440)* A market with few sellers.

Oligopsony *(page 358)* A market with few buyers.

Opportunity Cost *(page 206)* The cost associated with opportunities that are foregone by not putting the firm's resources to their highest value use.

Opportunity Cost of Capital *(page 556)* The rate of return that one could earn by investing in a different project with similar risk.

Ordinal Ranking of Utility *(page 67)* Values that denote relative levels of satisfaction, assigned when the particular unit of utility is unimportant.

P

Paasche Index *(page 96)* A cost-of-living index that calculates the amount of money at current year prices that an individual requires to purchase a bundle of goods and services *chosen in the current year*, divided by the cost of purchasing the same bundle in the base year.

Pareto Efficiency *(page 588)* An allocation is Pareto efficient if goods cannot be reallocated to make someone better off without making someone else worse off.

Partial Equilibrium Analysis *(page 295)* A determination of the equilibrium prices and quantities in a particular market that ignores effects from other markets.

Peak-Load Pricing *(page 390)* A form of intertemporal price discrimination in which peak users pay more than off-peak users because marginal cost is higher during peak periods.

Perfect Competition *(page 283)* A market in which all goods are perfect substitutes, there are no barriers to entry, and no firm can affect the market price.

Positive Analysis *(page 5)* An explanation or prediction of an economic activity.

Predatory Pricing *(page 368)* A pricing policy designed to drive one or more competitors out of business and/or discourage new entrants to a market.

Present Discounted Value *(page 547)* The current value of an expected future cash flow.

Price-Consumption Curve *(page 102)* A curve derived by tracing the utility-maximizing combinations of two goods as the price of one changes.

Price Discrimination *(page 376)* Charging different prices to different customers for similar goods.

Price Elasticity of Demand *(page 35)* The percentage change in the quantity demanded of a good resulting from a 1 percent increase in the price of that good.

Price Elasticity of Supply *(page 35)* The percentage change in the quantity supplied of a good resulting from a 1 percent increase in the price of that good.

Price Leadership *(page 459)* A form of implicit collusion, where one firm in the market sets the price and other firms follow suit.

Price Support *(page 305)* A policy by which the government sets the market price of a good, usually an agricultural product, above the free-market level and buys up whatever output is needed to maintain that price.

Price Taker *(page 255)* A firm with no influence over the market price.

Principal *(page 632)* An individual who employs one or more agents to achieve his or her objective.

Principal–Agent Problem *(page 633)* The problem that arises when managers (agents) pursue their own goals, even if that entails lower profits for the owners of the firm (the principals).

Prisoners' Dilemma *(page 455)* A game in which two prisoners must decide separately whether to confess to a crime; it is a parable for competition in which all firms would do better if they cooperated, but each has a strong incentive to undercut its competitors.

Producer Surplus *(page 267)* The sum over all units of production of the difference between the market price of the good and the marginal cost of production.

Production Possibilities Frontier *(page 599)* A curve that describes the various combinations of two goods that can be produced given fixed quantities of inputs.

Profit Maximization *(page 252)* The goal of a firm; it is achieved when the marginal revenue of the firm is equal to the marginal cost of production.

Prospective Sunk Cost *(page 207)* A cost that has not yet been incurred but that cannot be recovered once it is incurred.

Public Good *(page 672)* A nonexclusive and nonrival good.

Pure Bundling *(page 397)* When a firm sells two or more goods only as a package.

R

Rate of Return *(page 553)* The discount rate that makes the net present value of an investment equal to zero.

Rate-of-Return Regulation *(page 358)* Setting a price that gives a monopoly a competitive return on its assets.

Reaction Curve *(page 443)* The profit-maximizing production choices of one firm in a duopoly as a function of the other firm's output.

Real Discount Rate *(page 558)* The discount rate that applies when cash flows are in real terms, i.e., after netting out inflation.

Real Price *(page 12)* The price of a good relative to the aggregate price level; also called the "constant dollar" price.

Regulatory Lag *(page 358)* Delays that are usually required to change a regulated price.

Reservation Price *(page 378)* The maximum amount that a customer is willing to pay for a good.

Return *(page 165)* The total monetary flow an asset yields as a fraction of its price.

Revealed Preference *(page 85)* An approach to consumer theory in which preferences are determined by observing the choices consumers make.

Risk *(page 147)* The possibility of several different outcomes occurring when the probability of each outcome is known.

Risk-Averse Individual *(page 155)* A person who prefers a certain income to a risky alternative with the same expected income.

Risk-Free Return *(page 165)* A return which is free of risk, whether of default or interest rate fluctuations. An example is the return on U.S. Treasury bills.

Risk-Loving Individual *(page 155)* A person who prefers a risky alternative to a certain one even though both offer the same expected income.

Risk-Neutral Individual *(page 155)* A person who is indifferent between earning a certain income and earning a risky one with the same expected income.

Risk Premium *(page 155)* The amount of money that a risk-averse individual will pay to avoid taking a risk.

S

Second Theorem of Welfare Economics *(page 595)* If individual preferences are convex, then every efficient allocation is a competitive equilibrium for some initial allocation of goods.

Secondary Supply *(page 41)* The supply from recycled scrap material.

Second-Degree Price Discrimination *(page 380)* Charging different prices per unit for different quantities of the same good.

Sequential Game *(page 491)* A game in which players move in order, rather than simultaneously.

Sherman Act *(page 367)* A law that prohibits contracts, combinations, or conspiracies that restrain trade, and makes monopolizing or attempting to monopolize illegal.

Slutsky Equation *(page 145)* An equation that separates the effect of a price change on quantity demanded into an income and a substitution effect.

Snob Effect *(page 128)* A negative network externality in which an individual's demand for a good is higher the fewer are the other people who have it.

Stackelberg Model *(page 447)* A model of oligopoly in which one firm sets output before the other firms do.

Standard Deviation *(page 150)* A measure of variability, equal to the square root of the variance, which is the average of the deviations of outcomes from their expected value.

Strategic Move *(page 440)* An action that constrains one's own behavior in a way that yields a strategic advantage.

Substitutes *(page 34)* Goods that compete in the market, so that if the price of one good increases, the quantity demanded of the substitute will also increase.

Substitution Effect *(page 111)* The change in consumption of a good that is associated with a change in its price, while the level of satisfaction is held constant.

Sunk Cost *(page 207)* An expenditure that when made cannot be recovered.

Supply Curve *(page 21)* The amount producers are willing to sell as a function of the market price.

T

Technical Efficiency *(page 177)* When firms combine their inputs to produce a given output as inexpensively as possible.

Third-Degree Price Discrimination *(page 381)* Dividing consumers into two or more groups with different demands for a product in order to charge different prices to each group.

Tit-for-Tat Strategy *(page 487)* In a repeated game, a strategy that responds in kind to an opponent's previous play. The strategy cooperates with cooperative opponents and retaliates against uncooperative ones.

Total Cost *(page 208)* The total cost of production, composed of fixed and variable costs.

Transfer Prices *(page 421)* The internal prices at which the parts and components from a firm's upstream divisions are "sold" to downstream divisions.

Transferable Emissions Permits *(page 657)* Marketable permits, allocated among firms, that specify the maximum level of emissions that can be generated.

Transitivity of Preferences *(page 63)* If a consumer prefers basket A to basket B, and also prefers basket B to basket C, then he will prefer basket A to basket C.

Two-Part Tariff *(page 376)* A form of pricing in which consumers are charged both an entry fee and a usage fee.

Tying *(page 409)* Requiring the purchaser of a product to also purchase a second product from the same firm.

U

Uncertainty *(page 148)* The possibility of several different outcomes occurring when the probability of each is unknown.

User Cost *(page 568)* The opportunity cost of depletion when producing a unit of an exhaustible resource.

Utility *(page 88)* The level of satisfaction that a person gets from consuming a good or undertaking an activity.

Utility Possibilities Frontier *(page 593)* A curve that includes all efficient allocations of resources measured in terms of the utility levels of two individuals.

V

Variable Cost *(page 208)* A cost that varies with the level of output, such as expenditures on wages and raw materials.

W

Welfare Economics: *(page 592)* The normative evaluation of markets and economic policy.

Welfare Effects *(page 289)* Gains and losses brought about by government policy.

Answers to Selected Exercises

CHAPTER 2

2. If the Soviet Union had purchased an additional 200 million bushels, the new demand, Q_D' would have been equal to $200 + Q_D$: $200 + Q_D = 200 + 2580 - 194P = 2780 - 194P$. Equating quantity supplied with quantity demanded: $1800 + 240P = 2780 - 194P$. $P = \$2.26$, an increase of 46 cents per bushel.

4. a. Total demand, $Q_D = 3550 - 266P$, equals domestic demand, Q_{DD}, plus export demand, Q_{DE}, where $Q_{DD} = 1000 - 46P$ and $Q_{DE} = 2550 - 220P$. If export demand decreases by 40%, $Q_D = 1000 - 46P + 0.6 (2550 - 220P) = 2530 - 178P$. Domestic supply is $Q_S = 1800 + 240P$. Equating supply and demand, $1800 + 240P = 2530 - 178P$, implying $P = \$1.75$. The market-clearing quantity is 2220 million bushels.
b. With a price of \$3, the market is not in equilibrium. Demand $= 1000 - 46\cdot3 = 862$, Supply $= 1800 + 240\cdot3 = 2520$, and excess supply is, therefore, $2520 - 862 = 1658$ million bushels. The government must purchase this amount to support a price of \$3, and spend $\$3\cdot1.66$ million $= \$5.0$ billion.

6. a. First, considering non-OPEC supply: $S_C = Q^* = 13$. With $E_S = 0.10$ and $P^* = \$18$, $E_S = d(P^*/Q^*)$ implies $d = 0.07$. Substituting for d, S_C, and P in the supply equation, $c = 11.74$, and $S_C = 11.74 + 0.07P$. Similarly, since $Q_D = 23$, $E_D = -b(P^*/Q^*) = -0.05$, and $b = 0.06$. Substituting for b, $Q_D = 23$, and $P = 18$ in the demand equation gives $23 = a - 0.06(18)$, so that $a = 24.08$. Hence $Q_D = 24.08 - 0.06P$.
b. As above, $E_S = 0.4$ and $E_D = -0.4$: $E_S = d(P^*/Q^*)$ and $E_D = -b(P^*/Q^*)$, implying $0.4 = d(18/13)$ and $-0.4 = -b(18/23)$. So $d = 0.29$ and $b = 0.51$. Next solve for c and a: $S_C = c + dP$ and $Q_D = a - bP$, implying $13 = c + (0.29)(18)$ and $23 = a - (0.51)(18)$. So $c = 7.78$ and $a = 32.18$.
c. With OPEC's supply reduced from 10 bb/yr to 4 bb/yr, add this lower supply of 4 bb/yr to the short-run and long-run supply equations: $S_C' = 4 + S_C = 11.74 + 4 + 0.07P = 15.74 + 0.07P$ and $S_C'' = 4 + S_C = 11.78 + 0.29P$. These are equated with short-run and long-run demand, so that: $15.74 + 0.07P = 24.08 - 0.06P$, implying that $P = \$64.15$ in the short run; and $11.78 + 0.29P = 32.18 - 0.51P$, implying that $P = \$24.29$ in the long run.

CHAPTER 3

4. a. See Figure 3(a) where B represents the number of packages of butter and M the number of packages of margarine.

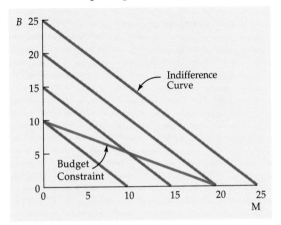

Figure 3(a)

b. Convexity means that the curve is "bowed inward." Here, the indifference curves are not "strictly convex," since they are straight lines.

c. The budget constraint is $Y = P_B B + P_M M$, $20 = 2B + M$, $B = 10 - 0.5M$. Given that Bill is indifferent between butter and margarine, and that the price of butter is greater than the price of margarine, Bill will only buy margarine.

5. **a.** See Figure 3(b), where "A" is the quantity of alcoholic drinks and "N" is the quantity of non-alcoholic drinks.
b. At any combination of A and N, Jones is willing to give up less of A to get some N than Smith is. Thus Jones has a *lower* MRS of A for N than Smith has. Jones' indifference curves are less steep than Smith's at any point on the graph.
c. To maximize satisfaction, each consumer must consume quantities such that the MRS between any two commodities equals the ratio of the prices. Their MRS's must be equal because they face the same prices. But because they have different preferences, they will consume different amounts of the two goods, A and N.

6. In Figure 3(c) we plot miles flown, M, against all other goods, G, in dollars. The slope of the budget line is $-P_M/P_G$. The price of miles flown changes as miles flown changes, so the budget curve is kinked at 25,000 and 50,000 miles. Suppose P_M is $1 per mile for $\leq 25,000$ miles, then $P_M = \$0.75$ for $25,000 < M \leq 50,000$, and $P_M = \$.50$ for $M > 50,000$.

Figure 3(b)

Figure 3(c)

Also, let $P_G = \$1$. Then the slope of the first segment is -1, the slope of the second segment is -0.75, and the slope of the last segment is -0.5.

CHAPTER 4

1. **a.** With a small change in price, the following point elasticity formula is appropriate: $E_p = \%\Delta Q/\%\Delta P$. For computer chips, $E_p = -2$, and for disk drives, $E_p = -1$. Let $TR_1 = P_1 Q_1$ be revenue before the price exchange and $TR_2 = P_2 Q_2$ be revenue after the price change. Then ΔTR would be $TR_2 - TR_1$. For computer chips, $\Delta TR = -12\%TR_1$. For disk drives, $\Delta TR = -1\%TR_1$.
b. Although we know the responsiveness of demand to changes in price, we need to know the quantities and the prices of the products to determine total sales revenues.

4. **a.** The demand curve is a straight line with a vertical intercept of $P = 12$ and a horizontal intercept of $Q = 6$ (since $Q = 6 - P/2$).
b. If there were no toll, the price P would be 0, so that $Q = 6$.
c. If the toll is $6, $Q = 3$. The consumer surplus lost is the difference between consumer surplus when $P = 0$ ($36) and consumer surplus when $P = 3$ ($9), or $27.

9. **a.** With small changes in price, the point elasticity formula would be appropriate. But here, the price of food doubles from $2 to $4, so arc elasticity should be used:

$E_P = (\Delta Q/\Delta P)(\overline{P}/\overline{Q})$. We know that $E_p = -1$, $P = 2$, $\Delta P = 2$, and $Q = 5000$. So, if there is no change in income, we can solve for ΔQ: $-1 = (\Delta Q/2)$ $[(2 + 1)/(5{,}000 + \Delta Q/2)] = (\Delta Q \cdot 3)/(10{,}000 + \Delta Q)$. We find that $\Delta Q = -2{,}500$: she decreases her consumption of food from 5000 to 2500 units.

b. A tax rebate of $5000 implies an income increase of $5000. To calculate the response of demand to the tax rebate, we use the definition of the arc income elasticity: $E_I = (\Delta Q/\Delta I)$ $(\overline{I}/\overline{Q})$. We know that $E_I = 0.5$, $I = 25{,}000$, $\Delta I = 5000$, $Q = 2500$. We solve for ΔQ: $0.5 = (\Delta Q/5000)$ $[(25{,}000 + 2500)/(2500 + \Delta Q/2)]$. Since $\Delta Q = 238$, she increases her consumption of food from 2500 to 2738 units.

c. On her final indifference curve, she chooses to consume 2738 units of food (for $10,952) and $19,048 worth of all other goods. At the original food price of $2, this combination would have cost her $2738 \cdot \$2 + \$19{,}048 = \$24{,}524$. So, she would have had an extra $476 to spend on either food or other consumption, and would have been better off.

CHAPTER 4—APPENDIX

1. The first utility function can be represented as a series of straight lines; the second as a series of hyperbolas in the positive quadrant; and the third as a series of "L"s. Only the second utility function meets the definition of a strictly convex shape.

3. The Slutsky equation is $dX/dP_X = \partial \chi / \partial P|_{U=U^*} - X(\Delta X/\Delta I)$, where the first term represents the substitution effect and the second term represents the income effect. With this type of utility function the consumer does not substitute one good for the other when the price changes, so the substitution effect is zero.

CHAPTER 5

2. The four mutually exclusive states are given in Table 5 below.

7. Consumers with income X^* will simultaneously purchase unfair insurance and take unfair gambles. They are risk averse against large losses, but risk loving for large income gains.

CHAPTER 6

1. **a.** The average product of labor, AP, is equal to Q/L. The marginal product of labor, MP, is equal to $\Delta Q/\Delta L$. The relevant calculations are given in the following table.

L	Q	AP	MP
0	0	—	—
1	10	10	10
2	17	8½	7
3	22	7⅓	5
4	25	6¼	3
5	26	5⅕	1
6	25	4⅙	−1
7	23	3²⁄₇	−2

b. This production process exhibits diminishing returns to labor, which is characteristic of all production functions with one fixed input. Each additional unit of labor yields a smaller increase in output than the last unit of labor.

Table 5	Congress Passes Tariff	Congress Does Not Pass Tariff
Slow growth rate	State 1: Slow growth with tariff	State 2: Slow growth without tariff
Fast growth rate	State 3: Fast growth with tariff	State 4: Fast growth without tariff

c. Labor's negative marginal product can arise from congestion in the chair manufacturer's factory. As more laborers are using a fixed amount of capital, they get in each other's way, decreasing output.

5. If the marginal product (MP) of labor is greater than the average product (AP) of labor, then each additional unit of labor is more productive than the average of all previous units. By adding the last unit, the average of all units increases. The AP is at a maximum when the productivity of the last unit is equal to the average of all previous units.

8. **a.** Let Q_1 be the output of DISK, Inc., Q_2 be the output of FLOPPY, Inc., and X be equal amounts of capital and labor for the two firms. Then, $Q_1 = 10X^{0.5}X^{0.5} = 10X^{(0.5 + 0.5)} = 10X$ and $Q_2 = 10X^{0.6}X^{0.4} = 10X^{(0.6 + 0.4)} = 10X$. Because $Q_1 = Q_2$, they both generate the same output with the same inputs.
b. With capital fixed at 9 machine units, the production functions become $Q_1 = 30L^{.5}$ and $Q_2 = 37.37L^{.4}$. Consider the following table:

L	Q Firm 1	MP Firm 1	Q Firm 2	MP Firm 2
0	0	—	0	—
1	30.00	30.00	37.37	37.37
2	42.43	12.43	49.31	11.94
3	51.96	9.53	57.99	8.68
4	60.00	8.04	65.06	7.07

For each unit of labor above 1 unit, the marginal product of labor is greater for DISK, Inc.

CHAPTER 7

3. **a.** Total cost, TC, is equal to fixed cost, FC, plus variable cost, VC. Since the franchise fee, FF, is a fixed sum, the firm's fixed costs increase by the fee. Then average cost, equal to $(FC + VC)/Q$, and average fixed cost, equal to (FC/Q), increase by the average franchise fee (FF/Q). Average variable cost is unaffected by the fee, as is marginal cost.
b. When a tax t is imposed, variable costs increase by tQ. Average variable cost in-

creases by t (fixed cost is constant), as does average (total) cost. Because total cost increases by t with each additional unit, marginal cost increases by t.

4. It is probably referring to accounting profit; this is the standard concept used in most discussions of how firms are doing financially. In this case, the article points to a substantial difference between accounting and economic profits. It claims that, under the current labor contract, automakers must pay many workers even if they are not working. This implies that their wages are *sunk* for the life of the contract. Accounting profits would subtract wages paid; economic profits would not, since they are sunk costs. Therefore automakers may be earning economic profits on these sales, even if they have accounting losses.

5. If the firm can produce one chair with either 4 hours of labor or 4 hours of machinery or any combination, then the isoquant is a straight line with a slope of -1 and intercepts at $K = 4$ and $L = 4$. The isocost line, $TC = 22L + 110K$, has a slope of $-1/5$ and intercepts at $K = TC/110$ and $L = TC/22$. The cost minimizing point is a corner solution, where $L = 4$ and $K = 0$, and $TC = 88$.

8. The production of gasoline involves distilling crude oil and refining the distillate into gasoline. Given that the marginal cost of production is constant up to the capacity constraint

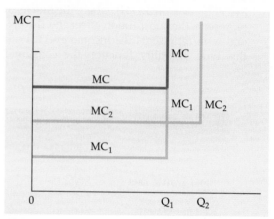

Figure 7

for both processes, the marginal cost curves are "mirror" L-shapes. Total marginal cost $MC = MC_1 + MC_2$, where MC_1 is the marginal cost of distilling crude oil up to the capacity constraint, Q_1 and MC_2 is the marginal cost of refining distillate up to the capacity constraint, Q_2. If the capacity constraint of the distilling unit is lower than that of the hydrocracking unit, total MC is vertical at Q_1. (See Figure 7.) If the capacity constraint of the hydrocracking unit is lower than that of the distilling unit, total MC is vertical at Q_2.

CHAPTER 7—APPENDIX

1. **a.** Returns to scale refers to the relationship between output and proportional increases in all inputs. If $F(\lambda L, \lambda K) > \lambda F(L,K)$, there are increasing returns to scale; if $F(\lambda L, \lambda K) = \lambda F(L,K)$, there are constant returns to scale; if $F(\lambda L, \lambda K) < \lambda F(L,K)$, there are decreasing returns to scale. Applying this to $F(L,K) = K^2 L$, $F(\lambda L, \lambda K) = (\lambda K)^2 (\lambda L) = \lambda^3 K^2 L = \lambda^3 F(L,K) > \lambda F(L,K)$. So, this production function exhibits increasing returns to scale.
    b. $F(\lambda L, \lambda K) = 10\lambda K + 5\lambda L = \lambda F(L,K)$. The production function exhibits constant returns to scale.

    c. $F(\lambda L, \lambda K) = (\lambda K \lambda L)^{0.5} = (\lambda^2)^{0.5} = (KL)^{0.5} = \lambda(KL)^{0.5} = \lambda F(L,K)$. The production function exhibits constant returns to scale.

2. The marginal product of labor is $100K$. The marginal product of capital is $100L$. The marginal rate of technical substitution is K/L. Set this equal to the ratio of the wage rate to the rental rate of capital: $K/L = 30/120$ or $L = 4K$. Then substitute for L in the production function and solve for a K that yields an output of 1000 units: $1000 = 100K \cdot 4K$. So, $K = 2.5^{0.5}$, $L = 4 \cdot 2.5^{0.5}$, and total cost is equal to $379.20.

CHAPTER 8

1. The table below shows the firm's revenue and cost information when the price falls to $35. At a price of $35 the firm should produce 7 units to maximize profit.

3. **a.** Profit is maximized where marginal cost (MC) is equal to marginal revenue (MR). Here, MR is equal to $60. Setting MC equal to 60 yields a profit-maximizing quantity of 30.
    b. Profit is equal to total revenue (PQ) minus total cost. So profit $= PQ - 100 - Q^2$. At $P = 60$ and $Q = 30$, profit $= 800$.

Output (units)	Price ($/unit) P = 40	Revenue ($) P = 40	Total Cost	Profit ($) P = 40	Marginal Cost P = 40	Marginal Revenue P = 40	Revenue ($/unit) P = 35	Marginal Revenue P = 35	Profit ($) P = 35
0	40	0	50	−50	—	—	0	—	−50
1	40	40	100	−60	50	40	35	35	−65
2	40	80	128	−48	28	40	70	35	−58
3	40	120	148	−28	20	40	105	35	−43
4	40	160	162	−2	14	40	140	35	−22
5	40	200	180	20	18	40	175	35	−5
6	40	240	200	40	20	40	210	35	10
7	40	280	222	58	22	40	245	35	23
8	40	320	260	60	38	40	280	25	20
9	40	360	305	55	45	40	315	35	10
10	40	400	360	40	55	40	350	35	−10
11	40	440	425	15	65	40	385	35	−40

c. The firm produces in the short run if its revenues are greater than its variable costs. The firm's short-run supply curve is its MC curve about minimum AVC. Here, AVC is equal to variable cost, Q^2, divided by quantity, Q. So, AVC = Q. Also, MC is equal to 2Q. So, MC is greater than AVC for any quantity greater than 0. This means that the firm produces in the short run as long as price is positive.

5. **a.** With the imposition of a $1 tax on a single firm, all its cost curves shift up by $1.
   b. Because the firm is a price taker, the imposition of the tax only on one firm does not change the market price. Given that the firm's short-run supply curve is its marginal cost curve (above average variable cost), and that the marginal cost curve has shifted up (or inward), the firm supplies less to the market at every price.
   c. If the tax is placed on a single firm, that firm will go out of business unless it was earning a positive economic profit before the tax.

CHAPTER 9

1. **a.** In free-market equilibrium, $L^S = L^D$. Solving, $w = \$4$ and $L^S = L^D = 40$. If the minimum wage is $5, then $L^S = 50$ and $L^D = 30$. The number of people employed will be given by the labor demand. So employers will hire 30 million workers.
   b. With the subsidy, only $w - 1$ is paid by the firm. The labor demand becomes $L^{D*} = 80 - 10(w - 1)$. So, $w = \$4.50$ and $L = 45$.

4. **a.** Equating demand and supply, $28 - 2P = 4 + 4P$. $P^* = 4$ and $Q^* = 20$.
   b. The 25% reduction required by the new Payment-In-Kind Program would imply that farmers produce 15 bushels. To encourage farmers to withdraw their land from cultivation, the government must give them 5 billion bushels that they sell on the market. Since the total supply to the market is still 20 billion bushels, the market price remains at $4 per bushel. The farmers gain $20 billion ($4 × 5 billion bushels) from the PIK Program, while consumers are not affected.
   c. Taxpayers gain because the government does not have to pay to store the wheat for a year and then ship it to an underdeveloped country. The PIK Program can last only as long as wheat reserves last. But PIK assumes that the land removed from production can be restored to production at such times as the stockpiles are exhausted. If this cannot be done, consumers may eventually pay more for wheat-based products. Finally, farmers enjoy a windfall profit because they have no production costs.

9. The supply and demand curves for natural gas can be approximated as follows: $Q^S = 14 + 2P_G + 0.25P_O$, $Q^D = -5P_G + 3.75P_O$. With the price of oil at $12 per barrel, these curves become $Q^S = 17 + 2P_G$, and $Q^D = 45 - 5P_G$. Setting $Q^D = Q^S$, $17 + 2P_G = 45 - 5P_G$, $P = \$4$. At this price, equilibrium quantity is 25 Tcf. If a ceiling of $1 is imposed, producers would supply 19 Tcf and consumers would demand 40 Tcf. Consumers gain area A − B = 57 − 3.6 = $53.4 billion in the figure. Producers lose area A − C = −57 −9 = $66.0 billion. Deadweight loss is equal to 53.4 − 66 = $12.6 billion.

13. No, it would not. The clearest case is where labor markets are competitive. With either design of the tax, the wedge between supply and demand must total 12.4 percent of the wage paid. It does not matter whether the tax is imposed entirely on the workers (shifting the effective supply curve up by 12.4%) or entirely on the employers (shifting the effective demand curve down by 12.4%). The same applies to any combination of the two that sums to 12.4%.

CHAPTER 10

2. There are three important factors: (1) How similar are the products offered by Caterpillar's competitors? If they are close substitutes, a small increase in price could induce customers to switch to the competition. (2) What is the age of the existing stock of tractors? A 5% price increase induces a smaller drop in demand with an older population of tractors. (3) As a capital input in agricultural production, what is the expected profitability of the agricultural sector? If expected farm incomes are falling, an

increase in tractor prices induces a greater decline in demand than one would estimate with information on past sales and prices.

4. **a.** Optimal production if found by setting marginal revenue equal to marginal cost. If the demand function is linear, $P = a - bQ$ (here, $a = 100$ and $b = 0.01$), so that $MR = a - 2bQ = 100 - 2(0.01)Q$.

Total cost $= 30,000 + 50Q$, so $MC = 50$. Setting $MR = MC$ implies $100 - 0.02Q = 50$, so $Q = 2,500$. Substituting into the demand function, $P = 100 - 0.01 \cdot 2,500 = 75$ cents. Total profit is $-30,000 + 50 \cdot 2,500 - 0.01 (2,500)^2 = -30,000 + 125,000 - 62,500$, or $325 per week.

b. Suppose initially that the consumers must pay the tax. Since the price (including the tax) that consumers would be willing to pay remains unchanged, the demand function can be written $P + t = 100 - 0.01Q - t$. Because the tax increases the price of each unit, total revenue for the monopolist decreases by tQ, and marginal revenue decreases by t: $MR = 100 - 0.02Q - t$, where $t = 10$ cents. To determine the profit-maximizing output with tax, equate marginal revenue and marginal cost: $100 - 0.02Q - 10 = 50$, or $Q = 2,000$ units.

From the demand function, average revenue $= 100 - 0.01 \cdot 2,000 - 10 = 70$ cents. Total profit is $70 (2000) - (30,000 + 50 (2000)) = 10,000$ cents or $100 per week.

8. **a. Pro:** Although Alcoa controlled about 90% of primary aluminum production in the United States, secondary aluminum production by recyclers accounted for 30% of the total aluminum supply. It should be possible for a much larger proportion of aluminum supply to come from secondary sources. Therefore the price elasticity of demand for Alcoa's primary aluminum is much higher than we would expect. In many applications, other metals, such as copper and steel, are feasible substitutes for aluminum. Here, the demand elasticity Alcoa faces may be lower than we would otherwise expect.

b. Con: The stock of potential supply is limited. Therefore, by keeping a stable high price, Alcoa could reap monopoly profits. Furthermore, since Alcoa had originally pro-

duced the metal reappearing as recycled scrap, it would have taken into account in its output decisions the effect of scrap reclamation on future prices. Hence, it exerted effective monopolistic control over the secondary metal supply.

c. Alcoa was not ordered to sell any of its U.S. production facilities. Rather, (1) it was barred from bidding for two primary aluminum plants constructed by the government during World War II; and (2) it was ordered to divest itself of its Canadian subsidiary, which became Alcan.

11. No, you should not. In a competitive market, a firm views price as being horizontal and equal to average revenue, which is equal to marginal revenue. If Connecticut's marginal cost increases, price will still be equal to Massachusetts's marginal cost, total marginal cost, and marginal revenue. Only Connecticut's quantity is reduced (which, in turn, reduces overall quantity), as shown in Figure 10 below.

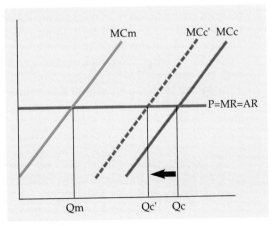

Figure 10

CHAPTER 11

1. **a.** The Saturday-night requirement separates business travelers, who prefer to return home for the weekend, from tourists, who travel on the weekend.

b. By basing prices on the buyer's location, sorting is done by geography. Then prices can reflect transportation charges, which the customer pays for whether delivery is received at the buyer's location or at the cement plant.

c. Rebate coupons with food processors separate consumers into two groups: (1) customers who are less price sensitive (those who have a lower elasticity of demand) do not request the rebate; and (2) customers who are more price sensitive (those who have a higher demand elasticity) request the rebate.

d. A temporary price cut on bathroom tissue is a form of intertemporal price discrimination. Price-sensitive customers buy more tissue than they would otherwise during the price cut, while non-price-sensitive consumers buy the same amount.

e. The plastic surgeon can distinguish a high-income patient from a low-income patient by negotiation. Arbitrage is no problem because plastic surgery cannot be transferred from low-income patients to high-income patients.

8. **a.** A monopolist with two markets should pick quantities in each market so that the marginal revenues in both markets are equal to one another and equal to marginal cost. Marginal cost is the slope of the total cost curve, 30. To determine marginal revenues in each market, we solve for price as a function of quantity. Then we substitute this expression for price into the equation for total revenue. $P_{NY} = 150 - 3Q_{NY}$, and $P_{LA} = 120 - (3/2)Q_{LA}$. Then total revenues are $TR_{NY} = Q_{NY}P_{NY} = Q_{NY}(150 - 3Q_{NY})$, and $TR_{LA} = Q_{LA}Q_{LA} = Q_{LA}(120 - (3/2)Q_{LA})$. The marginal revenues are the slopes of the total revenue curves: $MR_{NY} = 150 - 6Q_{NY}$, and $MR_{LA} = 120 - 3Q_{LA}$. Next, we set each marginal revenue to marginal cost ($= 30$), implying $Q_{NY} = 20$, and $Q_{LA} = 30$. With these quantities, we solve for price in each market: $P_{NY} = 150 - 3\cdot20 = 90$, and $P_{LA} = 120 - (3/2)\cdot30 = 75$.

b. With the new satellite, Sal can no longer separate the two markets. The total demand function is the horizontal summation of the two markets. Above a price of 120, the total demand is just the New York demand function. Below a price of 120, we add the two demands: $Q_T = 50 - (1/3)P + 80 - (2/3)P =$

$130 - P$. Sal maximizes profit by choosing a quantity so that MR = MC. Total revenue is QP, where $P = 130 - Q$. TR $= Q(130 - Q)$, so marginal revenue is $130 - 2Q$. Setting this equal to marginal cost implies a profit-maximizing quantity of 50 with a price of 80. In the New York market, quantity is equal to $50 - (1/3)80 = 23\frac{1}{3}$, and in the Los Angeles market, quantity is equal to $80 - (2/3)80 = 26\frac{2}{3}$. Together, 50 units are purchased at a price of 80.

c. Under the market conditions in (a) profit is equal to the sum of revenues from each market minus the cost of producing quantity for both markets: $Q_{NY}P_{NY} + Q_{LA}P_{LA} - 1000 - 30(Q_{NY} + Q_{LA}) = 20\cdot90 + 30\cdot75 - 1000 + 30(20 + 30) = 1,550$. Under the market conditions in (b) profit is equal to the total revenue minus the cost of producing quantity for both markets: $QP - (1000 + 30Q) = 50\cdot80 - (1000 + 30\cdot50) = 1500$. So Sal makes more money when the two markets are separated.

Under the market conditions in (a), in the New York market consumer surplus is $(150 - 90)\cdot20(1/2) = 600$, and in the Los Angeles market consumer surplus is $(120 - 75)\cdot30(1/2) = 675$. Under the conditions in (b), in the New York market consumer surplus is $(150 - 80)\cdot 23\frac{1}{3}(1/2) = 816$, and in the Los Angeles market consumer surplus is $(120 - 80)\cdot 26\frac{2}{3}(1/2) = 533$. The New Yorkers prefer (b) because the equilibrium price is 80 instead of 90, so their consumer surplus is higher. But the customers in Los Angeles prefer (a), because the equilibrium price is 75 instead of 80.

10. **a.** With individual demands of $Q_1 = 6 - P$, individual consumer surplus is equal to $18 per week, or $936 per year. An entry fee of $936 captures all consumer surplus, even though no court fee would be charged, since marginal cost is equal to zero. Weekly profits would be equal to the number of serious players, 1000, times the weekly entry fee, $18, minus $5000, the fixed costs, or $13,000 per week.

b. When there are two classes of customers the club owner maximizes profits by charging court fees above marginal cost and by setting the entry fee equal to the remaining consumer surplus of the consumer with the smaller demand—the occasional player. The entry fee, T, is equal to the consumer surplus remaining after the court fee is assessed: $T = (Q_2 - 0)(6 - P)(1/2)$, where $Q_2 = 3 - (1/2)P$, or $T = (3 - (1/2)P)(6 - P) (1/2) = 9 - 3P + P^2/4$. Entry fees for all players would be $2000(9 - 3P + P^2/4)$. Revenues from court fees equals $P(Q_1 + Q_2) = P[1000(6 - P) + 1000 (3 - P/2)] = 9000P - 1500P^2$. Then total revenue = TR = $2000 [(9 - 3P + P^2/4) + 9000P - 1500P^2 = 18,000 + 3000P - 1000P^2$. Marginal cost is zero, and marginal revenue is given by the slope of the total revenue curve: $\Delta TR/\Delta P = 3000 - 2000P$. Equating marginal revenue and marginal cost implies a price of $1.50 per hour. Total revenue is equal to $20,250. Total cost is equal to fixed costs of $5000. So, profit is $15,250 per week, which is greater than the $13,000 per week when only professional players become members. c. An entry fee of $18 per week would attract only serious players. With 3000 serious players, total revenues would be $54,000, and profits would be $49,000 per week. With both serious and occasional players, entry fees would be equal to 4000 times the consumer surplus of the occasional player: $T = 4000(9 - 3P + P^2/4)$. Court fees are $P[(6 - P)3000 + (3 - P/2)1000] = (21P - 3.5 P^2)1000$. Then TR = $[4(9 - 3P + P^2/4) + (21P - 3.5P^2)]1000 = (36 + 9P - 2.5P^2)1000$. Equating marginal revenue and marginal cost implies a price of (9/5), or $1.80 per hour. Then total revenue is equal to $44,100. Total cost is equal to fixed costs of $5000. Profit with a two-part tariff is $39,100 per week, which is less than the $49,000 per week with only professional players. The club owner should set annual dues at $936 and earn profits of $2.548 million per year.

11. Mixed bundling is often the ideal strategy when demands are only somewhat negatively correlated and/or when marginal production costs are significant. The following tables present the reservation prices of the three consumers and the profits from the three strategies:

	Reservation Price ($)		
	For 1	For 2	Total
Consumer A	$ 3.25	$ 6.00	$ 9.25
Consumer B	8.25	3.25	11.50
Consumer C	10.00	10.00	20.00

	Price 1	Price 2	Bundled	Profit
Sell separately	$ 8.25	$6.00	–	$28.50
Pure bundling	–	–	$ 9.25	27.75
Mixed bundling	10.00	6.00	11.50	29.00

The profit-maximizing strategy is to use mixed bundling.

15. a. For each strategy, the optimal prices and profits are

	Price 1	Price 2	Bundled	Profit
Sell separately	$40.00	$40.00	–	$240.00
Pure bundling	–	–	$100.00	400.00
Mixed bundling	59.95	59.95	100.00	319.90

Pure bundling dominates mixed bundling because with marginal costs of zero, there is no reason to exclude purchases of both goods by all customers.

b. With marginal cost of $35, the optimal prices and profits are

	Price 1	Price 2	Bundled	Profit
Sell separately	$90.00	$90.00	–	$110.00
Pure bundling	–	–	$100.00	120.00
Mixed bundling	59.95	59.95	100.00	110.00

Pure bundling still dominates all other strategies.

CHAPTER 11—APPENDIX

1. We examine each case, then compare profits. a. Optimal quantities and prices with no external market for engines are $Q_E = Q_A = 2000$, $P_E = \$8000$, and $P_A = \$18,000$. For the engine-building division,

TR = 2000·$8000 = $16M, TC = $2(2000)^2$ = $8M, and π = $8M. For the automobile-assembly division, TR = 2000 · $18,000 = $36M, TC = $8000 · 2000 + 16M = $32M, and π = $4M. Total profits are $12M.

b. Optimal quantities and prices with an external market for engines are Q_E = 1500, Q_A = 3000, P_E = $6,000, and P_A = $17,000. For the engine-building division, TR = 1500 ·$6000 = $9M, TC = $2(1500)^2$ = $4.5M, and π = $4.5M. For the automobile-assembly division, TR = 3000·$17,000 = $51M, TC = (8000 + 6000)3000 = $42M, and π = $9M. Total profits are $13.5M.

c. Optimal quantities and prices with a monopoly market for engines are Q_E = 2200, Q_A = 1600, P_E = $8800, and P_A = $18,400, with 600 engines sold in the monopolized market for $9400. For the engine-building division, TR = 1600·$8800 + 600·9400 = $19.72M, TC = $2(2200)^2$ = $9.68M, and π = $10.04M. For the automobile-assembly division, TR = 1600·$18,400 = $29.44M, TC = (8000 + 8800)1600 = $26.88M, and π = $2.56M. Total profits are $12.6M.

The upstream division, building engines, earns the most profit when it has a monopoly on engines. The downstream division, building automobiles, earns the most when there is a competitive market for engines. Given the high cost of engines, the firm does best when engines are produced at the lowest cost with an external, competitive market for engines.

CHAPTER 12

1. Each firm earns economic profit by distinguishing its brand from all other brands. If these competitors merge into a single firm, the resulting monopolist would not produce as many brands as would have been produced before the merger. But, producing several brands with different prices and characteristics is one method of splitting the market into sets of customers with different price elasticities.

3. a. To maximize profit $\pi = 53Q - Q^2 - 5Q$, we find $\Delta\pi/\Delta Q = -2Q + 48 = 0$. $Q = 24$, so P = 29. Profit is equal to 576.

b. $P = 53 - Q_1 - Q_2$, $\pi_1 = PQ_1 - C(Q_1)$ = $53Q_1 - Q_1^2 - Q_1Q_2 - 5Q_1$ and $\pi_2 = PQ_2 - C(Q_2) = 53Q_2 - Q_1Q_2 - Q_2^2 - 5Q_2$.

c. The problem facing Firm 1 is to maximize profit, given that the output of Firm 2 will not change in reaction to the output decision of Firm 1. Therefore, Firm 1 chooses Q_1 to maximize π_1, as above. The change in π_1 with respect to a change in Q_1 is $53 - 2Q_1 - Q_2 - 5 = 0$, implying $Q_1 = 24 - Q_2/2$. Since the problem is symmetric, the reaction function for Firm 2 is $Q_2 = 24 - Q_1/2$.

d. Solve for the values of Q_1 and Q_2 that satisfy both reaction functions: $Q_1 = 24 - (1/2)(24 - Q_1/2)$. So, $Q_1 = 16$ and $Q_2 = 16$. The price is $P = 53 - Q_1 - Q_2 = 21$. Profit is $\pi_1 = \pi_2 = P \cdot Q_i - C(Q_i) = 256$. Total profit in the industry is $\pi_1 + \pi_2 = 512$.

5. *True.* The reaction curve of Firm 2 will be $q_2 = 7.5 - 1/2\ q_1$ and the reaction curve of Firm 1 will be $q_1 = 15 - 1/2\ q_2$. Substituting yields $q_2 = 0$ and $q_1 = 15$. The price will be 15, which is the monopoly price.

10. a. To determine the Nash equilibrium we calculate the reaction function for each firm, then simultaneously solve for price. *Assuming marginal cost is zero,* profit for Firm 1 is $P_1Q_1 = P_1(20 - P_1 + P_2) = 20P_1 - P_1^2 + P_2P_1$. $MR_1 = 20 - 2P_1 + P_2$. At the profit-maximizing price, $MR_1 = 0$. So, $P_1 = (20 + P_2)/2$. Because Firm 2 is symmetric to Firm 1, its profit-maximizing price is $P_2 = (20 + P_1)/2$. We substitute Firm 2's reaction function into that of Firm 1: $P_1 = [20 + (20 + P_1)/2]/2 = 15 + P_1/4$. $P_1 = 20$. By symmetry $P_2 = 20$. Then $Q_1 = 20$, and by symmetry $Q_2 = 20$. Profit for Firm 1 is $P_1Q_1 = 400$, and profit for Firm 2 is also 400.

b. If Firm 1 sets its price first, it takes Firm 2's reaction function into account. Firm 1's profit is $\pi_1 = P_1[20 - P_1 + (20 + P_1)/2]$. Then, $d\pi_1/dP_1 = 20 - 2P_1 + 10 + P_1$. Setting this expression equal to zero, $P_1 = 30$. We substitute for P_1 in Firm 2's reaction function, $P_2 = 25$. At these prices, $Q_1 = 20 - 30 + 25 = 15$ and $Q_2 = 20 + 30 - 25 = 25$. Profit is $\pi_1 = 30 \cdot 15 = 450$ and $\pi_2 = 25 \cdot 25 = 625$.

c. Your first choice should be (iii), and your second choice should be (ii). Setting prices above the Cournot equilibrium values is optional for both firms when Stackelberg strategies are followed. From the reaction functions, we know that the price leader provokes a price increase in the follower. But the follower increases price less than the price leader, and hence undercuts the leader. Both firms enjoy increased profits, but the follower does best, and both do better than they would in the Cournot equilibrium.

CHAPTER 13

1. If games are repeated indefinitely and all players know all payoffs, rational behavior will lead to apparently collusive outcomes. But, sometimes the payoffs of other firms can only be known by engaging in extensive information exchanges.

   Perhaps the greatest problem to maintaining a collusive outcome is exogenous changes in demand and in the prices of inputs. When new information is not available to all players simultaneously, a rational reaction by one firm could be interpreted as a threat by another firm.

2. Excess capacity can arise in industries with easy entry and differentiated products. Because downward sloping demand curves for each firm lead to outputs with average cost above minimum average cost, increases in output result in decreases in average cost. The difference between the resulting output and the output at minimum long-run average cost is excess capacity, which can be used to deter new entry.

4. **a.** There are two Nash equilibria, (100,800) and (900,600).
   b. Both managers will follow a high-end strategy, and the resulting equilibrium will be (50,50), yielding less profit to both parties.
   c. The cooperative outcome (900,600) maximizes the joint profit of the two firms.
   d. Firm 1 benefits the most from cooperation. Compared to the next best opportunity, Firm 1 benefits by $900 - 100 = 800$, whereas Firm 2 loses $800 - 600 = 200$ under cooperation. Therefore, Firm 1 would need to offer

Firm 2 at least 200 to compensate for Firm 2's loss.

6. **a.** Yes, there are two: (1) Given Firm 2 chooses A, Firm 1 chooses C; given Firm 1 chooses C, Firm 2 chooses A. (2) Given Firm 2 chooses C, Firm 1 chooses A; given Firm 1 chooses A, Firm 2 chooses C.
   b. If both firms choose according to maximin, Firm 1 will choose Product A and Firm 2 will choose Product A, resulting in -10 payoff for both.
   c. Firm 2 will choose Product C in order to maximize payoffs at 10,20.

CHAPTER 14

1. The budget line for workers under this program is a straight line at $5000. There is no incentive to work under the new program. Only wages yielding incomes greater than $10,000 will yield a positive labor supply.

5. The demand for labor is given by the marginal revenue product of labor; $MRP_L = MR \cdot MP_L$. In a competitive market, price is equal to marginal revenue, so $MR = 10$. The marginal product of labor is equal to the slope of the production function $Q = 12L - L^2$. This slope is equal to $12 - 2L$. The firm's profit-maximizing quantity of labor occurs where $MRP_L = w$, the wage rate. If $w = 30$, solving for L yields 4.5 hours per day. Similarly, if $w = 60$, solving for L yields 3 hours per day.

8. Economic rent is the difference between total wages for all employed workers minus the amount that would have induced these workers to work. Total wages are equal to $wL_D = 1200w - 10w^2$. The total income that workers would have accepted is the area under the labor supply curve up to the labor demanded at w. From the supply function, we know that $L = 20w$, or $w = (1200 - 10w)/20$. Then this area is a triangle equal to $L_D \cdot w_s \cdot 1/2 = (1200 - 10w)[(1200 - 10w)/20] \cdot 1/2 = 36{,}000 - 600w + 2.5w^2$. If the union's goal is to maximize rent, then it would choose a w to maximize $(1200w - 10w^2) - (36{,}000 - 600w + 2.5w^2) = -36{,}000 = 1800w - 12.5w^2$. The slope with respect to w is $1800 - 25w$. The maximum occurs where

this slope is equal to zero, or $w = 72$. At a wage rate of $72, 480 union members are employed. They would have been willing to work for a total income of $5760 ($0.5 \cdot 480 \cdot 480/20$). They receive $34,560 and enjoy economic rents of $28,800 ($34,560 - 5760$).

CHAPTER 15

1. The present discounted value of the first $80 payment one year from now is $PDV = 80/(1 + 0.10)^1 = \$72.73$. The value of all these coupon payments can be found the same way: $PDV = 80[1/(1.10)^1 + 1/(1.10)^2 + 1/(1.10)^3 + 1/(1.10)^4 + 1/(1.10)^5] = \$303.26$. The present value of the final payment of $1000 in the sixth year is $1000/1.1^6 = \$564.47$. So the present value of this bond is $303.26 + $564.47 = $867.73. With an interest rate of 15 percent, $PDV = \$700.49$.

3. Redefining terms, the net present value equation becomes $NPV = -5 - 5(1 + R)^{-1} -1(1+R)^{-2} - 0.5(1+R)^{-3} + 0.96[(1+R)^{-4} + (1 + R)^{-5} + (1 + R)^{-6} + (1 + R)^{-7}] + 0.96[(1 + R^{-8}) + (1 + R)^{-9} + (1 + R)^{-10} + (1+R)^{-11}] + 0.96[(1 + R)^{-12} + (1 + R)^{-13} + (1 + R)^{-14} + (1 + R)^{-15}] + 0.96[(1 + R)^{-16} + (1 + R)^{-17} + (1 + R)^{-18} + (1 + R)^{-19}] + 0.96(1 + R)^{-20} + 1(1 + R)^{-20}$. With an interest of 4 percent, the NPV becomes $-5 - 4.8075 - 0.9246 - 0.4445 + 3.0978 + 2.6482 + 2.2637 + 1.9349 + 0.4381 + 0.4564 = -\$338,000$. The investment is not worthwhile.

7. **a.** If we buy a bottle and sell it after t years, we pay $100 now and receive $100t^{0.5}$ when it is sold. The NPV of this investment is $NPV = -100 + e^{-rt}100t^{0.5} = -100 + e^{-0.1t}100t^{0.5}$.

   If we do buy a bottle, we will choose t to maximize the NPV. The necessary condition is $dNPV/dt = e^{-0.1t}(50 - t^{-0.5}) - 0.1e^{-0.1t} \cdot 100t^{0.5} = 0$. Solving, $t = 5$. If we hold the bottle 5 years, the NPV is $-100 + e^{-0.1 \cdot 5}100 \cdot 5^{0.5} = 35.67$. Since each bottle is a good investment, we should buy all 100 bottles.
   b. You get $130 now, but lose the $100 \cdot 5^{0.5}$ you would get for selling in five years. The NPV of the offer is $NPV = 130 - (e^{(-0.1)(5)})(100)(5^{(0.5)}) = -238 < 0$. Therefore, you should not sell.

c. If the interest rate changes from 10 percent to 5 percent the NPV calculation changes to $NPV = -100 + e^{-0.05t} \cdot 100t^{0.5}$. If we hold the bottle 10 years, the maximum NPV is $-100 + e^{-0.05 \cdot 10} \cdot 100 \cdot 10^{0.5} = \$91.80$.

CHAPTER 16

1. Even with identical preferences, the contract curve may or may not be a straight line. This can easily be shown graphically. For example, when both individuals have utility functions $U = x^2y$, the marginal rate of substitution is given by $2y/x$. It is not difficult to show that the MRS's of both individuals are equal for all points on the contract curve $y = (Y/X)/x$, where X and Y are the total quantities of both goods. One example in which the contract curve is not a straight line is when the two individuals have different incomes and one good is inferior.

2. The marginal rate of transformation is equal to the ratio of the marginal costs of producing the two goods. Most production possibilities frontiers are "bowed outward." However, if the two goods are produced with identical production functions, the production possibilities frontier is a straight line.

6. A change from a constant-returns-to-scale production process to a sharply-increasing-returns-to-scale process does not imply a change in the shape of the isoquants. One can simply redefine the quantities associated with each isoquant such that proportional increases in inputs yield greater than proportional increases in outputs. Under this assumption, the marginal rate of technical substitution would not change, and there would be no change in the production contract curve.

CHAPTER 17

5. **a.** In the recent past, American automobiles appeared to customers to be of lower quality. To reverse this trend, American companies invested in quality control, improving the potential repair records of their products. They signaled the improved quality of their products through improved warranties.

b. Moral hazard occurs when the party to be insured (the owner of an American automobile with an extensive warranty) can influence the probability or the magnitude of the event that triggers payment (the repair of the automobile). Covering all parts and labor associated with mechanical problems reduces the incentive to maintain the automobile. Hence, a moral hazard problem is created with extensive warranties.

6. Truth in advertising promotes competition by providing the information necessary for consumers to make optimal decisions. Honest advertising facilitates this process. In the absence of truthful advertising, buyers are unable to do these comparisons. Goods priced identically can be of unequal quality. Hence, there will be a tendency for buyers to "stick" with proven products, reducing competition between existing firms and discouraging entry.

CHAPTER 18

3. One needs to know the value to homeowners of swimming in the river, and the marginal cost of abatement. The choice of a policy tool will depend on the marginal benefits and costs of abatement. If firms are charged an equal rate effluent fee, the firms will reduce effluent to the point where the marginal cost of abatement is equal to the fee. If this reduction is not high enough to permit swimming, the fee could be increased.

The setting of a standard will be efficient only if the policy maker has complete information regarding the marginal costs and benefits of abatement. Further, the standard will not encourage firms to reduce effluent further if new filtering technologies become available. A transferable effluent permit system still requires the policy maker to determine the efficient effluent standard. Once the permits are distributed, a market will develop and firms with a higher cost of abatement will purchase permits from firms with lower abatement costs. However, unless permits are sold initially, no revenue will be generated.

5. **a.** Profit is maximized when marginal revenue is equal to marginal cost. With a constant marginal revenue of $20 and a marginal cost of $10 + 2Q$, $Q = 5$.
b. If bees are not forthcoming, the farmer must pay $10 per acre for artificial pollination. Since the farmer would be willing to pay up to $10 to the beekeeper to maintain each additional hive, the marginal social benefit of each is $30, which is greater than the marginal private benefit of $20. Equating the marginal social benefit to the marginal cost, $Q = 10$.
c. The most radical change that would lead to more efficient operations would be the merger of the farmer's business with the beekeeper's business. This merger would internalize the positive externality of bee pollination. Short of a merger, the farmer and beekeeper should enter into a contract for pollination services.

Index